LEADERSHIP

Enhancing the Lessons of Experience

LEADERSHIP
Enhancing the Lessons of Experience

Richard L. Hughes
Robert C. Ginnett
Gordon J. Curphy

McGraw-Hill
Irwin

Boston   Burr Ridge, IL   Dubuque, IA   Madison, WI   New York   San Francisco   St. Louis
Bangkok   Bogotá   Caracas   Kuala Lumpur   Lisbon   London   Madrid   Mexico City
Milan   Montreal   New Delhi   Santiago   Seoul   Singapore   Sydney   Taipei   Toronto

McGraw-Hill Higher Education

*A Division of The **McGraw-Hill** Companies*

LEADERSHIP: ENHANCING THE LESSONS OF EXPERIENCE

Published by McGraw-Hill/Irwin, an imprint of The McGraw-Hill Companies, Inc. 1221 Avenue of the Americas, New York, NY 10020. Copyright © 2002, 1999, 1996, 1993 by The McGraw-Hill Companies, Inc. All rights reserved. No part of this publication may be reproduced or distributed in any form or by any means, or stored in a database or retrieval system, without the prior written consent of The McGraw-Hill Companies, Inc., including, but not limited to, in any network or other electronic storage or transmission, or broadcast for distance learning.

Some ancillaries, including electronic and print components, may not be available to customers outside the United States.

This book is printed on acid-free paper.

domestic   2 3 4 5 6 7 8 9 0 DOC/DOC 0 9 8 7 6 5 4 3 2
international 1 2 3 4 5 6 7 8 9 0 DOC/DOC 0 9 8 7 6 5 4 3 2 1

ISBN 0-07-244529-7

Publisher: *John E. Biernat*
Senior sponsoring editor: *Andy Winston*
Editorial coordinator: *Sara E. Strand*
Senior marketing manager: *Ellen Cleary*
Project manager: *Anna M. Chan*
Production supervisor: *Susanne Riedell*
Designer: *Artemio Ortiz Jr.*
Producer, Media technology: *Jennifer Becka*
Supplement producer: *Nate Perry*
Typeface: *10/12 Palatino*
Compositor: *Carlisle Communications, Ltd.*
Printer: *R. R. Donnelley & Sons Company*

INTERNATIONAL EDITION ISBN 0-07-112360-1

Copyright © 2002. Exclusive rights by The McGraw-Hill Companies, Inc. for manufacture and export. This book cannot be reexported from the country to which it is sold by McGraw-Hill. The International Edition is not available in North America.

Library of Congress Cataloging-in-Publication Data

Hughes, Richard L.
     Leadership : enhancing the lessons of experience / Richard L. Hughes, Robert C. Ginnett, Gordon J. Curphy.—4th ed.
       p. cm.
     Includes bibliographical references and index.
     ISBN 0-07-244529-7 (alk. paper)
       1. Leadership. I. Ginnett, Robert C. II. Curphy, Gordon J. III. Title.
     HM1261 .H84 2002
     303.3'4—dc21

                                                                                2001052217

www.mhhe.com

We dedicate this book to the leaders of today and tomorrow whose behaviors and actions continuously shape our ever-changing world. Nothing makes this clearer than the leadership challenges we all face in light of the events of September 11, 2001.

Thanks also to our families for their support and grounding:
Georgeann, Anne, Amy, and Sarah
Sherry, Laura, and Brad
Dianne, Chelsea, Ian, and McLaren

Rich Hughes is Director of Sustainable Leadership Capacity at the Center for Creative Leadership (CCL), an international, nonprofit educational institution devoted to behavioral science research and leadership education. In this role, Rich leads CCL's effort to explore how cultural and systemic factors in organizations impact leadership and leadership development. He joined the Center in 1995 after having served for the previous decade as head of the Department of Behavioral Sciences and Leadership at the U.S. Air Force Academy. He is a clinical psychologist and a graduate of the U.S. Air Force Academy. He has an MA from the University of Texas and a PhD from the University of Wyoming.

Robert Ginnett is a senior fellow at the Center for Creative Leadership. Besides his ongoing research concerning the leadership of high-performance teams and organizations, Robert is a lead instructor in the Leadership at the Peak course for CEOs and Presidents, ranked no. 1 in executive education by *Bricker's* as reported in *The Wall Street Journal*. He has worked with hundreds of organizations including General Motors, Novartis, FMC, Prudential, Masterfoods, GlaxoSmithKlein, Daimler Benz, NASA, the Central Intelligence Agency, United Airlines, and Delta Airlines. Prior to joining the Center for Creative Leadership, Robert was a tenured professor at the U.S. Air Force Academy and served as the director of leadership

and counseling. He also served in numerous line and staff positions in the Air Force including leadership of an 875-man combat force during the Vietnam War. Robert is an organizational psychologist whose education includes master of business administration, master of arts, and master of philosophy degrees, and a PhD from Yale University.

Gordy Curphy is Vice President of Institutional Leadership for The Blandin Foundation, a nonprofit organization dedicated to the improvement of rural communities in Minnesota. In this role Gordy will be responsible for the design and delivery of leadership and change programs for school administrators, local and state government officials, hospital administrators, business leaders, and community citizens. Prior to his position at The Blandin Foundation, Gordy was a Vice President and General Manager for the Minneapolis and Denver offices of Personnel Decisions International. In these roles he developed and managed leadership selection, succession planning, and development interventions for clients such as Carlson Companies, Medtronic, Anheuser-Busch, Boeing, The Home Depot, Saudi Aramco, Qwest, NCR, Deluxe, Hewlett-Packard, Oppenheimer Funds, Xcel Energy, SmithKline-Beecham, and Charter Communications. He has his undergraduate degree from the U.S. Air Force Academy, an MA from St. Mary's University, and a PhD from the University of Minnesota.

Often the only difference between chaos and a smoothly functioning operation is leadership; this book is about that difference.

The authors are psychologists; therefore the book has a distinctly psychological tone. You, as a reader, are going to be asked to think about leadership the way psychologists do. There is much here about psychological tests and surveys, about studies done in psychological laboratories, and about psychological analyses of good (and poor) leadership. You will often run across common psychological concepts in these pages, such as personality, values, attitudes, perceptions, and self-esteem, plus some not-so-common "jargon-y" phrases like double-loop learning, expectancy theory, and perceived inequity. This is not the same kind of book that would be written by coaches, sales managers, economists, political scientists, or generals.

Be not dismayed. Because these authors are also teachers with a good eye and ear for what students find interesting, they write clearly and cleanly, and they have also included a host of entertaining, stimulating snapshots on leadership: cartoons, quotes, anecdotal highlights, and personal glimpses from a wide range of intriguing people, each offered as an illustration of some scholarly point.

Also, because the authors are, or have been at one time or another, together or singly, not only psychologists and teachers but also children, students, Boy Scouts, parents, professors (at the U.S. Air Force Academy), Air Force officers, pilots, church members, athletes, administrators, insatiable readers, and convivial raconteurs, their stories and examples are drawn from a wide range of personal sources, and their anecdotes ring true.

As psychologists and scholars, they have reviewed here a wide range of psychological studies, other scientific inquiries, personal reflections of leaders, and philosophic writings on the topic of leadership. In distilling this material, they have drawn many practical conclusions useful for current and potential leaders. There are suggestions here for goal setting, for running meetings, for negotiating, for managing conflict within groups, and for handling your own personal stress, to mention just a few.

All leaders, no matter what their age and station, can find some useful tips here, ranging over subjects such as body language, keeping a journal, and how to relax under tension.

In several ways the authors have tried to help you, the reader, feel what it would be like "to be in charge." For example, they have posed quandaries such as the following: You are in a leadership position with a budget provided by an outside funding source. You believe strongly in, say, Topic A, and have taken a strong, visible public stance on that topic. The head of your funding source takes you aside and says, "We disagree with your stance on Topic A. Please tone down your public statements, or we will have to take another look at your budget for next year."

What would you do? Quit? Speak up and lose your budget? Tone down your public statements and feel dishonest? There's no easy answer, and it's not an unusual situation for a leader to be in. Sooner or later, all leaders have to confront just how much outside interference they will tolerate in order to be able to carry out programs they believe in.

The authors emphasize the value of experience in leadership development, a conclusion I thoroughly agree with. Virtually every leader who makes it to the top of whatever pyramid he or she happens to be climbing does so by building on earlier experiences. The successful leaders are those who learn from these earlier experiences, by reflecting on and analyzing them to help solve larger future challenges.

In this vein, let me make a suggestion. Actually, let me assign you some homework. (I know, I know, this is a peculiar approach in a book foreword but stay with me, I have a point.)

YOUR ASSIGNMENT: To gain some useful leadership experience, persuade eight people to do some notable activity together for at least two hours that they would not otherwise do without your intervention. Your only restriction is that you cannot tell them why you are doing this.

It can be any eight people: friends, family, teammates, club members, neighbors, students, working colleagues. It can be any activity, except that it should be something more substantial than watching television, eating, going to a movie, or just sitting around talking. It could be a roller-skating party, an organized debate, a songfest, a long hike, a visit to a museum, or volunteer work such as picking up litter or visiting a nursing home.

If you will take it upon yourself to make something happen in the world that would not have otherwise happened without you, you will be engaging in an act of leadership with all of its attendant barriers, burdens, and pleasures, and you will quickly learn the relevance of many of the topics that the authors discuss in this book. If you try the eight-person-two-hour experience first and read this book later, you will have a much better understanding of how complicated an act of leadership can be. You will learn about the difficulties of developing a vision ("Now that we are together, what are we going to do?"), of motivating others, of setting agendas and timetables, of securing resources, of the need for follow-through. You may even learn about "loneliness at the top." However, if you are successful, you will also experience the thrill that comes from successful leadership. One person *can* make a difference by enriching the lives of others, if only for a few hours. And for all of the frustrations and complexities of leadership, the tingling satisfaction that comes from success can become almost addictive. The capacity for making things happen can become its own motivation. With an early success, even if it is only with eight people for two hours, you may well be on your way to a leadership future.

The authors believe that leadership development involves reflecting on one's own experiences. Reading this book in the context of your own leadership experience can aid in that process. Their book is comprehensive, scholarly, stimulating, entertaining, and relevant for anyone who wishes to better understand the dynamics of leadership, and to improve her or his own personal performance.

David P. Campbell

The fourth edition contains several significant changes we believe will further enhance the text's usefulness. An overarching goal was to reduce the length of the text, even knowing there would be new material added to this edition. This reduction was accomplished through certain formatting changes as well as by deletion of certain material deemed less central to the major sections of the book and its overall theme.

There have been two significant changes to Part I, "Leadership Is a Process, Not a Position." One change involved moving the chapter on contingency leadership. In the third edition, this chapter was in Part I. In this new edition, that chapter has been moved to Part IV (Chapter 12), similar to its placement in the book's second edition. Ironically, it was feedback from the second edition that led us to place the chapter in the introductory material. However, that chapter was so complex and integrative, that its early placement simply did not work. We believe the introduction to the book's overall perspective on leadership (i.e., Part I) will be clearer to the student with the contingency chapter appearing later, and we believe the chapter itself will be better understood and appreciated by students who will now have greater breadth in the subject matter before they get to it. The other significant change to Part I involved significant revision of the chapter on assessing leadership and measuring its effects (Chapter 4). This has been a problematic chapter in every edition of the book. We understand that a chapter on methodological issues is unlikely to be popular with either students or instructors. On the other hand — after serious consideration of simply doing away with the chapter entirely — we chose to revise and reframe it. Leadership is a topic about which seemingly everyone has an opinion, and we believe it essential to raise the question How do you — or others — know what you claim to know about leadership? We see that as the essential contribution of that chapter to the purpose of the text.

Part II, "Focus on the Leader," begins again with a chapter on power and influence (Chapter 5), and this chapter remains essentially unchanged from the second edition. The next chapter in Part II deals with leadership and values, and has expanded material on how globalization is making the issue of values ever more salient for leaders. We eliminated the section on attitudes from this chapter, which gives the chapter greater continuity and focus. The remaining chapters in Part II have changed considerably. There are now just two other chapters in "Focus on the Leader" whereas in the last edition there were four. The chapter on leadership behavior (Chapter 8) remains substantially the same, but this edition's chapter on leadership traits (Chapter 7) contains the best of material from the previous edition's chapters on personality, intelligence and creativity. Our treatment of transactional and transformational leadership now appears in Part IV, as part of Chapter 13.

Part III, "Focus on the Followers," has been shortened by eliminating a chapter that seemed somewhat redundant with the material on followers and followership in Part I. The two chapters remaining in Part III (new Chapters 9 and 10) have been updated but remain otherwise similar in structure and content.

There are two major changes to Part IV, "Focus on the Situation." One has been mentioned already: inclusion of the chapter on contingency theories of leadership here (Chapter 12) rather than in Part I. The other is an entirely new chapter covering the issues of leadership and change (Chapter 13). The impact of the nature and pace of change in our world today on the subject of leadership and how the nature of leadership itself is *about* change led us to believe this new chapter represents a significant contribution to the book, and we believe an appropriate subject with which to conclude this section of the book.

The book concludes, as did the third edition, with a lengthy section dealing with leadership skills. Other than an additional perspective on team development, few changes have been made to the content of this section. On the other hand, we believe the usefulness of this material is enhanced in the new edition by a brief section at the end of each chapter indicating the specific leadership skills that are most relevant to that particular chapter.

As we noted earlier, several important format changes have been made to the book. For example, outlines at the beginning of each chapter have been eliminated. The "Leadership Quotes" still appear in every chapter, but they are now interspersed through each chapter in the margins rather than in a dedicated highlight. The highlights themselves have been trimmed down wherever possible, again with the objective of reducing the book's length. Several new highlights have been added, and other highlights from the previous edition have been deleted entirely. One final change is more frequent reference in the fourth edition to the "three leaders" (Colin Powell, Madeleine Albright, and Konosuke Matsushita) throughout the text, indicated by special symbols in the text margins.

We wish to thank a number of individuals for their significant contributions to this edition. We deeply appreciate the enthusiastic encouragement, guidance, and support of our friends and colleagues at McGraw-Hill/Irwin, including Sara Strand, Andy Winston, John Biernat, Anna Chan, Ellen Cleary, and Dana Woo. And, of course, we thank our constant support at CCL, Carol Vallee.

We are also indebted to a number of individuals whose evaluations and constructive suggestions about the previous edition provided the foundations for our revisions. We are grateful for the scholarly and insightful comments of Donald Cassiday, Patricia Castelli, Ahmad Tootoonchi, David Day, and Diane Torry. And we thank all those who corrected our conceptual mistakes, particularly Kate Beatty.

C O N T E N T S   I N   B R I E F

C O N T E N T S

3   Leadership Is Developed through Education and Experience   48

4   Assessing Leadership and Measuring Its Effects   77

PART II

FOCUS ON THE LEADER

5 Power and Influence   107

6 Leadership and Values   132

7 Leadership Traits   166

10 Groups, Teams, and Their Leadership   288

PART IV

Focus on the Situation

11 Characteristics of the Situation   325

PART V

LEADERSHIP SKILLS

I LEADERSHIP IS A PROCESS, NOT A POSITION

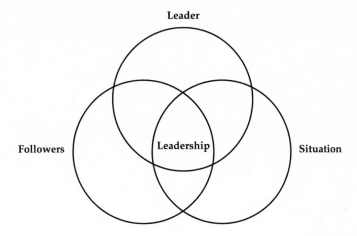

If any single idea is central to this book, it is that leadership is a process, not a position. The entire first part of the book explores that idea. One is not a leader—except perhaps in name only—merely because one holds a title or position. Leadership involves something happening as a result of the interaction between a leader and followers.

In Chapter 1 we define leadership and explore its relationship to concepts such as management and followership. We also suggest that better leadership is something everyone shares responsibility for. In Chapter 2 we discuss how leadership involves complex interactions between the leader, the followers, and the situation they are in. We also present an interactional framework for conceptualizing leadership which becomes an integrating theme throughout the rest of the book. Chapter 3 looks at how we can become better leaders by profiting more fully from our experiences, which is not to say that either the study or the practice of leadership is simple. Part I concludes with a chapter examining basic concepts and methods used in the scientific study of leaders and leadership.

1   LEADERSHIP IS EVERYONE'S BUSINESS

Introduction

I n the spring of 1972, an airplane flew across the Andes mountains carrying its crew and 40 passengers. Most of the passengers were members of an amateur Uruguayan rugby team en route to a game in Chile. The plane never arrived. It crashed in snow-covered mountains, breaking into several pieces on impact. The main part of the fuselage slid like a toboggan down a steep valley, finally coming to rest in waist-deep snow. Although a number of people died immediately or within a day of the impact, the picture for the 28 survivors was not much better. The fuselage initially offered little protection from the extreme cold, food supplies were scant, and a number of passengers had serious injuries from the crash. Over the next few days, several of the passengers became psychotic and several others died from their injuries. Those passengers who were relatively uninjured set out to do what they could to improve their chances of survival.

Several worked on "weatherproofing" the wreckage, others found ways to get water, and those with medical training took care of the injured. Although shaken from the crash, the survivors initially were confident they would be found. These feelings gradually gave way to despair, as search and rescue teams failed to find the wreckage. With the passing of several weeks and no sign of rescue in sight, the remaining passengers decided to mount several expeditions to determine the best way to escape. The most physically fit were chosen to go on the expeditions, as the thin mountain air and the deep snow made the trips extremely taxing. The results of the trips were both frustrating and demoralizing; the expeditionaries determined they were in the middle of the Andes mountains, and walking out to find help was believed to be impossible. Just when the survivors thought nothing worse could possibly happen, an avalanche hit the wreckage and killed several more of them.

The remaining survivors concluded they would not be rescued and their only hope was for someone to leave the wreckage and find help. Three of the fittest passengers were chosen for the final expedition, and everyone else's work was directed toward improving the expedition's chances of success. The three expeditionaries were given more food and were exempted from routine survival activities; the rest spent most of their energies securing supplies for the trip. Two months after the plane crash, the expeditionaries set out on their final attempt to find help. After hiking for 10 days through some of the most rugged terrain in the world, the expeditionaries stumbled across a group of Chilean peasants tending cattle. One of the expeditionaries stated, "I come from a plane that fell in the mountains. I am Uruguayan . . ." Eventually, 14 other survivors were rescued.

When the full account of their survival became known, it was not without controversy. It had required extreme and unsettling measures; the survivors had lived only by eating the flesh of their deceased comrades. Nonetheless, their story is one of the most moving survival dramas of all time, magnificently told by Piers Paul Read in *Alive* (1974). It is a story of tragedy and courage, and it is a story of leadership.

Perhaps a story of survival in the Andes is so far removed from everyday experience that it does not seem to hold any relevant lessons about leadership for you personally. But consider for a moment some of the basic issues the Andes survivors faced: tension between individual and group goals, dealing with the different needs and personalities of group members, and keeping hope alive in the face of adversity. These issues are not so very different from those facing many groups we're a part of. We can also look at the Andes experience for examples of the emergence of informal leaders in groups. Before the flight, a boy named Parrado was awkward and shy, a "second-stringer" both athletically and socially. Nonetheless, this unlikely hero became the best loved and most respected among the survivors for his courage, optimism, fairness, and emotional support. Persuasiveness in group decision making also was an important part of leadership among the Andes survivors. During the difficult discussions preceding the agonizing decision to survive on the flesh of their deceased comrades, one of the rugby players made his reasoning clear: "I know that if my dead body could help you stay alive, then I would want you to use it. In fact, if I do die and you don't eat me, then I'll come back from wherever I am and give you a good kick in the ass" (Read, 1974, p. 77).

The Purpose of This Book

Lives of great men all remind us
We can make our lives sublime
And, departing, leave behind us
Footprints on the sands of time.
    Henry Wadsworth Longfellow

Few of us will ever be confronted with a leadership challenge as dramatic as that faced by the Andes survivors. We may frequently face, however, opportunities for leadership that involve group dynamics which are just as complex. The purpose of this book is to help you be more effective in leadership situations by helping you better understand the complex challenges of leadership.

More specifically, we hope this book will serve as a sort of guide for interpreting leadership theory and research. The book describes and critically evaluates a number of leadership theories and research articles, and also offers practical advice on how to be a better leader. This book is designed to fill the gap between books that provide excellent summaries of leadership research but little practical advice on how to be a better leader and those that are not based on theory or research but primarily offer just one person's views on how to be a better leader (e.g., "how to" books, memoirs).

Three Leaders

One way we will bridge that gap between leadership research and more personalized accounts of leadership will be through personal glimpses of individual leaders. Dozens of different leaders are mentioned illustratively throughout the text, but three particular individuals will be a continuing focus across many chapters. They are Colin Powell, Madeleine Albright, and Konosuke Matsushita. Let us introduce you to them now.

Colin Powell

Colin Powell is the United States secretary of state. No African American has ever held a higher position in the U.S. government. He is also a former chairman of the Joint Chiefs of Staff, the highest-ranking officer in the U.S. armed forces. He has commanded soldiers, advised presidents, and led a national volunteer movement to improve the future for disadvantaged youth.

We might wonder whether his leadership of a national volunteer movement or the State Department differs in any way from his leadership of his country's military forces. We might also wonder what there is about him that inspired so many to hope he would run for elective office himself? And we might wonder, was he always a great leader, or did even Colin Powell need to learn a few things along the way? These are some of the questions we will consider ahead.

Madeleine Albright

Madeleine Albright was the U.S. secretary of state during the Clinton administration, becoming the highest-ranking woman official in the nation's history. A naturalized citizen, she was born in Czechoslovakia in the days immediately preceding World War II. Fleeing the tyranny of both Nazi Germany and Soviet communism, her family escaped to England and later emigrated to the United States. Remaining in Europe, her grandparents died in concentration camps.

Influencing others' views of foreign policy had always been an interest of Albright's, perhaps because she grew up in four different countries and speaks five languages. In the

> *The halls of fame are open wide and they are always full. Some go in by the door called "push" and some by the door called "pull."*
>
> Stanley Baldwin,
> British prime minister in 1930s

eighth grade she won a contest for correctly naming all the members of the United Nations, and as a ninth grader she started an international-relations club at her school, naming herself its president. As secretary of state she was known for her candor and charm as well as her grasp of complex issues. Before becoming secretary of state, Albright served in several other governmental roles. She also served on the faculty of Georgetown University, where she won numerous awards for outstanding teaching.

Konosuke Matsushita

Although you never may have heard of Konosuke Matsushita by name, John Kotter has called him the most remarkable entrepreneur of the 20th century. Despite only four years of formal education, he founded Matsushita Electric in 1917 and saw his company build revenues of nearly $50 billion. On a purely financial basis this exceeded the success of such other well-known entrepreneurs as Soichiro Honda, Sam Walton, J. C. Penney, Henry Ford, and Bill Gates. Matsushita's legacy, however, is far more than business success.

He was more than just wildly successful. He was an innovative leader who instituted radically unconventional management practices that even today are considered modern. He was a philanthropist, creating a Nobel Prize–like organization and an institute to develop leadership in government and politics for the 21st century. By comparison, graduates of the Matsushita Institute of Government and Management are 100 times more likely to serve in the Japanese Diet than graduates of the Kennedy School of Government at Harvard University are to serve in the U.S. Congress.

What accounts for the success of this remarkable man? Did he possess extraordinary qualities? Did certain unique circumstances or events favor him? We will examine these and other questions about Konosuke Matsushita.

What Is Leadership?

The Andes story and the lives of the three leaders we just introduced provide numerous examples of leadership. But just what *is* leadership? People who do research on leadership actually disagree more than you might think about what leadership really is. Most of this disagreement stems from the fact that **leadership** is a complex phenomenon involving the leader, the followers, and the situation. Some leadership researchers have focused on the personality, physical traits, or behaviors of the leader; others have studied the relationships between leaders and followers; still others have studied how aspects of the situation affect the ways leaders act. Some have extended the latter viewpoint so far as to suggest there is no such thing as leadership; they argue that organizational successes and failures often get falsely attributed to the leader, but the situation may have a much greater impact

Remember the difference between a boss and a leader: a boss says, "Go!"—a leader says, "Let's go!"
E. M. Kelly

on how the organization functions than does any individual, including the leader (Meindl & Ehrlich, 1987).

Perhaps the best way for you to begin to understand the complexities of leadership is to see some of the ways leadership has been defined. Leadership researchers have defined leadership in the following different ways:

- The creative and directive force of morale (Munson, 1921).
- The process by which an agent induces a subordinate to behave in a desired manner (Bennis, 1959).
- The presence of a particular influence relationship between two or more persons (Hollander & Julian, 1969).
- Directing and coordinating the work of group members (Fiedler, 1967).
- An interpersonal relation in which others comply because they want to, not because they have to (Merton, 1969; Hogan, Curphy, & Hogan, 1994).
- Transforming followers, creating visions of the goals that may be attained, and articulating for the followers the ways to attain those goals (Bass, 1985; Tichy & Devanna, 1986).
- The process of influencing an organized group toward accomplishing its goals (Roach & Behling, 1984).
- Actions that focus resources to create desirable opportunities (Campbell, 1991).
- The leader's job is to create conditions for the team to be effective (Ginnett, 1996).

As you can see, these definitions differ in many ways, and these differences have resulted in various researchers exploring very different aspects of leadership. For example, if we were to apply these definitions to the Andes survival scenario described earlier, researchers adopting Munson's definition would focus on the behaviors Parrado used to keep up the morale of the survivors. Researchers using Roach and Behling's definition would examine how Parrado managed to convince the group to stage and support the final expedition. One's definition of leadership might also influence just *who* is considered an appropriate leader for study. For example, researchers who adopted Merton's definition might not be interested in studying Colin Powell's leadership as an army general. They might reason that the enormous hierarchical power and authority of an army general makes every order or decision a "have to" response from subordinates. Thus, each group of researchers might focus on a different aspect of leadership, and each would tell a different story regarding the leader, the followers, and the situation.

Although such a large number of leadership definitions may seem confusing, it is important to understand that there is no single correct definition. The various definitions can help us appreciate the multitude of factors that affect leadership, as well as different perspectives from which to view it. For example, in Bennis's definition, the word *subordinate* seems to confine leadership to downward influence in hierarchical relationships; it seems to exclude informal leadership. Fiedler's definition emphasizes the directing and controlling aspects of leadership, and thereby may deemphasize emotional aspects of leadership. The emphasis Merton placed on subordinates' "wanting to" comply with a leader's wishes seems to exclude coercion of any kind as a leadership tool. Further, it becomes problematic to identify ways in which a leader's actions are really leadership if subordinates voluntarily comply when a leader with considerable potential coercive power merely asks others to do something without explicitly threatening them. Similarly, Campbell used the phrase *desirable opportunities* precisely to distinguish between leadership and tyranny.

All considered, we believe the definition provided by Roach and Behling (1984) to be a fairly comprehensive and helpful one. Therefore, this book also defines leadership as "the process of influencing an organized group toward accomplishing its goals." There are several implications of this definition which are worth further examination.

Leadership Is Both a Science and an Art

Saying leadership is both a science and an art emphasizes the subject of leadership as a field of scholarly inquiry, as well as certain aspects of the practice of leadership. The scope of the science of leadership is reflected in the number of studies—approximately 8,000—cited in an authoritative reference work, *Bass & Stogdill's Handbook of Leadership: Theory, Research, & Managerial Applications* (Bass, 1990). However, being an expert on leadership research is neither a necessary nor a sufficient condition for being a good leader. Some managers may be effective leaders without ever having taken a course or training program in leadership, and some scholars in the field of leadership may be relatively poor leaders themselves.

Any fool can keep a rule. God gave him a brain to know when to break the rule.

General Willard W. Scott

This is not to say that knowing something about leadership research is irrelevant to leadership effectiveness. Scholarship may not be a prerequisite for leadership effectiveness, but understanding some of the major research findings can help individuals better analyze situations using a variety of perspectives. That, in turn, can give leaders insight about how to be more effective. Even so, because the skill in analyzing and responding to situations varies greatly across leaders, leadership will always remain partly an art as well as a science.

Leadership Is Both Rational and Emotional

Leadership involves both the rational and emotional sides of human experience. Leadership includes actions and influences based on reason and logic as well as those based on inspiration and passion. We do not want to cultivate leaders like Commander Data of *Star Trek: The Next Generation*, who always responds with logical predictability. Because people differ in their thoughts and feelings, hopes and dreams, needs and fears, goals and ambitions, and strengths and weaknesses, leadership situations can be very complex. Because people are both rational and emotional, leaders can use rational techniques and/or emotional appeals in order to influence followers, but they must also weigh the rational and emotional consequences of their actions.

A full appreciation of leadership involves looking at both these sides of human nature. Good leadership is more than just calculation and planning, or following a "checklist," even though rational analysis can enhance good leadership. Good leadership also involves touching others' feelings; emotions play an important role in leadership too. Just one example of this is the civil rights movement of the 1960s. It was a movement based on emotions as well as on principles. Dr. Martin Luther King, Jr., *inspired* many people to action; he touched people's hearts as well as their heads.

> *A democracy cannot follow a leader unless he is dramatized. A man to be a hero must not content himself with heroic virtues and anonymous action. He must talk and explain as he acts—drama.*
>
> William Allen White,
> American writer and editor,
> *Emporia Gazette*

Aroused feelings, however, can be used either positively or negatively, constructively or destructively. Some leaders have been able to inspire others to deeds of great purpose and courage. On the other hand, as images of Adolf Hitler's mass rallies or present-day angry mobs attest, group frenzy can readily become group mindlessness. As another example, emotional appeals by the Reverend Jim Jones resulted in approximately 800 of his followers' volitionally committing suicide.

The mere presence of a group (even without heightened emotional levels) can also cause people to act differently than when they are alone. For example, in airline cockpit crews, there are clear lines of authority from the captain down to the first officer (second in command) and so on. So strong are the norms surrounding the authority of the captain that some first officers will not take control of the airplane from the captain even in the event of impending disaster. Foushee (1984) reported a study wherein airline captains in simulator training intentionally feigned incapacitation so that the response of the rest of the crew could be observed. The feigned incapacitations occurred at a predetermined point during the plane's final approach in landing, and the simulation involved conditions of poor weather and visibility. Approximately 25 percent of the first officers in these simulated flights allowed the plane to crash. For some reason, the first officers did not take control even when it was clear the captain was allowing the aircraft to deviate from the parameters of a safe approach. This example demonstrates how group dynamics can influence the behavior of group members even when emotional levels are *not* high. (Believe it or not, airline crews are so well trained, this is *not* an emotional situation.) In sum, it should be apparent that leadership involves followers' feelings and nonrational behavior as well as rational behavior. Leaders need to consider *both* the rational and the emotional consequences of their actions.

> *If you want some ham, you gotta go into the smokehouse.*
>
> Huey Long,
> Governor of Louisiana

Leadership and Management

In trying to answer "What is leadership?" it is natural to look at the relationship between leadership and management. To many, the word **management** suggests words like *efficiency, planning, paperwork, procedures, regulations, control,* and *consistency.* Leadership is often more associated with words like *risk taking, dynamic, creativity, change,* and *vision.* Some say leadership is fundamentally a value-choosing, and thus a value-laden, activity, whereas management is not. Leaders are thought to *do the right things,* whereas managers are thought to *do things right* (Bennis, 1985; Zaleznik, 1983). Here are some other distinctions between managers and leaders (Bennis, 1989):

- Managers administer; leaders innovate.
- Managers maintain; leaders develop.
- Managers control; leaders inspire.
- Managers have a short-term view; leaders, a long-term view.
- Managers ask how and when; leaders ask what and why.
- Managers imitate; leaders originate.
- Managers accept the status quo; leaders challenge it.

Zaleznik (1974, 1983) goes so far as to say these differences reflect fundamentally different personality types, that leaders and managers are basically different kinds of people. He says some people are managers *by nature;* other people are leaders *by nature.* This is not at all to say one is better than the other, only that they are different. Their differences, in fact, can be quite useful, since organizations typically need both functions performed well in order to be successful. For example, consider again the civil rights movement in the 1960s. Dr. Martin Luther King, Jr., gave life and direction to the civil rights movement in America. He gave dignity and hope of freer participation in our national life to people who before had little reason to expect it. He inspired the world with his vision and eloquence, and changed the way we live together. America is a different nation today because of him. Was Dr. Martin Luther King, Jr., a leader? Of course. Was he a manager? Somehow that does not seem to fit, and the civil rights movement might have failed if it had not been for the managerial talents of his supporting staff. Leadership and management complement each other, and both are vital to organizational success.

> *Stow this talk. Care killed a cat. Fetch ahead for the doubloons.*
>
> Long John Silver,
> in Robert Louis Stevenson's
> *Treasure Island*

> *Never try to teach a pig to sing, it wastes your time and it annoys the pig.*
>
> Paul Dickson,
> Baseball writer

With regard to the issue of leadership versus management, we take a middle-of-the-road position. We think of leadership and management as closely related but distinguishable functions. Our view of the relationship is depicted in Figure 1.1. It shows leadership and management as two over-lapping functions. Although some of the functions performed by leaders and managers may be unique, there is also an area of overlap.

FIGURE 1.1

*Leadership and
management overlap*

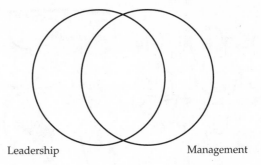

Leadership   Management

Leadership and Followership

One aspect of our text's definition of leadership is particularly worth noting:
Leadership is a social influence process shared among *all* members of a group.
Leadership is not restricted to the influence exerted by someone in a particular
position or role; followers are part of the leadership process, too. In recent years,
both practitioners and scholars have emphasized the relatedness of leadership
and **followership.** As Burns (1978) observed, the idea of "one-man leadership"
is a contradiction in terms.

Thus, the question *What is leadership?* cannot be separated from the question *What is followership?* There is no simple line dividing them; they merge.
The relationship between leadership and fol-
lowership can be represented by borrowing a
concept from topographical mathematics: the
Möbius strip. You are probably familiar with
the curious properties of the Möbius strip:
When a strip of paper is twisted and con-
nected in the manner depicted in Figure 1.2, it
proves to have only one side. You can prove this to yourself by putting a pencil to any point on the strip and tracing continuously. Your pencil will cover
the entire strip (i.e., both "sides"), eventually returning to the point at which
you started. In order to demonstrate the relevance of this curiosity to leadership, cut a strip of paper. On one side write *leadership,* and on the other side
write *followership.* Then twist the strip and connect the two ends in the manner of the figure. You will have created a leadership/followership Möbius
strip wherein the two concepts merge one into the other, just as leadership
and followership can become indistinguishable in organizations (adapted
from Macrorie, 1984).

This does not mean leadership and followership are the same thing. When
top-level executives were asked to list qualities they most look for and admire in
leaders and followers, the lists were similar but not identical (Kouzes & Posner,
1987). Ideal leaders were characterized as honest, competent, forward looking,
and inspiring; ideal followers were described as honest, competent, dependent,
and cooperative. The differences could become critical in certain situations, as

> *He who would eat the fruit must
> climb the tree.*
>
>   Scottish proverb

FIGURE 1.2

*The leadership/
followership
Möbius strip*

when a forward-looking and inspiring subordinate perceives a significant conflict between his own goals or ethics and those of his superiors. Such a situation could become a crisis for the individual and the organization, demanding choice between leading and following.

Leadership on Stages Large and Small

Great leaders sometimes seem larger than life. Charles de Gaulle, a leader of France during and after World War II, was such a figure (see Highlight 1.1). Not all good leaders are famous or powerful, however, and we believe leadership can be best understood if we study a broad range of leaders, some famous and some not so famous. Most leaders, after all, are not known outside their own particular sphere or activity, nor should they be. Here are a few examples of leadership on the small stage, where individuals influenced and helped their respective groups attain their goals.

• An elderly woman led an entire community's effort to organize an advocacy and support group for parents of mentally ill adult children and provide sheltered living arrangements for these people. She helped these families while also serving an invaluable role in educating state legislators and social agencies about the needs of this neglected constituency. There had been numerous parents with mentally ill children in this community before, but none had had the idea or took the initiative to organize among themselves. As a result of this woman's leadership, many adults live and work in more humane conditions than they did before.

• A seasoned air force sergeant took two young, "green" enlistees under her wing after they both coincidentally reported for duty on the same day. She taught them the ropes at work and took pride as they matured. One of them performed so well that he went on to be commissioned as an officer. Unfortunately, the sergeant discovered the other pilfering cash from the unit gift fund. Though it pained her to do so, the sergeant took action for the enlistee to be discharged from the service. Leadership involves significant intrinsic rewards such as seeing others blossom under your tutelage, but with its rewards also goes the responsibility to enforce standards of conduct.

• The office manager for a large advertising agency directed its entire administrative staff, most of whom worked in the reception area. His engaging

The Stateliness of Charles de Gaulle

Highlight 1.1

Certain men have, one might almost say from birth, the quality of exuding authority, as though it were a liquid, though it is impossible to say precisely of what it consists. In his fascinating book *Leaders,* former president Richard Nixon described the French president Charles de Gaulle as one of the great leaders he had met. Following are several aspects of de Gaulle's leadership based on Nixon's observations.

- *He conveyed stately dignity.* De Gaulle had a resolute bearing that conveyed distance and superiority to others. He was at ease with other heads of state but never informal with anyone, even close friends. His tall stature and imperious manner conveyed the message he was not a common man.
- *He was a masterful public speaker.* He had a deep, serene voice and a calm, self-assured manner. He used the French language grandly and eloquently. According to Nixon, "He spoke so articulately and with such precision that his message seemed to resonate apart from his words" (p. 59).
- *He played the part.* De Gaulle understood the role of theater in politics, and his meetings with the press (a thousand at a time!) were like audiences with royalty. He staged them in great and ornate halls, and he deftly crafted public statements that would be understood differently by different groups. In one sense, perhaps, this could be seen as a sort of falseness, but that may be too narrow a view. Nixon reflected on this aspect of de Gaulle's leadership: "General de Gaulle was a facade, but not a false one. Behind it was a man of incandescent intellect and a phenomenal discipline. The facade was like the ornamentation on a great cathedral, rather than the flimsy pretense of a Hollywood prop with nothing behind it" (p. 60).

Source: R. Nixon, *Leaders* (New York: Warner Books, 1982).

personality and concern for others made everyone feel important. Morale in the office was high, and many important customers credit their positive "first impression" of the whole agency to the congeniality and positive climate among the office staff. Leaders set the tone for the organization, and followers often model the behaviors displayed by the leader. This leader helped create an office mood of optimism and supportiveness that reached outward to everyone who visited.

These examples are representative of the opportunities every one of us has to be a leader. To paraphrase John Fitzgerald Kennedy, we all can make a difference and each of us should try. However, this book is more than an

The Romance of Leadership

Highlight 1.2

This text is predicated on the idea that leaders can make a difference. Interestingly, though, while people in the business world generally agree, not all scholars do.

People in the business world attribute much of a company's success or failure to its leadership. One study counted the number of articles appearing in *The Wall Street Journal* that dealt with leadership and found nearly 10 percent of the articles about representative target companies addressed that company's leadership. Furthermore, there was a significant positive relationship between company performance and the number of articles about its leadership; the more a company's leadership was emphasized in *The Wall Street Journal*, the better the company was doing. This might mean the more a company takes leadership seriously (as reflected by the emphasis in *The Wall Street Journal*), the better it does.

However, the authors were skeptical about the real utility of leadership as a concept. They suggested leadership is merely a romanticized notion, an obsession people want and need to believe in. Belief in the potency of leadership may be a sort of cultural myth, which has utility primarily insofar as it affects how people create meaning about causal events in complex social systems. The behavior of leaders, the authors contend, does not account for very much of the variance in an organization's performance. Nonetheless, people seem strongly committed to a sort of basic faith that individual leaders shape organizational destiny for good or ill.

Source: J. R. Meindl, S. B. Ehrlich, and J. M. Dukerich, "The Romance of Leadership." *Administrative Science Quarterly* 30 (1985), pp. 78–102.

exhortation for each of us to play a more active leadership role on the various stages of our lives. It is a review of what is known about leadership from available research, a review we hope is presented in a way that will foster leadership development. We are all more likely to make the kind of difference we want if we understand what leadership is and what it is not, how you get it, and what improves it (see Highlight 1.2 for a contrasting view of how much of a difference leaders really make). Toward that end, we will look at leaders on both the large and the small stages of life throughout the book. We will look at leaders on the world stage like Albright, Powell, and Matsushita; and we will look at leaders on those smaller stages closer to home like principals, coaches, and managers at the local store. You also might want to see Highlight 1.3 for a listing of women leaders throughout history from many different stages.

Women and Leadership A Few Women Leaders throughout History

Highlight 1.3

69 B.C.   Cleopatra, Queen of Egypt, is born and ascends the throne at age 17.

1429   Joan of Arc is finally granted an audience with Charles the Dauphin of France and subsequently captains the army at the siege of Orleans.

1492   Queen Isabella of Spain finances Columbus's voyage to the New World.

1638   Religious dissident Anne Hutchinson leads schismatic group from Massachusetts Bay Colony into wilderness and establishes Rhode Island.

1803–1806   Sacajawea leads the Lewis and Clark expedition.

1837   Educator Mary Lyons founds Mount Holyoke Female Seminary (later Mount Holyoke College), the first American college exclusively for women.

1843   Dorothea Dix reports to Massachusetts legislature on treatment of criminally insane, resulting in a significant reform of American mental institutions.

1849   Harriet Tubman escapes from slavery and becomes one of the most successful "conductors" on the Underground Railroad. She helps more than 300 slaves to freedom.

1854   Florence Nightingale, the founder of modern nursing, organizes a unit of women nurses to serve in the Crimean War.

1869   Susan B. Anthony is elected president of the National American Woman Suffrage Association.

1900   Carry Nation gains fame destroying saloons as head of the American Temperance Movement.

1919   Mary Pickford becomes the first top-level female executive of a major film studio.

1940   Margaret Chase Smith is the first woman elected to Congress.

1966   National Organization of Women (NOW) is founded by Betty Friedan.

1969   Golda Meir is elected prime minister of Israel.

1979   Mother Teresa receives Nobel Prize for her three decades of work leading the Congregation of Missions of Charity in Calcutta, India.

1979   Margaret Thatcher becomes the United Kingdom's first female prime minister.

1981   Jeane Kirkpatrick is appointed U.S. ambassador to the United Nations.

1981   Sandra Day O'Connor is first woman appointed to the U.S. Supreme Court.

1988   Benazir Bhutto is elected first female prime minister of Pakistan.

1994   Christine Todd Whitman becomes governor of New Jersey, later appointed to cabinet by President Bush in 2001.

1996   Madeleine Albright is appointed U.S. secretary of state.

Source: Originally adapted from the *Colorado Education Association Journal*, February–March 1991. Based on original work by the Arts and Entertainment Network.

Myths That Hinder Leadership Development

Few things pose a greater obstacle to leadership development than certain unsubstantiated and self-limiting beliefs about leadership. Therefore, before we begin examining what leadership and leadership development are in more detail, we will consider what they are not. We will examine several beliefs (we call them myths) that stand in the way of fully understanding and developing leadership.

Myth: *Good Leadership Is All Common Sense*

At face value, this myth says one needs only common sense to be a good leader. It also implies, however, that most if not all of the studies of leadership reported in scholarly journals and books only confirm what anyone with common sense already knows.

The problem, of course, is with the ambiguous term *common sense*. It implies a common body of practical knowledge about life that virtually any reasonable person with moderate experience has acquired. A simple experiment, however, may convince you that common sense may be less common than you think. Ask a few friends or acquaintances whether the old folk wisdom "Absence makes the heart grow fonder" is true or false. Most will say it is true. After that ask a different group whether the old folk wisdom "Out of sight, out of mind" is true or false. Most of that group will answer true as well, even though the two proverbs are contradictory.

A similar thing sometimes happens when people hear about the results of studies concerning human behavior. On hearing the results, people may say, "Who needed a study to learn that? I knew it all the time." However, several experiments by Slovic and Fischoff (1977) and Wood (1979) showed that events were much more surprising when subjects had to guess the outcome of an experiment than when subjects were told the outcome. What seems obvious after you know the results and what you (or anyone else) would have predicted beforehand are not the same thing. Hindsight is always 20/20.

> *Never reveal all of yourself to other people; hold back something in reserve so that people are never quite sure if they really know you.*
>
> Michael Korda,
> Author, editor

The point might become clearer with a specific example you may now try. Read the following paragraph:

> After World War II, the U.S. Army spent enormous sums of money on studies only to reach conclusions that, many believed, should have been apparent at the outset. One, for example, was that southern soldiers were better able to stand the climate in the hot South Sea islands than northern soldiers were.

This sounds reasonable, but there is just one problem; the statement above is exactly contrary to the actual findings. Southerners were no better than northerners in adapting to tropical climates (Lazarsfeld, 1949). Common sense can often play tricks on us.

Put a little differently, one of the challenges of understanding leadership may well be to know when common sense applies and when it does not. Do leaders need to act confidently? Of course. But they also need to be humble enough to recognize that others' views are useful, too. Do leaders need to persevere when times get tough? Yes. But they also need to recognize when times change and a new direction is called for. If leadership were nothing more than common sense, then there should be few, if any, problems in the workplace. However, we venture to guess you have noticed more than a few problems between leaders and followers. Effective leadership must be something more than just common sense.

Myth: Leaders Are Born, Not Made

Some people believe being a leader is either in one's genes or not; others believe that life experiences mold the individual, that no one is born a leader. Which

> *If you miss seven balls out of ten, you're batting three hundred and that's good enough for the Hall of Fame. You can't score if you keep the bat on your shoulder.*
>
> Walter B. Wriston,
> Chairman of Citicorp,
> 1970–1984

view is right? In a sense, both and neither. Both views are right in the sense that innate factors as well as formative experiences influence many sorts of behavior, including leadership. Yet both views are wrong to the extent they imply leadership is *either* innate *or* acquired; what matters more is how these factors *interact*. It does not seem useful, we believe, to think of the world as composed of two mutually exclusive types of people, leaders and nonleaders. It is more useful to address the ways in which each person can make the most of leadership opportunities he or she faces.

It may be easier to see the pointlessness of asking whether leaders are born or made by looking at an alternative question of far less popular interest: Are *college professors* born or made? Conceptually, the issues are the same, and here, too, the answer is that every college professor is both born *and* made. It seems clear enough that college professors are partly "born" since (among other factors) there is a genetic component to intelligence, and intelligence surely plays some part in becoming a college professor (well, at least a *minor* part!). But every college professor is also partly "made." One obvious way is that college professors must have advanced education in specialized fields; even with the right genes one could not become a college professor without certain requisite experiences. Becoming a college professor depends partly on what one is "born with" and partly on how that inheritance is shaped through experience. The same is true of leadership.

More specifically, research indicates that many cognitive abilities and personality traits are at least partly innate (McGue & Bouchard, 1990; Tellegen, Lykken, Bouchard, Wilcox, Segal, & Rich, 1988; McCrae & Foster, 1995). Thus, natural talents or characteristics may offer certain advantages or disadvantages to a leader. Take physical characteristics: A man's above-average height may increase others' tendency to think of him as a leader; it may also boost his own self-confidence. But it doesn't "make" him a leader. The same holds true for psychological characteristics which seem related to leadership. The very stability of certain characteristics over long periods of time (e.g., at school reunions people seem to have kept the same personalities we remember them as having years earlier) may reinforce the impression that our basic natures are fixed, but different environments nonetheless may nurture or suppress different leadership qualities.

Myth: The Only School You Learn Leadership from Is the School of Hard Knocks

Some people skeptically question whether leadership can develop through formal study, believing instead it can only be acquired through actual experience.

It is a mistake, however, to think of formal study and learning from experience as mutually exclusive or antagonistic. In fact, they complement each other. Rather than ask whether leadership develops from formal study or from real-life experience, it is better to ask what kind of study will help students learn to discern critical lessons about leadership from their own

> *Progress always involves risks. You can't steal second base and keep your foot on first.*
>
> Frederick B. Wilcox

experience. Approaching the issue in such a way recognizes the critical role of experience in leadership development, but it also admits that certain kinds of study and training can improve a person's ability to discern critical lessons about leadership from experience. It can, in other words, help accelerate the process of learning from experience.

We would argue that one of the advantages of formally studying leadership is that formal study provides students with a variety of ways of examining a particular leadership situation. By studying the different ways researchers have defined and examined leadership, students can use these definitions and theories to better understand what is going on in any leadership situation. For example, earlier in this chapter we used three different leadership definitions as a framework for describing or analyzing the situation facing Parrado and the remaining survivors of the plane crash, and each definition focused on a different aspect of leadership. These frameworks can similarly be applied to better understand the experiences one has as both a leader and a follower. We think it is very difficult for leaders, particularly novice leaders, to examine leadership situations from multiple perspectives, but we also believe developing this skill can help you become a better leader. Being able to analyze your experiences from multiple perspectives may be the greatest single contribution a formal course in leadership can give you.

An Overview of This Book

In order to fill the gaps between leadership research and practice, this book will critically review the major theories of leadership as well as provide practical advice about improving leadership. As our first steps in that journey, the next four chapters of the book describe how: (*a*) leadership is an interaction between the leader, the followers, and the situation; (*b*) various formal theories attempt to explain leadership effectiveness in terms of those interactions; (*c*) leadership develops through experience; and (*d*) leadership can be assessed and studied. The remainder of the book uses the leader–follower-situation interaction model described in Chapter 2 as a framework for organizing and discussing various theories and research findings related to leadership. The chapters in Part II focus on the leader, beginning with an examination of the issues of power and influence, then of ethics, values, and attitudes. Other chapters look at theories and research concerning the leader: how good and bad leaders differ in personality, intelligence, creativity, and behavior. Part II concludes by looking at charismatic leadership. Part III primarily focuses on the followers; it summarizes the research and provides practical advice on such topics as motivating subordinates and using delegation. Part IV examines how the situation affects the leadership process. Part V looks at several dozen specific leadership skills, including practical advice about handling specific leadership challenges. While Part V represents in one sense the "end" of the book, you may want to start reading about and practicing some of the skills right now.

> *Nurture your mind with great thoughts. To believe in the heroic makes heroes.*
> Benjamin Distaeli,
> British prime minister, 1874–1880

Summary

Although many definitions of leadership exist, we define leadership as the process of influencing others toward achieving group goals. The chapter also looks at the idea that leadership is both a science and an art. Because leadership is an immature science, researchers are still struggling to find out what the important questions in leadership are; we are far from finding conclusive answers to them. Even those individuals with extensive knowledge of the leadership research may be poor leaders. Knowing what to do is not the same as knowing when, where, and how to do it. The art of leadership concerns the skill of understanding leadership situations and influencing others to accomplish group goals. Formal leadership education may give individuals the skills to better understand leadership situations, and mentorships and experience may give individuals the skills to better influence others. Leaders must also weigh both rational and emotional considerations when attempting to influence others. Leadership sometimes can be accomplished through relatively rational, explicit, rule-based methods of assessing situations and determining actions. Nevertheless, there is also an emotional side of human nature that must be acknowledged. Leaders are often most effective when they affect people at both the emotional level and the rational level. The idea of leadership as a whole-person process can also be applied to the distinction often made between leaders and managers. Although leadership and management can be distinguished as separate functions, a more comprehensive picture of supervisory positions could be made by examining the overlapping functions of leaders and managers. Leadership does not occur without followers, and followership is an easily neglected component of the leadership process. Leadership is everyone's business and everyone's responsibility. Finally, learning certain conceptual frameworks for thinking about leadership can be helpful in making your own on-the-job experiences a particularly valuable part of your leadership development. Thinking about leadership can help you become a better leader than you are right now.

Key Terms

leadership   6
management   10

followership   11

Questions

1. We say leadership involves influencing organized groups toward goals. Do you see any disadvantages to restricting the definition to organized groups?
2. How would you define *leadership?*
3. Are some people the "leader type" and others not the "leader type"? If so, what in your judgment distinguishes them?
4. Identify several "commonsense" notions about leadership that, to you, are patently self-evident.
5. Does every successful leader have a valid theory of leadership?
6. Would you consider it a greater compliment for someone to call you a good manager or a good leader? Why? Do you believe you can be both?
7. Do you believe leadership can be studied scientifically? Why or why not?
8. To the extent leadership is an art, what methods come to mind for improving one's "art of leadership"?

Activity

"IF IT WAS

Describe the best leader you have personally -
known, or a favorite leader from history, a
novel, or a movie.

2 LEADERSHIP INVOLVES AN INTERACTION BETWEEN THE LEADER, THE FOLLOWERS, AND THE SITUATION

Introduction

I n Chapter 1, we defined leadership as the process of influencing an organized group toward accomplishing its goals. In this chapter, we will expand on this definition by introducing and describing a three-factor framework of the leadership process. We find this framework to be a useful heuristic both for analyzing various leadership situations and for organizing various leadership theories and supporting research. Therefore, the remainder of this chapter is devoted to providing an overview of the framework, and many of the remaining chapters of this book are devoted to describing the components of the framework in more detail.

Looking at Leadership through Several Lenses

In attempting to understand leadership, scholars understandably have spent much of their energy studying successful and unsuccessful leaders in government, business, athletics, and the military. Sometimes scholars have done this systematically by studying good leaders as a group (see Bennis & Nanus, 1985; Astin & Leland, 1991), and sometimes they have done this more subjectively, drawing lessons about leadership from the behavior or character of an individual leader such as Martin Luther King, Jr., Lee Iacocca, or Golda Meir. The latter approach is similar to drawing conclusions about leadership from observing individuals in one's own life, whether it be a high school coach, a mother or father, or one's boss. It may seem that studying the characteristics of effective leaders is the best way to learn about leadership, but such an approach tells only part of the story.

Consider an example. Suppose a senior minister was told by one of his church's wealthiest and consistently most generous members that he should not preach any more prochoice sermons on abortion. The wealthy man's contributions were a big reason a special mission project for the city's disadvantaged youth had been funded, and we might wonder whether the minister would be influenced by this outside pressure. Would he be a bad leader if he succumbed to this pressure and did not advocate what his conscience dictated? Would the minister be a bad leader if his continued public stand on abortion caused the wealthy man to leave the church and withdraw support for the youth program?

> *A leader is best*
> *When people barely know that he exists*
> *Not so good when people obey and acclaim him,*
> *Worst of all when they despise him.*
> *"Fail to honor people,*
> *They fail to honor you;"*
> *But of a good leader, who talks little,*
> *When his work is done, his aim fulfilled,*
> *They will all say, "We did this ourselves."*
>
> Lao-tzu

Although we can learn much about leadership by looking at leaders themselves, the preceding example suggests that studying only leaders provides just a partial view of the leadership process. Would we really know all we wanted to about the preceding example if we knew everything possible about the minister himself? His personality, his intelligence, his interpersonal skills, his theological training, his motivation? Is it not also relevant to understand a bit more, for example, about the community, his parishioners, the businessman, and so on? This points out how leadership depends on several factors, including the situation and the followers, not just the leader's qualities or characteristics. Leadership is more than just the kind of person the leader is or the things the leader does. Leadership is the process of influencing others toward the achievement of group goals; it is not just a person or a position.

If we use only leaders as the lens for understanding leadership, then we get a very limited view of the leadership process. We can expand our view of the leadership process by adding two other complementary lenses: the followers and the situation. However, using only the followers or the situation as a lens also would give us an equally limited view of the leadership process. In other words, the clearest picture of the leadership process occurs only when we use all three lenses to understand it.

The Interactional Framework for Analyzing Leadership

Perhaps the first researcher formally to recognize the importance of the leader, follower, and situation in the leadership process was Fred Fiedler (1967). Fiedler used these three components to develop his contingency model of leadership, a theory of leadership that will be discussed in more detail in Chapter 12. Although we recognize Fiedler's contributions, we owe perhaps even more to Hollander's (1978) transactional approach to leadership. We call our approach the **interactional framework.**

There are several aspects of this derivative of Hollander's (1978) approach that are worthy of additional comment. First, as seen in Figure 2.1, the framework

FIGURE 2.1

*An interactional
framework for
analyzing
leadership*

Source: Adapted from
E. P. Hollander,
Leadership Dynamics
(New York: Free Press,
1978).

> *The crowd will follow a leader who
> marches twenty steps in advance;
> but if he is a thousand steps in front
> of them, they do not see and do not
> follow him.*
>
> Georg Brandes

depicts leadership as a function of three elements—the **leader,** the **followers,** and the **situation.** Second, a particular leadership scenario can be examined using each level of analysis separately. Although this is a useful way to understand the leadership process, we can have an even better understanding of the process if we also examine the interactions among the three elements, or lenses, represented by the overlapping areas in the figure. For example, we can better understand the leadership process if we not only look at the leaders and the followers but also examine how leaders and followers affect each other in the leadership process. Similarly, we can examine the leader and the situation separately, but we can gain even further understanding of the leadership process by looking at how the situation can constrain or facilitate a leader's actions and how the leader can change different aspects of the situation in order to be more effective. Thus, a final important aspect of the framework is that leadership is the result of a complex set of interactions among the leader, the followers, and the situation. These complex interactions may be why broad generalizations about leadership are problematic; there are many factors that influence the leadership process (see Highlight 2.1).

An example of one such complex interaction between leaders and followers is evident in what has been called in-groups and out-groups. Sometimes there is a high degree of mutual influence and attraction between the leader and a few subordinates. These subordinates belong to the **in-group** and can be distinguished by their high degree of loyalty, commitment, and trust felt toward the leader. Other subordinates belong to the **out-group.** Leaders have considerably more influence with in-group followers than with out-group followers. However, this greater degree of influence also has a price. If leaders rely primarily on their formal authority to influence their followers (especially if they punish them), then leaders risk losing the high levels of loyalty and commitment followers feel toward them. There is even a theory of leadership called **Leader-Member Exchange Theory** that

Followership Styles

Highlight 2.1

The concept of different styles of leadership is reasonably familiar, but the idea of different styles of followership is relatively new. The very word *follower* has a negative connotation to many, evoking ideas of people who behave like sheep and need to be told what to do. Robert Kelly (1992), however, believes that followers, rather than representing the antithesis of leadership, are best viewed as collaborators with leaders in the work of organizations.

Kelly believes that different types of followers can be described in terms of two broad dimensions. One of them ranges from **independent, critical thinking** at one end to **dependent, uncritical thinking** on the other end. According to Kelly, the best followers think for themselves and offer constructive advice or even creative solutions. The worst followers need to be told what to do. Kelly's other dimension ranges from whether people are **active followers** or **passive followers** in the extent to which they are engaged in work. According to Kelly, the best followers are self-starters who take initiative for themselves, whereas the worst followers are passive, may even dodge responsibility, and need constant supervision.

Using these two dimensions, Kelly has suggested five basic styles of followership:

1. *Alienated followers* habitually point out all the negative aspects of the organization to others. While alienated followers may see themselves as mavericks who have a healthy skepticism of the organization, leaders often see them as cynical, negative, and adversarial.
2. *Conformist followers* are the "yes people" of organizations. While very active at doing the organization's work, they can be dangerous if their orders contradict societal standards of behavior or organizational policy. Often this style is the result of either the demanding and authoritarian style of the leader or the overly rigid structure of the organization.
3. *Pragmatist followers* are rarely committed to their group's work goals, but they have learned not to make waves. Because they do not like to stick out, pragmatists tend to be mediocre performers who can clog the arteries of many organizations. Because it can be difficult to discern just where they stand on issues, they present an ambiguous image with both positive and negative characteristics. In organizational settings, pragmatists may become experts in mastering the bureaucratic rules which can be used to protect them.
4. *Passive followers* display none of the characteristics of the exemplary follower (discussed next). They rely on the leader to do all the thinking. Furthermore, their work lacks enthusiasm. Lacking initiative and a sense of responsibility, passive followers require constant direction. Leaders may see them as lazy, incompetent, or even stupid. Sometimes, however, passive followers adopt

(continued)

this style to help them cope with a leader who expects followers to behave that way.

5. *Exemplary followers* present a consistent picture to both leaders and coworkers of being independent, innovative, and willing to stand up to superiors. They apply their talents for the benefit of the organization even when confronted with bureaucratic stumbling blocks or passive or pragmatist coworkers. Effective leaders appreciate the value of exemplary followers. When one of the authors was serving in a follower role in a staff position, he was introduced by his leader to a conference as "my favorite subordinate because he's a loyal 'No-Man.'"

Exemplary followers—high on both critical dimensions of followership—are critical to organizational success. Leaders, therefore, would be well advised to select people who have these characteristics and, perhaps even more importantly, *create the conditions that encourage these behaviors.*

describes these two kinds of relationships and how they affect the types of power and influence tactics leaders use (Graen & Cashman, 1975).

We will now examine each of the three main elements of the interactional framework in turn.

The Leader

This element primarily examines what the leader brings *as an individual* to the leadership equation. This can include unique personal history, interests, character traits, and motivation.

Madeleine Albright

For example, Madeleine Albright displayed an interest and ability in foreign affairs very early in her life. She was also always a hard-working and serious student, from her early school days, through her doctoral training, and as a junior member of the White House staff. In college, for example, she organized her meticulous notes into 15 different colored notebooks. Her self-discipline is further evident in the schedule she followed during her graduate school days. Already the mother of three daughters, she arose each day at 4:30 A.M. to work on her dissertation.

While the specific circumstances of her life were unique to Albright (as they are for each of us), perhaps the general portrait of her qualities may be fairly similar to that of many leaders. Leaders are *not* all alike, but they do tend to share many common characteristics. Research has shown that leaders differ from their followers, and effective leaders differ from ineffective leaders, on various personality traits, cognitive abilities, skills, and values (Stogdill, 1948, 1974;

Hogan, Curphy, & Hogan, 1994; Lord, DeVader, & Allinger, 1986; Kanter, 1983; Baltzell, 1980). Another way personality can affect leadership is through temperament, by which we mean whether the leader is generally calm or is instead prone to emotional outbursts. Leaders who have calm dispositions and do not attack or belittle others for bringing bad news are more likely to get complete and timely information from subordinates than are bosses who have explosive tempers and a reputation for killing the messenger.

Another important aspect of the leader is how he or she achieved leader status. Leaders who are appointed by superiors may have less credibility with subordinates and get less loyalty from them than leaders who are elected or emerge by consensus from the ranks of followers. Often, emergent or elected officials are better able to influence a group toward goal achievement because of the power conferred on them by their followers. However, both elected and emergent leaders need to be sensitive to their constituencies if they wish to remain in power.

Did Albright have instant credibility as secretary of state? Not with everyone, even though she'd already been serving as U.S. ambassador to the United Nations. Appointment, even by the president of the United States, does not free one from criticism. Many inside and outside the State Department believed a big reason she got the appointment was that Clinton wanted to appoint a woman to a very senior position. Albright may well have been the very best person for the position, but the varied interests of groups around her inevitably colored their opinions about her selection—for some positively, for others negatively.

More generally, a leader's experience or history in a particular organization is usually important to her or his effectiveness. For example, leaders promoted from within an organization, by virtue of being familiar with its culture and policies, may be ready to "hit the job running." In addition, leaders selected from within an organization are typically better known by others in the organization than are leaders selected from the outside. That is likely to affect, for better or worse, the latitude others in the organization are willing to give the leader; if the leader is widely respected for a history of accomplishment, then she may be given more latitude than a newcomer whose track record is less well known. On the other hand, many people tend to give new leaders a fair chance to succeed, and newcomers to an organization often take time to learn the organization's informal rules, norms, and "ropes" before they make any radical or potentially controversial decisions.

A leader's legitimacy also may be affected by the extent to which followers participated in the leader's selection. When followers have had a say in the selection or election of a leader they tend to have a heightened sense of psychological identification with her, but they also may have higher expectations and make more demands on her (Hollander & Offermann, 1990). We also might wonder what kind of support a leader has from his own boss. If followers sense their boss has a lot of influence with the higher-ups, then subordinates may be reluctant to take their complaints to higher levels. On the other hand, if the boss has little influence with higher-ups, subordinates may be more likely to make complaints to these levels.

BIZARRO   by DAN PIRARO

The foregoing examples highlight the sorts of insights one can gain about leadership by focusing on the individual leader as a level of analysis. Even if we were to examine the individual leader completely, however, our understanding of the leadership process would be incomplete. Consider another example, that of Konosuke Matsushita.

Konosuke Matsushita

Konosuke Matsushita began his company in 1917, its first product being a battery-powered electric bicycle lamp. By the 1930s Matsushita Electric had become a thriving corporation despite generally poor economic conditions in Japan. The company's success was due in large part to the fact that Matsushita himself was never one to become complacent with success. He always looked for ways to improve a product's quality or produce it at lower cost, and he always looked for ways to enhance the contribution of the people who worked at his company. Much of his success was due to his creative ways of involving employees in the leadership process. A half-century before concepts like

I'll be blunt, coach. I'm having a problem with this 'take a lap' thing of yours . . ."

Source:

employee empowerment and statements of corporate values became fashionable, he realized that a person's reason for working profoundly affects the quality of the person's work.

His own insight into this truth occurred during a visit in 1932 to a religious community in Japan. What caught his attention was the enthusiastic, reverent, and diligent work of people in the community despite the fact that they received no salary. He imagined what the impact on a corporation would be if work within it were made meaningful like a religion. He believed the employees would become both more satisfied and more productive (Kotter, 1997). This prompted deep personal reflection on the fundamental purposes of corporations, and just months later he made a historic speech to everyone in the company. In it he boldly proposed that "the mission of a manufacturer should be to overcome poverty, to relieve society as a whole from misery, and bring it wealth." He recognized such a mission might require even centuries to achieve, but he nonetheless challenged every person in the organization to accept what he considered a sacred calling. Just months later he went on to spell out a set of ideals which he urged all employees to commit themselves to. These were the ideals (Kotter, 1997):

> Service to the public.
> Fairness and honesty.
> Teamwork for the common cause.
> Untiring effort for improvement.
> Courtesy and humility.

Matsushita's speech was neither eloquent nor inspiring, but its message was consistent with how the organization had been run. More important, Matsushita's behavior following it was consistent with his vision and with the ideals he advocated. On an organizational level, he introduced systems like employee ownership of the company, and he encouraged what we now call empowerment among his workers. For example, in 1934 he told employees, "It's not enough to work conscientiously. No matter what kind of job [you have], you should think of yourself as being completely in charge of and responsible for your work, like being president of your own company" (Kotter, 1997, p. 124). Matsushita constantly stressed what he called "collective wisdom," the idea that decisions should be based on input from many employees, as an antidote to self-interested, arbitrary, or misguided actions by individual executives. And on a personal level, too, his interactions with others—his followers included—affirmed their importance and his concern for them.

The foregoing example highlights the sorts of insights one can gain about leadership by focusing on the followers as well as on the individual leader. Still another aspect of this level of analysis (i.e., The Leader) is reflected in Highlight 2.2. Even if we were to examine the individual leader completely, however, our understanding of the leadership process would be incomplete. Understanding leadership involves knowing about followers as well as about leaders.

The Followers

Matsushita knew that followers are a critical part of the leadership equation, but their role has not always been appreciated. For example, one can look at history and be struck by the contributions of extraordinary individual leaders. Even the major reviews of the leadership literature show that researchers have paid relatively little attention to the roles followers play in the leadership process (see Bass, 1981, 1990;

Changing Work Roles

Highlight 2.2

John Naisbitt called the 1990s the decade of women in leadership. Now, at the beginning of a new millennium, we might take stock of how women's roles at work have been changing. In the first place, in terms of sheer numbers women already are a large and indispensable element of contemporary work life. It is simply erroneous to think of women as a minority in the workforce. In fact, as many women in their 20s and 30s work as men; and while just 75 percent of men work, nearly 80 percent of women with no children under 18 do.

Furthermore, women not only compose a major portion of the workforce but also are assuming an increasingly significant place as leaders in it, and this will affect the nature of leadership and followership for everyone. Women are reaching a critical mass in all of the white-collar professions. For example, the percentage of women physicians has doubled in the past two decades. Women account for one-third of the MBA degrees and 40 percent of the law degrees awarded. They are advancing fastest in cutting-edge industries like computers and software, where in some cases women compose nearly one-third of a company's management force. And women are starting their own small businesses at a faster rate than men. Some have argued that for much of the 20th century, corporations have been based on a bureaucratic and authoritarian organizational model compatible with male psychology and that different structures and leadership styles necessarily will evolve as women assume an increasingly large role in corporate leadership. Whether and how men and women differ in their leadership and followership styles are open issues, but it is certain that women's roles in both arenas will keep growing.

Sources: J. Naisbitt and P. Aburdene, *Re-inventing the Corporation* (New York: Warner Books, 1985); and *Megatrends 2000* (New York: William Morrow, 1990).

Stogdill, 1974). However, we know that the followers' expectations, personality traits, maturity levels, levels of competence, and motivation affect the leadership process too (also see Highlight 2.3) (Sutton & Woodman, 1989; Burke, 1965; Moore, 1976; Scandura, Graen, & Novak, 1986; Sales, Levanoni, & Saleh, 1984).

The nature of followers' motivation to do their work is also important. Workers who share a leader's goals and values, and who feel intrinsically rewarded for performing a job well, might be more likely to work extra hours on a time-critical project than those whose motivation is solely monetary.

Even the number of followers reporting to a leader can have significant implications. For example, a store manager having three clerks working for him can spend more time with each of them (or on other things) than can a

Adjusting to New Roles

Highlight 2.3

Women are rapidly moving into leadership roles that previously had been occupied only by men. Such change, exciting and positive if also overdue, is accompanied by inevitable adjustments. The following is one contemporary woman's account of how it feels to be a trailblazer, a woman leader in a traditionally male-dominated field: the ministry.

"What do you do, Nancy?" the innocent, yet bold, six-year-old asked.

"I am a minister, Jason."

"You're not a ministerette?"

"No, just a minister, Jason. It doesn't matter if you are a girl or a boy . . . it is the same word."

"Oh," Jason replied. "I've never heard of that."

Jason is not alone. And his company is not only those in his age range. To most adults, youths, and children alike, a minister is a man. For anyone who is a pastor, a priest, a rabbi, or who is titled as "clergy," it is virtually assumed that person is male.

I am a woman and I am a minister. I could put those in reverse order, but I was indeed a woman first, and almost everyone I know uses the gender-then-title order: "Our lady minister," "Woman pastor," "Female clergy." Despite our seminaries and theological schools having an average female population of one-third, and despite the fact some Protestant denominations began ordaining women over 30 years ago, it seems strange that I am still a novelty to the average American. Yet, I am reminded of that constantly.

Part of the problem lies in the limitations of language, but even more, the problem lies in the limitations we place on ourselves and on those around us. Like it or not, clergy is not a traditional role for women. For most folks, there is really no good reason to restrict the ministry to males, only those seven words we hear all too often: "We have always done it that way." In being a minister, and in being female, I am breaking tradition. Not only am I breaking into a traditionally man's world; I am breaking out of a traditionally female world. And like so many women in nontraditional roles, I at times try to fill too many shoes. One of my greatest frustrations is the assumption that because I am female, I must be more sensitive, more caring, more concerned about cooking and our home, and so forth, than my husband. Those assumptions are almost as bad as those which assume I cannot be a good preacher because I am an alto and not a bass. Why cannot people accept me as a minister, as a human being—with all the talents, personality quirks, faults, gifts, and eccentricities thereof?

manager responsible for eight clerks and a separate delivery service; chairing a task force with 5 members is a different leadership activity than chairing a task force with 18 members. Still other relevant variables include followers' trust in the leader and their confidence (or not) that he or she is interested in their well-being.

Changing Roles for Followers

The preceding examples illustrate just a few ways in which followers compose an important and complementary level of analysis for understanding leadership. Such examples should point out how leadership must be understood in the context of a particular group of followers as well as in terms of an individual leader. Now, more than ever before, understanding followers is central to understanding leadership. That is because the leader–follower relationship is in a period

> *If you act like an ass, don't get insulted if people ride you.*
> Yiddish proverb

of dynamic change (Lippitt, 1982; Block, 1992; Hollander, 1994). One reason for this changing relationship is an increasing pressure on all kinds of organizations to function with reduced resources. Reduced resources and company downsizing have reduced the number of managers and increased their span of control, which in turn leaves followers to pick up many of the functions traditionally performed by leaders. Another reason is a trend toward greater power sharing and decentralized authority in organizations, which in turn creates greater interdependence among organizational subunits and increased need for collaboration among them. Furthermore, the nature of problems faced by many organizations is becoming so complex and the changes are becoming so rapid that more and more people are required to solve them.

These trends suggest several different ways in which followers can take on new leadership roles and responsibilities in the future. For one thing, followers can become much more proactive in their stance toward organizational problems. When facing the discrepancy between the way things are in an organization and the way they could or should be, followers can play an active and constructive role collaborating with leaders in solving problems. In general, making organizations better is a task that needs to be "owned" by followers as well as by leaders.

In addition to helping solve organizational problems, followers can better contribute to the leadership process by becoming better skilled at "influencing upward." Because followers are often at the level where many organizational problems occur, they can provide leaders with relevant information so that good solutions are implemented. Although it is true that some leaders need to become better listeners, it is also true that many followers need training in expressing ideas to superiors more clearly and positively. Still another way followers can assume a greater share of the leadership challenge in the future is by staying flexible and open to opportunities. The future portends more change, not less, and followers who face change with positive anticipation and an openness to self-development will be particularly valued and rewarded (Senge, 1990).

Thus, to an ever increasing degree, leadership must be understood in terms of both leader variables and follower variables, as well as the interactions among them. But even that is not enough. In addition to understanding the leader and the followers, we must also understand the particular situations in which leaders and followers find themselves.

The Situation

The situation is the third critical part of the leadership equation. Even if we knew all we could know about a given leader and a given set of followers, leadership makes sense only in the context of how the leader and followers interact in a given situation (see Highlight 2.4).

Berkeley in the 1960s

Highlight 2.4

The 1960s were a period of dissent and conflict, and perhaps even today no place epitomizes the decade more than Berkeley, California. But Berkeley did not always have a radical reputation.

The Berkeley campus of the huge University of California system had not always been a center of student protest and large-scale demonstrations. For a long time, it had been relatively sedate and conservative, even if also quite large; more than 20,000 students attended Berkeley in 1960. Campus leaders were clean-cut students who belonged to fraternities and sororities. Berkeley changed, however, in the fall of 1964 when a relatively small number of students launched what became known as the Free Speech Movement. Subsequent protests at other campuses across the country, and later globally, are traceable to the Free Speech Movement at Berkeley. One of its leaders was Mario Savio.

The sources of conflict and radicalism at Berkeley were many, including civil rights and the Vietnam War. But protest in Berkeley first erupted over the issue of whether students could solicit donations and distribute political materials near campus. Whether students could solicit donations or distribute materials on campus had been settled earlier; they could not. In response to having been ordered off campus, however, some student groups set up card tables just off campus, between the university's impressive Sproul Plaza and Berkeley's Telegraph Avenue, with its exciting and bohemian milieu of bookstores and coffeehouses.

Perhaps because their appearance so near the campus offended university officials—the student workers were rarely dressed or groomed in the clean-cut image favored by conservative administrators—even this activity eventually was prohibited. Outraged, a few students defiantly set up tables back in Sproul Plaza, right in the heart of the campus. Disturbed at this open rebuke to its authority, the university directed police to arrest one of the disobedient students. It was October 1, 1964, the birth of the Free Speech Movement.

Presumably, university officials believed this show of force on their part would dishearten the band of student protesters and break them up. As the arrested student got into the waiting police car, however, someone shouted, "Sit down!" and hundreds of other students immediately did just that. They sat down on the plaza right where they were, effectively blocking the car's movement. The police and administration had never before confronted such massive defiance, and for 32 hours the car stayed put (with the "prisoner," Jack Weinberg, inside) while demonstrators used its roof as a podium from which to speak to the crowd. One who climbed up to speak several times, and who clearly had a gift for energizing the crowd, was Mario Savio. In many ways, the Free Speech Movement, which pitted a rigid university bureaucracy against increasing numbers of alienated students, became a confrontation between just two people: Mario Savio and the university's brilliant but aloof president, Clark Kerr. It was not, however, a fair fight.

As W. J. Rorabaugh has observed, Kerr didn't stand a chance. The student activists were prepared for war, and Kerr wasn't. He was out of touch with the sentiments of increasing numbers of students, sentiments that in part were a direct result of the university's continuing neglect of undergraduate education at the expense of graduate study and government-sponsored research.

The students, on the other hand, had a clear objective—the freedom to be politically active on campus (i.e., free speech). Furthermore, many were politically experienced, seasoned by their participation in civil rights marches in the South. They understood the politics of protest, crowd psychology, the importance of the media, and how to maintain spirit and discipline in their own ranks. Thus, many ingredients for a successful social movement were present. All that was needed was a spark to ignite them and a leader to channel them.

Mario Savio was not a typical undergraduate. His commitment to social reform already was deep, and his experiences were broad. Raised in a devout Catholic family, he had worked in rural Mexico for a church relief organization and had taught in a school for black children in Mississippi. He was proud, cocky, and defiant. It was his ability to articulate his rage, however, that set Savio apart. He could give words and reason to the frustration and anger others were only feeling. Interestingly, Savio was a very different person in private than in public. In private, he seemed cold, hesitant, and self-doubting, but in front of a crowd he could be inspiring.

He may have been at his best at a protest rally in December 1964. Here is what it was like to be in Berkeley in the 60s, listening to a new kind of student leader, one giving voice to the sense of powerlessness and frustration with modern life, which would be a common theme in student revolts throughout the rest of the decade:

> There is a time when the operation of the machine becomes so odious, makes you so sick at heart, that you can't take part; you can't even passively take part, and you've got to put your bodies upon the gears and upon the wheels, upon the levers, upon all the apparatus and you've got to make it stop. And you've got to indicate to the people who run it, to the people that own it, that unless you're free, the machines will be prevented from working at all (Rorabaugh, p. 31).

Earlier that year, Savio had written, "I'm tired of reading history. Now I want to make it." He did. Try to analyze the emergence of Mario Savio in terms of the interactional framework.

Source: W. J. Rorabaugh, *Berkeley at War* (New York: Oxford University Press, 1989).

The situation may be the most ambiguous aspect of the leadership framework since it can refer to anything from the specific task a group is engaged in all the way to broad situational contexts such as the remote predicament of the Andes survivors. It can include the business challenges facing Matsushita Electric in the 1930s, the complex considerations a president weighs in selecting his cabinet, as in Madeleine Albright's case, or the challenge of establishing a working relationship with your new commander in chief, as in Colin Powell's case.

Madeleine Albright

Let's examine the situation surrounding Albright's selection as secretary of state a bit more closely. We've already noted that President Clinton was probably motivated, at least in part, by the desire to do something dramatic and symbolic—appoint a woman to be secretary of state for the first time ever. Thus, the larger political situation *around* Albright probably created a ripe opportunity for a woman of her talents and credentials to be appointed. On the other hand, there were also pressures from within the State Department working in the opposite direction. Albright had to overcome what may be the hardest "glass ceiling" for women anywhere, that in the State Department. Some saw the Albright appointment initially as mostly cosmetics, maybe good politics but not a choice of substance.

Not that we should consider gender a negative for Madeleine Albright. She certainly had not, except in the fact that she may have had to work harder than her male counterparts to rise to the level she did as secretary of state. She does not hide her gender, and sometimes uses it effectively to lighten situations, as when she said to the outgoing secretary of state, Warren Christopher, "I only hope that my heels can fill your shoes." This is not to say Albright was a "gentle" secretary, either in her diplomatic role internationally or in her managerial role within the State Department. Very early on in her tenure, she stunned State Department old-timers with her toughness (which may say as much about them as her!).

One other aspect of the situation surrounding Madeleine Albright's selection is interesting to consider: how she had expanded (perhaps even engineered) her network of professional associations over time, *increasing her visibility to others.* For many years before she became ambassador to the United Nations, Albright hosted high-powered dinner discussions at her home near Washington, D.C. Her home was a gathering place for power brokers in the Democratic Party and diplomatic establishments. Significantly, among those she hosted was then-governor of Arkansas Bill Clinton.

Colin Powell

We can also understand the interactional framework better by looking more closely at Colin Powell's situation (Powell, 1995). In November of 1992, Bill Clinton had been elected president but had not yet assumed office. He asked to see Colin Powell, then chairman of the Joint Chiefs of Staff. Powell's political affiliation and preferences at that time were unknown, but he had served faithfully under Presidents Reagan and Bush and had successfully orchestrated a wartime victory for President Bush in Operation Desert Storm.

The president-elect began by complimenting Powell about a speech he had made, and inquired about a few matters of national defense. Clinton particularly asked for Powell's thoughts about a possible nominee to secretary of defense; in other words, about the general's potential next boss. Clinton was inclined to name Congressman Les Aspin, pointedly complimenting Aspin's intelligence. Despite Clinton's evident intent to name Aspin, however, Powell said he had reservations about the nomination. He, too, complimented Aspin's intelligence but expressed concern that Aspin's disorganized management style would be inappropriate for a person having responsibility for such a large bureaucracy. The two went on to discuss other issues for over an hour, but when Powell rose to leave there was one more thing he needed to say. He felt he needed to address a political promise Clinton had made during the presidential campaign: a promise to end the ban on gays in the military. He said the senior military leadership didn't want it lifted, military people in general didn't want it lifted, and most in Congress didn't want it lifted. The concern, Powell stressed, was privacy. He wondered how the ban could be made to work in the close circumstances of living in army barracks or on naval ships. He asked the president-elect not to make this issue the first priority of the new administration.

> *You've got to give loyalty down, if you want loyalty up.*
>
> Donald T. Regan,
> Former CEO and White House chief of staff

Despite Powell's counsel, however, it did become so, and a highly controversial one at that. Through both private negotiation and public media questioning, both Powell and Clinton remained committed to their respective positions. Eventually, a compromise policy, popularly known as "don't ask, don't tell," was instituted that is still considered hopelessly flawed by many on both sides. But now let us look at this situation from the perspective of the interactional framework.

First of all, note how much more complex the situation of their meeting was than a mere first meeting between two successful men. One of them was the top military leader in the world at that time, the other would soon be his commander in chief by virtue of free election in a constitutional government which subordinates the military to civilian authority (just to be clear, this is *not* the case for most countries throughout history). In their first face-to-face meeting, which would set the tone for their future working relationship, Powell disagreed with several proposals favored by Clinton (frank and open disagreement, of course, is often the sign of a *constructive* relationship, and that is most likely the way the counsel was both given and received). Perhaps more significantly, both felt obligated to different courses of action and to different groups of stakeholders. Clinton, as a politician and new world leader, must also have been concerned about how the controversy would affect national and international perceptions of his leadership and credibility.

So just what was the situation here? It was the constitutionally mandated nature of their authority relationship. It was the interpersonal context of one person giving unpopular feedback or advice to someone else. It was the very real pressure being exerted on each man independently by different constituencies having different agendas. It was all these things, and more. Leadership, here as everywhere, involves the leader, the followers, and the complex situation they're a part of.

Leadership and Management Revisited

In Chapter 1 we looked at the relationship between leadership and management, and between leaders and managers. While these terms are not mutually exclusive, they do refer to a person's distinctive *style* and *approach.* Even in a particular role, two people may approach it differently; one more like a leader, the other more like a manager. The governor of one state, for example, may function more as a leader, whereas the governor of another state may function more as a manager (and not because there's anything different about the two states). It will be helpful to revisit those concepts in the context of the interactional framework.

Let's begin by reviewing some of the distinctions Bennis makes between leaders and managers.

Leaders	Managers
Innovate.	Administer.
Develop.	Maintain.
Inspire.	Control.
Long-term view.	Short-term view.
Ask what and why.	Ask how and when.
Originate.	Initiate.
Challenge the status quo.	Accept the status quo.
Do the right things.	Do things right.

Bennis is hardly alone in contrasting leaders and managers. Numerous other scholars echo the idea of a basic distinction between leadership and management. Kotter (1990), for example, described management in terms of coping with complexity, and leadership in terms of coping with change. Kotter noted how managerial practices and procedures can be traced to the 20th-century phenomenon of large organizations and the need to bring order and consistency to their functioning. Renewed interest in leadership, on the other hand, springs from the challenge of maintaining organizational success in an increasingly dynamic world. He said most U.S. corporations today, for example, are overmanaged and underled; but that "strong leadership with weak management is no better" (p. 103). Fairholm (1991) emphasized still other differences between leadership and management when he wrote that leadership and management are different in purpose, knowledge base, required skills, and goals. We distinguish leaders as more personal in their orientation to group members than managers. They are more global in their thinking. Leaders, we suggest, focus on values, expectations, and context. Managers, on the other hand, focus on control and results. Leaders impact followers and constituent groups in a way that allows volitional activity of followers, not through formal authority mechanisms . . . Managers give clear direction, make solitary assignments, and work hard for cooperation. The leader communicates indirectly, gives overlapping and ambiguous assignments, and sometimes sets employees up for internecine strife—to test loyalty and the leader's personal strength. Leaders value cooperation, not just coordination. They foster ideas of unity, equality, justice, and fairness in addition to efficiency and effectiveness, the bastions of management value. (p. 40)

Such differences are just what our framework is all about—**interactions.** In other words, the differences between leaders and managers, or between leadership and management, involve more than just differences between types of individuals. The differences extend to how such individuals *interact with* their followers and the situations they confront. Let's explore how these distinctions affect the other two elements of the framework.

Leader-Follower-Situation Interactions

Leaders create environments within which followers' innovations and creative contributions are welcome. Followers feel a stake in *shaping* something new, not just maintaining a status quo. Leaders also encourage growth and development in their followers in ways broader than what we might call mere job training (e.g., encouraging a follower to take on something really new, something that would stretch the follower but may involve failure on the task; or taking on a developmental experience not directly tied to the follower's present job requirements). Leaders generally are more interested in the big picture of followers' work, and tend to assess their followers' performance less formally and less in terms of specific criteria than managers, and more in terms of holistic, personal, idiosyncratic, or intuitive criteria. Leaders motivate followers more personally and through more personal and intangible factors (e.g., through inspiration, or the reward of just being able to work with the leader, or on a particular project). Leaders redefine the parameters of tasks and responsibilities, both for individual followers and for the entire group. In that sense, leaders actively *change* the situations they're in rather than just optimize their group's adaptation to it. They are forever "moving outside the constraints of structure" (Fairholm, p. 39). Such redefinitions also may occur through taking a long-term rather than a shorter-term perspective, through accentuating critical values or ends, or by marshaling energy to cope with some new threat.

Manager-Follower-Situation Interactions

Managers are more likely to emphasize routinization and control of followers' behavior. This might be expressed in terms of greater emphasis on making sure followers conform to policies or procedures ("doing it the way we've

> *All men have some weak points and the more vigorous and brilliant a person may be, the more strongly these weak points stand out. It is highly desirable, even essential, therefore, for the more influential members of a general's staff not to be too much like the general.*
>
> Major General Hugo Baron von Freytag-Loringhoven, Anti-Hitler conspirator

always done it") or in a tendency to assign narrower rather than broader tasks for followers to perform. It might be expressed in lesser degrees of decision-making discretion or autonomy given to followers, as in a manager's tendency to review *details* of work for them. Managers tend to assess their followers' performance in terms of explicit, fairly specific job descriptions. Managers motivate followers more with extrinsic, even contractual consequences, both positive and negative. Managers tend to accept the definitions of situations presented to them. They might be unlikely, for example, to reorient a group's task or mission in a whole new direction; or to change the whole culture of an organization. When managers do change things, they would be more likely to effect change officially, through control tactics such as developing new policies or procedures.

In reading the preceding paragraphs, it may seem to you that it's better to be a leader than a manager (or, perhaps, vice versa). But such a conclusion would ignore important characteristics of the followers. In some situations leaders are successful and managers are not, but in other situations the opposite is true. Consider, for example, one of Bennis's prototypical leaders: an inspiring individual having a vision of major institutional change that can be achieved only through the energy and creativity of committed followers. Such an inspiring individual may be thwarted, nonetheless, unless her followers share her value-based vision. If they are motivated primarily by economic incentives and are satisfied with their present lot, then the leader may fail to achieve her vision. The whole idea of *interaction* is that the effectiveness of any particular leader approach can be understood only in the context of certain follower and situational conditions. To return to Bennis's distinctions, managers emphasize *stability* whereas leaders emphasize *change*. Managers emphasize consistency and predictability in follower behavior (doing what's expected, doing things right), whereas leaders emphasize *changing* followers. That may mean transforming them or getting them to do more than they thought they could or thought they would. We'll see a similar distinction in Chapter 13 when we contrast transactional and transformational leadership (Bass, 1985).

Leadership, Management, and the Disney Brothers

Walt Disney is surely one of the most familiar names in the world (see Highlight 2.5). Roy Disney is not. Roy was Walt's brother, and he played a vital but different role in the success of the Disney enterprises. In many ways you can think of the differences between them in terms of the distinctions we've been making between leadership and management. In many ways Walt was the creative leader, Roy the manager or "financial guy." The success of the Disney enterprises was due to their *complementary* contributions, and their story provides an interesting illustration of how leaders interact with their followers and situations differently than managers do (Snyder, Dowd, & Houghton, 1994).

The Creative Genius of Walt Disney

Highlight 2.5

Walt Disney's creative genius has imprinted our cultural landscape with characters and stories more familiar to many people than their neighbors. Read through this brief description of his life and career, and as you do so think about what different factors contributed to his effectiveness as a creative leader.

Disney built a major studio that produced motion picture masterpieces like *Snow White* and *Fantasia*. Throughout his career, he pioneered technical innovations that set new standards for the industry. These innovations included introducing sound and color to cartoons, inventing special cameras to create new effects in films, and developing sophisticated robotics. He changed the nature of amusement parks in America with Disneyland and Walt Disney World. In fact, these parks are so visionary they've been required study at many schools of architecture. Far more than "fun places," they are serious experiments in urban design, testing radical ideas for solving the problems facing our cities.

For example, the Magic Kingdom at Walt Disney World is really a small city built on top of a huge service-and-utility tunneled infrastructure. The entire park was designed from the start with a quiet and efficient monorail system for mass transit. The area is unique, probably in the world, for setting nearly one-third of its acreage aside for conservation of natural habitat. It is, in sum, a city built with people in mind and a plan for the future. Disney originally intended that EPCOT be a test bed of concepts of planning and living that would always be 25 years ahead of its time and always evolving (EPCOT stands for Experimental Prototype Community of Tomorrow). Walt Disney, who once experimented with drawings that move, became a designer of communities for the 21st century (P. Blake, 1972, 1973).

What kind of a person was Walt Disney? What enabled him to accomplish all this? Certainly his creativity and resourcefulness were apparent early in his life. He was a cartoonist for his school paper, and while serving overseas as an ambulance driver during World War I (he was too young for actual military duty), he built a small business selling souvenir German helmets that appeared to have weathered rough combat. (He actually used new helmets painted to look old and used. A partner pounded dents in the helmets and shot holes in them; they even got human hair from a barber to put in the holes!) (Miller, 1956).

Disney always was committed to making his product the best, from souvenir war helmets to his films. He continuously experimented with new ways of doing things, innovating new technologies to produce the effects he wanted. In the 1930s, he had his special effects staffs make slow-motion pictures of bubbles popping, smoke blowing, and balls bouncing to improve their animation of such actions. He developed rigorous training programs for his animation staffs to help them draw more lifelike cartoons, like learning to blur fast-moving figures. And he had an uncanny sense of timing. For example, Disney profited from the emergence of

(continued)

sound and color in live-action film by seeing their potential application to ani-mated subjects sooner and more clearly than others. He acquired exclusive rights to the Technicolor process because he showed commitment to the new technique when other cartoon producers were skeptical (Thomas, 1976).

Disney had a genius for spotting talent, and he surrounded himself with other creative people, even eccentric ones. After he found them, though, he was a taskmaster. At work, he was all business, not what you might call a people person. He did not like dealing with others' personal problems, and he had a well-known temper. One of Disney's biographers wrote the following:

> He was incapable of small talk. His employees learned not to engage him in the banter that animators used as relief from the tedium of drawing. His mind was too involved with the problems of the moment—a storyline that defied solution, a cartoon that failed to evoke laughs at the preview, an overdue check from Columbia Pictures that threatened next week's payroll. His workers learned not to be offended if he passed them in the hallway without a word; they knew that he was preoccupied with a studio problem. (Thomas, 1976, p. 111)

Disney also had a sixth sense about what would appeal broadly to the Ameri-can culture, young and old. He trusted his intuition and judgment to an extraordi-nary degree, and took great risks with his studio to back them up. Furthermore, he made sure that every project had his personal stamp on it, including such details as what voices to use for the various characters. He was unique in Hollywood for the close personal supervision he gave his work. Walt Disney's name on a film meant it had received his individual touch (Thomas, 1976).

One of Walt's distinctive qualities was his drive to experiment and find new ways to improve motion picture quality. He was an innovator himself, but even more importantly he encouraged his staff to be innovative. His studio was always "on the move." He wanted it to be on the technological cutting edge of animation art and never fall prey to a cut-and-dried way of doing things. From the early days, Walt handled the creative side of Disney productions whereas Roy handled the job of securing financing for their cartoons. Walt was never interested in making money as an end in itself, but rather as a means to pro-ducing ever-better films. He would not compromise his sense of film quality to increase profit. In fact, he was a gambler willing to risk all for an idea he believed in. Walt's enthusiasm for the creative process was infectious and spread to his staff, who themselves were more dedicated to their art than to the bottom line. Walt's staff believed they were pioneers who were changing the very nature of mass media. He created an energetic and informal environment; he resisted rigid procedures and bureaucracy, yet his staff believed he ran the best studio in the world. One way Walt inspired such commitment among his followers was through his own commitment to *their* development and creative involvement in the studio's work. He brought out the best in them, a quality of work beyond what they believed themselves capable of. He wanted all the people working for him to feel they were making indispensable contributions to the overall project.

He encouraged his staff to use their *own* skills to devise original solutions to challenges rather than merely find out what he wanted them to do.

An interesting case in point of the difference between a leader's and manager's orientation may be in the disagreement Walt and Roy Disney had over Walt's idea of a new amusement park. What we now know as Disneyland, and may incorrectly assume looked like a surefire success as soon as Walt proposed it, was initially opposed by Roy. Roy thought it was just another one of Walt's crazy ideas, and was only willing to risk $10,000 of studio money on what he thought was a harebrained project. Trusting his own vision more than his brother's risk-averse conservatism, Walt scraped together the money needed to finance Disneyland—in part by borrowing on his own life insurance. Even after Walt's death the differences between him and his brother illustrate what's different between leadership and management. Without Walt's creative leadership, the studio fell under the management of "Roy men" who produced moderately successful but uninspired formula pieces for two decades. Only under Michael Eisner, a "Walt man" who understands popular culture, has the studio regained a leading place in American business (see Highlight 2.6).

A Final Word

Fairholm (1991) argued that organizations may need *two different kinds of people at the helm:* good leaders *and* good managers. He wrote, "We need competent, dedicated managers to provide continuity of process, to insure program productivity, and to control and schedule the materials needed for production or service delivery. We also need people who can infuse the organization with common values that define the organization, determine its character, link it to the larger society, and ensure its long-term survival" (p. 41). This view is certainly consistent with the success the two Disney brothers had bringing distinctive but complementary sets of competencies and values to their studio. But do examples like this prove that leaders and managers represent inherently different sorts of talents and interests? We think Kotter (1990) is on solid ground when he advises organizations preparing people for executive jobs to "ignore the recent literature that says people cannot manage and lead" (p. 104). He said they should try to develop leader-managers. In other words, it may be useful to distinguish between the functions of leadership and management but still *develop* those complementary functions in the same individuals.

This point may be particularly important with regard to developing the talents of *younger* leader-managers. It would seem inappropriately narrow and limiting for a young person to define himself or herself as "the manager type" or "the leader type." Premature self-definitions of being a leader *or* manager present such *reductio ad absurdum* eventualities as foreclosing real developmental opportunities (e.g., "I guess I shouldn't seek that student body position since it's a leadership role, and I'm really more the management type") or as inappropriate reactions to the sorts of job responsibilities typical for a person early in her career (e.g., "Boss, you've been giving me too many management-type

Passing the Reins at Disney

Highlight 2.6

The mantle of leadership at the Walt Disney Company is now in the hands of Michael Eisner. What was his path to that position, and what has been his imprint on the Disney tradition?

In upbringing, Eisner's personal history was quite different from Walt Disney's. Whereas Disney's family struggled financially, Eisner was born into affluence. Still, Eisner's family stressed discipline and thrift. Family connections did, however, help Eisner secure his first job in show business, as an usher for NBC in 1963. After graduating from college, he did such things for the network as keeping track of how frequently different commercials aired, and giving weekend traffic reports.

Eisner's big opportunity came in 1966, when he was picked by 24-year-old Barry Diller, a vice president at ABC (a relatively young network at the time), to refashion the network's children's programming on Saturday mornings. As it turned out, Eisner had a natural aptitude for selecting popular TV programs. He didn't study kids' viewing tastes, he simply trusted his own. It was a successful strategy; in five years he had taken charge of determining ABC's prime time schedule. Eisner succeeded there, too, but eventually both he and Diller left ABC to join Paramount Pictures. Among many successful films he launched at Paramount were those in the Indiana Jones series, beginning with *Raiders of the Lost Ark.*

With his demonstrated grasp of mass appeal, the board of Walt Disney Productions believed Eisner might be the creative genius to return the company to glory. It also brought on another new face, Frank Wells, known for his business savvy. The Eisner-Wells team represented a chemistry of talent echoing the earlier partnership of Walt and Roy Disney.

That is not to say their first days at Disney felt comfortable to the old-timers. In fact, Eisner and Wells shook things up, believing the organization had grown too soft and comfortable, even lazy. They brought a new style of management and work to the company. For example, Eisner instituted marathon meetings for generating creative ideas. Eisner's philosophy was to get members of a group to become uninhibited in expressing ideas to each other, a purpose furthered by requiring everyone to work for grueling hours together with little food and water. Difficult and different as the meetings were at first, the approach worked. The management culture at Disney was changing. There were other changes, too. Eisner recruited filmmaker George Lucas, the genius behind the *Star Wars* series, to develop a new ride for the parks that would appeal to teenagers. On other fronts he has vastly expanded the company's hotel operations, and broadened the company's film productions. The result? The company is again regarded as one of the most successful and visionary in the world.

Source: R. Grover, *The Disney Touch* (Burr Ridge: Irwin, 1997).

tasks, and I see myself more as a leader around here"). It seems prudent to note the commonalities—as shown in Figure 1.1—between leadership and management and not focus exclusively on the differences between them, *especially in the early stages of a person's professional development.*

There Is No Simple Recipe for Effective Leadership

As noted above, it is important to understand how the three domains of leadership interact—how the leader, the followers, and the situation are all part of the leadership process. Understanding their interaction is necessary before you can draw valid conclusions from the leadership you observe around you. When you see a leader's behavior (even when it may appear obviously effective or ineffective to you), you should not automatically conclude something good or bad about the leader, or what is the right way or wrong way leaders should act. You need to think about the effectiveness of that behavior in *that* context with *those* followers.

As obvious as the above sounds, we often ignore it. Too frequently, we just look at the leader's behavior and conclude that he or she is a good leader or a bad leader apart from the context. For example, suppose you observe a leader soliciting advice from subordinates. Obviously, it seems unreasonable to conclude that good leaders always ask for advice or that leaders who do not frequently ask for advice are not such good leaders. The appropriateness of seeking input from subordinates depends on many factors, such as the nature of the problem or the subordinates' familiarity with the problem. It may be that the subordinates have a lot more experience with this particular problem, and soliciting their input is the correct action to take in this situation.

> *Little things affect little minds.*
> Benjamin Disraeli

Consider another example. Suppose you hear that a leader disapproved a subordinate's request to take time off to attend to family matters. Was this bad leadership because the leader did not appear to be "taking care of her people"? Was it good leadership because she did not let personal matters interfere with the mission? Again, you cannot make an intelligent decision about the leader's actions by just looking at the behavior itself. You must always assess leadership in the context of the leader, the followers, and the situation.

The following statements about leaders, followers, and the situation make the above points a bit more systematically.

- A leader may need to respond to various followers differently in the same situation.
- A leader may need to respond to the same follower differently in different situations.
- Followers may respond to various leaders quite differently.

- Followers may respond to each other differently with different leaders.
- Two leaders may have different perceptions of the same followers or situations.

Conclusion: Drawing Lessons from Experience

All of the above leads to one conclusion: The right behavior in one situation is not necessarily the right behavior in another situation. It does *not* follow, however, that any behavior is appropriate in any situation. Although we may not be able to agree on the one best behavior in a given situation, we often can agree on some clearly inappropriate behaviors. Saying that the right behavior for a leader depends on the situation is not the same thing as saying it does not matter what the leader does. It merely recognizes the complexity among leaders, followers, and situations. This recognition is a helpful first step in drawing meaningful lessons about leadership from experience.

Summary

Leadership is a process in which leaders and followers interact dynamically in a particular situation or environment. Leadership is a broader concept than that of leaders, and the study of leadership must involve more than just the study of leaders as individuals. The study of leadership must also include two other areas: the followers and the situation. In addition, the interactive nature of these three domains has become increasingly important in recent years and can help us to better understand the changing nature of leader–follower relationships and the increasingly greater complexity of situations leaders and followers face. Because of this complexity, now, more than ever before, effective leadership cannot be boiled down to a simple and constant recipe. It is still true, however, that good leadership makes a difference, and it can be enhanced through greater awareness of the important factors influencing the leadership process.

Key Terms

interactional framework 23
leader 24
followers 24
situation 24
in-group 24
out-group 24

Leader-Member Exchange Theory 24
independent, critical thinking 25
dependent, uncritical thinking 25
active followers 25
passive followers 25
interactions 39

Questions

1. According to the interactional framework, effective leader behavior depends on many variables. It follows there is no simple prescription for effective leader behavior. Does this mean effective leadership is merely a matter of opinion or subjective preference?

2. Generally, leaders get most of the credit for a group's or an organization's success. Do you believe this is warranted or fair?

3. What are some of the other characteristics of leaders, followers, and situations you could add to those listed in Figure 2–1?

Skills

Leadership skills relevant to this chapter include:
- Building effective relationships with superiors.

- Building effective relationships with peers.

Activity

In this activity you will explore connotations to the words *leadership* and *management.* Divide yourselves into small groups and have each group brainstorm different word associations to the terms *leader* and *leadership* or *manager* and *management.* In addition, each group should discuss whether they would prefer to work for a manager or for a leader, and why. Then the whole group should discuss similarities and differences among the respective perceptions and feelings about the two concepts.

3 LEADERSHIP IS DEVELOPED THROUGH EDUCATION AND EXPERIENCE

Introduction

In Chapter 1, we discussed the importance of using multiple perspectives to analyze various leadership situations. Moreover, we argued that it is relatively difficult for leaders to develop this method of analysis on their own and that formal education is one of the best ways to develop multiple perspectives on leadership. Given the importance of formal education and experience in leadership development, this chapter reviews some of the ways you can better learn about leadership. As an overview, we begin this chapter by presenting a general model that describes how we learn from experience. Next, we describe how perceptions can affect a leader's interpretation of, and actions in response to, a particular leadership situation and why reflection is important to leadership development. In addition, this chapter reveals how the people you work with and the task itself can help you become a better leader, and reviews some of the typical content and pedagogy found in many formal leadership education programs. Finally, we discuss how to evaluate and choose between the many different kinds of leadership programs available.

> Leadership and learning are indispensable to each other.
>
> John F. Kennedy

The Action-Observation-Reflection Model

Consider for a moment what a young person might learn from spending a year working in two very different environments: as a staff assistant in the U.S. Congress or as a carpenter on a house construction crew. Each activity has a rich store of leadership lessons there for the taking. Working in Congress, for example, would provide opportunities to observe political leaders both onstage in the public eye and backstage in more private moments. It would provide opportunities to see members of Congress interacting with different constituencies, to see them in political defeat and political victory, and to see a range of leadership styles. A young person could also learn a lot by working on a building crew as it turned plans and materials into the reality of a finished house: watching the coordination with subcontractors, watching skilled craftsmen train younger ones, watching the leader's reactions to problems and delays, watching the leader set standards and assure quality work. At the same time, a person could work in either environment and *not* grow much if he or she is not disposed to. Making the most of experience is key to developing one's leadership ability. In other words, leadership development depends not just on the kinds of experiences one has but also on how one uses them to foster growth. A study of successful executives found that one key quality that characterized them was an "extraordinary tenacity in extracting something worthwhile from their experience and in seeking experiences rich in opportunities for growth" (McCall, Lombardo, & Morrison, 1988, p. 122).

But how does one do that? Is someone really more likely to get the lessons of experience by looking for them? Why is it not enough just to be there? Experiential learning theorists, such as Kolb (1983), believe people learn more from their experiences when they spend time thinking about them. These ideas are extended to leadership in the **action-observation-reflection** (A-O-R) **model**, depicted in Figure 3.1, which shows that leadership development is enhanced when the experience involves three different processes: action, observation, and reflection. If a person acts but does not observe the consequences of her actions or reflect on their

FIGURE 3.1

The spiral of experience

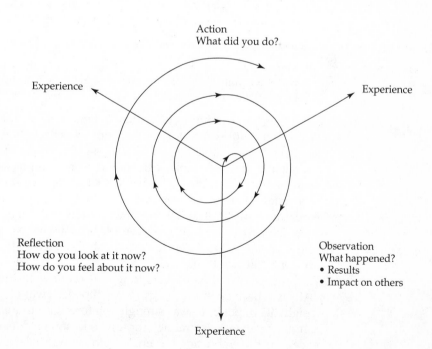

Action
What did you do?

Experience

Experience

Reflection
How do you look at it now?
How do you feel about it now?

Observation
What happened?
• Results
• Impact on others

Experience

*We shall not cease from exploration
And the end of all our exploring
Will be to arrive where we started
And know the place for the first
time.*

                    T. S. Eliot

significance and meaning, then it makes little sense to say she has learned from an experience. Because some people neither observe the consequences of their actions nor reflect on how they could change their actions to become better leaders, leadership development through experience may be better understood as the growth resulting from repeated movements through all three phases rather than merely in terms of some objective dimension like time (e.g., how long one has been on the job). We believe the most productive way to develop as a leader is to travel along the **spiral of experience** depicted in Figure 3.1.

Perhaps an example from Colin Powell's life will clarify how the spiral of experience pertains to leadership development. In 1963, Powell was a 26-year-old officer who had just returned to the United States from a combat tour in Vietnam. His next assignment would be to attend a month-long advanced airborne Ranger course. Near the end of the course, he was to parachute with other troops from a helicopter. As the senior officer on the helicopter, Powell had responsibility for assuring it went well. Early in the flight he hollered for everyone to make sure their static lines were secure, the cables which automatically pulled the chutes open when you jump. Nearing the jump site, he yelled for the men to check their hook-ups one more time. Here are his words describing what happened next:

> Then, like a fussy old woman, I started checking each line myself, pushing my way through the crowded bodies, running my hand along the cable and up to each man's chute. To my alarm, one hook belonging to a sergeant was loose. I shoved the dangling line in his face, and he gasped . . . This man would have stepped out of the door of the helo and dropped like a rock. (Powell, 1995, p. 109)

So what did Powell learn from this experience? Again, in his own words:

> Moments of stress, confusion, and fatigue are exactly when mistakes happen. And when everyone else's mind is dulled or distracted the leader must be doubly vigilant. "Always check small things" was becoming another one of my rules. (p. 109)

Let us now examine this incident in light of the A-O-R model. *Action* refers to Powell's multiple calls for the parachutists to check their lines. We might speculate from his self-description ("like a fussy old woman") that Powell might have felt slightly uncomfortable with such repeated emphasis on checking the lines, even though he persisted in the behavior. Perhaps you, too, sometimes have acted in a certain manner (or were forced to by your parents!) despite feeling a little embarrassed about it; and then, if it was successful, felt more comfortable the next time acting the same way. That seems to be just what happened with Powell here. The *observation* phase refers to Powell's shocked realization of the potentially fatal accident that would have occurred had he *not* double-checked the static lines. And the *reflection* phase refers to the lesson Powell drew from the experience: "Always check the small things." Even though it was obviously not a totally new insight, its importance was strongly reinforced by this experience. In a very real sense, Powell was "spiraling" through a lesson he'd learned from other experiences too, but embracing it even more this time, making it part of his style.

We also should note how Powell himself described his learning in a manner consistent with our interactional framework. He emphasized the situational importance of the leader's attention to detail, especially during moments of stress, confusion, and fatigue, when mistakes may be most likely to happen. Finally, it's worth noting that throughout Powell's autobiography he discusses many lessons he learned from experience. One of the keys to his success was his ability to keep learning throughout his career.

The Key Role of Perception in the Spiral of Experience

Experience is not just a matter of what events happen to you; it also depends on how you perceive those events. Perception affects all three phases of the action-observation-reflection model and thus plays a very important role in what any-one will extract from a leadership course or from any leadership situation. Human beings are not passive recorders of experiences that happen to them; rather, people actively shape and construct their experiences. In order to better understand how perception affects experience, we will examine its role in each part of the action-observation-reflection model. We will begin with the stage that seems to correspond most directly with perception—the observation phase.

Perception and Observation

Observation and perception both deal with attending to events around us. Both seem to take place spontaneously and effortlessly, so it is easy to regard them as passive processes. Our common mental images of the perceptual process reflect this implicit view. For example, it is a common misconception that the eye oper-ates essentially like the film in a continuously running camera. The fallacy of this passive view of perception is that it assumes we attend to all aspects of a sit-uation equally. However, we do not see everything that happens in a particular leadership situation, nor do we hear everything. Instead, we are selective in what we attend to and what we, in turn, perceive. One phenomenon that demonstrates this selectivity is called **perceptual set.** Perceptual sets can influ-ence any of our senses, and they are the tendency or bias to perceive one thing and not another. Many factors can trigger a perceptual set, such as feelings, needs, prior experience, and expectations. Its role in distorting what one hears proved a costly lesson when a sympathetic airline pilot told his depressed copi-lot, "Cheer up!" The copilot thought the pilot had said, "Gear up," and raised the wheels while the plane was still on the ground (Reason & Mycielska, 1982). Try your own ability to overcome perceptual set with the following exercise. Read through the narrative passage below several times:

> FINISHED FILES ARE THE RESULT
> OF YEARS OF SCIENTIFIC STUDY
> COMBINED WITH THE
> EXPERIENCE OF MANY YEARS.

Make sure you have read it to yourself several times *before going any further.* Now, go back to the text and count the number of times the letter *F* appears.

How many did you count? Three? Four? Five? Six? Most people do not get the correct answer (six) the first time. The most frequent count is three; perhaps that was how many you saw. If you did not find six, go back and try it again. The most common error in this seemingly trivial task is overlooking the three times the word *of* appears. People easily overlook it because the word *of* has a *v* sound, not an *f* sound. Most people unconsciously make the task an auditory search task and listen for the sound of *F* rather than look for the shape of *F;* hence, they find three *F*s rather than six. Listening for the sound constitutes a counterproductive perceptual set for this task, and having read the passage through several times before counting the *F*s only exaggerates this tendency. Another reason people overlook the word *of* in this passage is that the first task was to *read* the passage several times. Because most of us are fairly accomplished readers, we tend to ignore little words like *of.* It disappears from our perceptual set. Then, when we are asked to count the number of *F*s, we have already defined the passage as a reading task, so the word *of* is really not there for us to count.

> It's not what we don't know that hurts, it's what we know that ain't so.
>
> Will Rogers

There are strong parallels between the example of perceptual set above and the perceptual sets that come into play when we are enrolled in a leadership course or observe a leadership situation. For example, your instructor for this class may dress unstylishly, and you may be prejudiced in thinking that poor dressers generally do not make good leaders. Because of your biases, you may discount or not attend to some things your instructor has to say about leadership. This is unfortunate, as your instructor's taste in clothes has little to do with his or her ability to teach (which is, after all, a kind of leadership).

A similar phenomenon takes place when one expects to find mostly negative things about another person (e.g., a problem employee). Such an expectation becomes a perceptual set to look for the negative and look past the positive things in the process. For example, if you do not believe women and/or minorities are as successful as white males in influencing others, then you may be biased to identify or remember only those instances where a woman or minority leader failed, and discount or forget those instances where women or minority members succeeded as leaders. Unfortunately, we all have similar biases, although we are usually unaware of them. Often, we only become aware of our perceptual sets when we spend time reflecting about the content of a leadership training program or a particular leadership situation.

Perception and Reflection

Perceptual sets influence what we attend to or do not attend to, what we observe or do not observe. In addition, perception also influences the next stage of the spiral of experience—reflection—since reflection deals with how we interpret our observations. Perception is inherently an interpretive, or a meaning-making, activity. One important aspect of this deals with a process called **attribution.**

"Just don't make any personal appearances until after the election."
Source: Reprinted from *The Saturday Evening Post* © 1964.

Attributions are the explanations we develop for the behaviors or actions we attend to. For example, if you see Julie fail in an attempt to get others to form a study group, you are likely to attribute the cause of the failure to dispositional factors within Julie. In other words, you are likely to attribute the failure to form a study group to Julie's intelligence, personality, physical appearance, or some other factor even though factors beyond her control could have played a major part. This tendency to overestimate the dispositional causes of behavior and underestimate the environmental causes when others fail is called the **fundamental attribution error** (Nisbett & Ross, 1980). People prefer to explain others' behavior on the basis of personal attributions, even when obvious situational factors may fully account for the behavior.

On the other hand, if *you* attempted to get others to form a study group and failed, you would be more likely to blame factors in the situation for the failure (e.g., there was not enough time, or the others were not interested, or they would not be good to study with). This reflects a **self-serving bias** (Miller & Ross, 1975), the tendency to make external attributions (i.e., blame the situation) for one's own failures, yet make internal attributions (i.e., take credit) for one's successes. A third factor which affects the attribution process is called the **actor/observer difference** (Jones & Nisbett, 1972). It refers to the fact that people who are

> *Common sense is the collection of prejudices acquired by age 18.*
> Albert Einstein

observing an action are much more likely than the actor to make the funda-mental attribution error. Consider, for example, a student who gets a bad score on an exam. The person sitting *next* to her (i.e., an observer) would tend to attribute the bad score to *internal* characteristics (e.g., not very bright, weak in this subject) whereas the student herself would be more likely to attribute the bad score to *external* factors (e.g., the professor graded unfairly). Putting all these factors together, each of us tends to see our own success as due to our intelligence, personality, or physical abilities, but others' success as more attrib-utable to situational factors or to luck.

We hasten to note in concluding this section that reflection also involves higher functions like evaluation and judgment, not just perception and attribu-tion. We will address these broader aspects of reflection, which are crucial to learning from experience, just ahead.

Perception and Action

We have seen ways perception influences both the observation and reflection stages in the spiral of experience. It also affects the actions we take. For exam-ple, Mitchell and his associates (Green & Mitchell, 1979; Mitchell, Green, & Wood, 1981; Mitchell & Wood, 1980) have examined how perceptions and biases affect supervisors' actions in response to poorly performing subordinates. In general, these researchers found that supervisors were biased toward making dispositional attributions about a subordinate's substandard performance and, as a result of these attributions, often recommended that punishment be used to remedy the performance deficit.

Another perceptual variable that can affect our actions is the **self-fulfilling prophecy.** The self-fulfilling prophecy occurs when our expectations or predic-tions play a causal role in bringing about the events we predict. It is not difficult to see how certain large-scale social phenomena may be affected this way. For example, economists' predictions of an economic downturn may, via the conse-quent decreased investor confidence, precipitate an economic crisis. But the self-fulfilling prophecy occurs at the interpersonal level, too. A person's expectations about another may influence how he acts toward her, and in reaction to his behavior she may act in a way that confirms his expectations (Jones, 1986). One typical interaction sequence is shown in Figure 3.2.

Some of the best evidence to support the effects of the self-fulfilling prophecy on leadership training was collected by Eden and Shani (1982). Eden and Shani conducted a field experiment where they told leadership instructors their students had either unknown, regular, or high command potential. How-ever, the students' actual command potential was never assessed, and unbe-knownst to the instructors, the students were actually randomly assigned to the unknown, regular, or high command potential conditions. Nevertheless, stu-dents in the high-potential condition had significantly better objective test scores and attitudes than the students in the unknown- or regular-potential con-ditions, even though instructors simultaneously taught all three types of stu-

FIGURE 3.2

The role of expectations in social interaction

Source: Abstracted with permission from E. E. Jones, "Interpreting Interpersonal Behavior: The Effects of Expectancies," *Science* 234, no. 3 (October 1986), p. 43. Copyright 1986, American Association for the Advancement of Science.

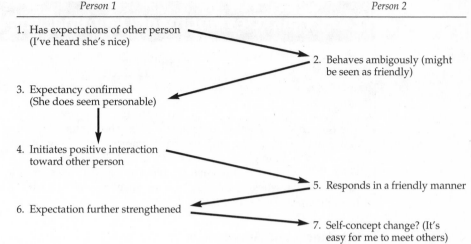

Person 1

1. Has expectations of other person (I've heard she's nice)

3. Expectancy confirmed (She does seem personable)

4. Initiates positive interaction toward other person

6. Expectation further strengthened

Person 2

2. Behaves ambiguously (might be seen as friendly)

5. Responds in a friendly manner

7. Self-concept change? (It's easy for me to meet others)

dents. Somehow the students picked up on their instructor's expectations and responded accordingly. Thus, just having expectations (positive or negative) about others can subtly influence our actions, and these actions can, in turn, affect the way others behave.

Reflection and Leadership Development

Perhaps the most important yet most neglected component of the action-observation-reflection model is reflection. Reflection is important because it can provide leaders with a variety of insights into how to frame problems differently, look at situations from multiple perspectives, or better understand subordinates. However, most managers spend relatively little time on this activity, even though the time spent reflecting about leadership can be quite fruitful.

One reason the reflection component is often neglected may be time pressure at work. Leaders are usually very busy people working in pressure-filled situations and often do not have time to ponder all the possible consequences of their actions or reflect on how they could have accomplished a particular action better. Sometimes it takes an out-of-the-ordinary experience to focus one's attention on developmental challenges (see Highlight 3.1). In addition, some leaders may not be aware of the value of reflection in leadership development. Hopefully, this section will clarify the value of reflection, and in so doing can complement the emphasis, throughout the remainder of the book, on looking at leadership from different perspectives.

Leadership Development Dilemmas for Women

Highlight 3.1

The Women's Leadership Program, offered by The Center for Creative Leadership (CCL), emphasizes receiving feedback, improving self-awareness, and setting leadership and life goals. Members of the CCL staff conducted a series of interviews with 60 executive women who had attended the program, and identified several salient issues these women were struggling with (Ohlott, 1999). Four particular themes stood out:

Wholeness and Authenticity

These executive women desired to have a whole and full life. They felt job demands had forced their lives to become one-dimensional. Often they felt they had given up an important part of themselves: a creative self, friendly self, musical self, athletic self, and so forth. Sometimes they felt their organizations required them to ignore or suppress some part of their true selves in order to succeed.

Clarity

After the program, many women developed great clarity about their own strengths, weaknesses, values, needs, priorities, and goals as leaders.

Connection

Many women expressed concerns that they did not have the degree of interpersonal connectedness with others they would have preferred. They expressed a desire for closer friendships and family ties. Many said they felt isolated in their organizations, with few confidants of either gender.

Control

One of the strongest themes identified in the interviews was the need to feel more in control. This need was manifested in a number of different ways, including the need to feel more comfortable exercising authority and a need to deal differently with organizational situations that made them feel helpless. Many women also expressed a desire to become more politically sophisticated.

To reflect upon the overall findings of the study, it is encouraging that virtually all of these executive women believed they were continuing to grow both personally and professionally. The experiences of this group of executive women certainly support the view that development persists throughout life.

Single- and Double-Loop Learning

It is difficult for leaders to fundamentally change their leadership style without engaging in some kind of reflection. Along these lines, Argyris (1976) described an intensive effort with a group of highly successful chief executive officers who became even better leaders through increased self-awareness. Argyris's model for conceptualizing this growth is applicable to any level of leader and is worth considering in more detail.

Argyris (1976) said that most people interact with others and the environment on the basis of a belief system geared to manipulate or control others, and to minimize one's own emotionality and the negative feelings elicited from others. This belief system also tends to create defensive interpersonal relationships and limits risk taking. People "programmed" with this view of life (as most of us are, according to Argyris) produce group and organizational dynamics characterized by avoidance of conflict, mistrust, conformity, intergroup rivalry, misperceptions and miscommunications with others, ineffective problem solving, and poor decision making. Most important for our purposes here, it generates a certain kind of learning that Argyris called **single-loop learning.**

Single-loop learning describes a kind of learning between the individual and the environment in which learners seek relatively little feedback that may significantly confront their fundamental ideas or actions. There is relatively little public testing of ideas against valid information. Consequently, an actor's belief system becomes self-sealing and self-fulfilling, and little time is spent reflecting about the beliefs. Argyris used the term *single-loop learning* because it operates somewhat like a thermostat; individuals learn only about subjects within the "comfort zone" of their belief systems. They might, for example, learn how well they are achieving a designated goal. They are far less likely, however, to question the validity of the goal or the values implicit in the situation, just as a thermostat does not question its temperature setting. That kind of self-confrontation would involve **double-loop learning.**

Double-loop learning involves a willingness to confront one's own views and an invitation to others to do so, too. It springs from an appreciation that openness to information and power sharing with others can lead to better recognition and definition of problems, improved communication, and increased decision-making effectiveness. Mastering double-loop learning can be thought of as learning how to learn. With considerable collective work, including the difficult task of working through personal blind spots, Argyris's group of leaders did move to this stage. In other words, through reflection they learned how to change their leadership styles by questioning their assumptions about others, their roles in the organization, and their underlying assumptions about the importance of their own goals and those of the organization.

Konosuke Matsushita seems to have perfected the art of double-loop learning despite never thinking of it in such a formal way. Early in his career Matsushita learned, as he said, to "subject my own methods of management to careful scrutiny, finding that there were many ways in which they could be improved" (quoted in Kotter, 1997, p. 83). He always stressed the importance of an open mind, expecting that he could learn something valuable from everyone he met. He was also quite successful in infusing his whole company with a similar value, which made it an extremely adaptive organization. He pushed not only himself but others as well out of comfortable routines. He believed that his company's success depended upon a humble commitment to continuous improvement rather than a corporate culture that was arrogant and rigid.

Thinking Frames and Multiple Perspectives

Another way to conceptualize reflection in leadership development involves **thinking frames,** which refer to the tactics and strategies people use to organize their thinking and to construe the meaning of events (Perkins, 1986). Thinking frames are our mental tools, and they may or may not be useful, just as a hammer or saw may or may not be useful depending on the task at hand. In addition, just as a child with a hammer perceives that the whole world needs hammering, our thinking frames can also represent limits on the ways we can (conceptually) operate on our environment. Leadership development can be thought of as the process of developing more complex and differentiated frames for organizing one's thinking (and hence action) about leadership. Moreover, because some thinking frames are relatively subtle, their development may be better assisted through structured educational experiences. For example, most people would not have thought of the action-observation-reflection model on their own. The development of multiple frames, or perspectives, may be one of the greatest contributions a formal course in leadership can make to a leader's development. The overarching idea in discussing the different definitions and theories of leadership in this text is to help you to develop different frames or perspectives for interpreting leadership situations, which in turn may help you to better influence others to achieve organizational goals. Perhaps one key to leadership success is having a variety of tools to choose from and knowing when and where to use them. We hope the theories and concepts described in this text will give you the tools, and by reflecting about your experiences as a leader, you should begin to gain some insight on when and where to use them.

Leadership Development through Experience

Although using the action-observation-reflection model will help you make the most of your leadership experiences and mature into a better leader, it is also important to realize that some situations are developmentally richer than others. In this section, we will review two developmental factors that make any given experience potent in fostering managerial growth: the people you work with and the characteristics of the task itself (Kouzes & Posner, 1987; Lombardo & Eichinger, 1989). These factors are important because they pro-

Good flutists learn from experience; unfortunately, so do bad flutists.

Anonymous

vide opportunities for a leader or a leader-to-be to apply the action-observation-reflection model and reflect on how to be a better leader.

The People You Work With

The people you associate with can stimulate development in many ways. Kouzes and Posner (1987) noted the diverse ways others nurture our growth:

> Other people have always been essential sources of guidance. We all remember the parent we looked to for advice and support; the special teacher who filled us with curiosity for our favorite subject; the neighbor who always let us watch, even take part in, the tinkering in the garage; the coach who believed that we had promise and inspired us to give our best; the counselor who gave us valuable feedback about our behavior and its impact; the master artisan who instructed us in the fundamentals of a craft; or the first boss who taught us the ropes to skip and the hoops to jump. (p. 286)

Others play an especially important role in personal and professional development at work, so we will focus attention there.

A boss, especially a very good or very bad one, can be a powerful catalyst for growth. Exceptional bosses are vivid examples of how to (or how not to) put values into action. However, bosses are not the only people who contribute to growth and development at work. Working with others who have different backgrounds, perspectives, or agendas can often be a growth experience. Working with problem subordinates can stimulate managerial growth, but so can the need to influence others over whom you have no direct authority or control. You may work on a project and report to a superior other than your own boss, or you may head a team of peers; such situations are particularly helpful in developing negotiation and other informal influence skills. Finally, different management skills are called on when you must make major changes to a group or project such as downsizing it, restructuring it, or starting it from scratch (Lombardo & Eichinger, 1989).

You can learn about effective and ineffective leadership by paying attention to the positive and negative models around you beyond your immediate boss. Watching others in leadership roles may suggest what to do as well as what not to do. Peers, especially, can be a great resource for developing one's effectiveness as a leader. In one program of peer coaching, school principals observed each other interacting in feedback conferences with their respective teachers and then met together afterward to share ideas about how well the conferences went (Gibble & Lawrence, 1987). Such principal-to-principal interaction is especially valuable in that it is rare for any supervisor to get feedback on his or her skill in providing feedback to subordinates. The principals praised their peer coaching as an extremely effective mechanism for enhancing their effectiveness as supervisors.

In an organization, you also can gain valuable perspectives and insights through close association with an experienced person willing to take you under his wing. Such an individual is often called a **mentor,** after the character in Greek mythology whom Odysseus trusted to run his household and see to his son's education when Odysseus went off to fight the Trojans. Now, 3,000 years later, Mentor's name is used to describe the process by which an older and more experienced person helps to socialize and encourage younger organizational colleagues (Wilson & Elman, 1990).

Generally, mentors are highly placed, powerful individuals who develop relatively long-lasting relationships with younger colleagues whose professional careers are influenced and furthered as a result (Hunt & Michael, 1983; Uecker & Dilla, 1985). Typically, the mentoring relationship is informal, though its value has encouraged some to recommend its use formally and systematically in organizations (Clutterbuck, 1982). In terms of value, both mentors and mentorees benefit from having this relationship. Mentors benefit by the greater influence they accrue by having former mentorees in various positions across the organization. Mentors also benefit by having a younger replacement ready to fill their position if they are promoted (Bass, 1990). The mentoree benefits from this relationship by gaining an influential ally and by learning through the mentor's tutoring about the subtler aspects of organizational ethics, influence, and leadership. Having a mentor can also result in more career opportunities for the mentoree (Whitely, Dougherty, & Dreher, 1988; Zey, 1984), and the lack of mentors for women has been cited as one reason there are relatively few women in executive positions (Astin & Leland, 1991). Although some may advocate systematizing mentorship programs to improve the career opportunities for all employees, it remains to be seen whether a formalized program would preserve the essence and qualities of more informal, self-selected mentoring relationships (Rosenbach, 1989).

According to strict definitions of mentoring, perhaps none of our three leaders had a true mentor throughout their careers. Yet Madeleine Albright, for example, was sharpened and toughened by several of her bosses. Two in particular stand out: Zbigniev Brzezinski, a former national security adviser in the Carter White House, and Ed Muskie, former senator from Maine. Both were brilliant, but also had tough-as-nails reputations. Although Ms. Albright was already a person meticulously prepared in advance for anything, her skills and self-confidence were further honed by working for these two very demanding leaders.

An idea somewhat related to mentoring is that of **executive coaching.** Increasingly, executive coaching is seen as a general responsibility of all executives toward managers who report to them. The failure to coach managers in their professional development makes as little sense as a football team composed of the best recruited players going through an entire season without a practice session or coach (Witherspoon & White, 1996). More simply, good coaching is nothing more than good management. It is investment that can help change counterproductive behavior, often interpersonal, that threatens to derail an otherwise valued manager (Waldroop and Butler, 1996).

The Task Itself

In addition to the various sorts of relationships with other people, certain kinds of work-related tasks can also be particularly developmental. Developmental tasks are often more complex and ambiguous than those one has faced before. In addition, leadership development can be enhanced if the environment one works in is changing, dynamic, uncontrollable, and unpredictable. The nature of the task may require new and creative solutions; old answers may not work anymore. Projects involving strategic planning and projections into an uncertain future can be quite challenging intellectually and can contribute to a leader's development (Lombardo & Eichinger, 1989).

> *I took a great deal o' pains with his education, sir; let him run the streets when he was very young, and shift for his-self. It's the only way to make a boy sharp, sir.*
> Charles Dickens, *Pickwick Papers*

Although we have emphasized the importance of applying the action-observation-reflection model to enhance one's learning from experience, the developmental value of the challenging tasks themselves cannot be denied. The best developmental opportunities are those that stretch individuals and allow them to test themselves against new and difficult tasks (Kouzes & Posner, 1987). Of course, the difficulty level of tasks and how much one will be stretched by doing them is meaningful mostly in the context of a given individual's maturity and experience. The following are the words of one college student who was in charge of the flag section of her school's marching band:

> I have 30 people under me broken into four sections. I am responsible for conducting our rehearsals, teaching flag routines, taking care of any problems, recruiting new members, and motivating my people. I do some of this through my four section leaders, so I have to make sure they are doing their jobs properly. The biggest challenge of all this is keeping motivation high and making sure that everyone learns what they are supposed to and performs it well. It is really giving me a lot of experience in interacting with people.

Another student described his own best leadership experience in terms of his unique background as an instructor on his collegiate parachute team:

> During this period I learned a lot about what it takes to teach a person to jump out of an airplane successfully and injury free. The foremost concern and responsibility is the welfare of the student, so I had to be certain that they learned the procedures correctly, and be thoroughly convinced that they would be safe once out the door no matter what situation may arise. I was responsible for someone else's life. I had to be very patient and understanding many times when they would not grasp an idea or a procedure properly, spending a lot of time in certain areas until they were proficient. Other times I had to be stern and strict to emphasize certain emergency procedures and safety hazards in order to be sure they were aware of the seriousness of the situation. During this period I experienced everything that goes into leadership. I had to work with many people. Many of them were my peers, which makes things more difficult in some cases.

Feeling responsible for someone else's life certainly increases one's personal pressure, and it was partly this pressure that made this student-instructor's role such a valuable leadership experience. Whether or not a particular task is perceived as developmentally challenging and generates a high level of personal pressure depends on several factors. The most commonly cited developmental challenge mentioned by managers was a task where both success and failure were possible and would be obvious to others. The risk of possible failure is a strong incentive for managers to learn. Managers also mentioned deadlines, travel requirements, and longer hours as factors that, while adding to personal pressure, also contributed to professional growth (Lombardo & Eichinger, 1989).

One last aspect of leadership-developing tasks should be mentioned. Just as mentoring relationships fail to develop for all members, organizations may not provide the same developmental opportunities for all their members. In particular, there is a striking difference between large and small organizations in the opportunities they offer. This is apparent, for example, in the chances of having a significant responsibility in the school play in schools with either large or small student bodies. In small schools, virtually anyone who wants to have a significant part in putting on the play will be able to do so. In large schools, though, the number of students far exceeds the number of important functions; many motivated students will miss out on the chance to participate and grow from the experience. As John Gardner (1990) has pointed out, the sheer size and impersonalness of some of our organizations does not provide the soil in which a young person's leadership can grow.

Making the Most of Your Leadership Experiences: Learning to Learn from Experience

This section builds on the ideas previously introduced in this chapter by providing leadership practitioners with a few suggestions to enhance learning from experience (see Highlight 3.2 for a description of some executives who apparently did not learn enough from experience). For well over a decade, researchers at the Center for Creative Leadership have been studying the role of learning from experience as an important developmental behavior for people in executive positions. While this research has contributed a great deal to *what* people need to learn to be successful (see Highlight 3.3 for a comparison of lessons men and women managers learn from experience), less is known about the process of learning or *how* we learn to be successful. Bunker and Webb (1992) asked successful executives to list adjectives describing how they felt while working through powerful learning events and potent developmental experiences. Their typical responses were a combination of both positive and negative feelings.

> *What would a man be wise; let him drink of the river*
> *That bears on its bosom the record of time;*
> *A message to him every wave can deliver.*
> *To teach him to creep till he knows how to climb.*
>
> John Boyle O'Reilly

Negatives	Positives
Pained	Challenged
Fearful	Successful
Frustrated	Proud
Stressed	Capable
Anxious	Growing
Overwhelmed	Exhilarated
Uncertain	Talented
Angry	Resourceful
Hurt	Learning

Executive Derailment: Knocking Yourself off the Track to Success

Highlight 3.2

Some executives on an apparently clear track to the top never make it. They become derailed. For more than a decade, researchers at the Center for Creative Leadership have studied executives who had fallen short of the levels of success predicted of them earlier in their careers. Typically, their derailments were the result of several factors, though insensitivity to others was the most frequent problem. Sometimes styles that served them well earlier became liabilities in new circumstances, and sometimes long-standing liabilities, previously outweighed by other aspects, eventually took their career toll. A 1996 study expanded the work and included samples of European as well as North American executives. In general, the derailment themes in Europe and North America were consistent:

Characteristics of Successful Leaders	Characteristics of Derailed Leaders
Ability to develop or adapt.	Inability to develop or adapt.
Ability to establish collaborative relations.	Poor working relations.
Ability to build and lead a team.	Inability to build and lead a team.
Nonauthoritarian.	Authoritarian.
Consistent exceptional performance.	Poor performance.
Ambitious.	Too ambitious.

How would you interpret these executives' derailments in terms of the action-observation-reflection model? Do you think the problem was in their actions? Their observation or awareness of the consequences of their actions? Or something else?

Source: Adapted from J. B. Leslie and E. Van Velsor, *A Look at Derailment Today: North America and Europe* (Greensboro, NC: Center for Creative Leadership, 1996).

This pattern strongly supports the long-hypothesized notion of a meaningful link between stress and learning (Janis, 1971). The learning events and developmental experiences that punctuate one's life are usually, perhaps always, stressful (Grey & Gordon, 1978; Hambrick, 1981; Jennings, 1971; Schein, 1978).

Bunker and Webb (1992) note that executives try to be successful without experiencing stress. They are most comfortable when they can draw upon a proven repertoire of operating skills to tackle a challenge they have conquered

Teach a highly educated person that it is not a disgrace to fail and that he must analyze every failure to find its cause. He must learn how to fail intelligently, for failing is one of the greatest arts in the world.

Charles F. Kettering, Inventor, automotive pioneer, and corporate leader

What Do Men and Women Managers Learn from Experience?

Highlight 3.3

For a quarter century or so, significant numbers of women have been represented in the management ranks of companies. During that period companies have promoted large pools of high-potential women, but relatively few of them have achieved truly top-level positions. Several factors probably account for this, but one possibility is that men and women learn differently from their work experiences. Researchers at the Center for Creative Leadership have studied how male and female executives describe the important lessons they've learned from their career experiences, and there are some interesting differences between the genders as well as significant overlap.

Most Frequent Lessons for Men and Women
Directing and motivating employees.
Self-confidence.
Basic management values.
How to work with executives.
Understanding other people's perspective.
Dealing with people over whom you have no authority.
Handling political situations.

For Men Only	For Women Only
Technical/professional skills.	Personal limits and blind spots.
All about the business.	Taking charge of career.
Coping with ambiguous situations.	Recognizing and seizing opportunities.
Shouldering full responsibility.	Coping with situations beyond your control.
Persevering through adversity.	Knowing what excites you.

Why would there be any learning differences between the genders? One hypothesis is that men and women managers tend to have somewhat different career patterns. For example, there is some evidence that women receive fewer truly challenging developmental opportunities.

Source: Adapted from E. Van Velsor, and M. W. Hughes, *Gender Differences in the Development of Managers: How Women Managers Learn from Experience* (Technical Report No. 145), Greensboro, NC: Center for Creative Leadership, 1990.

FIGURE 3.3

Anatomy of a learning experience

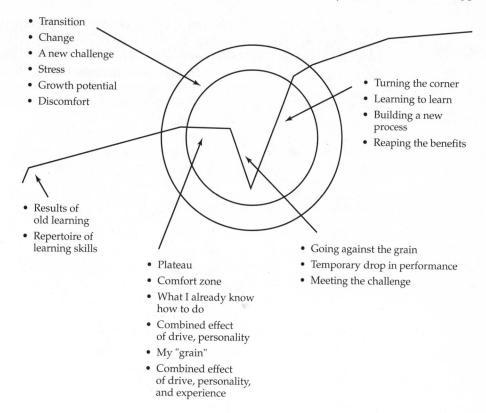

- Transition
- Change
- A new challenge
- Stress
- Growth potential
- Discomfort

- Turning the corner
- Learning to learn
- Building a new process
- Reaping the benefits

- Results of old learning
- Repertoire of learning skills

- Plateau
- Comfort zone
- What I already know how to do
- Combined effect of drive, personality
- My "grain"
- Combined effect of drive, personality, and experience

- Going against the grain
- Temporary drop in performance
- Meeting the challenge

in the past. Combined with the organizational pressure to have "proven performers" in important positions, there is a tremendous initial pressure to "continue to do what we've always done." In stressful situations, this tendency may become even more powerful. What results is one of the great Catch-22s of adult development: The times when people most need to break out of the mold created by past learning patterns are the times when they are most unwilling to do so. Being able to *go against the grain* of one's personal historical success requires an unwavering commitment to learning and a relentless willingness to let go of the fear of failure and the unknown.

Figure 3.3 depicts the Center for Creative Leadership's work on the process of "learning to learn from experience." Bunker and Webb (1992) describe the figure as a segment of life containing a series of learning opportunities. The circled segment represents a stressful episode of life—a potentially dramatic learning-to-learn event. The left side of the curve represents the growth and development that was stimulated by prior learning experiences. Also represented is a flattening out of learned skill value that often occurs; over time, new skills often become mere routinized habits. People operating in this stabilizing period, called the comfort zone, must overcome the caution generated by ongoing success and the fear of challenging what they already know how to do. The smaller concentric circle represents the tension created by the appearance of a new learning challenge—often arising out of a transition or a stressful experience that requires a response. The sharp dip in success depicts the performance regression that generally accompanies attempts at learning a new set of responses and strategies. One gets through this period (and thus performs at a higher level with broader skills) by coping with the stress or letting go of short-term expectations in favor of more long-term learning. Of course, if one is not willing to go against the grain and tolerate a small dip in performance, then the learning curve becomes flat—no learning.

> *Anyone who stops learning is old, whether at 20 or 80. Anyone who keeps learning stays young. The greatest thing in life is to keep your mind young.*
>
> Henry Ford

To be successful, learning must continue throughout life, beyond the completion of one's formal education.

> The end of extrinsically applied education should be the start of an education that is motivated intrinsically. At that point the goal of studying is no longer to make the grade, earn a diploma, and find a good job. Rather, it is to understand what is happening around one, to develop a personally meaningful sense of what one's experience is all about. (Csikszentmihalyi, 1990, p. 142)

There may be no better way to conclude this section than by turning again to the life of Konosuke Matsushita. John Kotter (1997) characterized Matsushita's whole life as one of continual learning, and suggested it may well be the future model for all of us:

> Forget . . . naive notions about success being a simple linear journey upward. KM's economic fortunes crashed twice, in 1899 and 1946. His health, psychological well-being, and personal happiness also fluctuated many times. In a volatile 21st century, this pattern could become more common.
>
> Most of all, forget the mid-20th-century model of learning, careers, and growth. If current trends continue, the success stories of the next few decades will not be about people who are educated from age five to twenty-five and who then apply that schooling until they retire forty years later. Winners will be those who are both willing and able to grow throughout their lifetimes.
>
> If there is any single lesson from his life that Matsushita himself seems to have thought would be particularly applicable and important in the future, it was this: don't assume that we cannot continue to develop, and develop greatly, as we age. (pp. 245–46)

Leadership Development through Education and Training

Although we believe experience plays a large role in leadership development, we believe formal education can play an important role, too. For example, Bray, Campbell, and Grant (1974), Howard (1986), and Wakabayashi and Graen (1984) all found that education level or academic performance in college was positively related to future managerial success. Furthermore, in a major review of the effectiveness of managerial training programs, Burke and Day (1986) found that educational programs generally had a positive effect on leadership development. Thus, formal education and training programs can help one become a better leader. However, it is important to note that these programs vary substantially in both content and pedagogy, and not all programs are appropriate for all leaders. The content of different leadership programs varies considerably, depending on the target audience; university-level courses generally provide a survey of the major leadership findings, programs for first-level supervisors often focus on how to train subordinates and give them feedback about their progress, and programs for senior executives often focus on strategic planning and public relations. In this regard, Brungardt (1996) helpfully distinguished between leadership development and leadership education, the latter being a component of the former. Programs also vary in the extent to which they are based on well-established and professionally accepted practices and standards. Some leadership training programs represent little more than fads or popularized pseudoscience. In the following pages, we will review some of the more common educational and training techniques used to teach and develop leadership.

University Courses in Leadership

Spitzberg (1987) estimated that over 500 colleges or universities offer some type of leadership training program. Often these programs consist of extracurricular leadership activities run out of the student development office or are courses much like the one for which you are using this book. The extracurricular activities can vary greatly, but the leadership courses often have a high degree of overlap in both content and pedagogy. In terms of content, the topics covered in most leadership courses are similar to the subjects addressed in this book and include how personality traits, cognitive abilities, values, behaviors, motivation, group dynamics, communication, situational factors, and different theories of leadership can all be used to describe the leadership process. In addition, many universities offer specialized courses that focus primarily on historical, business, minority, or female leaders.

> *An educated man can experience more in a day than an uneducated man in a lifetime.*
>
> Seneca, Roman statesman, 1st century A.D.

The techniques, or pedagogy, used to impart these different leadership concepts to students can vary greatly. Many courses use the standard lecture method, and Burke and Day (1986) found this method to be an effective way of imparting knowledge about leadership. Some courses also provide **individualized feedback** to students in the form of personality, intelligence, values, or interests test scores or leadership behavior ratings. A relatively new twist to individualized feedback is to have subjects compare the results of their personality or behavior self-ratings with those given to them by their peers (Curphy, 1991). **Case studies** consist of descriptions of various leadership situations and are used as a vehicle for leadership discussions. **Role playing** is also a popular methodology. In role playing, participants are assigned parts to play (e.g., a supervisor and an unmotivated subordinate) in a job-related scenario. Role playing has the advantage of letting trainees actually practice relevant skills and thus has greater transferability to the workplace than do didactic lectures or abstract discussions about leadership. **Simulations** and **games** are other methods of training. These are relatively structured activities designed to mirror some of the challenges or decisions commonly faced in the work environment. One of the better-known leadership simulations is the Center for Creative Leadership's "Looking Glass" (McCall & Lombardo, 1982), in which participants play different leadership roles in a glass manufacturing plant. A newer approach to leadership development puts participants in relatively unfamiliar territory (e.g., outdoors rather than offices) and presents them physical, emotionally arousing, and often team-oriented challenges.

Leadership Training Programs

There are numerous leadership training programs aimed particularly toward leaders and supervisors in industry or public service. In many ways, these have strong parallels to both the content and techniques used in university-level courses on leadership. However, these programs are usually much shorter (typically less than a week), and the content tends to be more focused than that of a university course. The content of these programs also depends on the organizational level of the recipients; programs for first-level supervisors focus on developing supervisory skills such as training, monitoring, giving feedback, and conducting performance reviews with subordinates. Generally, these programs use lectures, case studies, and role-playing exercises to improve leadership skills.

> *All rising to a great place is by a winding stair.*
>
> Francis Bacon,
> Philosopher

The programs for midlevel managers often focus on improving interpersonal, oral-communication, and written-communication skills, as well as giving tips on time management, planning, and goal setting. These programs rely more heavily on individualized feedback, case studies, presentations, role playing, simulations, **in-basket exercises,** and **leaderless group discussions** as techniques to help leaders develop. In in-basket exercises, participants are given a limited amount of time to prioritize and respond to a number of notes, letters, and phone messages from a fictitious manager's in-basket. This technique is particularly useful in assessing and improving a manager's planning and time management skills. In leaderless group discussions, facilitators and observers rate participants on the degree of persuasiveness, leadership, followership, or conflict each member manifests in a group that has no appointed leader. These ratings are used to provide managers with feedback about their interpersonal and oral-communication skills.

In reviewing the general field of leadership development and training, Conger (1996) offered this assessment: "Leadership programs can work, and work well, if they use a multi-tiered approach. Effective training depends on the combined use of four different teaching methods which I call personal growth, skill building, feedback, and conceptual awareness" (p. 52). Some programs seek to stimulate leadership development by means of oftentimes emotionally intense personal growth experiences such as river rafting, wilderness survival, and so forth. Leadership development through skill building involves structured activities focusing upon the sorts of leadership skills featured in the final section of this book. Some approaches to leadership development emphasize individualized feedback about each person's strengths and weaknesses, typically based upon standardized assessment methods. Feedback-based approaches can help identify "blind spots" an individual may be unaware of, as well as help prioritize which aspects of leadership development represent the highest priorities for development focus. Still other sorts of programs develop leadership by emphasizing its conceptual or intellectual components. An example of this approach would be an emphasis on theory and the use of case studies, common in many MBA programs. There are merits in each of these approaches, but Conger was on solid ground when he emphasized the value of combining elements of each.

In a related vein, Nevins and Stumpf (1999) emphasized that leadership development in the 21st century must occur in more lifelike situations and contexts. Toward that end, they advocated creating better practice fields for leadership development analogous to the practice fields whereon skills in competitive sports are honed, or practice sessions analogous to those in music training wherein those skills are sharpened.

Leadership programs for senior executives and CEOs tend to focus on strategic planning, public relations, and interpersonal skills. Many times, the entire senior leadership of a company will go through a leadership program at the same time. One goal of such a group might be to learn how to develop a strategic plan for their organization. In order to improve public relations skills, some programs have CEOs undergo simulated, unannounced interviews with television reporters and receive feedback on how they could have done better.

Designing and Evaluating Leadership Development Programs

Although a number of leadership training programs are based on sound theory and research, some other programs have no basis in science and should be considered speculative at best. Still others are based on unwarranted and simplistic extensions of scientific findings. Perhaps the best way to guarantee that a leadership program will be useful to you or your organization is to adopt a systematic approach to leadership training. There is value in being an informed consumer, and this is just as true in investing one's time, energy, and money in leadership programs as it is in other products and services. To this end, Peterson and Hicks (1995, 1996), Peterson (2001), and Campbell (1988) have described systematic models of training that can be combined into a framework for designing and evaluating any leadership development program. The major steps in this framework, known as the **Development Pipeline**™, can be found

FIGURE 3.4

The Development Pipeline™

in Figure 3.4. These steps include (1) determining training content; (2) providing insight; (3) determining motivation levels; (4) providing training on new knowledge and skills; (5) providing opportunities to practice new knowledge and skills; and (6) holding people accountable for using what they have learned. In this model, learning is analogous to water flowing through a pipeline. We know from physics that all things being equal, water meets less resistance in larger sections of a pipeline. Similarly, learning is thought to take place more easily in the more expanded sections of the Development Pipeline; less learning takes place in those sections of the pipeline that are narrow or constricted. The trick is to design leadership development programs that maximize the various sections of the Development Pipeline in a cost-effective manner. You can also evaluate the effectiveness of a leadership development program (or any training and development program) by systematically evaluating the level of constriction in each section of the pipeline. The following discussion is an application of the Development Pipeline to a typical university course in leadership.

The first section of the Development Pipeline is essentially concerned with the question *what needs to be learned?* In many university programs the professor determines the content and course objectives based on his or her knowledge of the leadership literature and the students in the program. However, professors can have very idiosyncratic views on leadership and leadership development. If they wish to expand this section of the Development Pipeline, then they must ensure that the leadership course content and objectives are aligned with organizational needs. Because most universities have the development of new leaders with qualities such as integrity, lifelong learning, critical thinking, and teamwork as part of their overall mission, professors will need to ensure their course objectives are aligned with their university's mission. For example, the course objectives for any leadership class or program at one of the military academies in the United States should be aligned with the knowledge and skills needed by new leaders in the U.S. Army, Navy, Air Force, or Coast Guard.

The same is true for leadership training programs in corporate settings. To expand this first section of the pipeline, course designers need to ensure that the training content supports the corporation's mission and objectives. If the com-

> *Tell me and I'll forget; show me and I may remember; involve me and I'll understand.*
>
> Chinese proverb

pany's mission is concerned with empowering employees, supporting innovation, and getting results, then the course content for a first-line supervisor should address these topics. Unfortunately, this section of the pipeline is very constricted for many leadership training programs because many organizations send employees to leadership development programs because (1) other companies are sending their employees (and may be gaining some advantage), (2) the senior staff went to the program and liked it, or (3) the employees deserve a reward for good work.

Another important component of the Development Pipeline concerns insight. This section of the pipeline is concerned with the question *how proficient are people on the objectives and skills that will be taught in the program?* People will be much more likely to spend the time to acquire knowledge or learn a new skill if they believe they lack proficiency in the skill. Conversely, it is very difficult to teach a new skill to someone who believes they already possess the skill. Well-designed leadership development programs provide participants with extensive feedback on where they currently stand on the skills being taught in the program. This is usually accomplished by having participants review the results of in-basket exercises, personality inventories), multi-rater instruments, or individual assessments. University courses can expand the insight section of the pipeline by having students take an exam on the course objectives the very first day of class. The results of the exam will provide students with insight on their level of proficiency with the course content and give them an idea of where they need to concentrate their efforts if they want to improve.

Once people have some insight on where they stand on the knowledge and skills taught in the course, the next question to be answered is *how motivated are people to learn the information in the program?* Just because someone does poorly on a precourse exam does not mean they will be motivated to learn the information. To maximize this section of the pipeline, course designers need to ensure that the training content is personally relevant to the participant. Professors must help students to see the connection between the course content and their ability to find a leadership position after graduation or to get promoted into a leadership position. It is important to note that well-designed insight tools can help to expand this section of the pipeline. For example, if a participant is getting poor scores on delegation and communication skills from her followers on a multirater instrument, and followers' perceptions are important to her, then it is very likely that she will pay extra attention to the delegation and communication modules in a leadership development program.

Most training design efforts focus on the next section of the Development Pipeline, which is new knowledge and skills. This section of the pipeline is concerned with the question *what are the best methods for teaching these new skills?* There are many ways to teach new leadership skills, some of which include lectures, group exercises or discussions, cases studies, **e-learning, action learning** (Margerison, 1988; Berry, 1990; Clover, 1991; Curphy, 2001), and **active learning** (Hill & Semler, 2001). With respect to e-learning, some companies are providing a number of training programs on CD ROM, Internet, or intranet formats. For example,

NCR offers over 3,600 electronic courses in 17 languages for its associates through NCR University (Ganzel, 2001). Some of these programs are specifically designed for first-line and midlevel leaders and include such topics as performance management, conflict management, six sigma, and change management skills (G. Brennan, 2001). Solving real organizational problems is at the core of action learning. Here cross-functional teams work over a three- to six-month period to solve a real issue facing an organization, such as reducing overall operating expenses by 30 percent or determining what new products to bring to the market. These teams work with a facilitator who helps them to acquire critical thinking, project management, problem-solving, business strategy, team, conflict management, and formal presentation skills throughout the course of the project. Coca-Cola, TRW, Pentair, Husky Oil, and the Saint Paul Companies are just a few of the organizations using an action learning approach to leadership development. Simulation-based learning is the hallmark of active learning programs. Five- to eight-person teams work with a facilitator and go through two to four days of in-depth leadership simulations modeled after their respective organizations. The facilitators are responsible for teaching new skills and models that the teams must then apply to the different leadership simulations. Companies such as Boeing, HJ Heinz, Anheuser-Busch, and Charter Communications all use active leader programs to improve the leadership skills of their employees.

Although there are many different ways to teach leadership, it is very important that the training content drive the methodology and not vice versa. Too often, professors use a combination of lecture and case study methodology to teach leadership, when an e-learning or simulation approach may be a more effective way to teach the course content. The same is true in the corporate world; many companies buy leadership development programs for their employees simply because the program makes heavy use of the latest technology. Whether or not this high-tech training actually results in improved knowledge and skill acquisition has yet to be seen. However, we do know that if e-learning, action learning, or active learning programs do not pay attention to all the sections of the Development Pipeline, then it is very unlikely that new knowledge and skills will be acquired and applied back at the workplace. The methodology used to teach new knowledge and skills is less important than ensuring that all the sections of the Development Pipeline are adequately addressed.

In the real-world practice section of the Development Pipeline, the fundamental question asked is *do people get the opportunity to practice new skills?* Well-designed training programs provide participants with opportunities to practice newly acquired skills; content alone is often not enough for people to successfully apply a skill in the workplace. University courses provide an ideal setting to practice new knowledge and skills, as the practice sessions can take place outside the workplace. Many corporate training programs are spread out over a three- to six-month period so that participants can practice new skills between sessions. For example, supervisors at Colorado Springs Utilities attend one day of training content and then have about a month to carry out various back-home applications before the next training session. These back-home applications (known in university courses as homework) often consist of practicing newly acquired skills in the workplace. Professors using the Development Pipeline to design a university course on leadership should ensure that more time is built in to practice more complex leadership skills.

The last section of the development pipeline asks, *how are participants held accountable for what they have learned?* In university settings final exams and term papers are good ways to maximize this section of the pipeline. A relatively easy way to expand this section of the pipeline in corporate settings is to have managers hold their followers responsible for behaving differently as a result of a training program. Although this sounds fairly simple, it is rarely if ever done in most companies today. Many managers maintain that they are either too busy to develop their people or state that it is the responsibility of the human resources department. Ensuring that your followers are continuing to develop and holding them accountable for applying what they have learned is an important responsibility for leaders. Some companies, such as Western Union, think that people development is so important that 20 percent of a sales manager's bonus is contingent upon the development of his or her followers.

This section of the pipeline is also concerned with evaluating the effectiveness of a leadership development program. At a minimum, one should ask whether the training successfully accomplished all of the course objectives. According to Kirkpatrick (1967), reaction, learning, behavioral, and results criteria can be used to evaluate a training program's success. Asking students to subjectively rate a course on overall value, enjoyment, and effectiveness exemplifies reaction criteria. Midterm and final exams are good examples of learning criteria, and asking peers whether participants have changed their behavior as a result of a university course in leadership would be an example of behavioral criteria. Examples of results criteria would include managers with work groups reporting increased sales, higher production or quality rates, improved customer satisfaction, or decreased repair times as a consequence of a leadership development program.

Although reaction, learning, and even behavioral data can be collected fairly easily for a university course or corporate leadership program, collecting results criteria has proven to be very difficult. There are often a number of factors that affect the output of a work group, and some (e.g., market forces, a strike, or an economic downturn) can have a much bigger effect on work group results than any leadership development program. It is important to note that more and more organizations are looking for the return on investment (ROI) for their leadership development dollars. What should the company expect in return for investing large amounts of money to develop their leadership bench strength? In many cases companies are looking for either behavior change or improved results to justify the cost of training their leaders. Because most corporate leadership development programs do not address all sections of the Development Pipeline, it is very unlikely that participants will have significantly improved capabilities as a result of these programs. And because the leadership capabilities of the participants were not significantly improved, it has so far proven to be very difficult to demonstrate a good return for a company's leadership development dollars (Curphy, 2001).

Finally, it is important to note that few university or corporate leadership development programs address all sections of the Development Pipeline. This does not mean that no learning takes place in these programs, but rather that learning could be substantially enhanced if some action was taken to expand the more constricted sections of the pipeline. Many times these actions cost little in time or money, but the payoff for learning can be quite high. For example, having participants simply complete a self-rated proficiency quiz on the course objectives as prework can enhance insight. Similarly, ensuring that participants meet with their boss to discuss what they have learned and how they will apply it at work can improve accountability. As we see in the Development Pipeline, training plays a key but not the only role in leadership development. Having insight into what skills to learn and the motivation to acquire them and being held accountable for learning are just as important as training program method and content. Organizations will not realize the full potential of their development interventions unless their programs address all sections of the Development Pipeline.

Building Your Leadership Self-Image

This chapter has explored how leadership develops through experience and formal education. Before concluding, however, we should acknowledge that not everyone wants to be a leader or believes he can be. John Gardner (1965) has argued that many of our best and brightest young people actually have been immunized against, and dissuaded from, seeking leadership opportunities and responsibilities. Other young people, even if they want to be leaders, may not believe they have what it takes. Both groups, we believe, are selling themselves short.

For those who merely want to avoid the responsibilities of leadership, we encourage an openness of mind about leadership's importance and pervasiveness. We hope this book offers ways of thinking about leadership that make it at once more immediate, more relevant, and more interesting than it may have seemed before. For others, we encourage flexibility in self-image. Do not stay out of the leadership arena based on some global and self-defeating generalization such as "I am not the leader type." Experiment and take a few risks with different leadership roles. This will help you appreciate new facets of yourself as well as broaden your leadership self-image.

Summary

This chapter reviews several major points regarding how leadership can be developed through both formal education and experience. One way to get more out of your leadership courses and experiences is through the application of the action-observation-reflection model. This model provides a framework for better understanding of leadership situations. In addition, being aware of the role perception plays in leadership development is also important, as it affects what you observe, how you interpret your observations, and what actions you take as a leader. Finally, it is important to remember that both education and experience can contribute to your development as a leader by enhancing your ability to reflect on and analyze leadership situations. Exposure to formal leadership education programs can help you to develop thinking frames or multiple perspectives to analyze leadership situations, and the people you work with and the task itself can also provide you with insights on how to be a better leader. However, what you gain from any leadership program or experience is a function of what you make of it. Successful leaders are those who have "an extraordinary tenacity in extracting something worthwhile from their experience and in seeking experiences rich in opportunities for growth" (McCall, Lombardo, & Morrison, 1988, p. 122). If you want to become a better leader, then you must seek challenges and try to get all you can from any leadership situation or opportunity.

Key Terms

action-observation-reflection model   49
spiral of experience   50
perceptual set   51
attribution   52
fundamental attribution error   53
self-serving bias   53
actor/observer difference   53
self-fulfilling prophecy   54
single-loop learning   57
double-loop learning   57
thinking frames   58
mentor   59

executive coaching   60
individualized feedback   67
case studies   67
role playing   68
simulations   68
games   68
in-basket exercises   68
leaderless group discussions   68
Development Pipeline   69
e-learning   71
action learning   71
active learning   71

Questions

1. Not all effective leaders seem to be reflective by nature. How do you reconcile that with the concept of the spiral of experience and its role in leadership development?

2. Explain how you can use knowledge about each of the following to enrich the benefits of your own present leadership experiences:

   a. The action-observation-reflection model.

  b. The people you interact and work
     with.
  c. The activities you're involved in.
3. Using the role of teacher as a specific
   instance of leadership, discuss how a
   teacher's perceptual set, expectations of
   students, and attributions may affect
   student motivation and performance. Do
   you think some teachers could become
   more effective by becoming more aware
   of these processes? Would that be true for
   leaders in general?
4. If you were to design the perfect
   leadership development experience for
   yourself, how would you do so and what
   would it include? How would you know
   it was effective?

5. Do you think people have a need for
   growth and development?
6. One important aspect of learning from
   experience is observing the consequences
   of one's actions. Sometimes, however, the
   most significant consequences of a
   leader's actions do not occur for several
   years (e.g., the ultimate impact of certain
   personnel decisions or a strategic decision
   to change a product line). If that is so,
   then is there any way individuals can
   learn from the consequences of those
   actions in a way to modify their behavior?
   If consequences are so delayed, is there a
   danger they might draw the wrong
   lessons from their experiences?

Skills

Leadership skills relevant to this chapter
include:
- Learning from experience
- Communication
- Listening
- Building technical competence
- Building effective relationships with
  superiors

- Building effective relationships with peers
- Problem solving
- Improving creativity
- Diagnosing performance problems in
  individuals, teams and organizations

Activity

Divide yourselves into groups and in each
group contrast what attributions you might
make about the leadership style of two

different individuals. All you know about
either of them is the following:

	Person A	*Person B*
Favorite TV show	*60 Minutes*	*Survivor*
Car	Ford Mustang	Volkswagen Beetle
Favorite sport	American football	Mountain biking
Political affiliation	Republican	Democrat
Favorite music	Country & western	New Age

4 ASSESSING LEADERSHIP AND MEASURING ITS EFFECTS

Introduction

I On a practical level, leadership is a topic that almost everyone is interested in at one time or another. For political scientists this interest manifests itself in the question "Who shall rule?" Psychologists take a different slant on the question and ask, "Who should rule?" People do have a vested interest in who is running their government, schools, company, or church; and because of this interest thousands of books and articles have been written about the topic of leadership. And just as computers and cars differ in terms of quality, so do the books and articles written about leadership. Some leadership books are built on solid research and can add tremendous value to readers, whereas others seem to be based on nothing more than opinions and hearsay. They say you can never judge a book by its cover, but unfortunately the uninformed find it extremely difficult to differentiate research findings from opinion. There are numerous examples where the conventional wisdom about leadership proved to be wrong once it was properly investigated. For example, only 70 years ago it was assumed that people who were taller and more athletic were better leaders. As a result, a number of books and articles were written about the importance of these attributes to leadership success. Not until the 1940s did leadership researchers systematically investigate these two attributes and show that the conventional wisdom was wrong (Stogdill, 1948).

> *Only 8 percent of Fortune 1000 executive directors rate their leadership capacity as excellent, while 47 percent rated their leadership capacity as fair to poor.*
>
> The Conference Board

Although the example above is fairly dated, there are more recent examples where the research findings ran contrary to the conventional wisdom about leadership. For a long time many people thought smarter people made better leaders; people who were not as smart were believed to be less effective leaders. On the surface this seems to make sense, because if given a choice most people would rather work for a smart than a dull leader. But research by Fiedler and his colleagues showed that in some situations smarter leaders consistently performed less well than those who were less smart. This was the case when smart, inexperienced leaders were asked to perform in highly ambiguous and stressful situations. Leaders who were less smart but more experienced often performed at a much higher level than their more gifted counterparts because they had already learned how to operate effectively under high levels of stress.

Until fairly recently the conventional wisdom also maintained that leaders who were stable and predictable were more effective than those who were less

One-fifth of large American companies will lose at least 48 percent of their top talent to retirement between 2000 and 2005.
Development Dimensions International

stable and predictable. However, research on the use of power shows that the most effective leaders use different bases of power to meet situational demands. Similarly, research on charismatic leadership shows that many charismatic leaders are unconventional and unpredictable in their behavior. They often come from the fringes of society, do all they can to change the status quo, and have a bigger impact on the people, organizations, and societies that they touch than their more stable and predictable counterparts. Examples might include Herb Kelleher, of Southwest Airlines, Martin Luther King, Jr., and Mahatma Gandhi. Once again, it is the only systematic investigation of the airlines industry that allows us to separate leadership fact from fiction.

Perhaps the biggest challenge to improving the practice of leadership is to provide practitioners with timely, easily digestible, research-grounded advice on how to effectively lead others. Leadership *practitioners* often want fast answers about how to be more effective or successful. Paradoxically, another challenge is that high-quality leadership research is difficult, expensive, and time consuming to conduct. For example, it often takes five years or more for a leadership study to be conducted and published (Fiedler, 1995). Obviously, leadership practitioners cannot wait this long for answers.

This tension between discovering the "truth" about a leadership question and being able to apply what is learned is what we call the **practice-research gap.** Leadership practitioners often seek information about how to improve their leadership skills, but typically find little help in the work of leadership researchers whose studies may seem untimely or of little practical value (Rynes, Bartunek, & Daft, 2001). Hogan, Curphy, and Hogan (1994) pointed out that the knowledge accumulated from 80 years of leadership research is of tremendous value, yet scientists have paid little attention to the ultimate consumers of their work—leaders and leaders to be. As a result, "real" leaders understandably turn to popular books and articles that *appear* to provide timely answers to their practical concerns. Unfortunately, however, the claims in the popular or "trade" literature are rarely based on sound research; they oversimplify the complexities of the leadership process; and many times they actually offer bad advice. Relatively little weight is given to well-researched leadership studies, primarily because the arcane requirements of publishing articles in scholarly journals make their content virtually unreadable (and certainly uninteresting) to actual leadership practitioners.

One key objective of this book is to make the results of leadership research more usable to leaders and leaders to be. This chapter is specifically designed to help readers better understand how leadership research is conducted, gain an appreciation for some of the practical applications of this research, and sharpen critical thinking skills about leadership and leadership research. However, it is also worth noting that this entire book is dedicated to bridging the practice-research gap. This book reviews what researchers know about various leadership topics, translates these findings into useful advice for practitioners, describes how practitioners might apply these findings in the work setting, and predicts what results practitioners should see if they apply this information at work.

At the same time, however, we stress that this book is *not* intended to be a guide for conducting leadership research; rather, it is a guide to help leadership students and budding practitioners *be* better leaders by helping them understand the complex relationships among many factors affecting leadership. This book provides multiple frameworks for conceptualizing leadership in order to help practitioners maximize what they learn from experience. As an overview, this chapter uses several practical examples to review the major techniques leadership researchers have used to assess or measure leadership. When assessing leadership, researchers are looking at the ways that leaders are different from followers or how successful leaders differ from unsuccessful leaders in terms of variables such as their values, personality traits, intelligence, job knowledge, experience, or behavior. Next, the chapter continues with these practical examples to discuss the major indicators used to measure leadership effectiveness. After that, we look at several methodologies that are used to study leadership. This section explores the empirical foundations of studying the *relationship* between leadership and other variables. In other words, this section looks at different ways to study the relationship between leadership (e.g., what leaders do) and its effects (e.g., what happens as a result).

Assessing Leadership

Because this chapter is about assessing leadership, it seems appropriate to begin with an example from research. The research in this case deals with leadership in commercial airline crews. Many airline crews consist of three positions with very distinct responsibilities. The aircraft captain is the final authority for all decisions regarding the aircraft and is ultimately responsible for the safety of the passengers and crew. The copilot helps the captain fly the aircraft, and the flight engineer is primarily responsible for the aircraft's preflight inspections and operation of systems (e.g., electrical, hydraulic, fuel, communication). Since airline

By and large, executives make poor promotion and staffing decisions. By all accounts, their batting average is no better than .333. At most, one-third of such decisions turn out right; one-third are minimally effective; and one-third are outright failures. In no other area would we put up with such miserable performance; indeed, we need not and should not. Managers making people decisions will never be perfect, of course, but they should come pretty close to batting 1.000.

Peter Drucker

crews must work together as a coordinated team to successfully complete a flight, one of the authors of this text studied factors affecting crew coordination (Ginnett, 1988). As a part of this project, he flew with a number of different airline crews and recorded conversations between crew members. The following is an excerpt of an interview between a copilot and the researcher:

> *Researcher:* Are all the captains you fly with pretty much the same?
> *Aircrew member:* Oh, no. Some guys are the greatest guys in the world to fly with. I mean they may not have the greatest hands in the world but that doesn't matter. When you fly with them, you feel like you can work together to get the job done. You really want to do a good job for them. Some other captains are just the opposite . . . you just can't stand to work with them. That doesn't mean you'll do anything that's unsafe or dangerous but you won't go out of your way to keep him or her out of trouble either. So you'll just sit back and do what you have to and just hope he or she screws up.
> *Researcher:* How can you tell which kind of captain you're working with?
> *Aircrew member:* Oh, you can tell.
> *Researcher:* How?
> *Aircrew member:* I don't know how you tell but it doesn't take very long. Just a couple of minutes and you'll know.

The above conversation details some of the difficulties in assessing leadership. Although it was the airline pilot's personal opinion that it was relatively easy to recognize good captains, personal opinions about leadership effectiveness can vary substantially across individuals. Thus the copilot may feel that the captain may not be a good leader, but the flight attendants and ground crews might think this captain is very effective. Who is right or whose opinion carries more weight in this situation? Moreover, the copilot thought he could tell good from bad leaders once they were on the job, but many organizations want to know this information *before* they make a hiring decision. Putting the wrong people into key leadership positions can literally cost stockholders billions of dollars and lead to organizational ruin (Leib, 1998). There are a number of ways to improve the odds of making good leadership hiring decisions, and some hiring techniques are much more effective than others in predicting leadership success. How do we know this? We know this because researchers have systematically determined which leadership assessment techniques yield more valid and accurate predictions than other techniques. Because the identification of leadership talent is so important to organizations these days, many of them have capitalized on these research findings to create practical tools and processes for assessing the leadership capabilities of potential first-line supervisors through CEOs (Lewis, Robie, Nilsen, & Curphy, 2001).

Another practical example might help to illuminate the various techniques organizations use to assess leadership. Suppose you were the mayor of a midsized city and you had fired the chief of police a little over two months ago. The chief was let go because of an increase in the city's crime rate, allegations of racial profiling, rumors of evidence tampering and department corruption, and reports of favoritism and poor morale in the police department. You want the new police chief to substantially reduce crime, clean up the police department, improve morale, and restore citizens' confidence in the department. Because your political future might depend on hiring the right police chief, you have begun a national search to find the right candidate. Over 50 people have formally applied for the position by the application cutoff date. So what would you do to pick the best candidate from this pool of 50 applicants?

When doctors make a poor diagnosis, their patients die and they don't have to deal with it anymore. When lawyers fail to present a good case, their clients go to jail and they don't have to deal with it anymore. But when hiring managers make a mistake, they have to say "good morning" to it every day.

Pete Ramstad,
Personnel Decisions International

If you didn't know anything about hiring new police chiefs, then you would probably do what most other organizations do when hiring new leaders. You would begin the process of hiring a police chief by reviewing the resumes of the 50 candidates (see Highlight 4.1). You would use the results of this resume screening to identify who

---

Resume Screening

Highlight 4.1

A common technique many organizations use to hire new employees is resume screening. A **resume** is a brief summary of a candidate's work and educational experiences. It is very likely that you will be asked to submit your resume when applying for a job. Hiring managers or human resource representatives then screen candidates' resumes to determine who should be tested or interviewed for the position. Because resumes often represent the first step in the hiring process and are an opportunity for candidates to put their best foot forward, you would expect them to be closely edited before they are submitted. However, some errors always seem to get through the editing process. Excerpts of some hilarious mistakes found on resumes include:

1. "Instrumental for ruining the entire operation of a Midwest chain store."
2. "Note: Please don't misconstrue my 14 jobs as 'job hopping.' I have never quit a job."
3. "The company made me a scapegoat, just like my three previous employers."
4. "Am a perfectionist and rarely if if ever forget details."
5. "I have lurnt Word Perfect 6.0, computor and spreadsheat progroms."
6. "References: None. I've left a path of destruction behind me."

Source: A. Fisher, "Stupid Resume Tricks: How to Avoid Getting Hired," *Fortune*, July 21, 1997.

you believe are the top 5 to 10 candidates. You would bring this narrower pool of candidates in for one or more interviews and perhaps narrow the pool down to the top two candidates. At this point you would probably call the references of the top two candidates and make a final hiring decision based on the candidate who seemed to have the best "chemistry" or "job fit." Although this hiring process appears to make perfect sense, it is very unlikely that you would pick a police chief who will be able to successfully reduce crime, build bridges with the community, and turn the department around. It may be that the odds of picking a good police chief through this process are not much better than picking one of the 50 applicants at random. But how do we know this? As seen in Table 4–1, we know this because leadership research shows that application blanks, unstructured interviews, and reference checks are very poor predictors of leadership effectiveness. Yet these techniques are among the most frequently used by organizations making leadership hiring decisions. That the most frequently used leadership hiring techniques are also the least valid shows how wide the practice-research gap truly is (see Highlight 4.2 for more information about the negative consequences of using poor leadership assessment techniques).

Best Practices in Assessing Leadership Potential

So what should you do if you want to improve the odds of hiring the right police chief? Research has shown that the best place to start is to clearly define what you are looking for in a prospective police chief. To do this, you would need to build

TABLE 4–1 Typical Correlations between Different Assessment Techniques and Job Performance in the United States

Assessment Technique	Correlation	U.S. Companies Using This Technique (percent)
Work sample/skill test	.54	1–20%
Mental abilities test	.53	1–20
Assessment center/job simulation	.50	1–20
Job knowledge test	.48	20–30
Job tryout	.44	1–20
Biographical questionnaire	.40	1–20
Structured interview[a]	.40	unknown
Personality test	.30	1–20
Unstructured interview	.20	90+
Reference check	.14	80+
Application blank	.10	90+

[a]Although interviews are among the most popular assessment techniques, it is uncertain how many are structured versus unstructured interviews.

Sources: K. Pearlman, "Validity Generalization: From Theory to Application" (paper presented at the Center for Human Resources Programs, Institute of Industrial Relations, University of California–Berkeley, 1985); T.A. Judge, "The Impact of I/O Psychology," *The Industrial and Organizational Psychologist* 35 (1997), pp. 108–110; A. M. Ryan, L. McFarland, H. Baron, and R. Page, "An International Look at Selection Practices: Nation and Culture as Explanations for Variability in Practices," *Personnel Psychology* 52, no. 2 (1999), pp. 359–92; American Management Association, *Job Skill Testing and Psychological Measurement*, June 2000.

The Glass Ceiling Effect

Highlight 4.2

Research has shown that significantly fewer women than men make it to the top leadership positions in corporate America. For example, women make up more than 40 percent of the workforce, but only 10 percent of the executive positions in Fortune 500 companies are held by women. Moreover, only 2 percent of women hold one of the top five jobs in these organizations; about 100 of the Fortune 500 companies have no women at all in top positions. The percentage of women in top leadership positions is no better in Japan, where only 9 percent of midlevel managers are women. However, research has shown that there are few developmental differences between male and female executives, and at least at midmanagement level there seem to be few practical differences in performance between men and women. This underrepresentation at the executive level is also known as the **glass ceiling effect.** So, if there are few performance and developmental differences between men and women at the midmanagement level, then why aren't a higher percentage of underrepresented groups filling executive positions? It may well be that top executives hire people in their own image, and if that image is one of a white male, then it is likely white males will be chosen to become their successors. Perhaps the first step in breaking this cycle is to adopt best-practice leadership assessment systems. In all likelihood these systems will reveal few practical performance differences between gender groups. If there are few performance differences at the midmanagement level, and if executive successors are coming primarily from midmanagement ranks, then over time a higher percentage of women should reach the executive level.

Sources: J. R. Renshaw, *Kimono in the Boardroom: The Invisible Revolution of Japanese Women Managers* (New York, Oxford University Press, 1999); S. Gebelein, "As Leaders, Women Rule," *Business Week,* November 24, 2000, p. 74; E. A. Powell, "Women Hit a 'Glass Wall,'" *Denver Post,* November 12, 1999, p. C-1.

a **competency model** for the police chief position. A competency model is the set of skills, knowledge, abilities, or other attributes that are relevant to successful performance in a particular job. In this situation the competency model for a police chief might consist of the following: problem-solving and decision-making skills, visioning skills, planning and coordinating skills, budgeting skills, delegation skills, organizational change skills, coaching skills, performance management skills, the ability to create high-performing teams, conflict management skills, the ability to build relationships with and earn the trust of key internal and external

> *If you don't know where you are going, you'll probably end up somewhere else.*
>
> David Campbell, The Center for Creative Leadership

stakeholders, communication skills, the ability to motivate others, honesty and integrity, the ability to cope with high levels of stress, and in-depth knowledge of the judicial system and various law enforcement techniques. The best candidate would be the person who possessed most if not all of these skills and attributes. How would you go about determining how many of these skills and attributes each of the 50 applicants possessed? And wouldn't it be even more important to know how well developed these skills and attributes are in each candidate? Fortunately, leadership researchers have collected a wealth of data that provide answers to these two questions.

> *The best predictor of future leadership behavior is past leadership behavior in similar circumstances.*
> Personnel Decisions International

Once the competency model for police chiefs had been finalized, leadership research shows that a **multiple hurdles approach** would be the most cost-effective and valid way to identify the best candidate from the applicant talent pool (Saal & Knight, 1988; Lewis, Nilsen, Robie, & Curphy, 2001). In a multiple hurdles approach, applicants are put through a series of leadership assessment techniques and only the applicants who "pass" one assessment are allowed to move on to the next, and so forth. Typically the most inexpensive leadership assessment techniques are used first, with the most expensive (and often most valid) techniques used as the last hurdles in the hiring process.

We would begin the multiple hurdle approach for our candidates by having the pool of 50 applicants take various **paper-and-pencil measures** of leadership effectiveness. As shown in Table 4–1, leadership researchers have indicated that biographical questionnaires, personality inventories, mental abilities tests, and interest inventories can do a very good job predicting future leadership effectiveness. Moreover, these measures are inexpensive and relatively easy to administer. In the case of identifying the right police chief, we would begin the hiring process by having all 50 candidates fill out a biographical questionnaire (McElreath & Bass, 1999). This questionnaire would ask candidates to identify what they had done in the past that was related to the police chief competencies, such as solving problems, making decisions, managing budgets, coaching others, and so forth. The responses to the questionnaire would be scored and only the top 10 scoring candidates would be allowed to proceed to the next hurdle.

The next step in the multiple hurdles approach would be to interview the remaining talent pool. In **structured interviews,** the interviewer asks the leader a predetermined set of questions; in **unstructured interviews** the interviewer does not follow a predetermined set of questions (Campion, Palmer, & Campion, 1997; Ganzach, Kluger, & Klayman, 2000). In an unstructured format, the interviewer has the latitude to allow the interview to proceed in whatever direction seems appropriate. The conversation between the researcher and aircrew member earlier in this chapter is an excerpt from an unstructured interview. Although unstructured interviews can provide interesting insights into the leadership process, it is difficult to compare the results of interviews from different leaders. Structured interviews, with their common set of questions and rating scales, usu-

TABLE 4–2   Selection Practices in Europe, Africa, Asia, and Australia

Americans alone cannot be blamed for making poor leadership selection decisions. People all over the world seem to make many of the same leadership selection mistakes. For example, consider the popularity of the assessment techniques used by the following countries:

Assessment Technique	Percent Usage						
	Australia	France	Germany	Hong Kong	Japan	South Africa	Sweden
Work sample/skill test	>5%	>5%	>5%	>5%	0%	>5%	>5%
Mental abilities test	20–50	20–50	1–20	1–20	0	50–80	20–50
Assessment center/ job simulation	1–20	1–20	1–20	1–20	0	20–50	1–20
Job tryout	1–20	20–50	1–20	1–20	0	20–50	1–20
Biographical form	1–20	1–20	20–50	1–20	1–20	1–20	1–20
One-on-one interviews	50–80	80–100	80–100	50–80	50–80	80–100	80–100
Reference check	80–100	50–80	20–50	50–80	50–80	80–100	80–100
Application blank	50–80	80–100	50–80	80–100	80–100	80–100	1–20
Personality test	20–50	50–80	1–20	20–50	0	50–80	50–80
Graphology (Handwriting analysis)	>5	50–80	>5	>5	0	1–20	1–20
Foreign language test	>5	20–50	1–20	20–50	0	1–20	20–50

This table provides a nice overview of the process a person would likely go through if hired for a leadership position in another country; those of you with poor handwriting may not want to apply for a leadership position in France. Although French companies seem to believe that graphology can be used to accurately predict leadership potential, there has yet to be a single shred of evidence to support this notion.

Source: A. M. Ryan, L. McFarland, H. Baron, and R. Page, "An International Look at Selection Practices: Nation and Culture as Explanations for Variability in Practices," *Personnel Psychology* 52, no. 2 (1999), pp. 359–92.

ally make it much easier to compare different leaders' attributes and skills. To use structured interviews for hiring a new police chief, you would begin by asking each candidate the same set of questions. These questions would ask participants to describe situations in the past where they had to exhibit the skills and attributes identified in the police chief competency model. The answers to the questions would then be evaluated using common rating scales. Examples of some of the police chief structured interview questions can be found in Highlight 4.3; more in-depth information about unstructured leadership interviews and examples of what not to do in an interview can be found in Highlights 4.4 and 4.5. Selection practices in different countries are summarized in Table 4–2.

The last step in the multiple hurdles approach would be to put the top three candidates through a police chief assessment center. **Assessment centers** probably represent the most sophisticated and expensive method for assessing leadership potential. The historical underpinnings of assessment centers lie in Europe where they were used in the 1920s to select officers for the German military (Simoneit, 1944) and civil servants and foreign service officers for the British government (Garforth, 1945). In the United States, assessment centers were first used to select special agents and spies for the Office of Strategic Services, now known

Interviewing: The Good, the Bad, and the Ugly

Highlight 4.3

The Good: Structured Interviews

Hiring managers make much better hiring decisions if they use structured interviews. Structured interviews are based on two premises: *Past behavior is the best predictor of future behavior, and recent behavior is a better predictor than distant past behavior.* Thus, the interviewer is using questions that ask applicants to describe situations similar to those they may encounter on the job, how they reacted or behaved in those situations, and what the impact of those behaviors was. Moreover, good interviewers probe for examples from the recent past. Some of the structured interview questions an applicant for a police chief position would be asked might include:

1. Ability to Motivate Others: Describe a situation where you had to motivate a group of people to do something they didn't want to do. What did you do, and what was the outcome of those behaviors?
2. Conflict Management Skills: Describe the last time you had to resolve a conflict between you and one of your peers. What was the situation, what did you do, and what were the consequences of those behaviors?
3. Performance Management Skills: Describe the last time you had to deal with a performance problem with a subordinate. What was the situation, how did you handle the problem, and how was the problem actually resolved?

As you might imagine, it takes considerable training to be a good structured interviewer. However, this investment in time can have a big payoff. Research has shown that skilled structured interviewers make substantially better hiring decisions than unskilled unstructured interviewers (see Table 4–1).

Sources: T. Janz, L. W. Hellervik, and D. C. Gilmore, *Behavior Description Interviewing* (Boston: Allyn and Bacon, 1986); V. Arnold, "Management and Executive Assessment" (paper presented at Personnel Decisions International, Denver, September 1997).

as the Central Intelligence Agency (Murray & MacKinnon, 1946). The purpose of modern-day assessment centers is to assess, identify, and develop leadership potential, and well over 200 institutions utilize this process (Spychalski, Quinones, Gaugler, & Pohley, 1997; Personnel Decisions International, 2001).

The three candidates attending an assessment center would go through a "virtual reality" experience specifically designed for police chiefs. They would begin the process by completing personality inventories and mental abilities tests while attending the assessment center. They would also spend one to two days in a simulated police department where they would be put in a number of difficult, com-

Interviewing: The Good, the Bad, and the Ugly

Highlight 4.4

The Bad: Unstructured Interviews

In unstructured interviews the applicant is asked whatever questions the interviewer deems necessary. This is probably the most popular leadership selection technique, and it gets even more popular the higher in the organization you go. At best, many of the questions in an unstructured interview lack job relevance; at worst they are just plain offensive or illegal. Some of the unstructured interview questions for a leadership position might include:

1. If you were any part of a car, what part would you be and why?
2. If you could go out to dinner with anyone, who would it be with and why?
3. Do you plan on having any more children?
4. How do you feel about women in leadership positions?

As ridiculous as these questions may seem, all too many people use them to hire or promote leaders. However, research has shown that unstructured interviews are poor predictors of future leadership success. So why do so many people use this approach when hiring leaders? One reason is that many leaders are absolutely convinced that they know how to pick other leaders. Yet an in-depth analysis of their past hires would reveal that they had more "misses" than "hits," but most leaders can recall only the times they made the right hiring decisions. Another reason is that most leaders are unfamiliar with the leadership assessment research. Because of this selective recall and lack of knowledge, unstructured interviews are likely to be around for a long time.

plex situations and their behaviors recorded by highly trained observers. Some of the simulations used in an assessment center include in-basket exercises and role plays. An **in-basket exercise** is a work simulation that requires candidates to read an overview of a fictitious police department and organizational charts. The candidates are then given two hours to indicate how they would handle various articles, e-mails, letters, voice mails, and memos in a typical police chief's in-basket. Candidates would then participate in a series of **role-play simulations,** of work, some of which might include a 30-minute meeting with a fictitious follower who is having performance problems, a mock interview with a TV reporter, a meeting with an angry citizen, and a presentation to the city council. The actors in the role-play simulations are trained assessors who observe and rate the performance of each candidate on the competencies embedded in each

> *Assessing leadership is like using a micrometer to measure jello.*
>
> Rex Blake,
> Independent consultant

Interviewing: The Good, the Bad, and the Ugly

Highlight 4.5

The Ugly: Examples of Stupid Interviewing Tricks

A survey of some of the top personnel executives in corporate America yielded the following behaviors in the people they had interviewed:

1. She wore a Walkman and said she could listen to me and the music at the same time.
2. The interviewee said he was so well qualified that if he didn't get the job, it would prove that the company's management was incompetent.
3. The candidate interrupted the interview so that he could phone his therapist for advice on answering questions.
4. During the interview he took off his right shoe and sock and sprinkled medicated foot powder on his foot. While he was putting his shoe back on, he mentioned that he had to use the powder four times a day, and this was one of those times.
5. Pointing to the picture on the interviewer's desk, the interviewee asked who the lovely babe was. When the interviewer said it was his wife, the interviewee asked if she was home right now and wanted her phone number.

Sources: B. Byham, *Landing the Job You Want: How to Have the Best Job Interview of Your Life* (Pittsburgh: DDI Press, 1997); L. Littlewood, "First Impression: Honesty, Attitude Turn Interviews into Jobs," *Denver Post*, May 24, 1998, p. E-3.

simulation. The assessors would then look across all of the instruments and simulations to create overall competency scores for each candidate, which would then be summarized in a written report. The mayor would then review the report and make a final hiring decision.

It is to be hoped that the process makes sense: first defining what you want in a leader, using job-relevant paper-and-pencil measures as an initial screen for leadership candidates, and then using structured interviews and high-fidelity work simulations to identify those candidates with the most potential for a leadership position. The first step in improving the bench strength of the leaders within an organization is to hire or promote the right people to begin with, and this process provides a road map for doing just that. Not only will organizations see an increase in their leadership bench strength, but also they will see improved organizational performance by using these leadership assessment processes (Heine, 2000; Hogan & Hogan, 2000; Curphy, 2000; Lewis, Nilsen, Robie, & Curphy, 2001). This does not mean that organizations need to adopt all of these steps in the multiple-hurdles process to hire and promote people with leadership potential. Many times having a clearly defined competency model and a biographical form and structured interview questions linked to the model will do a fairly good job of improving the odds of hiring good leaders. This is particularly true when hiring lower-level leaders, such as first-line supervisors. However, research has shown that work simulations are better predictors of leadership potential for midlevel managers and executives because candidates at these levels possess many of the same personality traits and are all fairly bright; therefore these measures do not do as good a job differentiating people with high versus low leadership potential (Curphy, 2000, 2001). In addition, the work simulations also provide hiring managers with better information about the development needs of newly hired leaders. This information can in turn be used to accelerate the assimilation process so that new leaders are making a greater contribution to organizational success shortly after being hired.

Although there are important organizational benefits to hiring the right leaders, perhaps the most important point to be made about the preceding section is that there would be little to write about if it weren't for the efforts of leadership researchers. Research is the only way we know which leadership techniques are the most valid for which leadership positions. Leadership researchers have conducted thousands of studies to determine how well various assessment techniques work for predicting future leadership effectiveness. Not only has this research helped companies to hire the right leaders, it has also leveled the playing field for candidates by creating fairer hiring processes. Unfortunately, Tables 4–1 and 4–2 show that most of this research continues to be ignored by the people making leadership hiring decisions. Organizations will continue to experience a shortfall in leadership talent as long as they continue to use assessment techniques that essentially result in little more than random selection.

Measuring the Effects of Leadership

After investment of time, energy, and money to hire the right candidate, the next key question is whether the new police chief has truly had any positive impact on the organization. After the chief's one year on the job, has the crime rate been reduced? Has department morale improved? Has racial profiling decreased, and has there been a commensurate increase in the public's trust in the police department? What information would you need to collect in order to evaluate the performance of the police chief on these issues? And if there are any changes in these performance indicators, are they the direct result of, in spite of, or completely independent of the efforts of the new police chief? Similarly, how would you compare the performances of Madeleine Albright and Colin Powell as secretary of state? Would you look at the level of morale in the State Department, the number of peace treaties or trade negotiations signed, the number of resolutions passed in the United 1Nations, and so on? Just as various techniques are used to assess leaders, there also are various ways to measure their *effects* on subordinates, organizations, or in the case of our two secretaries of state, the world. But what do we mean by "effects on subordinates"? A useful way to think about this is in terms of the ways that we typically define leadership success. We usually do not differentiate between successful and unsuccessful leaders by the behaviors they exhibit or the attributes they possess; rather, we are more likely to consider whether their followers are productive or satisfied. For example, we could make judgments about the success of a leader by looking at the police chief's ability to reduce crime rates, a coach's win-loss record, a college professor's end-of-course student ratings, or the production or quality rates for a production manager's work unit. Although the leader's behavior or personality traits will probably play a key role in these indices, when making judgments about the relative success of a leader we are examining the *consequences* or *impact* of these behaviors and not the behaviors per se. The material in this section describes how researchers typically measure leadership impact and their respective strengths and limitations.

Common Measures of Successful and Unsuccessful Leadership

Half of the CEOs in the world are below average.

David Campbell, The Center for Creative Leadership

In reality, there are a vast number of measures available to judge successful and unsuccessful leaders (see, for example, Highlight 4.6). Some of the more commonly used measures include a superior's effectiveness or promotion ratings, subordinates' ratings of their job satisfaction and morale or of their leader's effectiveness, and various work-unit performance indices. We will use the police chief example to discuss each of these in further detail below.

Superiors' Effectiveness and Performance Ratings.   One way to judge Colin Powell, Madeleine Albright, or any leader's success is in terms of his or her performance appraisal ratings. Most **superiors' performance ratings** are arrived at by a leader's superior and include ratings of performance on several relevant dimensions, as well as a recommendation (or not) for promotion. For example, Bass and Yammarino (1988) used superiors' overall performance ratings and promotion recommendations as criteria for judging the leadership effectiveness of navy surface fleet officers.

Because almost all organizations use some type of performance appraisal system, it may be worthwhile to briefly describe a typical performance appraisal form. The better performance appraisal forms typically include several features. First, superiors use some type of scale to rate how well a target leader accomplished several key objectives. Superiors also rate the leader on several key dimensions the organization believes are important, such as integrity, leadership, administrative skills, communication impact, and so forth. Finally, superiors then rate the overall performance and/or the promotability of the leader (Arvey & Murphy, 1998; Marentette, 2000). In our police chief example, you as the mayor would rate the police chief on *what* he or she actually accomplished over the past year. In other words, how successful was the police chief in reducing crime rates, improving department morale, reducing the number of employee grievances, reducing the number of

The Impact of Best Practice Leadership Selection Techniques

Highlight 4.6

Recently a very large manufacturer acquired two other large manufacturing firms. The top leaders of the combined organization were faced with several key leadership dilemmas. The first was to determine which individuals would fill the top leadership positions in the combined company, as there was no particularly good information about the leadership talent in any of the three organizations. The second was to create a new culture for the combined organization that emphasized financial acumen, customer service, global perspective, attracting and developing talent, and a new business strategy that focused on services rather than production. Working against this new culture was the frequent emphasis of the three heritage organizations on technical excellence to the exclusion of profitability and customer service. The third was that many of the top 300 leaders in all three organizations were due to retire in the next three years and top leadership was uncertain how it could start to identify and build its leadership talent to fill these gaps.

To address these three needs, the combined organization started by having the top 250 executives go through a two-day customized assessment center. The results of the center were used to place people in key leadership positions, identify strengths and weaknesses of individual leaders and leadership teams, and help executives understand the demands, challenges, and expectations of leaders in the new organizational culture. The next 750 leaders in the combined organization are currently going through another customized assessment center in order to identify and build replacement leaders for those executives who will soon be retiring. The results of the assessment center process on some of the key unit performance indices of the company have been nothing short of remarkable. In the year after the assessment center was used to identify and deploy the top 250 executives in the company:

- Sales increased from $35 to $38 billion.
- Earnings improved from $-$277 million to $1.902 billion.
- On-time deliveries improved from 48 percent to 100 percent.
- Stock price increased 27 percent.

Source: D. Heine, "Using I/O Psychology to Turn Around a Business," in G. J. Curphy (chair), *The Role of I/O Psychology in Executive Assessment and Development.* (symposium at the 15th Annual Conference of the Society for Industrial and Organizational Psychology, New Orleans, 2000).

lawsuits filed against the department, and improving trust with the local community? You would also rate *how* the police chief went about accomplishing these objectives. This usually involves rating each of the police chief competencies, such as the ability to solve problems and make decisions, meet budgets, coach others, create high-performing teams, manage conflict, and build relationships with and earn the trust of key internal and external stakeholders. These what and how ratings would then be combined to provide an overall rating of the police chief's performance over the past year.

As the mayor you would probably want to complete a performance appraisal on the police chief. However, you should also know that many times performance appraisal ratings might not be an accurate reflection of the police chief's true impact on his or her followers or the organization. Sometimes superiors simply do not take the time to provide accurate and comprehensive performance appraisal ratings; at other times superiors may be largely unaware or unfamiliar with a target leader's performance. This latter phenomenon is becoming more prevalent as organizations move toward virtual teams or increase the number of people any one superior may supervise. Some superiors have difficulty dealing with conflict and would rather give average ratings than consider the emotions and distress associated with unflattering ratings. In addition, friendships, perceptual sets, and attribution errors can bias superiors' ratings of a leader's true performance. Some performance appraisal systems do such a poor job measuring a leader's true impact that superiors find them to be virtually useless when making promotion or compensation decisions.

Subordinates' Ratings of Satisfaction, Organizational Climate, Morale, Motivation, and Leadership Effectiveness.   If leadership is defined partly in the eyes of followers, then perhaps a better way to judge the police chief's success is through **subordinates' ratings of effectiveness.** In this method subordinates are asked to rate their level of satisfaction or the effectiveness of the chief. Subordinates may be relatively satisfied or dissatisfied, may be motivated or unmotivated, may feel relatively committed or uncommitted to the organization, or may believe their leader is relatively effective or ineffective. Fostering a sense of motivation, cohesiveness, cooperation, and morale among unit members is a goal toward which most leaders will strive, yet several cautions may be in order when using subordinates' motivation or cohesiveness ratings to judge a leader's effectiveness. For one thing, some subordinates may be relatively unmotivated toward work no matter what the leader does. For example, it may be relatively difficult for the police chief to motivate a highly unionized police force or for a plant manager to motivate assembly line workers. For another, success in instilling a strong sense of motivation and cohesiveness in subordinates does not guarantee effective performance. It often is also necessary, for example, to ensure that subordinates are adequately trained and have the necessary equipment and resources to do the job. Without training and equipment, subordinates' performance still might be relatively low even if the subordinates are motivated. In addition, subordinates may be performing at a low level yet rate their leader as being relatively effective because he or she does not make them work very hard. Conversely, some subordinates may rate the leader as relatively ineffective if he or she does make them work hard.

Despite these cautions, there are two reasons why followers' ratings may be a more accurate reflection of a leader's impact than superiors' ratings of performance. First, followers are often in a better position to make these judgments. They usually are the direct recipients of their boss's day-to-day leadership behaviors. Second, although subordinates' ratings can also suffer from distortion or bias, such effects tend to cancel each other out when multiple raters are used. In our example, you could collect this information by asking direct reports to rate the police chief on the police chief competencies. These ratings would be averaged and used as another source of information for evaluating the performance of the police chief.

Unit Performance Indices.   Rather than use ratings to judge a leader's effectiveness, we could use **unit performance indices** to examine what impact leaders have on the "bottom lines" of their organizations. In other words, we could make judgments about leadership success by examining store sales, profit margins, the number of defective products returned, the number of on-time deliveries, crime rates, high school graduation rates, the dollar amount of charitable contributions collected, win-loss records, or days lost due to accidents. Like the two other sets of measures described earlier, none of these measures are perfect. The biggest qualification to remember in using them as measures of leadership is that these measures are often affected by factors beyond a leader's control. For example, many different factors can affect annual crime rates. These can include economic conditions, how crimes are categorized, how officers are given an incentive (or punished) for reporting crimes, changing demographics, the sudden popularity of new "designer drugs," and so on. Conceivably, the police chief could do "all the right things," yet still not reduce the crime rate from one year to the next, primarily due to circumstances beyond his or her control. Conversely, the chief may make a number of mistakes but may work in a city that sees an economic uptick due to the arrival of several new companies. These companies could provide hundreds of new jobs, which in turn would reduce the number of people unemployed and more likely to be involved in crime. Leadership practitioners need to remember that unit performance indices are often affected by several factors, some of which have more impact than anything a leader might do. It is important to estimate how much a leader's behavior might affect a particular unit performance index before using that index to judge the leader's effectiveness.

Best Practices in Measuring Leadership Success

Right about now you may be wondering if it is even possible to develop accurate measures of leadership success. Ratings by superiors and subordinates have their inherent problems, as do unit performance indices. Despite such problems, these measures generally yield useful information about a leader's effectiveness. Moreover, these measures get at different aspects of effectiveness. It is entirely possible for a leader to get strong ratings from his or her superiors but poor ratings from subordinates. This may be the case if a leader was brought in to turn around a poorly

> *If you can't measure it, then you can't manage it.*
>
> Peter Drucker

performing police department or if a leader has spent a considerable amount of time engaging in "strategic sucking up" with the mayor and city council. On the other hand, leaders could have poor relationships with their boss and great relationships with their subordinates, and such relationships would be reflected in the ratings they get from these two groups. Practitioners need to understand the advantages and problems associated with the different measures, and that multiple measures often yield the best information about leadership success.

Practitioners also need to think critically about how their behavior affects the measures used to judge leadership success. Leaders may perform relatively poorly on several unit performance indices yet also realize that performance on these indices is both relatively insensitive to their behavior and largely a function of, say, local economic conditions or inadequate resources. Leaders instead may choose to focus on improving their effectiveness in terms of criteria more sensitive to their actions, such as improving subordinates' perceptions of motivation, climate, or satisfaction.

Another concern for leadership practitioners might be the degree to which leadership success measures are biased. A study of over a million performance appraisals from the British National Health Service revealed that women received significantly lower performance appraisal evaluations than men (Alimo-Metcalfe, 1994). Females receive less pay for the same job as their male counterparts in both the United Kingdom and the United States (Alimo-Metcalfe, 1994; Jackson, 1996), and minority female managers make only 57 percent of the earnings of their white male counterparts in the United States (*Denver Post*, October 23, 1997). These results imply that females receive lower performance appraisal ratings across most jobs in these two countries. Because males make up the majority of managers in both countries, it may be some time before both genders receive the same level of effectiveness and performance ratings from their superiors (see Highlight 4.2). It is important to remember, however, that not all male managers automatically give all female subordinates lower performance appraisal ratings. The research cited above represents overall trends; individual male managers may or may not give female subordinates lower performance or effectiveness ratings.

Methodologies Used to Study Leadership

So far we have discussed the techniques used to assess a leader's personality traits or behaviors. We have also gone over the measures commonly used to evaluate a leader's success. What we have not discussed is how researchers determine whether there is a *relationship* between a leader's personality traits, behaviors, or values and their win-loss records, sales results, percentage of on-time takeoffs, subordinates' level of satisfaction, and so forth. Do leaders who are more outgoing, better problem solvers, or good listeners, or can handle stress well really have happier and more productive subordinates? The nature and strength of the relationships between various leadership attributes and performance or effectiveness measures is of

The color of leadership is bright orange. The color of leadership research is slate gray.

Jerry Hunt,
Texas Tech University

primary importance to researchers and practitioners alike. If there is little or no relationship between a leader's personality traits or behaviors and subordinates' satisfaction levels, then organizations would be wasting their time and money to assess these values and traits as part of their hiring or promotion processes. However, a large body of research shows that certain leadership attributes can be reliably assessed and are related to a number of positive leadership outcomes. How do leadership researchers systematically determine whether there is a relationship? The techniques used by researchers to determine these relationships can generally be grouped into either qualitative or quantitative approaches.

The Qualitative Approach

The most common qualitative approach is the case study. **Case studies** are an in-depth analysis of a particular leader's activities. A common form of the case study is the biography, such as *My American Journey* (Powell & Persico, 1995). Biographies usually provide detailed descriptions of the various situations facing the leader, the actions taken in response to these situations, and the results of the leader's actions (see Highlight 4.7). Case studies can provide leadership

Colin Powell's Rules

Highlight 4.7

1. It ain't as bad as you think. It will look better in the morning.
2. Get mad, then get over it.
3. Avoid having your ego so close to your position that when your position falls, your ego goes with it.
4. It can be done!
5. Be careful what you choose. You may get it.
6. Don't let adverse facts stand in the way of a good decision.
7. You can't make someone else's choices. You shouldn't let someone else make yours.
8. Check small things.
9. Share credit.
10. Remain calm. Be kind.
11. Have a vision. Be demanding.
12. Don't take counsel of your fears or naysayers.
13. Perpetual optimism is a force multiplier.

Source: C. Powell and J. E. Persico, *My American Journey* (New York: Random House, 1995).

practitioners with valuable ideas on what to do in different leadership situations, particularly if the situations facing the practitioner are similar to those described in a biography. However, there is no objective way to determine whether the actions taken actually caused the results described in a case study. Often factors beyond the leader's actions have a greater role in determining outcomes. Because of these problems, caution should always be used when trying to apply lessons discerned from a case study or biography; they may not fit your particular leadership style or apply to your leadership situation. Nevertheless, case studies often provide interesting and valuable reading, and offer leadership practitioners alternative perspectives for analyzing leadership situations. Case studies can also provide researchers with hypotheses to test further using more precise quantitative methods (Conger, 1998).

Quantitative Approaches

The two major quantitative approaches include correlational studies and experiments. **Correlational studies** are used to determine the statistical relationship between leaders' traits, mental abilities, or behaviors and various measures of leadership effectiveness such as subordinates' satisfaction or climate ratings. An example of a correlational study would be to identify a group of leaders (e.g., police chiefs in 100 midsized cities), collect their scores on some type of paper-and-pencil test (a mental abilities test), and also collect satisfaction ratings from their respective subordinates. A **correlation coefficient** would then be calculated between the intelligence test scores and subordinates' satisfaction ratings. A correlation coefficient is a statistical index of the strength of the relationship between two variables and can range between -1.00 and $+1.00$. Correlation coefficients close to 1.00 would indicate a strong, positive relationship, those close to .00 would indicate no relationship, and those close to -1.00 would indicate a strong inverse relationship between mental ability scores and subordinates' satisfaction ratings. A good example of a correlation study was published by Dorfman, Howell, Hibino, Lee, Tate, and Bautista (1997). These authors found that leaders who exhibited higher levels of supportive, contingent reward, and charismatic behaviors had more satisfied and motivated subordinates in the United States, Mexico, Japan, South Korea, and Taiwan (all correlations were in the .3–.6 range).

Correlational studies are among the most common methods used to study leadership. Both the ease of data collection and the ability of correlational studies to illuminate relationships between leader characteristics and effectiveness measures are major advantages of these studies. However, they do have one major drawback. It is usually difficult (though it is often tempting) to make **causal inferences** based on correlational data. A causal inference occurs when leadership researchers can definitely say that certain leadership behaviors or attributes *cause* various kinds of leadership outcomes. Although correlational studies help researchers to determine the relationship between leadership attributes and outcomes, they cannot be used to make causal inferences. For example, in the study by Dorfman and his coauthors we cannot tell if a leader's supportive behaviors cause their subordinates to be more satisfied, or if more satisfied subordinates cause their leaders to exhibit more supportive leadership behaviors. Indeed, some of the most common erroneous reasoning from research results involves inferring causal relationships between variables when only a correlational relationship has been established.

Experiments allow researchers to make causal inferences about leadership, and experimental designs are often based on the results of earlier case and correlational studies. Experiments generally consist of both independent and dependent variables. The **independent variable** is what the researcher manipulates or varies to test the hypothesis; it causes change in the dependent variable. In leadership research, the independent variable is often some type of leadership behavior and the **dependent variable** is usually some measure of leadership effectiveness, such as work-unit performance or subordinates' satisfaction ratings.

A description of a "laboratory" experiment on leadership may help make the distinction between independent and dependent variables a bit clearer. Howell and Frost (1988) were interested in determining whether charismatic leaders caused subordinates to perform at a higher level than supportive or directive leaders. These researchers trained two actresses to manifest either charismatic, directive, or supportive leadership styles. Thus, the style of leadership exhibited by the actress-leader for different groups of subordinates was the independent variable in this experiment; with some groups the actress-leaders exhibited charismatic behaviors, with others they exhibited only supportive or directive behaviors. The dependent variable was subordinates' performance, which in this case was measured by the number of memos subordinates successfully completed during a 45-minute in-basket exercise. As you can see, the researchers manipulated or changed the independent variable (the actresses' leadership styles varied across different groups of subordinates), but they merely recorded the subordinates' performance on the dependent variable (the number of memos successfully completed) at the end of each 45-minute session. The researchers reported that subordinates' performance levels were highest when leaders exhibited charismatic behaviors and as a result concluded that these leadership behaviors caused subordinates to perform at the highest levels.

Although experiments allow us to make causal inferences about leadership, experiments have drawbacks of their own. One is that the effects obtained in many laboratory experiments are stronger than the effects obtained when the same experiments are conducted in organizations. This is primarily due to the tightly controlled conditions under which laboratory experiments are run, whereas experiments in organizations cannot be so tightly controlled. Extraneous influences often minimize or distort the effects of the independent variable on the dependent variable when the experiment is conducted in an organizational setting. Another problem concerns the subjects used in many laboratory experiments. Many times, college undergraduates are used as subjects in leadership experiments, and these individuals may have little leadership or followership experience. For such reasons it becomes legitimate to ask how much the results of any particular laboratory experiment can be generalized to actual organizations.

TABLE 4–3   Some Common and Uncommon Variations of Leadership Studies

Feature	Common	Uncommon
Research method	Surveys	Experiments
Time frame	Static	Longitudinal
Research objective	Replication	Explore new issues
Locus of leadership	Heroic individual	Shared/distributed
Causality	Unidirectional	Reciprocal
Data sources	Single	Multiple
Level of leader	Supervisor	Executive

Source: G. Yukl, *Reflections and Directions in Leadership Research* (presentation made at the 14th Annual Conference of the Society of Industrial and Organizational Psychologists, Atlanta, May 1999).

Literally thousands of qualitative and quantitative studies have looked at what leaders do and how their actions affect important team or organizational outcomes. Organizations that have capitalized on this accumulation of knowledge and successfully bridged the practice-research gap have been able to design better hiring, performance management, training and development, and succession planning systems for their leaders. These systems almost always result in stronger leadership bench strength and in turn better organizational performance. Nevertheless, there are a number of important leadership questions that still need to be answered. Gary Yukl, one of the world's premier leadership researchers, maintained that although there is much we still need to learn about leadership, a great deal of the leadership research being conducted these days misses the mark. Leadership researchers appear to be too obsessed with surveys, too ready to replicate previous research, think only of leadership as a one-way relationship, or use the same quantitative designs too frequently for this research to be of much use (see Table 4–3). Yukl (1999) maintained that the yield rate of current research is only 11 percent; this is the percentage of studies that actually add something over and above what we already know about leadership. And as stated earlier, much of this leadership research provides little if any useful advice to leadership practitioners. So if the leadership research is not adding to our body of scientific knowledge and practitioners cannot use any of the findings, then what is truly driving leadership research? Unfortunately, it appears that the requirements for tenure are resulting in leadership research that is of little use to anyone.

Maxims and Theories of Leadership

Most of what people read about leadership amounts to little more than someone else's opinion about it. Often, such material is both anecdotal and prescriptive: anecdotal in the sense it reflects just one leader's views, and prescriptive in advising others how to be more effective. For example, although Colin Powell is an outstanding leader whose rules make intuitive sense (see Highlight 4.7), it is nonetheless uncertain whether his maxims would apply equally well for very different leaders in very different situations. **Maxims** are personal opinions that can give leaders valueable advice about leadership. It is important to be mindful of the difference between this kind of literature about leadership and more scientific or empirical approaches to understanding it. The latter are represented by data-based studies and theories reported in this book. Although both approaches have legitimate purposes, it is vital to understand the differences between them.

> *Everything you do at work counts.*
> Mike Watkins, Western Area Power Administration

The scientific alternative to leadership maxims is leadership theory. A leadership **theory** is a framework for conceptualizing relationships between variables and guiding research toward a fuller understanding of phenomena. With a theory a researcher makes public predictions about how certain leadership attributes or behaviors will systematically impact certain leadership effectiveness measures. Then the researcher collects the leadership assessment and effectiveness data prescribed by the theory, and conducts statistical analyses to determine whether his or her predictions are supported or refuted. For example, suppose a researcher predicted that the personality traits of dominance (wanting to be in charge of others) and dependability (being a reliable, trustworthy, and hard-working employee) were positively related to sales results in the computer retail industry. The researcher could use a paper-and-pencil measure of personality to assess store managers' standings on the traits of dominance and dependability. The researcher could then collect annual sales results for each store and conduct a correlational study to determine the nature and strength of the relationships between these three variables. The researcher might then publish the results of his or her findings in a scientific journal so that other researchers can gather more information that would support or refute the original theory and findings.

The public predictions of how leadership variables are interrelated, the systematic gathering and analysis of data, and the peer review of results are what make theories so central to scientific research. Theories are often modified to take new findings into account as researchers collect, analyze, and publish their findings about the theory. For example, other researchers may find that store managers' intelligence levels also are related to store performance. The original theory would then need to be modified so that dominance, dependability, and intelligence could all be used to predict sales managers' success. These findings could in turn be used to develop a competency model and selection system for future store managers in the computer retail industry.

The essence of theories of leadership, then, is to provide a reasonably coherent conceptual structure of how critical variables interact, involving ideas that can be put to the test and revised as new data accumulate. Simply put, theories of leadership involve testable ideas, whereas prescriptive approaches to leadership involve no such intended testability. Although both leadership maxims and theories are useful for understanding leadership situations, in general only leadership theories add to the body of knowledge concerning the science of leadership and help in the development of universal laws of leadership. It is also important to understand that theory building is hard, painstaking work. It is fairly easy to state one's opinions on how one should act as a leader; it is an entirely different matter to design a study, collect data, analyze, and finally publish the results.

Despite all of the advantages of conducting systematic research around the topic of leadership, there remains the question of why case studies and maxims carry so much weight among leadership practitioners. Academicians may be prompted to wonder why books such as *Who Moved My Cheese?* (Johnson, 1998), *Doing Business the GE Way* (Slater, 1998), or *It Doesn't Take a Hero* (Schwarzkopf, 1993) are so popular among practitioners? Perhaps the more central question, however, is why research-based articles in leadership and management journals are not more popular themselves. One reason is probably that the very format of research articles, with their emphasis on statistical results and so forth, is fairly dull and inaccessible to anyone but university professors and graduate students. However, we also suspect that leadership researchers themselves sometimes forget that other academicians should not be their only important audience. Leadership researchers need to do a better job of making the findings from their studies more relevant and accessible to practicing managers and leaders (see Highlight 4.8).

Summary

Although this chapter focused on leadership research, there are several reasons it is relevant for leadership practitioners even though they are unlikely to actually conduct leadership research themselves. First, organizations can and do use a number of techniques to assess the values, personality, intelligence, and behaviors for any applicant pool. Although none of these techniques are perfect, they can help hiring managers make substantially better staffing decisions, and many organizations are using fairly sophisticated assessment techniques to improve the odds of hiring good leaders. In all likelihood most of the people applying for any type of management position will go through one or more of the assessment techniques described in this chapter.

Second, practitioners need to understand that there are multiple ways to measure success. Additionally, superiors' ratings, subordinates' ratings, and unit performance measures can many times paint different pictures about the relative success of a leader. Practitioners need to understand which of these measures are the most important to their long-term success, which are the most sensitive to their efforts, and which may be more strongly influenced by factors beyond their control.

Third, practitioners also should know that there are three methods commonly used to study the linkage between what leaders do with different success measures. Case studies have the advantage of helping practitioners better

The Top Five Critical Thinking Questions Practitioners Should Ask When Reading about Leadership

1. *Who is in the sample?*

   - How big is the sample?
   - Is the sample representative of most leaders?
   - How similar are the leaders to you?

2. *What is the situation?*

   - What challenges and opportunities do the leaders face?
   - If reading about an experiment, how generalizable are the conditions to the "real world"?
   - What situational factors could affect the results of the experiment?
   - Is the situation similar to the one you currently face?

3. *What leadership qualities, characteristics, or behaviors are being assessed?*

   - Are the right attributes being assessed?
   - Are the best assessment techniques being used?

4. *How is leadership success being determined?*

   - By means of superiors' ratings, subordinates' ratings, or unit performance indices?
   - Are the best measures being used, or would alternative measures paint a different picture?
   - How might these measures be affected by factors beyond the leader's control?

5. *How do the writers link leadership assessment to success?*

   - By means of case studies, correlational studies, or experiments?
   - Are the right conclusions being drawn?
   - Are there any other plausible alternative explanations?
   - Did the writers acknowledge these alternative explanations?

understand the context in which a leader acts. However, they usually only describe the actions of one leader in one situation, and the generalizability of their findings to the reader may be questionable. Correlational studies have the advantage of using larger sample sizes and describe the statistical relationships between the results of different assessment techniques and success measures. These studies cannot tell us much about cause and effect relationships, however. Leadership experiments do yield valuable information about the cause and effect relationships between independent and dependent variables. Thus, experiments can tell us how different leadership behaviors affect group performance, subordinates' satisfaction levels, and so forth. But experiments are hard to conduct in field settings, and most laboratory experiments of leadership use college students as subjects; the generalizability of the findings for the latter experiments is always questionable.

Finally, leadership practitioners should understand the difference between maxims and theories of leadership. Maxims may represent valid advice, but they are ultimately no more than personal opinion. Since they amount to little more than personal opinion, different maxims sometimes give conflicting advice, and by their very nature there is no systematic way to "test" maxims. Theories, on the other hand, are a collection of testable predictions about the relationships between certain variables. Theories are developed on the basis of observations, and their corresponding hypotheses are tested and refined by means of correlational and experimental studies. Theories are useful in that they guide research and make predictions about how different variables interact. Theories add to our collective leadership knowledge, whereas maxims do not. Because we will describe a number of different leadership theories throughout this book, practitioners need to be able to think critically about leadership theories and determine how these theories can help them be better leaders.

Key Terms

practice-research gap   78
resume   81
competency model   83
glass ceiling effect   83
multiple hurdles effect   84
paper-and-pencil measures   84
structured interviews   84
unstructured interviews   84
assessment centers   85
in-basket exercise   87
role-play simulations   87
superiors' performance ratings   90

subordinates' ratings of effectiveness   92
unit performance indices   93
case studies   95
correlational studies   96
correlation coefficient   96
causal inferences   96
experiments   97
independent variable   97
dependent variable   97
maxims   99
theory   99

Questions

1. How do you react to the phrase *assessing leadership*? What positive and negative connotations does it have for you?
2. Some organizations are using graphology, or handwriting analysis, to make selection decisions. What do you think about this technique?
3. What are some of the measures you could use to judge the performance of a coach? A teacher? A student? What are the advantages and disadvantages with each of these measures? How much impact would the leader's behaviors have on each of these measures?
4. If you were to design an interview for hiring a restaurant manager, what questions would you include, and why?
5. How could you design a correlational study or an experiment to test one of Colin Powell's Rules in Highlight 4.7?
6. What is the single best work you have ever read about leadership or being a leader? What does this book or article say about assessing leadership, measuring leadership effectiveness, methods used to study leadership, or leadership maxims and theories?

Skills

Leadership skills relevant to this chapter include:
- Communication

- Building Effective Relationships with Superiors
- Building Effective Relationships with Peers

Activity

1. Assign groups of students the task of identifying various criteria by which any one of the following leaders (or any others) might be evaluated: an assistant coach, a teacher, a minister, an army general. Then each group should try to achieve consensus about the prioritization of these different criteria. The class as a whole can share views about each group's prioritization, as well as the extent to which there are unique or similar criteria across the different roles or the extent to which the various criteria are measurable.

2. Interview one or two midlevel managers and ask them to explain the process they use to hire new supervisors. What process did they use? According to Table 4-1 are they using mostly valid or invalid processes? Of the last 10 supervisors they had hired, how many top, solid, and low performers were in this group? How successful is this leader's process for identifying top-performing supervisors?

II Focus on the Leader

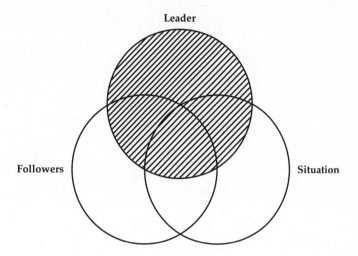

Part II focuses on the leader. The effectiveness of leadership, good or bad, is typically attributed to the leader much more than to the other elements of the framework. Sometimes the leader is the only element of leadership we even think of. One great leader's views were clear enough about the relative importance of leaders and followers:

> *Men are nothing; it is the man who is everything. . . It was not the Roman army that conquered Gaul, but Caesar; it was not the Carthaginian army that made Rome tremble in her gates, but Hannibal; it was not the Macedonian army that reached the Indus, but Alexander.*

Napoleon

Because the leader plays such an important role in the leadership process, the next four chapters of this book review research related to the characteristics of leaders, and what makes leaders effective. Part II begins with a chapter on power and influence since those concepts provide the most fundamental way to understand the process of leadership. Chapter 6 then looks at the closely related issues of leadership and values. In Chapter 7 we consider what aspects of personality are related to leadership, and in Chapter 8 we examine how all these preceding variables are manifested in effective or ineffective leader behavior.

5 POWER AND INFLUENCE

Introduction

We begin this part, called "Focus on the Leader," by examining the phenomenon of power. Some of history's earliest characterizations of leaders concerned their use of power. Shakespeare's plays were concerned with the acquisition and failing of power (Hill, 1985), and Machiavelli's *The Prince* has been described as the "classic handbook on power politics" (Donno, 1966). Current scholars have also emphasized the need to conceptualize leadership as a power phenomenon (Gardner, 1986; Hinkin & Schriesheim, 1989). Power may be the single most important concept in all the social sciences (Burns, 1978), though scholars today disagree on precisely how to define power or influence. But it's not just scholars who have different ideas about power. The concept of power is so pervasive and complex that each one of us probably thinks about it a little differently.

What comes to *your* mind when *you* think about power? Do you think of a person wielding enormous authority over others? Do you think of high office? Do you think of making others do things against their will? Is power ethically neutral, or is it inherently dangerous as Lord Acton said? ("Power corrupts, and absolute power corrupts absolutely.") Do you think a leader's real power is always obvious to others? What sorts of things might enhance or detract from a leader's power? What are the pros and cons of different ways of trying to influence people? These are the kinds of issues we will explore in this chapter.

Some Important Distinctions

Power has been defined as the capacity to produce effects on others (House, 1984), or the potential to influence others (Bass, 1990). While we usually think of power belonging to the leader, it is actually a function of the leader, the followers, and the situation. Leaders have the potential to influence their followers' behaviors and attitudes. However, followers also can affect the leader's behavior and attitudes. Even the situation itself can affect a leader's capacity to influence his followers (and vice versa). For example, leaders who can reward and punish followers may have a greater capacity to influence followers than those leaders who cannot use rewards or punishments. Similarly, follower or situational characteristics may diminish a leader's potential to influence followers, as when the latter belong to a strong, active union.

Several other aspects of power also are worth noting. Gardner (1986) made an important point about the exercise of power and its effects. He stated that "power does not need to be exercised in order to have its effect—as any hold-up man can tell you" (Gardner, 1986, p. 5). Thus, merely having the capacity to exert influence can often bring about intended effects, even though the leader may not take any action to influence his or her followers. For example, some months after the end of his term, Eisenhower was asked if leaving the White House had affected his golf game. "Yes," he replied, "a lot more people beat me now." Alternatively, power represents an inference or attribution made on the basis of an agent's observable acts of influence (Schriesheim & Hinkin, 1990). Power is never directly observed but rather attributed to others on the basis and frequency of influence tactics they use and on their outcomes.

Many people use the the terms *power, influence,* and *influence tactics* synonymously (Bass, 1990), but it is useful to distinguish between them. **Influence** can be defined as the change in a target agent's attitudes, values, beliefs, or behaviors as the result of influence tactics. **Influence tactics** refer to one person's actual behaviors designed to change another person's attitudes, beliefs, values, or behaviors. Although these concepts are typically examined from the leader's perspective (e.g., how a leader influences followers), we should remember that followers can also wield power and influence over leaders as well as over each other. Leadership practitioners can improve their effectiveness by reflecting on the types of power they and their followers have and the types of influence tactics that they may use or that may be used *on* them.

Whereas power is the *capacity* to cause change, influence is the degree of *actual change* in a target person's attitudes, values, beliefs, or behaviors. Influence can be measured by the behaviors or attitudes manifested by followers as the result of a leader's *influence tactics.* For example, a leader may ask a follower to accomplish a particular task, and whether or not the task is accomplished is partly a function of the leader's request. (The follower's ability and skill as well as access to the necessary equipment and resources are also important factors.) Such things as subordinates' satisfaction or motivation, group cohesiveness and climate, or unit performance indices can be used to measure the effectiveness of leaders' influence attempts. The degree to which leaders can change the level of satisfaction, motivation, or cohesiveness among followers is a function of the amount of power available to both leaders and followers. On the one hand, leaders with relatively

> *The true leader must submerge himself in the fountain of the people.*
>
> V. I. Lenin

high amounts of power can cause fairly substantial changes in subordinates' attitudes and behaviors; for example, a new and respected leader who uses rewards and punishments judiciously may cause a dramatic change in followers' perceptions about organizational climate and the amount of time followers spend on work-related behaviors. On the other hand, the amount of power followers have in work situations can also vary dramatically, and in some situations particular followers may exert relatively more influence over the rest of the group than the leader does. For example, a follower with a high level of knowledge and experience may have more influence on the attitudes, opinions, and behaviors of the rest of the followers than a brand-new leader. Thus, the amount of change in the attitudes or behaviors of the targets of influence is a function of the agent's capacity to exert influence and the targets' capacity to resist this influence.

Leaders and followers typically use a variety of tactics to influence each other's attitudes or behaviors (see Highlight 5.1 for a description of some nonverbal power cues common to humans). Influence tactics are the overt behaviors exhibited by one person to influence another. They range from emotional appeals, to the exchange of favors, to threats. The particular tactic used in a leadership situation is probably a function of the power possessed by both parties. Individuals with a relatively large amount of power may successfully employ a wider variety of influence tactics than individuals with little power. For example, a well-respected leader could make an emotional appeal, a rational appeal, a personal appeal, a legitimate request, or a threat to try to modify a follower's behavior. The follower in this situation may only be able to use ingratiation or personal appeals in order to change the leader's attitude or behavior.

At the same time, because the formal leader is not always the person who possesses the most power in a leadership situation, followers often can use a wider variety of influence tactics than the leader to modify the attitudes and behaviors of others. This would be the case if a new leader were brought into an organization in which one of his or her subordinates was extremely well liked and respected. In this situation, the subordinate may be able to make personal appeals, emotional appeals, or even threats to change the attitudes or behaviors of the leader, whereas the new leader may be limited to making only legitimate requests to change the attitudes and behaviors of the followers.

Power and Leadership

We began this chapter by noting how an understanding of power has long been seen as an integral part of leadership. Several perspectives and theories have been developed to explain the acquisition and exercise of power. In this section we will first examine various *sources* of power. Then we will look at how individuals vary in their personal *need* for power.

Gestures of Power and Dominance

Highlight 5.1

We can often get clues about relative power just by paying attention to behaviors between two people. There are a number of nonverbal cues we might want to pay attention to.

The phrase **pecking order** refers to the status differential between members of a group. It reminds us that many aspects of human social organization have roots, or at least parallels, in the behavior of other species. The animal kingdom presents diverse and fascinating examples of stylized behaviors by which one member of a species shows its relative dominance or submissiveness to another. There is adaptive significance to such behavioral mechanisms since they tend to minimize actual physical struggle and maintain a stable social order. For example, lower-ranking baboons step aside to let a higher-status male pass; they become nervous if he stares at them. The highest-status male can choose where he wants to sleep and whom he wants to mate with. Baboons "know their place." As with humans, rank has its privileges.

Our own stylized power rituals are usually so second-nature we aren't conscious of them. Yet there is a "dance" of power relations among humans just as among other animals. The following are some of the ways power is expressed nonverbally in humans.

Staring. In American society, it is disrespectful for a person of lower status to stare at a superior, though superiors are not bound by a similar restriction. Children, for example, are taught not to stare at parents. And it's an interesting comment on the power relationship between sexes that women are more likely to avert their gaze from men than vice versa.

Pointing. Children are also taught it's not nice to point. However, adults rarely correct each other for pointing because more than mere etiquette, pointing seems to be a behavior that is acceptable for high-status figures or those attempting to assert dominance. An angry boss may point an index finger accusingly at an employee; few employees who wanted to keep their jobs would respond in kind. The same restrictions apply to frowning.

Touching. Invading another person's space by touching the person without invitation is acceptable when one is of superior status but not when one is of subordinate status. It's acceptable, for example, for bosses or teachers to put a hand on an employee's or a student's shoulder, but not vice versa. The disparity also applies to socioeconomic status; someone with higher socioeconomic status is more likely to touch a person of lower socioeconomic status than vice versa.

Interrupting. Virtually all of us have interrupted others, and we have all been interrupted ourselves. Again, however, the issue is who was interrupting whom? Higher-power or -status persons interrupt; lower-power or -status persons are interrupted. A vast difference in frequency of behaviors also exists between the sexes in American society. Men interrupt much more frequently than women do.

Source: D. A. Karp and W. C. Yoels, *Symbols, Selves, and Society* (New York: Lippincott, 1979).

Sources of Leader Power

Where does a leader's power come from? Do leaders *have* it, or do followers *give* it to them? As we shall see, the answer may be both . . . and more.

Something as seemingly trivial as the arrangement of furniture in an office can affect perceptions of another person's power. One vivid example comes from John Ehrlichman's (1982) book, *Witness to Power*. Ehrlichman described his first visit to J. Edgar Hoover's office at the Department of Justice. The legendary director of the FBI had long been one of the most powerful men in Washington, D.C., and as Ehrlichman's impressions reveal, Hoover took every opportunity to reinforce that image. Ehrlichman was first led through double doors into a room replete with plaques, citations, trophies, medals, and certificates jamming every wall. He was then led through a second room, similarly decorated, then into a third trophy room, and finally to a large but bare desk backed by several flags and still no J. Edgar Hoover. The guide opened a door behind the desk, and Ehrlichman went into a smaller office, which Hoover dominated from an impressive chair and desk that stood on a dais about six inches high. Erhlichman was instructed to take a seat on a lower couch, and Mr. Hoover peered down on Ehrlichman from his own loftier and intimidating place.

> *And when we think we lead, we are most led.*
>
> Lord Byron

On a more mundane level, many people have experienced a time when they were called in to talk to a boss and left standing while the boss sat behind the desk. Probably few people in that situation misunderstand the power messages there. In addition to the factors just described, other aspects of office arrangements also can affect a leader's or follower's power. One factor is the shape of the table used for meetings. Individuals sitting at the ends of rectangular tables often wield more power, whereas circular tables facilitate communication and minimize status differentials. However, specific seating arrangements even at circular tables can affect participants' interactions; often individuals belonging to the same cliques and coalitions will sit next to each other. By sitting next to each other, members of the same coalition may exert more power as a collective group than they would sitting apart from each other. Also, having a private or more open office may not only *reflect* but also *affect* power differentials between people. Individuals with private offices can dictate to a greater degree when they want to interact with others by opening or closing their doors or by giving instructions about interruptions. Individuals with more open offices have much less power to control access to them. By being aware of dynamics like these, leaders can somewhat influence others' perceptions of their power relationship.

Prominently displaying symbols like diplomas, awards, and titles also can increase one's power. This was shown in an experiment in a college setting where a guest lecturer to several different classes was introduced in a different way to each. To one group he was

> *He who has great power should use it lightly.*
>
> Seneca

introduced as a student; to other groups he was introduced as a lecturer, senior lecturer, or professor, respectively. After the presentation, when he was no longer in the room, the class estimated his height. Interestingly, the same man was perceived by different groups as increasingly taller with each increase in academic status. The "professor" was remembered as being several inches taller than the "student" (Wilson, 1968).

This finding demonstrates the generalized impact a seemingly minor matter like one's title can have on others. Another study points out more dramatically how dangerous it can be when followers are overly responsive to the *appearances* of title and authority. This study took place in a medical setting and arose from concern among medical staff that nurses were responding mechanically to doctors' orders. A researcher made telephone calls to nurses' stations in numerous different medical wards. In each, he identified himself as a hospital physician and directed the nurse answering the phone to prescribe a particular medication for a patient in that ward. Many nurses complied with the request despite the fact it was against hospital policy to transmit prescriptions by phone. Many did so despite never even having talked to the particular "physician" before the call—and despite the fact that the prescribed medication was dangerously excessive, not to mention unauthorized. In fact, 95 percent of the nurses complied with the request made by the most easily falsifiable symbol of authority, a bare title (Cialdini, 1984). (Also see Highlight 5.2.)

Even choice of clothing can affect one's power and influence. Uniforms and other specialized clothing have long been associated with authority and status, including their use by the military, police, hospital staffs, clergy, and so on. In one experiment, people walking along a city sidewalk were stopped by someone dressed either in regular clothes or in the uniform of a security guard and told this: "You see that guy over there by the meter? He's overparked but doesn't have any change. Give him a dime!" Whereas fewer than half complied when the requestor was dressed in regular clothes, over 90 percent did when he was in uniform (Bickman, 1974). This same rationale is given for having personnel in certain occupations (e.g., airline crew members) wear uniforms. Besides more easily identifying them to others, the uniforms increase the likelihood that in emergency situations their instructions will be followed. Similarly, even the presence of something as trivial as tattoos can affect the amount of power wielded in a group. One of the authors of this text had a friend named Del who was a manager in an international book-publishing company. Del was a former merchant marine whose forearms were adorned with tattoos. Del would often take off his suit coat and roll up his sleeves when meetings were not going his way, and he often exerted considerably more influence by merely exposing his tattoos to the rest of the group.

A final situational factor that can affect one's potential to influence others is the presence or absence of a crisis. Leaders usually can exert more power during a crisis than during periods of relative calm. Perhaps this is because during a crisis leaders are willing to draw on bases of power they normally forgo. For example, a leader who has developed close interpersonal relationships with followers generally uses her referent power to influence them. During crises or emergency

The Milgram Studies

One intriguing way to understand power, influence, and influence tactics is to read a synopsis of Stanley Milgram's classic work on obedience and to think about how this work relates to the concepts and theories discussed in the present chapter. Milgram's research explored how far people will go when directed by an authority figure to do something that might injure another person. More specifically, Milgram wanted to know what happens when the dictates of authority and the dictates of one's conscience seem incompatible.

The participants were men from the communities surrounding Yale University. They were led to believe they were helping in a study concerning the effect of punishment on learning; the study's legitimacy was certainly enhanced by being conducted on the Yale campus itself. Two subjects at a time participated in the study, one as a teacher and the other as learner. The roles apparently were assigned randomly. The teacher's task was to help the learner memorize a set of word pairs by providing electric shocks whenever the learner (who would be in an adjacent room) made a mistake.

A stern experimenter described procedures and showed participants the equipment for administering punishment. This "shock generator" looked ominous, with rows of switches, lights, and warnings labeled in 15-volt increments all the way to 450 volts. Various points along the array were marked with increasingly dire warnings such as *extreme intensity* and *danger: severe*. The switch at the highest level of shock simply was marked XXX. Every time the learner made a mistake, the teacher was ordered by the experimenter to administer the next-higher level of electric shock.

In actuality, there was only one true subject in the experiment—the teacher. The learner was really a confederate of the experimenter. The supposed random assignment of participants to teacher and learner conditions had been rigged in advance. The real purpose of the experiment was to assess how much electric shock the teachers would administer to the learners in the face of the latter's increasingly adamant protestations to stop. This included numerous realistic cries of agony and complaints of a heart condition, all standardized, predetermined, tape-recorded messages delivered via the intercom from the learner's to the teacher's room. If the subject (i.e., the teacher) refused to deliver any further shocks, the experimenter prodded him with comments such as "The experiment requires that you go on" and "You have no other choice; you must go on."

Before Milgram conducted his experiment, he asked mental health professionals what proportion of the subjects would administer apparently dangerous levels of shock. The consensus was that only a negligible percentage would do so, perhaps 1 or 2 percent of the population. Milgram's actual results were dramatically inconsistent with what any of the experts had predicted. Fully 70 percent of the subjects carried through with their orders, albeit sometimes with great personal anguish, and delivered the maximum shock possible—450 volts!

Source: S. Milgram, "Behavioral Study of Obedience," *Journal of Abnormal and Social Psychology* 67 (1963), pp. 371–78.

FIGURE 5.1

Sources of leader power in the leader-follower-situation framework

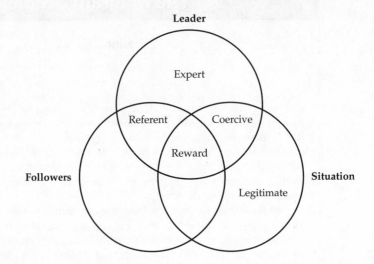

situations, however, leaders may be more apt to draw on their legitimate and coercive bases of power to influence subordinates. That was precisely the finding in a study of bank managers' actions; the bank managers were more apt to use legitimate and coercive power during crises than during noncrisis situations (Mulder, de Jong, Koppelar, & Verhage, 1986). This same phenomenon is observable in many dramatizations. In the television series *Star Trek, the Next Generation,* for example, Captain Picard normally uses his referent and expert power to influence subordinates. During emergencies, however, he will often rely on his legitimate and coercive power. Another factor may be that during crises followers are more willing to accept greater direction, control, and structure from leaders, whatever power base may be involved.

A Taxonomy of Social Power.   French and Raven (1959) identified five sources, or bases, of power by which an individual can potentially influence others. As seen in Figure 5.1, these five sources include one that is primarily a function of the leader; one that is a function of the relationship between leaders and followers; one that is primarily a function of the leader and the situation; one that is primarily a function of the situation; and finally, one that involves aspects of all three elements. Understanding these bases of power can give leadership practitioners greater insight about the predictable effects—positive or negative—of various sorts of influence attempts. Following is a more detailed discussion of French and Raven's (1959) five bases of social power.

Expert Power.   Expert power is the power of knowledge. Some people are able to influence others through their relative expertise in particular areas. A surgeon may wield considerable influence in a hospital because others depend on her knowledge, skill, and judgment, even though she may not have any formal authority over them. A mechanic may be influential among his peers because he is widely recognized as the best in the city. A longtime employee may be influential because his corporate memory provides a useful historical perspective to newer personnel. Legislators who are expert in the intricacies of parliamentary procedure, athletes who have played in championship games, and soldiers who have been in combat before are valued for the lessons learned and wisdom they can share with others.

Because expert power is a function of the amount of knowledge one possesses relative to the rest of the members of the group, it is possible for followers to have considerably more expert power than leaders in certain situations. For example, new leaders often possess less knowledge of the jobs and tasks performed in a particular work unit than the followers do, and in this case the followers can potentially wield considerable influence when decisions are made regarding work procedures, new equipment, or the hiring of additional workers. Probably the best advice for leaders in this situation is to ask a lot of questions and perhaps seek additional training to help fill this knowledge gap. So long as different followers have considerably greater amounts of expert power, it will be difficult for a leader to influence the work unit on the basis of expert power alone.

Referent Power.   One way to counteract the problems stemming from a lack of expertise is to build strong interpersonal ties with subordinates. Referent power refers to the potential influence one has due to the strength of the relationship between the leader and the followers. When people admire a leader and see her as a role model, we say she has referent power. For example, students may respond positively to advice or requests from teachers who are well liked and respected, while the same students might be unresponsive to less-popular teachers. This relative degree of responsiveness is primarily a function of the strength of the relationship between the students and the different teachers. We knew one young lieutenant who had enormous referent power with the military security guards working for him due to his selfless concern for them, evident in such habits as bringing them hot chocolate and homemade cookies on their late-night shifts. The guards, sometimes taken for granted by other superiors, understood and valued the extra effort and sacrifice this young supervisor put forth for them. When Buddy Ryan was fired as head coach of the Philadelphia Eagles football team, many of the players expressed fierce loyalty to him. One said, "We'd do things for Buddy that we wouldn't do for another coach. I'd sell my body for Buddy" (Associated Press, January 9, 1991). That is referent power.

Another way to look at referent power is in terms of the role friendships play in making things happen. It is frequently said, for example, that many people get jobs based on who they know, not what they know. The fact is, there is some truth to that. But we think the best perspective on this issue was offered by David Campbell, who said, "It's not who you know that counts. It's what who you know *knows about you* that counts!" (personal communication).

Referent power often takes time to develop. Furthermore, it can have a downside in that a desire to *maintain* referent power may limit a leader's actions in particular situations. For example, a leader who has developed a strong relationship with a follower may be reluctant to discipline the follower for poor

Power in an organization is the capacity generated by relationships.

Margaret A. Wheatley,
Futurist

work or chronic tardiness, as these actions could disrupt the nature of the relationship between the leader and the follower. Thus, referent power is a two-way street; the stronger the relationship, the more influence leaders and followers exert over each other. Moreover, just as it is possible for leaders to develop strong relationships with followers and, in turn, acquire more referent power, it is also possible for followers to develop strong relationships with other followers and acquire more referent power. Followers with relatively more referent power than their peers are often the spokespersons for their work units and generally have more latitude to deviate from work-unit norms. Followers with little referent power have little opportunity to deviate from group norms. For example, in an episode of the television show *The Simpsons*, Homer Simpson was fired for wearing a pink shirt to work (everybody else at the Springfield nuclear power plant had always worn white shirts). Homer was fired partly because he "was not popular enough to be different."

Legitimate Power.   Legitimate power depends on a person's organizational role. It can be thought of as one's formal or official authority. Some people make things happen because they have the power or authority to do so. The boss can assign projects; the coach can decide who plays; the colonel can order compliance with uniform standards; the teacher assigns the homework and awards the grades. Individuals with legitimate power exert influence through requests or demands deemed appropriate by virtue of their role and position. In other words, legitimate power means a leader has authority because he or she has been assigned a particular role in an organization (and the leader has this authority only as long as he or she occupies that position and operates within the proper bounds of that role).

It is important to note that legitimate authority and leadership are not the same thing. Holding a position and being a leader are not synonymous, despite the relatively common practice of calling position holders in bureaucracies the leaders. The head of an organization may be a true leader, but he also may not be. Effective leaders often intuitively realize they need more than legitimate power to be successful. Before he became president, Dwight Eisenhower commanded all Allied troops in Europe during World War II. In a meeting with his staff before the Normandy invasion, Eisenhower pulled a string across a table to make a point about leadership. He was demonstrating that just as you can pull a string, not push it, officers must lead soldiers and not push them from the rear.

Unreviewable power is the most likely to self-indulge itself and the least likely to engage in dispassionate self-analysis.

Warren E. Burger,
Chief justice, U.S. Supreme
Court, 1969–1986

It is also possible for followers to use their legitimate power to influence leaders. In these cases, followers can actively resist a leader's influence attempt by only doing work specifically prescribed in job descriptions, bureaucratic rules, or union policies. For example, many organizations have job descriptions that limit both the time spent at work and the types of tasks and activities performed. Similarly, bureaucratic rules and union policies can be invoked by followers to resist a leader's influence attempts. Often the leader will need to change the nature of his or her request or find another way to resolve the problem if these rules and policies are invoked by followers. If this is the case, then the followers will have successfully used legitimate power to influence their leader.

Reward Power.   Reward power involves the potential to influence others due to one's control over desired resources. This can include the power to give raises, bonuses, and promotions; to grant tenure; to select people for special assignments or desirable activities; to distribute desired resources like computers, offices, parking places, or travel money; to intercede positively on another's behalf; to recognize with awards and praise; and so on. Many corporations use rewards extensively to motivate employees. At McDonald's, for example, there is great status accorded the All-American Hamburger Maker, the cook who makes the fastest, highest-quality hamburgers in the country. At individual fast-food restaurants, managers may reward salespersons who handle the most customers during rush periods. Tupperware holds rallies for its salespeople. Almost everyone wins something, ranging from pins and badges to lucrative prizes for top performers (Peters & Waterman, 1982). Schools pick teachers of the year, and professional athletes are rewarded by selection to all-star teams for their superior performance.

The potential to influence others through the ability to administer rewards is a joint function of the leader, the followers, and the situation. Leaders vary considerably in the types and frequency in which they mete out rewards, but the position they fill also helps to determine the frequency and types of rewards administered. For example, employees of the month at Kentucky Fried Chicken are not given new cars; the managers of these franchises do not have the resources to offer such awards. Similarly, leaders in other organizations are limited to some extent in the types of and frequency with which they can administer awards. Nevertheless, leadership practitioners can enhance their reward power by spending some time reflecting on the followers and the situation. Often a number of alternative or innovative rewards can be created, and these rewards, along with ample doses of praise, can help a leader overcome the constraints his or her position puts on reward power.

Although using the power to administer rewards can be an effective way to change the attitudes and behaviors of others, there are several situations where a leader's use of reward power can be problematic. For example, the perception that a company's monetary bonus policy is handled equitably may be as important in motivating good work (or avoiding morale problems) as the amount of the bonus itself. Moreover, a superior may mistakenly assume that a particular reward is valued when it is not. This would be the case if a particular subordinate were publicly recognized for her good work when she actually dislikes public recognition. Leadership practitioners can avoid the latter problem by developing good relationships with subordinates and administering rewards that they, not the leader, value. Another potential problem with reward power is that it may produce compliance but not other desirable outcomes like commitment

Reprinted with special permission of King Features Syndicate

(Yukl, 1989). In other words, subordinates may perform only at the level necessary to receive a reward and may not be willing to put forth the extra effort needed to make the organization better. An overemphasis on rewards as payoff for performance may also lead to resentment and feelings by workers of being manipulated, especially if it occurs in the context of relatively cold and distant superior-subordinate relationships. Extrinsic rewards like praise, compensation, promotion, privileges, and time off may not have the same effects on behavior as intrinsic rewards such as feelings of accomplishment, personal growth, and development. There is evidence that under some conditions extrinsic rewards can decrease intrinsic motivation toward a task and make the desired behavior less likely to persist when extrinsic rewards are not available (Deci, 1972; Ryan, Mims, & Koestner, 1983). Overemphasis on extrinsic rewards may instill an essentially contractual or economic relationship between superiors and subordinates, diluting important aspects of the relationship like mutual loyalty or shared commitment to higher ideals (Wakin, 1981).

All these cautions about reward power should not cloud its usefulness and effectiveness, which is very real. As noted previously, top organizations make extensive use of both tangible and symbolic rewards in motivating their workers. Furthermore, some of the most important rewards are readily available to all leaders—sincere praise and thanks to others for their loyalty and work. The bottom line is that leadership practitioners can enhance their ability to influence others based on reward power if they (*a*) determine what rewards are available, (*b*) determine what rewards are valued by their subordinates, and (*c*) establish clear policies for the equitable and consistent administration of rewards for good performance.

Finally, because reward power is partly determined by one's position in the organization, some people may believe followers have little, if any, reward power. This may not be the case. If followers have control over scarce resources, then they may use the administration of these resources as a way of getting leaders to act in the manner they want. Moreover, followers may reward their leader by putting out a high level of effort when they feel their leader is doing a good job, and they may put forth less effort when they feel their leader is doing a poor job. By modifying their level of effort, followers may in turn modify a leader's attitudes and behaviors. And when followers compliment their leader (e.g., for running a constructive meeting), it is no less an example of reward power than when a leader compliments a follower. Thus, leadership practitioners should be aware that followers can also use reward power to influence leaders.

Coercive Power.   Coercive power, the opposite of reward power, is the potential to influence others through the administration of negative sanctions or the removal of positive events. In other words, it is the ability to control others through the fear of punishment or the loss of valued outcomes. Like reward power, coercive power is partly a function of the leader, but the situation often limits the coercive actions a leader can take. Examples of coercive power include policemen giving tickets for speeding, the army court-martialing AWOL

You do not lead by hitting people over the head—that's assault, not leadership.

Dwight D. Eisenhower

soldiers, a teacher detaining disruptive students after school, employers firing lazy workers, and parents spanking children (Klein, 1991). Even presidents resort to their coercive powers. Historian Arthur Schlesinger, Jr., for example, described Lyndon Johnson as having a "devastating instinct for the weaknesses of others." Lyndon Johnson was familiar and comfortable with the use of coercion; he once told a White House staff member, "Just you remember this. There's only two kinds at the White House. There's elephants and there's ants. And I'm the only elephant" (Barnes, 1989).

Coercive power, like reward power, can be used appropriately or inappropriately. It is carried to its extreme in harsh and repressive totalitarian societies. One of the most tragic instances of coercive power was in the cult led by Jim Jones, which tragically and unbelievably self-exterminated in an incident known as the Jonestown massacre (Conway & Siegelman, 1979). Virtually all of the 912 who died there drank, at Jones's direction, from large vats of a flavored drink containing cyanide. The submissiveness and suicidal obedience of Jones's followers during the massacre were due largely to the long history of rule by fear Jones had practiced. For example, teenagers caught holding hands were beaten, and adults judged slacking in their work were forced to box for hours in marathon public matches against as many as three or four bigger and stronger opponents. Jim Jones ruled by fear, and his followers became self-destructively compliant.

Perhaps the preceding example is so extreme that we can dismiss its relevance to our own lives and leadership activities. On the other hand, it does provide a dramatic reminder that reliance on coercive power has inherent limitations and drawbacks. This is not to say the willingness to use disciplinary sanctions is never necessary. Sometimes it is. Informal coercion, as opposed to the threat of formal punishment, can also be used to change the attitudes and behaviors of others. Informal coercion is usually expressed implicitly, and often nonverbally, rather than explicitly. It may be the pressure employees feel to donate to the boss's favorite charity, or it may be his glare when they bring up an unpopular idea. One of the most common forms of coercion is simply a superior's temperamental outbursts. The intimidation caused by a leader's poorly controlled anger is usually, in its long-term effects, a dysfunctional style of behavior for leaders.

It is also possible for followers to use coercive power to influence their leader's behavior. For example, a leader may be hesitant to take disciplinary action against a large, emotionally unstable follower. Followers can threaten leaders with physical assaults, industrial sabotage, or work slowdowns and strikes, and these threats can serve to modify a leader's behavior. In all likelihood, followers will be more likely to use coercive power to change their leader's behavior if they have a relatively high amount of referent power with their fellow co-workers. This may be particularly true if threats of work slowdowns or strikes are used to influence a leader's behavior.

Concluding Thoughts about French and Raven's Power Taxonomy.   On the basis of all this, can we reach any conclusions about what base of power is best for a leader to use? As you might have anticipated, we must say that's an unanswerable question without knowing more facts about a particular situation. For example, consider the single factor of whether or not a group is facing a crisis. This might affect the leader's exercise of power simply because leaders usually can exert *more* power during crises than during periods of relative calm. Perhaps this is because during a crisis leaders are willing to draw on bases of power they normally forgo. For example, a leader who has developed close interpersonal relationships with followers generally uses her referent power to influence them, but during crises or emergency situations leaders may be more apt to draw on their legitimate and coercive bases of power to influence subordinates. That was precisely the finding in a study of bank managers' actions; the bank managers were more apt to use legitimate and coercive power during crises than during noncrisis situations (Mulder, de Jong, Koppelar, & Verhage, 1986). Furthermore, it may be that during crises followers are more *eager* to receive direction and control from leaders.

But can't we make *any* generalizations about using various sources of power? Actually, there has been considerable research looking at French and Raven's ideas, and generally the findings indicate that leaders who relied primarily on referent and expert power had subordinates who were more motivated and satisfied, were absent less, and performed better (Yukl, 1981). However, Yukl (1981) and Podsakoff and Schriesheim (1985) have criticized these findings, and much of their criticism centers on the instrument used to assess a leader's bases of power. Hinkin and Schriesheim (1989) developed an instrument that overcomes many of the criticisms, and future research should more clearly delineate the relationship between the five bases of power and various leadership effectiveness criteria.

Even though much of the research to date about the five bases of power may be flawed, four generalizations about power and influence still seem warranted. First, effective leaders typically take advantage of *all* their sources of power. Effective leaders understand the relative advantages and disadvantages of different sources of power, and they selectively emphasize one or another depending on their particular objectives in a given situation. Second, whereas leaders in well-functioning organizations have strong influence over their subordinates, *they are also open to being influenced by them.* High degrees of reciprocal influence between leaders and followers characterize the most effective organizations (Yukl, 1989). Third, leaders vary in the extent to which they share power with subordinates. Some leaders seem to view their power as a fixed resource that, when shared with others (like cutting a pie into pieces), reduces their own portion. They see power in zero-sum terms. Other leaders see power as an expandable pie. They see the possibility of increasing a subordinate's power without reducing their own. Needless to say, which view a leader subscribes to can have a major impact on the leader's support for power-sharing activities like delegation and participative management. A leader's support for power-sharing activities (or, in today's popular language, *empowerment*) is also affected by the practice of holding leaders responsible for subordinates' decisions and actions as well as their own. It is, after all, the coach or manager who often gets fired when the team loses (Hollander & Offermann, 1990; Pfeffer, 1977). Fourth, effective leaders generally work to *increase* their various power bases (i.e., whether expert, referent, reward, or legitimate) or become more willing to *use* their coercive power.

Leader Motives

Thus far we have been looking at how different *sources* of power can affect others, but that's only one perspective. Another way of looking at the relationship between power and leadership involves focusing on the individual leader's personality. We will look most closely at the role personality plays in leadership in an upcoming chapter, but it will be nonetheless useful now to briefly examine how all people (including leaders) vary in their personal motivation to have or wield power.

People vary in their motivation to influence or control others. McClelland (1975) called this the **need for power,** and individuals with a high need for power derive psychological satisfaction from influencing others. They seek positions where they can influence others, and they are often involved concurrently in influencing people in many different organizations or decision-making bodies. In such activities they readily offer ideas, suggestions, and opinions, and also seek information they can use in influencing others. They are often astute at building trusting relationships and assessing power networks, though they can also be quite outspoken and forceful. They value the tangible signs of their authority and status as well as the more intangible indications of others' deference to them. Two different ways of expressing the need for power have been identified: **personalized power** and **socialized power.** Individuals who have a high need for personalized power are relatively selfish, impulsive, uninhibited, and lacking in self-control. These individuals exercise power for their own self-centered needs, not for the good of the group or the organization. Socialized power, on the other hand, implies a more emotionally mature expression of the motive. Socialized power is exercised in the service of higher goals to others or organizations and often involves self-sacrifice toward those ends. It often involves an empowering, rather than an autocratic, style of management and leadership.

Although the need for power has been measured using questionnaires and more traditional personality inventories, McClelland and his associates have used the Thematic Apperception Test (TAT) to assess need for power. The TAT is a **projective personality test** consisting of pictures such as a woman staring out a window or a boy holding a violin. Subjects are asked to make up a story about each picture, and the stories are then interpreted in terms of the strengths of various needs imputed to the characters, one of which is the need for power. Since the pictures are somewhat ambiguous, the sorts of needs projected onto the characters are presumed to reflect needs (perhaps at an unconscious level) of the storyteller. Stories concerned with influencing or controlling others would receive high scores for the need for power.

The need for power has been found to be positively related to various leadership effectiveness criteria. For example, McClelland and Boyatzis (1982) found the need for power to be positively related to success for nontechnical managers at

AT&T, and Stahl (1983) found that the need for power was positively related to managers' performance ratings and promotion rates. In addition, Fodor (1987) reported that small groups of ROTC students were more likely to successfully solve a subarctic survival situation if their leader had a strong need for power. Although these findings appear promising, several cautions should be kept in mind. First, McClelland and Boyatzis (1982) also reported that the need for power was unrelated to the success of technical managers at AT&T. Apparently, the level of knowledge (i.e., expert power) played a more important role in the success of the technical managers versus the nontechnical managers. Second, McClelland (1985) concluded that although some need for power was necessary for leadership potential, successful leaders also have the ability to inhibit their manifestation of this need. Leaders who are relatively uninhibited in their need for power will act like a dictator; such individuals use power impulsively, to manipulate or control others, or to achieve at another's expense. Leaders with a high need for power but low activity inhibition may be successful in the short term, but their followers, as well as the remainder of the organization, may pay high costs for this success. Some of these costs may include perceptions by fellow members of the organization that they are untrustworthy, uncooperative, overly competitive, and looking out primarily for themselves. Finally, it may be worth pointing out that some followers have a high need for power too. This can lead to tension between leader and follower when a follower with a high need for power is directed to do something.

Individuals vary in their motivation to manage, just as in their need for power. Miner (1974) described **motivation to manage** in terms of six composites:

- Maintaining good relationships with authority figures.
- Wanting to compete for recognition and advancement.
- Being active and assertive.
- Wanting to exercise influence over subordinates.
- Being visibly different from followers.
- Being willing to do routine administrative tasks.

Like McClelland, Miner also used a projective test to measure a person's motivation to manage. Miner's Sentence Completion Scale (MSCS) consists of a series of incomplete sentences dealing with the six components described above (e.g., "My relationship with my boss . . ."). Respondents are asked to complete the sentences, which are then scored according to established criteria. The overall composite MSCS score (though not component scores) has consistently been found to predict leadership success in hierarchical or bureaucratic organizations (Miner, 1978). Thus, individuals who maintained respect for authority figures, wanted to be recognized, acted assertively, actively influenced subordinates, maintained "psychological distance" between themselves and their followers, and readily took on routine administrative tasks were more apt to be successful in bureaucratic organizations. However, Miner also claimed that different qualities were needed in flatter, nonbureaucratic organizations, and his (1978) review of the MSCS supports this view.

Findings concerning both the need for power and the motivation to manage have several implications for leadership practitioners. First, not all individuals like being leaders. One reason may be that some have a relatively low need for power or motivation to manage. Because these scores are relatively stable and fairly difficult to change, leaders who do not enjoy their role may want to seek positions where they have fewer supervisory responsibilities.

Second, a high need for power or motivation to manage does not guarantee leadership success. The situation can play a crucial role in determining whether the need for power or the motivation to manage is related to leadership success. For example, McClelland and Boyatzis (1982) found the need for power to be related to leadership success for nontechnical managers only, and Miner (1978) found motivation to manage was related to leadership success only in hierarchical or bureaucratic organizations.

Third, in order to be successful in the long term, leaders may have to have both a high need for socialized power and a high level of activity inhibition. Leaders who impulsively exercise power merely to satisfy their own selfish needs will probably be ineffective in the long term. Finally, it is important to remember that followers, as well as leaders, differ in the need for power, activity inhibition, and motivation to manage. Certain followers may have stronger needs or motives in this area. Leaders may need to behave differently toward these followers than they might toward followers having a low need for power or motivation to manage.

Influence Tactics

Whereas power is the capacity or potential to influence others, influence tactics are the actual behaviors used by an agent to change the attitudes, opinions, or behaviors of a target person. Kipnis and his associates accomplished much of the early work on the types of influence tactics one person uses to influence another (Kipnis & Schmidt, 1982). Various instruments have been developed to study influence tactics, but the Influence Behavior Questionnaire, or IBQ (Yukl, Lepsinger, & Lucia, 1992), seems to be the most promising. Here is a detailed discussion of the different influence tactics assessed by the IBQ.

Types of Influence Tactics

The IBQ is designed to assess nine types of influence tactics, and its scales provide us with a convenient overview of various methods of influencing others. **Rational persuasion** occurs when an agent uses logical arguments or factual evidence to influence others. An example of rational persuasion would be when a politician's advisor explains how demographic changes in the politician's district make it important for the politician to spend relatively more time in the district seeing constituents than she has needed to in the recent past. Agents make **inspirational appeals** when they make a request or proposal designed to arouse enthusiasm or emotions in targets. An example here might be when a minister makes an impassioned plea to members of his congregation about the good works which could be accomplished if a proposed addition to the church were built. **Consultation** occurs when agents ask targets to participate in planning an activity. An example of consultation would be if the minister in the preceding example established a committee of church members to help plan the layout and uses of that new church addition. In this case the consultative work might not only lead to a better building plan but also *strengthen member commitment* to the very idea of a new addition. **Ingratiation** occurs when the agent attempts to get you in a good mood before making a request. A familiar example here would be a salesperson's good-natured or flattering banter with you before you make a decision about purchasing a product. Agents use **personal appeals** when they ask another to do a favor out of friendship. A sentence that opens with, "Bill, we've known each other a long time and I've never asked anything of you before" represents the beginning of a personal appeal, whereas influencing a target through the exchange of favors is labeled **exchange.** If two politicians agree to vote for each other's pet legislation despite minor misgivings about each other's bills, that is exchange. **Coalition tactics** are different from consultation in that they are used when agents seek the aid or support of others to influence the target. A dramatic example of coalition tactics occurs when several key significant people in an alcoholic's life (e.g., spouse, children, employer, neighbor) agree to confront the alcoholic in unison about the many dimensions of his problem. Threats or persistent reminders used to influence targets are known as **pressure tactics.** A judge who gives a convicted prisoner a suspended sentence but tells him to consider the suspension a "sword hanging over your head" if he breaks the law again is using pressure tactics. Finally, **legitimizing tactics** occur when agents make requests based on their position or authority. A principal may ask a teacher to be on the school's curriculum committee, and the teacher may accede to the request despite reservations just because it is the principal's prerogative to appoint any teacher to that role. In practice, of course, actual tactics often reflect combinations of these different approaches. Rarely, for example, is an effective appeal purely inspirational, without any rational elements at all.

Influence Tactics and Power

As alluded to throughout this chapter, a strong relationship exists between the relative power of agents and targets and the types of influence tactics used. Because leaders with relatively high amounts of referent power have built up close relationships with followers, they may be more able to use a wide variety of influence tactics to modify the attitudes and behaviors of their followers. For example, leaders with a lot of referent power could use inspirational appeals, consultations, ingratiation, personal appeals, exchanges, and even coalition tactics to increase the amount of time a particular follower spends doing work-related activities. Note, however, that leaders with high referent power generally do not use legitimizing or pressure tactics to influence followers since by threatening followers, leaders risk some loss of referent power. Leaders who have only coercive or legitimate power may be able to use only coalition, legitimizing, or pressure tactics to influence followers.

Other factors also can affect the choice of influence tactics (Kipnis & Schmidt, 1985). People typically use hard tactics (i.e., legitimizing or pressure tactics) when an influencer has the upper hand, when she anticipates resistance, or when the other person's behavior violates important norms. People typically use soft tactics (e.g., ingratiation) when they are at a disadvantage, when they expect resistance, or when they will personally benefit if the attempt is successful. People typically use rational tactics (i.e., the exchange and rational appeal) when parties are relatively equal in power, when resistance is not anticipated, and when the benefits are organizational as well as personal.

Other studies, too, have shown that influence attempts based on factual, logical analyses are the most frequently reported method by which middle managers exert lateral influence (Keys, Case, Miller, Curran, & Jones, 1987) and upward influence (Case, Dosier, Murkison, & Keys, 1988). Other important components of successful influence of one's superiors include thoroughly preparing beforehand, involving others for support (i.e., coalition tactics), and persisting through a combination of approaches (Case, Dosier, Murkison, & Keys, 1988).

> *Don't threaten. I know it's done by some of our people, but I don't go for it. If people are running scared, they're not going to make the right decisions. They'll make decisions to please the boss rather than recommend what has to be done.*
>
> Charles Pilliod

Findings about who uses different tactics, and when, provide interesting insights into the influence process. It is clear that one's influence tactic of choice depends on many factors, including intended outcomes and one's power relative to the target person. Whereas it may not be very surprising that people select influence tactics as a function of their power relationship with another person, it is striking that the relationship holds true so universally across different social domains. The relationship holds true for business executives, for parents and children, and for spouses. There is a strong tendency for people to resort to hard tactics whenever they have an advantage in clout if other tactics fail to get results (Kipnis & Schmidt, 1985). As the bank robber Willie Sutton once said, "A gun and a smile are more effective than a smile by itself." This sentiment is apparently familiar to bank managers, too. The latter reported greater satisfaction in handling subordinates' poor performance when they were relatively more punishing (Green, Fairhurst, & Snavely, 1986). Highlight 5.3 offers thoughts on how men and women managers sometimes use different techniques in "managing upward." It would be interesting to contrast the uses of power and influence of Madeleine Albright and Colin Powell, not only because of their gender but also because of their differing bases of power.

Although hard tactics can be effective, relying on them can change the way we see others. This was demonstrated in an experiment wherein leaders' perceptions and evaluations of subordinates were assessed after they exercised different sorts of authority over the subordinates (Kipnis, 1984). Several hundred business students acted as managers of small work groups assembling model cars. Some of the students were told to act in an authoritarian manner, exercising complete control over the group's work; others were told to act as demo-

Gender Differences in Managing Upward: How Male and Female Managers Get Their Way

Highlight 5.3

Both male and female managers in a Fortune 100 company were interviewed and completed surveys about how they influence upward—how they influence their own bosses. The results generally supported the idea that female managers' influence attempts showed greater concern for others, while male managers' influence attempts showed greater concern for self. Female managers were more likely to act with the organization's broad interests in mind, consider how others felt about the influence attempt, involve others in planning, and focus on both the task and interpersonal aspects of the situation. Male managers, on the other hand, were more likely to act out of self-interest, show less consideration for how others might feel about the influence attempt, work alone in developing their strategy, and focus primarily on the task alone.

One of the most surprising findings of the study was that, contrary to prediction, female managers were less likely than male managers to compromise or negotiate during their influence attempts. The female managers were actually more likely to persist in trying to persuade their superiors, even to the point of open opposition. At first this may seem inconsistent with the idea that the female managers' influence style involved greater concern for their relatedness to others. However, it does seem consistent with the higher value placed by the women managers on involvement. Perhaps female managers demonstrate more commitment to their issue, and greater self-confidence that they are doing the "right thing," precisely because they have interacted with others in the organization more already and know they have others' support.

While male and female managers emphasized different influence techniques, it is important to note neither group overall was more effective than the other. Nonetheless, there may be significant implications of the various techniques for a manager's career advancement. At increasingly higher management levels in an organization, effectiveness may be defined primarily by its fit with the organization's own norms and values. Managers whose style matches most closely that of their superior's may have an advantage in evaluations and promotion decisions. This may be a significant factor for women, given the highly skewed representation of males in the most senior executive ranks.

Source: K. E. Lauterbach and B. J. Weiner, "Dynamics of Upward Influence: How Male and Female Managers Get Their Way," *Leadership Quarterly* 7, no. 1 (1996), pp. 87–107.

cratic leaders, letting group members participate fully in decisions about the work. As expected, authoritarian leaders used more hard tactics, whereas democratic leaders influenced subordinates more through rational methods. More interesting was the finding that subordinates were evaluated by the two types of leaders in dramatically different ways even though the subordinates of both types did equally good work. Authoritarian leaders judged their subordinates as less motivated, less skilled, and less suited for promotion. Apparently, bosses who use hard tactics to control others' behavior tend not to attribute any resultant good performance to the subordinates themselves. Ironically, the act of using hard tactics leads to negative attributions about others, which, in turn, tend to corroborate the use of hard tactics in the first place.

Finally, we should remember that using influence tactics can be thought of as a social skill. Choosing the right tactic to use may not always be enough to ensure good results; the behavior must be *skillfully executed.* We are not encouraging deviousness or a manipulative attitude toward others, merely recognizing the obvious fact that clumsy attempts to influence do often come across as phoney. They may be counterproductive in the end. See Highlight 5.4 for some interesting ways skills are applied in the political arena.

To Be or Not to Be . . . a Porcupine

Highlight 5.4

We said before that there are no simple recipes for leadership. This is perfectly evident in the various ways power and influence are exercised in the halls of Congress. In *The Power Game,* author Hedrick Smith offers numerous examples of how Washington, D.C., actually works. For example, it is true that interpersonal relationships play a key part in one's effectiveness, but there are many paths to interpersonal power and influence in government, as the following anecdotes point out.

Barney Frank, a Democratic congressman from Massachusetts, likens success in the House of Representatives to high school. Nobody in the House can give any other member an order, not even the Speaker of the House. Neither can anyone be fired except by his or her own constituencies. That means, therefore, that those in Congress become influential by persuading people and having others respect but not resent them. In that sense it's like high school.

Sometimes, however, it may pay to be *unlikable,* at least in some situations. Former senator (and later secretary of state) Ed Muskie had a reputation for being a "porcupine," for being difficult in the conference committees where final versions of legislation were hammered out. A former staff member said Muskie was the best porcupine of them all because nobody wanted to tangle with him. Muskie will "be gross. He'll smoke a god-awful cigar. He'll just be difficult, cantankerous." One of the reasons Muskie was so successful as a legislator was precisely that he could be nearly impossible to deal with. People would rather ignore him, try to avoid fights or confrontations with his notorious temper. Muskie knew how to be a porcupine, and he used that behavior to advantage in authoring critical legislation.

Source: H. Smith, *The Power Game* (New York: Random House, 1988).

A Concluding Thought about Influence Tactics.   In the above discussion, an implicit lesson for leaders is the value of being conscious of what influence tactics one uses and what effects are typically associated with each tactic. Knowledge of such effects can help a leader make better decisions about her manner of influencing others. It might also be helpful for leaders to think more carefully about why they believe a particular influence tactic might be effective.

Research indicates that some reasons for selecting among various possible influence tactics lead to successful outcomes more frequently than others. More specifically, thinking an act would improve an employee's self-esteem or morale was frequently associated with successful influence attempts. On the other hand, choosing an influence tactic because it followed company policy and choosing one because it was a way to put a subordinate in his place were frequently mentioned as reasons for unsuccessful influence attempts (Dosier, Case, & Keys, 1988). In a nutshell, these results suggest that leaders should pay attention not only to the actual influence tactics they use—to *how* they are influencing others—but also to *why* they believe such methods are called for. It is perhaps an obvious but nonetheless important conclusion to reach from these results that influence efforts intended to build others up more frequently lead to positive outcomes than influence efforts intended to put others down.

> *All forms of tampering with human beings, getting at them, shaping them against their will to your own pattern, all thought control and conditioning, is, therefore, a denial of that in men which makes them men and their values ultimate.*
>
> A. A. Berle, Jr.,
> Writer on corporations

Summary

This chapter has defined power as the capacity or potential to exert influence, influence tactics as the behaviors used by one person to modify the attitudes and behaviors of another, and influence as the degree of change in a person's attitudes, values, or behaviors as the result of another's influence tactic. Because power, influence, and influence tactics play such important roles in the leadership process, this chapter provides ideas to help leaders improve their effectiveness. By reflecting on their different bases of power, leaders may better understand how they can affect followers and even expand their power. The five bases of power also offer clues as to why subordinates are able to influence leaders and successfully resist leaders' influence attempts.

Leaders also may gain insight into why they may not enjoy certain aspects of their responsibilities by reflecting on their own need for power or motivation to manage; they may also better understand why some leaders exercise power selfishly by considering McClelland's concepts of personalized power and activity inhibition. Leaders can improve their effectiveness by finding ways to enhance their idiosyncratic credit and not permitting in-group and out-group rivalries to develop in the work unit.

Although power is an extremely important concept, having power is relatively meaningless unless a leader is willing to exercise it. The exercise of power occurs primarily through the influence tactics leaders and followers use to modify the attitudes and behaviors of each other. The type of influence tactics used seems to depend on the amount of different types of power possessed, the degree of resistance expected, and the rationale behind the different influence tactics. Because influence tactics designed to build up others are generally more successful than those that tear down others, leadership practitioners should always consider why they are using a particular influence attempt before they actually use it. By carefully considering the rationale behind the tactic, leaders may be able to avoid using pressure and legitimizing tactics and to find ways to influence followers that build them up rather than tear them down. Being able to use influence tactics that modify followers' attitudes and behaviors in the desired direction at the same time they build up followers' self-esteem and self-confidence should be a skill all leaders strive to master.

Key Terms

power   107
influence   108
influence tactics   108
pecking order   110
expert power   114
referent power   115
legitimate power   116
reward power   117
coercive power   119
need for power   122
personalized power   122
socialized power   122

projective personality test   122
motivation to manage   123
rational persuasion   124
inspirational appeals   124
consultation   125
ingratiation   125
personal appeals   125
exchange   125
coalition tactics   125
pressure tactics   125
legitimizing tactics   125

Questions

1. The following questions all pertain to the Milgram studies (Highlight 5.2).
   a. What bases of power were available to the experimenter, and what bases of power were available to the subjects?

   b. Do you think subjects with a low need for power would act differently from those subjects with a high need for power? What about subjects with differing levels of the motivation to manage?

    c. What situational factors contributed to the experimenter's power?

    d. What influence tactics did the experimenter use to change the behavior of the subjects, and how were these tactics related to the experimenter's power base?

    e. What actually was influenced? In other words, if influence is the change in another's attitudes, values, or behaviors as the result of an influence tactic, then what changes occurred in the subject as the result of the experimenter's influence tactics?

    f. Many people have criticized the Milgram study on ethical grounds. Assuming that some socially useful information was gained from the studies, do you believe this experiment could or should be replicated today?

2. Some definitions of leadership exclude reliance on formal authority or coercion (i.e., certain actions by a person in authority may work but should not be considered leadership). What are the pros and cons of such a view?

3. Does power, as Lord Acton suggested, tend to "corrupt" the power holder? If so, what are some of the ways it happens? Is it also possible subordinates are corrupted by a superior's power? How? Or is it even possible that superiors can be corrupted by a subordinate's power?

4. Some people say it dilutes a leader's authority if subordinates are allowed to give feedback to the leader concerning their perceptions of the leader's performance. Do you agree?

5. Is leadership just another word for influence? Can you think of some examples of influence that you would *not* consider leadership?

6. Compare and contrast Colin Powell, Madeleine Albright, and Konosuke Matsushita in their respective sources of power.

Skills

Leadership skills relevant to this chapter include:

- Assertiveness
- Building technical competence
- Building effective relationships
- Punishment
- Negotiation

Activity

This activity will demonstrate how the five bases of power are manifest in behavior. Write the five bases of power on the blackboard or put them on an overhead. Break students into five groups, and give each group a 3 × 5 card which lists one of the five bases of power. Give the group 10 minutes to plan and practice a 1-minute skit which will be presented to the rest of the class. The skit should demonstrate the base of power listed on the 3 × 5 card. After the skit is presented, the remaining groups should guess which base of power is being used in the skit. As an alternative, you might choose a project for out-of-class work. Another variation is to assign the groups the task of finding a 3–4 minute segment from a movie or video and bring that in to the class.

6   LEADERSHIP AND VALUES

Introduction

I n the previous chapter, we examined many different facets of power and its use in leadership. The topics in this chapter go hand in hand with understanding the role of power in leadership. That is because leaders can use power for good or ill, and the leader's personal code of ethics and values may be one of the most important determinants of how power is exercised or constrained. For example, a political leader may be able to stir a group into a frenzy (and become even more popular) by identifying a scapegoat to blame for a community's or nation's problems, but would it be right? A business executive may be able to earn her company millions of dollars by selling unsafe drugs to patients desperate for something to cure their malady, but would it be right?

But perhaps you find those examples too obvious and simplistic. Therefore, let us slightly modify them. Is it *ever* right for a political leader to stir a populace into a frenzy? And what standards should govern the application of such power? In the second example, because a drug may not yet have passed the strict and lengthy requirements of U.S. Federal Drug Administration approval, should it also be withheld from use in other countries which—facing very different medical challenges than the United States—seek its availability? These are more difficult questions to answer, but the general point should be clear: The mere possession of power, of any kind, leads inevitably to ethical questions about how that power should and should not be used. The challenge of leadership becomes even more complex when we consider how individuals of different backgrounds, cultures, and nationalities may hold quite different values yet be thrown into increasingly closer interaction with each other as our world becomes both smaller and more diverse. This chapter will explore these fascinating and important aspects of leadership.

Ethics and Values

Leaders face ethical dilemmas at all levels, and the best leaders recognize and face them with a commitment to doing what is right, not just what is expedient. Of course, the phrase *doing what is right* sounds deceptively simple. Sometimes it will take great moral courage to do what is right, even when the right action seems clear. At other times, though, leaders face ethically complex issues that lack simple black-and-white answers. Whichever the case, leaders set a moral example to others that becomes the model for an entire group or organization, for good or bad. Leaders who themselves do not honor truth do not inspire it in others. Leaders mostly concerned with their own advancement do not inspire selflessness in others. Leaders should internalize a strong set of **ethics,** principles of right conduct or a system of moral values.

> *Leadership cannot just go along to get along . . . Leadership must meet the moral challenge of the day.*
>
> Jesse Jackson

Both Gardner (1990) and Burns (1978) have stressed the centrality and importance of the moral dimension of leadership. Gardner said leaders ultimately must be judged on the basis of a framework of values, not just in terms of their effectiveness. He put the question of a leader's relations with his or her followers or constituents on the moral plane, arguing (with the philosopher Immanuel Kant) that leaders should always treat others as ends in themselves, not as objects or mere means to the leader's ends (which, however, does not necessarily imply that leaders need to be gentle in interpersonal demeanor or "democratic" in style). Burns (1978) took an even more extreme view regarding the moral dimension of leadership, maintaining that leaders who do not behave ethically do not demonstrate true leadership.

One behavior common to many good leaders is that they tend to align the values of their followers with those of the organization or movement; they make the links between the two sets more explicit. But just what are values? How do values and ethical behavior develop? Is one person's set of standards better or higher than another's? These are the sorts of questions we will address in this section.

What Are Values?

Values are "constructs representing generalized behaviors or states of affairs that are considered by the individual to be important" (Gordon, 1975, p. 2). When Patrick Henry said, "Give me liberty, or give me death," he was expressing the value he placed upon political freedom. The opportunity to constantly study and learn may be the fundamental value or "state of affairs" leading a person to pursue a career in academia. Someone who values personal integrity may be forced to resign from an unethical company. Thus, values play a fairly central role in one's overall psychological makeup and can affect behavior in a variety

TABLE 6–1 People Vary in the Relative Importance They Place on Values like the Following

Terminal Values	Instrumental Values
An exciting life	Being courageous
A sense of accomplishment	Being helpful
Family security	Being honest
Inner harmony	Being imaginative
Social recognition	Being logical
Friendship	Being responsible

Source: Adapted from M. Rokeach, *The Nature of Human Values* (New York: Free Press, 1973).

of situations. In work settings, values can affect decisions about joining an organization, organizational commitment, relationships with co-workers, and decisions about leaving an organization (Boyatzis & Skelly, 1989). It is important for leaders to realize that individuals in the same work unit can have considerably different values, especially since we cannot see values directly. We can only make inferences about people's values based on their behavior.

Some of the major values that may be considered important by individuals in an organization are listed in Table 6–1. The instrumental values found in Table 6–1 refer to modes of behavior, and the terminal values refer to desired end states (Rokeach, 1973). For example, some individuals value equality, freedom, and having a comfortable life above all else; others may believe that family security and salvation are important goals to strive for. In terms of instrumental values, such individuals may think that it is important always to act in an ambitious, capable, and honest manner, whereas others may think it is important only to be ambitious and capable. We should add that the instrumental and terminal values in Table 6–1 are only a few of those Rokeach has identified.

How Do Values Develop?

According to Massey (1979), each person's values reflect the contributions of diverse inputs, including family, peers, the educational system, religion, the media, science and technology, geography, and current events (see Figure 6.1). Although one's values can change throughout one's life, they are relatively firmly established by young adulthood. Figure 6.2 represents the building blocks of leadership skills as a pyramid, and you can see that values are on the bottom of the pyramid (along with interests, motives, lifelong goals, personality traits and preferences, and intelligence). All of the attributes in that bottom row are relatively enduring and permanent; they serve as a foundation to other attributes of leadership that are less enduring and thus more modifiable. At the top of the pyramid are leadership skills and competencies that can be developed through practice.

Massey used the term **value programming** to highlight the extent to which forces outside the individual shape and mold personal values. He analyzed

FIGURE 6.1

Some influences on the development of personal values

Source: Adapted from M. Massey, *The People Puzzle* (Reston, VA.: Reston Publishing, 1979).

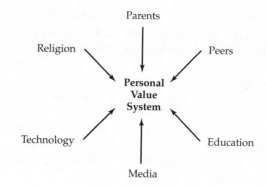

FIGURE 6.2

The building blocks of skills

changes in the value-programming inputs that characterized each of the decades since the 1920s and related them to dominant and distinctive values held among people who were value-programmed during those respective periods. For example, he said the monumental event of the 1930s, the Great Depression, programmed people growing up then to especially value economic security. People growing up in the 1960s, however, were value-programmed quite differently. Dramatic shifts and changes in American society occurred during the 1960s. There were violent social protests, experimentation with new lifestyles, and pervasive questioning of establishment values.

Boyatzis and Skelly (1989), Maccoby (1983), and Massey (1979) have all said that the pervasive influence of broad forces like these tend to create common value systems among people growing up at a particular time that distinguish them from people who grow up at different times. There are, of course, significant differences among individuals *within* any generational group, but these authors emphasized differences *between* groups. For example, people who grew up prior to World War II valued authority, job security, and stability; people who grew up in the 1960s valued participation, informality, and personal growth; and those who grew up in the 1980s valued competitiveness, entrepreneurialism, and cost-effectiveness.

These authors attributed much of the misunderstanding between older leaders and younger followers to the fact that their basic value systems were formulated during quite different social and cultural conditions, and these analyses offer a helpful perspective for understanding how differences in values can add tension to the interaction between some leaders and followers. Do you think there are any basic differences in values between the "Baby Boomer" generation (now in their 40s and 50s) and "Generation X" which might affect the leadership process? In thinking about that question, you may be interested in an ongoing research project at the Center for Creative Leadership, which has been studying emerging leaders ranging between 25 and 35 years of age. On the basis of interviews with emerging leaders themselves, their managers, and human resource staff in their organizations, they are perceived as being technologically savvy, independent, skeptical of institutions, entrepreneurial, adventuresome, efficient, embracing change, and focused on outcomes.

Lest we overemphasize the significance of intergenerational differences, however, we should consider the results of a recent scientific sampling of over 1,000 people living in the United States (Ladd, 1994) which found *little* evidence of a generation gap in basic values. Indeed, the director of one of the largest polling organizations in the world called the results some of the most powerful he had seen in 30 years of public-opinion research. They showed, he said, "that even though young people buy different CDs and clothes, they do *not* buy into a set of values different from their elders" (Ladd, p. 50).

> *Question authority, but raise your hand first.*
>
> Bob Thaues

Thus, while it's true that experiences unique to particular generations help explain certain values characteristic of people in one generation, people from different generations still share many of the same values. But what might explain value differences *within* a given age group? Actually, they're the same factors depicted in Figure 6.1 which Massey used to explain value differences *across* generations. There may be significant differences in the value-programming experiences of teenagers from the same generation based on factors like their family's religious affiliation and involvement, the norms of the particular peer group they associate with, their formal education, and so on.

Up to this point the discussion has focused on the *content* of a person's values. Equally important, however, is the question of how one *thinks about* value-laden issues or ethical dilemmas. **Moral reasoning** refers to the process leaders use to make decisions about ethical and unethical behaviors. Moral reasoning does not refer to the morality of individuals per se, or their espoused values, but rather to the *manner by which they solve moral problems*. Values play a key role in the moral reasoning process, since value differences among individuals often result in different judgments regarding ethical and unethical behavior.

Kohlberg (1969) theorized that people progress through a series of *developmental stages* in their moral reasoning. Each stage reflects a more cognitively complex way of analyzing moral situations than the preceding one, and the sequence of stages is fixed, or invariant. Moral reasoning is assessed using ethical dilemmas such as whether a man is morally justified in stealing an overpriced drug to save his dying wife, and an individual's stage of moral reasoning is based on the *way the answer is explained* rather than the particular answer given. Two individuals, for example, may each argue that the husband was morally wrong to steal the drug—even in those extenuating circumstances—yet offer qualitatively different kinds of reasons as to *why* the action was wrong. Similarly, two individuals may each argue the husband was morally justified in stealing the drug, yet offer different reasons as to why it was justifiable. The focus is on the reasoning process rather than on the decision per se. You may find it interesting to reflect on the moral issues raised in Highlight 6.1. Obviously, different individuals may have quite different points of view on these ethical questions.

That distinction may be clearer by looking in greater detail at different ways of evaluating the husband's behavior. Table 6–2 outlines Kohlberg's six stages of

---

What Would You Do?

Highlight 6.1

Here are several situations having ethical dimensions. How would you act in each one, and by what principles or reasoning process do you reach each decision?

- Would you vote for a political candidate who was honest, competent, and agreed with you on most issues if you also knew that person was alcoholic, sexually promiscuous, and twice divorced?
- Assume that as a teenager you smoked marijuana once or twice, but that was years ago. Would you answer truthfully on an employment questionnaire if it asked whether you had ever used marijuana?
- Your military unit has been ambushed by enemy soldiers and suffered heavy casualties. Several of your soldiers have been captured, but you also captured one of the enemy soldiers. Would you torture the captured enemy soldier if that were the only way of saving the lives of your own soldiers?
- Terrorists have captured a planeload of tourists and threatened to kill them unless ransom demands are met. You believe that meeting the ransom demands is likely to lead to the safe release of those passengers, but also likely to inspire future terrorist acts. Would you meet the terrorists' demands (and probably save the hostages) or refuse to meet the terrorists' demands (and reduce the likelihood of future incidents).
- If you were an elementary school principal, would you feel it was part of your school's responsibility to teach moral values, or only academic subject matter?
- Assume that you have been elected to your state's legislature, and that you are about to cast the deciding vote in determining whether abortions will be legally available to women in your state. What would you do if your own strong personal convictions on this issue were contrary to the views of the majority of the people you represent?

Source: Adapted from Stock (1991).

TABLE 6–2 Developmental Levels and Stages of Moral Reasoning

Description of Stages	Examples of Moral Reasoning in Support of Stealing the Drug	Examples of Moral Reasoning against Stealing the Drug
Preconventional Level		
Stage 1: "Bad" behavior is that which is punished	"If you let your wife die you will get in trouble."	"If you steal the drug you will get in trouble."
Stage 2: "Good" behavior is that which is concretely rewarded	"If you do happen to get caught, you could give the drug back and not get much of a sentence."	"Even if you were caught and didn't get much of a sentence, your wife would probably die while you were in jail and it wouldn't do you much good."
Conventional Level		
Stage 3: "Good" behavior is that which is approved by others; "bad" behavior is that which is disapproved by others	"If you don't steal the drug you'll never be able to look anyone in the face again."	"Everyone would know you are a thief."
Stage 4: "Good" behavior conforms to standards set by social institutions; transgressions lead to feelings of guilt or dishonor	"If you have any sense of honor, you'd do your duty as a husband and steal the drug."	"If you stole the drug, however desperate you felt, you'd never be able to look at yourself in the mirror again."
Postconventional Level		
Stage 5: "Good" behavior conforms to community standards set through democratic participation; concern with maintaining self-respect and the respect of equals	"If you don't steal the drug you'd lose your own respect and everyone else's too."	"We've all agreed to live by common rules, and any form of stealing breaks that bond."
Stage 6: "Good" behavior is a matter of individual conscience based on responsibly chosen commitments to ethical principles.	"If you didn't steal it, you might have satisfied the letter of the law, but you wouldn't have lived up to your own standards of conscience."	"Maybe others would have approved of your behavior, but stealing the drug would still have violated your own conscience and standards of honesty."

Source: Adapted from Kohlberg (1984).

> *So near is a falsehood to truth that a wise man would do well not to trust himself on the narrow edge.*
>
> Cicero

moral development, as well as how a person at each stage might evaluate the husband's behavior. Note that the six stages themselves are organized into three higher-order levels: the **preconventional level,** in which a person's criteria for moral behavior are based primarily on *self-interest* such as avoiding punishment or being rewarded; the **conventional level,** in which the criteria for moral behavior are based primarily on *gaining others' approval* and behaving (as the name implies) *conventionally;* and the **postconventional level,** in which the criteria are based on universal, abstract principles which may even transcend the laws of a particular society. Finally, to say moral development progresses in invariant stages does not imply that all individuals actually achieve the highest stages. Few adults do. How do you think, in that regard, a political leader at the conventional level may differ in behavior (e.g., in the "stands" he or she takes on issues) from one at the postconventional level?

But what is it that actually *moves* an individual from one level to the next? In summarizing several decades of research on moral judgment, Rest (1993) highlighted fundamental, dramatic, and extensive changes which occur in young adulthood (the 20s and 30s) in how people define what is morally right or wrong. Rest noted that formal education is strongly correlated with these, though no specific academic or personal experiences proved pivotal. Moral judgment is part of each person's *general* personal and social development, and those individuals whose moral judgment develop most are those who "love to learn, seek new challenges, who enjoy intellectually stimulating environments, who are reflective, who make plans and set goals, who take risks, who see themselves in the larger social contexts of history and institutions, and who take responsibility for themselves and their environs" (p. 209). At the same time, deliberate curricular attempts to affect moral judgment have been shown to be effective. Interestingly, though, some of the largest gains from formal moral education programs have occurred with participants in their 20s and 30s rather than with more traditionally school-age students. This should not be surprising. It may be beneficial to have struggled with certain life experiences before the lessons of moral education make complete sense.

Values and Leadership

How Values Affect Leadership.   According to England and Lee (1974), values can affect leaders in six different ways. First, values affect leaders' perceptions of situations and the problems at hand. Leaders who value occupational success above all else may see a work-related problem as an obstacle to their achievement, whereas leaders who value helping others may see a work-related problem as an opportunity to help a subordinate or another work unit. Second, leaders' values affect the solutions generated and the decisions reached about problems. If leaders believe being courageous and standing up for one's beliefs are important, then they may be more likely to generate solutions or make decisions not considered politically correct in their organizations. Third, values play an extremely important role in interpersonal relationships; they influence how leaders perceive different individuals and groups. For example, leaders who value self-control may have a difficult time dealing with followers who are very emotionally demonstrative and, in turn, may choose to have fairly distant relationships with these followers. Fourth, values often influence leaders' perceptions of individual and organizational successes as well as the manner in which these successes are to be achieved. Leaders who primarily value competitiveness, independence, and imagination may assess leadership effectiveness differently from leaders who value helpfulness, logic, and cheerfulness. Fifth, values provide a basis for leaders to differentiate between right and wrong, and between ethical and unethical behavior. Sixth, values also may affect the extent to which leaders accept or reject organizational pressures and goals. Leaders who place a premium on being obedient may never question the goals of the organization. However, leaders who believe being independent is important may often question and even actively resist the implementation of some organizational goals in their work units.

Values may be expressed by whole organizations as well as by individuals. Many organizations are adopting and disseminating formal statements of their corporate core values to assure their widespread understanding and practice. One example of this is seen in Highlight 6.2. Not all organizations, however,

---

Compaq's Values

Highlight 6.2

More and more organizations are developing formal statements of corporate values. Here are Compaq's values as highlighted in a letter to Compaq employees and contractors by the CEO, Eckhard Pfeiffer:

Committed to Our Customers We exist because of our customers. We are so committed to them that customer satisfaction and quality are used as benchmarks for every employee's performance.

People Make the Difference Our success relates directly to our employees. We seek the best people and provide them with the best environments in which to work, learn, and develop.

Competitive and Results-Oriented We achieve more than other companies because we identify stretch goals, mobilize quickly, act boldly, and reward results.

Fast-Moving and Adaptable We reinvent ourselves and change quickly, adapting with a sense of urgency to the changing needs of our customers.

Partner for Success We are excellent at partnering. We form relationships that build on the best skills and resources to benefit partners, Compaq, and most importantly, customers.

Everyone Contributes to the Team We achieve greater results faster through collaboration, reflecting our belief in diversity and our ability to work across the organization. Anyone, regardless of position or background, can make a difference.

Innovate Like an Enterpreneur We think innovatively and take risks to benefit our customers. We strive to create the most efficient and cost-effective processes, products, and solutions possible.

Communicate Openly We communicate directly and openly with one another and listen attentively.

Accountable for Performance Each of us takes ownership for quality performance and results. We solve problems rather than assign blame.

Demonstrate Integrity We act honestly and respectfully when dealing with each other, our community, and our environment, and we adhere to the highest ethical standards.

Enjoy Work We take work seriously, but enjoy what we do and value a sense of humor.

embrace such lofty aspirations. What role do you think shared values play in the membership and leadership of extremist groups such as the assorted "patriot" or militia movements in the United States? Of skinheads? Of religious terrorist groups? Of cults like Heaven's Gate, whose members committed mass suicide in 1996 in the belief they would be transported to an alien spacecraft? Of the Jonestown commune described in the preceding chapter?

Empirical Studies of the Ethical Dimension of Leadership.   Empirical studies of the ethical dimension of leadership have looked at factors affecting moral reasoning and ethical versus unethical behavior, the frequency or prevalence of unethical behaviors in the workplace, the relationship between values and leadership success, and tolerating unethical conduct in others.

Several researchers have reported that individuals with strong value systems tend to behave more ethically, which at first may seem like a classic case of discovering the obvious. However, certain kinds of situations increased the likelihood of unethical behavior from people regardless of their value systems. Such situations tended to be highly competitive and unsupervised. Unethical behavior also was more likely to occur when there was no formal ethics policy governing behavior, when there was no threat of punishment for unethical behavior, or when unethical behavior actually was rewarded (Hegarty & Sims, 1978, 1979; Malinkowski & Smith, 1985; Trevino & Youngblood, 1990).

Studies exploring opinions about unethical behaviors or practices in the workplace have yielded fairly disturbing results. For example, a 1988 Harris Poll reported that 89 percent of the 1,200 workers and managers surveyed believed it was important for leaders to be upright, honest, and ethical in their dealings. However, only 41 percent indicated their current supervisor had these characteristics. Another Harris Poll conducted in 1989 reported that many individuals believed businesses would purposely sell unsafe products, risk employee health and safety, and harm the environment (see Figure 6.3). In addition, Pitt (1985)

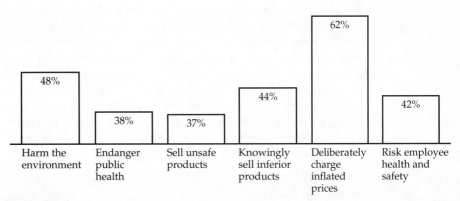

FIGURE 6.3

Perceptions of unethical business practices—Percent of people expressing belief business would. . .

Source: Harris Poll, reported in *Business Week*, May 29, 1989, p. 29.

> *Beware of the man who had no regard for his own reputation, since it is not likely he should have any for yours.*
>
> George Shelley

asked middle and senior managers in South Africa to rate the corruptness of various business practices and then indicate how frequently they believed colleagues and friends engaged in such acts. A representative finding was that although approximately 95 percent of the respondents said taking a large bribe was definitely wrong, they believed one-third of their friends and colleagues would do so. Furthermore, even in the case of such a clearly corrupt act as bribery, only one-third of the respondents said they believed legal action against the individual afterward would be appropriate. Among other things, data like these suggest that ethical practices do not receive a high enough priority in many organizations. On the contrary, there are numerous examples of organizations that have been financially rewarded for unethical behavior (e.g., bribes to secure lucrative contracts, defense industries' padding contracts with the government).

Other studies also have examined how leaders' values are related to leadership style or success. Some have shown that men and women differ in the values they emphasize in moral reasoning; men are more concerned about equity and justice, whereas women show more care for others and social responsibility in their moral reasoning (Brockner & Adsit, 1986; Gilligan, 1982; Powell, Posner, & Schmidt, 1984). In addition, Schmidt and Posner (1986) reported that both public and private administrators were relatively more concerned with their obligations to their organizations than with their obligations to society, and Weber (1989) reported that managers often used majority opinion rather than universal principles of justice when making decisions with ethical implications. Despite the cynicism that exists about the ethical practices of people in some leadership positions, managers with a strong sense of right and wrong do appear to be better leaders. Both Ghiselli (1968) and Gordon (1975) reported that leaders' personal values correlated positively with leadership effectiveness.

An important new line of research deals with efforts to develop a scale for assessing a leader's integrity. It has been well documented that a leader's success is powerfully affected by perceptions of his or her integrity. For example, one study found that honesty was the single attribute most diagnostic of the category "leader," as distinguished from "nonleader" (Lord, Foti, & DeVader, 1984). On the other hand, it is not well understood how impressions of a leader's integrity develop, how such perceptions change over time, nor what leader behaviors are most critical in impacting perceptions of their integrity. A key step in fostering such understanding would be the development of a measure of leader integrity in organizational settings. The Perceived Leader Integrity Scale (PLIS) represents a preliminary effort to do just that (Craig and Gustafson, 1998). It asks subordinates to rate the extent to which various statements accurately describe their supervisor. Here is a sampling of items from the scale:

Always gets even.

Would lie to me.

Would allow me to be blamed for his/her mistake.

Would deliberately distort what I say.

Would take credit for my ideas.

Lacks high morals.

Gives special favors to "pet" employees, but not to me.

Important as this preliminary work on the PLIS is, however, it does not represent the first attempt to develop a standardized scale of leader integrity. See Highlight 6.3 for an interesting reflection on the challenges of developing psychological scales.

A slightly different question than behaving unethically oneself is that of tolerating unethical behavior in others. It seems that reporting or confronting individuals whose behavior violated ethical or organizational norms depends on at least two situational variables: the seriousness of the infraction and the emotional relationship of the violator (Curphy, Gibson, Macomber, Calhoun, Wilbanks, &

The Average Self-Rating on "Ethical Behavior" Is Way above Average

Highlight 6.3

David Campbell, a senior fellow at the Center for Creative Leadership, is one of the most prolific reseachers in the world in the field of leadership. Among other things, he has authored numerous widely used surveys to assess various facets of leadership. The following story relates his efforts to develop an ethics scale for the Campbell Leadership Index (CLI).

In preliminary work on the CLI, it seemed obvious that "ethics" was central to the practice of good leadership and, therefore, should be one of the scales on the instrument (the CLI now includes 17 scales, including ambitious, enterprising, considerate, entertaining, organized, and productive). Consequently, in the early versions of the survey Campbell included adjectives such as *ethical, honest, trustworthy,* and *candid,* and negative adjectives such as *deceptive* and *scheming.* As with other CLI scales, this one was normed so that the average person would receive a score of 50 on the ethics scale; obviously some would get higher scores and some lower scores.

During the CLI testing period, however, a major problem emerged because almost no one wanted to believe that he or she was merely "average" in ethical behavior, let alone "below average." To soften the impact of such feedback, Campbell changed the name of the scale to "trustworthy" in the hope that this would retain the meaning but lessen the adverse reaction. But that change helped little. Eventually Campbell changed the name of the scale to "credible," which is more acceptable and also better captures the reasons why some executives may get low ratings on the scale despite self-perceptions of scrupulous honesty.

Burger, 1995). Individuals appear less likely to blow the whistle on another's ethical infraction if the violation did not seem serious and if the offender was a close friend of the potential whistleblower.

Group and Organizational Dimensions of Moral Reasoning and Ethical Conduct.   From a leadership perspective, we might well ask what happens when you combine individuals from different levels of development together into one group: What level does the group as a whole manifest? Researchers have found that group decisions about ethical dilemmas can be at lower levels of moral reasoning than the decisions made by individual members if the leader of the group is a less-principled moral reasoner (Dukerich, Nichols, Elm, & Vollrath, 1990). This finding has significant implications for what a group's collective morality may be when the leader is relatively unprincipled. What, for example, is likely to happen to a group's collective behavior if its leader is intelligent, quite domineering, and supremely unprincipled? Do you know of any leaders like that?

Even whole organizations may have characteristic levels of "moral sense" analogous to levels of personal moral development in individuals (Stevens, 1981; Petrick & Manning, 1990). Organizationally speaking, the preconventional level of moral development refers to organizations characterized by rampant fear and manipulation among organization members; life is a moral jungle where all that counts is surviving, even if through treachery, manipulation, or deceit. In organizations at the conventional level of moral development, good behavior is defined by satisfying others, complying with proper authority, and following the rules. The highest level of ethical climate in organizations (i.e., the postconventional level) is characterized by norms of principled and open decision making, including "respect for justice and the minority rights of productive and creative individuals: searching for consensus rather than relying on majority vote" (Petrick & Manning, 1990, p. 15). Bill O'Brien (1994), the former CEO of a major insurance company, likened an organization's poor ethical climate to a bad odor one gets used to:

> *Subordinates cannot be left to speculate as to the values of the organization. Top leadership must give forth clear and explicit signals, lest any confusion or uncertainty exist over what is and is not permissible conduct. To do otherwise allows informal and potentially subversive "codes of conduct" to be transmitted with a wink and a nod, and encourages an inferior ethical system based on "going along to get along" or the notion that "everybody's doing it.*
>
> Richard Thornburgh,
> Former U.S. attorney general

> Organizations oriented to power, I realized, also have strong smells, and even if people are too inured to notice, that smell has implications. It affects performance, productivity, and innovation. The worse aspect of this environment is that it stunts the growth of personality and character of everyone who works there. (p. 306)

And just as we asked what moves individuals from one level of moral reasoning to the next, we might also ask what moves *organizations* from one level to the next. One approach suggests five concerted steps. (1) Improve the quality of the leader-follower relationship so that genuine support for ethical conduct and initiative is provided. (2) Have explicit ethical guidelines and systems in place to deal quickly with unethical conduct. (3) Have an organizational ombudsman appointed to address ethical conflicts. (4) Have a formal ethics education program for all organizational members. (5) Most important, ensure that both formal and informal leaders model high standards of ethical conduct (Petrick & Manning, 1990). Recommendations like these reflect increasing recognition that ethical behavior is an organizational responsibility, not just an individual responsibility; and that standards of ethical conduct are not synonymous with standards of legal conduct—they are higher. Something can be unethical even though it is legal, so no leader should be content merely to ensure organizational members avoid breaking the law. Here are a few examples of the kinds of actions that may be legal yet are clearly unethical (Brumback, 1991):

- Scapegoating personal failures.
- Shirking unpleasant responsibilities.
- Knowingly making unreasonable demands of others.
- Breaking promises.
- Slacking off.
- Favoring friends for desirable assignments when others are more qualified.

Others, too, are calling attention to the organizational dimensions of ethical behavior. It seems clear that ethical behavior within an organization (or *by* it) is not simply the sum of the collective moralities of its members. Covey (1990), for example, has developed and popularized an approach called **principle-centered leadership.** This approach postulates a fundamental interdependence between the personal, the interpersonal, the managerial, and the organizational levels of leadership. The unique role of each level may be thought of like this:

> *It's important that people know what you stand for. It's equally important that they know what you won't stand for.*
>
> Mary Waldrop

Personal: The first imperative is to be a trustworthy person, and that depends on both one's character *and* competence. Only if one is trustworthy can one have trusting relationships with others.

Interpersonal: Relationships that lack trust are characterized by self-protective efforts to control and verify each other's behavior.

Managerial: Only in the context of trusting relationships will a manager risk empowering others to make full use of their talents and energies. But even with an empowering style, leading a high-performing group depends on skills such as team building, delegation, communication, negotiation, and self-management.

Organizational: An organization will be most creative and productive when its structure, systems (e.g., training, communication, reward), strategy, and vision are aligned and mutually supportive. Put differently, certain organizational alignments are more likely to nurture and reinforce ethical behavior among its members than others.

Much of the preceding discussion revolved around the issue of trust. Another perspective on a leader's trust in others is presented in Highlight 6.4.

When Good People Do Bad Things.   An important aspect of ethical conduct involves the mental gymnastics by which people can dissociate their moral thinking from their moral acting. One's ability to reason about hypothetical moral issues, after all, does not assure that one will *act* morally. Furthermore, one's moral actions may not always be consistent with one's espoused values. Bandura (1986, 1990), in particular, has pointed out several ways people with

---

Theory X and Theory Y: Two Views of Human Nature

Highlight 6.4

Several decades ago, Douglas McGregor (1966) explained different styles of managerial behavior on the basis of their implicit attitudes about human nature. His work remains influential today. McGregor identified two contrasting sets of assumptions people make about human nature, calling these **Theory X** and **Theory Y.**

In the simplest sense, Theory X reflects a more pessimistic view of others. Managers with this orientation rely heavily on coercive, external-control methods, such as pay, disciplinary techniques, punishments, and threats, to motivate workers. Such managers assume people are not naturally industrious or motivated to work. Hence, it is the manager's job to minimize the harmful effects of workers' natural laziness and irresponsibility by closely overseeing their work and creating external incentives to do well and disincentives to avoid slacking off.

Theory Y, on the other hand, reflects the view that most people are intrinsically motivated by their work. Rather than needing to be coaxed or coerced to work productively, such people value a sense of achievement, personal growth, pride in contributing to their organization, and respect for a job well done. Konosuke Matsushita's leadership was clearly consistent with the Theory Y view of human nature; he believed that human beings are by nature good and responsible.

But are there practical advantages to holding a Theory X or Theory Y view? Evidently there are. There is evidence that success comes more frequently to leaders who, like Matsushita, share a positive view of human nature. Hall and Donnell (1979) reported findings of five separate studies involving over 12,000 managers that explored the relationship between managerial achievement and attitudes toward subordinates. Overall, they found that managers who strongly subscribed to Theory X beliefs were far more likely to be in their lower-achieving group.

firm moral principles nonetheless may behave badly without feeling guilt or remorse over their behavior. We should look at each of these.

Moral justification involves reinterpreting otherwise immoral behavior in terms of a higher purpose. This is most dramatically revealed in the behavior of combatants in war.

> Moral reconstrual of killing is dramatically illustrated by the case of Sergeant York, one of the phenomenal fighters in the history of modern warfare. Because of his deep religious convictions, Sergeant York registered as a conscientious objector, but his numerous appeals were denied. At camp, his battalion commander quoted chapter and verse from the Bible to persuade him that under appropriate conditions it was Christian to fight and kill. A marathon mountainside prayer finally convinced him that he could serve both God and country by becoming a dedicated fighter. (Bandura, 1990, p. 164)

Another way to dissociate behavior from one's espoused moral principles is through **euphemistic labeling.** This involves using "cosmetic" words to defuse or disguise the offensiveness of otherwise morally repugnant or distasteful behavior. Terrorists, for example, may call themselves "freedom fighters," and firing someone may be referred to as "letting him go." **Advantageous comparison** lets one avoid self-contempt for one's behavior by comparing it to even more heinous behavior by others ("If you think *we're* insensitive to subordinates' needs, you should see what it's like working for *Acme*"). Through **displacement of responsibility** people may violate personal moral standards by attributing responsibility to others. Nazi concentration camp guards, for example, attempted to avoid moral responsibility for their behavior by claiming they were merely "carrying out orders."

A related mechanism is **diffusion of responsibility,** whereby reprehensible behavior becomes easier to engage in and live with if others are behaving the same way. When everyone is responsible, it seems, no one is responsible. This way of minimizing individual moral responsibility for collective action can be one negative effect of group decision making. Through **disregard or distortion of consequences,** people minimize the harm caused by their behavior. This can be a problem in bureaucracies when decision-makers are relatively insulated by their position from directly observing the consequences of their decisions. **Dehumanization** is still another way of avoiding the moral consequences of one's behavior. It is easier to treat others badly when they are dehumanized, as evidenced in epithets like "gooks" or "satan-worshippers." Finally, people sometimes try to justify immoral behavior by claiming it was caused by someone else's actions. This is known as **attribution of blame.**

How widespread are such methods of minimizing personal moral responsibility? When people behave badly, Bandura (1977) said, it is *not* typically because of a basic character flaw; rather, it is because they use methods like these to construe their behavior in a self-protective way.

Darley (1994) suggested still another way people justify seemingly unethical conduct, and his observations illuminate certain common leadership practices. Darley said *ethical problems are almost inherent in systems designed to measure performance.*

The more any quantitative performance measure is used to determine a group's or an individual's rewards and punishments, the more subject it will be to corruption pressures and the more apt it will be to distort and corrupt the action patterns and thoughts of the group or individual it is intended to monitor. . . The criterial control system unleashes enormous human ingenuity. People will maximize the criteria set. However, they may do so in ways that are not anticipated by the criterion setters, in ways that destroy the validity of the criteria. The people "make their numbers" but the numbers no longer mean what you thought they did. (Darley, 1994)

> *Only mediocrities rise to the top in a system that won't tolerate wave making.*
>
> Lawrence J. Peter,
> Author of *The Peter Principle*

This has been called **Darley's law,** and it is exemplified in a story from Joseph Heller's novel *Catch-22.* You can read about it in Highlight 6.5, though Darley's law is not limited to fiction. Halberstam (1986) described another organization in which the "numbers game" had a corrupting effect. In this case, it was in the Ford Motor Company. In the eyes of those who worked in Ford plants around the country in the 1950s, Detroit "number crunchers" like Robert McNamara (later a secretary of defense during the Vietnam War) did not want to know the truth. McNamara and his people in Detroit were the ones who kept making liberal agreements with the unions and at the same time setting higher and higher levels of production while always demanding increased quality. They talked about quality, but they did not give the plant managers the means for quality; what they really wanted was production. So the plant managers were giving them what they wanted, numbers, while playing lip service to quality. Years later in Vietnam, some American officers, knowing McNamara's love of numbers, cleverly juggled the numbers and played games with body counts in order to make a stalemated war look more successful than it was. They did this not because they were dishonest, but because they thought if Washington really wanted the truth it would have sought the truth in an honest way. In doing so they were the spiritual descendants of the Ford factory managers of the 1950s (p. 220).

Darley described three general problems that can arise when performance measurement systems are put in place. A person might cheat on the measurement system by exploiting its weaknesses either in hopes of advancement or through fear of falling behind. Or, even with the best will in the world, a person might act in a way that optimizes his or her performance measurements without realizing that this outcome was not what the system really intended. Finally, a person may even have the best interests of the system in mind and yet manipulate the performance measurement system to allow continuation of the actions that best fulfill his or her reading of the system goals. One major disadvantage of this particular approach is that it "takes underground" constructive dialogue about system goals or modifications in system measurements.

What, ethically, should one do when one is part of a performance measurement system? Darley suggested "that the time for the individual to raise the moral issue is when he or she feels the pressure to substitute accountability for morality, to act wrongly, because that is what the system requires. And that intervention might then be directed at the system, by honorably protesting its design." For those who are governed by a performance measurement system, a constant moral vigilance is necessary—it is needed most of all by those in leadership positions.

Catch-22

Highlight 6.5

This story is about Yossarian, the central character of Joseph Heller's novel *Catch 22*. It demonstrates how a performance measurement system can create forces that morally corrupt the individuals functioning within that system.

During World War II, the allied high command needed some measure of when each bomber crew flying over Germany had "done enough." The answer they came up with was simply to count the number of bombing missions each crew had flown. It seemed to demand a commensurate risk among all concerned, and also seemed correlated with other primary objectives like the number of enemy factories destroyed. After flying a certain number of missions, crews expected to be rotated back to the states.

What was Yossarian's story? Terrified of flying the dangerous combat missions assigned to him, he flew his B-29 on different and infinitely safer routes over the open ocean. He simply dropped the plane's entire payload of bombs there over water. *From the point of view of the military indicator of missions flown, these were successful missions* which even earned Yossarian points toward a safe follow-on assignment. Driven by fear, Yossarian had corrupted the indicator from one that was correlated with organizational success to one that was arguably negatively correlated with organizational success.

You might wonder whether this proves the indicator was inherently flawed. Wasn't the bomber command justified in designing the measurement system without consideration of this particular possibility? Was it not entitled to assume American soldiers would not commit acts of treasonous cowardice? The intriguing point of Heller's novel is that *Yossarian's act was a perfectly normal response to the particular dynamics in which it arose.* In Heller's novel, *Yossarian's commanders were cheating on the system themselves*! Some, for example, were trying to gain promotion by raising the number of missions required to go home while not flying any missions themselves. Other commanders let friends and favorites accumulate missions by flying "milk runs" in which little enemy opposition was experienced. Still other leaders tried to get credit for bombing missions even though, in fact, they had not flown any. The leadership itself, in other words, destroyed any possibility that pilots like Yossarian would see any moral barriers to cheating. *Corruption is contagious*, and Darley suggests that performance measurement systems inherently invite widespread corruption.

Souce: Adapted from Darley (1994).

The Impact of Sex Role Stereotypes on Leadership

Leadership Emergence among Women and Men

Gaining entry to and investing in a career are the first steps in the leadership development process. The most typical route to occupational leadership for women and men involves starting at an entry level in a formal organization (often in a technical or specialized function), then moving up to manage others in the function, then managing managers of the function, and finally becoming a general manager of the groups of functions that form the business. It does appear that women are increasingly in the "pipeline" for becoming leaders in the world of work. In 1992, for example, it was estimated that 40 percent of midlevel managers and 2.9 percent of senior-level managers in Fortune 1,000 companies were women. In many countries there are also significant numbers of women in government roles (see Figure 6.4). Nonetheless, there still are obstacles ahead for women moving into leadership roles even as

> *Children are likely to live up to what you believe of them.*
>
> Lady Bird Johnson

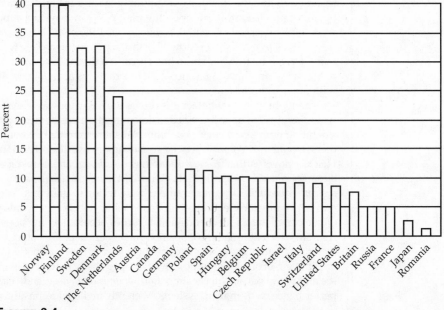

FIGURE 6.4

Women's membership in parliaments

In 1994, women occupied only 10 percent of the parliamentary seats around the world. In Denmark, Sweden, Finland, and Norway, however, they occupied more than one-third of the seats. What is different about these countries? It's not just their views toward women; they all have proportional representation, a rule that provides party representation in parliamentary bodies based on the proportion of total votes the party receives (different, for example, from the "winner take all" rule practiced in U.S. congressional elections). Women have done much more poorly in countries without proportional representation, including Japan, Britain, and the United States.

Source: *The Economist,* November 19, 1994.

we see women entering law, medicine, sciences, the arts, and commerce in numbers equal to, if not greater than, white males (also see Highlight 6.6). What problems still exist?

In a classic study of sex roles, Schein (1973, 1975) demonstrated how bias in sex role stereotypes created problems for women moving up through these managerial roles. Schein asked male ($n = 300$) and female ($n = 167$) middle managers to complete a survey on which they rated various items on a five-point scale in terms of how characteristic they were of (*a*) men in general, (*b*) women in general, or (*c*) successful managers. Schein found a high correlation between the ways both male and female respondents perceived "males" and "managers," but no correlation between the ways the respondents perceived "females" and "managers." It was as though being a manager was defined by attributes thought of as masculine. Furthermore, it does not appear that the situation has changed much over the past two decades. In 1990, management students in the United States, Germany and

Female Executives on the Fast Track: You Can Take This Job and Shove It . . .

Highlight 6.6

Although a higher percentage of females are filling positions in the executive suite, many of the best and brightest female managers are choosing to leave their parent organizations. Many are doing so because they have seen less-qualified males get promoted ahead of them, were frustrated with the slow pace of advancement, or had finally moved to a position where they could observe the top level of management and did not like what they saw. Few left their organizations for monetary reasons (many were making well over $150,000 per year) but instead left the comfort and security of their parent organizations in order to form their own small businesses. These females had all the requisite skills needed to be successful in the corporate world, but many of these skills were also precisely those needed to start up and maintain a small business. Many of these businesses have been phenomenal success stories, not only in terms of the bottom-line results but also as places where people prefer to work. These companies were often modeled after the values of their leaders—competitive and ambitious but also collaborative, affiliative, and supportive. Although these women are playing a key role in the American economy (over 70 percent of all workers are employed in companies with less than 50 people), one wonders how much more successful large organizations would be if they could stem the hemorrhaging of this talent. Moreover, because there is a real shortage of good leaders in our companies and institutions, organizations can ill afford to lose this talent.

Source: L. Baum, "Corporate Women: What It Takes to Get to the Top," *Business Week,* June 22, 1987, pp. 72–78.

Great Britain, for example, still perceived successful middle managers in terms of characteristics more commonly ascribed to men than to women (Schein & Mueller, 1990). One area where views *do* seem to have changed over time involves women's perceptions of their own roles. In contrast to the earlier studies, women today see as much similarity between "female" and "manager" as between "male" and "manager" (Brenner, Tomkiewicz, & Schein, 1989). To women, at least, being a woman and being a manager are not a contradiction in terms.

There also have been many other studies of the role of women in management. In one of these, *Breaking the Glass Ceiling* (Morrison, White, & Van Velsor, 1987), researchers documented the lives and careers of 78 of the highest-level women in corporate America. A few years later the researchers followed up with a small sample of those women to discuss any changes that had taken place in their leadership paths. The researchers were struck by the fact that the women were much like the senior men they had worked with in other studies. Qualitatively, they had the same fears: They wanted the best for themselves and for their families. They wanted their company to succeed. And, not surprisingly, they still had a drive to succeed. In some cases (also true for the men) they were beginning to ask questions about life balance—was all the sacrifice and hard work worth it? Were 60-hour workweeks worth the cost to family and self?

Looking more quantitatively, however, the researchers expected to find significant differences between the women who had broken the glass ceiling and the men who were already there. After all, the popular literature and some social scientific literature had conditioned them to expect that there is a feminine versus a masculine style of leadership, the feminine style being an outgrowth of a consensus/team-oriented leadership approach. Women, in this view, are depicted as leaders who, when compared to men, are better listeners, more empathic, less analytical, more people oriented, and less aggressive in pursuit of goals.

In examining women in leadership positions, the researchers collected behavioral data, including ratings by both self and others, assessment center data (gathered from leadership development programs at the Center for Creative Leadership), and their scores on the California Psychological Inventory. Contrary to the stereotypes and popular views, however, there were no statistically significant differences between men's and women's leadership styles. Women and men were equally analytical, people oriented, forceful, goal oriented, empathic, and skilled at listening. There were other differences between the men and women, however, beyond the question of leadership styles. The researchers did find (and these results must be interpreted cautiously because of the relatively small numbers involved) that women had significantly lower well-being scores, their commitment to the organizations they worked for was more guarded than that of their male counterparts, and the women were much more likely to be willing to take career risks associated with going to new or unfamiliar areas of the company where women had not been before.

Continued work with women in corporate leadership positions has both reinforced and somewhat clarified these findings. For example, the lower scores for women with regard to their ratings of general well-being may reflect the inadequacy of their support system for dealing with day-to-day issues of living.

This is tied to the reality for many women that in addition to having roles in their companies they remain chief caretakers for their families. Further, there may be additional pressures of being visibly identified as proof that the organization has women at the top.

Other types of differences—particularly those around "people issues"—are still not evident. In fact, the hypothesis is that such supposed differences may hinder the opportunities for leadership development of women in the future. For example, turning around a business that is in trouble or starting a new business are two of the most exciting opportunities a developing leader has to test her leadership abilities. If we apply the "women are different" hypothesis, then the type of leadership skills needed for successful completion of either of these assignments may well leave women off the list of candidates. However, if we accept the hypothesis that women and men are more alike as leaders than they are different, then women will be found in equal numbers on the candidate list.

The Narrow Band of Acceptable Behavior

One of the most important factors which seems to impede the advance of women and other minorities into leadership roles is bias, a bias that might be labeled the **narrow band of acceptable behavior** (Morrison, White, & Van Velsor, 1987a &1987b). The narrow band of acceptable behavior is depicted in Figure 6.5. The

FIGURE 6.5

The narrow band of acceptable behavior

Source: Adapted from A. M. Morrison, R. P. White, and E. Van Velsor, *Breaking the Glass Ceiling* (Reading, MA: Addison-Wesley, 1987).

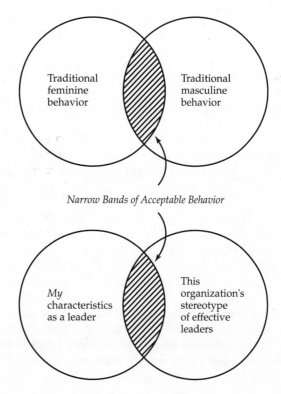

characteristics and behaviors in the right-hand circle are those associated with traditional masculine behavior, and the characteristics and behaviors in the left-hand circle are those associated with traditional feminine behavior. The narrow band of overlap between the two circles can be thought of as a "hoop" women executives needed to pass through. Women executives in the *Glass Ceiling* project

> had to show their toughness and independence and at the same time count on others. It was essential that they contradict the stereotypes that their male executives and coworkers had about women—they had to be seen as different, "better than women" as a group. But they couldn't go too far, to forfeit all traces of femininity, because that would make them too alien to their superiors and colleagues. In essence, their mission was to do what *wasn't* expected of them as women to gain acceptance. The capacity to combine the two consistently, to stay within a narrow band of acceptable behavior, is the real key to success.

The concept of a narrow band of acceptable behavior is not limited to women. It may be applied to any individual's deviation from organizationally defined standards. The more a person looks like, acts like, dresses like, and talks like other leaders in the organization, the wider the band of acceptable behavior (the greater the overlap of the two circles). The less one looks like, acts like, dresses like, and talks like others—some of which, like gender, race, or nationality, are beyond a person's control—the narrower the band of acceptable behavior. One implication of this view is that an individual who differs in obvious ways from the prototypical image of leader (as with gender) has less "wiggle room" available; it's as though there are already one or two strikes against that person. To put it differently, a narrower band of acceptable behavior is like walking a tightrope. The tightrope for the women executives in the *Glass Ceiling* study, for example, involved balancing the following inherently contradictory sets of expectations:

> *Neither shall you allege the example of the many as an excuse for doing wrong.*
>
> Exodus 23:2

- Taking risks, but being consistently outstanding.
- Being tough but not macho.
- Being ambitious, but knowing you will not receive equal treatment.
- Taking responsibility, but following others' advice.

Even today, this active bias—some would call it a comfort factor of having leaders in the organization sharing common modes of behavior, values, looks, and attitudes—is still the basis for excluding women and other minorities from leadership ranks and from development opportunities. But is such bias inevitable? Must all women leaders pass the narrow band of acceptable behavior? Maybe not.

Research on second-generation managerial women suggest many of them appear to be succeeding *because of* characteristics heretofore considered too feminine for effective leadership (Rosener, 1990). Rosener's survey research identified several differences in how men and women described their leadership experi-

"That's what they all say, honey."

ences. Men tended to describe themselves in somewhat transactional terms, viewing leadership as an exchange with subordinates for services rendered. They influenced others primarily through their organizational position and authority. The women, on the other hand, tended to describe themselves in transformational terms. They helped subordinates develop commitment for broader goals than their own self-interest, and described their influence more in terms of personal characteristics like charisma and interpersonal skill than mere organizational position.

According to Rosener such women leaders encouraged participation and shared power and information, but went far beyond what is commonly thought of as participative management. She called it **interactive leadership.** Their leadership self-descriptions reflected an approach based on enhancing others' self-worth and believing that the best performance results when people are excited about their work and feel good about themselves.

How did this interactive leadership style develop? Rosener concluded it was due to these women's socialization experiences and career paths. As we indicated above, the social role expected of women has emphasized they be cooperative, supportive, understanding, gentle, and service-oriented. As they entered the business world, they still found themselves in roles emphasizing these same behaviors. They found themselves in staff, rather than line, positions, and in roles lacking formal authority over others such that they had to accomplish their work without reliance on formal power. What they had to do, in other words, was employ their socially acceptable behavioral repertoire in order to survive organizationally.

What came easily to women turned out to be a survival tactic. Although leaders often begin their careers doing what comes naturally and what fits within the constraints of the job, they also develop their skills and styles over time. The women's use of interactive leadership has its roots in socialization, and the women interviewees firmly believe that it benefits their organizations. Through the course of their careers, they have gained conviction that their style is effective. In fact, for some it was their own success that caused them to formulate their philosophies about what motivates people, how to make good decisions, and what it takes to maximize business performance. (p. 124)

Such women's success, however, does not mean the narrow band of acceptable behavior has disappeared. The women in the survey were for the most part *not* from large, traditional companies, like those in the *Glass Ceiling* project. Rosener called for organizations to expand their definitions of effective leadership—to create a *wider* band of acceptable behavior so that both men and women will be freer to lead in ways which take advantage of their true talents (see Highlight 6.6). The extent of the problem is suggested by data from a recent study looking at how CEOs, almost all male, and senior female executives explained the paucity of women in corporate leadership roles. Figure 6.6 com-

FIGURE 6.6

What prevents women from advancing to corporate leadership?

pares the percentages of CEOs versus female executives who endorsed various possible explanations of the situation. It is clear that the CEOs attributed it primarily to inadequacies in the quantity and quality of experience of potential women candidates for the top spots, while the females themselves attributed it to various forms of stereotyping and bias.

Leading across Cultures

A rather common problem for office managers in the United States is controlling the use of the office copier. Frequently, office managers publish policies and procedures to govern use of the machines, and hence control administrative costs. When a U.S. manager of a water resources project in Indonesia did the same thing, however, an action he considered routine, he was accused of insensitivity to Indonesian ways—in fact, accused not just of unfriendliness but of unethical behavior. After a series of similar incidents, he lost his job. Leading across cultures requires an appreciation of the sometimes profound differences in the value systems of other cultures.

What Is Culture?

A good starting place for understanding differences in cultural value systems is with the concept of culture itself. **Culture** refers to those learned behaviors characterizing the total way of life of members within any given society. Cultures differ from one another just as individuals differ from one another. To outsiders, the most salient aspect of any culture typically involves behavior—the distinctive actions, mannerisms, and gestures characteristic of that culture. Americans visiting Thailand, for example, may find it curious and even bothersome to see male Thais hold hands with each other in public. They may react negatively to such behavior since it is untypical to *them*, and laden with *North American* meaning (e.g., "It's okay for women to hold hands in public, but men just shouldn't do that!"). Salient as such behaviors are, however, they are also just the tip of the iceberg. The "mass" of culture is *not* so readily visible, just as most of an iceberg lies beneath the water. Hidden from view are the beliefs, values, and myths that provide context to manifest behaviors (Kohls, 1984). A clear implication for business leaders in the global context, therefore, is the need to become aware and respectful of cultural differences and cultural perspectives. Barnum (1992) pointed out the importance of being able to look at one's own culture through the eyes of another:

> Consciously or unconsciously they will be using their own beliefs as the yardsticks for judging you, so know how to compare those yardsticks by ferreting out their values and noting where they differ the least and most from yours. For example, if their belief in fatalism outweighs your belief in accountability, there will be conflicts down the road. This is a severe problem in the Middle East, for instance, and affects management styles in companies and even the ability to market life insurance, which is frowned upon in communities where Muslim observances are strong. (p. 153)

A Framework for Understanding Cultural Differences

Thus, it can be helpful to see one's own culture through the eyes of another; just as it also can be helpful to see other cultures through eyes unbiased (or at least less biased) by one's own filters. Hofstede (1980) described four dimensions of cultural values and beliefs: individualism versus collectivism, masculinity versus femininity, tolerance versus intolerance of uncertainty, and power distance versus power equalization. More recently, researchers at the Center for Creative Leadership have developed a conceptual framework for analyzing cultural differences based on seven fundamental dilemmas that people of all cultures face (Wilson, Hoppe, & Sayles, 1996). Let us look at each of these seven dilemmas in greater detail.

Source of Identity: Individual–Collective. This deals with the degree to which individuals should pursue their own interests and goals or contribute to a larger group, whether extended family, ethnic group, or company.

Goals and Means of Achievement: Tough–Tender. This deals with how success is defined in a culture. Is it defined by tangible rewards like financial success and material well-being or by intangible rewards such as good relationships with others or spiritual satisfaction?

Orientation to Authority: Equal–Unequal. How should people of different status, authority, or power behave toward each other—as equals or unequals?

Response to Ambiguity: Dynamic–Stable. To what extent is uncertainty accepted or tolerated? In running an organization, are tight controls and structure imposed to ensure certainty, or is greater tolerance for ambiguity and uncertainty evident via loose or nonexistent control systems?

Means of Knowledge Acquisition: Active–Reflective. Is action or reflection more valued as a means of acquiring information and knowledge?

Perspective on Time: Scarce–Plentiful. Is the sense or experience of time urgent or relaxed?

Outlook on Life: Doing–Being. Which is preferred—mastery over nature or living in harmony with nature? Is the outcome of life more dependent upon human effort or on the expression of divine will?

You probably can see how misunderstandings and slights can occur when people from different cultures are working together, but let us look at two specific applications of this scheme. First, consider the historic U.S. emphasis on individualism (e.g., the focus on *self*-confidence, *self*-control, *self*-concept, *self*-expression, or the way rugged individualists are heroically portrayed in film, television, and literature) and how it might impact work. Given an individualist perspective, certain management practices and expectations seem self-evident, such as the idea of individual accountability for work. When individual accountability is valued, for example, decision-making authority tends to be delegated to individual managers. What's more, those same managers may be inclined to take personal credit when the job is well done. A different norm, however, applies in industrialized Japan. Decision making is often very time-consuming, to assure that everyone who will be impacted by a decision has input on it beforehand. Konosuke Matsushita's leadership epitomized this aspect of Japanese culture. For example, he constantly stressed "collective wisdom." He believed decisions should be based on input from many employees, and implemented only after everyone had a say. Another "self-evident" principle to the U.S. mind is that individual career progress is desirable and "good." In some other cultures, however, managers resist competing with peers for rewards or promotions so as not to disturb the harmony of the group or appear self-interested.

Another example of potential conflict or misunderstanding can be seen in the case of orientation to authority, how people should handle power and authority relationships with others. The United States is a relatively young and mobile country, populated mostly by immigrants. Relative to other countries, there is little concern with family origin or class background. There is a belief that success should come through an individual's hard work and talent, not by birthright or class standing. This all leads to a relative informality at work, even among individuals of strikingly different position within a company. Subordinates expect their bosses to be accessible, even responsive in some ways to their subordinates. In some other cultures, however, higher status in a company confers nearly unchallengeable authority, and an expectation as well that most decisions will be referred *up* to them (as distinguished from delegated down to others). You can see even from these two examples that the seven dimensions of cultural values create quite an array of possible tensions between people from different cultures working together.

The Universality of Leadership Attributes

It is an interesting question whether the attributes of effective leaders are shared universally around the world, or whether different attributes of leadership are valued more in some cultures than in others. A very ambitious project known as the GLOBE research program is addressing that question. Its goal is to develop an empirically based theory of leadership to help predict the effectiveness of leader and organizational practices in different countries. The GLOBE program has been going on since 1993, collecting data from over 17,00 middle managers from 92 different countries. So far, the project has identified 21 specific attributes and behaviors that are viewed universally across cultures as contributing to leadership effectiveness (House et al., 1999). They are listed in Table 6–3. In addition, the project has identified eight characteristics that were universally viewed as impediments to leader effectiveness (see Table 6–4). And GLOBE has identified 35 leader characteristics that are viewed as positive in some cultures but negative in others (see Table 6–5).

TABLE 6–3   Leader Attributes and Behaviors Universally Viewed as Positive

Trustworthy	Positive	Intelligent
Just	Dynamic	Decisive
Honest	Motive arouser	Effective bargainer
Foresighted	Confidence builder	Win-win problem solver
Plans ahead	Motivational	Administratively skilled
Encouraging	Dependable	Communicative
Informed	Coordinator	Team builder
Excellence oriented		

Adapted from House et al., 1999, *Cultural Influences on Leadership and Organizations: Project Globe. Advances in Global Leadership*, Vol. 1, pp. 171–233. JAI Press Inc.

TABLE 6–4   Leader Attributes and Behaviors Universally Viewed as Negative

Loner	Nonexplicit
Asocial	Egocentric
Noncooperative	Ruthless
Irritable	Dictatorial

Adapted from House et al., 1999, *Cultural Influences on Leadership and Organizations: Project Globe. Advances in Global Leadership*, Vol. 1, pp. 171–233. JAI Press Inc.

TABLE 6–5   Examples of Leader Behaviors and Attributes That Are Culturally Contingent

Ambitious	Logical
Cautious	Orderly
Compassionate	Sincere
Domineering	Worldly
Independent	Formal
Individualistic	Sensitive

Adapted from House et al., 1999, *Cultural Influences on Leadership and Organizations: Project Globe. Advances in Global Leadership*, Vol. 1, pp. 171–233. JAI Press Inc.

Implications for Leadership Practitioners

The perspectives and findings presented in this chapter have significant implications for leadership practitioners. Perhaps most important, leadership practitioners should *expect* to face a variety of challenges to their own system of ethics, values, or attitudes during their careers. Additionally, values often are a source of interpersonal conflict. Although we sometimes say two people don't get along because of a personality conflict, often these conflicts are due to differences in value systems, not personality traits. Often, people on either side of an issue see *only* themselves and their own side as morally justifiable. Nonetheless, people holding seemingly antithetical values may still need to work together, and dealing with diverse and divergent values will be an increasingly common challenge for leaders. As noted earlier, interacting with individuals and groups holding divergent and conflicting values will be an inevitable fact of life for future leaders (see Highlight 6.7). This does not mean, however, that increased levels of interpersonal conflict are inevitable. Both leaders and followers might be well advised to minimize the conflict and tension often associated with value differences. Leaders in particular have a responsibility not to let their own personal values interfere with professional leader–subordinate relationships unless the conflicts pertain to issues clearly relevant to the work and the organization. (See Highlight 6.8 for a perspective on how subordinates' values may or may not affect the evaluation of a leader.)

Louis Farrakhan and the Million Man March

Highlight 6.7

Louis Farrakhan, leader of the Nation of Islam, assembled the largest black audience ever in America for his Million Man March in 1995. Farrakhan is a highly visible yet unsettling figure in contemporary America. After all, what should people make of a religious leader who calls those of other faiths "bloodsuckers," and is implicated by rumor in the assassination of Malcolm X, his predecessor? Without question, Farrakhan evokes strikingly different reactions in others.

To some extent, perceptions of Louis Farrakhan are skewed by race, much as perceptions of O. J. Simpson's guilt or innocence are skewed by race. In a *Time* magazine poll, for example, 48 percent of whites (compared to 36 percent of blacks) believed the phrase "a bigot and racist" accurately applied to Farrakhan. Forty-eight percent of blacks said the phrase did not apply at all to Farrakhan, whereas only 12 percent of whites said it did not apply. Even within the black community, however, there are widely divergent views of Farrakhan. Eldridge Cleaver, for

(continued)

example, a black leader who gained notoriety as a radical in the 1960s, said that after Malcolm X's murder, "Farrakhan gravitated to the top of the heap as the slime-ball, scheming, renegade bandwagoner that he is."

Sometimes Farrakhan seems paranoid as well as racist. For example, he believes that Jewish financiers manipulate world events. And he was infuriated by television reports that claimed the actual attendance at his Million Man March fell far short of the number he claimed were there. Such deceitful media reports, he said, were a racist plot. Despite such wild claims, however, Farrakhan did make the Million Man March a reality. Although he has been criticized by other black leaders for his failure to use the march as a stimulus for corrective political action, perhaps no other contemporary black leader could have orchestrated the march at all, Jesse Jackson and Colin Powell included.

The comparison between Farrakhan and Powell is an interesting one. There are several parallels between them. Both were born in New York in the 1930s to West Indian immigrants. Both were raised in the Episcopal church. Both are extremely intelligent, articulate, and recognizable. But they followed different paths to prominence: Powell sought success in white society via the integrated U.S. Army, Farrakhan among the troops of racial separatism.

It remains to be seen which of them will have the greater long-term impact on the country.

Sources: H. L. Gates, Jr., "The Charmer," *The New Yorker,* April 29, 1996, pp. 116–31; H. Fineman and V. E. Smith, "An Angry Charmer," *Newsweek,* October 30, 1995, pp. 32–37; S. Monroe, "The Mirage of Farrakhan," *Time,* October 30, 1995, p. 52.

Does Character Count?

Highlight 6.8

Does one's character make a difference in the kind of leader she or he will be? Decades ago, Richard Nixon's critics frequently asked, "Would you buy a used car from this man?" The obvious implication was whether a person who seemed "shifty" was suited for high political office.

More recently, the United States painfully confronted the relationship between private and public character, and even after several years of public angst the answers are anything but clear. Despite being embroiled in one of the most notorious scandals in recent American political history, President Clinton's approval ratings remained high. For example, a Time/CNN survey in March 1998 indicated an approval rating of 67 percent, just a point below his own all-time high, even while a majority (52 percent) also expressed belief he had engaged in a pattern of sexual misconduct while president. On the surface, it would seem that "mere" sexual misconduct is not enough to tarnish a president's job performance. On a more fundamental level, however, do these results really imply that people do not care whether their leaders demonstrate integrity and trustworthiness?

We gain some insight into this issue by examining the polling data in further detail. The 67 percent who approved of Clinton's job performance despite accusations of his sexual misconduct explained their rationale in the following ways (percentages represent those who said reasons were "extremely" or "very" important factors in their judgment):

- A president is a human being, with all the temptations the rest of us have. (68 percent)
- A president's private life has no bearing on his suitability for the job. (57 percent)
- Clinton's performance in running the country is so good that I'm willing to put up with his failings. (52 percent)
- While lying is seldom acceptable, lying about sex is something that most of us do. (40 percent)

In reviewing public sentiment on this issue, we might appear to have drastically lowered our expectations that leaders should exemplify outstanding character. Others, though, might counter that we are finally becoming realistic in our expectations of leaders. Another reason might be a distinction some make between public and private morality. Such factors might partially explain why the impeachment of President Clinton by the House of Representatives itself met with a fairly high level of public disapproval.

And the issue was not settled by President Clinton's departure from office. Indeed, his final-hour pardoning of financier Mark Rich produced a firestorm of protest, even from former Clinton supporters. Was this the case of an act that differed in moral gravity from the previous incidents? Was it a final confirmation that the deficiencies in character alleged by many finally became clear to all? Or was it simply a lapse in judgment on Clinton's part during the final hours of his presidency?

What do *you* think about whether character counts? Rather than focusing on the fairly distant world of presidential politics, however, answer the following questions with reference to *your own boss (or professor!):*

- If you found this person lied to you about something in his or her personal life, would it have any impact whatsoever in your estimation of the individual as a leader?
- If that person had a pattern of sexual misconduct with very junior members of the staff or students, would that seem "harmless" to you, and irrelevant to the person's leadership effectiveness?

Source: Time/CNN polling data, *Time*, March 30, 1998, pp. 21–25.

Summary

This chapter reviews evidence regarding the relationships between values and leadership. Values are constructs that represent general sets of behaviors or states of affairs that individuals consider to be important, and they are a central part of a leader's psychological makeup. Values are an important component of the moral reasoning process, which is the process people use to resolve moral or ethical dilemmas. This is important since leaders undoubtedly will face a variety of ethical dilemmas during their careers. Values also impact leadership through a cultural context within which various attributes and behaviors are regarded differentially—positively or negatively. Finally, despite the significant progress women have made in moving into managerial and leadership ranks in their organizations, sex role stereotypes still adversely impact the opportunity of women—and other minority groups too—to exercise the full range of their talents and behavioral repertoire and be rewarded for it.

Key Terms

ethics   133
values   133
value programming   134
moral reasoning   136
preconventional level   138
conventional level   138
postconventional level   138
principle-centered leadership   145
Theory X   146
Theory Y   146
moral justification   147

euphemistic labeling   147
advantageous comparison   147
displacement of responsibility   147
diffusion of responsibility   147
distortion of consequences   147
dehumanization   147
attribution of blame   147
Darley's law   148
narrow band of acceptable behavior   153
interactive leadership   155
culture   157

Questions

1. Do you think it always must be "lonely at the top" (or that if it is not, you are doing something wrong)?
2. How do you believe one's basic philosophy of human nature affects one's approach to leadership?
3. Identify several values you think might be the basis of conflict or misunderstanding between leaders and followers.
4. Can a leader's public and private morality be distinguished? Should they be?
5. Can a bad person be a good leader?
6. Are there any leadership roles men and women should not have equal opportunity to compete for?

Skills

Leadership skills relevant to this chapter include:
- Communication
- Listening

- Managing conflict
- Credibility

Activity

1. Each person should select his or her own 10 most important values from the following list, and then rank-order those 10 from most important (1) to least important (10). Then have an open discussion about how a person's approach to leadership might be influenced by having different "highest priority" values. The values are: Achievement, Activity (keeping busy), Advancement, Adventure, Aesthetics (appreciation of beauty), Affiliation, Affluence, Authority, Autonomy, Balance, Challenge, Change/Variety, Collaboration, Community, Competence, Competition, Courage, Creativity, Economic Security, Enjoyment, Fame, Family, Friendship, Happiness, Helping Others, Humor, Influence, Integrity, Justice, Knowledge, Location, Love, Loyalty, Order, Personal Development, Physical Fitness, Recognition, Reflection, Responsibility, Self-Respect, Spirituality, Status, Wisdom.

2. Explore how the experiences of different generations might have influenced the development of their values. Divide into several groups and assign each group the task of selecting representative popular music from a specific era. One group, for example, might have the 1950s, another the Vietnam War era, and another the 1990s. Using representative music from that era, highlight what seem to be dominant concerns, values, or views of life during that period.

7 LEADERSHIP TRAITS

Introduction

P owell's Rules for Picking People: Look for intelligence and judgment and, most
critically, a capacity to anticipate, to see around corners. Also look for loyalty,
integrity, a high energy drive, a balanced ego, and the drive to get things done.
Colin Powell

In Chapter 1 leadership was defined as "the process of influencing an organized
group toward accomplishing its goals." Given this definition, one question that
leadership researchers have tried to answer over the past 100 years is whether
certain personal attributes or characteristics help or hinder the leadership
process. In other words, does athletic ability, height, personality, intelligence, or
creativity help a leader to influence a group? Put in the context of our three leaders, are Colin Powell, Madeleine Albright, or Konosuke Matsushita smarter,
more creative, more ambitious, or more outgoing than their less successful
counterparts? Do these three leaders act in fundamentally different ways than
their followers, and are these differences in behavior due to differences in their
innate intelligence, certain personality traits, or creative ability? If so, then could
these same characteristics also be used to differentiate successful from unsuccessful leaders, executives from first-line supervisors, or leaders from individual contributors? It was questions like these that led to what was perhaps the
earliest theory of leadership, the **Great Man theory** (Stogdill, 1974).

The roots of the Great Man theory can be traced back to the early 1900s,
when many leadership researchers and the popular press maintained that leaders and followers were fundamentally different. This led to hundreds of
research studies that looked at whether certain personality traits, physical
attributes, intelligence, or personal values differentiated leaders from followers.
Stogdill (1948) was the first leadership researcher to summarize the results of
these studies, and he came to two major conclusions. First, leaders were not
qualitatively different than followers; many followers were just as tall, smart,

outgoing, and ambitious as the people who were leading them. Second, some characteristics, such as intelligence, initiative, stress tolerance, responsibility, friendliness, and dominance, were modestly related to leadership success. In other words, people who were smart, hardworking, conscientious, friendly, or willing to take charge were often more successful in influencing a group to accomplish its goals than people who were less smart, lazy, impulsive, grumpy, or did not like giving orders. Having "the right stuff" in and of itself was no guarantee of leadership success, but it did improve the odds of successfully influencing a group toward the accomplishment of its goals.

Subsequent reviews by Mann (1959) and Stogdill (1974) involving hundreds of more sophisticated studies came to the same two conclusions. Although these three reviews provided ample evidence that people with the right stuff were more likely to be successful as leaders, many leadership researchers focused solely on the point that leaders were not fundamentally different than followers. They erroneously concluded that personal characteristics could not be used to predict future leadership success; as a result most of the subsequent research shifted toward other leadership phenomena. It was not until the publication of seminal articles by Lord, DeVader, and Allinger (1986) and Hogan, Curphy, and Hogan (1994) that intelligence and personality regained popularity with leadership researchers. Because of these two articles and subsequent leadership research, we now know a lot about how intelligence and various personality traits help or hinder leaders in their efforts to influence others. This research also provided insight on the role that various situational and follower characteristics have in affecting how a leader's intelligence and personality play out in the workplace. The purpose of this chapter is to summarize what we currently know about personality, intelligence, and leadership. As an overview, this chapter defines personality, intelligence, creativity, and emotional intelligence, reviews some of the key research findings for these concepts, and discusses the implications of this research for leadership practitioners.

Personality Traits and Leadership

What Is Personality?

> *There is an optical illusion about every person we ever meet. In truth, they are all creatures of a given temperament, which will appear in a given character, whose boundaries they will never pass: but we look at them, they seem alive, and we presume there is impulse in them. In the moment, it seems like an impulse, in the year, in the lifetime, it turns out to be a certain uniform tune, which the revolving barrel of the music box must play.*
>
> Ralph Waldo Emerson

Despite its common usage, Robert Hogan (1991) noted that the term **personality** is fairly ambiguous, and has at least two quite different meanings. One meaning refers to the impression a person makes on others. This view of personality emphasizes a person's *social reputation* and reflects not only a description but also an evaluation of the person in the eyes of others. From the standpoint of leadership, this view of personality addresses two distinct issues: "What kind of leader or person is this?" and "Is this somebody I would like to work for or be associated with?" In a practical sense, this view of personality comes into play whenever you describe the person you work for to a roommate or friend. For example, you might describe him or her as pushy, honest, outgoing, impulsive, decisive, friendly, and independent. Furthermore, whatever impression this leader made on you, chances are others would use many of the same terms of description. In that same vein, many people would probably say that Colin Powell is self-confident, friendly, conventional, outgoing, and achievement-oriented, and that he handles pressure well.

The second meaning of personality emphasizes the underlying, unseen structures and processes inside a person that explain why we behave the way we do; why each person's behavior tends to be relatively *similar across different situations,* yet also *different from another person's behavior.* Over the years psychologists have developed many theories to explain how such unseen structures may cause individuals to act in their characteristic manner. For example, Sigmund Freud (1913) believed that the intrapsychic tensions among the id, ego, and superego caused one to behave in characteristic ways even if the real motives behind the behaviors were unknown (i.e., unconscious) to the person. Although useful insights about personality have come from many different theories, most of the research addressing the relationship between personality and leadership success has been based on the **trait approach,** and that emphasis is most appropriate here.

"**Traits** refer to recurring regularities or trends in a person's behavior" (R. Hogan, 1991, p. 875), and the trait approach to personality maintains that people behave the way they do because of the strengths of the traits they possess. Although traits cannot be seen, they can be inferred from consistent patterns of behavior and reliably measured by personality inventories. For example, the personality trait of dependability differentiates leaders who tend to be hard-working and rule abiding from those who do not like to work hard and are more prone to break rules. Leaders getting higher scores on the trait of dependability on a personality inventory would be more likely to come to work on time, do a thorough job in completing work assignments, and rarely leave work early. We would also infer that leaders getting lower scores on the trait of dependability would be late to work more often, make impulsive decisions, or fail to follow through with commitments.

Personality traits are useful concepts for explaining why people act fairly consistently from one situation to the next. This cross-situational consistency in behavior may be thought of as analogous to the seasonal weather patterns in different cities (Hogan, Hogan, & Roberts, 1996; Roberts, 1996). We know that it is extremely cold and dry in Minneapolis in January, and hot and humid in Hong Kong in August. Therefore, we can do a pretty good job predicting what the weather will generally be like in Minneapolis in January, even though our predictions for any particular day will not be perfect. Although the average temperature in Minneapolis hovers around 20°F, the temperature ranges from

−30°F to 30°F on any single day in January. Similarly, knowing how two people differ on a particular personality trait can help us predict more accurately how they will tend to act in a variety of situations.

Just as various climate factors can affect the temperature on any single day, so can external factors affect a leader's behavior in any given situation. The trait approach maintains that a leader's behavior reflects an interaction between his or her personality traits and various situational factors (see, for example, Highlight 7.1. Traits play a particularly important role in determining how people behave in unfamiliar, ambiguous, or what we might call **weak situations.**

Personality and the Presidency

Highlight 7.1

Traits are unseen dispositions that can affect the way people act. Their existence can be inferred by a leader's consistent pattern of behaviors. One way of examining a leader's standing on the trait of achievement orientation is to examine one's achievements and accomplishments over the life span. Leaders with higher levels of achievement orientation tend to set high personal goals and are persistent in the pursuit of these goals. When considering the following leader's achievements and accomplishments, think about this person's standing on this personality trait, and try to guess who this person might be:

Age 23: lost a job.
Age 23: was defeated in bid for state legislature.
Age 24: failed in business venture.
Age 25: was elected to legislature.
Age 26: sweetheart died.
Age 27: experienced several emotional problems.
Age 27: was defeated in bid to be speaker of the house.
Age 34: was defeated for nomination to Congress.
Age 37: was elected to Congress.
Age 39: lost renomination to Congress.
Age 40: was defeated in bid for land office.
Age 45: was defeated in bid for U.S. Senate.
Age 47: was defeated for nomination to be vice president.
Age 49: was defeated in bid for Senate a second time.
Age 51: was elected president of the United States.

The person was Abraham Lincoln.

On the other hand, situations that are governed by clearly specified rules, demands, or organizational policies—**strong situations**—often minimize the effects traits have on behavior (Curphy, 1997a, c; 1996b).

The strength of the relationship between personality traits and leadership effectiveness relationship is often inversely related to the relative strength of the situation (i.e., leadership traits are more closely related to leadership effectiveness in weak situations). Given the accelerated pace of change in most organizations today, it is likely that leaders will be facing even more unfamiliar and ambiguous situations in the future. Therefore, personality traits may play an increasingly important role in a leader's behavior. If organizations can accurately identify those personality traits and the individuals who possess them, then they should be able to do a better job promoting the right people into leadership positions. And if the right people are in leadership positions, the odds of achieving organizational success should be dramatically improved. The next section describes some of the efforts researchers have taken to identify those personality traits related to leadership effectiveness.

The Five Factor Model of Personality

Although personality traits provide a useful approach to describing distinctive, cross-situational behavioral patterns, one potential problem is the sheer number of traitlike terms available to describe another's stereotypical behaviors. As early as 1936 Allport and Odbert identified over 18,000 trait-related adjectives in a standard English dictionary. Despite this large number of adjectives, research has shown that most of the traitlike terms people use to describe others' behavioral patterns could be reliably categorized into five broad personality dimensions. Historically, this five-dimension model was first identified by Webb in 1915 (Deary, 1996) and independently verified by Thurstone (1934), but over the years a number of researchers using very diverse samples and assessment instruments have noted similar results (see Hogan, Curphy, & Hogan, 1994). Given the robustness of the findings, there appears to be a compelling body of evidence to support these five dimensions of personality. These dimensions are referred to in the personality literature as the **Five Factor Model (FFM) of personality**, and most modern personality researchers endorse some version of this model (Azar, 1995; Barrick & Mount, 1996; Curphy, 1998b; Hogan, 1991; Hogan, Hogan, & Roberts, 1996; Barrick, 1999; Quirk & Fondt, 2000).

At its core, the FFM of personality is a categorization scheme. Most, if not all, of the personality traits that you would use to describe someone else could be reliably categorized into one of the FFM personality dimensions. A description of the model can be found in Table 7–1. The five major dimensions include surgency, dependability, agreeableness, adjustment, and intellectance. Perhaps the easiest way to understand this categorization scheme is to describe how our three world leaders would fall into each of the FFM categories.

Rule 13: When put into a position of command, take charge.

Norman Schwarzkopf

TABLE 7–1   The Five Factor Model of Personality

Five Factor Dimensions	Traits	Behaviors/Items
Surgency	Dominance	I like having responsibility for others.
	Sociability	I have a large group of friends.
Agreeableness	Empathy	I am a sympathetic person.
	Friendly	I am usually in a good mood.
Dependability	Organization	I usually make "to do" lists.
	Credibility	I practice what I preach.
	Conformity	I rarely get into trouble.
	Achievement orientation	I am a high achiever.
Adjustment	Steadiness	I remain calm in pressure situations.
	Self-acceptance	I take personal criticism well.
Intellectance		I like traveling to foreign countries.

Surgency (also referred to as dominance, self-confidence, the need for power, or dynamic) involves patterns of behavior often exhibited in group settings and generally concerned with getting ahead in life (Michel & Hogan 1996; Hogan, 2000). Such behavioral patterns often appear when someone is trying to influence or control others. Individuals higher in surgency are outgoing, competitive, decisive, impactful, and self-confident. Individuals lower in surgency prefer to work by themselves and have relatively little interest in influencing or competing with others.

Because leaders' decisiveness, competitiveness, and self-confidence can affect their ability to successfully influence a group, it is not surprising that leaders often have higher surgency scores than nonleaders (Barrick, 1999; Hurtz & Donovan, 2000). Given the behaviors associated with surgency, it is likely that our three world leaders would have higher surgency scores than most other people. Moreover, Colin Powell, and Madeleine Albright would probably have higher surgency scores than Konosuke Matsushita because the former two leaders appear outwardly more assertive and outspoken than Matsushita.

Another FFM personality dimension is **agreeableness** (also known as empathy, friendliness, or the need for affiliation). This personality dimension concerns how one gets along with, as opposed to getting ahead of, others (Hogan, 2000). Individuals high in agreeableness tend to be empathetic, approachable, and optimistic; those lower in agreeableness are more apt to appear insensitive, distant, and pessimistic.

> If you need a friend in Washington, get a dog.
>
> Harry Truman

Because teamwork and cooperation are important components of group functioning, it should not be surprising that leaders often have higher agreeableness scores than people in individual contributor roles (Barrick, 1999; Sandal, Endressen, Vaernes, & Ursin, 1999). Chances are that Colin Powell and Konosuke Matsushita have fairly high agreeableness scores—both project warm, down-to-earth, and approachable images and appear to be genuinely concerned about others. Madeleine Albright would probably have average agreeableness scores—she can be extremely charming when she wants to, but at other times can appear distant, aloof, and difficult to get along with.

Dependability (also known as conscientiousness) does not involve interacting with others but rather concerns those behavioral patterns related to one's approach to work. Leaders who are higher in dependability tend to be planful and hardworking, follow through with their commitments, and rarely get into trouble. Those who are lower in dependability tend to be more spontaneous, creative, and rule bending, and less concerned with following through with commitments.

In many ways dependability may be more concerned with management than leadership tendencies. Although leaders with higher scores are planful,

organized, goal oriented, and prefer structure, they also tend to be risk averse, uncreative, somewhat boring, and dislike change. Again, the situation will determine whether these tendencies can help or hinder a leader's ability to influence a group toward the accomplishment of its goals. For our three world leaders, Colin Powell would likely have the highest dependability scores; Madeleine Albright and Konosuke Matsushita might have somehat lower scores.

Adjustment (also known as emotional stability or self-control) is concerned with how people react to stress, failure, or personal criticism. Leaders higher in adjustment tend to be calm and tend not to take mistakes or failures personally, whereas those lower in adjustment may become tense, anxious, or exhibit emotional outbursts when stressed or criticized.

Followers often mimic a leader's emotions or behaviors under periods of high stress, so leaders who are calm under pressure and thick-skinned can often help a group stay on task and work through difficult issues. Unfortunately, the opposite is also true. With his calm demeanor and high stress tolerance, Konosuke Matsushita would probably have the highest adjustment scores of our three world leaders. Colin Powell would also have fairly high scores. Madeleine Albright is known to have a temper and be prone to occasional emotional outbursts; therefore, she would likely have lower than average adjustment scores.

Those behavioral patterns dealing with how one reacts to new experiences are related to the personality dimension of **intellectance** (also known as openness to experience). Leaders higher in intellectance tend to be imaginative, broad-minded, and curious; they seek out new experiences through travel, the arts, movies, sports, reading, going to new restaurants, or learning about new cultures. Individuals lower in intellectance tend to be more practical and have narrower interests; they like doing things the tried-and-true way rather than experimenting with new ways. It is important to note that intellectance is not the same thing as intelligence—smart people are not necessarily intellectually curious. Our three world leaders all appear to be open to new experiences and intellectually curious. All are well traveled and seem to have a broad set of interests; therefore, they would all have higher than average intellectance scores.

Implications of the Five Factor Model

The trait approach and the FFM provide leadership researchers and practitioners with several useful tools and insights. For one, personality traits provide researchers and practitioners with an explanation for leaders' and followers' tendencies to act in consistent ways over time. They help us to understand why some leaders are dominant versus deferent, outspoken versus quiet, planful versus spontaneous, warm versus cold, and so forth. It is also important to note that the behavioral manifestations of personality traits are often exhibited automatically and without much conscious thought. People high in surgency, for example, will often maneuver to influence or lead whatever groups or teams they are a part of without even thinking about it. Although personality traits predispose us to act in certain ways, we can nonetheless learn to modify our behaviors through experience, feedback, and reflection.

As seen in Figure 7.1, personality traits are one of the key components of behavior and are relatively difficult to change. Moreover, because personality traits tend to be stable over the years and the behavioral manifestations of traits occur somewhat automatically, it is extremely important for leaders, and leaders to be, to have insight into their personalities. For example, consider a leader who is relatively low in the trait of adjustment, but also is deciding whether to accept a high-stress/high-visibility job. On the basis of his personality trait scores alone, we might predict that this leader could be especially sensitive to criticism, as well as moody and prone to emotional outbursts. If the leader understood that he may have issues dealing with stress and criticism, then he

FIGURE 7.1

The building blocks of skills

could choose not to take the position, modify the situation to reduce the level of stress, or learn techniques for effectively dealing with these issues. A leader who lacked this self-insight would probably make poorer choices and have more difficulties coping with the demands of this position (Curphy, 1996a).

The FFM has proved to be very useful in several different ways. It is fairly robust, and most personality researchers currently embrace some form of the Big Five model (Azar, 1995; Barrick, 1999; Mount, Barrick, & Strauss, 1994; Barrick & Mount, 1996; Curphy, 1998b; Hogan, Hogan, & Roberts, 1996; Howard & Howard, 1995; Hurtz & Donovan, 2000). Furthermore, the model has proved to be a very useful scheme for categorizing the findings of the personality-leadership performance research.

Another advantage of the FFM is that it is a useful method for profiling people. For example, Mumford, Zaccaro, Johnson, Diana, Gilbert, and Threlfall (2000) reported that a unique set of personality traits differentiated senior leaders in operational units compared with those in staff functions in the U.S. Army. Heckman and Roberts (1997) showed that engineers and accountants tended to be lower in the trait of surgency but higher in the trait of dependability. On the other hand, marketing and sales place a premium on creativity and on influencing others, and people in these occupations tended to be higher in surgency but lower in dependability. There is a compelling body of evidence showing that surgency, agreeableness, dependability, and adjustment are all positively correlated with leadership success—the higher the scores on these four FFM dimensions, the more likely an individual will be an effective leader (Curphy, 2001; Hogan, Curphy, & Hogan, 1994; Barrick, 1999; Quirk & Fandt, 2000; Hurtz & Donovan, 2000; Judge, Higgens, Thoresen, & Barrick, 1999). The intellectance–leadership performance relationship is more tenuous; higher scores on intellectance are related to a leader's willingness to learn and look for a new job when downsized (Barrick, 1999; Boudreau, Boswell, Judge, & Bretz, 2001), but do not appear to be consistently related to leadership success (Hogan, Curphy, & Hogan, 1994). Some of the more recent research also showed that surgency is the best predictor of a leadership job offer after an interview and successful completion of an overseas leadership assignment (Caldwell & Burger, 1998; Caliguiri, 2000). Agreeableness is also a key factor in completing an overseas leadership assignment and working in tightly confined team situations, such as submarine crews (Sandal, Endressen, Vaernes, & Ursin, 1999). Dependability is related to the amount of time people take to prepare for an interview and their overall job satisfaction; lower scores increase their likelihood of engaging in counterproductive work behaviors (Barrick, 1999, Caldwell & Burger, 1998; Hurtz & Donovan, 2000; Sarchione, Cuttler, Muchinsky, & Nelson-Grey, 1998). Higher adjustment scores also helped leaders to complete an overseas assignment, successfully cope with change, and report positive earnings per share after an initial public offering (Judge, Thoresen, Pucik, & Welbourne, 1999; Welbourne & Cyr, 1999). In a similar vein, Blake (1996) reported some interesting findings for military cadets who were higher in agreeableness and surgency. His research indicated that higher agreeableness was positively related to performance ratings during the freshman and sophomore years but that higher surgency was more strongly related to performance ratings over the last two years at the U.S. Coast Guard Academy. Apparently getting along with others and developing strong social supports are very important during the first two years of a military cadet's life, but getting ahead becomes more important over the last two years. It may be that it takes a couple of years to develop strong social networks and supports, and once they have been established, other personality traits, such as surgency, become more important.

Another advantage of the Five Factor Model is that it appears universally applicable across cultures (Curphy, 1997a, 1996b; Hogan, Hogan, & Roberts, 1996; Schmidt, Kihm, & Robie, 2000; Salgado, 1997). People from Asian, Western European, Middle Eastern, Eastern European, or South American cultures seem to use the same five personality dimensions to categorize, profile, or describe others.

While the categorization schemes seem to be the same, however, some cultures do place varying importance on different personality dimensions. For example, Barrick and Mount (1996; Barrick, 1999) reported that dependability was positively related to job performance across *all* jobs in the United States. No matter what the job, it seems that people who are more planful, rule abiding, goal oriented, and reliable are generally higher performers than people who lack these attributes. These same findings for dependability hold true for employees in European countries, but in Europe higher-performing employees also had higher adjustment scores (Salgado, 1997).

Why Do Some Leaders Fail? The Dark Side of Personality

It goes without saying that not all leaders are successful, and some fail miserably. Why do leaders fail? Failure can occur for a variety of reasons, some of which are beyond the leader's or anyone else's control. Sometimes, however, leaders fail for personal, rather than situational, reasons—they may simply lack the abilities or experience needed to be successful. At other times, they may possess these assets but still fail. When this happens it is often because the leaders have been promoted to positions where they can no longer rely on themselves to do all the work but must instead succeed through others. Such leaders generally lack the ability to form cohesive, goal-oriented teams, and this deficit can be the result of one or more dark-side personality traits. **Dark-side personality traits** are irritating or counterproductive behavioral tendencies that interfere with a leader's ability to form cohesive teams and that cause followers to exert less effort toward goal accomplishment. Several aspects of dark-side traits are worth noting. First, typical measures of personality are designed to detect bright-side traits, and dark-side traits are usually not assessed or detected with interviews, personality inventories, or assessment center techniquese (Brinkmeyer & Hogan,

> *I did not have sexual relations with that woman.*
>
> Bill Clinton

TABLE 7–2   Dark-Side Personality Traits

Argumentative. This trait identifies leaders who are suspicious, are overly sensitive to criticism, and expect to be mistreated. Leaders possessing this trait do not take personal criticism well and are apt to start arguments and have a hard time ending them.

Interpersonal Insensitivity. Leaders possessing this trait tend to be aloof and unaware of how they come across to others, and to have difficulties putting themselves in "other peoples' shoes."

Narcissism. Leaders with this trait tend to be overly self-confident, self-centered, and extremely ambitious. They grossly overestimate their abilities, have a strong sense of entitlement, and often hold others in contempt. Extremely arrogant, they are always right and not afraid to tell you so. Such individuals often exploit followers for their own self-aggrandizement.

Fear of Failure. These individuals make poor leaders because they dread being criticized. As a result, they tend to be overly cautious and reluctant decision-makers. When forced to make decisions, they often impose old solutions to problems even when it is obvious that they will not work.

Perfectionism. This dark-side trait identifies leaders who are conscientious and methodical but also attend so closely to details that they have trouble setting and maintaining priorities. They maintain extremely high standards for themselves and their followers, and their inflexibility, nit-picking, and micromanaging tendencies can be extremely irritating.

Impulsivity. As leaders, these individuals are hedonistic and often ignore the feelings of followers when in pursuit of their own pleasure. They enjoy testing limits, may fail to keep promises and commitments, and often neglect to consider the consequences of their actions.

1997; Brown, 1997; Curphy, 1997d; Curphy, Gibson, Asiu, Horn, & Macomber, 1994; Hogan, Curphy, & Hogan, 1994; McDaniel, 1999; Rybicki & Klippel, 1997). Second, some dark-side traits are strongly related to higher FFM dimension scores. For example, perfectionism is often associated with very high dependability scores. Argumentativeness, impulsivity, and narcissism are related to higher surgency scores (McDaniel, 1999). Although higher surgency, agreeableness, dependability, and adjustment scores are related to leadership success, companies may also have a greater proportion of leaders with dark-side tendencies if they use FFM personality inventories as part of the hiring process. Third, these counterproductive tendencies typically become apparent only after a leader has been in the position for some period of time. Candidates possessing dark-side traits may do very well in interviews but be poor performers once on the job. Table 7–2 provides descriptions of some of the more common dark-side traits.

The behaviors associated with dark-side traits can occur anywhere in an organization. Many times organizations put up with these tendencies because an individual is smart, is experienced, or possesses unique skills. Nevertheless, leaders manifesting dark-side traits tend to leave a longer and longer trail of bruised people, and it is often only a matter of time before these tendencies catch up with them. As seen in Highlight 7.2, these tendencies can and often do have tragic consequences. See if you can pick out which dark-side traits this individual exhibited.

An Example of Dark-Side Personality Traits

Highlight 7.2

The subject in this case is a CEO of a $2 billion book publishing company who was dismissed as part of a corporate buyout. The individual started his career with the company as a book salesman over 30 years ago and reigned as the CEO for over 15 years. His leadership credo was "business is conflict. . . You don't get excellence by saying yes. You get love, but you don't get excellence. This company has raised the hurdles of excellence every bloody day."

According to his staff, the subject ruled by intimidation and fear. His profane harangues were an industry legend. Scores of former employees tell of meetings at which he publicly threatened to lop off people's hands or private body parts or tear out their throats for failure to perform. Whenever something went wrong or a goal wasn't achieved, the subject always saw it as a personal matter rather than the result of the business situation. As a result, the subject always placed personal blame for failure and the staff quickly learned not to come forward with problems. He rarely went through a single meeting without going after someone, and people saw his use of degradation and humiliation as a way of controlling his staff.

Many of his staff saw the buyout as the only way to get rid of the CEO. He had been in place for over 15 years and played a key role in making the company a multi-billion-dollar organization. Nevertheless, after the buyout the parent organization faced the specter of mass resignations if the subject was allowed to remain as CEO. As a result of the discontent of his staff, the CEO was asked to resign. Unfortunately, even to this day the CEO has no idea why he was let go, and seems genuinely despondent over the decision. When confronted with stories of abuse and intimidation, he either denies that they ever took place or claims that they were blown all out of proportion.

Source: R. T. Hogan, G. J. Curphy, and J. Hogan, "What Do We Know about Leadership: Effectiveness and Personality," *American Psychologist* 49 (1994) pp. 493–504.

Personality Types and Leadership

The Differences between Traits and Types

Traits are not the only way to describe personality. An alternative way to describe how leaders and followers differ in their day-to-day behavioral patterns is through **types,** or in terms of a **personality typology.** Superficially, there may appear to be little difference between traits and types. Even some of the same words are used to name them. Extroversion, for example, may be the name of a trait in one theory, but another theory may talk about extroverted *types.*

By their very nature, financial analysts tend to be defensive, conservative, and pessimistic. On the other side of the fence are the guys in sales and marketing—aggressive, speculative, and optimistic. They're always saying, "Let's do it," while the bean counters are always cautioning you on why you shouldn't do it. In any company you need both sides of the equation, because the natural tension between the two groups creates its own system of checks and balances.

Lee Iacocca

And, as it turns out, the differences here are more than skin-deep. We will only emphasize one aspect of the differences, the one we believe is most fundamental conceptually. Each trait (e.g., dominance) is conceptualized as a *continuum* along which people vary, typically in a bell-curve distribution. A person may be relatively lower or relatively higher on that trait, and the differences in behavioral patterns between any two people may be thought of as roughly proportional to how close or far apart their scores fall on the scale. Types, on the other hand, are usually thought of as relatively *discrete categories*.

This distinction may be clearer with an example. Let us take the trait of dominance, and compare it with a hypothetical construct we will call a "dominant type." Psychological typologies are often expressed in terms of polar opposites, so let us further suppose that our typology also refers to the bipolar opposite of dominant types, which we'll call submissive types. Importantly, people are considered to be *one or the other*, just as everyone is either male or female. If you are a dominant type you are considered to be more like all other dominant types than you are like any submissive type; if you are a submissive type you are considered to be more like every other submissive type than you are like any dominant type. In other words, typologies tend to put people into discrete psychological categories and emphasize the *similarities* among all people in the same category regardless of actual score (as long as it is in the right "direction"). Furthermore, typologies tend to emphasize *differences* between people of different types (e.g., between dominant and submissive types) regardless of actual score.

This point may become even clearer by looking at Figure 7.2. The upper line refers to the continuum of the trait defined at one end by submissiveness and at

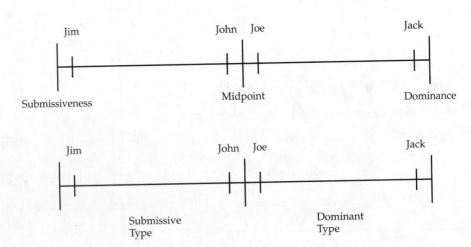

FIGURE 7.2

Traits and types

the other end by dominance. The trait scores of four different leaders—Jim, John, Joe, and Jack—are indicated on the scale. You can infer from their relative positions on the scale that John is more like Joe than he is like either Jim or Jack. But now look at the lower line. This refers to a typology of submissive types and dominant types. The theory behind personality types suggests that John is more like Jim than Joe, and Joe is more like Jack than John.

Psychological Preferences as a Personality Typology

One very popular personality typology involves psychological preferences, or what might be called "mental habits." Like traits, our **preferences** play a role in the characteristic and unique ways we behave from day to day. According to Jung (1971), preferences influence our choice of careers, ways of thinking, relationships, and work habits. Nearly 2 million people take the **Myers-Briggs Type Indicator (MBTI)** every year (Myers, 1976, 1977, 1980; Myers & Briggs, 1943/1962; Myers & McCaulley, 1985), which is not only the most popular measure of preferences but also one of the most popular psychological tests around (Quast & Hansen, 1996; Thayer, 1988). The MBTI is often used in college-level leadership and adult education courses, formal leadership training programs, organizational personnel programs, and by consultants as a part of various organizational interventions. Moreover, numerous books and articles have been published about how the MBTI can be used to better understand oneself, coworkers, partners in intimate relationships, children, and educational or occupational preferences.

According to Myers and McCaulley (1985), there are four basic preference dimensions in which people can differ. These four dimensions are **extraversion–introversion, sensing–intuition, thinking–feeling,** and **judging–perceiving.** The four dimensions are bipolar, meaning that individuals generally prefer being either, say, extraverted or introverted. A more in-depth description of the day-to-day behavioral patterns of these four dimensions can be found below.

The *extraversion-and-introversion* dimension is fundamentally concerned with where people get their energy. Some leaders are naturally gregarious and outgoing. Their spontaneous sociability makes it easy for them to strike up conversations with anyone about almost anything. Not surprisingly, such extraverts have a breadth of interests and a large circle of acquaintances. They are energized by being around others, but their tendency to "think out loud" and speak whatever is on their mind can sometimes get them into trouble. Introverted leaders prefer to think things through and only announce their final decisions, and followers may have a difficult time understanding the process the leader used to reach his or her conclusions. Because introverts find being around others to be draining, they may come across as less approachable than extraverts.

The *sensing-and-intuition* dimension is concerned with how people look at data. Leaders who prefer their sensing mode like facts and details; the focus of information gathering concerns the real, the actual, the literal, the specific, and the present. Hence, sensing leaders tend to be practical, orderly, and down-to-earth decision-makers. By contrast, leaders who rely on their intuition look for the big picture beyond particular facts or details; information is most meaningful for its pattern, framework, figurative meaning, and future possibilities. Intuitive leaders tend to be innovative and conceptual (though sometimes impractical), and are more comfortable with their hunches and inspirations.

Whereas the sensing-and-intuition dimension is concerned with how leaders and followers look at data, the *thinking-and-feeling* dimension is concerned with the considerations leaders prefer when making decisions. Thinking leaders like to analyze, criticize, and approach decisions impersonally and objectively. They use their heads to adopt a relatively detached stance toward decisions and pay more attention to operational, bottom-line considerations. Feeling leaders naturally empathize and appreciate, and prefer to approach decisions personally and subjectively. They value humaneness and social harmony and use their hearts to weigh the impact of any decision on particular people.

The *judging-and-perceiving* dimension has to do with the amount of information a leader needs before feeling comfortable making a decision. Judging leaders strive for closure; they like things to be settled and come across as decisive, methodical, and organized. Judgers get nervous *before* decisions are made and only want a minimal amount of information when making decisions. Although they make up their minds quickly, they may not have all relevant facts and as a result make poorer decisions. Perceiving leaders like to keep their options open; they are curious, spontaneous, and flexible. Perceivers prefer to collect as much information as possible before making a decision or a commitment. Perceivers often get nervous *after* a decision is made, as they may not feel that enough information was collected or data were analyzed. Although perceivers are good at gathering and analyzing additional data, they sometimes are accused of suffering from "analysis-paralysis."

As with personality traits, many leaders and followers exhibit the behaviors associated with their preference dimension almost automatically, particularly in weak or stressful situations. However, it is important to note that people are not locked into exhibiting only those behaviors associated with their preferences. Leaders can and do exhibit those behaviors associated with the opposite side of any preference dimension, but it takes personal insight and conscious energy and effort to do so. Moreover, the more extreme the preference score, the more likely the associated behavioral patterns will be exhibited, and the more focused will be the effort needed to exhibit nonpreference behaviors.

On the basis of descriptions provided above, you could make judgments about whether you are an extravert versus introvert, sensor versus intuitor, thinker versus feeler, or judger versus perceiver. The predominant preference scores for each of the four dimensions can be used to create one of 16 **psychological types**. For example, someone with high preferences for introversion, sensing, thinking, and judging would be categorized as an ISTJ (see Highlight 7.3 for a more in-depth description). Myers and McCaulley (1985) and Hirsh and Kummerow (1990) maintained that individuals within a particular type were more similar to each other than they were to individuals of a different type. Thus, ESTJ leaders are more like other ESTJ leaders than they are like INTJ or ESFP leaders.

Personality Preferences and Types for Mutual Fund Managers

Highlight 7.3

The portfolio managers for mutual funds often control billions of dollars of assets. These individuals and their staffs closely scrutinize different companies' financial reports, industry and business trends, local and global economic indicators, political and governmental activity, technological advances, and so on, to determine which stocks or bonds their mutual fund should invest in, hold, or sell. Obviously, most mutual fund managers are very bright and good with numbers, but what kind of personality preferences are associated with successful mutual fund managers? It turns out that most mutual fund managers are ISTJs. They are introverted, which means that they are introspective and tend to keep to themselves. Mutual fund managers are also strong sensors; they are data driven and not driven to acting on hunches that are contradicted by information. As thinkers their decisions are not swayed by emotion and have a strong bottom-line focus. And as judgers they are likely to focus on and reach closure on one issue before moving to the next. Psychologists who have used the MBTI to assess mutual fund managers also report that many mutual fund managers are ineffective team players—they are loners and consummate individual contributors. So even though they may make very good financial decisions, they may not be a whole lot of fun to work with or for. Unless, of course, you also happen to be an ISTJ.

Source: B. O'Reilly, "Does Your Fund Manager Play the Piano?" *Fortune,* December 29, 1997, pp. 139-44.

Implications for Leaders: Types and Preferences

As stated earlier, the preference scores for the four basic dimensions are combined to form 1 of 16 different types. Kroeger and Thuesen (1988) maintained that no one type was necessarily better than another in terms of leadership success, and that each type had unique strengths and potential weaknesses. Although there appears to be little published evidence to support this claim, there is evidence to show that leaders are disproportionately represented by certain types far more than others. Table 7–3 shows that a majority of leaders preferred thinking and judging activities over feeling and perceiving activities. Leaders were more likely to be ISTJs, INTJs, ESTJs, or ENTJs than any of the other 12 types (McCaulley, 1988). If we were to apply the 16 types to our three world leaders, what would you speculate might be Colin Powell's MBTI type? Or Konosuke Matsushita? Or Madeleine Albright?

Although the MBTI is an extremely popular and potentially useful instrument, leadership practitioners need to be aware of its limitations and possible misuses. The four preference dimensions can provide useful insights about

TABLE 7–3 **The 16 Personality Types of the MBTI**

Characteristics Frequently Associated with Each Myers-Briggs Type

ISTJ (14%)[a]
Serious, quiet, earn success by concentration and thoroughness. Practical, orderly, matter-of-fact, logical, realistic, and dependable. See to it that everything is well organized. Take responsibility. Make up their own minds as to what should be accomplished and work toward it steadily, regardless of protest or distractions.

ISTP (2%)
Cool onlookers—quiet, reserved, observing, and analyzing life with detached curiosity and unexpected flashes of original humor. Usually interested in impersonal principles, cause and effect, how and why mechanical things work. Exert themselves no more than they think necessary, because any waste of energy would be inefficient.

ESTP (2%)
Matter-of-fact, do not worry or hurry, enjoy whatever comes along. Tend to like mechanical things and sports, with friends on the side. May be a bit blunt or insensitive. Adaptable, tolerant, generally conservative in values. Dislike long explanations. Are best with real things that can be worked, handled, taken apart, or put together.

ESTJ (23%)
Practical, realistic, matter-of-fact, with a natural head for business or mechanics. Not interested in subjects they see no use for, but can apply themselves when necessary. Like to organize and run activities. May make good administrators, especially if they remember to consider others' feelings and points of view.

ISFJ (2%)
Quiet, friendly, responsible, and conscientious. Work devotedly to meet their obligations. Lend stability to any project or group. Thorough, painstaking, accurate. May need time to master technical subjects, as their interests are usually not technical. Patient with detail and routine. Loyal, considerate, concerned with how other people feel.

ISFP (1%)
Retiring, quietly friendly, sensitive, kind, modest about their abilities. Shun disagreements, do not force their opinions or values on others, usually do not care to lead but are often loyal followers. Often relaxed about getting things done, because they enjoy the present moment and do not want to spoil it by undue haste or exertion.

ESFP (1%)
Outgoing, easygoing, accepting, friendly, enjoy everything and make things more fun for others by their enjoyment. Like sports and making things. Know what's going on and join in eagerly. Find remembering facts easier than mastering theories. Are best in situations that need sound common sense and practical ability with people as well as with things.

ESFJ (2%)
Warm-hearted, talkative, popular, conscientious, born cooperators, active committee members. Need harmony and may be good at creating it. Always doing something nice for someone. Work best with encouragement and praise. Little interest in abstract thinking or technical subjects. Main interest is in things that directly and visibly affect people's lives.

---

oneself and others, but the fundamental concept of being a type is problematic. First, types are not completely stable over time. Some research indicates at least one letter in the four-letter type may change in half the people taking the test in as little as five weeks (McCarley & Carskadon, 1983; Myers & McCaulley, 1985). There also are data showing major developmental changes in distribution of types with age (Cummings, 1992). It is difficult to see how one should select individuals for teams or provide career guidance to others based on types if the types (or at least type scores) change, in some cases seemingly quickly. Furthermore, since the behavior of two people of the same type may vary as greatly as that of people of different types, the utility of typing systems remains uncertain.

INFJ (1%)

Succeed by perseverance, originality, and desire to do whatever is needed or wanted. Put their best efforts into their work. Quietly forceful, conscientious, concerned for others. Respected for their firm principles. Likely to be honored and followed for their clear convictions as to how best to serve the common good.

INFP (1%)

Full of enthusiasms and loyalties, but seldom talk of these until they know you well. Care about learning, ideas, language, and independent projects of their own. Tend to undertake too much, then somehow get it done. Friendly, but often too absorbed in what they are doing to be sociable. Little concern with possessions or physical surroundings.

ENFP (2%)

Warmly enthusiastic, high-spirited, ingenious, imaginative. Able to do almost anything that interests them. Quick with a solution for any difficulty and ready to help anyone with a problem. Often rely on their ability to improvise instead of preparing in advance. Can usually find compelling reasons for whatever they want.

ENFJ (4%)

Responsive and responsible. Generally feel real concern for what others think or want, and try to handle things with due regard for other person's feelings. Can present a proposal or lead group discussion with ease and tact. Sociable, popular, sympathetic. Responsive to praise and criticism.

INTJ (9%)

Usually have original minds and great drive for their own ideas and purposes. In fields that appeal to them, they have a fine power to organize a job and carry it through with or without help. Skeptical, critical, independent, determined, often stubborn. Must learn to yield less important points in order to win the most important.

INTP (5%)

Quiet, reserved, impersonal. Enjoy especially theoretical or scientific subjects, logical to the point of hair splitting. Usually interested mainly in ideas, with little liking for parties or small talk. Tend to have sharply defined interests. Need careers where some strong interest can be used and useful.

ENTP (9%)

Quick, ingenious, good at many things. Stimulating company, alert, and outspoken. May argue for fun on either side of a question. Resourceful in solving new and challenging problems, but may neglect routine assignments. Apt to turn to one new interest after another. Skillful in finding logical reasons for what they want.

ENTJ (22%)

Hearty, frank, decisive, leaders in activities. Usually good in anything that requires reasoning and intelligent talk, such as public speaking. Are usually well-informed and enjoy adding to their fund of knowledge. May sometimes be more positive and confident than their experience in an area warrants.

[a] The percentage of managers falling into each of the 16 types.

Consulting Psychologists Press Inc. *Manual: A Guide to the Development and Use of the Myers-Briggs Type Indicator.* Palo Alto, CA: Author, 1993.

But perhaps the most serious problem of all in using typologies concerns the way they are sometimes *misused* (Gibson & Curphy, 1996). Unfortunately, some people become so enamored with simple systems of classifying human behavior that they begin to see *everything* through "type" glasses. Some people habitually categorize their friends, spouses, and co-workers into types. Knowledge of type should be a basis for appreciating the richness and diversity of behavior, and the capabilities in others and ourselves. It is not meant to be a system of categorization that oversimplifies our own and others' behavior by seemingly putting people into neat and tidy little boxes (i.e., types). Believing someone is a particular type (e.g., "He's an ISTJ") can become a sort of perceptual filter that keeps us from actually recognizing when that person is acting in a manner contrary to that type's characteristic style. Another misuse occurs when someone uses "knowledge" of type as an excuse or a rationalization for his own counterproductive behaviors ("I know I'm talking on and on and dominating the conversation, but after all, I'm an extravert!"). In this case, the misuse of type can become a self-fulfilling prophecy that may make it very difficult for a leader to change a follower's behavior. The MBTI is a useful tool in enhancing awareness of oneself and others, but leadership practitioners need to understand that, like any tool, it can be misused too.

Intelligence and Leadership

What Is Intelligence?

The first formal linkage between intelligence and leadership was established around 1115 B.C. in China, where the dynasties used standardized tests to determine which citizens would play key leadership roles in the institutions they had set up to run the country (DuBois, 1964). Using intelligence tests to identify potential leaders in the United States goes back to World War I, and to a large extent this use of intelligence testing continues today. Over 100 years of very comprehensive and systematic research provides overwhelming evidence to support the notion that general intelligence plays a substantial role in human affairs (Arvey et al., 1994; Humphreys, 1984; Neisser et al., 1996; Ree & Earles, 1992, 1993; Schmidt & Hunter, 1992; Scarr, 1989; Sternberg, 1997). Still, intelligence and intelligence testing are among the most controversial topics in the social sciences today. There is contentious debate over questions like how heredity and the environment affect intelligence, whether intelligence tests should be used in public schools, and whether ethnic groups differ in average intelligence test scores. For the most part, however, we will bypass such controversies here. Our focus will be on the relationship between intelligence and leadership. (See Arvey et al., 1994; Azar, 1995; Brody, 1992; Cronbach, 1984; Humphreys, 1984; Linn, 1989; Neisser et al., 1996; and Sternberg, 1997, for reviews of these controversies.)

> *Perhaps no concept in the history of psychology has had or continues to have as great an impact on everyday life in the Western world as that of general intelligence.*
>
> Sandra Scarr

We define **intelligence** as a person's all-around effectiveness in activities directed by thought (Arvey et al., 1994; Cronbach, 1984). So what does this definition of intelligence have to do with leadership? Research has shown that more intelligent leaders are faster learners; make better assumptions, deductions, and inferences; are better at creating a compelling vision and developing strategies to make their vision a reality; can develop better solutions to problems; can see more of the primary and secondary implications of their decisions; and are

FIGURE 7.3

*The building
blocks of skills*

Source: © Personnel
Decisions
International, 1997.

quicker on their feet than leaders who are less intelligent (Herrnstein & Murray, 1994; Lord, DeVader, & Allinger, 1986; Curphy, 2000, 2001; Sternberg, 1997; Nutt, 1999). To a large extent people get placed into leadership positions to solve problems, be they customer, financial, operational, interpersonal, performance, political, educational, or social in nature. Therefore, given the behaviors associated with higher intelligence, it is easy to see how a more intelligent leader will oftentimes be more successful in influencing a group to accomplish its goals than a less intelligent leader. Like personality traits, however, intelligence alone is not enough to guarantee leadership success. There are plenty of smart people who make poor leaders just as there are less intelligent people who are great leaders. Nevertheless, many leadership activities do seem to involve some degree of decision-making and problem-solving ability, which means that a leader's intelligence can affect the odds of leadership success in many situations.

As seen in Figure 7.3, intelligence is relatively difficult to change. Like personality, it is also an unseen quality and can only be inferred by observing behavior. Moreover, intelligence does not affect behavior equally across all situations. Some activities, such as following simple routines, put less of a premium on intelligence than others. Finally, we should point out that our definition of intelligence does not imply that intelligence is a fixed quantity. Although heredity plays a role, intelligence can be and is modified through education and experience (Arvey et al., 1994; Brody, 1997; Cronbach, 1984; Humphreys, 1989; Neisser et al., 1996; Rushton, 1997).

The Triarchic Theory of Intelligence

Although there is a strong, positive relationship between intelligence and leadership effectiveness, there is still an ongoing debate about the nature of intelligence. Many psychologists have tried to determine the structure of intelligence; is intelligence a unitary ability, or does it

> *The first method for estimating the intelligence of a ruler is to look at the men he has around him.*
>
> Niccolò Machiavelli

involve a collection of related mental abilities (Azar, 1995; Gardner, 1983; Herrnstein & Murray, 1994)? Other psychologists have said that the *process* by which people do complex mental work is much more important than determining the number of mental abilities (Sternberg, 1985, 1997). Perhaps the most comprehensive and compelling theory of intelligence developed and tested over the past 20 years is Sternberg's (1985, 1997) **triarchic theory of intelligence.** It also offers some of the most significant implications for leadership. The triarchic theory focuses on what a leader *does* when solving complex mental problems, such as how information is combined and synthesized when solving problems, what assumptions and errors are made, and the like. According to this theory, there are three basic types of intelligence. **Analytic intelligence** is general problem-solving ability and can be assessed using standardized mental abilities tests. Leaders and followers with higher levels of analytic intelligence tend to be quick learners, do well in school, see connections between issues, and have the ability to make accurate deductions, assumptions, and inferences with relatively unfamiliar information.

There is still much, however, that analytic intelligence does not explain. There are a number of people who do well on standardized tests but not in life (Sternberg, Wagner, Williams, & Horvath, 1995). At the same time, some people do relatively poorly on standardized intelligence tests but often develop ingenious solutions to practical problems. For example, Sternberg and his associates described a situation where students in a school for the mentally retarded did very poorly on standardized tests yet consistently found ways to defeat the school's elaborate security system. In this situation the students possessed a relatively high level of **practical intelligence,** or "street smarts." People with street smarts know how to adapt to, shape, or select new situations in order to get their needs met better than people lacking street smarts (e.g., think of a stereotypical computer nerd and an inner-city kid both lost in downtown New York). In other words, practical intelligence involves knowing how things get done and how to do them. For leaders, practical intelligence involves knowing what to do and how to do it when confronted with a particular leadership situation, such as dealing with a poorly performing subordinate, resolving a problem with a customer, or getting a team to work better together (see Highlight 7.4).

Everyone is ignorant, only on different subjects.

Will Rogers

Because of its potential importance to leadership effectiveness, there are several other aspects of practical intelligence worth noting. First, practical intelligence is much more concerned with knowledge and experience than analytic intelligence (see Figure 7–3). Leaders can build their practical intelligence by building their leadership knowledge and experience. Thus, textbooks such as this one can help you to build your practical intelligence. Getting a variety of leadership experiences, and perhaps more important, reflecting on these experiences, will also help you to build practical intelligence. Second, practical intelligence is *domain specific.* A leader who has a lot of knowledge and experience in leading a pharmaceutical research team may feel like a duck out of water when

Is There a Military Mind?

Highlight 7.4

To many, the word *leadership* is synonymous with military authority. It evokes images of uniforms, salutes, rank and insignia, and discipline. To some it suggests positive associations like the chain of command's clear lines of authority and responsibility, decisiveness, respect for authority, camaraderie, selfless commitment to a higher mission, and good discipline. Others, however, do not have such a positive view. They may agree with Groucho Marx that military intelligence is a contradiction in terms.

So what are military leaders really like? For more than a decade, all newly promoted generals in the U.S. Army have attended a special leadership development course at the Center for Creative Leadership. It included a significant emphasis on individual psychological feedback to the generals based on a comprehensive battery of psychological tests. Psychologist David Campbell has extensively analyzed these test results, and his conclusions provide perhaps the best answers to questions about the psychological characteristics of military leaders. In terms of analytic intelligence, the generals proved to be an extremely bright group, averaging at the 95th percentile of IQ for the general population. They scored higher than a sample of corporate CEOs. They also had over 20 years of experience in the U.S. Army, so they had a high level of practical intelligence for warfare. In terms of personality, they have extremely high dependability scores; they are socially mature, alert to ethical and moral issues, and more conventional (i.e., less innovative) in their approach to problem solving than other executive groups, but they still score right at the average for the overall population. The generals also attained very high dominance and achievement orientation scores. In considering data from all sources, Campbell identified a common personality profile among the generals, which he termed "The Aggressive Adventurer." This profile describes dominant, competitive, action-oriented, patriotic men drawn to physically adventurous activities.

Source: D. P. Campbell, "The Psychological Test Profiles of Brigadier Generals: Warmongers or Decisive Warriors?" Invited address presented to Division 14 of the American Psychological Association, New York, 1987.

asked to lead a major fund-raising effort for a charitable institution. As another example, one of the authors worked with a highly successful retail company having over 100,000 employees. All of the key leaders had over 20 years of retail operations and merchandising experience, but they also did very poorly on standardized intelligence tests. The company had successfully expanded in the United States (which capitalized on their practical intelligence), but their attempt to expand to foreign markets was a failure. This failure was due in part to the leaders' inability to learn, appreciate, or understand the intricacies of other cultures (analytic intelligence), their lack of knowledge and experience in

The Triarchic Theory of Intelligence and Executive Decision Making

Highlight 7.5

A study of 356 major organizational decisions revealed that about half were outright failures (Nutt, 1999). Many of these failures were the result of the process used by executives to make and implement their decisions. Executives were more likely to make a poor organizational decision when they limited the search for alternatives, imposed solutions to problems too readily, and used position power rather than referent power to get their decisions implemented. Decisions were more likely to be successful when they made the need for action clear at the outset, set objectives (but not the methods for achieving them), carried out an unrestricted search for solutions, and got key people to participate in the decision-making process. It appears that successful decision-makers used a combination of analytic, practical, and creative intelligence and capitalized on these same three qualities of the group to make better organizational level decisions.

The importance of all three types of intelligence seems to also play a key role in the number of U.S. executives being asked to run companies in Europe, Latin America, and Asia. Cox (2000) maintained that executives trained in the United States are a hot commodity, as they often have the high levels of analytic and creative intelligence many foreign organizations are seeking and, more important, seem to have more practical intelligence than their foreign counterparts. This practical intelligence stems from the fact that U.S. executives are more likely to have attended one of the better business schools, more operational and management experience, and more experience in e-commerce and implementing technological solutions to solve business problems. Some examples of U.S.–trained executives running large overseas companies include Marjorie Scardino, CEO of Pearson, a large London-based publishing firm; Barbara Lundberg, CEO of Elektrim, a large Polish telecommunications firm; and Jeffrey Katz, the CEO of SwissAir.

Sources: P. T Nutt, "Surprising but True: Half the Decisions in Organizations Fail," *Academy of Management Executive* 1999 (no. 4), pp. 75–90; J. Cox, "Tech Savvy U.S. Executives a Hot Commodity Abroad: Foreign Firms Mine USA for Leadership," *USA Today*, April 24, 2000, p. 10B.

foreign markets (practical intelligence), and in turn their development of inappropriate strategies for running the business in other countries (a combination of analytic and practical intelligence). Thus, practical intelligence is extremely useful when leading in familiar situations, but analytic intelligence may play a more important role when leaders are facing new or novel situations.

Third, this example points out the importance of having both types of intelligence. As seen in Highlight 7.5, organizations today are looking for leaders and followers who have the necessary knowledge and skills to succeed (practical intelligence) and the ability to learn (analytic intelligence) (Stamps, 1996; Connelly, Gilbert, Ziccaro, Threlfell, Marks, & Mumford, 2000; Cox, 2000). Fourth, it may be that high levels of practical intelligence may compensate for lower levels of analytic intelligence. Leaders having lower analytic abilities may still be able to solve complex work problems or make good decisions provided they have plenty of job-relevant knowledge or experience. But leaders with more analytic intelligence, all things being equal, may develop their street smarts more quickly than leaders with less analytic intelligence. Analytic intelligence may play a lesser role once a domain of knowledge is mastered, but a more important role when encountering new situations.

The third component of the triarchic theory of intelligence is **creative intelligence.** Creative intelligence is the ability to produce work that is both novel and useful (Sternberg, 1997, 2001; Sternberg & Lubart, 1996). Using *both* criteria (novel and useful) as components of creative intelligence helps to eliminate many of the more outlandish solutions to a potential problem by ensuring that

> *The best way to have a good idea is to have a lot of ideas.*
>
> Dr. Linus Pauling

adopted solutions can be realistically implemented or have some type of practical payoff. Several examples might help to clarify the novel and practical components of creative intelligence. The inventor of Velcro got his idea while picking countless thistles out of his socks; he realized that the same principle that produced his frustration might be translated into a useful fastener. The inventor of 3M's Post-it notes was frustrated because bookmarks in his church hymnal were continually sliding out of place, and he saw a solution in a low-tack adhesive discovered by a fellow 3M scientist. The scientists who designed the *Pathfinder* mission to Mars were given a budget that was one-tenth that of the previous mission to Mars, the *Viking Lander.* Yet the scientists were challenged to develop a spacecraft that had more capabilities than the *Viking Lander.* Their efforts with *Pathfinder* were a resounding success, due in part to some of the novel solutions used both to land the spacecraft (an inflatable balloon system) and to explore the surrounding area (the *Sojourner* rover).

Two of the more-interesting questions surrounding creativity concern the role of intelligence and the assessment of creative ability. Research by Sternberg and Lubart (1996) shows that analytic intelligence correlates at about the .5 level with creative intelligence. Thus, the best research available indicates that analytic intelligence and creativity are related, but the relationship is far from perfect. Some level of analytic intelligence seems necessary for creativity, but having a high level of analytic intelligence is no guarantee that a leader will be creative. And like practical intelligence, creativity seems to be specific to certain fields and subfields: Most composers are not architects, and most writers are not mathematicians (Cronbach, 1984; Sternberg & Lubart, 1996).

In addition, actually assessing creativity is no simple matter. Tests of creativity, or **divergent thinking** are very different from tests that assess **convergent thinking.** Tests of convergent thinking usually have a single best answer; good examples here are most intelligence and aptitude tests. Conversely, tests of creativity or divergent thinking have many possible answers (Guilford, 1967). Although Sternberg and Lubart (1996), Sternberg and Dees (2001), and Sternberg (2001) all showed that it is possible to reliably judge the relative creativity of different responses, the fact remains that judging creativity is more difficult than scoring convergent tests. For example, there are no set answers or standards for determining whether a movie, a marketing ad, or a new manufacturing process is truly creative. Another difficulty in assessing creativity is that it may wax and wane over time; many of the most creative people seem to have occasional dry spells or writer's block. This is very different from analytic intelligence, where performance on mental abilities tests remains fairly constant over time.

The Components of Creative Intelligence

So far we have discussed creative intelligence as a unitary ability. However, research suggests that creativity appears to be made up of seven components: *synthetic ability, analytic intelligence, practical intelligence, thinking style, personality factors, intrinsic motivation,* and *environmental factors* (Amabile, 2001; Amabile & Conti, 1995; Kohn, 1987; Oldham & Cummings, 1996; Sternberg, 1985, 2001; Sternberg & Grigorenko, 1997; Sternberg & Lubart, 1996). **Synthetic ability** is what we traditionally view as creativity; these skills help people see things in new ways or recognize novel patterns or connections. Analytic intelligence helps people to evaluate solutions, and practical intelligence provides the knowledge and experience base from which novel solutions are developed. According to Sternberg and Lubart, these first three components are very important to the creative process, and leaders lacking in any one of them will be less creative than those possessing all three.

> *The "untrapped mind" is open enough to see many possibilities, humble enough to learn from anyone and anything, forbearing enough to forgive all, perceptive enough to see things as they really are, and reasonable enough to judge their true value.*
>
> Konosuke Matsushita

Thinking style is somewhat related to synthetic ability. Thinking styles are not abilities per se, but rather are the preferred ways for using the abilities one has (Sternberg & Grigorenko, 1997). For example, some people seem to prefer improving or adapting already existing products or processes. A first-line supervisor in a manufacturing facility may be very adept at modifying existing production schedules or equipment in order to better meet customers' needs. Other people seem to prefer developing completely new products. A team leader tasked with developing a new ad campaign for a major brewer might come up with a series of promotional ads using novel attention-getting devices, such as frogs or chameleons. According to Kirton (1987), these two examples illustrate the difference between **adaptive** and **innovative thinking styles.** Adaptors prefer to modify or change existing products or processes; innovators prefer to create entirely new processes or products. Adaptors and innovators may have the same level of synthetic ability, but they just seem to use this ability in different ways. It is important to note that U.S. companies seem particularly adept at developing new technology (i.e., innovation), whereas Japanese industries are very good at improving the technology and finding efficient ways to bring it to the marketplace (i.e., adaptation).

Several personality factors also seem to play a role in creativity. More specifically, people having higher levels of self-confidence, energy, risk taking, independence, impulsiveness, and intellectance seem to be more creative than people who lack self-confidence, are more conforming, and are less open to new and novel experiences (Amabile, 2001; Amabile & Gryskiewicz, 1987; Hogan & Morrison, 1993; Oldham & Cummings, 1996; Sternberg & Lubart, 1996). People will also be more creative when they are intrinsically motivated or feel challenged by the subject matter or problem itself (Amabile, 2001; Amabile & Hennessey, 1988; Tierney, Farmer, & Graen, 1999). Creative people are more likely to focus attention on solving the problem at hand, not on the need to meet deadlines, make money, or impress others.

Finally, several situational or environmental factors appear related to creativity. People who have more complex or challenging jobs and who have supportive, noncontrolling leaders seem to be more creative than people in uninteresting jobs who also have highly controlling supervisors (Oldham & Cummings, 1996). Several aspects of work groups also seem to affect creativity. Although the size of the group did not seem to matter, teams that were given clear goals, stayed task focused, and provided mutual support and participation often developed more innovative solutions than teams lacking these qualities (West & Anderson, 1996).

Team stability also seems to play a role in creativity. Amabile and Conti (1995; 1997) studied companies before, during, and after going through a large downsizing, and reported that teams that remained relatively intact during this process were substantially more creative in terms of patent applications than teams that were broken up. These authors also reported that an organization's support for creativity, in terms of time and resources, was a key factor in the creativity of individual employees.

The story of Chester Carlson provides a good example of how some of the seven components play important roles in developing a creative and useful solution to a problem. Chester Carlson invented the photocopy duplicating process, which revolutionized office work. Duplicating machines are relied on so much today that most people probably assume the invention was met with instant acceptance. That was not the case, however. Most people do not realize that it was 22 years from the time Carlson got the idea to the time his product became commercially available—or that refining and "selling" his concept was an uphill battle primarily because of the existence of carbon paper. (With carbon paper, people thought, why would you need anything else?) His solution for making copies of documents was certainly imaginative, but it was also derived from his considerable technical expertise. Moreover, his persistence in developing and persuading others of the potential of his process is a testament to the importance of intrinsic motivation in creativity.

Creative thinking is not an entirely rational or conscious process. Many times we do our most imaginative thinking unconsciously; people often gain sudden insights to an old problem out of the blue. There are interesting anecdotal accounts of how different creative thinkers recognized and even harnessed these unconscious processes. Albert Einstein, for example, once remarked that he got his best ideas in the morning when he was shaving. The great inventor Thomas Edison reportedly developed a technique to awaken himself and capture the typically unusual imagery and mental activity occurring as one falls asleep. These thinkers recognized the mind's fertility during its resting periods. Einstein's and Edison's receptivity to ideas emerging from their nonlogical mental processes was surely an important part of their genius. They were able to harness their unconscious rather than censor it, as many of us may do by suppressing or discounting mental activity that seems purposeless, nonsensical, or threatening.

Implications of the Triarchic Theory of Intelligence

The three types of intelligence in Sternberg's theory correspond nicely with the three leaders identified in Chapter 1. Although the three leaders probably possess high levels of all three types of intelligence, it may be that Madeleine Albright has particularly strong analytic intelligence. She not only has her doctorate, but she is known for her ability to learn new information, see connections between various world events, and think through the implications of foreign policy decisions. Colin Powell has highly developed practical intelligence for leading in the military. He has commanded a number of large and small military units and held line and staff positions during times of peace and war. An open question is the relevance of his extensive military knowledge and experience to his role as secretary of state. Konosuke Matsushita may have the highest level of creative intelligence, as he and his company are known for developing new and useful consumer products.

> If I had to sum up in one word what makes a good manager, I'd say decisiveness. You can use the fanciest computers to gather the numbers, but in the end you have to set a timetable and act.
>
> Lee Iacocca

Some 200 separate studies have examined the relationship between intelligence test scores and leadership effectiveness or emergence, and these studies have been the topic of major reviews by Stogdill (1948); Mann (1959); Ghiselli (1963); Stogdill (1974); Bray, Campbell, and Grant (1974); Cornwell (1983); Bray and Howard (1983); Lord, DeVader, and Allinger (1986); Bass (1990); and Fiedler (1992). These 10 reviews provided overwhelming support for the idea that leadership effectiveness or emergence is positively correlated with analytic intelligence. Nonetheless, it is important to recognize that the correlation between analytic intelligence and leadership success is far from perfect. Leadership situations that are relatively routine, unchanging, or require specific indepth product or process knowledge may place more importance on practical intelligence than analytic intelligence. Having a high level of analytic intelligence seems more important when solving ambiguous, complex problems, such as those encountered by executives at the top levels of an organization. Here leaders must be able to detect themes and patterns in seemingly unrelated information, make accurate assumptions about market conditions, or make wise merger, acquisition, or divestiture decisions. Further evidence that higher levels of analytic intelligence are associated with top leaders can be found in Figure 7.4.

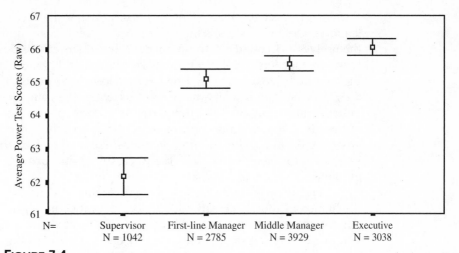

FIGURE 7.4

Average intelligence test scores by management level

Source: N. Kuncel, "Personality and Cognitive Differences among Management Levels" (Unpublished manuscript, Personnel Decisions International, Minneapolis, 1996).

Although a high level of analytic intelligence is usually an asset to a leader, research also suggests that in some situations analytic intelligence may have a *curvilinear* relationship with leadership effectiveness (Ghiselli, 1963; Stogdill, 1974). When differences in analytic intelligence between leader and followers are too great, communication can be impaired; a leader's intelligence can become an impediment to being understood by subordinates (Bass, 1990). An alternative explanation for the curvilinear relationship between analytic intelligence and leadership effectiveness may have to do with how stress affects leader–subordinate interactions. Fiedler (1992) and Gibson (1992) found that smart but inexperienced leaders were less effective in stressful situations than less intelligent, experienced leaders. An example of this finding was clearly demonstrated in the movie *Platoon*. In one frantic scene, an American platoon is ambushed by the Vietcong, and an inexperienced, college-educated lieutenant calls for artillery support from friendly units. He calls in the wrong coordinates, however, and as a result artillery shells are dropped on his own platoon's position rather than the enemy's position. The situation comes under control only after an experienced sergeant sizes up the situation and tells the artillery units to cease firing. This example points out the importance of practical intelligence in stressful situations. Leaders revert to well-practiced behaviors under periods of high stress and change, and leaders with high levels of practical intelligence have a relatively broad set of coping and problem-solving behaviors to draw upon in these situations. Because of the level of stress and change associated with many leadership positions today, systematically improving practical leadership skills through education and experience is extremely important for leaders and leaders-to-be.

With respect to creative intelligence, perhaps the most important point leaders should remember is that their primary role is not so much to be creative themselves as to build an environment where others can be creative. This is not to say that leaders should be uncreative, but rather that most innovations have their roots in ideas developed by people closest to a problem or opportunity (i.e., the workers). Leaders can boost the creativity throughout their groups or organizations in many ways, but particularly through selecting creative people in the first place, and providing opportunities for others to develop their creativity, and through broader interventions like making sure the motivation or incentives for others are conducive to creativity and providing at least some guidance or vision about what the creative product or output should look like.

There are several things leaders can do to improve the group and organizational factors affecting creativity. Leaders should be mindful of the effect various sorts of incentives or rewards can have on creativity; certain types of motivation to work are more conducive to creativity than others. Research has shown that people tend to generate more creative solutions when they are told to focus on their intrinsic motivation for doing so (i.e., the pleasure of solving the task itself) rather than focusing on the extrinsic motivation (i.e., public recognition or pay) (Amabile, 1985, 2001; Amabile & Hennessey, 1988; Tierney, Farmer, & Graen, 1999). When they need to foster creativity, leaders may find it more effective to select followers who truly enjoy working on the task at hand (i.e., are intrinsically motivated) rather than relying on rewards (i.e., extrinsic motivation) to foster creativity.

It is also helpful to remember that synthetic abilities can also be hindered if people believe that their ideas will be evaluated. The experiments of Amabile 1983, 1987 and Zhou (1998) showed that students who were told their projects were to be judged by experts produced less creative projects than students who were not told their projects would be judged. A similar sort of phenomenon can occur in groups. Even when a group knows its work must ultimately be evaluated, there is a pronounced tendency for members to be evaluative and judgmental too early in the solution-generating process. This tends to reduce the number of creative solutions generated, perhaps because of a generally shared belief in the value of critical thinking (and in some groups the norm seems to be the more criticism the better) and of subjecting ideas to intense scrutiny and evaluation. When members of a group judge ideas as soon as they are offered, two dysfunctional things can happen. People in the group may censor themselves (i.e., not share all their ideas with the group), as even mild rejection or criticism has a significant dampening effect (Prince, 1972), or they may prematurely reject others' ideas through negativistic focus on an idea's flaws rather than its possibilities. Given these findings, leaders may want to hold off on evaluating new ideas until they are all on the table, and should also encourage their followers to so the same.

Finally, leaders who need to develop new products and services should try to minimize the level of turnover in their teams and provide them with clear goals. Teams having unclear goals may successfully develop new or novel products, but these products may have low marketability or usefulness. Two examples might help illustrate this point. In the 1980s Texas Instruments (TI) decided to delve into the personal computer business. TI had a reputation for technical excellence, and one of the best managers in the company was asked to head up the project. The manager did not have a clear sense of what customers wanted or what a personal computer should be able to do. This lack of clarity had some fairly dramatic effects. As more and more engineers were added to the project, more and more innovative hardware ideas were added to the computer design. These additions caused the project to take much longer and cost a lot more than planned, but the TI personal computer ended up winning a number of major engineering awards. Unfortunately, it was also a business disaster, as the product ultimately failed to meet customer needs. Although Compaq computers arose from the ashes of TI's failure, the TI project serves as a good example for a concept called **creeping elegance.** Leaders not having a clear vision of what a final project should look like may end up with something that fails to meet customer needs. Leaders need to provide enough room for creativity to flourish, but enough direction for effort to be focused.

One industry that places a premium on creativity is the motion picture industry. Because creativity is so important to the commercial success of a movie, it is relatively easy for a movie to succumb to creeping elegance. But how do movie directors successfully avoid creeping elegance when dealing with highly creative people having huge egos? Part of the answer may be in the approach of two of Hollywood's most successful directors. Steven Speilberg and Ron Howard said that before they ever shot a scene they first had a very clear picture of it in their own minds. If they did not have a clear picture, then they sat down with the relevant parties and worked it out. Both situations point out the importance of having a clear vision when managing creativity.

Intelligence and Stress: Cognitive Resources Theory

In the preceding section we noted that intelligence may be a more important quality for leaders in some situations than others. You may be surprised to learn, however, that recent research actually suggests there are times when intelligence may be a disadvantage. A key variable affecting this paradoxical finding seems to be whether or not the leader is in a stressful situation. Recent research suggests that stress plays a key role in determining just how a leader's intelligence affects his or her effectiveness. While it is not surprising that stress affects behavior in various ways, Fiedler and Garcia (1987) developed the **cognitive resources theory (CRT)** to explain the interesting relationships between leader intelligence and experience levels, and group performance in stressful versus nonstressful conditions.

As first described in Chapter 4, CRT consists of several key concepts. Certainly one of these is intelligence. Fiedler and Garcia (1987) and Fiedler (1995) defined intelligence as we have earlier—it is one's all-around effectiveness in activities directed by thought and is typically measured using standardized intelligence tests (i.e., analytic intelligence). Another key concept is experience, which represents the habitual behavior patterns, overlearned knowledge, and skills acquired for effectively dealing with task-related problems (i.e., practical intelligence). Although experience is often gained under stressful and unpleasant conditions, experience also provides a "crash plan" to revert back to when under stress (Fiedler, 1992, 1995). As Fiedler observed, people often act differently when stressed, and the crash plan describes this change in behavior patterns. For most of the CRT studies, experience has been defined as time in the job or organization. A third key concept in CRT is stress. Stress is often defined as the result of conflicts with superiors or the apprehension associated with performance evaluation (Fiedler, 1995; Gibson, 1992). This interpersonal stress is believed to be emotionally disturbing and can divert attention from problem-solving activities (Sarason, 1986). In other words, people can get so concerned about how their performance is being evaluated that they may fail to perform at an optimal level. In sum, cognitive resources theory provides a conceptual scheme for explaining how leader behavior changes under stress levels to impact group performance.

Cognitive resources theory makes two major predictions with respect to intelligence, experience, stress, and group performance. First, because experienced leaders have a greater repertoire of behaviors to fall back on, leaders with greater experience but lower intelligence are hypothesized to have higher-performing groups under conditions of high stress. Experienced leaders have "been there before" and better know what to do and how to get it done when faced with high-stress situations. Leaders' experience levels can interfere with performance under low-stress conditions, however.

That leads to a second hypothesis. Because experience leads to habitual behavior patterns, leaders with high levels of experience will have a tendency to misapply old solutions to problems when creative solutions are called for (Fiedler, 1992, 1995). Experienced leaders overrely on the tried and true when faced with new problems, even when under relatively low periods of stress. Thus, leaders with higher levels of intelligence but less experience are not constrained by previously acquired behavior patterns and should have higher-performing groups under low-stress conditions. In other words, experience is helpful when one is under stress but is often a hindrance to performance in the absence of stress.

These two major predictions of CRT can be readily seen in everyday life. For the most part, it is not the most intelligent but the most experienced members of sporting teams, marching bands, acting troops, or volunteer organizations who are selected to be leaders. These leaders are often chosen because other members recognize their ability to perform well under the high levels of stress associated with sporting events and public performances. In addition, research with combat troops, firefighters, senior executives, and students has provided reasonably strong support for the two major tenets of CRT (Fiedler & Garcia, 1987; Fiedler, 1992, 1995; Gibson, 1992).

Despite this initial empirical support, one problem with CRT concerns the apparent dichotomy between intelligence and experience. Fiedler and Garcia's (1987) initial investigations of CRT did not examine the possibility that leaders could be both intelligent and experienced. Subsequent research by Gibson (1992) showed not only that many leaders were both intelligent and experienced, but also that these leaders would fall back on their experience in stressful situations and use their intelligence to solve group problems in less-stressful situations.

Another issue with CRT concerns the leader's ability to tolerate stress. As Schonpflug (1995) and Zaccaro (1995) correctly pointed out, some leaders may be better able to tolerate high levels of stress than others. Some leaders may have personalities characterized by considerable emotional stability or adjustment, and it may be that such leaders may do well in high-stress situations even when they lack experience because of their inherent ability to handle stress. Further research on this issue seems warranted.

In general, Fiedler and his colleagues have provided solid evidence to support the major tenets of CRT. Because of this research, CRT has several important implications for leaders. First, it may be that the best leaders are often smart *and* experienced. Although intelligence tests are good indicators of raw mental horsepower, it is just as important for leaders to broaden their leadership knowledge and experience if they want to be successful in high-stress situations. This latter point may be very important today, where the additional stress of organizational downsizing and "delayering" may cause the performance of leaders to be scrutinized even more closely than in the past. In fact, this additional scrutiny may well cause leaders who were previously successful to perform rather poorly in this high-stress environment.

Second, leaders may not be aware of the degree to which they are causing stress in their followers. If followers perceive that their performance is being closely watched, then they are likely to revert to their crash plans in order to perform. If the situation calls for new and novel solutions to problems, however, the leaders' behavior may be counterproductive. A key point here is that leaders may be unaware of their impact on followers. For example, they may want to review their followers' work more closely in order to be helpful, but followers may not perceive it this way.

Third, the level of stress inherent in the position needs to be understood before selection of leaders. Those doing the selection to fill high-stress leadership positions can either look for experienced leaders or reduce the stress in the situation so that more intelligent leaders can be more successful (Levy-Leboyer, 1995). Another alternative could be to hire more intelligent leaders and put them through some type of stress management program so that the effects of stress are minimized (Fielder, 1995). It is also possible that experienced leaders may get bored if placed into low-stress positions (Ganzach, 1998).

Emotional Intelligence and Leadership

What Is Emotional Intelligence?

More and more has been written about the positive attributes of a leader's emotional quotient, or EQ. The term has become so popular that the American Dialect Society voted EQ as the most useful phrase of 1995. But what is EQ, and how is it

> *There is no single entity called EQ (emotional intelligence quotient) as people have defined it. One sympathetic interpretation of what journalists were saying is that there were a dozen unrelated things, which collectively might predict more than intelligence, things like warmth, optimism, and empathy. But there was nothing new about that. Instead, the story became this fabulous new variable that is going to outpredict intelligence. There is no rational basis for saying that.*
>
> John Mayer

the same as or different from personality or the three types of intelligence described in this chapter? Unfortunately, there appears to be at least four major definitions of **emotional intelligence.** The term *emotional intelligence* can be attributed to two psychologists, Peter Salovey and John Mayer, who studied why some bright people fail to be successful. Salovey and Mayer (1990) discovered that many of them ran into trouble because of their lack of interpersonal sensitivity and skills, and defined emotional intelligence as a group of mental abilities that help people to recognize their own feelings and those of others. Bar-On (1996) believed that emotional intelligence was another way of measuring human effectiveness and defined it as a set of 15 abilities necessary to cope with daily situations and get along in the world. Aberman (2000) defined emotional intelligence as the degree to which thoughts, feelings, and actions were aligned. According to Aberman, leaders are more effective and "in the zone" when their thoughts, feelings, and actions were perfectly aligned. Daniel Goleman, a science writer for the *New York Times,* substantially broadened these definitions and summarized some of this work in his books *Emotional Intelligence* (1995) and *Working with Emotional Intelligence* (1998). Goleman argued that success in life is based more on one's self-motivation, persistence in the face of frustration, mood management, ability to adapt, and ability to empathize and get along with others than on one's analytic intelligence or IQ. Table 7–4 lists Goleman's 25 attributes of emotional intelligence. It is interesting to note that many of his emotional intelligence attributes look remarkably similar to the FFM personality dimensions and traits discussed earlier in this chapter.

Can Emotional Intelligence Be Measured and Developed?

Both Goleman and Bar-On have developed measures of emotional intelligence. Bar-On's measure is self-rated and called the Emotional Quotient Inventory (EQi). The Emotional Competence Inventory (ECI) was developed by Goleman and consists of 10 questionnaires. These questionnaires are completed by the individual and nine others; the responses are aggregated and given to the participant in a feedback report. Because both of these researchers have defined emotional intelligence differently and use a different process to assess EQ, it is not surprising that the two instruments often provide leaders with conflicting results (Schwartz, 2000). Nevertheless, the Air Force Recruiting Service has used the EQi to screen potential recruiters; it found that candidates scoring higher on the attributes of assertiveness, empathy, happiness, self-awareness, and problem solving were much less likely to turn over prematurely in the position and had a 90 percent chance of meeting their recruiting quotas (Schwartz, 2000).

TABLE 7–4 The 25 Attributes of Emotional Intelligence

Self-awareness	Emotional awareness
	Accurate self-assessment
	Self-confidence
Self-regulation	Self-control
	Trustworthiness
	Conscientiousness
	Adaptability
	Innovation
Motivation	Achievement drive
	Commitment
	Initiative
	Optimism
Empathy	Service orientation
	Developing others
	Leveraging diversity
	Political awareness
	Understanding others
Social skills	Influence
	Communication
	Leadership
	Change catalyst
	Conflict management
	Building bonds
	Collaboration and cooperation
	Team capabilities

Source: D. Goleman, *Working with Emotional Intelligence* (New York: Bantam Doubleday Dell, 1998).

One issue that most EQ researchers do agree upon is that emotional intelligence can be developed. Goleman and Aberman have developed one- to five-day training programs to help leaders improve their emotional intelligence; Bar-On has developed 15 e-learning modules that are available at EQ University.com. One of the big adopters of EQ training has been the sales staff at American Express Financial Advisors (AEFA). Leaders at AEFA discovered that the company had a well-respected set of investment and insurance products for customers, but many sales staff were struggling with how to respond to the emotions exhibited by clients during sales calls. Moreover, the best salespeople seem to be better able to "read" their clients' emotions and respond in a more empathetic manner. Since 1993 more than 5,500 sales staff and 850 sales managers at AEFA have attended a five-day training program to better recognize and respond to the emotions exhibited by clients. AEFA found that sales staff attending this program increased annual sales by an average of 18.1 percent, whereas those who did not attend training only achieved a 16.1 percent increase. However, the sample was very small and the comparison somewhat unfair because the control group did not receive any kind of sales training in lieu of the EQ training (Schwartz, 2000). Therefore, it is uncertain whether the EQ training content actually adds value over and above five days of sales training.

Implications of Emotional Intelligence

Aberman (2000) maintained that people can be extremely ineffective when their thoughts, feelings, and actions are misaligned—for example, arguing with someone on your cellular phone when driving on the interstate highway. It seems likely that leaders who are thinking or feeling one thing and actually doing something else are probably less effective in their ability to influence groups toward the accomplishment of their goals. The EQ literature should also be credited with popularizing the idea that noncognitive abilities, such as stress tolerance, assertiveness, and empathy, can play important roles in leadership success. Today, many organizations are using *both* cognitive and noncognitive measures as part of the process of hiring or promoting leaders. Finally, the EQ literature has also helped to bring emotion back to the workplace. Human emotions are very important aspects of one-on-one interactions and teamwork (Druskat & Wolff, 2001), but too many leadership practitioners and researchers have chosen to ignore the role they play. When recognized and leveraged properly, emotions can be the motivational fuel that help individuals and groups to accomplish their goals. When ignored or discounted, emotions can significantly impede a leader's ability to influence a group. As discussed in the FFM section of this chapter, leaders who can empathize and get along with others are often more successful than those who cannot.

Despite these positive contributions, emotional intelligence has several limitations. First, some researchers, Goleman in particular, have maintained that EQ is more important than intelligence when it comes to leadership success. Unfortunately, none of the research bears this out. The simple fact of the matter is that leaders will not be successful if they have lots of EQ but little IQ; the most effective leaders have both of these qualities. Second, few EQ researchers have acknowledged the existence of personality, much less 100 years of personality–leadership effectiveness research. As stated earlier, Tables 7–1 and 7–4 look very similar, and Goleman and Bar-On have talked about the attributes of their theories much like other researchers have talked about personality traits. At least as conceptualized by these two authors, it is difficult to see how EQ is any different from personality. Third, if the EQ attributes are essentially personality traits, then it is difficult to see how they will change as a result of a training intervention. Personality traits are very difficult to change, and the likelihood of changing 20 to 40 years of day-to-day behavioral patterns as the result of some e-learning modules or a five-day training program seems highly suspect. As we will see in the next chapter, people can change their behavior, but it takes considerable effort and coaching over the long term to make it happen. Finally, an important question to ask is whether EQ is really something new, or simply a repackaging of old ideas and findings? Leaders do benefit from good interpersonal skills, achievement motivation, and emotional self-control. But is this a new insight? Probably not.

Summary

This chapter examined the relationships between personality traits, personality types, intelligence, and emotional intelligence with leadership success. In general, all of these attributes can help a leader to influence a group toward the accomplishment of its goals, but in and of themselves they are no guarantee of leadership success. Oftentimes the situation will dictate which personality traits, components of intelligence, or emotional intelligence attributes will positively affect a leader's ability to influence a group.

Although the term *personality* has many different meanings, we use the term to describe one's typical or characteristic patterns of behavior. There are several different theories to describe why people act in characteristic ways, but the trait approach to personality has been the most thoroughly researched, and as such plays a key role in the chapter. The adoption of the Five Factor Model (FFM) of personality has helped to clarify the personality–leadership relationships, and researchers have noted that leadership success is positively correlated with the FFM personality dimensions of surgency, dependability, agreeableness, and adjustment.

Personality types are another way of looking at distinctive behavioral patterns. The most popular test of types is the Myers-Briggs Type Indicator (MBTI), which measures a person's preferences on four major dimensions. Individuals' scores for these four dimensions are typically combined to define a psychological type.

The most recent theory for understanding intelligence divides it into three related components: analytic intelligence, practical intelligence, and creative intelligence. All three components are interrelated. Most research shows that leaders possess higher levels of analytic intelligence than the general population, and that more intelligent leaders often make better leaders. Analytic intelligence appears to confer two primary benefits upon leaders. First, leaders who are smarter seem to be better problem solvers. Second, and perhaps more important, smarter leaders seem to profit more from experience.

The roles of practical and creative intelligence in leadership are receiving increasing attention. Practical intelligence, or one's relevant job knowledge or experience, is proving to be extremely important for leaders. Leaders with higher levels of practical intelligence seem to be better at solving problems under stress. Moreover, practical intelligence seems to be the easiest of the three components to change. This implies that leaders should use techniques such as the action-observation-reflection model, described in Chapter 3, to extract the most learning from their experiences.

Creative intelligence involves developing new and useful products and processes, and creativity is extremely important to the success of many businesses today. Creativity consists of seven components, including synthetic abilities, analytic intelligence, practical intelligence, thinking skills, relevant personality traits, intrinsic motivation, and several environmental factors. Understanding the seven components of creativity is important as the factors can give leaders ideas about how to improve their own and their followers' creativity. It is important that leaders learn how to successfully stimulate and manage creativity, even more than being creative themselves.

In some ways emotional intelligence is a relatively new concept, and there are at least four different definitions of emotional intelligence. Generally, emotional intelligence has to do with understanding and responding to one's own and others' emotions. Leaders who can better align their thoughts and feelings with their actions may be more effective than leaders who think and feel one way about something but then do something different about it. Although emotional intelligence has helped to point out the role emotions and noncognitive abilities play in leadership success, much of it seems to be nothing more than another label for personality. If this is the case, then emotional intelligence may be a leadership fad that will fade away over time.

Key Terms

Questions

1. What FFM and dark-side personality traits do you think would help professional sports players be more successful? Would successful coaches need the same or different personality traits and preferences? Would successful players and coaches need different traits and preferences for different sports?

2. Do you think personality is a helpful dimension for understanding the effectiveness of political leaders? Does this question necessarily imply that successful political leaders have good personalities, and unsuccessful ones bad personalities? (Hint: explore this issue by considering both the bright and the dark side of personality.)

3. Describe the situational factors that constrain or limit your behavior. Describe the situational factors that constrain or limit the effects personality has on some specific leader's behavior.

4. Individuals may well be attracted to, selected for, or successful in leadership roles early in their lives and careers based on their analytic intelligence. But what happens over time and with experience? Do you think *wisdom*, for example, is just another word for intelligence, or is it something else?

5. What role would downsizing play in an organization's overall level of practical intelligence?

6. We usually think of creativity as a characteristic of individuals, but might some organizations be more creative than others? What factors do you think might affect an organization's level of creativity?

7. How is Goleman's Conceptualization of EQ the same as or different from the FFM of personality?

Skills

The leadership skills relevant to this chapter include:

- Learning from experience
- Problem solving
- Improving creativity
- Diagnosing performance problems in individuals, groups, and organizations

Activity

1. Your instructor has access to an instrument designed to assess personality types. The instrument takes about 10 minutes to complete and could be given to you as homework. Follow the instructions at the top of the instrument, and determine which of the 16 personality types you fall into. Review Table 7–3 to get a brief description of your type and how what percentage of leaders share this type with you.

2. Your instructor could suspend a 30-foot rope approximately 3 feet off the ground. You and the rest of the class would get on one side of the rope. The rope represents an electrified fence, and your task is to get everyone successfully *over* the rope without touching it. You may not touch, lower, raise, or adjust the rope in any manner. You may not let any part of your skin or clothing touch the rope, nor can you drape anything over the rope to protect you from the current. There are two rules you must follow to successfully navigate the rope. First, before starting to cross the fence, everyone in the group must form a line parallel to the rope and hold hands with the people on either side. These links with the other people in the group cannot be broken. Second, a quality

error is committed if any group member touches the fence. If the group detects their own error, then only the person currently attempting to navigate the fence needs to start over. If the instructor catches the error but the group does not, then the instructor has the right to have the entire group start over. This is analagous to catching a bad product before it is delivered to a customer instead of delivering defecting products to customers. You will have about 25 minutes to plan and execute this exercise.

8   LEADERSHIP BEHAVIOR

Introduction

> T he leader sets the example. Whether in the Army or in civilian life, the other
> people in the organization take their cue from the leader—not from what the
> leader says, but what the leader does.
>
> Colin Powell

In the preceding chapters of Part II, we examined the relationships between leadership success and variables such as a leader's intelligence, personality traits and types, values, and attitudes. Important as they may be, however, variables like these may have only an indirect relationship with leadership effectiveness. Their effect presumably comes from the impact they have on leader behavior, which appears to have a more direct relationship with leader's ability to successfully influence a group toward the accomplishment of its goals.

One advantage of looking at leaders in terms of behavior instead of, say, personality is that behavior is often easier to measure; leadership behaviors can be observed whereas personality traits, values, or intelligence must be inferred from behavior or measured with tests. Another advantage of looking at leader behavior is that many people are less defensive about, and feel in more control of, specific behaviors than they do about their personalities or intelligence. This point has significant implications for developing leadership skills, a topic we will take up in detail at the end of this book.

Leaders with certain traits, values, or attitudes may find it easier to effectively perform some leadership behaviors than others. For example, leaders with higher agreeableness scores (as defined in Chapter 7) may find it relatively easy to show concern and support for followers but may also find it difficult to discipline followers. Leaders on a committee who are judgers and prefer planning out activities may have a difficult time learning to tolerate team members who feel that plans tie them down (i.e., perceivers). Leaders can learn new behaviors but, depending on their leadership traits, may take more or less practice to develop ease and competence in performing in new situations.

This chapter begins with a discussion on why it is important to study leadership behavior. We then review some of the early research on leader behavior, and discuss several ways to categorize or conceptualize different leadership behaviors. Next, we briefly summarize what is currently known about an increasingly common leadership behavior assessment technique, the 360-degree, or multirater, feedback questionnaire. The last section provides both a research perspective and some practical advice on behavioral change. It includes such topics as development planning, coaching, and mentoring.

Studies of Leadership Behavior

Why Study Leadership Behavior?

Thus far, we have reviewed research on a number of key variables affecting leadership behavior, but we have not directly examined fundamentally what leaders actually do to successfully influence a group. For example, what did Colin Powell do as a lieutenant to influence his platoon in Vietnam, and were the behaviors needed to be successful as the chief of the Joint Chiefs of Staff or secretary of state the same as or different from those needed in Vietnam? Further, did Madeleine Albright exhibit the same behaviors as secretary of state as Colin Powell, and are these essentially the same as those exhibited by Konosuke Matsushita as he grew his company into a multibillion-dollar organization? Because of these questions,

> *For every person who's a manager and wants to know how to manage people, there are 10 people who are being managed and would like to figure out how to make it stop.*
>
> Scott Adams,
> the creator of "Dilbert"

it is appropriate to turn our attention to leader behavior itself, for if we could identify how successful leaders act compared with unsuccessful leaders, then we could design systems that would allow us to hire, develop, and promote the skills necessary for organizations to succeed in the future. Unfortunately, given the success of the Dilbert comic strip and the explosive growth of management consulting firms, it appears that there are a number of leaders (or persons in positions of leadership) who either do not know what to do and how to do it, or do not realize how their behavior is affecting the people who work for them (Curphy, 1996a, 1998a; Chavan & Colvin; 1999).

Before we go into the different ways to categorize what leaders do to influence a group, it might be good to review what we know so far about leadership skills and behaviors. As seen in Figure 8.1, leadership behaviors (which include skills and competencies) are a function of intelligence, personality traits and preferences, values, attitudes, interests, knowledge, and experience. The factors in the bottom layer of blocks are relatively difficult to change, and they predispose a leader to act in distinctive ways. As described in Chapter 7, one's personality traits and preferences are pervasive and almost automatic, occurring typically without much conscious attention. The same could be said about how

FIGURE 8.1

The building blocks of skills

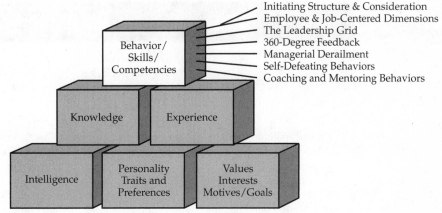

values, attitudes, and intelligence affect behaviors. Over time, however, it is to be hoped that leaders learn and discern which behaviors are more appropriate and effective than others. In addition, it is always useful to remember the pivotal roles individual difference and situational variables can play in a leader's actions (see Highlight 8.1).

The Early Studies

If you were asked how to study and identify the behaviors that best differentiated effective from ineffective leaders, how would you do it? Interviews, behavioral observation, and paper-and-pencil techniques (e.g., questionnaires) would seem to be the most likely approaches. You could ask leaders what they do, follow the leaders around to see how they actually behave, or administer questionnaires to ask them and those they work with how often the leaders exhibited certain behaviors. These three approaches have been used extensively in past and present leadership research.

Much of the initial leader behavior research was conducted at Ohio State University and the University of Michigan. Collectively, the Ohio State University studies developed a series of questionnaires to measure different leader behaviors in work settings. Hemphill (1949) began this development effort by collecting over 1,800 questionnaire items that described different types of leadership behaviors. These items were collapsed into 150 statements, and these statements were then used to develop a questionnaire called the **Leader Behavior Description Questionnaire (LBDQ)** (Hemphill & Coons, 1957). In order to obtain information about a particular leader's behavior, subordinates were asked to rate the extent to which their leader performed behaviors like the following:

He lets subordinates know when they've done a good job.

He sets clear expectations about performance.

Behaviors versus Skills

Highlight 8.1

Leadership behaviors are somewhat different from leadership skills. A leadership behavior concerns a specific action, whereas a leadership skill consists of three components, which include a well-defined body of knowledge, a set of related behaviors, and clear criteria of competent performance. Perhaps leadership skills may be better understood by using an analogy from basketball. People differ considerably in their basketball skills; good basketball players know when to pass and when to shoot, and are adept at making layups, shots from the field, and free throws. Knowing when to pass and when to shoot is an example of the knowledge component, and hitting layups and free throws is an example of the behavioral component of skills. In addition, shooting percentages can be used as one criterion for evaluating basketball skills. Leadership skills, such as delegating, can be seen much the same way. Good leaders know when and to whom a particular task should be delegated (i.e., knowledge), they effectively communicate their expectations concerning a delegated task (i.e., behavior), and they check to see whether the task was accomplished in a satisfactory manner (i.e., criteria). Thus, a skill is knowing when to act, acting in an manner appropriate to the situation, and acting in such a way that it helps the leader accomplish team goals.

He shows concern for subordinates as individuals.

He makes subordinates feel at ease.

In analyzing the questionnaires from thousands of subordinates, the statistical pattern of responses to all the different items indicated leaders could be described in terms of two independent dimensions of behavior called consideration and initiating structure (Fleishman, 1973; Halpin & Winer, 1957). **Consideration** refers to how much a leader is friendly and supportive toward subordinates. Leaders high in consideration engage in many different behaviors that show supportiveness and concern, such as speaking up for subordinates' interests, caring about their personal situations, and showing appreciation for their work. **Initiating structure** refers to how much a leader emphasizes meeting work goals and accomplishing tasks. Leaders high in initiating structure engage in many different task-related behaviors, such as assigning deadlines, establishing performance standards, and monitoring performance levels.

The LBDQ was not the only leadership questionnaire developed by the Ohio State researchers. They also developed, for example, the Supervisory Descriptive Behavior Questionnaire (SBDQ), which measured the extent to which leaders in industrial settings exhibited consideration and initiating structure behaviors (Fleishman, 1972). The Leadership Opinion Questionnaire (LOQ) asked leaders to indicate the extent to which they believed different consideration and initiating behaviors were important to leadership success (Fleishman, 1989). The LBDQ-XII was developed to assess 10 other categories of leadership behaviors in addition to consideration and initiating structure (Stogdill, 1959). Some of the additional leadership behaviors assessed by the LBDQ-XII included acting as a representative for the group, being able to tolerate uncertainty, emphasizing production, and reconciling conflicting organizational demands.

Rather than trying to describe the variety of behaviors leaders exhibit in work settings, the researchers at the University of Michigan sought to identify leader behaviors that contributed to effective group performance (Likert, 1961). They concluded that four categories of leadership behaviors are related to effective group performance: leader support, interaction facilitation, goal emphasis, and work facilitation (Bowers & Seashore, 1966).

Both goal emphasis and work facilitation are **job-centered dimensions** of behavior similar to the initiating structure behaviors described earlier. **Goal emphasis** behaviors are concerned with motivating subordinates to accomplish the task at hand, and **work facilitation** behaviors are concerned with clarifying roles, acquiring and allocating resources, and reconciling organizational conflicts. Leader support and interaction facilitation are **employee-centered dimensions** of behavior similar to the consideration dimension of the various Ohio State questionnaires. **Leader support** includes behaviors where the leader shows concern for subordinates; **interaction facilitation** includes those behaviors where leaders act to smooth over and minimize conflicts among followers. Like the researchers at Ohio State, those at the University of Michigan also developed a questionnaire, the Survey of Organizations, to assess the degree to which leaders exhibit these four dimensions of leadership behaviors (Bowers & Seashore, 1966).

Although the behaviors composing the task-oriented and people-oriented leadership dimensions were similar across the two research programs, there was a fundamental difference in assumption underlying the work at the University of Michigan and that at Ohio State. Researchers at the University of Michigan considered job-centered and employee-centered behaviors to be at *opposite ends of a single continuum of leadership behavior.* Leaders could theoretically manifest either strong employee *or* job-centered behaviors, but not both. On the other hand, researchers at Ohio State believed that consideration and initiating structure were *independent continuums.* Thus, leaders could be high in both initiating structure and consideration, low in both dimensions, or high in one and low in the other.

The key assumption underlying both research programs was that certain behaviors could be identified that are universally associated with a leader's ability to successfully influence a group toward the accomplishment of its goals. Here are the kinds of questions researchers were interested in:

From the University of Michigan perspective, who tends to be more effective in helping a group to accomplish its goals, job- or employee-centered leaders?

From the Ohio State perspective, are leaders who exhibit high levels of *both* task- and people-oriented behaviors more effective than those who exhibit *only* task or people behaviors?

What role do situational factors play in leadership effectiveness? Are employee-centered leadership behaviors more important in nonprofit organizations or downsizing situations, whereas job-centered behaviors are more important in manufacturing organizations or start-up situations?

The answers to these questions have several practical implications. If leaders need to exhibit only job- or employee-centered behaviors, then selection and training systems need to focus only on these behaviors. But if situational factors play a role, then researchers need to identify which variables are the most important, and to train leaders how to modify their behavior accordingly.

As you might suspect, the answer to all of these questions is, "It depends." In general, researchers have reported that leaders exhibiting a high level of consideration or employee-centered behaviors had more satisfied subordinates. Leaders who set clear goals, explained what followers were to do and how to get tasks accomplished, and monitored results (i.e., initiating structure or job-centered) often had higher-performing work units if the group faced relatively ambiguous or ill-defined tasks (Bass, 1990). At the same time, however, leaders whose behavior was highly autocratic (an aspect of initiating structure) were more likely to have relatively dissatisfied subordinates (Bass, 1990). Findings like these suggest that *there is no universal set of leader behaviors always associated with leadership success.* Often the degree to which leaders need to exhibit task- or people-oriented behaviors depends upon the situation, and it is precisely this finding that prompted the research underlying the contingency theories of leadership described in Chapter 12. If you review these theories you will see strong links to the job- and employee-centered behaviors identified 40 years ago.

Alternative Conceptualizations of Leadership Behaviors

The Ohio State and University of Michigan studies were a good first step in describing what leaders actually do. Other researchers have extended these findings into more user-friendly formats or developed different schemes for categorizing leadership behaviors. Like the earlier research, these alternative conceptualizations are generally concerned with: *(a)* identifying key leadership behaviors, *(b)* determining whether these behaviors have positive relationships with leadership success, and *(c)* developing those behaviors related to leadership success. One popular conceptualization of leadership is really an extension of the findings reported by the University of Michigan and Ohio State leadership researchers. The **Leadership Grid**® profiles leader behavior on two dimensions: **concern for people** and **concern for production** (Blake & McCanse, 1991; Blake & Mouton, 1964). The word *concern* reflects how a leader's underlying assumptions about people at work and the importance of the bottom line affect leadership style. In that sense, then, the Leadership Grid deals with more than just behavior. Nonetheless, it is included in this chapter because it is such a direct descendant of earlier behavioral studies.

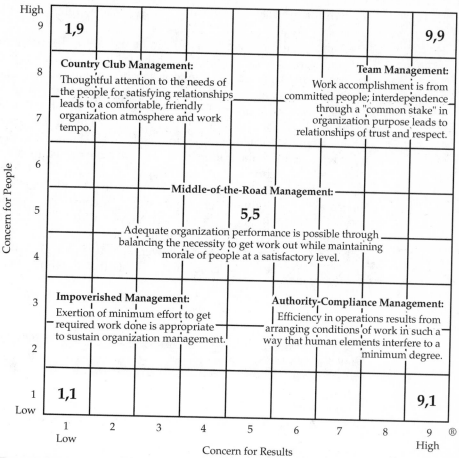

FIGURE 8.2

The Leadership Grid figure

Source: Robert R. Blake and Anne Adams McCanse, *Leadership Dilemmas—Grid Solutions* (Houston: Gulf Publishing, 1991), p. 29. Copyright 1991, by Scientific Methods, Inc. Reproduced by permission of the owners.

As Figure 8.2 shows, leaders can get scores ranging from 1 to 9 on both concern for people and concern for production depending on their responses to a leadership questionnaire. These two scores are then plotted on the Leadership Grid, and the two score combinations represent different leadership orientations. Each orientation reflects a "unique set of assumptions for using power and authority to link people to production" (Blake & McCanse, 1991, p. 29). Amid the different leadership styles, the most effective leaders are claimed to have both high concern for people and high concern for production, and Leadership Grid training programs are designed to move leaders to a 9,9 leadership style. Whereas this objective seems intuitively appealing, where do you think Madeleine Albright, Colin Powell, or Konosuke Matsushita score on these two dimensions? Do all three of them show a high concern for production and people? Are there differences between the three leaders, or are all three 9,9 leaders?

Although the Leadership Grid can be useful for describing or categorizing different leaders, we should note that the evidence to support the assertion that 9,9 leaders are the most effective comes primarily from Blake, Mouton, and their associates. However, other more recent research might shed some light on whether 9,9 leaders are really the most effective. Robie, Johnson, Nilsen, and Hazucha (2001) conducted a study of 1,400 managers in the United States, Germany, Denmark, the United Kingdom, Italy, Spain, France, and Belgium to determine whether the same leadership behaviors were related to effectiveness across countries. They reported that leadership behaviors associated with problem solving and driving for results (initiating structure or 9,1 leadership) were consistently related to successfully influencing a group to accomplish its goals, regardless of country. Using 800 managers in a U.S. high-tech firm, Goff (2000) reported that managers who spent more time building relationships (consideration or 1,9 leadership) also had more satisfied followers (i.e., they were less likely to leave the organization). These results seem to indicate that the most effective leadership style might just depend on the criteria used to judge effectiveness. The context and style of a leader's behavior are factors which affect impact (see Highlight 8.2).

Does Humor Matter?

Highlight 8.2

Does a leader's sense of humor affect his or her ability to influence a group toward the accomplishment of its goals? Several researchers examined this question and discovered the answer is not a simple yes or no. Laissez-faire leaders (1,1) who used humor reported having more satisfied followers, but did not have higher performing work groups. Task-focused leaders (9,1) who used humor actually had less satisfied and lower performing work units. Apparently their use of humor seemed out of sync with their constant focus on goal setting, productivity, and cost-cutting initiatives. Transformational leaders (9,9) who used humor seemed to have higher performing work groups. The key lesson from this research appears to be that the impact of a leader's humor will depend on the leader's style and the context in which it is delivered. Task-focused leaders should be keenly attuned to followers' needs when the company is facing an economic downturn or a difficult organizational dilemma, and also be aware that the use of humor in these situations will probably have just the opposite effect as intended.

Source: B. J. Avolio, J. M. Howell, and J. J. Sosik, "A Funny Thing Happened on the Way to the Bottom Line: Humor as a Moderator of Leadership Style Effects," *Academy of Management Journal* 42, no. 2 (1999), pp. 219–27.

So far in this section we have described several ways to categorize leaders or leadership behaviors, but what are the implications of this research for leadership practitioners? Believe it or not, you can see the practical application of this leadership behavior research in just about every Global 1000 company. As first discussed in Chapter 4, competency models describe the behaviors and skills managers need to exhibit if an organization is to be successful (King, Fowler, & Zeithaml, 2001). Just as leaders in different countries may need to exhibit behaviors uniquely appropriate to that setting to be successful, different businesses and industries within any one country often emphasize different leadership behaviors. Therefore, it is not unusual to see different organizations having distinct competency models depending upon the nature and size of the business, its level of globalization, or the role of technology or teams in the business (Peterson, 1998; Ulrich, Zenger & Smallwood, 1999). An example of a competency model for a major high-tech firm can be found in Figure 8.3. The inside wheel represents the general competencies, and the outside wheel represents

FIGURE 8.3

An example of a management competency model for a Fortune 500 high-tech firm

Source: Personnel Decisions. Copyright 1991, *Personnel Decisions*. All rights reserved. Used with permission.

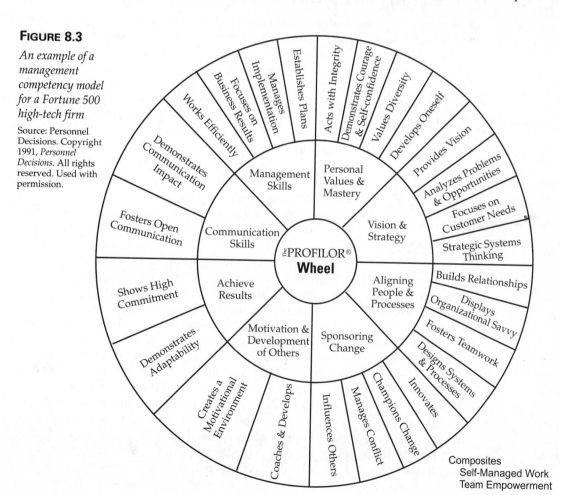

the more specific skills managers in this company need to carry it successfully through the 21st century.

Many of the best organizations now have competency models for different levels of management. For example, the behaviors and skills needed by department supervisors, store managers, district managers, regional vice presidents, and division presidents at The Home Depot vary considerably, and these differences are reflected in the competency models for each management group. These models help to clarify expectations of performance and describe the skills necessary for promotion. They also help human resource professionals to design selection, development, performance management, and succession planning programs so that organizations have a steady supply of leadership talent (Bracken, 1994; Curphy, 2001; Gebelein, 1994, 1996; Schippmann, Ash, Battista, Carr, Eyde, Hesketh, Kehoe, Pearlman, Prien, & Sanchez, 2000; Tett, Guterman, Bleier, & Murphy (in press).

Assessing Leadership Behaviors: Multirater Feedback Instruments

One way to improve leadership effectiveness is to provide leadership practitioners with feedback regarding the frequency and skill with which they perform various types of leadership behaviors. A $200-million industry has developed over the past decade to meet this need. This is the **360-degree,** or **multirater feedback,** instrument industry, and it is difficult to overestimate the importance it has had on management development both in the United States and overseas. Jack Welch, the CEO of General Electric, has stated that these tools have been critical to GE's success (Gebelein, 1994; Tichy & Cohen, 1997). Practically all of the Global 1000 companies are using some type of multirater feedback instrument for managers and key individual contributors (Edward & Ewen, 1996; Campbell, Curphy, & Tuggle, 1995; Lepsinger & Lucia, 1997; Tornow & London, 1998; Collins, 1999; Morical, 1999; Bracken, Timmreck, & Church, 2000). Multirater feedback instruments have been translated into 16 different languages, and well over five million managers have now received feedback on their leadership skills and behaviors from these instruments (Curphy, 2001). Because of the pervasiveness of multirater feedback in both the public and private sectors, it will be useful to examine some of the issues surrounding these instruments.

Every ten years or so a new management innovation comes along that generates much enthusiasm in organizations. Three hundred and sixty degree feedback has perhaps been the most notable management innovation of the 1990s.

LeeAnn Atwater and
David Waldman

Bracken, Timmreck & Church (2000) pointed out that many managers and human resource professionals have assumed that a manager's self-appraisal was the most accurate source of information regarding leadership strengths and weaknesses. This view has changed, however, with the introduction of multirater feedback instruments. These tools show that direct reports, peers, and superiors can have very different perceptions about a target leader's behavior, and these perspectives can paint a more accurate picture of the strengths and development needs of the leader than self-appraisals alone (see Figure 8.4). A manager may think he or she gets along exceptionally well with others, but if 360-degree feedback ratings from peers and direct reports indicate that the manager is very difficult to

FIGURE 8.4

Sources for 360-degree feedback

work with, then the manager should gain new insights on what to do to improve his leadership effectiveness. Prior to the introduction of 360-degree instruments, it was difficult for managers to get accurate information about how others perceived their on-the-job behaviors since the feedback they received from others in face-to-face meetings tended to be adulterated or watered down (Campbell, Curphy, & Tuggle, 1995; Peiperl, 2001). Moreover, as described in Chapter 7, many of the most frequent behaviors exhibited by leaders occur almost automatically, and many leaders do not understand or appreciate their impact on others. As a result, for a long time it was difficult for managers to determine how to leverage leadership strengths and overcome behavioral deficits. Today, most organizations use 360-degree tools for management development, as a part of a training or coaching program, in succession planning, or even as a part of the performance appraisal process (Lepsinger & Lucia, 1997; Ghorpede, 2000; DeNisi & Kluger, 2000; Bracken, Timmreck, & Church, 2000; Church & Waclawski, 2001).

Given the pervasive role 360-degree feedback plays in many organizations today, it is interesting to note that research is just starting to catch up with the use of these tools.

Much of this research has explored whether 360-degree feedback even matters, whether self-observer perceptual gaps matter, whether leaders' ratings can improve over time, and whether there are meaningful culture/gender/race issues with 360-degree feedback ratings. With respect to the first issue, Atwater, Waldman, Atwater, and Cartier (2000) reported that leaders who received 360-degree feedback had higher performing work units than leaders who did not receive this type of feedback. Church (1997, 2000) looked at independent measures of performance and reported that leaders receiving higher other (i.e., boss, peer, and direct report) ratings did get more accomplished than those who received lower ratings. These results indicate that 360-degree feedback ratings do matter (Ghorpade, 2000). They also point out the importance of developing leadership skills. Leaders with a broad set of highly developed leadership skills will be much more effective than leaders with a narrow set of underdeveloped skills.

> *Three hundred and sixty degree feedback results show that there are plenty of leaders who are leadership legends in their own minds but are also charismatically challenged in the eyes of others.*
>
> Gordy Curphy

As stated earlier, one of the advantages of 360-degree feedback is that it provides insight into self-perceptions and others' perceptions of leadership skills. But do self-observer gaps matter? Are leaders more effective if they have a high level of insight (i.e., rate their strengths and weaknesses as a leader the same as others do)? Some level of disagreement is to be expected, as bosses, peers, and direct reports may each have different expectations for a leader (Chueng, 1999; Hooijberg & Choi, 2000; Greguras & Robie, 1998; Mount, Judge, Scullen, Sytsma, & Hezlett, 1998). Nevertheless, insight does not seem to matter as far as leadership effectiveness is concerned. Even leaders with large self-observer gaps were effective as long as they had high observer ratings. On the other hand, the least effective leaders were those with high self and low others' ratings (Fleenor, McCauley & Brutus, 1996; Church, 1997; Atwater, Ostroff, Yammarino, & Fleenor, 1998). The important lesson here is that leadership is in the eyes of others. And the key to high observer ratings is to develop a broad set of leadership skills that will help groups to accomplish their goals. Highlight 8.3 illustrates the responses of leaders who rejected their 360-degree feedback.

> *In many cases the only person who is surprised by his or her 360-degree feedback results is the feedback recipient.*
>
> Gordy Curphy

Some of the Top Reasons for Rejecting Observer Feedback

Highlight 8.3

Being a leader is a tough job. Being a good leader is even tougher. Everyone you work with believes he or she is an expert on the subject of leadership, and it is difficult to keep everyone happy all of the time. Most leaders put forth considerable effort to be effective only to discover that they may be coming up short in the eyes of others. As a result, many leaders find 360-degree feedback to be a very valuable but somewhat unpleasant experience. The most effective leaders are those who accept unflattering feedback and do something about it. Less effective leaders are those who refuse to accept their 360-degree feedback results. The following are actual quotes of leaders who rejected their 360-degree feedback results:

- "My former boss told me to act this way. I'm actually nicer."
- "These ratings are biased because some of my observers are jealous of my promotion."
- "Human resources should have given this survey to more conscientious people."
- "The strengths are accurate, but the weaknesses are overstated."
- "I think my observers had the rating scale backwards when they completed the questionnaires."
- "These people aren't aware that I have changed those behaviors"

Another line of research has looked at whether 360-degree feedback ratings improve over time. In other words, is it possible to change others' perceptions of a leader's skills? One would hope that this would be the case, given the relationship between others' ratings and leadership effectiveness. Walker and Smither (1999) reported that managers who shared their 360-degree feedback results with their followers and worked on an action plan to improve their ratings had a dramatic improvement in others' ratings over a five-year period. Johnson and Johnson (2001) looked at 360-degree ratings over a two-year period and reported leadership productivity improvements of 9.5 percent for 515 managers in a manufacturing company. DeNisi and Kluger (2000) and Church and Waclawski (2001) aptly pointed out that 360-degree feedback alone is often not enough to improve leadership skills. Leaders must set development goals and commit to a development plan to improve skills if they want to see improvement in others' ratings (and, in turn, leadership effectiveness) over time.

The last line of research has explored whether there are important cultural, racial, or gender issues with 360-degree feedback. In terms of cultural issues, some countries, such as Japan, do not believe that peers or followers should provide leaders with feedback (Tornow & London, 1998). Other countries, such as Saudi Arabia, tend more to avoid conflict and provide only positive feedback to leaders (Curphy, 2001). The latter phenomenon is not limited to other countries, but appears also in the United States where leaders working in small organizations or in companies with many of the employees related often report similar results. People seem more hesitant to provide leaders with constructive feedback if they have to deal with the consequences of this feedback both on and off work (Curphy, 2001). The implication of these findings is that 360-degree feedback is not a management panacea; societal or organizational culture plays a key role in the accuracy and utility of the 360-degree feedback process.

With respect to racial differences, comprehensive study by Mount, Sytsma, Hazucha, and Holt (1997) looked at the pattern of responses from bosses, peers, and subordinates for over 20,000 managers from a variety of U.S. companies. In general, these researchers reported that blacks tended to give higher ratings to other blacks, irrespective of whether they were asked to provide peer, subordinate, or boss ratings. However, the overall size of this effect was rather small. White peers and subordinates generally gave about the same level of ratings for both black and white peers and bosses. This was not the case for white bosses, however, who tended to give significantly higher ratings to whites who reported directly to them. These findings imply that black leaders are likely to advance at a slower pace than their white counterparts, as 80–90 percent of salary, bonus, and promotion decisions are made solely by bosses (Bernardin & Beatty, 1984). Later this chapter Thomas (2001) will describe now these racial differences play out in mentoring programs.

With respect to gender issues, research indicates that there are some gender differences, though these differences tend to be slight. Female managers tend to get higher ratings on the majority of skills, yet their male counterparts are generally perceived as having higher advancement potential. There does not appear to be any same-sex bias in 360-degree feedback ratings, and female managers tend to be lower self-raters. Male managers tend to have less accurate self-insight and a higher number of blind spots when compared to their female counterparts (Personnel Decisions International, 1995).

So what should a leadership practitioner take away from all of this 360-degree feedback research? First, given the popularity of the technique, it is likely that you will receive 360-degree feedback sometime in your career. Second, 360-degree feedback should be built around an organization's competency model, which in turn describes the leadership behaviors needed to achieve organizational goals (Ulrich, Zenger, & Smallwood, 1999). Third, 360-degree feedback may be one of the best sources of "how" feedback for leadership practitioners. Leaders get plenty of "what" feedback—what progress they are making toward group goals, what level of customer service is being achieved, win–loss records, and so on, but they get very little feedback on "how" they should act to get better results. Multirater instruments provide this feedback. Fourth, effective leaders seem to have a broad set of well-developed leadership skills. Fifth, leaders need to create specific goals and development plans in order to improve leadership skills—360-degree feedback results give leaders ideas on what to improve but may not be enough in and of themselves to affect behavioral change. Sixth, leadership behavior can change over time, but it may take a year or two to acquire new skills and for the changes to be reflected in 360-degree feedback ratings. Finally, there are some cultural, racial, and gender issues associated with 360-degree feedback, and practitioners should be aware of these issues before implementing any 360-degree feedback process.

Managerial Derailment and Self-Defeating Behaviors

So far we have talked about what leaders can do in order to improve their effectiveness. The first lesson might be to determine which behaviors are most closely aligned with success, perhaps by identifying key behaviors by means of a competency model. Another lesson might be to get 360-degree feedback on these key behaviors. This feedback helps identify strengths and potential development needs. Not all leaders, however, truly learn such lessons. It might behoove us to look not just at how leaders succeed, but at the complementary question: why some leaders *fail*? We can learn valuable lessons about what *not* to do as a leader by studying them.

> CEOs are three times more likely to get booted than a generation ago.
>
> Ram Charan and
> Geoffrey Colvin

There is a growing body of research that indicates that somewhere between 30 and 50 percent of managers and executives fail (Charan & Colvin, 1999; Hogan, Curphy, & Hogan, 1994; Sloane, Hezlett, Kuncel, & Sytsma, 1996). These figures imply that up to half of the leaders in any organization are not going to be able to build cohesive teams or achieve business results, which unfortunately lends some weight to Scott Adams's quote at the beginning of the chapter. Initial research on **managerial derailment**—whereby individuals who at one time were on the fast track now had their careers derailed—was conducted in the early 1980s by researchers at the Center for Creative Leadership. The researchers went to the human resource departments in a number of Fortune 100 companies seeking lists of their "high-potential" managers. McCall and Lombardo (1983) defined high potentials as those individuals who had been identified as eventually becoming either the CEO/president or one of his or her direct reports sometime in the future. They waited for three years and then returned to these organizations to ask what had happened to the people on the lists. They discovered that roughly a quarter of the high potentials had been promoted to one of the top two levels in the organization, and an equal percentage had not yet been promoted but would be as soon as a position became available. Another 25 percent had left the company; some had quit to form their own company and others were given a better offer somewhere else. Finally, about a quarter of the people on the list were no longer being considered for promotion. If they were still with the company, then they had been moved to a less influential and visible position. Many others had been asked to leave the company. These individuals represented cases of managerial derailment.

Several other researchers have investigated the managerial derailment phenomenon (Hazucha, 1992; Lombardo, Ruderman, & McCauley, 1987; Peterson, 1993a, 1993b; Van Velsor & Leslie, 1995). This more recent research used much larger samples (Peterson examined over 600 derailed managers), European samples, and more sophisticated assessment tools (i.e., 360-degree feedback instruments). Moreover, a substantially higher percentage of women and minorities were represented in this more recent research, as the initial high-potential list was dominated by white males. As Van Veslor and Leslie (1995) pointed out, this research focused on identifying those factors which helped derailment candidates get initially identified as high potentials, as well as on those factors contributing to their ultimate professional demise. Although these studies varied in many ways, there are many consistent findings across them. Both groups were smart, ambitious, willing to do whatever it took to get the job done, and had considerable technical expertise. In other words, all of the high-potential candidates had impressive track records in their organizations.

On the other hand, the derailed candidates exhibited one or more behavioral patterns not evident in the high potentials who succeeded. The derailment themes can be found in Table 8–1 and are described in more detail below. It is important to note that four of the derailment themes included in Table 8–1 have been consistently reported in the research both in the United States and Europe, and that apparently a new theme is emerging and another is disappearing over time. The first derailment pattern has to do with an **inability to build relationships** with co-workers. The derailed managers exhibiting this pattern of behavior were very insensitive to the needs and plights of their followers and co-workers, and were often overly competitive, demanding, and domineering. They embraced the "my way or the highway" school of management. Many were also extremely arrogant and truly believed no one in their organizations was as good as they were, and they let their co-workers know it every chance they could. Some of these derailed managers also did whatever they felt

TABLE 8–1   Themes in Derailment Research

Four Enduring Themes	McCall & Lombardo (1983)	Morrison et al. (1987)	Lombardo & McCauley (1988)	United States (1993–94)	Europe (1993–94)
Problems with interpersonal relationships	Insensitive to others; cold, aloof, arrogant; overly ambitious	Poor relationships, too ambitious	Problems with interpersonal relationships, isolates self	Poor working relations	Poor working relations, organizational isolation, authoritarian, too ambitious
Failure to meet business objectives	Betrayal of trust; poor performance	Performance problems	Lack of follow-through	Too ambitious, lack of hard work	Too ambitious, poor performance
Inability to build and lead a team	Failing to staff effectively	Can't manage subordinates	Difficulty molding a staff	Inability to build and lead a team	Inability to build and lead a team
Inability to develop or adapt	Unable to adapt to a boss with a different style, unable to think strategically	Unable to adapt to a boss or culture, not strategic	Strategic differences with management, difficulty making strategic transitions	Unable to develop or adapt,t conflic with upper management	Unable to develop or adapt
Emergent themes	—	Too narrow business experience	—	Not prepared for promotion, narrow functional orientation	Not prepared for promotion, narrow functional orientation
Disappearing themes	Overdependent on advocate or mentor	—	Overdependence	—	—

Source: E. Van Velsor and J. B. Leslie, "Why Executives Derail: Perspectives across Time and Cultures," *Academy of Management Executive* 9, no. 4 (1995), pp. 62–71.

necessary to get the job done, even if it meant stepping on a few toes in the process. Unfortunately, this is not one of the recommended techniques for winning friends and influencing people. It's better to remember the old adage that you should be careful whom you step on going up the ladder, because you may meet them again on your way down. Many of these managers left a trail of bruised people who were just waiting for the right opportunity to bring these leaders down. Highlight 8.4 illustrates the case of a sales manager with derailment potential.

An Example of a Derailed Leader

Highlight 8.4

The following is a story about a sales manager who seems to have derailment potential. See if you can pick out which derailment factors may be at play in this story. In addition, what advice would you give to the writer to "fix" the problem?

I've been working in a medium-sized manufacturing company for the past 20 years. I'm not in sales, but interact with salespeople on a daily basis. Over the past year or so, I have noticed the sales force has been frustrated. After numerous conversations not only with the sales force, but also with other people in all aspects of the company, I have realized that the poison is coming from one person: Mike, the sales manager. Mike has been with the company for over 10 years and has successfully maneuvered his way to the position of sales manager. All of his promotions were given to him because of his own self-promotion. He has an enormous ego. His tactics of bulldog management, double standards, and outright lying is driving his sales force out and is frustrating people all over the company. He is disliked, even hated, by almost everyone in the company. Amazingly, Mike doesn't realize what people think of him. I believe the owners tolerate Mike's behavior because he has produced decent sales over the years. This year sales are substantially down. I believe the company is going to start to lose good salespeople because of Mike. Here's why: Nobody will confront him because if they do, he threatens them or makes them do some ridiculous assignment. All conversations with Mike are one-sided. If you bring up a concern that involves him, he will change the subject and dismiss you. It's like he is afraid of the truth. He is dishonest and essentially a loose cannon. I believe the owners know the truth about Mike but they continue to let him act this way. I believe Mike will never leave because he knows he could never get away with the things he does anywhere else. My concern is that if the owners don't fix the "Mike problem" they will start to lose good salespeople. Any advice?

Source: J. Lloyd, "Good Firms Work to Find Out Truth about Bad Managers," *Milwaukee Journal Sentinel,* August 20, 2000, p. 20.

According to Van Velsor and Leslie (1995), approximately two-thirds of European and one-third of American derailment candidates fall into this pattern. For example, a female vice president of marketing and sales for a cellular phone company was fired from her $200,000 a year job for exhibiting many of the behaviors just listed. She was very bright, had an excellent technical background (an engineer by training), had already been the CEO for several smaller organizations, and worked very long hours. Her in-depth managerial assessment results

(Chapter 4) indicated that she also had a strong leaderlike personality, with higher scores in surgency and dependability and average scores in agreeableness and adjustment. This assessment also indicated she had extremely high narcissism scores, and at work this dark-side trait would manifest itself by her talking down to people, quickly identifying and capitalizing on others' faults, constantly commenting on their incompetence, running over her peers when she needed resources or support, promoting infighting among her peers and subordinates, and expecting to be pampered. Interestingly, she had no idea she was having such a debilitating effect on those she worked with until she received her 360-degree feedback. Had she received this feedback sooner, she might have been able to stop her career from derailing.

Charan and Colvin (1999) stated that people problems are one of the primary reasons why CEOs fail. However, unlike derailed midlevel managers, most CEOs get along with others in the company. The problem with CEOs is that they get along with some of their direct reports too well and do not take timely action to address problem performers. More specifically, some CEOs fail because they place loyal subordinates into jobs they are incapable of handling, falsely believe they can help poorly performing subordinates to change ineffective behavior, do not want to offend Wall Street or the board by letting popular (but ineffective) executives go, or do not feel comfortable hiring outsiders to fill key executive positions.

> *The devil that you know is better than the one you do not know.*
>
> Old folk saying

Another derailment pattern identified in Table 8–1 is a **failure to meet business objectives.** Although both successful and derailed managers experience business downturns, the groups handled setbacks quite differently. Successful managers took personal responsibility for their mistakes and sought ways to solve the problem. Derailed managers tended to engage in finger-pointing and blaming others for the downturn. *But as long as things were going well,* it was difficult to differentiate these two groups on this factor. Some of these managers were also untrustworthy. They either blatantly lied about business results or failed to keep promises, commitments, or deadlines. The most common reason for CEO failure is the inability to meet earnings projections (Charan & Colvin, 1999). However, this inability to meet financial projections is not the result of a poor business strategy, unwanted products and services, or inadequate distribution channels. Most CEOs have well-above-average analytic and practical intelligence, so they usually do not have a problem developing a vision or strategy for the company, nor do they make poor decisions concerning which markets to pursue and products to develop. In many cases, CEOs fail to get results because of their inability to execute according to the business strategy. They tend to get distracted and lose focus or do not hold their direct reports accountable for getting the results outlined in their business plans.

> *When the dog is dead, the fleas are gone.*
>
> Puerto Rican folk saying

The third derailment pattern identified by Van Velsor and Leslie (1995) was an **inability to lead and build a team.** Some managers derailed because they hired staff who were just like themselves, which in turn only served to magnify their own strengths and weaknesses. Others wanted to stay in the limelight and hired staff less capable than they were. Still others micromanaged their staffs, even when not expert themselves in the tasks (not that it's ever recommended). These bosses wanted their followers to "check their brains at the door" before coming to work. One thing that often underlies this pattern is a lack of trust and high perfectionism scores (Chapter 7).

Another derailment profile has to do with a leader's **inability to adapt** to new bosses, businesses, cultures, or structures. As pointed out earlier in this chapter, many business situations require different leadership behaviors and skills, and some derailed managers could not adapt or adjust their styles to changing bosses, followers, and situations. They persisted in acting the same way, even when it was no longer appropriate to new circumstances. When solving problems, they often imposed past solutions that were no longer viable. For example, a first-line supervisor for an electronics firm that built video poker machines was having a very difficult time transitioning from his old job as a missile guidance repairman in the U.S. Air Force. He thought he should lead his subordinates the way he led others in the military: his staff should be willing to work long hours and over the weekends without being told, and to travel for extended periods of time with short notice. Their thoughts or opinions on ways to improve work processes did not matter to him, and he expected everyone to maintain cool and professional attitudes at work. After half of his staff quit as a direct result of his supervision, he was demoted and replaced by one of his subordinates.

In the past, organizations could afford to take their time in identifying and developing leadership talent. Many of the best organizations today have strong programs for systematically developing leadership bench strength (Curphy, 1998a; Cheran, Drotter & Noel, 2001; Tichy & Cohen, 1997). However, more and more organizations today are under increasing pressure to find good leaders quickly, and they are increasingly asking their own high-potential but inexperienced leadership talent to step up to the plate and fill these key roles. Although these new leaders are bright and motivated, they often have narrow technical backgrounds and lack the leadership breadth and depth necessary for the new positions. The unfortunate result is that many of these leaders leave the organization because of **inadequate preparation for promotion.**

For example, a relatively young woman attorney was promoted to be the vice president of human resources in a large telecommunications firm. Although she was extremely bright and ambitious, it soon became apparent that she lacked much of the necessary skill or knowledge. Although she tried very hard to be successful, she made a number of poor decisions and failed to earn the respect of her staff. After six months she was given a generous separation package and asked to leave the company. According to Van Velsor and Leslie (1995), this is a relatively new derailment theme. Given the contributing factors, it is also a theme that is likely to be more prevalent in the future.

Most derailed managers manifested several of these themes; the presence of only one of these behavioral patterns was usually not enough for derailment.

The first and paramount responsibility of anyone who purports to manage is to manage the self: one's own integrity, character, ethics, knowledge, wisdom, temperament, words, and acts. It is a complex, unending, incredibly difficult, oft-shunned task. We spend little time and rarely excel at self-management precisely because it is so much more difficult than prescribing and controlling the behavior of others. However, without management of self, people are not fit for authority no matter how much they acquire, for the more authority they acquire the more dangerous they become. It is management of the self that should occupy 50 percent of our time and the best of our ability. And when we do that, the ethical, moral, and spiritual elements of management are inescapable.

Dee Hock

The only exception to this rule was a failure to meet business objectives. Managers who did not follow through with commitments, broke promises, lied, were unethical, and did not get results did not stay on the high-potential list for long. Although this research has not identified any unique derailment patterns for minorities, some male-female differences have been noted. Females were more likely to derail because of their inability to deal with broader and more complex organizational issues or to lead people from different technical backgrounds than their own. Males were more likely to derail because of their arrogance, inflexibility, or abrasive interpersonal style.

One might think that most managers exhibiting derailment behavioral patterns would be aware of the negative impact they have on others. Unfortunately, this is not always so. Many managers on the path to derailment are simply unaware of the way they come across to others. Recent research on self-defeating behaviors may explain how these counterproductive behavior patterns develop and why some managers lack insight into their behavior. According to Cudney and Hardy (1993), a **self-defeating behavior** is an action or attitude that once helped an individual cope with a stressful experience but interferes with the individual's ability to cope in new situations.

A list of some of the more common self-defeating behaviors can be found in Table 8–2. You can also see that the behaviors in Table 8–2 are similar to the derailment themes and the dark-side personality traits previously identified in Chapter 7. Like the behaviors associated with dark-side personality traits, a big part of the problem with self-defeating behaviors is that they are highly practiced and often performed automatically, with little conscious thought. Furthermore, a person may rationalize the appropriateness of a self-defeating behavior by recalling some particular situation where the behavior *was* adaptive (or seemed so). But problems may occur when such behaviors get generalized from *unusual* circumstances to *most* circumstances. For example, everyone worries about some things sometimes (e.g., how an interview is going to go; whether your

TABLE 8–2   Common Self-Defeating Behaviors

Procrastination	Suspiciousness
Defensiveness	Overcommitted
Worrying	Overly critical
Alienating	Rigidity
Hostility	Overcontrolling
Perfectionism	Inability to trust others

Source: M. R. Cudney and R. E. Hardy, *Self-Defeating Behaviors* (San Francisco: HarperCollins. 1993).

presentation made a good impression on the audience, whom to select for an important assignment, whether to major in this subject or that). Worrying becomes a problem, however, when it becomes habitual and consuming—when it keeps you from *doing* anything else or from actually *making* a decision. It may never be particularly helpful, but that's when it becomes truly self-defeating.

How could such a seemingly irrational and counterproductive behavior ever become a habit for some people? Strange as it may seem, it can happen through reinforcement. The head of a management consulting firm was asked to open a new office in a large U.S. city. He worked an average of 70–80 hours a week identifying and building relationships with and delivering products and services to key clients. These efforts paid off, and in less than three years the office had grown from 1 to 15 people and from $50,000 to $2,500,000 in annual revenue. As staff and revenues grew, the head of the firm was reinforced through bonus and salary increases to continue to build relationships with, and deliver services to, clients. Unfortunately, this leader failed to acknowledge the importance of supporting, coaching, and developing his people—he was a classic task-focused, 9,1 leader. Although this style of leadership was effective for opening the office, his overcommitment to task performance began to have a debilitating effect on the morale of the office. The leader in this case was fortunate enough to recognize the impact of his self-defeating behaviors, and was able to utilize some of the techniques in the next section to change these behaviors, improve morale, and continue to obtain good business results. Another example of the potential consequences of self-defeating behaviors is in Highlight 8.5.

Changing Behavior

Why Change Behavior?

The material covered so far can help leadership practitioners better understand the key behaviors associated with success; how successful leadership behaviors may vary depending on the country, culture, or business; what kind of behaviors could get them into trouble; and how to get feedback on these behaviors. But the fact of the matter is that knowing this information is not enough. Ultimately, some of the leader's behavior needs to *change*. But changing behavior, especially long-standing patterns of behavior, can be quite difficult.

> *Organizations don't change; people change. If you want your organization to do something differently, then you'll have to figure out how to get people to change their behavior.*
>
> David B. Peterson

How many times have you asked yourself how you could possibly change your own or another's behavior? Learning how to change your own and others' behaviors is a key leadership skill, given that situations, technology, organizational structure, followers, bosses, products, rules and regulations, and competitors seem to be in a constant state of flux. Moreover, think about the new behaviors and skills

The Invisible Barrier—What Precludes Black Managers from Advancement?

Highlight 8.5

Herdie Baisden, a black general manager and vice president of a management consulting firm, has investigated why black managers failed to advance in many organizations. Working with a variety of psychological assessment instruments as well as 360-degree feedback tools, Baisden noted that black managers tended to react differently to negative feedback than white managers. Baisden stated that blacks tended to dismiss this information as a product of racism rather than viewing it as a springboard for improvement. Blacks also tended to avoid feedback because they felt they needed to be exceptionally competent to succeed and wanted to project an image that "everything is under control and I don't need any help." When black managers did seek feedback from others, they often turned to others they could trust—other blacks. Blacks make up only 6 percent of management but they turned to blacks 22 percent of the time when soliciting feedback. These reactions often resulted in distorted 360-degree feedback ratings for black managers. These individuals tended to overrate their own performance and have bigger self-other gaps between their own ratings and their bosses' ratings of them when compared to white managers.

Baisden stated that some of these protective behaviors may be natural outgrowths of the work situations facing black managers. If a black manager perceives that a work environment is nonsupportive at best or hostile at worst, then these behaviors make sense. Unfortunately, these reactions ultimately become self-defeating behaviors, as they prevent black managers from getting the feedback they need in order to improve. Baisden maintains that blacks wishing to advance need to be receptive to feedback from others. This not only provides them with developmental ideas, it also tells the organization that the manager is willing to take risks and grow.

Source: H. Baisden, *PDI Indicator: The Rise of Black Managers* (Minneapolis: Personnel Decisions, 1993).

you will need to acquire as you move from individual contributor, first-line supervisor, midlevel manager to executive roles. Just as the head of the management consulting firm learned to add more supportive or employee-centered behaviors to his repertoire, so must you learn how to adapt your behavior to meet the changing demands of the role or situation (see Highlight 8.6). But learning how to change your own behavior is often not enough. Good leaders also know how to change and modify the behaviors of their followers so that they can be more effective team members and better achieve team goals. In the next section we discuss research

Traits and Behavior Change

Highlight 8.6

Just as basketball skills can improve with practice, so too can leadership skills. For example, shooting 200 free throws a day should improve a player's free throw shooting percentages in games, and taking advantage of public-speaking opportunities can improve a leader's public-speaking skills. The degree of practice needed to develop proficiency in a skill will, of course, vary from person to person. Almost everyone can learn the skill of solving algebraic problems. However, people with relatively greater quantitative ability will learn how to solve more difficult algebraic problems, will solve them faster, and will be more likely to apply them in novel situations than people with weaker quantitative ability. Similarly, leaders with higher dominance, sociability, and emotional stability scores may benefit more from a relatively brief public-speaking course than introverted leaders who do not have a strong desire to influence others. This does not mean the latter cannot benefit from a public-speaking course, only that they may need to work longer at developing the skill than others. Thus, just as natural athleticism can make learning a new sport less difficult, so too can traits, cognitive abilities, values, or preferences help or hinder the development of a new leadership skill. Both initial individual differences and practice play important roles in the acquisition and development of leadership skills.

surrounding three common methods of behavioral change: development planning, coaching, and mentoring. While this section is primarily research focused, practical tips on how to change behavior through development planning and coaching can be found in Part V of this book.

Development Planning

How many times have you made a resolution to change a habit, only to discover two months later that you are still exhibiting the same behaviors? This is often the fate of well-intentioned New Year's resolutions. Most people do not even make such resolutions since the failure rate is so high. Given this track record, you might wonder if it is even possible to change one's behavior, particularly if it has been reinforced over time and is exhibited almost automatically. Fortunately, however, it *is* possible to change behavior, even long-standing habits. For example, many people permanently quit smoking or

> *When you're in a new job where you're stretched, your focus should be on learning, not getting an A.*
> Mary Dee Hicks

drinking without going through any type of formal program (Miller & Rollnick, 1991). Others may change after they gain insight into how their behavior affects others. Some will need support to maintain a behavioral change over time, while still others seem destined to never change.

Managers seem to fall into the same categories; some managers change once they gain insight, others change with support, and others may not ever change. But do people just fall into one of these groups by accident? Is there any way to stack the odds in favor of driving behavioral change? Research by Hazucha, Hezlett, & Schneider (1993); McCauley, Ruderman, Ohlott, & Morrow (1994); Hezlett & Koonce (1995); Peterson & Hicks (1995, 1996); Dalton (1998); DeNisi & Kluger (2000); Behar, Arvidson, Omilusik, Ellsworth, & Morrow (2000); and Peterson (2001) provides several suggestions that leaders can take to accelerate the development of their own leadership skills. We can use the Development Pipeline described in Chapter 3 as a way to categorize these suggestions. As seen in Figure 8.5, the first step in changing behavior is knowing what to work on. Leaders need to have insight about their development needs, and 360-degree feedback can provide very useful information in this regard. Other sources of information about development needs can come from the results of an assessment center, a performance appraisal, or direct feedback from others.

> *Nine out of 10 information technology workers said they would feel more loyal to their employer if they had an individual development plan, but only 30 percent reported having any kind of development plan.*
>
> Jeff Stoner

The next step in developing one's own leadership skills is working on development goals that matter. No leader has all of the knowledge and skills necessary to be successful; as a result most leaders have multiple development needs. Leaders need to determine which new skills will have the highest personal and organizational payoffs and build development plans that address these needs. The development plan should be focused on only one or two needs; plans addressing more than this tend to be overwhelming and unachievable. If leaders have more than two development needs, then they should first work to acquire one or two skills before moving on to the next set of development needs.

Figure 8–5 indicates that acquiring new knowledge and skills is the next step in the Development Pipeline. For leaders, this means creating a written

FIGURE 8.5

The Development Pipeline

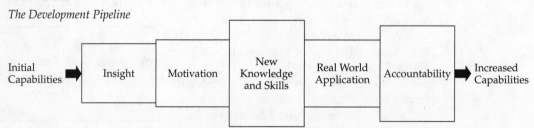

development plan that capitalizes on available books, seminars, college courses, e-learning modules, and so forth, to acquire the knowledge underlying a particular development need (see Figure 8.6). For example, you can either learn how to delegate through the school

> The more you crash, the more you learn.
>
> David B. Peterson

of hard knocks or take a seminar to learn the best practices of delegation skills. As we will see, knowledge alone is not enough to develop a new skill, but relevant books and courses can accelerate the learning process. In addition, it is

FIGURE 8.6

A sample development plan

FOCUS: Career and Development Objectives
Career Objectives: To become a senior manager *Strategies: Advancement, mastery* *One Development Objective: To improve my active listening skills*

Criteria for Success
I will have successfully improved my active listening skills when I can go an entire week without interrupting anyone.

IMPLEMENT: Action Steps	SEEK FEEDBACK & SUPPORT: Whom to Involve	Reassess Date
- *I will listen to the entire message before sharing my thoughts at staff meetings.* - *I will not interrupt my direct reports in our morning operations meetings.* - *I will use one paraphrase, open-ended question, or a reflecting statement in my conversations with peers and direct reports I see daily.*	- *Bob (peer), Steve (peer)* - *Ann, Carl, Tim (direct reports)* - *Bob (peer), Lisa (direct report)*	- *Weekly* - *Daily* - *Daily*
Stretch Assignments	Whom to Involve	Reassess Date
Operations Project Team (this is a highly contentious team that will really challenge my listening skills)	*Dianne (peer)* *Frank (peer)*	*15 February*
Resources: Books or Seminars		Reassess Date
- *Read the chapter in the Successful Manager's Handbook; Listen to Others* - *Attend the Organizational Communication module training on interpersonal and communication skills*		*15 December* *15 January*
REFLECT WITH A PARTNER		When
- *I will get monthly feedback on my progress with Steve (boss)*		*Monthly*

important not to underestimate the power of having a written development plan. Leaders (and followers) who have a written plan seem more likely to keep development on their radar screens and take the actions necessary to acquire new skills.

Taking courses and reading books are good ways for leaders to acquire foundational knowledge, but new skills will only be acquired when they are practiced on the job. Just as surgeons can read about and watch a surgery but will only perfect a surgical technique through repeated practice, so too will leaders only acquire needed skills if they practice them on the job. Therefore, good development plans capitalize upon on-the-job experiences to hone needed leadership skills. Peterson (2001) wrote that most leadership positions offer ample opportunities to develop new skills, provided that leaders leverage all of the experiences available to them. These on-the-job activities are so important to development that 70 to 80 percent of the action steps in a development plan should be job related.

The last step in acquiring new skills is accountability, and there are several ways to make this happen with a development plan. One way to build in accountability is to have different people provide ongoing feedback on the action steps taken to develop a skill. For example, leaders could ask for feedback from a peer or direct report on their listening skills immediately after staff meetings. Another way to build accountability is to periodically review progress on development plans with the boss. This way the boss can look for opportunities to help the leader further practice developing skills and determine when it is time to add new development needs to the plan.

It is important to realize that **development planning** is more than a plan—it is really a process (Peterson & Hicks, 1995). Good development plans are constantly being revised as new skills are learned or new opportunities to develop skills become available. Leaders who take the time to write out and execute best-practice development plans usually report the most improvement in later 360-degree feedback ratings. Development planning provides a methodology for leaders to improve their behavior, and much of this development can occur as they go about their daily work activities.

Coaching

Development plans tend to be self-focused; leaders and followers use them as a road map for changing their own behaviors. When trying to change the behavior of followers, however, leaders can often do more than review a follower's development plan, provide ongoing feedback, or review plans periodically with followers. The next step in followers' development often involves coaching. Coaching is a key leadership skill, as it can help leaders to improve the bench strength of the group, which in turn should help the group to accomplish its goals. Because of its role in development, coaching can also help to retain high-quality followers

Coaching is the quickest, most customized, and most powerful behavior change technique available to a leader.

David B. Peterson

(Wenzel, 2000). Because of these outcomes, coaching is a popular topic these days, but it is also a frequently misunderstood one. It is hoped that the material in this section will help to clarify what coaching is, and identify some best-coaching practices.

Coaching is the "process of equipping people with the tools, knowledge, and opportunities they need to develop themselves and become more success-ful" (Peterson & Hicks, 1996, p. 14). In general, there are two types of coaching, informal and formal coaching. **Informal coaching** can occur anywhere in an organization, and occurs whenever a leader helps followers to change their behaviors. According to Peterson and Hicks (1996), informal coaching generally consists of five steps. In *forging a partnership,* leaders build a trusting relationship with their followers, identify followers' career goals and motivators, and learn how their followers view the organization and their situation. The key question to be answered in this first step of coaching is "development for what?" Where do the followers want to go with their careers? Why do they want to go there? The answers to these questions help to create a target or end goal as well as a personal payoff for development. Nevertheless, if a leader fails to build a rela-tionship based on mutual trust with a follower, then chances are the follower will not heed the leader's guidance and advice. Therefore, it is important that coaches also *determine the level of mutual trust,* and then improve the relationship if necessary before targeting development needs or providing feedback and advice. Too many inexperienced coaches either fail to build trust, or take the relationship for granted, with the long-term end result being little, if any, behav-ioral change, and a frustrated leader and follower.

Once career goals have been identified and a solid, trusting relationship has been built, leaders then need to *inspire commitment.* In this step, leaders work closely with followers to gather and analyze data to determine development needs. A leader and a follower may review appraisals of past performance, feed-back from peers or former bosses, project reports, 360-degree feedback reports, and any organizational standards that pertain to the follower's career goals. By reviewing this data, the leader and the follower should be able to identify and prioritize those development needs most closely aligned with career goals.

The next step in the coaching process involves *growing skills.* Followers use their prioritized development needs to create a development plan, and leaders in turn develop a **coaching plan** that spells out precisely what they will do to support the followers' development plan. Leaders and followers then review and discuss the development and coaching plans, make necessary adjustments, and execute the plans.

Just because a plan is developed does not mean it will be executed flaw-lessly. Learning often is a series of fits and starts, and sometimes followers either get distracted by operational requirements or get into developmental ruts. In the step called *promote persistence,* leaders help followers to manage the mundane, day-to-day aspects of development. Leaders can help followers refocus on their development by capitalizing on opportunities to give followers relevant, on-the-spot feedback. Once the new behavior has been practiced a number of times and becomes part of the follower's behavioral repertoire, then leaders help followers to *transfer the skills to new environments* by applying the skills in new settings and revising their development plans. In this step, leaders need to also ask themselves how they themselves are role-modeling development and whether they are creating an environment that fosters individual development.

There are several points about informal coaching worth additional comment. First, the five-step process identified by Peterson and Hicks (1996) can be used by leadership practitioners to diagnose why behavioral change is *not* occurring and what can be done about it. Second, informal coaching can and does occur anywhere in the organization. Senior executives can use this model to develop their staffs, peers can use it to help each other, and so forth. Third, this process is just as effective for high-performing followers as it is for low-performing followers. Leadership practitioners have a tendency to forget to coach their solid or top followers, yet these individuals are often making the greatest contributions to team or organizational success. Moreover, research has shown that the top performers in a job often produce 20–50 percent more than the average performer, depending on the complexity of the job (Hunter, Schmidt, & Judiesch, 1990). So if leaders would focus on moving their solid performers into the highest-performing ranks and making their top performers even better, chances are their teams might be substantially more effective than if they only focused on coaching those doing most poorly (see Figure 8.7).

Fourth, both "remote" coaching of people and coaching of individuals from other cultures can be particularly difficult (Curphy, 1996a; Peterson & Hicks, 1996, 1997). It is more difficult for leaders to build trusting relationships with followers when they are physically separated by great distances. The same may be true with followers from other cultures—what may be important to, say, a

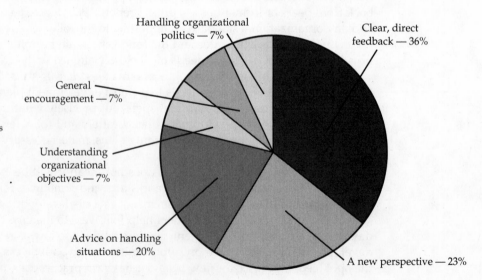

FIGURE 8.7

What were the most useful factors in the coaching you received?

Source: "The Business Leader as Development Coach," *PDI Portfolio*, Winter 1996, p. 6.

Handling organizational politics — 7%

Clear, direct feedback — 36%

General encouragement — 7%

Understanding organizational objectives — 7%

Advice on handling situations — 20%

A new perspective — 23%

Kenyan follower and how this person views the world may be very different from what his or her Dutch or Singaporean leader believes.

The kinds of behaviors that need to be developed can also vary considerably by culture. For example, one senior executive for a high-tech firm was coaching one of his Japanese direct reports on how to do better presentations to superiors. The follower's style was formal, stiff, and somewhat wooden, and the leader wanted the follower to add some humor and informality to his presentations. However, the follower said that by doing so he would lose the respect of his Japanese colleagues, so his commitment to this change was understandably low. What was agreed upon was that his style was very effective in Japan, but that it needed to change when he was giving presentations in the United States.

Informal coaching can help groups to be successful as well as to reduce turnover among employees, but what does it take to be a good informal coach? Research by Wenzel (2000) showed that the most effective informal coaches had a unique combination of leadership traits and skills. Leaders with higher levels of intelligence, surgency, and agreeableness were often more effective as coaches than those with lower scores. These leadership traits were the foundation for the relationship building, listening, assertiveness, and feedback skills associated with effective informal coaches. Good informal coaches use these traits and skills to build trusting relationships with their followers, build best-practice coaching and development plans, and deliver tough and honest feedback when necessary. Suggestions on how to improve relationship building, listening, assertiveness, feedback, and informal coaching skills can be found in Part V of this book.

Most people are familiar with the idea of a personal fitness trainer, a person who helps design a fitness program tailored to a specific individual's needs and goals. **Formal coaching** programs provide a similar kind of service for executives and managers in leadership positions (Curphy, 1996a; Peterson, 1996, 1999; Witherspoon & White, 1996, 1997; Peterson & Hicks, 1998). Approximately 65 percent of the Global 1000 companies use some form of formal coaching (Peterson & Hicks, 1998). Formal coaching programs are quite individualized by their very nature, but several common features deserve mention. There is a one-on-one relationship between the manager and the coach (i.e., consultant) which lasts from six months to more than a year. The process usually begins with the manager's completion of an extensive battery of personality, intelligence, interests, value, and 360-degree feedback instruments, as well as with interviews by the coach of other individuals in the manager's world of work. As the result of the assessment phase of this process, both the manager and the coach have a clear picture of development needs and how the different components of the building-block model interact and affect these needs. The coach and the manager meet regularly (roughly monthly) to review the results of the feedback instruments and work on building skills and practicing target behaviors. Role plays and videotape are used extensively during these sessions, and coaches provide immediate feedback to clients practicing new behaviors in realistic work situations. Another valuable outcome of coaching programs can involve clarification of managers' values, and identification of discrepancies between their espoused values and their actual behaviors and devising strategies to better align their behaviors with their values.

Approximately 6,000 managers and executives have been through one of the coaching programs designed by Peterson and his associates (Peterson, 1993a, 1993b, 1996; Peterson & Hicks, 1996, 1998). Some were derailment candidates, but many were not. Some were high potentials with a few rough edges, and others were successful managers and executives who needed leadership or skill training in one or two key areas. This large sample and PDI's commitment to research have produced some interesting findings.

A formal coaching program can cost more than $30,000 (Smith, 1993; Curphy, 1996a), and it is reasonable to ask, Is it worth it? The answer seems to be an unqualified yes. A solid body of research shows that well-designed and well-executed coaching programs result in three times more behavioral change than more traditional learning and training approaches (Peterson, 1993a, 1993b, 1996; Witherspoon & White, 1997). Moreover, the behavioral changes appear to be in place one year after the termination of a coaching program, indicating permanent behavioral change (Peterson, 1999). Such changes can be particularly important if the person making them—that is, the leader being coached—is in a highly placed or very responsible position. Most coaching candidates have hundreds, if not thousands, of subordinates, and usually oversee multimillion- or multibillion-dollar budgets. Thus, the money spent on a coaching program can be relatively small in comparison to the budgets and resources the candidates control. Many organizations believe if a coaching program helps a leader better utilize resources or get higher productivity from workers, then it is likely that they will see a high return on investment from a coaching program.

Mentoring

Mentoring is a personal relationship in which a more experienced mentor (usually someone two to four levels higher in an organization) acts as a guide, role model, and sponsor of a less experienced protégé. Mentors provide protégés with knowledge, advice, challenge, counsel, and support about career opportunities, organizational strategy and policy, office politics, and so forth (Murray & Owen, 1991; Lall, 1999; Ragins & Cotton, 1999; Ragins, Cotton, & Miller, 2000; Thomas, 2001). Although mentoring has a strong developmental component, it is not the same as coaching. One key difference is that mentoring may not target specific development needs. Protégés often meet with their mentors to get a different perspective of the organization or for advice on potential committee and task force assignments or promotion opportunities. Another difference is that this guidance is not coming from the protégé's immediate supervisor. Protégés often do receive informal coaching from their boss, but may be more apt to seek career guidance and personal advice from their mentors. Another difference is that the mentor may not even be part of the organization. Some mentors may have retired from the organization, or may have been someone for whom the protégé worked a number of years earlier.

> *Parents are the first leadership trainers in life.*
>
> Bruce Avolio

As in coaching, there are both formal and informal mentoring programs. *Informal mentoring* occurs when a protégé and mentor build a long-term relationship based on friendship, similar interests, and mutual respect. These relationships often begin with the protégé working in some part of the mentor's organization or on a high-visibility project for the mentor. *Formal mentoring* programs occur when the organization assigns a relatively inexperienced but high-potential leader to one of the top executives in the company. The protégé and mentor get together on a regular basis so that the protégé can gain exposure and learn more about how decisions are made at the top of the organization. Oftentimes organizations implement formal mentoring programs to accelerate the development of female or minority protégés (Thomas, 2001; Raggins, Cotton, & Miller, 2000).

Mentoring is quite prevalent in many organizations today. Steinberg and Foley (1999) reported that 74 percent of the noncommissioned officers and officers in the U.S. Army had mentors, and Lall (1999) reported that 67 percent of all U.S. Navy admirals had mentors sometime in their career. Moreover, many admirals reported having an average of 3.5 mentors by the time they retired. Raggins, Cotton, and Miller (2000) found formal mentoring programs, although well intended, were much less effective than informal mentoring for protégé compensation and promotion. The reason for this is that most formal mentoring programs have a difficult time replicating the strong emotional bonds found in informal programs. In addition, most formal mentoring programs only lasted a year, whereas many informal mentoring relationships can last a lifetime.

Thomas (2001) examined the role mentoring played in the careers of minority leaders. He reported that minority leaders who made it to the top of their organizations often had two key qualities. First, successful minority executives were concerned with getting the right experiences and developing the right foundation of leadership skills when they first joined the organization. Their focus was more on personal growth than with titles and rewards. Second, they had an extensive set of mentors and corporate sponsors who provided guidance and support over their careers. These mentors and sponsors helped the executives to develop the three Cs critical to advancement: confidence, competence, and credibility. Thomas (2001) also stated that the most successful white mentor–minority protégé relationships recognized that race was a potential barrier to advancement but were still able to bring up and work through touchy issues. Less successful white mentor–minority protégé relationships engaged in "protective hesitation," in which race or sensitive issues were avoided, ignored, or discounted.

Because of the benefits of informal mentoring, leadership practitioners should look for opportunities to build mentoring relationships with senior leaders whenever possible. However, Lall (1999) aptly pointed out that protégés cannot make these relationships happen by themselves. In many cases, mentors seek out protégés, or mentors and protégés seek out each other to build relationships. But leaders and leaders-to-be can do a couple of things to improve the odds of finding a mentor. The first step is to do one's current job extremely well. Mentors are always looking for talent, and they are very unlikely to take someone under their wing who appears unmotivated or incompetent. The second step is to look for opportunities to gain visibility and build social relationships with potential mentors.

Working on a key task force, doing presentations for the executive committee, or signing up for community activities sponsored by a top executive are just a few of the pathways one could take to gain the attention of potential mentors.

Summary

Leaders can benefit from the leadership behavior research in several ways. First, the behavioral approach has served the important purpose of directing attention to identifying types of leadership behavior critical to success. Second, the behavioral approach allows leadership practitioners to focus on concrete and specific examples of leader behavior. Third, an outgrowth of the behavioral approach has been the development of competency models and 360-degree feedback instruments. The 360-degree feedback instruments can be used to provide valuable feedback to leadership practitioners and often play important roles in many training, coaching, and succession-planning programs.

Research has also helped to identify factors that can cause high-potential managers to fail. This research on managerial derailment has identified "fatal flaws," including such counterproductive leadership behaviors as arrogance, insensitivity, or untrustworthiness. Another body of research indicates that many of these derailment factors may be self-defeating behaviors, behaviors that developed as a way of coping with a stressful situation but are misapplied in other situations.

The chapter also examined the process of behavior change. Research shows that some managers seem to be able to change on their own after gaining insight on how their behavior affects others. This insight is often gained through reflection, in-depth assessments, or 360-degree feedback. Nevertheless, more managers will change if some formal system or process of behavioral change is put into place; these systems include development planning, informal and formal coaching programs, and mentorships. Development planning is the process of pinpointing development needs, creating development plans, implementing plans, and reflecting on and revising plans on a regular bases. A development plan is a written document that specifies strategies and tactics for exploiting behavioral strengths and overcoming weaknesses. Good action plans focus on one or two development needs, capitalize upon on-the-job experiences, and specify sources of feedback. Organizations with formal development systems are likely to realize greater behavioral changes from a greater number of managers than organizations having no system or only an informal one.

Leaders can create development plans for themselves, and they can also help their followers with behavioral change through coaching or mentoring programs. Informal coaching programs often consist of a series of steps designed to create permanent behavioral changes in followers, and both leaders and followers play active roles in informal coaching programs. Mentoring programs have many of the same objectives as coaching programs but take place between an individual (the protégé) and a leader several levels higher in the organization (the mentor).

Key Terms

Questions

1. Could you create a competency model for college professors? For college students? If you used these competency models to create 360-degree feedback tools, who would be in the best position to give professors and students feedback?
2. Do you know anyone who has derailed from a leadership position? What did this person do? Use the leader-follower-situation model to better understand why this individual derailed.
3. Can you identify any self-defeating behaviors in yourself ? In what situations are these behaviors likely to be exhibited? How could you ensure these behaviors are not misapplied?
4. What would a development plan for students look like? How could you capitalize on school experiences as part of a development plan?
5. What would a leadership coaching or mentoring program for students look like? How could you tell whether the program worked?

Skills

The leadership skills relevant to this chapter include:
• Providing constructive feedback
• Setting goals

• Development planning
• Coaching
• Empowerment

Activity

1. Read the Development Planning material in Part V of this book. Complete a GAPS analysis and create your own development plan. Share your development plan with someone in class. Your partner should use the Development Planning Checklist found in the Coaching section of Part V to critique your plan. Check with your partner in two to four weeks to review progress on your plans.

2. Read the Coaching material in Part V of this book. Complete a GAPS analysis for someone you would like to coach. Use the results of the GAPS analysis to create development and coaching plans for this individual.

III FOCUS ON THE FOLLOWERS

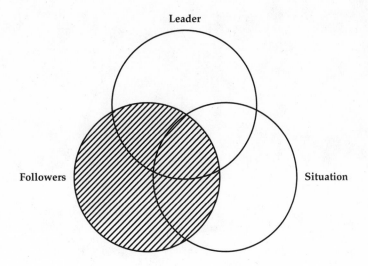

W e began Part II with Napoleon's belief that the individual leader is the crucial element of leadership. We begin Part III by qualifying that sentiment. Although the importance of a good leader cannot be denied, followers also play an equally important, if often overlooked, role in the success of any group or organization. It was not, after all, Napoleon by himself who won or lost battles; his soldiers obviously played some part too. In Part III we look at the vital role played by followers in affecting the leadership process.

9 Motivation, Satisfaction, and Performance

Introduction

P olls estimate that if companies could get 3.7 percent more work out of each employee, the equivalent of 18 more minutes of work for each eight-hour shift, the gross domestic product in the U.S. would swell by $355 billion, twice the total GDP of Greece.

The Gallup Organization

If you go back to Chapter 1, we defined leadership as "the process of influencing an organized group toward accomplishing its goals." Implicit in this definition is the ability to motivate others, and many people believe this may be one of the most important qualities of a good leader. The importance of follower motivation is suggested in findings from diverse work groups that most people believe they could give as much as 15 percent or 20 percent more effort at work than they now do with no one, including their own bosses, recognizing any difference. Perhaps even more startling, these workers also believed they could give 15 percent or 20 percent *less* effort with no one noticing any difference (Kinlaw, 1991). Moreover, variation in work output varies significantly across leaders and followers. Hunter, Schmidt, and Judiesch (1990) estimated the top 15 percent of workers in any particular job produced from 20 to 50 percent more output than the average worker, depending on the complexity of the job. Put another way, the best computer programmers or salesclerks might write up to 50 percent more programs or process 50 percent more customer orders. Might better methods of motivating workers lead to higher productivity from *all* the workers? And are more motivated workers happier or more satisfied workers? What can leaders do to increase the motivation and satisfaction levels of their followers?

Creating highly motivated and satisfied followers depends, most of all, on understanding others. Therefore, whereas motivation is an essential part of leadership, it is appropriate to include it in this part of the book, which focuses

241

on the followers. As an overview, this chapter will address three key areas. First, we will examine the links between leadership, satisfaction, motivation, and performance—four closely related concepts. Second, we will review the major theories and research for motivation and satisfaction. Last, and perhaps most important, we will discuss what leaders can do to enhance the motivation and satisfaction of their followers if they implement these different theories.

Defining Motivation, Satisfaction, and Performance

Motivation, satisfaction, and performance seem clearly related. For example, Colin Powell probably could have pursued a number of different vocations, but was *motivated* to complete ROTC and join the army. He was also motivated to put in extra time, energy, and effort in his various positions in the army, and he was judged or rated by his superiors as being an exceptional performer. His outstanding *performance* as an officer was crucial to his promotion as the head of the Joint Chiefs of Staff during the Reagan and Bush administrations and his later appointment as secretary of state. We could also infer that he was happy or *satisfied* with military life, as he was a career officer in the army. Figure 9.1 provides an overview of the relationships between leadership, motivation, satisfaction, and performance. As we can see, various leadership behaviors often result in more satisfied followers. Some of these leadership behaviors are related to building relationships or consideration (see Chapter 8) and properly implementing different motivational techniques. More satisfied followers are more likely to remain with the company and engage in activities that help others at work (i.e., organizational citizenship behaviors), and are less likely to retaliate against the leader or the organization. Followers who work for leaders who effectively solve problems and successfully implement various motivational techniques also tend to exert higher levels of effort toward the accomplishment of group goals. Research has shown that these follower behaviors result in higher levels of customer satisfaction and loyalty, which in turn leads to better team performance in retail, sales, or restaurant settings (Huselid, 1995; Sirota Consulting, 1998; Koys, 2001). Thus, the leader's ability to motivate followers is vitally important to both the morale and the performance of the work group. However, it is important to understand that the leader's use of good motivational techniques is not the only factor affecting group performance. Selecting the right people for the team (Chapter 4), correctly using power and influence tactics (Chapter 5), being seen as ethical and credible (Chapter 6), possessing many of the bright-side and none of the dark-side personality traits (Chapter 7), and acquiring the necessary resources and developing follower skills (Chapter 8) are other leadership factors affecting a group's ability to accomplish its goals.

Most people probably think of motivation as dealing with choices about what we do and how much effort we put into doing it. According to Kanfer

The real challenge [for leaders] is to manage human resources as effectively as possible in order to attain world-class performance.

Fred Luthans and
Alexander Stajkovic

FIGURE 9.1

Relationships between leadership, job satisfaction, and performance

Sources: M.A. Huselid, "The Impact of Human Resource Management Practices on Turnover, Productivity, and Corporate Financial Performance," *Academy of Management Journal* 38, no. 4 (1995), pp. 635–72; T. Butorac, *Recruitment and Retention: The Keys to Profitability at Carlson Companies*, presentation given at Personnel Decisions International, Minneapolis, MN, June 11, 2001; D.J. Koys, "The Effects of Employee Satisfaction, Organizational Citizenship Behavior, and Turnover on Organizational Effectiveness: A Unit Level, Longitudinal Study, *Personnel Psychology* 54, no. 1 (2001), pp. 101–14; J. Husserl, "Allied's Organizational Life Cycle," *Management Education & Development* 24, no. 3 (1998), p. 8; Sirota Consulting, *Establishing the Linkages between Employee Attitudes, Customer Attitudes, and Bottom-Line Results* (Chicago, IL: Author, 1998).

(1990), **motivation** is anything that provides *direction, intensity,* and *persistence* to behavior. Another definition considers the term *motivation* a sort of shorthand to describe choosing an activity or task to engage in, establishing the level of effort to put forth on it, and determining the degree of persistence in it over time (Campbell & Pritchard, 1976). Other researchers define motivation as a behavior probability; it is the likelihood an individual will initiate and continue exhibiting certain behaviors (Miller & Rollnick, 1991). Like personality traits and types, motivation is not directly observable; it must be inferred from behavior. We would infer that one person would be highly motivated to do well in school if she spent a lot of time studying for exams. She could choose to spend her time and energy on socializing, intramurals, or volunteer work, but because she is spending time outlining readings and reviewing class notes we say she is motivated to do well in school. At work, if one person regularly assembles twice

> *Only the mediocre are always at their best.*
>
> Jonathan Winters

as many radios as any other person in his work group—assuming all have the same abilities, skills, and resources—then we likely would say this first person is more motivated than the others. We use the concept of motivation to explain differences we see among people in the energy and direction of their behavior. Thus, the energy and effort Madeleine Albright expended advancing her career in the academic and the diplomatic communities or Konosuke Matsushita expended to grow his company would be examples of the direction, intensity, and persistence components of motivation.

Performance, on the other hand, concerns those behaviors directed toward the organization's mission or goals, or the products and services resulting from those behaviors. At work or school we can choose to perform a wide variety of behaviors, but performance would only include those behaviors related to the production of goods or services or obtaining good grades. Performance differs from **effectiveness,** which generally involves making judgments about the adequacy of behavior with respect to certain criteria such as work-group or organizational goals. Konosuke Matsushita was motivated to start and grow his company and performed those behaviors associated with building successful companies, and many people would judge these behaviors to be effective given the phenomenal growth of his business conglomerate. However, it is important to understand that performance is affected by more than a follower's motivation. Factors such as intelligence, skill, and the availability of key resources can affect a follower's behavior in accomplishing organizational goals (i.e., performance) independently of that person's level of motivation. *Thus, an adequate level of motivation may be a necessary but insufficient condition of effective performance.*

Fifty-five percent of workers are unengaged; 19 percent are so uninterested and negative about their jobs that they poison the workplace to the point that companies might be better off if they called in sick.

The Gallup Organization

Job satisfaction is not how *hard* one works or how *well* one works, but rather how much one *likes* a specific kind of job or work activity. Job satisfaction deals with one's attitudes or feelings about the job itself, pay, promotion or educational opportunities, supervision, co-workers, workload, and so on (Saal & Knight, 1988). Various polls over the past half century have consistently shown the vast majority of men and women report liking their jobs (see Campbell &

Source: Reprinted with special permission of King Features Syndicate.

Hyne, 1995; Health, Education, & Welfare Task Force, 1973; Hoppock, 1935; Smith, Scott, & Hulin, 1977; or Staines & Quinn, 1979). Research has also shown that people who are more satisfied with their jobs are more likely to engage in **organizational citizenship behaviors**—behaviors not directly related to one's job that are helpful to others at work. Organizational citizenship behaviors make for a more supportive workplace. Examples might include volunteering to help another employee with a task or project, or filling in for another employee when asked (Organ & Ryan, 1995; Chen, Mui, & Sego, 1998; Bettercourt, Gwinner, & Meuter, 2001). Happier workers tend to be more helpful workers.

Although people generally like the work they do, two related events have caused a downturn in job satisfaction levels among employees in the United States. Over the past 10 years, many organizations have downsized or substantially reduced the number of people on the company payroll. For example, Kodak and Digital Equipment Corporation have each eliminated over 25,000 positions, AT&T eliminated 60,000 jobs, and the U.S. military has shrunk by over a million positions since the early 1990s. These positions were eliminated to reduce costs and improve profitability, but they also dramatically increased the workload for the remaining workers (i.e., the same amount of work was being performed by fewer people), and severed the implicit contract between workers and employers (i.e., if workers performed at a high level, then employers guaranteed a job for life). The end result is that job dissatisfaction among workers is at an all-time high. Although people report being satisfied with what they do for a living, the forced overtime, increased workload, and erosion of trust between employers and employees has significantly lowered levels of job satisfaction (Howard, 1996; Curphy, 1998b; Mills, 1999; Quigley, 2001; Hales & Hales, 2001). As a result, more workers are leaving their jobs than ever before, and it is has been very difficult to maintain various indices of organizational effectiveness when many of the best and brightest employees are leaving the company. Job satisfaction may not have as direct an effect on the accomplishment of organizational goals as motivation or performance, but the indirect effects of reduced organizational citizenship behaviors or increased turnover are so important that leaders can ill afford to ignore them.

> *People don't leave companies, they leave bad bosses.*
>
> Beverly Kaye

As a result of the economic downturn, many leaders today are facing the dual challenges of having to achieve increasingly difficult unit performance goals while having fewer followers available to do the work. The best leaders and organizations understand that one way to meet these challenges is to recruit, develop, and retain top leadership and technical talent. Savvy companies that spend considerably more time and effort attracting, developing, and retaining the best people often report superior financial results (Butorac, 2001; Charan, Drotter, & Noel, 2001). For example, many of the organizations appearing in *Fortune* magazine's "The 100 Best Companies to Work For" also do very well when compared to the S&P 500 Index. *The best leaders may well be those who can motivate workers to perform at a high level while maintaining an equally high level of job satisfaction.*

Having now defined motivation, performance, and job satisfaction, we can explore their relationships a bit further. We have already noted how motivation does not always assure good performance. If followers lack the necessary skills or resources to accomplish a group task, then trying to "motivate them more" could be unproductive and even frustrating (Campbell, 1977; 1988). For example, no high school basketball team is likely to defeat the Los Angeles Lakers, however motivated the players may be. The players on the high school team simply lack the abilities and skills of the Lakers players. Higher motivation will usually only affect performance if followers already have the abilities, skills, and resources to get the job done. Motivating others is an important part of leadership, but not all of it; pep talks and rewards are not always enough.

The relationships between motivation and job satisfaction are a bit more straightforward—as a matter of fact, many theories of motivation are also theories of job satisfaction. The implicit link between satisfaction and motivation is that satisfaction increases when people accomplish a task, particularly when the task requires a lot of effort. It might also seem logical that *performance* must be higher among more satisfied workers, but actually this is not always so (Iaffaldano & Muchinsky, 1985; Podsakoff & Williams, 1986). It is just not true that happy workers are always the most productive ones, nor is it true that unhappy or dissatisfied workers are always the poorest performers. It is entirely possible, for example, for poorly performing workers to be fairly satisfied with their jobs (maybe because they are paid well yet do not have to work very hard, like Homer Simpson in the television show "The Simpsons"). It is also possible for dissatisfied workers to be relatively high performers (they may have a strong work ethic, or they may be trying to improve chances to get out of their current job). Despite the intuitive appeal of believing that satisfied workers usually perform better, it may be that satisfaction has only an indirect effect on performance (Locke & Latham, 1990). Nevertheless, having both satisfied *and* high-performance followers is a goal leaders should usually strive to achieve.

Understanding and Influencing Follower Motivation

So what do leaders do to "motivate" followers to accomplish group goals? Are all leaders and followers motivated the same way? Is there a universal theory of motivation? In other words, did Madeleine Albright, Colin Powell, or Konosuke Matsushita use the same or different techniques to motivate their followers? As seen in Highlight 9.1, organizations spend billions on motivating the troops, but do these interventions actually help to improve job satisfaction, retention, and performance? Research can provide the answers to these questions, and few topics of human behavior have been the subject of so much attention as that of motivation. So much has been written about motivation that a comprehensive review of the subject is beyond the scope of this book. We will, however, survey several major approaches to understanding worker motivation, as well as address the implications of these approaches for follower satisfaction and performance. (See

Organizations Spend Billions on Motivational Programs for Employees, and All They Get Are Burned Feet

Highlight 9.1

The past five years has seen a virtual explosion in the motivation industry. Top speakers, such as Spencer Johnson *(Who Moved My Cheese?)*, Norman Schwarzkopf, or Tom Peters often command $60,000 for a one-hour speaking engagement, and they are often booked for months in advance. In addition, companies are now using more extreme activities, such as firewalking, skydiving, whitewater rafting, rock climbing, and bungee jumping to motivate the troops. Software consulting firm EMC has spent $625,000 to have 5,000 employees walk over burning coals. But do these expensive speakers and extreme activities actually help to improve organizational performance? Unfortunately, exhaustive research has shown there is virtually no link between motivational spending and company revenues, profitability, or market share. Perhaps the biggest problem is that employees may find it difficult to see the link between walking over a bed of hot coals and making another 20 sales calls every week. Other than bankrolling the motivation industry, these programs do seem to have another benefit. Nine U.S. Air Force recruiters had to go to the emergency room after they received second- and third-degree burns on their feet after one of these "motivational" programs.

Sources: D. Jones, "Firms Spend Billions to Fire Up Workers—With Little Luck," *USA Today*, May 10, 2001, pp. 1–2A; P.G. Chronis, "9 Burn Feet in National Guard Recruiters' Fire Walk," *Denver Post*, December 28, 1998, pp. 1A, 17A.

Kanfer, 1990; Campbell & Pritchard, 1976; and Personnel Decisions International, 2000 for more comprehensive reviews.) These motivational theories and approaches provide leadership practitioners with a number of suggestions to get followers to engage in and persist with different behaviors. It is important to understand that some motivational theories are particularly useful in certain situations but are not as applicable in others. Just as a carpenter can successfully build better wooden structures or furniture by having a larger set of tools, so can leadership practitioners solve a greater number of motivational problems among followers by becoming familiar with different motivational theories and approaches. People who have only hammers in their tool kits are more likely to

> *Some players you pat their butts, other players you kick their butts, and some players you leave alone.*
>
> Pete Rose

see every problem as a nail needing hammering, and it is not unusual for less effective leaders to call on a very limited number of approaches to any motivational problem. *Leaders who are knowledgeable about different motivational theories are more likely to choose the right theory for a particular follower and situation, and often have higher-performing and more satisfied employees as a result.*

It is important to understand that most performance problems can be attributed to unclear expectations, skill deficits, resource/equipment shortages, or a lack of motivation. Of these underlying causes, leaders seem to have the most difficulty recognizing and rectifying motivation problems. An example might help to illustrate this point. A major airline was having serious problems with the customer service of its flight attendants. Passenger complaints were on the rise and airplane loading (the average number of people per flight) was decreasing. The perceived lack of customer service was beginning to cost the airline market share and revenues; to fix the problem they decided to have all 10,000 flight attendants go through a two-day customer service training program. Unfortunately, passenger complaints only got worse after the training. A thorough investigation of the underlying cause of the problem revealed that flight attendants knew what they were supposed to do, had all of the skills necessary to perform the behaviors, and usually had the resources and equipment necessary to serve customers. The root cause was a lack of motivation to "go the extra mile" for customers. When asked what they found to be the most motivating aspect of being a flight attendant, most stated "time off." In other words the flight attendants were most motivated when they were *not* at work. Given that a strong union represented the flight attendants, how would you go about solving this dilemma? The next section will give you some ideas on how to resolve this and other motivation problems that you may face as a leader.

In this section we will discuss the key aspects of 10 different approaches to understanding motivation in a work or leadership context. We have organized the approaches into four broad categories: need theories, individual-difference approaches, cognitive theories, and situational approaches. This categorization seems helpful for explanatory purposes, even though it is admittedly atheoretical. These theories and approaches are listed in Table 9–1. For illustrative purposes we will also discuss how leadership practitioners could apply these approaches to motivate two fictitious followers, Julie and Ling Ling. Julie is a 21-year-old ski lift operator in Banff, Alberta. Her primary job is to ensure that people get on and off her ski lift safely. She also does periodic equipment safety checks and maintains the lift lines and associated areas. Julie works from 7:30 A.M. to 5:00 P.M. five days a week, gets paid a salary, and has a pass that allows her to ski for free whenever she is off work. Ling Ling is a 35-year-old real estate agent in Hong Kong. She works for an agency that locates and rents apartments for people on one- to three-year business assignments for various multinational companies. She works many evenings and weekends showing apartments, and gets paid a salary plus a commission for every apartment she rents. How the 10 approaches could be used to motivate Julie and Ling Ling will be discussed periodically throughout this section.

TABLE 9–1   Ten Motivational Approaches

Category	Theory or Approach	Major Themes or Characteristics
Need	Maslow's hierarchy of needs	Satisfy needs to change behavior.
	Alderfer's ERG theory	Can satisfy multiple needs simultaneously.
	Herzberg's two-factor theory	Hygiene factors result in dissatisfaction; motivators result in satisfaction.
Individual difference	Achievement orientation	Personality trait.
	Intrinsic motivation	People are more motivated to do some activities than others.
Cognitive	Goal setting	Set goals to change behavior.
	Expectancy theory	Motivate others by clarifying links between behaviors, performance, and rewards.
	ProMES	Motivate others by clarifying links between behaviors, performance, evaluations, rewards, and personal needs.
Situational	Job characteristics model	Modify task or job to increase motivation.
	Operant approach	Change rewards and punishments to change behavior.

Need Theories

One way to get followers to engage and persist with the behaviors needed to accomplish group goals is to appeal to their needs. What underlying needs do flight attendants have, and would they exhibit higher levels of customer service behaviors if leaders satisfied these needs? The three major need theories include Maslow's (1954) hierarchy of needs, Alderfer's (1969) existence-relatedness-growth (ERG) theory, and Herzberg's (1964, 1966) two-factor theory. These theories assume that all people share a common set of basic needs; the theories primarily differ in the types of needs that supposedly underlie or drive people's behavior. **Needs** refer to internal states of tension or arousal, or uncomfortable states of deficiency people are motivated to change (Kanfer, 1990). Hunger would be a good example of a need, as people are motivated to eat when they get hungry. Other needs might include the need to live in a safe and secure place, to belong to a group with common interests or social ties, or to do interesting and challenging work. If these needs were not being met, then people would choose to engage in and persist with certain behaviors until they were satisfied. According to these motivational approaches, leadership practitioners can get followers to engage in and persist with certain behaviors by correctly identifying and appeasing their needs.

Maslow's Hierarchy of Needs.   According to Maslow (1954), people are motivated by five basic sorts of needs. These include the need to survive physiologically, the need for security, the need for affiliation with other people (i.e., belongingness), the need for self-esteem, and the need for self-actualization.

FIGURE 9.2

Maslow's hierarchy of needs

Self-actualization needs

Esteem needs

Belongingness needs

Security needs

Physiological needs

Maslow's conceptualization of needs is usually represented by a triangle with the five levels of needs arranged in a hierarchy (see Figure 9.2) called, not surprisingly, the **hierarchy of needs.** According to Maslow, any person's behavior can be understood primarily as the effort directed to satisfy one particular level of need in the hierarchy. Which level happens to be motivating a person's behavior at any time depends on whether or not lower needs in the hierarchy have been satisfied. According to Maslow, lower-level needs must be satisfied before the next-higher level becomes salient in motivating behavior.

Maslow (1954) said higher-level needs like those for self-esteem or self-actualization would not become salient (even when unfulfilled) until lower needs were satisfied. Thus, a practical implication of his theory is that leaders may only be successful in motivating follower behavior by taking account of the follower's position on the needs hierarchy. Applying Maslow's hierarchy to Julie, it might be relatively inefficient to try to motivate our ski lift operator by appealing to how much pride she could take in a job well done (i.e., to her self-esteem) if she was underdressed for weather conditions. If her boss wanted Julie to do more, then she should first make sure that Julie's physiological (i.e., clothing) needs were met, that she worked and lived in a secure place, and that she had ample opportunities to socialize with other employees. Only after these lower needs have been met should the boss try to increase Julie's self-esteem. Thus, if leadership practitioners want to use Maslow's hierarchy of needs to motivate employees to work harder, then they need to determine where their followers fall on the needs hierarchy and ensure all lower-order needs are satisfied before appealing to their followers' self-esteem or self-actualization needs. Leadership practitioners should watch for "mismatches" between their motivational efforts and followers' *lowest* (on the hierarchy) unsatisfied needs.

ERG Theory.   Alderfer's (1969) **existence-relatedness-growth (ERG) theory** is similar to Maslow's hierarchy of needs. In the terms of ERG theory, *existence* needs basically correspond to Maslow's physiological and security needs; *relatedness* needs are like Maslow's social and esteem needs; and *growth* needs are similar to the need for self-actualization. Beyond those similarities, however, are two important differences.

First, Alderfer (1969) reported that people sometimes try to satisfy *more than one need at a time*. For example, even though a follower's existence needs may not be entirely satisfied, she may still be motivated to grow as a person. Second, he claimed *frustration of a higher-level need can lead to efforts to satisfy a lower-level need*. In other words, a follower who is continually frustrated in achieving some need might regress and exert effort to satisfy a lower need that has already been satisfied. For example, if Ling Ling had strong relatedness needs but was unable to build friendships with her co-workers, she might regress to satisfying her existence needs. Some of these behaviors might include moving to an upscale neighborhood; buying a more expensive wardrobe, a new sportscar, or new stereo equipment; or demanding more pay. Alderfer called this the **frustration regression hypothesis.**

The practical implications for motivating followers using ERG theory are threefold. First, leadership practitioners should identify the degree of need for existence, relatedness, and growth for their followers. Followers having relatively unmet existence or relatedness needs will focus their behaviors on satisfying these needs, and leadership practitioners may be able to help with these endeavors. Second, followers having relatively satisfied existence and relatedness needs are more apt to focus on growth needs. Leadership practitioners can get a lot of motivational "mileage" by helping followers satisfy their growth needs, as these followers are more willing to develop and master new skills, apply skills in new situations, look for more responsibility and independence, and strive to achieve greater personal and organizational challenges. Third, leadership practitioners should also be on the lookout for the frustration regression hypothesis among followers. If followers are repeatedly thwarted in satisfying a need, and have shifted their efforts to oversatisfying a lower-level need, then appealing to the need that was thwarted may be relatively fruitless. For instance, trying to motivate Ling Ling to work harder by stating the real estate agency is a team and needs to work together to get results will probably not result in substantial behavioral change for Ling Ling. Instead, the leader may need to work closely with Ling Ling to determine why she has been unable to satisfy her relatedness needs, and coach her on how to build relationships with others in the agency. Only after these relationships are established will the leader be able to motivate Ling Ling to work as a part of a team to get results.

Herzberg's Two-Factor Theory.   Herzberg (1964, 1966) developed the **two-factor theory** from a series of interviews he conducted with accountants and engineers. More specifically, he asked what satisfied them about their work and found that their answers usually could be sorted into five consistent categories.

TABLE 9–2   Motivators and Hygiene Factors of the Two-Factor Theory

Hygiene Factors	Motivators
Supervision	Achievement
Working conditions	Recognition
Co-workers	The work itself
Pay	Responsibility
Policies/procedures	Advancement and growth
Job security	

Source: Adapted from F. Herzberg, *Work and the Nature of Men* (Cleveland, OH: World Publishing, 1966).

Furthermore, rather than assuming that what dissatisfied people was always just the opposite of what satisfied them, he also specifically asked what *dissatisfied* people about their jobs. Surprisingly, the list of satisfiers and dissatisfiers represented entirely different aspects of work.

Herzberg labeled the factors that led to *satisfaction* at work **motivators,** and he labeled the factors that led to *dissatisfaction* at work **hygiene factors.** The most common motivators and hygiene factors can be found in Table 9–2. According to the two-factor theory, efforts directed toward improving hygiene factors will not increase followers' motivation. No matter how much leaders improve working conditions, pay, or sick-leave policies, for example, followers *will not* exert any additional effort or persist any longer at a task. For example, followers will probably be no more motivated to do a dull and boring job merely by being given pleasant office furniture. On the other hand, followers may be asked to work in conditions so poor as to create dissatisfaction, which can distract them from constructive work.

Given limited resources on the leader's part, the key to increasing followers' effort levels according to two-factor theory is to just adequately satisfy the hygiene factors while maximizing the motivators for a particular job. It is important for working conditions to be adequate, but it is even more important (for enhancing motivation and satisfaction) to provide plenty of recognition, responsibility, and possibilities for advancement (see Figure 9.3). In the words of Fred Herzberg, "If you don't want people to have Mickey Mouse attitudes, then don't give them Mickey Mouse work" (unpublished comments).

Two-factor theory suggests that there are several actions Julie's boss could take if she wanted Julie to work harder as a ski lift operator. Although improving the hygiene factors will not get Julie to work harder, they can serve as demotivators if not adequately addressed. Thus, Julie's boss should first determine how satisfied Julie is with pay, co-workers, working conditions, and her actions as a supervisor, and do all she can to improve these factors. Once these factors are addressed, then Julie's boss should focus on Julie's need to do a good job by getting her some recognition for being one of the best ski lift operators at the

FIGURE 9.3

Herzberg's two-factor theory

resort, increasing her responsibility, or providing her with opportunities for advancement. According to the theory, leaders appealing to motivators before addressing hygiene factors are unlikely to get their followers to exert extra effort toward team or organizational goals.

Although the two-factor theory offers leaders ideas about how to, and how not to, bolster followers' satisfaction, it has received little empirical support beyond Herzberg's (1964) own results. In other words, it just may not be an accurate explanation for job satisfaction despite its apparent grounding in data. We present it here in part because it has become such a well-known approach to work motivation and job satisfaction that the present account would appear incomplete if we ignore it. The problem with two-factor theory, however, seems to lie in the very aspect that at first seemed its strength: the original data on which it was based. For one thing, as noted earlier, Herzberg developed his theory after interviewing only accountants and engineers, two groups who are hardly representative of workers in other lines of work or activity. Furthermore, his subjects typically attributed job satisfaction to *their* skill or effort, yet blamed their dissatisfaction on circumstances beyond their control. This sounds suspiciously like the fundamental attribution error described earlier in this book. Despite such limitations, however, Landy (1985) concluded that the two-factor theory has provided useful insight into what followers find satisfying and dissatisfying about work.

Concluding Thoughts on Need Theories. According to these three theories, leaders should start by determining if lower-level needs or hygiene factors are being satisfied. In most cases it will be difficult for followers to exhibit the behaviors necessary for group success if these lower-level needs are not being met; therefore, leaders should do all they can to help followers meet these needs. Once the lower-level needs or hygiene factors are satisfied, leaders can then work to satisfy higher-level needs, which in turn should improve the odds of group success. So how would you apply the need theories to improve the customer service of flight attendants? How would you go about determining the needs of flight attendants, and what kind of program would you implement to improve customer service? Although the three need theories do provide some useful ideas on how to improve customer service, it is important to note that they have several limitations. For one thing, none of the theories makes specific predictions about what an individual will do to satisfy a particular need (Betz,

1984; Kanfer, 1990). In the example, Ling Ling may exert considerable effort to establish new friendships at work, try to make friends outside work, or even spend a lot of money on a new car or stereo equipment (the frustration regression hypothesis). The theories' lack of specificity and predictive power severely limits their practical applicability in real-life settings. On the other hand, awareness of the general nature of the various sorts of basic human needs described in these theories seems fundamentally useful to leaders. Leaders will have a difficult time getting followers to maintain various work behaviors by emphasizing good relationships with co-workers or appealing to their sense of pride if the job pays only minimum wage and followers are having a difficult time making ends meet. A person may be reluctant to volunteer for a self-actualizing opportunity in support of a political campaign if such participation may risk that person's financial security. Perhaps the greatest insight provided by these three theories is that leadership practitioners may need to address some basic, fundamental areas before their attempts to get followers to expend more effort on work-related behaviors will be successful (see Highlight 9.2).

Individual Differences in Motivation

The body of every organization is made up of four kinds of bones. There are the wishbones, who spend all of their time wishing someone would do the work. Then there are the jawbones, who do all the talking, but little else. The knucklebones knock everything anybody else tries to do. Fortunately, in every organization there are also the backbones, who get under the load and do most of the work.

Leo Aikman, *On Bones*

Is it possible that some people are naturally more "motivated" than others? Do some people automatically put forth a higher level of effort toward group goals simply because of who they are or because they enjoy what they do? Unlike the three need theories that claimed all people share some fundamental needs, the individual difference approach to motivation assumes that people vary substantially in their achievement orientation or intrinsic motivation. This approach to motivation is rather simple. To improve group performance, leaders should select only those followers who possess both the right skills and have a higher level of achievement orientation or find the work to be intrinsically motivating.

Achievement Orientation.   Atkinson (1957) proposed that an individual's tendency to exert effort toward task accomplishment depended partly on the strength of his or her motive to achieve success, or, as Atkinson called it, **achievement orientation.** McClelland (1975) further developed Atkinson's ideas and said that individuals with a strong achievement orientation (or in McClelland's terms, a strong *need for achievement*) strived to accomplish socially acceptable endeavors and activities. These individuals also preferred tasks that provided immediate and ample feedback and were moderately difficult (i.e., tasks that required a considerable amount of effort but were accomplishable). Additionally, individuals with a strong need to achieve felt satisfied when they successfully solved work problems or accomplished job tasks (McClelland, 1975). Individuals with a relatively low need to achieve generally preferred easier tasks and did not feel satisfied by solving problems or accomplishing assigned tasks. McClelland (1975) maintained that differences in achievement orientation were a pri-

The Best Companies to Work for in America

Highlight 9.2

Each year *Fortune* magazine publishes a list of the 100 best companies to work for in America. Starting with a database of more than 1,000 companies, the top 100 companies are those that achieve the highest score on the Great Place to Work Trust Index, a survey given to 225 random employees. Some of the companies consistently making this top 100 list include:

Southwest Airlines	Federal Express	Whole Foods Market
Merck	S.C. Johnson Wax	Honda of America
Harley-Davidson	Hallmark Cards	Deloitte & Touche
USAA Insurance	Microsoft	J.M. Smucker
Medtronic	Goldman-Sachs	3M
SAS Institute	Procter & Gamble	L.L. Bean
Hewlett-Packard	Marriott International	REI

So what makes each of these companies such a great place to work? Although these companies represent very different industries, many of them share three common attributes. First, they are led by an inspiring leader. Herb Kelleher of Southwest Airlines spends a considerable amount of time making sure that employees believe in his vision of the company. Second, many of the 100 best companies have great facilities. USAA Insurance has company-sponsored van pools and on-site ATMs, baseball fields, tennis courts, gyms, a dry-cleaning service, a store, a bank, and a top-notch cafeteria. Third, many employees felt their companies allowed them to pursue a higher sense of purpose. Many people work at Medtronic because its pacemakers substantially improve patients' lives. So how do the three need theories map onto the common attributes of the 100 best companies to work for? What would you need to do as a leader if you wanted your company to become one of the best to work for?

Sources: R.B. Leiber, "100 Best Companies to Work for in America: Why Employees Love These Companies," *Fortune*, January 12, 1998, pp. 72–74; L. Grant, "Happy Workers, High Returns," *Fortune*, January 12, 1998, p. 81; R. Levering, and M. Moskowitz, "100 Best Companies to Work for in America." *Fortune*, January 12, 1998, pp. 84–95.

mary reason people differed in the levels of effort they exerted to accomplish assignments, objectives, or goals. Thus, achievement orientation is a bit like "fire in the belly"; people with more achievement orientation are likely to set higher personal and work goals and are more likely to expend the effort needed to accomplish them. People with low levels of achievement motivation tend to set lower personal and work goals, and are less likely to accomplish them.

Achievement orientation is also a component of the Five Factor personality dimension of dependability (see Chapter 7). Like intelligence, dependability has been found to be positively related to performance across virtually all jobs (Barrick & Mount, 1991; Ones, Mount, Barrick, & Hunter, 1994; Tett, Jackson, & Rothstein, 1991; Tett, Jackson, Rothstein, & Reddon, 1994). Achievement orientation has been found to predict success in school (Gough, 1987), in the military (Curphy & Osten, 1993; Hough, 1992), in blue-collar and retail workers (Hogan & Hogan, 1992; Paajanen, Hansen, & McLellan, 1993), and in managers (Nilsen, 1995; Curphy, 1998b, 2000, 2001). All things being equal, people with higher levels of achievement orientation are likely to do better in school, pursue postgraduate degrees, get promoted more quickly, and get paid higher salaries and bonuses than their lower-scoring counterparts.

Given that individuals with higher achievement orientation scores set high personal goals and put in the time and effort necessary to achieve them, it is hardly surprising that achievement orientation is often a key success factor for people who advance to the highest levels of the organization. For example, achievement orientation appears to be a common success factor underlying the careers of Madeleine Albright, Colin Powell, and Konosuke Matsushita.

So how could a leader apply this knowledge of achievement motivation to improve the performance of Julie, Ling Ling, and the flight attendants? Perhaps the first step would be to ensure the hiring process selected those individuals with higher levels of achievement orientation. Assuming they had higher scores, we would expect Ling Ling to work with her boss to set aggressive goals for renting apartments and then work as many nights and weekends as are needed to achieve them. We might also expect Ling Ling to obtain her MBA from Hong Kong University over the next few years. Julie could also be expected to set high personal and work goals, but she may find that her job limits her ability to pursue these goals. Unlike Ling Ling, who can control the number of nights and weekends she wants to work, Julie has no control over the number of people who ride on her lift. The job itself may limit Julie's ability to fulfill her high level of achievement orientation. As a result, she may pursue other activities, such as becoming an expert skier, joining the ski patrol, doing ski racing, looking for additional responsibilities or opportunities for advancement, or finding another job where she has the opportunity to achieve and get rewarded for her efforts. Because Julie will set and work toward high personal goals, a good boss would work closely with Julie to find work-related ways to capitalize on her achievement orientation. Thus, achievement orientation may be a dual-edged sword. Leadership practitioners may be able to hire a group of highly motivated followers, but they also need to set clear expectations, provide opportunities for followers to set and achieve work-related goals, and provide feedback on progress toward goals. Otherwise followers may find different ways to fulfill their high levels of achievement orientation.

> *People go to work to succeed.*
> Norman Schwarzkopf

Intrinsic Motivation.   Work behavior is motivated by both internal and external factors. In this section, we will focus on the former, although we also will examine how the two factors interact. We use the term **intrinsic motivation** to describe behavior seemingly motivated for its own sake, for the personal satisfaction and increased feelings of competence or control one gets from doing it. In other words, some people are motivated to persist in certain behaviors for the simple reason that they like to do them. Julie or Ling Ling might spend a lot of time operating ski lifts or showing apartments simply because they enjoy these activities. What is intrinsically motivating for one person, however, may not be for someone else. Hobbies, for example, are almost by definition intrinsically motivating, yet they also reflect the diversity of human tastes for different activities. Stamp collecting may be intrinsically motivating to one person, yet exceedingly boring to many others. The key for leadership practitioners is to identify the activities their followers like to perform (within reason), and increase their job opportunities to do them.

Deci (1975) and Dawes (1991) observed that individuals often voluntarily put forth effort toward activities they enjoy doing. If an individual is already engaged in an intrinsically motivating activity, we might ask what would result if extrinsic rewards were added to the intrinsic reward of just performing the activity. It might seem at first as though the activity would be even further strengthened if external rewards were added to the internal rewards. Sometimes, though, that is not the case. Some research has shown that external rewards or incentives may backfire if they are given to people already intrinsically motivated to perform the tasks. That can result in a *decrease* in the person's intrinsic motivation toward the tasks (Calder & Staw, 1975; Deci, 1972; Kohn, 1993). Further study of this **overjustification effect** has shown that external rewards can result in a decrease in intrinsic motivation when they are perceived to be "controlling"; however, rewards seen as providing "informational" value (e.g., letting a person know how well he or she is doing) or those that are consistent with societal norms concerning pay and benefits typically do not result in a decrease in intrinsic motivation for the task (Deci, 1975; Eisenberger & Cameron, 1996; Fisher, 1973; Lepper, Greene, & Nisbett, 1973). After reviewing the results of approximately 100 studies, Eisenberger and Cameron (1996) went on to say that the overjustification effect is more of a myth than reality; the number of situations where this occurs is so limited and so easily avoided that it rarely, if ever, happens in the real world. Despite this preponderance of evidence, however, many educators and leaders continue to believe in the notion that rewards reduce the intrinsic motivation of tasks.

So how would intrinsic motivation and the overjustification effect work with Julie and Ling Ling? In both cases, the leaders would need to spend time with both individuals to find out what they enjoy doing at work. Not only might the boss learn that Julie really likes to work outdoors; she might also like the social nature of interacting with the crowds waiting in lift lines. This might indicate Julie would particularly enjoy working in the largest and most crowded lifts, something other lift operators may not enjoy so much. Ling Ling might really like sales but hate the paperwork associated with closing leases. Her boss could assign the administrative aspects of Ling Ling's job to an administrative support person, or find other ways (such as using technology) to reduce her administrative workload.

Although followers will almost always have to perform activities they may not like, the more a leader aligns her followers' intrinsic interests with their work activities, the more motivated her team is likely to be.

Concluding Thoughts on Individual Differences in Motivation.   Because people vary in their achievement orientation and in the tasks they find intrinsically motivating, one way to ensure that followers will exert the effort needed to accomplish their tasks is to select individuals already high in these motives. Although McClelland (1985) has reported successfully training people to be higher in achievement orientation, this can be a relatively expensive and inefficient process; putting more emphasis on selecting the right people for the job in the first place may be a preferable approach for leaders to take.

It is also important to remember that perhaps the most effective way to determine what followers find to be intrinsically motivating is to simply ask them what they like to do. However, many leaders either do not have particularly good relationships with their followers or assume they know what motivates them, so they often fail to ask this simple question. While it may not be possible to completely align tasks with followers' intrinsic interests, leaders may be able to reassign or periodically rotate tasks to increase the level of follower motivation. Leaders often assume that jobs and task assignments are static and unchangeable, but most organizations do not care who does the work as long as it gets done. Leaders may be able to get higher-quality work and have more satisfied employees by reassigning work according to intrinsic interests. As the head of customer service, how would you use this information about individual differences in motivation to improve the customer service levels of flight attendants?

Cognitive Theories

Another way to get followers to engage and persist with the behaviors associated with group success is to persuade them to think differently about their efforts. Rather than appealing to needs or hiring individuals who are naturally more "motivated," the cognitive theories look at whether followers will exert more effort toward group goals when the expectations for performance and the links between the level of effort and desirable outcomes are clear. Should leaders set goals for their teams or simply tell them to do their best? Similarly, should leaders explicitly point out what rewards a group will get if they achieve certain outcomes, or will followers exert more effort if rewards are vague and only loosely tied to performance? The research underlying the cognitive theories provides leadership practitioners with the answers to these two important questions.

> *Goals drive behavior.*
> David B. Peterson, Personnel
> Decisions International

Goal Setting.   One of the most familiar and easiest formal systems of motivation to use with followers is **goal setting.** From the leader's perspective, it involves helping followers see how a goal might be attained by following a systematic plan to achieve it. According to Locke and Latham (1990), goals are the most powerful determinants of task behaviors. Goals serve to direct attention, mobilize effort, help people develop strategies for goal achievement, and help people continue exerting effort until the goal is reached. That leads, in turn, to even higher goals (see Highlight 9.3).

Locke and Latham (1990) reported that nearly 400 studies across individuals, groups, and organizations in eight different countries have provided consistent support for several aspects of goal setting. First, this research showed goals that were both *specific* and *difficult* resulted in consistently higher effort and performance when contrasted to "do your best" goals. Second, *goal commitment* is critical. Merely having goals is not enough. Although follower participation in setting goals is one way to increase commitment, goals set either by leaders unilaterally or through participation with followers can lead to necessary levels of commitment. Commitment to assigned goals was often as high as commitment to goals followers helped to set, provided the leader was perceived to have legitimate authority, expressed confidence in followers, and provided clear standards for performance (Locke & Latham, 1990; Klein, Wesson, Hollenbeck, & Alge, 1999). Third, followers exerted the greatest effort when goals were accompanied by *feedback*; followers getting goals or feedback alone generally exerted less effort.

Several other aspects of goal setting are also worth noting. First, goals can be set for any aspect of performance, be it reducing costs, improving the quality of services and products, increasing voter registration, or winning a league

The High-Performance Cycle

Highlight 9.3

According to Locke and Latham (1990), leaders can have both high-performing and highly satisfied workers by implementing the high-performance cycle in their work groups. Leaders start the high-performance cycle by first setting high expectations for followers and giving them specific, difficult goals to achieve. Specific, difficult goals will energize followers to develop task strategies, exert a certain level of effort, and persist on the task. Given this effort, followers will successfully accomplish the goal if they are committed to the goal, are given timely feedback, and have the necessary resources and abilities. Successful goal accomplishment leads to valued rewards, which in turn leads to increased job satisfaction and organizational commitment. Higher organizational commitment will allow leaders to set more difficult goals and to expect higher levels of performance and satisfaction from followers.

Every substandard organization I have ever seen had low performance standards. If you want superior performance, then you have got to set high standards for your employees.

            Norman Schwarzkopf

championship. Nevertheless, leaders need to ensure that they do not set conflicting goals, as followers can only exert so much effort over a given period of time. Second, determining just how challenging to make goals creates a bit of a dilemma for leaders. Successfully completed goals provide followers with a sense of job satisfaction, and easy goals are more likely to be completed than difficult goals. However, easily attainable goals result in lower levels of effort (and, in turn, performance) than do more difficult goals. Locke and Latham (1990) suggested that leaders might motivate followers most effectively by setting moderately difficult goals, recognizing partial goal accomplishment, and making use of a continuous-improvement philosophy by making goals incrementally more difficult (Imai, 1986).

A leader's implicit and explicit expectations about goal accomplishment can also affect the performance of followers and teams. Research by Dov Eden and his associates in Israel provided fairly consistent support for the Pygmalion and Golem effects (Davidson & Eden, 2000; Eden, Geller, Gewirtz, Gordon-Terner, Inbir, Liberman, Pass, Salomen-Segev, & Shalit, 2000). The **Pygmalion Effect** occurs when leaders articulate high expectations for followers; in many cases these expectations alone will lead to higher performing followers and teams. Unfortunately, the **Golem Effect** is also true—leaders who have little faith in their followers' ability to accomplish a goal are rarely disappointed. Thus a leader's expectations for a follower or team have a good chance of becoming a self-fulfilling prophecy (Chapter 3). These results indicate that leaders wanting to improve team performance should set high but achievable goals and express confidence and support that the followers can get the job done (White & Locke, 2000; McNatt, 2000).

How could leadership practitioners apply goal setting to Julie and Ling Ling in order to increase their motivation levels? Given the research findings just described, Julie and Ling Ling's bosses should work with these two followers to set specific and moderately difficult goals, express confidence that they can achieve their goals, and provide regular feedback on goal progress. Julie and her boss could look at Julie's past performance or other lift operators' performance as a baseline, and then set specific and measurable goals around the number of hours worked, the number of people who fall off the lift during a shift, customer satisfaction survey ratings from skiers, the length of lift lines, or the number of complaints from customers. Similarly, Ling Ling and her boss could look at some real estate baseline measures and set goals around the number of apartments rented for the year, the total monetary value of these rentals, the time it takes to close a lease and complete the necessary paperwork, customer complaints, and sales expenses. Note that both Ling Ling and Julie's bosses would need to take care that they do not set conflicting goals. For example, if Julie had a goal only for the number of people who fell off the lift, then she might be more likely to run the lift very slowly, resulting in long lift lines and numerous customer complaints. In a similar vein, bosses need to ensure that individual goals do not conflict with team or organizational goals. Ling Ling's boss would need to make sure that Ling Ling's goals did not interfere with those of the other real estate agents in the firm. If Ling Ling's goals did not specify territorial limits, then she might rent properties in other agents' territories, which in turn might cause a high level of interoffice conflict. Both bosses should also take care to set measurable goals; that way they could provide Julie and Ling Ling with the feedback they need to stay on track. More information on the specific steps of goal setting can be found in Part V of this book.

Expectancy Theory.   The next two cognitive theories are concerned with clarifying the links between what people do and the rewards or outcomes they will obtain. First described by Tolman (1932), **expectancy theory** has been modified for use in work settings (Vroom, 1964; Porter & Lawler, 1968; Lawler, 1973). It involves two fundamental assumptions: (*a*) motivated performance is the result of conscious choice, and (*b*) people will do what they believe will provide them the highest (or surest) rewards. Thus, expectancy theory is a highly *rational* approach to understanding motivation. It assumes that people act in ways that maximize their expectations of attaining valued outcomes, and that reliable predictions of behavior are possible if the factors that influence those expectations can be quantified. In this model, there are three such factors to be quantified. The first two are probability estimates (expectancies), and the third is a vector sum of predicted positive and negative outcomes. Expectancy theory maintains that leadership practitioners will be able to motivate followers if they understand the process followers use to determine whether certain behaviors will lead to valued rewards.

The first probability estimate is the **effort-to-performance expectancy.** Like all probabilities, it ranges from no chance of the event occurring to absolute certainty of its occurring; or, in decimal form, from 0.0 to 1.0. Here, the follower estimates the likelihood of performing the desired behavior adequately, assuming she puts forth the required effort. The second probability estimate is the **performance-to-outcome expectancy.** In this case, our follower estimates the likelihood of receiving a reward, given that she achieves the desired level of performance. This is a necessary step in the sequence since it is not uncommon for people to actually do good work yet not be rewarded for it (e.g., someone else may be the teacher's pet). Finally, the follower must determine the likely outcomes, assuming that the previous conditions have been met, and determine whether their weighted algebraic sum (**valence**) is sufficiently positive to be worth the time and effort. To put it more simply, expectancy theory says that people will be motivated to do a task if three conditions are met: (1) they can perform the task adequately if they put forth enough effort, (2) they will be rewarded if they do it, and (3) they value the reward (see Figure 9.4).

Applying these three concepts to Ling Ling might be helpful here. Since the Chinese government takeover in 1997 and the collapse of the Asian economy, the real estate rental market has been depressed in Hong Kong. Even though Ling Ling has been working three weekday evenings a week and all day Saturday

FIGURE 9.4

An example of expectancy theory

(showing an average of 12 apartments per week), she is 25 percent behind her sales quota. According to expectancy theory, Ling Ling would first determine if working the additional two weekday evenings a week would enable her to rent more apartments—effort-to-performance expectancy. Second, Ling Ling would have to determine if renting these additional apartments would be sufficient to reach her sales quota by the end of the year—performance-to-outcome expectancy. Finally, Ling Ling would have to weigh the advantages of reaching her sales quota (sales bonus, job security) relative to the disadvantages (stress, loss of free time, loss of sleep, etc.)—valences. Notice that if Ling Ling did not believe that (a) working additional weekday evenings would help her to rent more apartments, (b) renting these additional apartments would be enough to reach her annual sales quota, or (c) the benefits of reaching her sales quota outweighed the costs, then Ling Ling would choose not to put forth the effort to rent additional apartments. She may feel that the real estate market is in such bad shape or her bonus so low that even if she were to meet her quota, it would not be worth the additional effort. As seen in Figure 9.4, all three components must have a relatively high probability or be favorably weighted in order for Ling Ling to exert further effort in renting additional apartments.

Leadership practitioners using expectancy theory to motivate a follower to do a work project would need to take three steps. First, the leader would have to increase effort-to-performance expectancy by clarifying the links between the follower's level of effort and project completion. To do this, the leader and follower might discuss what the follower would need to do, and the amount of time and resources it would take to complete the project. Second, the leader would need to increase the performance-to-reward expectancy by discussing the positive outcomes to the follower and the organization if the project were completed on time and at cost. This might involve such things as a year-end bonus, increased recognition by upper management, or reduced costs or increased market share for the organization. Finally, the leader would need to clarify all of the potential valences for successfully completing the project. This may not be obvious to the follower, so the leader would need to clearly describe both the pros and the cons but emphasize the positive aspects of the project.

> *A company is always perfectly designed to produce what it is producing. If it has quality problems, cost problems, or productivity problems, then the behaviors associated with these outcomes are being reinforced. This is not conjecture. This is the cold, hard reality of human behavior.*
>
> Anonymous

ProMES.   Another cognitive theory of motivation that can be used with individuals, groups, and organizations is called the **Productivity Measurement and Enhancement System (ProMES)** (Pritchard, Jones, Roth, Stuebing, & Ekeberg, 1988). Like expectancy theory, ProMES takes a very rational approach to motivation, and focuses on the decision-making process followers use when choosing to perform specific behaviors. In this process, followers are more motivated when they see clear links between: (1) the behaviors they exhibit, (2) the products and services they produce, (3) the evaluations they receive, (4) the rewards they earn, and (5) their personal needs. To motivate followers, leaders set goals and provide feedback on followers' behaviors, they clarify and provide feedback on how these behaviors are creating valued products and services for the team or organization, and they describe how these products and services are in turn related to followers' performance evaluations, rewards, and personal needs. According to Pritchard and his colleagues, any break in the motivational sequence will have a dramatic effect on followers' motivational levels. For example, if leaders have not set clear goals, then followers may not see how their behaviors are creating value-added products and services. Similarly, if leaders do not provide feedback on the number or quality of the products and services produced, or have not explained how different performance levels will lead to different evaluations and rewards, then followers are likely to be much less motivated to perform.

ProMES is a very data-driven, metrics-based theory of motivation. Workers must be given regular feedback on the products and services they are producing, and how they are doing with respect to performance evaluations and rewards. To implement a ProMES program, leaders and followers work together to develop measures of productivity, evaluation, and reward for their work groups. This process helps to clarify what tasks followers will need to perform and how well or frequently they need to do them. Identifying the type, frequency, and format of the feedback for each task is also part of this process (feedback is often provided using various graphs or charts). Care is taken so that followers' behaviors are aligned with team or organizational objectives. Pritchard and his colleagues have implemented ProMES in nine different countries at dozens of manufacturing, service, sales, and military organizations, and the results have been very impressive. In almost all cases, ProMES has led to productivity gains that have far outstripped those associated with individual organizational interventions, such as goal setting, training, or personnel selection (Azar, 1997). Pritchard believes these results are due to the fact that ProMES addresses *all* the links in the motivational sequence. Rewards alone may be motivating if rewards are the problem, but they may not be particularly effective in situations where the rewards are not valued or where the links between what people do and what they produce are not clear.

So how might we apply ProMES to increase Julie's level of motivation as a ski lift operator? The first step would be to have Julie and her boss set several areas of goals for various ski lift operator tasks, such as running the lift safely, minimizing lift line lengths, or maintaining a high level of customer service. Next, Julie and her boss would select what metrics to use to provide feedback and measure progress. These might include weekly customer service surveys or the number of times the ski lift was slowed down or stopped for safety reasons. Julie could review her progress using daily lift stoppage charts and weekly graphs for the survey results. Julie and her boss would then need to decide how certain levels of performance would link to various performance evaluation ratings. Having customer satisfaction ratings above 70 percent may be a "4," above 80 percent a "3," above 90 percent a "2," and above 95 percent a "1." Next, Julie and her boss would also decide how different evaluation ratings would result in different rewards. For example, Julie could be eligible for an additional $300 per month if her performance evaluations averaged 1.0–1.5, $150 per month for evaluations averaging 1.5–2.0, and so on. Finally, the boss would need to ensure that these monetary rewards were valued by Julie. It may turn out that Julie would rather have time off, substitute her operator shifts to ski patrol shifts, or be sponsored as a ski racer by the resort. In this case, the boss would have to link Julie's performance evaluations to the more valued rewards.

Concluding Thoughts on Cognitive Theories of Motivation.   All three of the preceding cognitive theories assume that people make rational, conscious decisions about what to put their energies into. Unfortunately (or fortunately?), human behavior does not always correspond to what rational analysis might predict. Human motivation is often affected by nonrational or emotional considerations as well as by rational ones; behavior does not follow a simple and logical formula. For example, while it may be very logical for Julie to work five days a week, she may nonetheless decide to "blow off" work one day and go skiing at another resort instead. It is worth recalling our earlier discussion about how people always operate in both rational and emotional realms of behavior. Because people make choices to exert effort based on both rational and emotional considerations, predictions based on rational modeling alone are inexact. For example, the highest levels of follower motivation are often noted with charismatic or transformational leaders (Chapter 13), and none of these three models can adequately explain why followers are so willing to put forth high levels of energy and effort for these leaders. Still, they may provide leadership practitioners with several useful ideas on how to better motivate followers in a broad variety of situations, and they are more helpful than having no theories at all. Just because rational approaches do not reflect the full complexity of being human does not mean leaders should ignore the insights they offer.

Perhaps more than the other theories and approaches described in this section, the cognitive theories place a strong premium on leader–follower communication. It is hard to imagine how goal setting, expectancy theory, or ProMES would work if the leader did not articulate goals, provide ongoing feedback, and continually clarify motivational links with followers. If leader–follower communication is poor, then it is unlikely that leaders will realize the benefits of these three approaches. The research shows that these theories can effectively increase worker motivation; when they fail it often has more to do with how the theory was implemented than with inadequacy of the theory. Thus, leaders with poor interpersonal communication and feedback skills might have a difficult time using these theories to increase follower motivation levels.

Let's assume that as the head of customer service, you have good communication and feedback skills. After reading this section you know that ProMES is the most comprehensive cognitive theory of motivation, as it combines elements of goal setting, expectancy theory, and operant conditioning (which is described more fully in the next section). As a leader, how would you design and implement a ProMES intervention in order to improve the customer service levels of flight attendants?

Situational Approaches

So far we have discussed how underlying needs, individual differences in achievement orientation, or goals or performance-to-reward links can affect follower motivation levels. However, these motivational techniques are mainly follower- or leader-centric; they pertain to certain follower qualities or leader actions. From Chapter 2 we know that leadership is an interaction between the leader, followers, and the situation, and the theories of motivation can be categorized using the same framework. The two approaches described in this section show how it is possible to change the situation in order to improve followers' motivation levels. In other words, this research shows that some jobs are more motivating than others and that it is possible to reengineer jobs to improve followers' motivation levels. These two situational approaches to motivation include the job characteristics model and the operant approach.

The Job Characteristics Model.   According to the **job characteristics model,** jobs or tasks having certain kinds of characteristics provide inherently greater motivation and job satisfaction than others. Hackman and Oldham (1976, 1980) said that followers will work harder and be more satisfied if their tasks are meaningful, provide ample feedback, allow considerable latitude in deciding how to accomplish them, and require use of a variety of skills. The Hackman and Oldham model is based on five critical job characteristics: task identity, task significance, feedback, autonomy, and skill variety. Note that while a job high in all these characteristics might seem intrinsically motivating, this model is *not* just another way of looking at intrinsic motivation. *Individuals* differ in their intrinsic motivation, whereas the job characteristics model says some *jobs* are, by their nature, more motivating and satisfying than others.

This is not to say that individual differences are unimportant in the job characteristics model. They actually do play a key role in the model by means of a concept called **growth-need strength.** This refers to the degree to which an individual is motivated by the need to fulfill herself (in Maslow's terms, to increase her self-esteem or self-actualization). Hackman and Oldham (1976, 1980) said that individuals with high growth-need strength especially desire jobs high on the five characteristics in the model; they are even more motivated and satisfied than others with such jobs, and even less motivated and satisfied than others with jobs very low on those characteristics. Thus, if leaders were to follow the tenets of the job characteristics model to increase followers' satisfaction and motivation, then they would hire followers with high growth-need strength, and they would restructure followers' jobs to have more favorable task characteristics.

Research has provided mixed support for the job characteristics model. The 28 studies reviewed by Loher, Noe, Moeller, and Fitzgerald (1985) provided evidence that strongly confirmed the satisfaction hypothesis. Other research, however, has called into question the satisfaction and motivation predictions of the model. There is even some evidence calling into question the presumed causal relationship between job satisfaction and job characteristics. While Hackman and Oldham (1976, 1980) presumed higher job satisfaction *resulted from* working in a job that had certain characteristics, other research indicated that people may, in fact, rate their job characteristics higher *as a result* of being satisfied in those jobs. For example, one study provided false satisfaction feedback to workers who had similar and equally satisfying jobs. Those who were given higher job satisfaction feedback rated their job characteristics higher than workers given lower job feedback (Adler, Skov, & Salvemini, 1985). Moreover, Griffin, Welsh, and Moorhead (1981) reported that there was little evidence to show that workers with favorable job characteristics and high growth-need strength actually exerted more effort or persisted at tasks longer than workers with less favorable job characteristics and lower growth-need strength. Despite these mixed findings, the job characteristics theory does provide an alternative perspective for improving followers' motivation levels and has been used extensively in designing or redesigning jobs.

There are several other aspects of the job characteristics model worthy of comment. First, it is important to remember what work was like when this model was developed. In the mid-1970s, a number of jobs were highly routinized and people were essentially doing a small number of highly repeatable tasks. This was particularly true in the manufacturing and service sectors, where, for example, assembly line workers or phone operators did the same tasks over and over. However, technology and organizational downsizing has changed the nature of work in the United States and many other Western countries. Technology has made jobs either more simple or substantially more complex. For example, workers at McDonald's no longer have to enter the dollar amount of items or calculate change; they now merely push buttons with item or meal symbols, and the register automatically calculates the total amount due and change. On the other hand, many assembly line workers now need to have a much higher level of knowledge of electronics, pneumatics, robotics, and advanced materials to successfully perform their jobs. Furthermore, economic downturns and downsizing have required the people remaining in an organization to assume the responsibilities and tasks previously done by those who were let go.

These three changes probably have made most jobs more complex, and according to the job characteristics model people should be happier and more productive than they were 25 years ago. Although national statistics report worker productivity is at an all-time high, other research shows that people are much less happy with work now than they have ever been (Kleiman, 1997; Jones, 2001). Perhaps the biggest reason for this relatively high level of worker dissatisfaction is organizational downsizing and worker burnout. People with higher growth-need strength may welcome these additional responsibilities and duties, but those with lower growth-need strength may be the most vocal about the changes, and the most susceptible to long-term exhaustion and burnout. Xie and Johns (1995) reported that there is a point where job scope exceeds capabilities, and the total direct and indirect costs of burnout may exceed $100 *billion* per year. Of course, the job characteristics model is not responsible for this high level of burnout. As a matter of fact, if job redesign for the survivors is done according to the model, then it may be possible to boost employee motivation and minimize the debilitating effects of stress associated with most downsizings. Unfortunately, however, top management usually assigns new responsibilities and tasks with little regard to the knowledge, skills, training, or resources needed to successfully carry them out (Bedeian & Armenakis, 1998). Cascio's (1995) longitudinal analysis of approximately 500 organizational downsizings showed that most gain some short-term financial benefits, but fail to boost stock prices over the long haul. This failure to gain long-term benefits may be due to employee burnout. Moreover, as Tom Peters so aptly pointed out, most organizations do not shrink to greatness (Peters, 1997).

Despite the mixed findings, a boss could use the job characteristics model to make Julie's job more motivating. Given that Julie spends most of her working day operating a ski lift, task identity is probably not an issue. Her actions affect the number of people getting on and off the lift. Task significance could be an issue, however, if the boss has not explained how Julie's job is a highly visible and important part of the ski resort. It may be worth the boss's time to point out the importance of Julie's role in ski resort operations and how her actions could impact the reputation and financial well-being of the resort, particularly if a skier got hurt due to an unsafe ski lift. The feedback component of Julie's job could also be lacking, and the boss might implement some of the feedback mechanisms discussed earlier with ProMES to enhance this aspect of Julie's job. In terms of autonomy, however, it may be difficult for the boss to change this aspect of Julie's job to increase her motivation levels. The boss may get the biggest motivational increase by increasing the skill variety of Julie's job. In general, operating a ski lift is fairly routine and monotonous. The boss may be able to increase Julie's skill variety by having her rotate through regular shifts of trail grooming with the snow cat, working in the gift shop, handling customer complaints at the resort, or doing ski patrol duties. Given these possible interventions, the job characteristics model can provide leadership practitioners with another perspective on how to change certain aspects of the situation to increase followers' motivation levels. However, this model also assumes that leaders have some control over situational variables, but in some situations, such as union environments, leaders may be very limited in their ability to restructure work to improve followers' motivation.

> *You get what you reinforce, but you do not necessarily get what you pay for.*
>
> Fred Luthans,
> University of Nebraska, and
> Alexander Stajkovic,
> University of California, Irvine

The Operant Approach.   One very popular way to change the direction, intensity, or persistence of behavior is through rewards and punishments. It will help at the outset of this discussion of the **operant approach** to define several terms. A **reward** is any consequence that *increases* the likelihood that a particular behavior will be repeated. For example, if Julie gets a cash award for a suggestion to improve customer service at the ski resort, then she will be more likely to forward additional suggestions. **Punishment** is the administration of an aversive stimulus or the withdrawal of something desirable, each of which *decreases* the likelihood a particular behavior will be repeated (Arvey & Ivancevich, 1980). Thus, if Ling Ling loses her bonus for not getting her paperwork in on time, then she will be less likely to do so again in the future. Both rewards and punishments can be administered in a contingent or noncontingent manner. **Contingent** rewards or punishments are administered as *consequences of a particular behavior.* Giving Julie a medal immediately after she won a skiing race or giving Ling Ling a bonus check for exceeding her sales quota might be good examples here. **Noncontingent** rewards and punishments are not associated with particular behaviors. Monthly paychecks might be an example here, if both Julie and Ling Ling receive the same amount of base pay every month whatever their actual effort or output. Finally, behaviors that are not rewarded will eventually be eliminated through the process of **extinction.**

When properly implemented, there is ample evidence to show that the operant approach can be a very effective way to improve follower motivation and performance (Stajkovic & Luthans, 2001; Luthans & Stajkovic, 1999; Bloom & Milkovich, 1998; Jenkins, Mitra, Gupta, & Shaw, 1998; Curphy, 1991a; Komacki, Zlotnick, & Jensen, 1986; Luthans & Kreitner, 1985; Pritchard, Hollenback, & DeLeo, 1976). Some of this research has also shown that rewards work better than punishments, particularly if administered in a contingent manner

(Stajkovic & Luthans, 2001; Jenkins, Mitra, Gupta, & Shaw, 1998; Luthans & Kreitner, 1985; Podsakoff & Todor, 1985; Arvey, Davis, & Nelson, 1984; Podsakoff, Todor, & Skov, 1982). When comparing the relative impact of different types of rewards, Stajkovic and Luthans (2001) reported that incentive pay targeted at specific follower behaviors was the most effective, followed by social recognition and performance feedback for improving follower performance in credit card processing centers. Although Kohn (1993) has gained attention by arguing that incentive pay programs do not work, his statements appear to be based on nothing more than his own opinions. The research clearly shows that leaders who properly design and implement contingent reward systems do indeed increase follower productivity and performance.

So how does a leader properly design and implement an operant system for improving followers' motivation and performance levels?

Using operant principles properly to improve followers' motivation and hence performance requires several steps. First, *leadership practitioners need to clearly specify what behaviors are important.* This means that Julie's and Ling Ling's leaders will need to specify what they want them to do, how often they should do it, and the level of performance required. Second, *leadership practitioners need to determine if those behaviors are currently being punished, rewarded, or ignored.* Believe it or not, sometimes followers are actually rewarded for behaviors that leaders are trying to extinguish, and punished for behaviors that leaders want to increase. For example, Julie may get considerable positive attention from peers by talking back to her leader or for violating the ski resort dress code. Similarly, Ling Ling may be overly competitive and get promoted ahead of her peers (e.g., by renting apartments in her peers' territories), even when her boss extols the need for cooperation and teamwork. It also may be the case that leaders sometimes just ignore the very behaviors they would like to see strengthened. An example here would be if Julie's boss consistently failed to provide rewards when Julie worked hard to achieve impressive safety and customer service ratings (see Highlight 9.4).

Third, *leadership practitioners need to find out what followers actually find rewarding and punishing.* Leaders should *not* make the mistake of assuming that followers will find the same things rewarding and punishing as they do, nor should they assume that all followers will find the same things to be rewarding and punishing. What may be one follower's punishment may be another follower's reward. For example, Ling Ling may dislike public attention and actually exert less effort after being publicly recognized, yet some of her peers may find public attention to be extremely rewarding. Fourth, *leadership practitioners need to be wary of creating perceptions of inequity when administering individually tailored rewards.* A peer may feel that she got the same results as Ling Ling, yet she received a smaller bonus check for the quarter. Leaders can minimize inequities by being clear and consistent with rewards and punishments. Fifth, *leadership practitioners should not limit themselves to administering organizationally sanctioned rewards and punishments.* Oftentimes leaders are limited in the amount of money they can give followers for good

The Folly of Rewarding A While Hoping for B

Highlight 9.4

Steven Kerr has written a compelling article detailing how many of the reward systems found in government, sports, universities, businesses, medicine, and politics often *compel people to act in a manner contrary to that intended.* For example, voters want politicians to provide the specifics of their programs or platform, yet politicians often get punished for doing so. Some constituency is bound to get hurt or offended whenever the specifics of a program are revealed, which in turn will cost the politician votes. If a politician keeps overall goals vague, more voters are likely to agree with the politician and vote for him or her in the next election.

Businesses, like universities and politicians, often utilize inappropriate reward systems. According to Kerr, the following are some of the more common management reward follies:

We hope for . . .	But we often reward . . .
Long-term growth	Quarterly earnings
Teamwork	Individual effort
Commitment to total quality	Shipping on schedule, even with defects
Reporting bad news	Reporting good news, whether it is true or not

Kerr states that managers who complain about unmotivated workers should consider the possibility that their current reward system is incongruent with the performance they desire.

Source: S. Kerr, "On the Folly of Rewarding A, While Hoping for B," *Academy of Management Executive* 9, no. 1 (1995), pp. 7–14.

performance. However, research by Stajkovic and Luthans (2001) showed that social recognition and performance feedback resulted in productivity improvements in followers of 24 percent and 20 percent, respectively, and these rewards do not cost any money. Using a bit of ingenuity, leaders can often come up with an array of potential rewards and punishments that are effective and inexpensive, and do not violate organizational norms or policies. Julie might find driving the snow cat to be extremely enjoyable, and her boss could use this reward to maintain or increase Julie's motivation levels for operating the ski lift. Finally, because the administration of noncontingent consequences has relatively little impact, *leadership practitioners should administer rewards and punishments in a contingent manner whenever possible.* Highlight 9.5 is an example of the positive results that can come from implementing the operant approach systematically.

Emery Air Freight

Highlight 9.5

Emery Air Freight is one of the most successful examples of how leaders can change the direction, intensity, and persistence of followers' behaviors through the operant approach. Emery Air Freight discovered that it was using the full capacity of its air freight containers only 45 percent of the time and, because of the highly competitive nature of the air freight shipping business, wanted to reduce costs and increase profits by making better use of its air freight containers. The company initially had given employees detailed instructions on how to better use air freight containers. However, this intervention met with little success, and the senior executives at Emery Air Freight consequently decided to implement an operant motivational strategy.

Emery Air Freight's operant strategy consisted of several different steps. First, checklists for air freight container usage were developed. These checklists consisted of the specific behaviors or actions workers could take when preparing an air container for delivery. Second, workers recorded their performance on the checklists, which provided them with information on their own performance with respect to organizational goals. Third, supervisors were trained to provide positive reinforcement on a contingent basis, and in turn praised and rewarded workers for meeting goals or showing improvement over time. In terms of results, Emery Air Freight credited the operant strategy with $2 million in reduced costs after only three years.

Concluding Thoughts on Situational Approaches to Motivation.   The job characteristics model and the operant approach make an important point that is often overlooked by other theories of motivation: By changing the situation, leaders can enhance followers' motivation, performance, and satisfaction. Unfortunately, many leaders naively assume it is easier to change an *individual* than it is to change the *situation*, but this is often not the case. It is important to remember that the situation is not always fixed, and followers are not the only variable in the performance equation. Leaders can often see positive changes in followers' motivation levels by restructuring work processes and procedures, which in turn can increase task identity and significance or skill variety. Tying these changes with a well-designed and well-implemented reward system can result in further increases in motivation. However, leaders are likely to encounter some resistance whenever they change the processes, procedures, and rewards for work, even if these changes are for the better. As noted by Peterson and Hicks (1996), doing things the old way is easy, as followers know the expectations for performance and usually have developed the skills needed to achieve results. Followers often find that doing things a new way can be frustrating, as expectations may be unclear and they may not have the requisite skills. Leadership practitioners can help followers work through this initial resistance to new processes and procedures by showing support, providing training and coaching on new skills, and capitalizing on opportunities to reward progress. If the processes, procedures, and rewards are properly designed and administered, then in many cases followers will successfully work through their resistance and, over time, wonder how they ever got work done using the old systems. The successful transition to new work processes and procedures will rest squarely on the shoulders of leaders. So, given the implications of the situational approach to motivation, how could you use job reengineering and the operant approach to improve the customer service levels of flight attendants? What information would you need to gather, how would you implement the program, and what would be the potential pitfalls of your program?

Motivation Summary

We hope that, after reading this chapter, you will have a better understanding of how follower characteristics (needs, intrinsic motivation), leader actions (goal setting, ProMES), and situational factors (contingent rewards) affect how you and your followers are motivated (and demotivated). Moreover, you should be able to start recognizing situations where some theories provide better insights about problems in motivation levels than others. For example, if we go back to the survival situation described in Chapter 1, then we can see that the need theories (Maslow and Alderfer) provide better explanations for the behavior of the survivors than the job characteristics model or intrinsic motivation. On the other hand, if we think about the reasons we might not be doing well in a particular class, then we may see that we have not set specific goals for our grades or that the links between our efforts and our grades are not very clear. Or if we are working in a bureaucratic organization, then we may see that there are few consequences for either substandard or superior performance; thus, there is little reason to exert any extra effort. Perhaps the best strategy for leaders is to be flexible in the types of interventions they consider to affect follower motivation. That will require, of course, familiarity with the strengths and weaknesses of the different theories and approaches presented here. Just as a carpenter can more effectively build a house by using a variety of tools, a leader can be more effective by using a variety of motivational interventions to resolve work problems.

At this point it is also important to note that one of the most important tools for motivating followers has not been addressed in this chapter. As described in Chapter 13, charismatic or transformational leadership is often associated with extraordinarily high levels of follower motivation, yet none of the theories described in this chapter can adequately explain how these leaders can get their followers to do more than they ever thought possible. Perhaps this is due to the fact that the theories in this chapter take a very rational or logical approach to motivation, yet transformational leadership uses emotion as the fuel to drive followers' heightened motivational levels. Just as our needs, thoughts, personality traits, intrinsic interests, and rewards can motivate us to do something different, so can our emotions drive us to engage in and persist with a particular activity. A good example here may be political campaigns. Do people volunteer to work for these campaigns because of some underlying need, personal goals, or their intrinsic interests in politics? Although these are potential reasons for some followers, the emotions generated by political campaigns, particularly where the two lead candidates represent different value systems, often seem to provide a better explanation for the large amount of time and effort people contribute. Leadership practitioners should not overlook the interplay between emotions and motivation, and the better able they are to address and capitalize on emotions when introducing change, the more successful they are likely to be.

A final point concerns the relationship between motivation and performance. Many leadership practitioners equate the two, but as we pointed out earlier in this chapter, they are not the same concepts. Getting followers to put in more time, energy, and effort on certain behaviors will not help the team to be more successful if they are the wrong behaviors to begin with. Similarly, followers may not know how and when to exhibit those behaviors associated with performance. Leadership practitioners must clearly identify those behaviors related to performance, coach and train their followers on how and when to exhibit these behaviors, and then use one or more of the theories described in this chapter to get followers to exhibit and persist with those behaviors associated with higher performance levels.

Understanding and Influencing Follower Satisfaction

As stated earlier, job satisfaction concerns one's attitudes about work, and there are several practical reasons why job satisfaction is an important concept for leaders to think about. According to Locke and Latham (1990; Ross and Curphy (2000); Sutherland (2000); Armour (2000); and Butorac (2001), satisfied workers are more likely to continue working for an organization. Satisfied workers are also more likely to engage in organizational citizenship behaviors, behaviors that go beyond job descriptions and role requirements and help reduce the workload or stress of others in the organization (Organ & Ryan, 1995; Bettencourt, Gwinner, & Meuter (2001)). Dissatisfied workers are more likely to be adversarial in their relations with leadership (e.g., file grievances) and engage in diverse sorts of counterproductive behaviors (Strauss, 1998; Quigley, 2001). Dissatisfaction is one of the key reasons people leave organizations (Tett & Meyer, 1993; Sutherland, 2000; Armour, 2000; Tepper, 2000; Butorac, 2001), and many of the reasons people are satisfied or dissatisfied with work are within the leader's control (see Table 9–3). Although the total costs of dissatisfaction are difficult to measure, the direct costs

> *One of the symptoms of approaching a nervous breakdown is the belief that one's work is terribly important. If I were a medical man, I would prescribe a holiday to any patient who considered his work important.*
>
> Bertrand Russell

TABLE 9–3   Why People Leave or Stay with Organizations

Why Do People Leave Organizations?		Why Do People Stay with Organizations?	
Limited recognition and praise	34%	Promises of long-term employment	82%
Compensation	29%	Supports training and education	78%
Limited authority	13%	Hires/keeps hard-working, smart people	76%
Personality conflicts	8%	Encourages fun, collegial relationships	74%
Other	16%	Bases job evaluation on innovation	72%

Sources: Pace Communication, Inc., *Hemispheres Magazine*, November 1994, p. 155; and "Keeping Workers Happy," *USA Today*, February 10, 1998, p. 1B.

of replacing a first-line supervisor or an executive can range from $5,000 to $200,000 per hire, depending on recruiting, relocation, and training fees, and these costs do not include those associated with the productivity lost as a result of unfilled positions (Curphy, 1998a). Employee dissatisfaction can also affect revenue and capital available for organizational expansion and upgrades. A survey of major corporations showed that 49 percent switched to another vendor because of poor customer service (Peters, 1997). Barry Gibbons, the former CEO of Burger King, stated that "70–90 percent of the decisions not to repeat purchase of anything are not about product or price. They are about dimensions of service" (McKay, 1998). McKay stated that employees are probably not going to provide world-class service if they are unhappy with their job, boss, or company. The inability to retain customers will directly affect revenues and make investors think twice about buying stock in a company. Relatedly, Schellenbarger (1997) reported that 35 percent of investor decisions are driven by nonfinancial factors. Number 5 on a list of 39 factors investors weighed before buying stock was the company's ability to attract and retain talent. These findings imply that a company's stock price is driven not only by market share and profitability, but also by service and bench strength considerations. Thus, employee satisfaction (or dissatisfaction) can have a major impact on the organization's bottom line.

Of these outcomes, perhaps employee turnover has the most immediate impact on leadership practitioners. It would be very hard for Julie's or Ling Ling's bosses to achieve results if ski resort or real estate personnel were constantly having to be replaced, and the leader was spending an inordinate amount of time recruiting, hiring, and training replacements. Although some level of **functional turnover** is healthy for an organization (i.e., these followers are retiring, did not fit into the organization, or were substandard performers), dysfunctional turnover is not. **Dysfunctional turnover** occurs when the "best and brightest" in an organization become dissatisfied and leave it. Bedeian and Armenakis (1998) pointed out that dysfunctional turnover is most likely to occur when downsizing is the response to organizational decline (i.e., increased costs or decreased revenues, market web share, or earnings). In these situations, dysfunctional turnover may have several devastating effects. First, those individuals in the best position to turn the company around are no longer there. Second, those who remain are even less capable of successfully dealing with the additional workload associated with the downsizings. Compounding this problem is that training budgets also tend to be slashed during downsizings. Third, organizations that downsize have a very difficult time recruiting people with the skills needed to turn the company around. Either competent candidates avoid applying for jobs within the organization because of the uncertainties of job security, or the less competent managers remaining with the company may decide not to hire anyone who could potentially replace them (Bedeian & Armenakis, 1998). Because leaders can play an important role in followers' satisfaction levels, and because followers' satisfaction levels can have a substantial impact on various organizational outcomes, it is worth going into the topic in greater detail (see Highlights 9.6 and 9.7).

A Recipe for Success: How to Get Better Results by Keeping Employees Happy

Highlight 9.6

More and more organizations are beginning to realize that their overall success depends on how they treat their employees. Hiring good people, setting high goals and expectations, providing needed resources, developing new skills, and holding people accountable for results seem to be important ingredients in organizational success. Employees who work in organizations with these qualities often exert more effort toward organizational goals, report higher levels of job satisfaction, and are more likely to stay with their company over the next three years than employees working for organizations that do not possess these qualities. Support for these success factors can be found in surveys of 80,000 managers conducted by the Gallup Organization, a study of 110 midsized companies in the United Kingdom, and an examination of the 100 Best Companies to Work For. Although the ingredients for organizational success appear straightforward, few companies appear able to implement them on a consistent and comprehensive basis because many managers believe they do not have time to interview potential employees, much less set clear expectations and develop skills. Nor are they much better at holding their employees accountable for results, as many managers do not take the time to complete annual performance reviews. If research has shown that these leadership activities are related to an organization's ability to attract and retain key talent and in turn obtain superior results, and if managers are not doing them, then what other things are they spending their time on?

Sources: T. Butorac, "Recruitment and Retention: The Keys to Profitability at Carlson Companies," presentation given at Personnel Decisions International, Minneapolis, MN, June 11, 2001; S. Hallam, *Leadership Matters: Research about Leadership Is Important* (Akron, OH: University of Akron, 2001); L. Grant, "Happy Workers, High Returns," *Fortune*, January 12, 1998, p. 81; Institute of Personnel and Development. *Impact of People Management Practices on Business Performance Costs* (London: Plymbridge Distributors, 1998).

A Recipe for Failure: Abusive Bosses = Workplace Anger and Violence

Highlight 9.7

What did I tell you the first day? Your thoughts are nothing; you are nothing. . . if you were in my toilet bowl I wouldn't bother flushing it. My bath mat means more to me than you . . . you don't like it here, leave!

—George Huang, *Swimming with Sharks*

Workplace anger and violence seem to be on the rise. A recent Gallup survey showed that 25 percent of employees report themselves as being "somewhat angry" at work. One in 20 employees has been assaulted at work, 1 in 6 has been sexually harassed, and 1 in 3 has been the subject of verbal abuse. Workplace homicides are now the second most prevalent reason for death at work, with 709 homicides occurring in 1998. Unfortunately, poor leadership practices appear to be a leading cause of workplace anger; and workers are four times more likely to leave a company if they have an abusive boss. But what can a leader do to control anger and violence in the workplace? First, given that many people are working longer hours than ever before, leaders need to be especially vigilant of follower stress and strain. Second, leaders must be willing to let people take some time off when things start to get out of hand. The work will still be there tomorrow—few people have jobs where things really have to be done at a certain time. Third, never, ever abuse followers. There are many more of them than there are of you, and they can make your life miserable with various acts of computer sabotage, work slowdowns, and other passive-aggressive acts. More important, they are the people who are closest to the customer and do most of the work. If you have a performance problem, counsel the individuals in private and if necessary put them on some kind of performance plan. You could also use some of the development planning and coaching techniques described in Part V of this text to turn their performance around.

Sources: A. Quigley, "Organizational Consequences of Workplace Aggression," in R.T. Hogan and D.K. Sheldon (chairs), *Aggression in the Workplace: The Forgotten Problem*, symposium conducted at the 14th Annual Conference of the Society of Industrial & Organizational Psychology, Atlanta, GA, May 1999; B. J. Tepper, "Consequences of Abusive Supervision," *Academy of Management Journal* 43, no. 2 (2000), pp. 178–89; D. Hales and R.E. Hales, "Is Work Driving You Mad?" *Parade Magazine*, March 18, 2001, pp. 8–9; and G. Strauss, "Workers Hone the Fine Art of Revenge: Acts of Violence, Harassment toward Boss on Rise in Corporate World," *Denver Post*, August 24, 1998, p. 6E.

Global, Facet, and Life Satisfaction

There are different ways to look at a person's attitudes about work, but researchers usually collect this data using some type of job satisfaction survey (Bracken, 1992; Butorac, 2001; Curphy, 2001). Such surveys typically include items such as those found in Table 9–4, and they are usually sent to a representative sample of employ-

TABLE 9–4   Typical Items on a Satisfaction Questionnaire

1. Overall, I am satisfied with my job.
2. I feel the workload is about equal for everyone in the organization.
3. My supervisor handles conflict well.
4. My pay and benefits are comparable to those in other organizations.
5. There is a real future for people in this organization if they apply themselves.
6. Exceptional performance is rewarded in this organization.
7. We have a good health care plan in this organization.
8. In general, I am satisfied with my life and where it is going.

These items are often rated on a scale ranging from *strongly disagree* (1) to *strongly agree* (5).

ees in the organization. Their responses are collected and tabulated, and the results are usually disseminated throughout the organization. Table 9.4 presents examples of three different types of items typically found on a job satisfaction survey. Item 1 is a **global satisfaction** item, which assesses the overall degree to which employees are satisfied with their organization and their job. Items 2 through 7 are **facet satisfaction** items, which assess the degree to which employees are satisfied with different aspects of work, such as pay, benefits, promotion policies, working hours and conditions, and the like. People may be relatively satisfied overall but still dissatisfied with certain aspects of work. For example, a study of junior officers in the army revealed that overall satisfaction among them has been in decline over the past 10 years, and this decline is beginning to negatively impact reenlistment rates. A higher percentage of junior officers are choosing to leave the army than ever before; the two primary reasons for this high level of dysfunctional turnover seem to be dissatisfaction with immediate supervisors and top leadership. Many junior officers reported that they were tired of working for career-obsessed supervisors who had a strong tendency to micromanage and would just as soon throw them under a bus if it would advance their career (Stone, 2000). This decline in global satisfaction is not limited only to the army. Unfortunately, it is happening in many companies today. Much of this decline can be attributed to higher follower expectations, greater follower access to information through technology, economic downturns, organizational downsizings, and incompetent bosses (Curphy, 2001). The following quote summarizes what many followers are feeling today.

The question: If you had to describe your office environment as a type of television show, what would it be? The responses: "Survivor," 38 percent; soap opera, 27 percent; medical emergency, 18 percent; courtroom drama, 10 percent; science fiction, 7 percent.

Andrea Nierenberg,
New York University

Would life on a slave ship be much better if the galley master first asked the rowers to help write a mission statement? What employers need to come to terms with is the economic, cultural, and societal benefits of being loyal to their employees. If they don't, eventually their abuses will bite them on the ass.

Daniel Levine, *Disgruntled: The Darker Side of the World of Work*

Leadership practitioners should be aware of several other important findings regarding global and facet satisfaction. The first finding is that people generally tend to be very happy with their vocation or occupation. They may not like the pay, benefits, or their boss, but they do seem to be satisfied with what they do for a living (Campbell & Hyne, 1995). This points out the importance of intrinsic motivation, as most people gravitate to tasks or jobs they find interesting and enjoyable. The second finding pertains to the **hierarchy effect.** In general, persons with longer tenure or in higher positions tend to have higher global and facet satisfaction ratings than those new or lower in the organization (Campbell & Hyne, 1995). Because people higher in the organization are happier at work, they may not understand or appreciate why people at lower levels are less satisfied. From below, leaders at the top can appear somewhat naive and out of touch. From above, the complaints about morale, pay, or resources are often perceived as whining. One of the authors once worked with a utilities company that had downsized and was suffering from all of the ill effects associated with high levels of dysfunctional turnover. Unfortunately, the executive vice president responsible for attracting and retaining talent and making the company "an employer of choice" stated that he had no idea why employees were complaining, and that things would be a lot better if they just quit whining. Because the executive did not understand or appreciate the sources of employee complaints, the programs to improve employee morale completely missed the mark, and the high levels of dysfunctional turnover continued. The hierarchy effect also implies that it will take a considerable amount of top leaders' focus and energy to increase the satisfaction levels of nonmanagement employees—lip service alone is never enough.

Compensation is another facet of job satisfaction that can have important implications for leadership practitioners. As you might expect, the hierarchy effect is alive and well with pay: A survey of 3 million employees reported that 71 percent of senior management, 58 percent of middle management, and only 46 percent of nonmanagers rate their pay as "very good." Of nonmanagers, 33 percent rate their pay as "so-so" and 20 percent rate their pay as "very poor" (Kleiman, 1998). Given the wage gap between males and females, it may be correct to assume that a disproportionate amount of females can be found in these less satisfied groups. Many of these females may be the highest performers in their positions; therefore, this wage discrepancy, in combination with relatively small annual pay increases over the past few years, may contribute to disproportionately high levels of dysfunctional turnover among females.

People who are happier with their jobs also tend to have higher life satisfaction ratings (Judge, Boudreau, & Bretz, 1994; Judge & Watanabe, 1993; Hart, 1999). **Life satisfaction** concerns one's attitudes about life in general, and Item 8 in Table 9–4 is an example of a typical life satisfaction question. Since leaders are often some of the most influential people in their followers' lives, they should never underestimate the impact they have on their followers' overall well-being. Unfortunately, at least some of the increasing violence at home and in the workplace may be exacerbated by poor leadership (Ferlise, 1995; Hogan, Curphy, & Hogan, 1994; Curphy, 2001; Hales & Hales, 2001; Quigley, 2001).

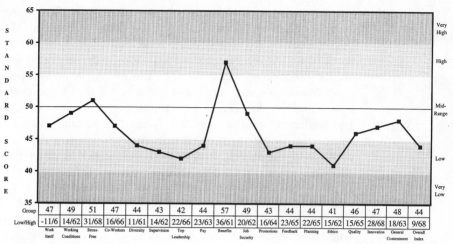

FIGURE 9.5

Results of a facet satisfaction survey

Source: D. P. Campbell and S. Hyne, *Manual for the Revised Campbell Organizational Survey* (Minneapolis, MN: National Computing Systems, 1995).

Job satisfaction surveys are used extensively in both public and private institutions. Organizations using these instruments typically administer them every one or two years to assess workers' attitudes about different aspects of work, changes in policies or work procedures, or other initiatives. Such survey results are most useful when they can be compared with those from some **reference group.** The organization's past results can be used as one kind of reference group—are people's ratings of pay, promotion, or overall satisfaction rising or falling over time? Job satisfaction ratings from similar organizations can be another reference group—are satisfaction ratings of leadership and working conditions higher or lower than those in similar organizations?

Figure 9.5 shows the facet and global satisfaction results for approximately 80 employees working at a medium-sized airport in the western United States. Employees completing the survey included the director of aviation and his supervisory staff ($n = 11$), the operations department ($n = 6$), the airfield maintenance department ($n = 15$), the communications department ($n = 6$), the airport facilities staff ($n = 12$), the administration department ($n = 10$), and the custodial staff ($n = 20$). The airport is owned by the city and has seen tremendous growth since the opening of the new terminal in 1995. By 1997 aircraft emplanements had already reached the level projected for the year 2010, and had exceeded the capacity of the new terminal. Unfortunately, staffing had remained at the 1995 levels, and the resulting workload and stress were thought to be adversely affecting morale and job satisfaction. Because of these concerns, the director of aviation decided to do a job satisfaction survey to pinpoint problems areas and develop action plans to resolve them.

Scores above 50 on Figure 9–5 are areas of satisfaction, scores below 50 are areas of dissatisfaction when compared to national norms. Here we see that airport employees are very satisfied with their benefits, are fairly satisfied with the work itself, but are dissatisfied with top leadership, ethics, supervision, feedback, promotion opportunities, and the like. All airport employees got to review these results, and each department discussed the factors underlying the survey results and developed and implemented action plans to address problem areas. Top leadership, in this case the director of aviation, was seen as the biggest source of dissatisfaction by all departments. The director was a genuinely nice person and meant well, but he never articulated his vision for the airport, never explained how employees' actions were related to this mission, failed to set goals for each department, did not provide feedback, never clarified roles or areas of responsibilities for his staff, delegated action items to whomever he happened to see in the hall, often changed his mind with key decisions, and failed to keep his staff informed of airline tenant or city council decisions. When confronted with this information, the director placed the blame on the rapid growth of the airport and the lack of staffing support from the city (the fundamental attribution error in action again). The city manager then gave the director six months to substantially improve employee satisfaction levels. The director did not take the problem very seriously so, not surprisingly, the survey results six months later were no different for top leadership. The director was subsequently removed from his position because of his failure to improve the morale at the airport.

It is important to point out that rarely is it enough to merely administer surveys. Leaders must also be willing to take action on the basis of survey results, or risk losing credibility and actually increasing job dissatisfaction. Upon receiving the results of these surveys, leaders with bad results may feel tempted to not share any results with their followers, but this is almost always a mistake. Although the results may not be flattering, the rumors are likely to be much worse than the results themselves. Also, followers will be less than willing to fill out subsequent satisfaction surveys if they see denial of the results and little if any change to the workplace. Furthermore, leaders feeling defensive about such results and tempted to hide them should remember that the bad results may not be a surprise to anyone but themselves; therefore, what's to hide? On a practical level, leaders should never assess employees' attitudes about work unless they are willing to share the results and take action.

Three Theories of Job Satisfaction

All of the theories of motivation described earlier provide insight into followers' levels of job satisfaction too. For example, it would be difficult for Julie to be satisfied with her job if she was consistently underdressed for weather conditions, or for Ling Ling to be satisfied if her goals were unclear, she was not provided feedback, or she failed to be rewarded for good performance. Nonetheless, several other theories offer even better explanations for job satisfaction.

Affectivity.   Affectivity refers to one's tendency to react to stimuli in a consistent emotional manner (Judge & Hulin, 1993; Judge & Locke, 1993; Judge, Locke, Durham, & Kluger, 1998). People with a disposition for **negative affectivity** consistently react to changes, events, or situations in a negative manner. They tend to be unhappy with themselves and their lives, and are more likely to focus on the downside or disadvantages of a situation. People with a disposition for **positive affectivity** consistently react to changes, events, or situations in a positive manner. They are happy with their lives, and tend to take an upbeat, optimistic approach when faced with new situations. People with a positive affective disposition tend to see a cup as half full; people with a negative affective disposition are more likely to describe a glass as half empty. These two groups of individuals are thought to attend to, process, and recall information differently, and these differences affect both job satisfaction and satisfaction with life itself. Researchers have found that negative affectivity was related to job dissatisfaction, and positive affectivity to job satisfaction (Judge & Hulin, 1993; Judge, Bono, & Locke, 2000). Of course, such results are hardly surprising—we all know individuals who never seem happy whatever their circumstances, and others who seem to maintain a positive outlook even in the most adverse circumstances.

These findings suggest that leadership initiatives may have little impact on a person's job satisfaction if their affective disposition is either extremely positive or negative. For example, if Ling Ling has a negative affective disposition, she may remain dissatisfied with her pay, working conditions, and so forth, *no matter what her leader does.* This is consistent with the findings of a study of identical twins reared apart and together which discovered that affectivity has a strong genetic component (Arvey, Bouchard, Segal, & Abraham, 1989; Connolly & Viswesvaran, 1998). Given that leaders can do little to change followers' genetic makeup, these findings again highlight the importance of using good selection procedures when hiring employees. Trying to increase followers' job satisfaction is a reasonable goal, but some followers may be hard (impossible?) to please, no matter what the leader does.

From a leader perspective, affectivity can have several implications in the workplace. First and foremost, one's own affectivity can have a strong influence on followers' morale or satisfaction levels. Say you worked for a leader with negative affectivity. Chances are he or she would find fault in your work, and constantly complain about organizational policies, resources, and so on. The opposite might be true if you worked for someone having positive affectivity. Second, leading a high percentage of followers having either positive or negative affectivity would likely result in very different leadership experiences. The positive group may be much more tolerant and willing to put up with organizational changes; the negative group would likely find fault in any change the leader made. Increasing job satisfaction through affectivity means hiring those with positive affectivity. However, few, if any, selection systems address this important workplace variable. Because negative affectivity may not be assessed or even apparent until a follower has been on the job for a period of time, perhaps the best advice for leadership practitioners is that some followers might well have a permanent chip on their shoulders, and there may be little you can do to change it.

Equity Theory.   This cognitive approach assumes that people value fairness in leader–follower exchange relationships (Kanfer, 1990). Followers are said to be most satisfied when they believe that what they put into an activity or a job and what they get out of it are roughly equivalent to what others put into and get out of it (Adams, 1963; Vecchio, 1982). **Equity theory** proposes a very rational model for how followers assess these issues. Followers presumably reach decisions about equitable relationships by assigning values to the four elements in Figure 9.6 and then comparing the two ratios (Adams, 1963). Regarding the specific elements in each ratio, personal outcomes refer to what one is receiving for one's efforts, such as pay, recognition, job satisfaction, opportunity for advancement, and personal growth. Personal inputs refer to all those things one contributes to an activity or a job, such as time, effort, knowledge, and skills.

A key aspect of equity theory is that Figure 9.6 contains *two* ratios. Judgments of equity are always based on a comparison to some reference group. It is the *relationship between the two ratios* that is important in equity theory, not the absolute value of either one's own or another's outcomes or inputs, considered by themselves. What matters most is the comparison between one's own ratio and that of a reference group such as one's co-workers or workers holding similar jobs in other organizations. Consider, for example, the story of an investment banker who was making over $400,000 per year but was extremely dissatisfied with her pay. The banker stated that, on the one hand, she got paid a "ridiculously high" amount of money for what she did, but on the other hand, she knew investment bankers who were making considerably more than she was. Similarly, Ling Ling may make more money than her peers, but she may also work longer hours, have more skills, and lease more apartments. In other words, although her outcomes are greater, so are her inputs, and thus the ratios may still be equal; there is equity.

In essence, equity theory does not try to evaluate equality of inputs or equality of outcomes. It is concerned with fairness of inputs relative to outcomes. The perception of inequity creates a state of tension and an inherent pressure for change. As long as there is general equality between the two ratios, there is no motivation (at least based on inequity) to change anything, and people are reasonably satisfied. If, however, the ratios are significantly different, a follower will be motivated to take action likely to restore the balance. Exactly what the follower will be motivated to do depends on the direction of the inequality. Adams (1965) suggested six ways people might restore balance: (*a*) changing their inputs, (*b*) changing their outcomes, (*c*) altering their self-perceptions,

FIGURE 9.6

Equity theory ratios

$$\frac{\text{Personal outcomes}}{\text{Personal inputs}} = \frac{\text{Reference group outcomes}}{\text{Reference group inputs}}$$

(*d*) altering their perceptions of their reference group, (*e*) changing their reference group, or, if all else fails, (*f*) leaving the situation. Thus, if Julie believed her ratio was lower than her co-worker's, she might reduce her level of effort or seek higher pay elsewhere. She could also change her reference group to that of ski lift operators at other resorts, or even quit. Research has shown that perceptions of underpayment generally resulted in actions in support of the model, but perceptions of overpayment did not. Instead of working harder in an overpayment condition (to make their own ratio more equitable), subjects often rationalized that they really deserved the higher pay (Campbell & Pritchard, 1976). An example of how equity theory might affect some salary negotiations is presented in Highlight 9.8.

Leadership, Equity Theory, and Professional Athlete Salary Demands

Highlight 9.8

General managers are responsible for the overall performance of their professional sports teams. They help select players and coaches; negotiate media, player, coach, and stadium contracts; keep team morale at a high level; and take action to ensure the team wins the championship and makes money. One of the most difficult issues general managers deal with is negotiating contracts with players. Many of the difficulties here involve equity theory. Players look at their own pay and performance and compare them to that of other athletes in the league. If they feel their compensation is not consistent with that of other players, they usually ask to be traded or for a new contract to be negotiated. These comparisons have led to the $100 million-plus salaries now commanded by marquee players in basketball, football, and baseball. But what happens to team morale, the win–loss record, and financial performance when one or two players make substantially more money than the rest of the team? Research on professional baseball teams over an eight-year period indicated that teams with high pay dispersion levels (i.e., large gaps between the highest and lowest paid starting player) did less well financially and were less likely to win division championships. Researchers surmised that this drop in team performance was due to the high levels of pay dispersion which eroded team performance and increased inequity for other players on the team. The trick for general managers seems to be to find enough financial rewards to induce higher levels of performance but not create inequity situations for the rest of the team.

Source: M. Bloom, "The Performance Effects of Pay Dispersions on Individuals and Organizations," *Academy of Management Journal* 42, no. 1 (1999), pp. 25–40.

Organizational Justice.   Organizational justice is a cognitive approach based on the premise that people who are treated unfairly are less productive, satisfied, and committed to their organizations. Moreover, these individuals are more likely to initiate collective action and engage in various counterproductive work behaviors (Sheppard, Lewicki, & Minton, 1992). According to Trevino (1992), organizational justice is made up of three related components. **Interactional justice** reflects the degree to which people are given information about different reward procedures and are treated with dignity and respect. **Distributive justice** concerns followers' perceptions of whether the level of reward or punishment is commensurate with an individual's performance or infraction. Dissatisfaction occurs when followers believe someone has received too little or too much reward or punishment. Perceptions of **procedural justice** involve the process in which rewards or punishments are administered. If someone is to be punished, then followers will be more satisfied if the person being punished has been given adequate warnings and has had the opportunity to explain his or her actions, and if the punishment has been administered in a timely and consistent manner. Research has shown that these different components of organizational justice are related to satisfaction with the leader, pay, promotion, and the job itself (McFarlin & Sweeney, 1992; Sheppard, Lewicki, & Minton, 1992; Trevino, 1992; Moorman, 1991; Brockner & Wisenfeld, 1996; Ployhart & Ryan, 1998; Colquitt, 2001; Colquitt, Conlon, Wesson, Porter, & Ng, 2001; Elovainio, Kjvimaki, & Helkama, 2001; Phillips, Douthitt, & Hyland, 2001).

So what would leaders need to do if they wish to improve follower satisfaction and reduce turnover using organizational justice theory? The underlying principle for organizational justice is fairness—do Ling Ling or Julie feel that the process in which rewards or punishments are administered is fair? Are the potential rewards commensurate with performance? Do Julie and Ling Ling believe the reward system is unbiased? Leaders who want to improve job satisfaction using this approach need to ensure that followers answer yes to these three questions. If followers answer no to any of the questions, then leaders need to change the reward and punishment system if they want to improve job satisfaction using organizational justice theory.

Summary

This chapter has reviewed research concerning motivation, satisfaction, and performance. Motivation was defined as anything that provides direction, intensity, and persistence to behavior. Although motivation is an important aspect of performance, performance and motivation are not the same thing. Performance is a broader concept than motivation, as abilities, skills, group norms, and the availability of resources can all affect followers' levels of performance. Job satisfaction is a set of attitudes that people have about work. Although a majority of people are generally satisfied with their jobs, people often have varying levels of satisfaction for different aspects of their jobs, such as pay, working conditions, supervisors, or co-workers.

Many of the approaches to understanding motivation have distinct implications for increasing performance and satisfaction. Therefore, several different theories of motivation were reviewed in this chapter. The first three theories, Maslow's (1954) hierarchy of needs, Alderfer's (1969) existence-relatedness-growth (ERG) theory, and Herzberg's (1964, 1966) two-factor theory assume that people are motivated to satisfy a universal set of needs. The next two theories examined motivation in terms of individual differences, emphasizing a person's intrinsic motivation to perform a particular task or a person's general level of achievement orientation. The next set of theories, ProMES and expectancy theory, examined motivation from a cognitive perspective. These theories assume that people make rational, conscious choices about the direction, intensity, and persistence of their behaviors, and generally engage in behaviors that maximize payoffs and minimize costs. The last two theories, the job characteristics model and operant approach, examined motivation from a situational perspective. Leadership practitioners likely will be more effective if they learn to recognize situations where various approaches, or the insights particular to them, may be differentially useful. Just as a carpenter can more effectively build a house by using a variety of tools, a leader can be more effective by using a variety of motivational interventions to enhance work.

Several other theories seem to be more useful for explaining followers' attitudes about work. Some research suggests that individuals vary in the characteristic tenor of their affectivity; some people are generally affectively positive whereas others are generally affectively negative. Such differences may set limits on the extent to which initiatives by leaders will actually impact follower satisfaction. Leaders may also be able to increase satisfaction levels by clarifying followers' perceptions of equity and organizational justice. Followers (and leaders for that matter) are more likely to have positive attitudes about work if they believe that their compensation is similar to that of others and that the reward and disciplinary systems are fair and just.

Key Terms

Questions

1. Why do you think there are so many different theories or approaches to understanding motivation? Shouldn't it be possible to determine which one is best and just use it? Why or why not?
2. Many good leaders are thought of as good motivators. How would you rate Colin Powell, Madeleine Albright, and Konosuke Matsushita in terms of their ability to motivate others?
3. What is your own view of what motivates people to work hard and perform well?
4. Do you know of any examples where reward systems are inconsistent with desired behavior?
5. What do you find personally satisfying or dissatisfying at work or school? For those things you find dissatisfying, how could you make them more satisfying? What theory of job satisfaction best explains your actions?

Skills

Leadership skills relevant to this chapter include:
• Providing constructive feedback
• Setting goals

• Punishment
• Diagnosing performance problems in individuals, groups, and organizations

Activity

1. Earlier in this chapter you were asked how the four types of motivation theories could be used to improve the customer service levels of flight attendants. Break into four groups, and have each group discuss how they would design and implement a motivation program using either a need, individual difference, cognitive, and situational approach. Each group should then give a 15-minute presentation on their findings. The presentation should include the approach they used, how they would collect any needed additional data, the program design, program implementation, potential barriers to the program, and their evaluation of the effectiveness of their program.

2. Interview someone in a leadership position to determine how he or she motivates employees. Do they use some of the programs outlined in Highlight 9–1? How would you categorize their motivational techniques using the 10 approaches outlined in this chapter?

3. Interview someone in a leadership position on employee satisfaction and retention. Does the organization conduct regular satisfaction surveys? What do the survey results reveal about the organization? Is the organization having any turnover problems? Why or why not?

10 Groups, Teams, and Their Leadership

Introduction

Understanding the unique characteristics that make individual followers tick is useful to leaders, but not enough. Leaders also need to understand how followers *as a group* represent something that cannot be understood solely in terms of the group members' collective individual characteristics. While both leadership and followership often have been conceptualized in terms of characteristics of individuals, it is interesting to note that a survey of 35 texts on organizational behavior found that in each one, the chapter on leadership is in the section on group behavior, not in the section on individual behavior (Ginnett, 1992). This should not be terribly surprising since groups (even as small as two people) are essential if leaders are to impact anything beyond their own behavior. What may be surprising is that the concept of groups is sometimes omitted entirely from books on leadership. As stated earlier, the whole can be greater than the sum of its parts, and the **group perspective** looks at how different group characteristics can affect relationships both with the leader and among followers.

> *We are born for cooperation, as are the feet, the hands, the eyelids, and the upper and lower jaws.*
>
> Marcus Aurelius

This chapter will begin by examining some of the characteristic of groups that uniquely differentiate them from individual phenomena. Given the high interest in organizational team work, we will move from the group to the team and conclude with a model developed to help leaders design, diagnose, and leverage high-impact factors to create the conditions which foster team effectiveness.

The Nature of Groups

Perhaps we should begin by defining what a **group** is. A group can be thought of as "two or more persons who are interacting with one another in such a manner that each person influences and is influenced by each other person" (Shaw, 1981).

Three aspects of this definition are particularly important to the study of leadership. First, this definition incorporates the concept of reciprocal influence between leaders and followers, an idea considerably different from the one-way nature of influence implicit in the dictionary's definition of followers. Second, group members interact and influence each other. Thus, people waiting at a bus stop would not constitute a group, as there generally is neither interaction nor influence between the various individuals. On the other hand, eight people meeting to plan a school bond election would constitute a group, as there probably would be a high level of mutual interaction among the attendees. Third, the definition does not constrain individuals to only one group. Everyone belongs to a number of different groups; an individual could be a member of various service, production, sports, religious, parent, and volunteer groups simultaneously.

It is important to realize that though people belong to many groups, just as they do to many organizations, groups and organizations are not the same thing (groups, of course, can exist within organizations). Organizations can be so large that most members do not know most of the other people in the organization. In such cases there is relatively little intermember interaction and reciprocal influence. Similarly, organizations typically are just too large and impersonal to have much effect on anyone's feelings, whereas groups are small and immediate enough to impact both feelings and self-image. People often tend to identify more with the groups they belong to than with the organizations they belong to; they are more psychologically "invested" in their groups. Also, certain important psychological needs (e.g., social contact) are better satisfied by groups than by organizations.

Perhaps an example will clarify the distinction between groups and organizations. Consider a church so large that it may fairly be described as an organization: so large that multiple services must be offered on Sunday mornings; so large that dozens of different study classes are offered each week; so large there are numerous different choirs and musical ensembles. In so large a church, the members hardly could be said to interact with or influence each other except on an occasional basis. Such size often presents both advantages and disadvantages to the membership. On the one hand, it makes possible a rich diversity of activities; on the other hand, such size can make the church itself (i.e., the overall organization) seem relatively impersonal. It may be difficult to identity with a large organization other than in name only (e.g., "I belong to First Presbyterian Church"). In such cases many people identify more with particular groups within the church than with the church itself; it may be easier to *feel* a part of some smaller group such as the high school choir or a weekly study group.

Although groups play a pervasive role in society, in general people spend very little time thinking about the factors that affect group processes and intragroup relationships. Therefore, the rest of this section will describe some group characteristics that can affect both leaders and followers. Much of the research on groups goes well beyond the scope of this chapter (see Gibbard, Hartman, & Mann, 1978; Shaw, 1981; Hackman, 1990), but six concepts are so basic to the group perspective that they deserve our attention. These six concepts are group size, stages of group development, roles, norms, communication, and cohesion. Five of them will be addressed in sections below. The sixth, communication, permeates them all.

Group Size

The size of any group has implications for both leaders and followers. First, leader emergence is partly a function of group size. The greater number of people in a large versus a small group will affect the probability that any individual is likely to emerge as leader. Second, as groups become larger, **cliques** are more likely to develop (Yukl, 1981). Cliques are subgroups of individuals who often share the same goals, values, and expectations. Because cliques generally wield more influence than individual members, they are likely to exert considerable influence—positively or negatively—on the larger group. Leaders need to identify and deal with cliques within their groups, as many intragroup conflicts are the results of cliques having different values, goals, and expectations.

Third, group size also can affect a leader's behavioral style. Leaders with a large **span of control** tend to be more directive, spend less time with individual subordinates, and use more impersonal approaches when influencing followers. Leaders with a small span of control tend to display more consideration and use more personal approaches when influencing followers (Badin, 1974; Goodstadt & Kipnis, 1970; Kipnis, Schmidt, & Wilkinson, 1980; Udell, 1967). Fourth, group size also affects group effectiveness. Whereas some researchers have suggested the optimal number of workers for any task is between five and seven (Bass, 1960; Indik, 1965), it probably is wise to avoid such a simple generalization. The answer to the question of appropriate group size seems to be "just big enough to get the job done." Obviously, the larger the group, the more likely it is that it will involve differentiated skills, values, perceptions, and abilities among its members. Also, there certainly will be more "people power" available to do the work as group size increases.

There are, however, limits to the benefits of size. Consider the question, "If it takes 1 person two minutes to dig a 1-cubic-foot hole, how long will it take 20 people to dig the same size hole?" Actually, it probably will take the larger group considerably *longer*, especially if they all participate at the same time. Beyond the purely physical limitations of certain tasks, there also may be decreasing returns (on a per capita basis) as group size increases. This is true even when the efforts of all group members are combined on what is called an **additive task.** An additive task is one where the group's output simply involves the combination of individual outputs (Steiner, 1972). Such a case may be illustrated by the number of individuals needed to push a stalled truck from an intersection. One individual probably would not be enough—maybe not even two or three. At some point, though, as group size increases in this additive task, there will be enough combined force to move the truck. However, as the group size increases beyond that needed to move the truck, the individual

> *A committee is an animal with four back legs.*
>
> Jean le Carre

contribution of each member will appear to decrease. Steiner (1972) suggested this may be due to **process loss** resulting from factors such as some members not pushing in the right direction. Process losses can be thought of as the inefficiencies created by more and more people working together.

Group size can affect group effectiveness in a number of other ways. As group size increases, the diminishing returns of larger work groups may be due to **social loafing** (Latane, Williams, & Hawkins, 1979). Social loafing refers to the phenomenon of reduced effort by people when they are not individually accountable for their work. Experiments across different sorts of tasks have tended to demonstrate greater effort when every individual's work is monitored than when many individuals' outputs are anonymously pooled into a collective product. Recent evidence, however, suggests the process may be considerably more complicated than initially thought (Porter, Bird, & Wunder, 1991). The performance decrement may be affected more by the level of task complexity or the reward structure (e.g., cooperative versus competitive) than by outcome attribution.

Sometimes, working in the presence of others may actually increase effort or productivity through a phenomenon called **social facilitation.** Social facilitation was first documented in classic experiments at the Hawthorne plant of the Western Electric Company (see Highlight 10.1). However, social facilitation is not limited to research situations. It refers to any time people increase their level of work due to the presence of others. Typically this occurs when the presence of others increases individual accountability for work, in contrast to other

Social Facilitation and the Hawthorne Effect

Highlight 10.1

Social facilitation was first documented in experiments conducted at the Hawthorne plant of the Western Electric Company during the late 1920s and early 1930s. These classic studies were originally designed to evaluate the impact of different work environments (Mayo, 1933; Roethlisberger & Dickson, 1939). Among other things, researchers varied the levels of illumination in areas where workers were assembling electrical components and found production increased when lighting was increased. When lighting was subsequently decreased, however, production again increased. Faced with these rather confusing data, the researchers turned their attention from physical aspects of the work environment to its social aspects. As it turns out, one reason workers' production increased was simply because someone else (in this case, the researchers) had paid attention to them. The term *Hawthorne effect* is still used today to describe an artificial change in behavior due merely to the fact a person or group is being studied.

occasions when being in a group reinforces individual anonymity and social loafing (Zajonc, 1965).

Developmental Stages of Groups

Just as children go through different stages of development, so do groups. Tuckman's (1965) review of over 60 studies involving leaderless training, experimental, or therapeutic groups revealed that groups generally went through four distinct stages of development. The first stage, **forming,** was characterized by polite conversation, the gathering of superficial information about fellow members, and low trust. The group's rejection of emerging potential leaders with negative characteristics also took place during the forming stage. The second stage, **storming,** usually was marked by intragroup conflict, heightened emotional levels, and status differentiation as remaining contenders struggled to build alliances and fulfill the group's leadership role. The clear emergence of a leader and the development of group norms and cohesiveness were the key indicators of the **norming** stage of group development. Finally, groups reached the **performing** stage when group members played functional, interdependent roles that were focused on the performance of group tasks.

The four stages of group development identified by Tuckman (1965) are important for several reasons. First, people are in many more leaderless groups than they may realize. For example, many sports teams, committees, work groups, and clubs start out as leaderless teams. Team or club captains or committee spokespersons are likely to be the emergent leaders from their respective groups. On a larger scale, perhaps even many elected officials initially began their political careers as the emergent leaders of their cliques or groups, and were then able to convince the majority of the remaining members in their constituencies of their viability as candidates.

If you start yelling and becoming obtrusive and beboppin' around, you give the impression of insecurity, and that becomes infectious. It bleeds down into the actors, and they become nervous; then it bleeds down into the crew, and they become nervous, and you don't get much accomplished that way. You have to set a tone and just demand a certain amount of tranquility.

Clint Eastwood
on being a film director

Another reason it is important to understand stages of group development is the potential relationships between leadership behaviors and group cohesiveness and productivity. Some experts have maintained that leaders need to focus on consideration or group maintenance behaviors during the norming stage to improve group cohesiveness, and on task behaviors during the performing stage in order to improve group productivity (Stogdill, 1972; Terborg, Castore, & DeNinno, 1975). They also have suggested that leaders who reverse these behaviors during the norming and performing stages tend to have less cohesive and less productive groups. Thus, being able to recognize stages of group development may enhance the likelihood that one will emerge as a leader as well as increase the cohesiveness and productivity of the group being led.

While Tuckman's model is widely known if for no other reason than its components rhyme with each other, it is not without criticism. Recall that the subjects for Tuckman's research were training, experimental, or therapy groups. None of these particularly represent teams forming to do work in an organizational context. For example, Ginnett observed many surgical teams and never once saw them engage in storming behaviors as they formed. You wouldn't want to be the patient if there was a formation argument between the surgeon, the anesthesiologist, and the scrub nurse about who was going to get to use the scalpel today.

Gersick (1988, 1989) proposed a better model for teams in organizational settings. In studying **project teams,** she found that teams don't necessarily jump right in and get to work. Rather, they spend most of the first half of the team's life muddling through various ideas and strategies. Then, about midway into the project, the team seems to experience the equivalent of a midlife crisis where there is a flurry of activity and a reexamination of the strategy to see if it will allow them to complete their work. Gersick labeled this process **punctuated equilibrium,** which is obviously quite different from Tuckman's four-stage model.

Group Roles

Group roles are the sets of expected behaviors associated with particular jobs or positions. Most people have multiple roles stemming from the various groups with which they are associated. In addition, it is not uncommon for someone to occupy numerous roles within the same group as situations change. Ginnett (1990) found that members of airline crews have varying roles over the course of a day. Although some behaviors were universally associated with certain roles, effective team members on these airline crews generally were more flexible in changing their behavior as other role demands changed. For example, whereas the captain of an airplane is responsible for the overall operation and decision making during a flight, flight attendants often take over responsibility for planning and carrying out the crew's social activities in the evening (i.e., when the flight is over). One captain in the study, however, continued to make *all* the crew's decisions, including their evening social plans; he was inflexible with regard to the role of decision-maker. Not coincidentally, he was seen as a less-effective leader—even during the actual flights—than more flexible captains.

Some roles, like positions on athletic teams, have meaning only in relatively specific contexts. Generally speaking, for example, one only plays a lineman's role during football games (admittedly, one might argue that at many schools being an intercollegiate athlete is a role that extends to aspects of student life outside sports). Other roles are more general in nature, including certain common ones that play a part in making any group work—or not work—well. Highlight 10.2 presents a vivid example of how powerful roles can be as determinants of behavior.

In Chapter 8, leader behavior was characterized initially in terms of two broad functions. One deals with getting the task done (**task role**), and the other with supporting relationships within the work group (**relationship role**). Similarly, roles in groups can be categorized in terms of task and relationship

The Stanford Prison Experiment

Highlight 10.2

A fascinating demonstration of the power of roles occurred when social psychologist Philip Zimbardo and his colleagues (1973) created a simulated prison environment at Stanford University. From a larger group of volunteers, two dozen male college students were randomly assigned to be either "prisoners" or "guards." The simulation was quite realistic, with actual cells constructed in the basement of one of the university buildings. The guards wore uniforms, and carried nightsticks and whistles; their eyes were covered by sunglasses. The prisoners were "arrested" at their homes by police cars replete with blazing sirens. They were handcuffed, frisked, blindfolded, and brought to the "jail." They were fingerprinted, given prisoner outfits, and assigned numbers by which they would henceforth be addressed.

It did not take long for the students' normal behavior to be overcome by the roles they were playing. The guards became more and more abusive with their power. They held prisoners accountable for strict adherence to arbitrary rules of prison life (which the guards themselves created), and seemed to enjoy punishing them for even minor infractions. They increasingly seemed to think of the prisoners—truly just other college students—as bad people. The emotional stress on the prisoners became profound, and just six days into the two-week episode the experiment was halted. This unexpected outcome basically occurred because participants' roles had become their reality. They were not just students role-playing guards and prisoners; to a disconcerting degree they became guards and prisoners.

What should people conclude from the Stanford prison study? At an abstract level, the study dramatically points out how behavior is partly determined by social role. Additionally, it is clear how just being in the role of leader, especially to the extent it is attended by tangible and symbolic manifestations of power, can affect how leaders think and act toward followers. Still another lesson people might draw involves remembering the volunteers all had many different roles in life than those assigned to them in the study, though being a guard or a prisoner was certainly the salient one for a period of time. Whereas everyone has many roles, the salience of one or another often depends on the situation, and a person's behavior changes as his or her role changes in a group.

Source: P. Zimbardo, C. Haney, W. Banks, and D. Jaffe, "The Mind Is a Formidable Jailer: A Pirandellian Prison," *New York Times Magazine*, April 8, 1973, pp. 38–60.

functions (see Highlight 10.3). Many of the roles in Highlight 10.3 are appropriate for followers, not just the official group leader; all of these different roles are part of the leadership process and all contribute to a group's overall effectiveness. Moreover, it is important to recognize that the very distinction between task and relationship roles is somewhat arbitrary. It is sensible enough when

Task and Relationship Roles in Groups

Highlight 10.3

Task Roles

Initiating: Defining the problem, suggesting activities, assigning tasks.
Information Seeking: Asking questions, seeking relevant data or views.
Information Sharing: Providing data, offering opinions.
Summarizing: Reviewing and integrating others' points, checking for common understanding and readiness for action.
Evaluating: Assessing validity of assumptions, quality of information, reasonableness of recommendations.
Guiding: Keeping group on track.

Relationship Roles

Harmonizing: Resolving interpersonal conflicts, reducing tension.
Encouraging: Supporting and praising others, showing appreciation for others' contributions, being warm and friendly.
Gatekeeping: Assuring even participation by all group members, making sure that everyone has a chance to be heard and that no individual dominates.

Source: Adapted from K. D. Benne and P. Sheats, "Functional Roles of Group Members," *Journal of Social Issues* 4 (1948), pp. 41–49.

looking at the short-term impact of any given behavior, but in another sense relationship roles are task roles. After all, task-oriented behavior may be adequate for accomplishing short-term objectives, but an appropriately cohesive and supportive group increases the potential for long-term effectiveness at future tasks as well as present tasks.

Although the roles in Highlight 10.3 generally contribute to a group's overall effectiveness, several types of problems can occur with group roles that can impede group performance. One type of role problem concerns the **dysfunctional roles,** listed in Highlight 10.4. The common denominator among these roles is how the person's behavior primarily serves selfish or egocentric purposes rather than group purposes.

Another role problem is **role conflict.** Role conflict involves receiving contradictory messages about expected behavior and can in turn adversely affect a person's emotional well-being and performance (Jamal, 1984).

Role conflict can occur in several different ways. Perhaps most common is receiving inconsistent signals about expected behavior from the same person.

Dysfunctional Roles

Highlight 10.4

Dominating: Monopolizing group time, forcing views on others.
Blocking: Stubbornly obstructing and impeding group work, persistent negativism.
Attacking: Belittling others, creating a hostile or intimidating environment.
Distracting: Engaging in irrelevant behaviors, distracting others' attention.

Source: Adapted from K. D. Benne and P. Sheats, "Functional Roles of Group Members," *Journal of Social Issues* 4 (1948), pp. 41–49.

When the same person sends mixed signals, it is called **intrasender role conflict** ("I need this report back in five minutes, and it had better be perfect"). **Intersender role conflict** occurs when someone receives inconsistent signals from several others about expected behavior. Still another kind of role conflict is based on inconsistencies between different roles a person may have. Professional and family demands, for example, often create role conflicts. **Interrole conflict** occurs when someone is unable to perform all of his roles as well as he would like. A final type occurs when role expectations violate a person's values. This is known as **person-role conflict.** An example of person-role conflict might be when a store manager encourages a salesperson to mislead customers about the quality of the store's products when this behavior is inconsistent with the salesperson's values and beliefs.

A different sort of role problem is called **role ambiguity.** In role conflict, one receives clear messages about expectations, but the messages are not all congruent. With role ambiguity, the problem is lack of clarity about just what the expectations are (House, Schuler, & Levanoni, 1983; Rizzo, House, & Lirtzman, 1970). There may have been no role expectations established at all, or they may not have been clearly communicated. A person is experiencing role ambiguity if she wonders, "Just what am I supposed to be doing?" It is important for leaders to be able to minimize the degree to which dysfunctional roles, role conflict, and role ambiguity occur in their groups, as these problems have been found to have a negative impact on organizational commitment, job involvement, absenteeism, and satisfaction with co-workers and supervisors (Fisher & Gitelson, 1983).

Group Norms

Norms are the informal rules groups adopt to regulate and regularize group members' behaviors. Although norms are only infrequently written down or openly discussed, they nonetheless often have a powerful and consistent influence on behavior (Hackman, 1976). That is because most people are rather good at reading the social cues that inform them about existing norms. For example, most people easily discern the dress code in any new work environment without needing written guidance. People also are apt to notice when a norm is violated, even though they may have been unable to articulate the norm before its violation was apparent. For example, most students have expectations (norms) about creating extra work for other students. Imagine the reaction if a student in some class complained that not enough reading was being assigned each lesson or that the minimum length requirements for the term paper needed to be substantially raised.

Norms do not govern all behaviors, just those a group feels are important. Norms are more likely to be seen as important and apt to be enforced if they *(a)* facilitate group survival; *(b)* simplify, or make more predictable, what behavior is expected of group members; *(c)* help the group avoid embarrassing interpersonal problems; or *(d)* express the central values of the group and clarify what is distinctive about the group's identity (Feldman, 1984).

One irony about norms is that an outsider to a group often is able to learn more about norms than an insider. An outsider, not necessarily subject to the norms himself, is more apt to notice them. In fact, the more "foreign" an observer is, the more likely it is the norms will be perceived. If a man is accustomed to wearing a tie to work, he is less likely to notice that men in another organization also wear ties to work, but is *more* likely to note that the men in a third organization typically wear sweaters and sweatshirts around the office.

Group Cohesion

Group cohesion is the glue that keeps a group together. It is the sum of forces that attract members to a group, provide resistance to leaving it, and motivate them to be active in it. Highly cohesive groups interact with and influence each other more than do less cohesive groups. Furthermore, a highly cohesive group may have lower absenteeism and lower turnover than a less cohesive group, and low absenteeism and turnover often contribute to higher group performance; higher performance can, in turn, contribute to even higher cohesion, thus resulting in an increasingly positive spiral.

However, greater cohesiveness does not always lead to higher performance. A highly cohesive but unskilled team is still an unskilled team, and such teams will often lose to a less cohesive but more skilled one. Additionally, a highly cohesive group may sometimes develop goals that are contrary to the larger organization's goals. For example, members of a highly cohesive research team at a particular college committed themselves to working on a problem that seemed inherently interesting to them. Their nearly zealous commitment to the project, however, effectively kept them from asking, or even allowing others to ask, if the research aligned itself well with the college's stated objectives. Their quite narrow and basic research effort deviated significantly from the college's expressed commitment to emphasize applied research. As a result, the college lost some substantial outside financial support.

Other problems also can occur in highly cohesive groups. Researchers (Alderfer, 1977; Ginnett, 1987) have found that some groups can become so cohesive they erect what amount to fences or boundaries between themselves and others. Such **overbounding** can block the use of outside resources that could make them more effective. Competitive product development teams can become so overbounded (often rationalized by security concerns or inordinate fears of "idea thieves") that they will not ask for help from willing and able staff within their own organizations.

One example of this problem was the failed mission to rescue U.S. embassy personnel held hostage in Iran during the Carter presidency. The rescue itself was a rather complicated mission involving many different sorts of U.S. military forces. Some of these forces included sea-based helicopters. The helicopters and their crews were carried on regular naval vessels, though most sailors on the vessels knew nothing of the secret mission. Senior personnel were so concerned that some sailor might leak information, and thus compromise the mission's secrecy, that maintenance crews aboard the ships were not directed to perform increased levels of maintenance on the helicopters immediately before the critical mission. Even if a helicopter was scheduled for significant maintenance within the next 50 hours of flight time (which would be exceeded in the rescue mission), crews were not told to perform the maintenance. According to knowledgeable sources, this practice did impact the performance of at least one of the failed helicopters, and thus the overall mission.

Janis (1982) discovered still another disadvantage of highly cohesive groups. He found that people in a highly cohesive group often become more concerned with striving for unanimity than in objectively appraising different courses of action. Janis labeled this phenomenon **groupthink** and believed it accounted for a number of historic fiascoes, including Pearl Harbor and the Bay of Pigs invasion. It may have played a role in the *Challenger* disaster, and it also occurs in other cohesive groups ranging from business meetings to air crews, and from therapy groups to school boards.

What is groupthink? Cohesive groups tend to evolve strong informal norms to preserve friendly internal relations. Preserving a comfortable, harmonious group environment becomes a hidden agenda that tends to suppress dissent, conflict, and critical thinking. Unwise decisions may result when concurrence seeking among members overrides their willingness to express or tolerate deviant points of view and think critically. Janis (1982) identified a number of symptoms of groupthink, which can be found in Highlight 10.5.

A policy-making or decision-making group displaying most of the symptoms in Highlight 10.5 runs a big risk of being ineffective. It may do a poor job of clarifying objectives, searching for relevant information, evaluating alternatives, assessing risks, and anticipating the need for contingency plans. Janis (1982) offered the following suggestions as ways of reducing groupthink and thus of improving the quality of a group's input to policies or decisions. First, leaders should encourage all group members to take on the role of critical evaluator. Everyone in the group needs to appreciate the importance of airing

Symptoms of Groupthink

Highlight 10.5

An illusion of invulnerability, which leads to unwarranted optimism and excessive risk taking by the group.

Unquestioned assumption of the group's morality and therefore an absence of reflection on the ethical consequences of group action.

Collective rationalization to discount negative information or warnings.

Stereotypes of the opposition as evil, weak, or stupid.

Self-censorship by group members from expressing ideas that deviate from the group consensus due to doubts about their validity or importance.

An illusion of unanimity such that greater consensus is perceived than really exists.

Direct pressure on dissenting members, which reinforces the norm that disagreement represents disloyalty to the group.

Mindguards, who protect the group from adverse information.

Source: Adapted from I. L. Janis, *Groupthink,* 2nd ed. (Boston: Houghton Mifflin, 1982).

doubts and objections. This includes the leader's willingness to listen to criticisms of his or her own ideas. Second, leaders should create a climate of open inquiry through their own impartiality and objectivity. At the outset, leaders should refrain from stating personal preferences or expectations, which may bias group discussion. Third, the risk of groupthink can be reduced if independent groups are established to make recommendations on the same issue. Fourth, at least one member of the group should be assigned the role of devil's advocate, an assignment that should rotate from meeting to meeting.

One final problem with highly cohesive groups may be what Shephard (1991) has called **ollieism.** Ollieism, a variation of groupthink, occurs when illegal actions are taken by overly zealous and loyal subordinates who believe that what they are doing will please their leaders. It derives its name from the actions of Lieutenant-Colonel Oliver North, who among other things admitted he lied to the U.S. Congress about his actions while working on the White House staff during the Iran-Contra affair. Shephard cited the slaying of Thomas à Becket by four of Henry II's knights and the Watergate break-in as other prime examples of ollieism. Ollieism differs from groupthink in that the subordinates' illegal actions usually occur without the explicit knowledge or consent of the leader.

Nevertheless, Shephard pointed out that although the examples cited of ollieism were not officially sanctioned, the responsibility for them still falls squarely on the leader. It is the leader's responsibility to create an ethical climate within the group, and leaders who create highly cohesive yet unethical groups must bear the responsibility for the group's actions.

After reading about the uncertain relationships between group cohesion and performance, and the problems with overbounding, groupthink, and ollieism, one might think that cohesiveness should be something to avoid. Nothing, however, could be further from the truth. First of all, problems with overly cohesive groups occur relatively infrequently and, in general, leaders will be better off thinking of ways to create and maintain highly cohesive teams than not developing these teams out of concern for potential groupthink or overbounding situations. Second, perhaps the biggest argument for developing cohesive groups is to consider the alternative—groups with little or no cohesiveness. In the latter groups, followers would generally be dissatisfied with each other and the leader, commitment to accomplishing group and organizational goals may be reduced, intragroup communication may occur less frequently, and interdependent task performance may suffer (Robbins, 1986). Because of the problems associated with groups having low cohesiveness, leadership practitioners need to realize that developing functionally cohesive work groups is a goal they all should strive for.

In summary, the group perspective provides a complementary level of analysis to the individual perspective presented earlier in this chapter. A follower's behavior may be due to his or her values, traits, or experience (i.e., the individual perspective), or this behavior may be due to the followers' roles, the group norms, the group's stage of development, or the group's level of cohesiveness (i.e., the group perspective). Thus, the group perspective can also provide both leaders and followers with a number of explanations of why individuals in groups behave in certain ways. Moreover, the six group characteristics just described can give leaders and followers ideas about (a) factors that may be affecting their ability to influence other group members and (b) what to do to improve their level of influence in the group.

Groups versus Teams: Is There a Difference?

Virtually everyone has been involved in some group or other, often with the sort commonly called teams. But is there a difference between a group and a team? With *teams* and *teamwork* being the buzzwords of the new millennium, it is worth discussing the concept of teams and coordinated group work, or teamwork

As described earlier in this chapter, two identifying characteristics of groups are mutual interaction and reciprocal influence. Members of teams also have mutual interaction and reciprocal influence, but we generally distinguish teams from groups in four other ways. First, team members usually have a stronger sense of identification among themselves than group members do. Often, both team members and outsiders can readily identify who is and who is not on the team (athletic uniforms are one obvious example); identifying members of a group may be more difficult. Second, teams have common goals or tasks; these may range from the development of a new product to an athletic league championship. Group members, on the other hand, may not have the same degree of consensus about goals as team members do. Group members may belong to the group for a variety of personal reasons, and these may clash with the group's stated objectives. (This phenomenon probably happens with teams, too, although perhaps not to the same extent.)

Third, task interdependence typically is greater with teams than with groups. For example, basketball players usually are unable to take a shot unless other team members set picks or pass the ball to them. On the other hand, group members often can contribute to goal accomplishment by working independently; the successful completion of their assigned tasks may not be contingent on other group members. Of course, task interdependence can vary greatly even across teams. Among athletic teams, for example, softball, football, soccer, and hockey teams have a high level of task interdependence, whereas swimming, cross-country, and track teams have substantially lower levels of task interdependence. Fourth, team members often have more differentiated and specialized roles than group members. In the preceding section, we noted that group members often play a variety of roles within the group; however, team members often play a single, or primary, role on a team. Finally, it is important to bear in mind that the distinctions we have been highlighting probably reflect only matters of degree. One might consider teams to be highly specialized groups.

Effective Team Characteristics and Team Building

Not only do teams vary in the extent to which they have specialized roles or task interdependence; teams also vary in their effectiveness. Virtually identical teams can be dramatically different in terms of success or failure (see Highlight 10.6). We must ask, therefore, what makes one team successful and another unsuccessful? Although this is an area only recently studied, exploratory work at the Center for Creative Leadership has tentatively identified several key characteristics for effective team performance (see Highlight 10.7 for an astronaut's perspective on teamwork).

Examples of Effective and Ineffective Teams

Highlight 10.6

Most people can readily think up a number of examples of ineffective and effective teamwork. Consider the relative effectiveness of the teams depicted in the following two true stories:

Ineffective Teamwork: After an airline flight crew failed to get a "nose gear down and locked" indicator light to come on while making a landing approach into Miami, all three crew members became involved in trying to change the burned-out indicator bulb in the cockpit. Nobody was flying the airplane and none of them were monitoring the flight of the L-1011 as it descended into the Everglades and crashed.

Effective Teamwork: The crew of a DC-10, after having lost all capability to control the airplane through flight controls as a result of an engine explosion, realized they needed all the help they could get. Captain Al Haynes discovered another experienced captain was traveling in the passenger cabin and invited him to come up to the cabin to help the regular crew out. Miraculously, their combined abilities enabled the crew—using techniques developed on the spot—to control the plane to within a few feet of the ground. Even though there were fatalities, over 100 people survived a nearly hopeless situation.

The Center for Creative Leadership's research with teams indicated that successful and unsuccessful teams could be differentiated on the basis of eight key characteristics, the first six of which are primarily concerned with task accomplishment (Hallam & Campbell, 1992). First, effective teams had a *clear mission* and *high performance standards*. Everyone on the team knew what the team was trying to achieve and how well he or she had to perform in order to achieve the team's mission. Second, leaders of successful teams often *took stock* of their equipment, training facilities and opportunities, and outside resources available to help the team. Leaders of effective teams spent a considerable amount of time *assessing the technical skills* of the team members. After taking stock of available resources and skills, good leaders would work to *secure those resources and equipment* necessary for team effectiveness. Moreover, leaders of effective teams would spend a considerable amount of time *planning* and *organizing* in order to make optimal use of available resources, to select new members with needed technical skills, or to improve needed technical skills of existing members.

> *He that would be a leader must be a bridge.*
>
> Welsh proverb

The last two characteristics of effective teams were concerned with the group maintenance or interpersonal aspects of teams. Hallam and Campbell's (1992) research indicated that *high levels of communication* were often associated with effective teams. These authors believed this level of communication helped

Women in Leadership: Teamwork from an Astronaut's Perspective

Highlight 10.7

Dr. Bonnie J. Dunbar is an American astronaut. She has flown on four space shuttle missions. We asked her to share a few personal reflections about the meaning of teamwork and followership to her as she was growing up, as well as presently in her role in the space program. She wrote this during preparation for her flight in June 1992. She was payload commander for that space shuttle mission.

Above all, the success of a space flight depends upon teamwork: within the crew and between the ground controllers and the crew. Teamwork is a valued attribute among currently selected astronauts.

I was very fortunate as a young girl to have been exposed to that concept by my family. With four children and a multitude of chores to be performed, my mother and father impressed upon us our responsibilities within the family unit. Success of the farm (and our future) depended upon our contribution. As the oldest, I was expected to participate in all chores, including driving the tractor and "round-up" by horseback. There were no distinctions in these responsibilities between my brothers and me. Group experiences within the 4-H organization (showing steers, etc.) and playing on baseball, volleyball, and basketball teams reinforced the pride of sharing success together and consoling each other in defeat.

When I attended college, some of that team experience was missed. By virtue of my gender, I was considered an unwelcome minority by many in the engineering college. Therefore, I was never invited to the study groups or participated in group solution of the homework problems. Still, I found an outlet in group activities by belonging to Angel Flight (co-ed auxiliary to Air Force ROTC—I was elected Commander of 50 my junior year) and by continuing to play co-ed baseball. Ironically, my engineering classmates needed my athletic ability as first baseman on the playing field.

I was also supported by three very important individuals during this time: my father, my mother, and the chairman of the Ceramic Engineering Department, Dr. James I. Mueller. My parents always encouraged me to pursue my "dreams" and to be the best person I could be. The fact that I was the first in the family to attend college was a source of pride for them. That I subscribed to their principles of hard work, human compassion, and honesty was probably a source of greater pride. They were proud of my selection as an astronaut but my father was more concerned that I not forget how to get manure on my boots.

In my professional life, the closest I have come to real group esprit de corps has come through my association with the Astronaut Office. Perhaps it was due to the concept of "class training," or the similarity of individuals involved, but I consider those I work with as also my closest friends. Our successes are really those of a family team that extends out to the engineers, managers, and administrative support in the Space Shuttle program.

I am now on my third NASA Space Shuttle crew. As Payload Commander I have tried to convey to the noncareer payload specialists on my next flight the importance of

(continued)

being part of the crew . . . that we will share both the successes and the failures of the flight. It has been an interesting experience to assess others' ability to become "part of the team." I have seen what not being part of the team can do, and in a flight environment that can be highly risky. Not being a team member does more than cause internal friction within the crew; it can be hazardous.

So, what does being "part of the team" mean? It doesn't always mean being the smartest or the fastest. It does mean recognizing the big picture goal and the contribution that each individual brings to the whole. It may not mean being the life of the party, but it does mean being able to get along with people and to tread a fine line . . . knowing when to compromise and knowing when to stand firm. And, in an organization such as ours with competitive individuals used to being on top of the hill, it means knowing when to be a Chief and when to be an Indian. In the Astronaut Office, mission specialists rotate through technical jobs and different responsibilities during flights. Sometimes they are Indians instead of Chiefs. Those that perform best and appear to be well-regarded can do each equally well.

team members to stay focused on the mission and to take better advantage of the skills, knowledge, and resources available to the team. High levels of communication also helped to *minimize interpersonal conflicts* on the team, which often drained energy needed for team success and effectiveness. The characteristics of effective teams identified in this research provide leadership practitioners with a number of ideas about how they may be able to increase the effectiveness of their work units or teams.

A different avenue to group and team effectiveness has been to use a normative approach. One example of this technique is described in *Groups That Work (and Those That Don't)* (Hackman, 1990). Ginnett (1993, 1996) has developed an expanded model focusing specifically on team leadership, which we will examine in more detail later in this chapter. For now, our concern is with one of the three major leadership functions in Ginnett's model that focuses on team design. The model suggests four components of design of the team itself that help the team get off to a good start, whatever its task. This is important because it is not uncommon to find that a team's failure can be traced to its being set up inappropriately from the very beginning. If a team is to work effectively, the following four variables need to be in place from the beginning.

1. *Task structure:* Does the team know what its task is? Is the task reasonably unambiguous and consistent with the mission of the team? Does the team have a meaningful piece of work, sufficient autonomy to perform it, and access to knowledge of its results?

2. *Group boundaries:* Is the collective membership of the team appropriate for the task to be performed? Are there too few or too many members? Do the members collectively have sufficient knowledge and skills to perform the work? In addition to task skills, does the team have sufficient maturity and interpersonal skills to be able to work together and resolve conflicts? Is there an appropriate amount of diversity on the team (e.g., members are not so similar that they do not have differing perspectives and experiences, and yet not so diverse that they cannot communicate or relate to one another)?

FIGURE 10.1

Organizational shells

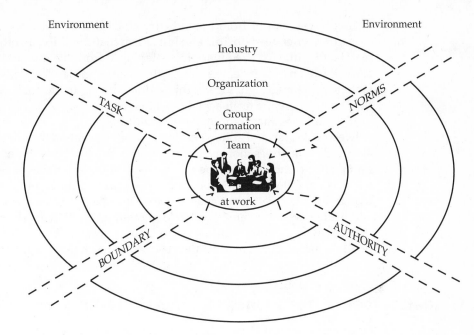

3. *Norms:* Does the team share an appropriate set of norms for working as a team? Norms can be acquired by the team in three ways: *(a)* They can be imported from the organization existing outside the team, *(b)* they can be instituted and reinforced by the leader or leaders of the team, or *(c)* they can be developed by the team itself as the situation demands. If the team is to have a strategy that works over time, then it must ensure that conflicting norms do not confuse team members. It also needs to regularly scan and review prevailing norms to ensure they support overall objectives.

4. *Authority:* Has the leader established a climate where her authority can be used in a flexible rather than a rigid manner? Has she, at one end of the authority continuum, established sufficient competence to allow the group to comply when conditions demand (such as in emergencies)? Has she also established a climate such that any member of the team feels empowered to provide expert assistance when appropriate? Do team members feel comfortable in questioning the leader on decisions where there are no clear right answers? In short, have conditions been created where authority can shift to appropriately match the demands of the situation?

As noted above, many of these team design components may be imported from preexisting conditions in the organization within which the team is form-ing, from the industry in which the organization operates, or even from the envi-ronment in which the industry exists. To help team leaders consider these vari-ous levels, Hackman and Ginnett (1986, 1993) developed the concept of **organizational shells** (see Figure 10.1). Notice that the four critical factors for team design (task, boundary, norms, and authority) are necessary for the group to work effectively. In some cases, all the information about one of these critical factors may be input from the industry or organizational shell level. In these cases, the leader need do little else but affirm that condition. In other cases, there may be too little (or even inappropriate) input from the organizational level to allow the team to work effectively. In these cases, the leader needs to modify the factors for team design. Ideally this is done during the formation process—the final shell before the team actually begins work.

These ideas may require a new way of thinking about the relationship between a leader and followers. In many organizational settings, leaders are assigned. Sometimes, however, the people who create conditions for improved group effectiveness are not the designated leaders at all; they may emerge from the ranks of followers. This model has been used to differentiate between effective and ineffective "self-managing work groups"—teams where the followers and leaders were the same people. Moreover, because the model is prescriptive, it also provides a number of suggestions about what ineffective work groups can do to be successful. That same purpose underlies the following model as well.

Ginnett's Team Effectiveness Leadership Model

Since we have emphasized that leadership is a group or team function and have suggested that one measure of leadership effectiveness may be whether the team achieves its objectives, it is reasonable to examine a model specifically designed to help teams perform more effectively: the **Team Effectiveness Leadership Model**, or **TELM** (Ginnett, 1993, 1996). Another way to think of this model is as a mechanism to first identify what a team needs to be effective, and then to point the leader either toward the roadblocks that are hindering the team or toward ways to make the team even more effective than it already is. This approach is similar to McGrath's (1964) description of leadership, which suggested that the leader's main job is to determine what needs the team is faced with and then take care of them. This approach also will require us to think about leadership not as a function of the leader and his or her characteristics but as a function of the team. As the title of the model suggests, team effectiveness is the underlying driver.

We have mentioned this model of group or team effectiveness briefly before, but now we will explore it in greater detail. The original model for examining the "engine of a group" was developed by Richard Hackman and has been the basis for much research on groups and teams over the last 20 years (Hackman, 1990). The model presented here includes major modifications by Ginnett and represents an example of a leadership model that has been developed primarily using field research. It provides the underlying structure for the "Leadership and High Performance Teams" course offered by the Center for Creative Leadership. While there have been controlled experimental studies validating portions of the model (K. W. Smith, Salas, & Brannick, 1994), the principal development and validation have been completed using actual high-performance teams operating in their own situational context. Examples of the teams studied in this process include commercial and military air crews in actual line flying operations, surgical teams

FIGURE 10.2

*General systems
theory applied to
teams*

in operating suites, top management teams, product development and manufacturing teams, and teams preparing the Space Shuttle fleet for launch. A complete illustration of the model will be shown later. Because of its complexity, it is easier to understand by starting with a few simpler illustrations.

At the most-basic level, this model (see Figure 10.2) resembles a systems theory approach with inputs on the left (i.e., individual, team, and organizational factors), processes or throughputs in the center (i.e., what one can tell about the team by actually observing team members at work), and outputs on the right (i.e., how well the team did in accomplishing its objectives). We will examine each of these stages. However, we will proceed through the model in reverse order—looking at outputs first, then the process stage, then inputs.

Outputs

What do we mean by outputs? Quite simply, **outputs** (see Figure 10.3) are the results of the team's work. For example, a football team scores 24 points. A production team produces 24 valves in a day. A tank crew hits 24 targets on an artillery range. Such raw data, however, are insufficient for assessing team effectiveness. How do we know if a team's output is good? How do we know if a team is effective? Even though it was possible for the three different teams mentioned above to measure some aspect of their work, these measurements are not very helpful in determining their effectiveness, either in an absolute sense or in a relative sense. For comparison and research purposes, it is desirable to have some measures of team effectiveness that can be applied across teams and tasks. Hackman (1990) argued that a group is effective if (*a*) the team's productive output (goods, services, decisions) meets the standards of quantity, quality, and timeliness of the people who use it; (*b*) the group process that occurs while the group is performing its task enhances the ability of the members to work as members of a team (either the one they were on or any new teams they may be assigned to) in the future; and (*c*) the group experience enhances the growth and personal well-being of the individuals who compose the team.

Process

It should be obvious why leaders should be concerned with the outputs listed in the preceding section. After all, if a team does not "produce" (output), then it could not be considered effective. But what is process? And why should a leader

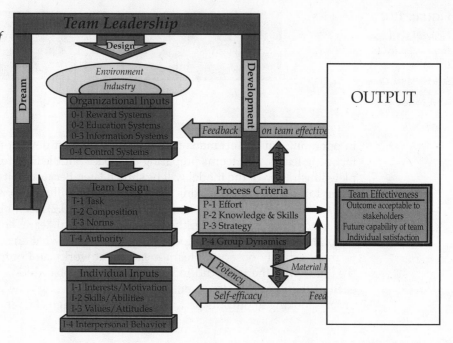

care about it? Actually, there are several reasons a leader might want to pay attention to the team's process—how the team goes about its work.

Some teams may have such a limited number of products that the leader can ill afford to wait until the product is delivered to assess its acceptability to the client. For example, a team whose task is to build one (and only one) satellite to be launched into orbit will have no second chances. There may be no opportunity to correct any problem once the satellite is launched (or, as was the case with the flawed Hubble Space Telescope, correction can be made only after great expense). Therefore, it may be desirable for the leader of such a team to assess his team's work while it is working rather than after the satellite is launched. Other kinds of teams have such high standards for routine work that there simply are not enough critical indicators in the end product to determine effectiveness from outcome measures. As an example of this situation, a team operating a nuclear power plant is surrounded by so many technical backup systems that it may be difficult to determine team effectiveness by looking at "safe operation" as a measurement criterion. But we have evidence that not all teams in nuclear power plants operate equally well (Chernobyl and Three Mile Island are but two examples). It would seem helpful to be able to assess real teams "in process" rather than learn of team problems only following disastrous outcomes. Even leaders of noncritical teams might like to be able to routinely monitor their teams for evidence of effective or ineffective processes. So it turns out that the way teams go about their work can provide some very useful information to the leader.

FIGURE 10.4

Process criteria of team effectiveness

Since process assessment is so important, let us focus for a moment on the block containing the four process measures of effectiveness in Figure 10.4. These four **process measures** of effectiveness provide criteria by which we can examine the ways in which teams work. If a team is to perform effectively, it must (*a*) work hard enough; (*b*) have sufficient knowledge and skills within the team to perform the task, *(c)* have an appropriate strategy to accomplish its work (or ways to approach the task at hand), and *(d)* have constructive and positive group dynamics among its members. The phrase *group dynamics* refers to interactions among team members, including such aspects as how they communicate with others, express feelings toward each other, and deal with conflict with each other, to name but a few of the characteristics. Assessing and improving group process is no trivial matter, as has been documented extensively in a comprehensive view of group process and its assessment by Wheelan (1994). The process measures are identified in the TELM by the labels P-1 through P-4 (P stands for process) in Figure 10.4. Last, it should be apparent that the process measure identified as group dynamics is depicted as the base or foundation for the other process measures. Our research over the last six years has consistently shown that to be precisely the case: Effective group dynamics are the foundation upon which other teamwork proceeds. If the team is ultimately to achieve the three valued outcome measures of effectiveness, a firm foundation of effective group dynamics will be critical. This foundation concept will appear in other sections of the model described later, as well.

What should the leader do if she discovers a problem with one of these four process measures? Paradoxically, the answer is not to focus her attention on that process per se. While the four process measures are fairly good diagnostic measures for a team's ultimate effectiveness, they are, unfortunately, not particularly good leverage points for fixing the problem. An analogy from medicine would be a doctor who diagnoses the symptoms of an infection (a fever) but who then treats the symptoms rather than attacking the true underlying cause (a nail in the patient's foot). Similarly at the team level, rather than trying to correct a lack of effort being applied to the task at hand (perhaps a motivation problem), the team leader would be better advised to discover the underlying problem and fix that than to assume that a motivational speech to the team will do the job. This is not to imply that teams cannot benefit from process help. It merely suggests that the leader should ensure that there are no design problems (at the input level) that should be fixed first.

Inputs

In a manufacturing plant, **inputs** are the raw materials that are processed into products for sale. Similarly in team situations, inputs are what is available for teams as they go about their work. However, an important difference between an industrial plant and a team is that for a plant, the inputs are physical resources. Often for team design, we are considering psychological factors. There is a variety of levels of inputs, ranging from the individual level to the environmental level. Some of the inputs provide little opportunity for the leader to have an influence—they are merely givens. Leaders are often put in charge of teams with little or no control over the environment, the industry, or even the organizational conditions. There are other inputs, however, that the leader can directly impact to create the conditions for effective teamwork.

> *Ask not what your country can do for you. Ask what you can do for your country.*
>
> John F. Kennedy

Figure 10.5 shows the multiple levels in the input stage of the model. Note that there are input factors at the individual and organizational levels and that both of these levels affect the team design level, as depicted by the direction of the arrows between these levels. Also note that there is a **leverage point I**(ndividual) 1–4, T(eam) 1–4, and O(rganization) 1–4 corresponding to each of the four process measures of effectiveness (P-1 through P-4). The meaning and importance of these leverage points will be clearer if we look at a few specific examples. Let us assume we have observed a team and discovered that its members are just not working very hard. They seem to be uninterested in the task, frequently wandering off or not even showing up for scheduled team work. We would diagnose this at the process level as a problem of effort (P-1). Rather than just encouraging them to work harder (or threatening them), we should first look at the input level to see if there is some underlying problem. The individual level (I-1, corresponding to a P-1 diagnosis) suggests that we look at the interests and motivations of the individual team members. These are referred to as **individual factors** in the model. If we have built a team to perform a mechanical assembly task but the individuals assigned have little or no interest in mechanical work, and instead prefer the performing arts, they may have little interest in contributing much

FIGURE 10.5

Inputs to team effectiveness

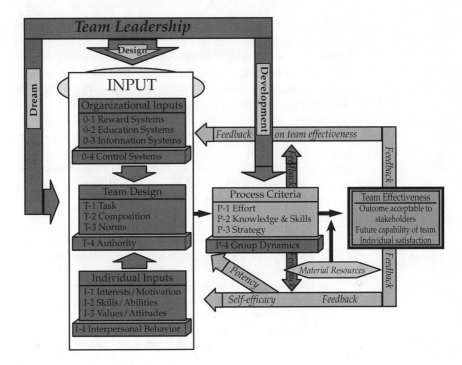

effort to the team task. Here, using instruments such as the Campbell Interest and Skills Survey to select personnel may help our team's effort level from an individual perspective (D. P. Campbell, Hyne, & Nilsen, 1992).

While it may seem tempting to move to the team-level inputs next, it is important to remember that this model emphasizes the way teams are influenced by both individual and organizational level inputs (again, note the direction of the arrows "leading into" the team design stage in Figure 10.5). Therefore, we will look at the **organizational level** next. At the organizational level (O-1), the model suggests that we should examine the reward system that may be impacting the team. If the individuals have no incentive provided by the organization for putting forth effort, they might not be inclined to work very hard, or perhaps, not to work at all. Similarly, the reward system may be solely structured to reward individual performance. Such a reward structure would be inconsistent with designs for a team task where interdependence and cooperation among members is often an underlying premise. If a professional basketball organization provides rewards for players based only on individual points scored, with no bonuses for team performance (games won or making the playoffs), you can expect little passing, setting picks for teammates, and so on.

Both the individual- and organizational-level variables contribute to the team's ability to perform the task. But there can also be problems at the **team design** level. Here (T-1), a poorly designed task is hypothesized to be unmotivating. If a job is meaningless, lacks sufficient autonomy, or provides no knowledge of results, we would not expect to see followers putting forth much effort.

Using the model, we found key leverage points at various levels of the input stage that would impact the way the team went about its work (team process). In the example cited, we diagnosed a process-level problem with effort (P-1), so we examined the 1-level variables at the individual, organizational, and team levels as the most likely location for finding input stage problems. By the way, the concept of leverage point does not imply that only factors at corresponding "numbers" should be considered. For example, a team's effort might be affected by an oppressive and authoritarian leader. As we have already seen, this "foundation-level variable" can have a tremendous impact on the other variables. Indeed, so powerful is this component, we should examine the process measure of group dynamics (P-4) and its corresponding leverage points in more detail. Consider the following two examples:

> **Surgical Team.** A surgical team composed of highly experienced members is involved in a surgical procedure that each member has participated in numerous times before. During one portion of the procedure, the surgeon asks for a particular instrument. The scrub nurse looks across the table at the assistant with a questioning gaze and then hands the surgeon the instrument he requested. Recognizing the instrument he has been handed (and asked for) is not correct for the current procedure, he throws it down on the table and curses at the scrub nurse. All members of the surgical team take a half-step back from the table and all casual conversation stops. No one offers any further voluntary assistance to the surgeon.
>
> **Commercial Airline Crew.** A commercial airline crew is making a routine approach into an uncrowded airport on a clear day. The captain is flying and has declared a visual approach. His final approach to the runway is not good, which greatly complicates the plane's landing, and the landing is poor. After taxiing to the gate, the captain and his entire crew debrief (discuss) the poor approach, and the team members talk about what they could have done individually and collectively to help the captain avoid or improve a poor approach in the future. The captain thanks the members for their help and encourages them to consider how they could implement their suggestions in other situations.

Obviously, the group dynamics are very different in these two cases. In the first example, the surgeon's behavior, coupled with his status, created a condition inappropriate for effective teamwork. The airline captain in the second example, even though not performing the task well, created a team environment where the team was much more likely to perform well in the future. In both of these cases, we would have observed unusual (one negative and one positive) group dynamics while the team was at work. These are examples of the group dynamics at the P-4 level.

Again returning to the model for determining points of leverage, we would check the I-4 variable at the individual level to determine if the team members involved had adequate interpersonal skills to interact appropriately. At the organizational level, the O-4 variable would suggest we check organizational components to determine if there are organizational control systems that inhibit or overly structure the way in which the team can make decisions or control its own fate. Such factors may include organizational design or structure limitations (a subject we will discuss in more detail in Chapter 11), or it may be a rigid computerized control system that specifies every minute detail of the tasks not only of the teams as a whole but of all the individuals composing the team. These excessive controls at the organizational level can inhibit effective team-work. Finally, at the team design level, the T-4 variable would have us examine authority dynamics created between the leader and the followers. Authority dynamics describe the various ways the team members, including the leader, relate and respond to authority. It is at the team level that the followers have opportunities to relate directly with the team's authority figure, the team leader. The intricacies of how these various authority dynamics can play themselves out in a team's life are more complex than this chapter warrants. Suffice it to say that there is a range of authority relationships that can be created, from auto-cratic to laissez-faire. For a more detailed explanation of this concept, see Gin-nett (1993). But even without further description, it should be no surprise that the varied group dynamics observed in the previous two examples were lever-aged by the leaders' use of authority in very different ways.

It would be simple if leaders could identify and specify in advance the ideal type of authority for themselves and their teams, and then work toward that objective. However, teams seldom can operate effectively under one fixed type of authority over time. The leader might prefer to use his or her favorite style, and

"Well, I guess I did it again guys? Missed a field goal in the final seconds. But hey, we're a team, right? Right, guys? Guys?"

Source: © Tribune Media Services. All rights reserved. Reprinted with permission.

the followers might also have an inherent preference for one type of authority or another; but if the team is to be effective, then the authority dynamics they are operating with should complement the demands of the situation. Since situations often change over time, so should the authority dynamics of the team. This idea is very similar to a point made earlier in the book—that effective leaders tend to use all five sources of leader power.

In research on the behavior of leaders in forming their teams, Ginnett (1993) found that highly effective leaders used a variety of authority dynamics in the first few minutes of the team's life. This does not mean that each highly effective leader used a single style that was different from the others (i.e., other leaders). It does mean that each one of the effective leaders used a variety of authority styles. At one point in the first meeting of the team, the leader would behave directively, which enabled him to establish his competence and hence his legitimate authority. At another time, he would engage the team in a very participative process and actively seek participation from each member of the team. By modeling a range of authority behaviors in the early stages of the team's life, the effective leaders laid the groundwork for continuing expectations of shifting authority as the situational demands changed.

Prescriptions of the Model

Having seen two examples of how this model uses team process measures to guide the search for critical input variables (or key leverage points) at the individual, organizational, and team design levels, we are ready to move on to the job of the leader. Following McGrath's (1964) view of the leader's role (the leader's main job is to identify and help satisfy team needs), and using Ginnett's TELM, it is possible to identify constructive approaches for the leader to pursue. As described earlier in this chapter, what leaders do depends on where a team is in its development. Ideally, leaders will have the opportunity to assume their leadership role at the very beginning of a team's life. With that luxury, the leader can proceed directly through the model from left to right. In this way, she can implement the three critical functions for team leadership: dream, design, and development.

Dream.   Obviously, the team needs to have a dream or sense of direction. In their book *The Wisdom of Teams* (1994), Katzenbach and Smith suggested that this may be the most important single step in teamwork. If the team has a challenging and demanding goal, teamwork may be necessary to accomplish the task. In highly effective work teams, the leader ensures that the team has a clear vision of where they are going. The communication of a vision frequently involves metaphorical language so that team members actually "paint their own picture" of where the team is headed. As one organizational leader told us, "It's hard to have a 'dream come true' if you haven't got a dream."

Design.   The importance of the design function of leadership cannot be overstated. Whether in the startup of a team or in the midstream assignment of leaders, designing the team is critical. It is also often the most frequently omitted step. Managers have long been trained to detect deviations and correct them. But what if the deviations are not detectable until the output stage? At their best, managers often detect deviations at the process stage and attempt to fix them "right where they are seen." Far too often, little time or attention is focused at the input level. Senior-level leaders may resist changing the organizational systems for a number of reasons, including having a vested interest in maintaining the status quo (whatever it is, it at least let them rise to their current position!). And while individual team leaders may have little control over the organizational context and systems, they always have the opportunity for making an impact in their own team's design.

This is a luxury few leaders get, however. If a leader takes over the reins of an in-place team, then she should (1) examine the team at work to determine if the process measures indicate potential problems, (2) back up to the appropriate level in the input stage to identify problems that may need to be corrected or redesigned, and (3) take appropriate action.

Development.   If the leader finds that the team has a clear sense of direction and vision, and the input variables at the individual, organizational, and team levels are contributing positively to team effectiveness (i.e., the design portion of the leader's job has been taken care of), then she can turn her attention to the development level. Development is the ongoing work done with the team at the process level to continue to find ways to improve an already well-designed team. Given our individualistic culture, we have identified many teams in organizations that are apparently well designed and supported at the input level, but that have had no training or experience in the concept of teamwork. There are times when effective teamwork is based on very different concepts than effective individual work. For example, for a team to do well, the individuals composing the team must sometimes not maximize their individual effort. Referred to as subsystem nonoptimization, this concept is at first not intuitively obvious to many newly assigned team members. Nevertheless, consider the example of a high school football team that has an extremely fast running back and some very good (but considerably slower) blocking linemen as members of the offense. Often, team members are told they all need to do their absolute best if the team is going to do well. If our running back does his absolute best on a sweep around the end, then he will run as fast as he can. By doing so, he will leave his blocking linemen behind. The team is not likely to gain much yardage on such a play, and the linemen and the back, who have done their individual best, are apt to learn an important experiential lesson about teamwork. Most important, after several such disastrous plays, all of the team members may be inclined to demonstrate poor team process (lower effort, poor strategy, poor use of knowledge, and poor group dynamics represented by intrateam strife). If we assume that all the input stage variables are satisfactorily in place, ongoing coaching may now be appropriate. The coach would get better results if he worked out a better coordination plan between the running back and the linemen. In this case, the fast running back

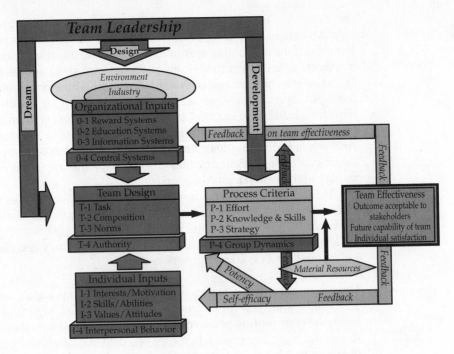

needs to slow down (i.e., not perform maximally) to give the slower but excellent blockers a chance to do their work. After they have been given a chance to contribute to the play, the running back will have a much better chance to then excel individually, and so will the team as a whole.

We are now in a position to consider the complete model (see Figure 10.6). It has been shown that leaders can influence team effectiveness by *(a)* ensuring the team has a clear sense of purpose and performance expectations; *(b)* designing or redesigning input stage variables at the individual, organizational, and team design levels; and *(c)* improving team performance through ongoing coaching at various stages, but particularly while the team is actually performing its task. These "midcourse corrections" should not only improve the team outcomes but also help to avoid many of the team-generated problems that can cause less-than-optimal team performance (Steiner, 1972).

Concluding Thoughts about Ginnett's Team Effectiveness Leadership Model

It is helpful to point out the few remaining items depicted in the model which have not been discussed (see Figure 10–6). Note first the box labeled **material resources** in the lower right-hand corner. Note that this is a physical requirement, not an issue for the design or coaching of the team itself. Even if a team is well designed, has superior organizational systems supporting its work, and has access to superior-quality ongoing development, without adequate physical resources it is not likely to do well on the output level. Also note that background shells representing the industry and the environment have been included, as discussed earlier in this chapter and shown in Figure 10.1. While the team leader may have little opportunity to influence these shells, the shells will certainly have an impact on the team.

Finally, there are several feedback loops which provide information to various levels of the organization. Usually, information is available to the organization as a whole (either formally or informally) about which teams are doing well and which are struggling. Whether leaders have access to this information is largely a function of whether they have created or stifled a safe climate. Feedback at the individual level can influence the perceived efficacy of the individual members of the team (Bandura, 1977; Lindsley, Brass, & Thomas, 1995), while the overall potency of the team is impacted even for tasks that the team has yet to attempt (Guzzo, Yost, Campbell, & Shea, 1993).

Lastly, let us reinforce a limitation noted earlier. For ease of use and guidance, this model has been presented as if it were a machine (e.g., if P-2 breaks, check I-2, O-2, and G-2). As with other models of leadership or other human systems, however, nothing is that simple. There are obviously other variables that impact teams and team effectiveness. There are also complex interactions between the variables described even in this model. But we have considerable evidence that the model can be useful for understanding teams (Hackman, 1990) and, in light of the relationship between teams and leadership, we are now using it as an underlying framework in courses to help leaders more effectively lead their teams.

Let us integrate the variables from this model into our L-F-S framework (see Figure 10.7). Clearly, there are variables of importance in each of the three arenas. However, in this model the characteristics of the leader play a lesser role because the leader's job is to work on what is not being provided for the team in order for it to perform its task. The focus thus has shifted from the leader to the followers and to the situation.

Geographically Dispersed Teams

Just as teams and teamwork have become essential to the accomplishment of work in organizations in the present (and as far as we can foresee into the future), so too will be an understanding of teams that are not in a single location. With the movement toward the global marketplace and the resultant globalization of organizations, it is appropriate to briefly consider the difficulties and recommended solutions for leading [geographically dispersed teams **(GDTs)**,] or as they are sometimes referred to, virtual teams. There is considerable discussion about the labeling of such teams (Kossler & Prestridge, 1996), but for simplicity we will call them GDTs here.

FIGURE 10.7

Factors from the normative model of group effectiveness and the interactional framework

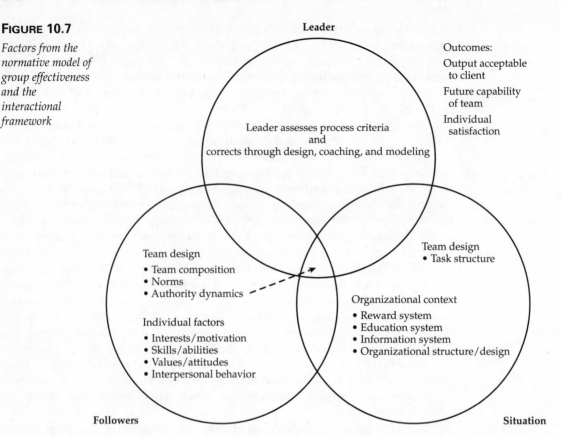

Leader

Leader assesses process criteria
and
corrects through design, coaching, and modeling

Outcomes:

Output acceptable to client

Future capability of team

Individual satisfaction

Team design
• Team composition
• Norms
• Authority dynamics

Individual factors
• Interests/motivation
• Skills/abilities
• Values/attitudes
• Interpersonal behavior

Team design
• Task structure

Organizational context
• Reward system
• Education system
• Information system
• Organizational structure/design

Followers

Situation

The marketplace is the globe (see Highlight 10.8). Western corporations are recognizing that growth and development opportunities are often much greater in Russia and other nations of the former Soviet Union, China, Latin America, and Africa than they are in their traditional markets of North America and Europe. But with this realization come new challenges for leading teams that are not only dispersed geographically but are often culturally different as well. Fortunately, information and communication technology is offering some new opportunities, if not solutions, for part of these problems. Early in this millennium, personal computer sales should top 100 million annually, or one PC for every 60 people on the planet; more than 60 million people will use cellular phones; and the Internet and World Wide Web are expanding at approximately 100 percent growth annually (Lipnack & Stamps, 1997). But is the mere opportunity to communicate electronically sufficient to ensure teamwork? Apparently not.

Researchers at the Conference Board (1996) reported that there were five major areas that needed to change if global teams were to work. The five listed were senior management leadership, innovative use of communication tech-

What Is the "Global Population" of Your Classroom?

Highlight 10.8

Your authors attended a training session conducted by a major corporation intended for its newly appointed executives. One session was devoted to demonstrating the need for a global perspective in today's environment. To illustrate the key point, the instructor divided the room into unequal groups representing the geographical distribution of the world's population and had each group stand up in turn. As each group stood, she told them the proportion of the global population they represented. The proportions she used are provided below. You might try it in your classroom—it makes the point dramatically.

Australia and New Zealand	2%
North America	5%
Former Soviet Union	5%
Latin America	7%
Western/Eastern Europe	10%
Africa	12%
Asia	56%

nology, adoption of an organization design that enhances global operations, the prevalence of trust among team members, and the ability to capture the strengths of diverse cultures, languages, and people.

Armstrong and Cole (1994) did in-depth studies of GDTs and have reported three conclusions which should be considered by leaders of these teams. First, the distance between members of a GDT is multidimensional. "Distance" includes not just geographical distance, but also organizational distance (e.g., different group or department cultures), temporal distance (e.g., different time zones), and differences in national culture. Second, the impact of such distances on the performance of a distributed work group is not directly proportional to objective measures of distance. In fact, Armstrong and Cole suggested that a new measure of distance between group members that reflects the degree of group cohesion and identity, a measure of psychological distance between members, would predict group performance better than geographical distance. Finally, the differences in the effects that distance seems to have on work groups is due at least partially to two intervening variables: (1) integrating practices *within* a GDT, and (2) integrating practices *between* a GDT and its larger host organization.

Finally, there are a number of frameworks under development to help leaders work with GDTs, and there may be specific factors that these frameworks provide which can be useful. However, in our admittedly limited exposure to GDTs in a pure research sense, a number of our clients have reported the TELM (discussed earlier) has been quite useful in considering the process problems that present themselves and in suggesting appropriate leverage points for intervention.

Summary

The group perspective showed that followers' behaviors can be the result of factors somewhat independent of the individual characteristics of followers. Group factors that can affect followers' behaviors include group size, stages of group development, roles, norms, and cohesion. Leadership practitioners should use these concepts to better understand followers' behaviors. Leaders should also use a team perspective for understanding follower behavior and group performance. Leadership practitioners need to bear in mind how a team's sense of identity, common goals or tasks, level of task interdependence, and differentiated roles affect functional and dysfunctional follower behavior. Additionally, because effective teams have several readily identifiable characteristics, leadership practitioners may want to use the suggestions provided by Hackman (1990), Ginnett (1992), or Hallam and Campbell (1992) to develop more effective teams.

The Team Effectiveness Leadership Model posited that team effectiveness can best be understood in terms of inputs, processes, and outcomes. The input level consists of the individual characteristics of the followers; the design of the team itself; and various organizational systems which create the context in which the teams will operate. The process level concerns the way in which teams behave while going about their tasks, and the output level concerns whether customers and clients are satisfied with the team's product, whether the team improves and develops as a performing unit, and whether followers are satisfied to be members of the team. By identifying certain process problems in teams, leaders can use the model to diagnose appropriate leverage points for action at the individual, team design, or organizational levels, or for ongoing development at the process level. Leaders concerned with teamwork in organizational settings have found this framework useful in helping them conceptualize factors affecting team effectiveness and identifying targets for change.

Key Terms

group perspective 288	additive task 290
group 288	process loss 291
cliques 290	social loafing 291
span of control 290	social facilitation 291

Questions

1. How do the tenets of Ginnett's Team Effectiveness Leadership Model compare with the components of team performance described earlier?
2. Not all group norms are positive or constructive from the leader's perspective. If a group holds counterproductive norms, what should the leader do?
3. On the basis of what you know about European, U.S., and Japanese cultures, which of our three leaders (Albright Powell and Matsushita) would be more comfortable with a group or team-based approach to work?

Skills

Leadership skills relevant to this chapter include:
- Diagnosing performance problems in individuals, groups, and organizations
- Team building for work teams
- Team building at the top.

Activity

NASA Exercise: Lost on the Moon

Your spaceship has crash-landed on the dark side of the moon and you are scheduled to rendezvous with the mother ship, which is 200 miles away on the lighted side of the moon. The crash has ruined the ship and destroyed all the equipment except for the 15 items listed below. Your crew's survival depends on reaching the mother ship, so you must choose the most critical items available to take on the 200-mile trip. Your task is to rank-order the 15 items in the order of their importance for your survival. Place a "1" beside the most important item, a "2" beside the second most important item, and so on until you have ranked all 15 items.

_____ Box of matches

_____ Food concentrate

_____ 50 feet of nylon rope

_____ Parachute silk

_____ Solar-powered portable heating unit

_____ Two .45 caliber pistols

_____ One case of dehydrated milk

_____ Two 100-pound tanks of oxygen

_____ Stellar map

_____ Self-inflating life raft

_____ Magnetic compass

_____ Five gallons of water

_____ Signal flares

_____ First-aid kit with hypodermic syringes

_____ Solar-powered FM transmitter/receiver

Your instructor has the "NASA Expert" answers and the instructions for completing the exercise.

IV FOCUS ON THE SITUATION

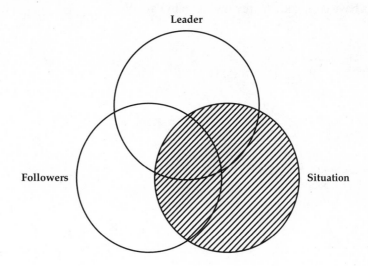

I n previous chapters we noted that understanding leaders and followers is much more complicated than many people first think. For example, we examined how leaders' personality
characteristics, behaviors, and attitudes affect the leadership process. Similarly, followers' attitudes, experience, personality characteristics, and behaviors, as well as group norms and cohesiveness, also affect the leadership process. Despite the complexities of leaders and followers,
however, perhaps no factor in the interactional framework is as complex as the situation. Not
only do a variety of task, organizational, and environmental factors affect behavior, but the relative salience or strength of these factors varies dramatically across people. What one person perceives to be the key situational factor affecting his or her behavior may be relatively unimportant to another person. Moreover, the relative importance of the situational factors also varies
over time. Even in the course of a single soccer game, for example, the situation changes constantly: The lead changes, the time remaining in the game changes, weather conditions change,
injuries occur, and so on. Given the dynamic nature of situations, it may be a misnomer to speak
of "the" situation in reference to leadership.

Because of the complex and dynamic nature of situations and the substantial role perceptions
play in the interpretation of situations, no one has been able to develop a comprehensive taxonomy describing all of the situational variables affecting a person's behavior. In all likelihood, no
one ever will. Nevertheless, considerable research about situational influences on leadership has
been accomplished. Leadership researchers have examined how different task, organizational,
and environmental factors affect both leaders' and followers' behavior, though most have examined only the effects of one or two situational variables on leaders' and followers' behavior. For
example, a study might have examined the effects of task difficulty on subordinates' performance

yet ignored how broader issues, such as organizational policy or structure, might also affect their performance. This is primarily due to the difficulty of studying the effects of organizational and environmental factors on behavior. As you might imagine, many of these factors, such as market conditions or crisis situations, do not easily lend themselves to realistic laboratory experiments where conditions can be controlled and interactions analyzed. Nonetheless, several consistent findings have emerged. We review them in Part IV.

11 CHARACTERISTICS OF THE SITUATION

Introduction

I n a book designed to introduce students to the subject of leadership, a chapter about "the situation" poses some challenging obstacles and dilemmas. The very breadth of the topic is daunting; it could include almost everything else in the world that has not been covered in the previous chapters! To the typical student who has not yet begun a professional career, pondering the magnitude of variables making up the situation is a formidable request. For one thing, the situation you find yourself in is often seen as completely beyond your control. For example, how many times have you heard someone say, "Hey, I don't make the rules around here. I just follow them." Furthermore, the subject is made more difficult by the fact

> When you've exhausted all possibilities, remember this: You haven't!
>
> Robert H. Schuller

that most students have limited organizational experience as a frame of reference. So why bother to introduce the material in this chapter? Because the situation we are in often explains far more about what is going on and what kinds of leadership behaviors will be best than any other single variable we have discussed so far!

In this chapter we will try to sort out some of the complexity and magnitude of this admittedly large topic. First, we will review some of the research which has led us to consider these issues. Then, after considering a huge situational change that is now occurring, we will present a model to help in considering key situational variables. Finally, we will take a look forward through one interesting lens. Throughout the chapter, though, our objective will be primarily to increase awareness rather than to prescribe specific courses of leader action.

Background

The appropriateness of a leader's behavior with a group of followers often makes sense only when you look at the situational context in which the behavior occurs. Whereas severely disciplining a follower might seem a poor way to lead, if the follower in question had just committed a safety violation endangering the lives of hundreds of people, then the leader's actions may be exactly right. In a similar fashion, the situation may be the primary reason personality traits, experience, or cognitive abilities are related less consistently to leadership effectiveness than to leadership emergence (R. T. Hogan, J. Hogan, & Curphy, 1992; Yukl, 1989). Most leadership emergence studies have involved leaderless discussion groups, and for the most part the situation is quite similar across such studies. In studies of leadership effectiveness, however, the situation can and does vary dramatically. The personal attributes needed to be an effective leader of a combat unit, chemical research-and-development division, community service organization, or fast-food restaurant may change considerably. Because the situations facing leaders of such groups may be so variable, it is hardly surprising that studies of leader characteristics have yielded inconsistent results when looking at leadership effectiveness across jobs or situations. Thus, the importance of the situation in the leadership process should not be overlooked.

Historically, some leadership researchers emphasized the importance of the situation in the leadership process in response to the Great Man theory of leadership. These researchers maintained that the situation, not someone's traits or abilities, plays the most important role in determining who emerges as a leader (Murphy, 1941; Person, 1928; Spiller, 1929). As support for the situational viewpoint, these researchers noted that great leaders typically emerged during economic crises, social upheavals, or revolutions; great leaders were generally not associated with periods of relative calm or quiet. For example, Schneider (1937) noted that the number of individuals identified as great military leaders in the British armed forces during any time period depended on how many conflicts the country was engaged in; the greater the number of conflicts, the greater the number of great military leaders. Moreover, researchers advocating the situational viewpoint believed leaders were made, not born, and that prior leadership experience helped forge effective leaders (Person, 1928). These early situational theories of leadership tended to be very popular in the United States, as they fit more closely with American ideals of equality and meritocracy, and ran counter to the genetic views of leadership that were more popular among European researchers at the time (Bass, 1990). (The fact that many of these European researchers had aristocratic backgrounds probably had something to do with the popularity of the Great Man theory in Europe.)

Trying to change individual and/or corporate behavior without addressing the larger organizational context is bound to disappoint. Sooner or later bureaucratic structures will consume even the most determined of collaborative processes. As Woody Allen once said, "The lion and the lamb may lie down together, but the lamb won't get much sleep." What to do? Work on the lion as well as the lamb designing teamwork into the organization . . . Although the Boston Celtics have won 16 championships, they have never had the league's leading scorer and never paid a player based on his individual statistics. The Celtics understand that virtually every aspect of basketball requires collaboration.

Robert W. Keidel

More recent leadership theories have explored how situational factors affect leaders' behaviors. In **role theory,** for example, a leader's behavior was said to depend on a leader's perceptions of several critical aspects of the situation: rules and regulations governing the job; role expectations of subordinates, peers, and superiors; the nature of the task; and feedback about subordinates' performance (Merton, 1957; Pfeffer & Salancik, 1975). Role theory clarified how these situational demands and constraints could cause role conflict and role ambiguity. Leaders may experience role conflict when subordinates and superiors have conflicting expectations about a leader's behavior or when company policies contradict how superiors expect tasks to be performed. A leader's ability to successfully resolve such conflicts may well determine leadership effectiveness (Tsui, 1984).

> The way of the superior is three-fold, but I am not equal to it. Virtuous, he is free from anxieties; wise, he is free from perplexities; bold, he is free from fear.
>
> Confucius

Another effort to incorporate situational variables into leadership theory was Hunt and Osborn's (1982) **multiple-influence model.** Hunt and Osborn distinguished between microvariables (e.g., task characteristics) and macrovariables (e.g., the external environment) in the situation. Although most researchers looked at the effects tasks had on leader behaviors, Hunt and Osborn believed macrovariables had a pervasive influence on the ways leaders act. Both role theory and the multiple-influence model highlight a major problem in addressing situational factors, which was noted previously: that situations can vary in countless ways. Because situations can vary in so many ways, it is helpful for leaders to have an abstract scheme for conceptualizing situations. This would be a step in knowing how to identify what may be most salient or critical to pay attention to in any particular instance.

One of the most basic abstractions is **situational levels.** The idea behind situational levels may best be conveyed with an example. Suppose someone asked you, "How are things going at work?" You might respond by commenting on the specific tasks you perform (e.g., "It is still pretty tough. I am under the gun for getting next year's budget prepared, and I have never done that before."). Or, you might respond by commenting on aspects of the overall organization (e.g., "It is really different. There are so many rules you have to follow. My old company was not like that at all."). Or, you might comment on factors affecting the organization itself (e.g., "I've been real worried about keeping my job—you know how many cutbacks there have been in our whole industry recently."). Each response deals with the situation, but each refers to a very different level of abstraction: the task level, the organizational level, and the environmental level. Each of these three levels provides a different perspective with which to examine the leadership process (see Figure 11.1).

These three levels certainly do not exhaust all the ways situations vary. Situations also differ in terms of physical variables like noise and temperature levels, workload demands, and the extent to which work groups interact with other groups. Organizations also have unique "corporate cultures," which define a

FIGURE 11.1

*An expanded
leader-follower-
situation model*

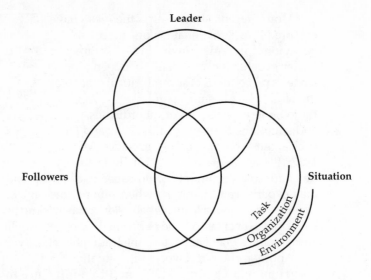

context for leadership. And there are always even broader economic, social, legal, and technological aspects of situations within which the leadership process occurs. What, amid all this situational complexity, should leaders pay attention to? We will try to provide some insights into this question by presenting a model which considers many of these factors. But first, let us consider an environmental aspect of the situation that is changing for virtually all of us as we move into the new millennium.

From the Industrial Age to the Information Age

All of us have grown up in the age of industry, but perhaps in its waning years. Starting just before the American Civil War and continuing up through the last quarter of the 20th century, the industrial age supplanted the age of agriculture. During the industrial age, companies succeeded according to how well they could capture the benefits from "economies of scale and scope" (Chandler, 1990). Technology mattered, but mostly to the extent that companies could increase the efficiencies of mass production. Now a new age is emerging, and in this information age many of the fundamental assumptions of the industrial age are becoming obsolete.

Kaplan and Norton (1996) described a new set of operating assumptions underlying the information age and contrasted them with their predecessors in the industrial age. They described changes in the following ways companies operate:

> **Cross Functions.** Industrial age organizations gained competitive advantage through specialization of functional skills in areas like manufacturing, distribution, marketing, and technology. This specialization yielded substantial benefits, but over time, also led to enormous inefficiencies, and slow response processes. The infor-

mation age organization operates with integrated business processes that cut across traditional business functions.

Links to Customers and Suppliers. Industrial age companies worked with customers and suppliers via arm's-length transactions. Information technology enables today's organizations to integrate supply, production, and delivery processes and to realize enormous improvements in cost, quality, and response time.

Customer Segmentation. Industrial age companies prospered by offering low-cost but standardized products and services (remember Henry Ford's comment that his customers "can have whatever color they want as long as it is black." Information age companies must learn to offer customized products and services to diverse customer segments.

Global Scale. Information age companies compete against the best companies throughout the entire world. In fact, the large investments required for new products and services may require customers worldwide to provide adequate returns on those costs.

Innovation. Product life cycles continue to shrink. Competitive advantage in one generation of a product's life is no guarantee of success for future generations of that product. Companies operating in an environment of rapid technological innovation must be masters at anticipating customers' future needs, innovating new products and services, and rapidly deploying new technologies into efficient delivery processes.

Knowledge Workers. Industrial companies created sharp distinctions between an intellectual elite on the one hand (especially managers and engineers), and a direct labor workforce on the other. The latter group performed tasks and processes under direct supervision of white-collar engineers and managers. This typically involved physical rather than mental capabilities. Now, all employees must contribute value by what they know and by the information they can provide.

One needs only to reflect upon Kaplan and Norton's list of changing operating assumptions to recognize that the situation leaders find themselves in today is different from the situation of 20 years ago. What's more, it is probably changing at an ever increasing rate. In a very real sense, the pace of change today is like trying to navigate white-water rapids; things are changing so rapidly it can be difficult to get one's bearings. Therefore, we believe it is helpful to use a model that identifies some of the key elements of the situation in an organizational setting.

The Congruence Model

Like Ginnett's Team Effectiveness Leadership Model (TELM) described in the previous chapter, the Congruence Model, presented most recently by Nadler and Tushman (1997), is a systems model with *inputs, processes,* and *outputs.* We will focus on the four factors making up the organizational processes in this chapter, but we should briefly discuss the inputs and outputs first. As can be seen in Figure 11.2, there are three components under inputs: the environment, the resources, and the history. Attention to these components must be kept to a minimum here, but their importance in impacting leaders and followers is

FIGURE 11.2

A Congruence Model

Source: *Competing by Design: The Power of Organizational Architecture,* by David Nadler and Michael Tushman. Copyright © 1997 Oxford University Press. Used by permission of Oxford University Press, Inc.

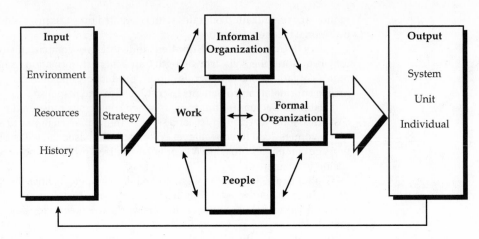

nonetheless significant. We already have noted the magnitude of changes resulting from the shift in environment from the industrial age to the information age. Beyond that, *environment* also includes market changes, governmental regulations and laws, competitors, financial institutions, and even changes in weather patterns (consider the impact of *El Niño* in 1998). We will return to examine some further ways to specify environmental factors later in the chapter. *Resources* are anything which the organization can use to its benefit, and may include not only material components such as capital or information, but also less tangible components such as perceptions of quality (e.g., Nikkon cameras or Mercedes automobiles). *History of the organization* includes not only the recent past that bears upon today's work but also myths about the organization's origin. For example, when taking important visitors on tours of the facilities at a large manufacturing plant, the guides would always stop and point out a series of visitor parking spots located near the executive wing of the building. The guides explained that the first plant manager and his team had decided to do away with executive parking slots by consensus, and that "consensus decision making was still the way everyone worked here"—25 years later.

Outputs are evaluated by the impact on the system as a whole, the unit, and the individual (again, very much like the TELM). At each of these levels, it is appropriate to ask how well the organization met its objectives, how efficient it was at achieving those outcomes, and how well the organization has scanned the horizon for new opportunities and threats. Before moving to the core process variables of the situation in this model, it is necessary to note that strategy is the collective set of business decisions about how to allocate scarce resources to maximize the strengths of the organization, given the external opportunities, while minimizing the organizational weaknesses, given the external threats.

The core of the Congruence Model has four components: the work, the people, the formal organization, and the informal organization. Note that each component relates to the other three. This is a key component of this model and is the basis of its name. Based upon a tenet of systems theory, the components of the model attempt to stay in balance or homeostasis. The better the fit of all the components, the more "congruence" there is between its various elements. Just one implication of this idea is that if a leader wanted to make changes in the outputs of his or her team, the model suggests it would be better to make small but equal changes in all the subsystems than it would be to make a substantial change in only one component. If only one element is changed, the other major components in the model, in trying to achieve homeostasis, would tend to resist and react to pull the "out-of-balance" element back in line.

The Work

At the most fundamental level, the work is "what is to be done" by the organization and its component parts. Given the variety of tasks people perform, it is natural for people to try to order and make sense of them. In thinking back across the many different tasks you have performed, you might categorize them as boring, challenging, dangerous, fun, interesting, and so on. However, labeling tasks is just a reaction to them and does not foster understanding about what aspects of any task may have caused a particular reaction. In looking at tasks, therefore, we want to get beyond subjective reactions to more objective ways of analyzing them.

> *The brain is a wonderful organ; it begins working the moment you get up in the morning and does not stop until you get to the office.*
>
> Robert Frost

There are several objective ways to categorize tasks performed by leaders and followers. Tasks can be categorized according to their function, the skills or abilities needed to perform them, the equipment needed to perform them, and so on. As seen in an earlier chapter, tasks also can be described in terms of the characteristics of the job itself: skill variety, task identity, task significance, autonomy, and feedback from the job. We will add to those characteristics two other dimensions: task structure and task interdependence.

Job Characteristics.   **Skill variety** and the next four dimensions of tasks are all components of the job characteristics model (Hackman & Oldham, 1976, 1980) described in Chapter 9. Skill variety refers to the degree to which a job involves performing a variety of different activities or skills. For example, if an individual attaches the left taillight to a car on an automobile assembly line by mechanically screwing in the fasteners, there would be increased work but no increased skill variety if he subsequently stepped over the line to the other side to install the right taillight. Skill variety involves using different skills, whether mechanical, cognitive, or physical. We might also add that there is a qualitative dimension to skill variety. In general, jobs requiring greater skill variety are more enjoyable than those requiring lesser skill variety, but it also matters whether any particular individual personally values the skills she performs.

Although satisfaction may also depend on growth-need strength (the individual's psychological need for personal accomplishment, for learning, and for personal development), typically jobs that require a low variety of skills are repetitive, monotonous, boring, and dissatisfying (Bass, 1990; Hackman & Oldham, 1980; House & Dressler, 1974). And like structured tasks, tasks with low levels of skill variety make it easier for leaders to use directive behaviors but, because followers already know how to do the job, also make directive leadership behavior somewhat redundant (Howell & Dorfman, 1981, 1986; Kerr & Jermier, 1978; Kipnis, 1984). In such situations, leaders might try to restructure a subordinate's job in order to increase the number of (valued) skills needed. If that is not possible, then high levels of support and consideration for followers are helpful (Hackman & Oldham, 1980; House & Dressler, 1974).

Task identity refers to the degree to which a situation or task requires completion of a whole unit of work from beginning to end with a visible outcome. For example, if one works on an assembly line where circuit boards for compact disc (CD) players are being produced, and the task is to solder one wire to one electronic component and then pass the circuit board on to the next assembly worker, then this job would lack task identity. At the other extreme, if one assembled an entire CD player, perhaps involving 30 or 40 different tasks, then the perception of task identity would increase dramatically as one could readily see the final results of one's efforts. Furthermore, the job's skill variety (as discussed above) would increase as well.

Task significance is the degree to which a job substantially impacts others' lives. Consider an individual whose task is to insert a bolt into a nut and tighten it down to a certain specification using a torque wrench. If that bolt is one of several that fasten a fender to other parts of an automobile body on an assembly line, then both skill variety and task identity would probably be very low. Moreover, if the assembly person leaves the entire bolt off, it may cause a squeak or a rattle, but probably would not cause the fender to fall off. In such a job, task significance would be quite low as well. However, if the worker tightens the only bolt securing a critical component of a brake assembly on the space shuttle, then skill variety and task identity would be exactly the same as for our fender installer. However, task significance would be substantially higher.

Autonomy is the degree to which a job provides an individual with some control over what he does and how he does it. Someone with considerable autonomy would have discretion in scheduling work and deciding the procedures used in accomplishing it. Autonomy often covaries with technical expertise, as workers with considerable expertise will be given more latitude, and those with few skills will be given more instruction and coaching when accomplishing tasks (Hersey & Blanchard, 1977, 1984). Moreover, responsibility and job satisfaction often increase when autonomy increases (Hackman & Oldham, 1980).

The last task component in the job characteristics model is **feedback,** which refers to the degree to which a person accomplishing a task receives information about performance *from performing the task itself.* In this context feedback does not refer to feedback received from supervisors but rather to what is intrinsic to the work activity itself. Driving a car is one example of feedback intrinsic to a task. If you are a skilled driver on a road with a number of twists and turns, then you get all the feedback you need about how well you are accomplishing the task merely by observing how the car responds to the inputs you make. This is feedback from the job itself as opposed to feedback from another person (who in this example would be a classic backseat driver). Extending this example to work or team settings, leaders sometimes may want to redesign tasks so that they (the tasks) provide more intrinsic feedback. Although this does not absolve the leader from giving periodic feedback about performance, it can help to free up some of the leader's time for other work-related activities. Additionally, leaders should understand that followers may eventually become dissatisfied if leaders provide high levels of feedback for tasks that already provide intrinsic feedback (House & Dressler, 1974; Howell & Dorfman, 1981; Kerr & Jermier, 1978).

> *If you want to give a man credit, put it in writing. If you want to give him hell, do it on the phone.*
>
> Charles Beacham

Task Structure.   Perhaps the easiest way to explain **task structure** is by using an example demonstrating the difference between a structured and an unstructured task. Assume the task to be accomplished is solving for x given the formula $3x + 2x = 15$. If that problem were given to a group of people who knew the fundamental rules of algebra, then everyone would arrive at the same answer. In this example there is a known procedure for accomplishing the task; there are rules governing how one goes about it; and if people follow those rules, there is one result. These features characterize a *structured task*.

On the other hand, if the task is to resolve a morale problem on a team, committee, or work group, then there may be no clear-cut method for solving it. There are many different ways, perhaps none of which is obvious or necessarily best for approaching a solution. It may even be that different observers would not see the problem in the same way; they may even have quite different ideas of *what morale is*. Solving a morale problem, therefore, exemplifies an *unstructured task*.

People vary in their preferences for, or ability to handle, structured versus unstructured tasks. With the Myers-Briggs Type Indicator (MBTI), for example, perceivers are believed to prefer unstructured situations, whereas judgers prefer activities that are planned and organized (Myers & McCaulley, 1985). Individuals with high tolerance for stress may handle ambiguous and unstructured tasks more easily than people with low tolerance for stress (Bass, 1990). Aside from these differences, however, we might ask whether there are any general rules for how leaders should interact with followers as a function of task structure. One consideration here is that while it is *easier* for a leader or coach to give instruction in structured tasks, it is not necessarily the most helpful thing to do.

We can see that by returning to the algebra problem described earlier. If a student had never seen such an algebra problem before, then it would be relatively easy for the teacher to teach the student the rules needed to solve the problem.

Once any student has learned the procedure, however, he can solve similar problems on his own. Extending this to other situations, once a subordinate knows or understands a task, a supervisor's continuing instruction (i.e., initiating structure or directive behavior) may provide superfluous information and eventually become irritating (Ford, 1981; House & Dressler, 1974; Kerr & Jermier, 1978; Yukl, 1989). Subordinates *need* help when a task is unstructured, when they do not know what the desired outcome looks like, and when they do not know how to achieve it. Anything a supervisor or leader can do to increase subordinates' ability to perform unstructured tasks is likely to increase their performance and job satisfaction (Siegall & Cummings, 1986). Paradoxically, though, unstructured tasks are by nature somewhat ill defined. Thus, they often are more difficult for leaders themselves to analyze and provide direction in accomplishing. Nonetheless, reducing the degree of ambiguity inherent in an unstructured situation is a leadership behavior usually appreciated by followers.

Task Interdependence.   **Task interdependence** concerns the degree to which tasks require coordination and synchronization in order for work groups or teams to accomplish desired goals. Task interdependence differs from autonomy in that workers or team members may be able to accomplish their tasks in an autonomous fashion, but the products of their efforts must be coordinated in order for the group or team to be successful. Tasks with high levels of interdependence place a premium on leaders' organizing and planning, directing, and communication skills (Curphy, 1991a, 1992; Galbraith, 1973). In one study, for example, coaches exhibiting high levels of initiating-structure behaviors had better-performing teams for sports requiring relatively interdependent effort, such as football, hockey, lacrosse, rugby, basketball, and volleyball; the same leader behaviors were unrelated to team performance for sports requiring relatively independent effort, such as swimming, track, cross-country, golf, and baseball (Fry, Kerr, & Lee, 1986). Like task structure and skill variety, task interdependence can also dictate which leader behaviors will be effective in a particular situation.

In summary, these seven task dimensions provide a variety of ways in which to categorize or describe tasks. For example, ironing a shirt would probably have high task structure, autonomy, task identification, and feedback, and low skill variety, task significance, and task interdependence. On the other hand, building your own home may garner high ratings on all seven dimensions. Still another familiar activity is evaluated on these dimensions in Highlight 11.1. These seven dimensions can provide leaders with insight about how their behavior and work assignments may either help or hinder followers' satisfaction and performance. At the same time, leaders should remember that these dimensions exist somewhat in the eye of the beholder. What one follower perceives as an unstructured task might be seen by another as fairly structured. Finally, as we have emphasized before, leaders should use their communication and listening skills to assure that they understand subordinates' feelings and beliefs about the work they perform.

Golf and the Task Factors of the Situation

Highlight 11.1

Golf provides a convenient skill for illustrating the seven task factors described in this chapter. Golf provides a reasonable amount of *task structure*, as there are basic rules and procedures for properly hitting woods, long irons, and short irons, and for putting.

Skill variety comes into play because golfers use a variety of skills and talents. These include deciding on a club, the method used to swing the club, how hard to swing it, what kind of equipment to use, where to target the ball, how to compensate for wind, when to putt, and so on.

Because one person does all of the driving, pitching, and putting and is solely responsible for his or her score, a round of golf has a high level of *task identity*.

Task significance may be a little more difficult to appreciate in this example. It may not be there at all unless one is a particularly poor golfer (where he or she endangers the lives of other people) or, in the case of the professional golfer, has a family who depends on his or her performance.

Autonomy is certainly present when playing golf. The golfer gets to decide when to do the "work," how to do it, which clubs to use, and what strategies and tactics to use.

Feedback from the job is also apparent. Shortly after a golfer strikes the ball, she receives feedback on how well her swing worked. Whether it slices, hooks, or goes straight down the fairway is a bit of information that tells the golfer immediately how well her work is being accomplished.

Finally, golf generally lacks *task interdependence*. Golfers are not dependent on the other members in their foursome for their own score.

The People

We can afford to be very brief here since much of the rest of the book has focused on this topic. Still, it is worth repeating that leaders should look at the followers in terms of skills, knowledge, experience, expectations, needs, and preferences. In an increasingly global society, leaders can no longer afford to be parochial in their selection of followers. Compounding the global nature of work is, as noted earlier, the increasing rate of change in the environment. In a stable environment, any species can select a niche and survive for eons. But in a rapidly changing environment, diversity allows the species to sense and adapt more quickly. The same is true in the leadership world as well. Diversity is no longer merely the politically correct facade of leadership—it is essential to quality and survival in a rapidly changing world.

The Formal Organization

As with tasks, there also are a variety of dimensions for conceptualizing the organizational level of situations. This section will address how level of authority, organizational structure, organizational design, lateral interdependence, and organizational culture affect leaders' and followers' behavior.

> *A man may speak very well in the House of Commons, and fail very complete in the House of Lords. There are two distinct styles requisite.*
>
> Benjamin Disraeli

Level of Authority.   **Level of authority** concerns one's hierarchical level in an organization. The types of behaviors most critical to leadership effectiveness can change substantially as one moves up an organizational ladder. First-line supervisors, lower-level leaders, and coaches spend a considerable amount of time training followers, resolving work-unit or team-performance problems, scheduling practices or arranging work schedules, and implementing policies. Leaders at higher organizational levels have more autonomy and spend relatively more time setting policies, coordinating activities, and making staffing decisions (Blankenship & Miles, 1968; Luthans, Rosenkrantz, & Hennessey, 1985; Mintzberg, 1973; Page & Tornow, 1987). Moreover, leaders at higher organizational levels often perform a greater variety of activities and are more apt to use participation and delegation (Chitayat & Venezia, 1984; Kurke & Aldrich, 1983). A quite different aspect of how level of authority affects leadership is presented in Highlight 11.2.

Organizational Structure.   **Organizational structure** refers to the way an organization's activities are coordinated and controlled, and represents another level of the situation in which leaders and followers must operate. Organizational structure is a conceptual or procedural reality, however, not a physical or tangible one. Typically, it is depicted in the form of a chart that clarifies formal authority relationships and patterns of communication within the organization. Most people take organizational structure for granted and fail to realize that structure is really just a tool for getting things done in organizations. Structure is not an end in itself, and different structures might exist for organizations performing similar work, each having unique advantages and disadvantages. There is nothing sacrosanct or permanent about any structure, and leaders may find that having a basic understanding of organizational structure is not only useful but imperative. Leaders may wish to design a structure to enhance the likelihood of attaining a desired outcome, or they may wish to change structure to meet future demands. There are a number of ways to describe organizational structures, but perhaps the simplest way is to think of structure in terms of complexity, formalization, and centralization.

Complexity.   Horizontal, vertical, and spatial elements make up organizational complexity. Concerning an organizational chart, **horizontal complexity** refers to the number of "boxes" at any particular organizational level. The greater the number of boxes at a given level, the greater the horizontal com-

The Glass Ceiling and the Wall

Highlight 11.2

While the past 15 years have been marked by increasing movement of women into leadership positions, women still occupy only a tiny percentage of the highest leadership positions. In Fortune 500 companies, for example, less than 5 percent of the corporate officers are women. Researchers at the Center for Creative Leadership embarked on the Executive Woman Project to understand why (Morrison, White, & Van Velsor, 1987).

They studied 76 women executives in 25 companies who had reached the general-management level or the one just below it. The average woman executive in the sample was 41 and married. More than half had at least one child, and the vast majority were white.

The researchers expected to find evidence of a "glass ceiling," an invisible barrier that keeps women from progressing higher than a certain level in their organizations *because they are women.* One reason the women in this particular sample were interesting was precisely because they had apparently "broken" the glass ceiling, thus entering the top 1 percent of the workforce. These women had successfully confronted three different sorts of pressure throughout their careers, a greater challenge than their male counterparts faced. One pressure was that from the job itself, and this was no different for women than for men. A second level of pressure, however, involved being a female executive, with attendant stresses such as being particularly visible, excessively scrutinized, and a role model for other women. A third level of pressure involved the demands of coordinating personal and professional life. It is still most people's expectation that women will take the greater responsibility in a family for managing the household and raising children. And beyond the sheer size of such demands, the roles of women in these two spheres of life are often at odds (e.g., being businesslike and efficient, maybe even tough, at work yet intimate and nurturing at home).

The Center for Creative Leadership researchers described the "lessons for success" of this group of women who had broken through the glass ceiling. They also reported, however, a somewhat unexpected finding. Breaking through the glass ceiling presented women executives with an even tougher obstacle. They "hit a wall" that kept them out of the very top positions. The researchers estimated that only a handful of the women executives in their sample would enter the topmost echelon, called senior management, and that none would become president of their corporation.

plexity. Typically, greater horizontal complexity is associated with more specialization within subunits and an increased likelihood for communication breakdowns between subunits. **Vertical complexity** refers to the number of hierarchical levels appearing on an organization chart. A vertically simple organization may have only two or three levels from the highest person to the lowest. A vertically complex organization, on the other hand, may have 10 or more. Vertical complexity can affect leadership by impacting other factors such as authority dynamics and communication networks. **Spatial complexity** describes geographical dispersion. An organization that has all of its people in one location is typically less spatially complex than an organization that is dispersed around the country or around the world. Obviously, spatial complexity makes it more difficult for leaders to have face-to-face communication with subordinates in geographically separated locations, and to personally administer rewards or provide support and encouragement. Generally, all three of these elements are partly a function of organizational size. Bigger organizations are more likely to have more specialized subunits (horizontal complexity) and a greater number of hierarchical levels (vertical complexity), and to have subunits that are geographically dispersed (spatial complexity).

Formalization. **Formalization** describes the degree of standardization in an organization. Organizations having written job descriptions and standardized operating procedures for each position have a high degree of formalization. The degree of formalization in an organization tends to vary with its size, just as complexity generally increases with size (Robbins, 1986). Formalization also varies with the nature of work performed. Manufacturing organizations, for example, tend to have fairly formalized structures, whereas research-and-development organizations tend to be less formalized. After all, how could there be a detailed job description for developing a nonexistent product or making a scientific discovery?

The degree of formalization in an organization poses both advantages and disadvantages for leaders and followers. Whereas formalizing procedures clarifies methods of operating and interacting, it also may constitute demands and constraints on leaders and followers. Leaders may be constrained in the ways they communicate requests, order supplies, or reward or discipline subordinates (Hammer & Turk, 1987; Podsaskoff, 1982). If followers belong to a union, then union rules may dictate work hours, the amount of work accomplished per day, or who will be the first to be laid off (Hammer & Turk, 1987). Other aspects of the impact of formalization and other situational variables on leadership are presented in Highlight 11.3.

Centralization. **Centralization** refers to the diffusion of decision making throughout an organization. An organization that allows decisions to be made by only one person is highly centralized. When decision making is dispersed to the lowest levels in the organization, the organization is very decentralized. Advantages of decentralized organizations include increased participation in the decision process and, consequently, greater acceptance and ownership of decision outcomes. These are both desirable outcomes. There are also, however, advantages to centralization, such as uniform policies and procedures (which can increase feelings of equity), and clearer coordination procedures (Bass, 1990). The task of balancing the degree of centralization necessary to achieve

Are There Substitutes for Leadership?

Highlight 11.3

Are leaders always necessary? Or are certain kinds of leader behaviors, at least, sometimes unnecessary? Kerr and Jermier (1978) proposed that certain situational or follower characteristics may well effectively neutralize or substitute for leaders' task or relationship behaviors. *Neutralizers* are characteristics that reduce or limit the effectiveness of a leader's behaviors. *Substitutes* are characteristics that make a leader's behaviors redundant or unnecessary.

Kerr and Jermier (1978) developed the idea of **substitutes for leadership** after comparing the correlations between leadership behaviors and follower perform- ance and satisfaction with correlations between various situational factors and fol- lower performance and satisfaction. Those subordinate, task, and organizational characteristics having higher correlations with follower performance and satisfac- tion than the two leadership behaviors were subsequently identified as substitutes or neutralizers. The following are a few examples of the situational factors Kerr and Jermier found to substitute for or neutralize leaders' task or relationship behaviors:

- A subordinate's ability and experience may well substitute for task-oriented leader behavior. A subordinate's indifference toward rewards overall may neutralize a leader's task and relationship behavior.
- Tasks that are routine or structured may substitute for task-oriented leader behavior, as can tasks that provide intrinsic feedback or are intrinsically sat- isfying.
- High levels of formalization in organizations may substitute for task- oriented leader behavior, and unbending rules and procedures may even neutralize the leader's task behavior. A cohesive work group may provide a substitute for the leader's task and relationship behavior.

Source: S. Kerr and J. M. Jermier, "Substitutes for Leadership: Their Meaning and Measurement," *Organizational Behavior and Human Performance* 22 (1978), pp. 375–403.

coordination and control, on the one hand, and gaining desirable participation and acceptance, on the other, is an ongoing challenge for the leader.

Organizational Design. In addition to being classified by their degree of com- plexity, formalization, and centralization, organizations can also be classified into several different kinds of organizational design. Organizational design can be thought of most easily in the following two questions: (1) How do I want to divide up the work? (2) How do I want the divisions to coordinate their work?

FIGURE 11.3

A manufacturing company with a functional design

Three of the most common kinds of **organizational designs** in the traditional (or industrial age) format include functional, product, and matrix organizations.

Functional.   Some organizations have their structures designed around certain important and continuing functions. For example, a manufacturing company with a **functional design** might have its organizational chart include one block for manufacturing, one for sales or marketing, one for research and development, and so on (see Figure 11.3). Advantages of functional organizations include efficient use of scarce resources, skill development for technical personnel, centralized decision making and control, and excellent coordination within each functional department. Disadvantages of functional organizations can include poor coordination across departments, slow responses to change, a piling up of decisions at the top of the hierarchy, and narrow or limited views by employees of overall organizational goals (Austin, Conlon, & Daft, 1986). In other words, in organizations structured functionally the very commonality within the various functional units can create problems. Functional groups can become so cohesive that they create rigid boundaries and dysfunctional competitiveness between themselves and other groups within the same organization.

Product.   In an organization with a **product design,** the blocks on the organization chart define the various products or services that are delivered ultimately to the consumer. One might consider an automobile organization such as General

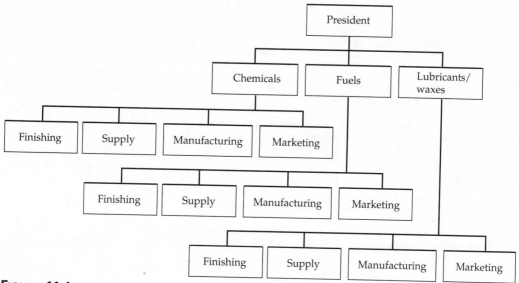

FIGURE 11.4

A petroleum company with a product design

Motors, where there are the Buick, Chevrolet, Cadillac, Saturn, and Pontiac divisions. These are identifiable products, and employees are assigned to these product groupings. A different product design is represented in Figure 11.4. A product organization design overcomes some of the problems associated with functional organizations, as a product organization has better coordination across functional skills, places a premium on organizational goals rather than functional goals, and has better control over diverse products or services. The disadvantages of product organizations include duplication of resources, less in-depth technical expertise, and weak coordination across different product groupings.

Matrix.   The **matrix design** is a combination of the product and functional designs. In this design, both product orientation and functional specialties are maintained (see Figure 11.5). In a matrix organization, there is a product manager for each product and one of his or her tasks is to obtain the resources necessary from the functional specialties as requirements demand. If the product will require the services of a computer software engineer, for example, then the product manager must acquire those services from the manager of the engineering function.

The greatest advantage of the matrix is efficient utilization of human resources. Imagine putting together a team to design a new product, and further suppose that a chemical engineer's services are among the team's needs. Also imagine, however, that the chemical engineer is required for only one month's work whereas the total product design phase encompasses a whole year. If our imaginary organization

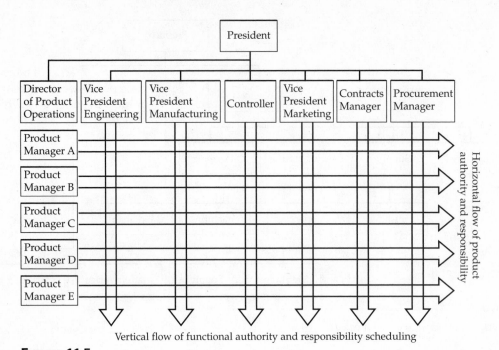

FIGURE 11.5

A manufacturing company with a matrix design

were designed according to a product orientation, the product manager would have to hire a full-time chemical engineer despite needing his or her services for only one month. In a matrix organization, on the other hand, the chemical engineer could be assigned to the engineering division, and the various product managers could arrange to acquire the engineer's time on an as-needed basis. Such an arrangement can create scheduling nightmares, but it also results in more efficient utilization of unusual or scarce resources. Another advantage of the matrix design includes increased lateral communication and coordination.

The greatest disadvantage of the matrix design is that employees end up working for two bosses. Such a dual-authority structure can create confusion and frustration. In the case above, the chemical engineer may have "professional loyalty" to the engineering group (which would dictate the highest-quality engineering possible) and "profitability loyalty" to the product group (which would dictate the most cost-effective engineering). Our chemical engineer might very well experience conflict over which loyalty to serve first. Additionally, matrix designs can lead to conflict and disagreements over the use of shared resources, and time is lost through frequent meetings to resolve such issues. Thus, administrative costs are high in matrix organizations. Finally, matrix designs can work well only if managers see the big picture and do not adopt narrow functional or product perspectives.

Lateral Interdependence.   The degree of **lateral interdependence** in an organization can also affect leaders' and followers' behaviors. Lateral interdependence concerns the degree of coordination or synchronization required between organizational units in order to accomplish work-group or organizational goals. Thus, lateral interdependence is similar to task interdependence but at a higher organizational level; lateral interdependence represents the degree to which a leader's work group is affected by the actions or activities of other subunits within the organization (Bass, 1990; Sayles, 1979). For example, a leader of a final assembly unit for personal computers will be very dependent on the activities of the power supply, cabinet, monitor, mother board, floppy drive, and hard drive manufacturing units in order to successfully meet production goals. On the other hand, the leader of a manufacturing unit that makes all of the products used to assemble backpacks has a much lower degree of lateral interdependence. As lateral interdependence increases, leaders usually spend more time building and maintaining contacts in other work units or on public relations activities (Hammer & Turk, 1987; Kaplan, 1986). Moreover, leaders are more likely to use rational persuasion as an influence tactic when the level of lateral interdependence is high (Kanter, 1982; Kaplan, 1986).

The Informal Organization

One word which sums up the informal organization better than any other is its culture. Although most people probably think of culture in terms of very large social groups, the concept also applies to organizations. **Organizational culture** has been defined as a system of shared backgrounds, norms, values, or beliefs among members of a group (Schein, 1985), and **organizational climate** concerns members' subjective reactions about the organization (Bass, 1990; Kozlowski & Doherty, 1989). These two concepts are distinct in that organizational climate is partly a function of, or reaction to, organizational culture; one's feelings or emotional reactions about an organization are probably affected by the degree to which a person shares the prevailing values, beliefs, and backgrounds of organizational members (Schneider, 1983). If a person does not share the values or beliefs of the majority of members, then in all likelihood this person would have a fairly negative reaction about the organization overall. Thus, organizational climate (and indirectly organizational culture) is related to how well organizational members get along with each other (Bass, 1990; Kozlowski & Doherty, 1989). It is also important to note that organizational climate is narrower in scope but highly related to job satisfaction. Generally, organizational climate has more to do with nontask perceptions of work, such as feelings about co-workers or company policies, whereas job satisfaction usually also includes perceptions of workload and the nature of the tasks performed.

Just as there are many cultures across the world, there are a great number of different cultures across organizations. Members of many military organizations have different norms, background experiences, values, and beliefs, for example, from those of the faculty at many colleges. Similarly, the culture of an

---

TABLE 11–1   Some Questions That Define Organizational Culture

---

- What can be talked about or not talked about?
- How do people wield power?
- How does one get ahead or stay out of trouble?
- What are the unwritten rules of the game?
- What are the organization's morality and ethics?
- What stories are told about the organization?

Source: Adapted from R. H. Kilmann and M. J. Saxton, *Organizational Cultures: Their Assessment and Change* (San Francisco: Jossey-Bass, 1983).

investment firm is very different from the culture of a research-and-development firm, a freight hauling company, or a college rugby team. Cultural differences can even exist between different organizations within any of these sectors. The culture of the U.S. Air Force is different from the culture of the U.S. Marine Corps, and Yale University has a different culture than the University of Colorado even though they are both fine institutions of higher learning.

One of the more fascinating aspects of organizational culture is that it often takes an outsider to recognize it; organizational culture becomes so second nature to many organizational members that they are unaware of how it affects their behaviors and perceptions (Bass, 1990). Despite this transparency to organizational members, a fairly consistent set of dimensions can be used to differentiate between organizational cultures. For example, Kilmann and Saxton (1983) stated that organizational cultures can be differentiated based on members' responses to questions like those found in Table 11–1. Another way to understand an organization's culture is in terms of myths and stories, symbols, rituals, and language (Schein, 1985). A more detailed description of the four key factors identified by Schein can be found in Highlight 11.4.

Here is an example of how stories contribute to organizational culture. A consultant was asked to help a plant that had been having morale and production problems for years. After talking with several individuals at the plant, the consultant believed he had located the problem. It seems everyone he talked to told him about Sam, the plant manager. He was a giant of a man with a terrible temper. He had demolished unacceptable products with a sledgehammer, stood on the plant roof screaming at workers, and done countless other things sure to intimidate everyone around. The consultant decided he needed to talk to this plant manager. When he did so, however, he met a very agreeable person named Paul. Sam, it seems, had been dead for nearly a decade, but his legacy lived on (Dumaine, 1990).

It is important for leaders to realize that they can play an active role in changing an organization's culture, not just be influenced by it (Bass, 1985; Kouzes & Posner, 1987; Schein, 1985; Tichy & Devanna, 1986). Leaders can

Schein's Four Key Organizational Culture Factors

Highlight 11.4

Myths and stories are the tales about the organization that are passed down over time and communicate a story of the organization's underlying values. Virtually any employee of Wal-Mart can tell you stories about Sam Walton and his behavior—how he rode around in his pickup truck, how he greeted people in the stores, and how he tended to "just show up" at different times. The Center for Creative Leadership has stories about its founder, H. Smith Richardson, who as a young man creatively used the mail to sell products. Sometimes stories and myths are transferred between organizations even though the truth may not lie wholly in either one. A story is told in AT&T about one of its founders and how he trudged miles and miles through a blizzard to repair a faulty component so that a woman living by herself in a rural community could get phone service. Interestingly enough, this same story is also told in MCI.

Symbols and artifacts are objects that can be seen and noticed and that describe various aspects of the culture. In almost any building, for example, symbols and artifacts provide information about the organization's culture. For example, an organization may believe in egalitarian principles, and that might be reflected in virtually everyone having the same-size office. Or there can be indications of opulence, which convey a very different message. Even signs might act as symbols or artifacts of underlying cultural values. At one university that believed students should have first priority for facilities, an interesting sign showed up occasionally to reinforce this value. It was not a road sign, but a sign appearing on computer monitors. When the university's main computer was being overused, the computer was programmed to identify nonstudent users, note the overload, and issue a warning to nonstudent users to sign off. This was a clear artifact, or symbol, underlying the priority placed on students at that school.

Rituals are recurring events or activities that reflect important aspects of the underlying culture. An organization may have spectacular sales meetings for its top performers and spouses every two years. This ritual would be an indication of the value placed on high sales and meeting high quotas. Another kind of ritual is the retirement ceremony. Elaborate or modest retirement ceremonies may signal the importance an organization places on its people.

Language concerns the jargon, or idiosyncratic terms, of an organization and can serve several different purposes relevant to culture. First, the mere fact that some know the language and some do not indicates who is in the culture and who is not. Second, language can also provide information about how people within a culture view others. Third, language can be used to help create a culture. A good

(continued)

example of the power of language in creating culture is in the words employees at Disneyland or Walt Disney World use in referring to themselves and park visitors. Employees—all employees, from the costumed Disney characters to popcorn vendors—are told to think of themselves as members of a cast, and never to be out of character. Everything happening at the park is part of the "show," and those who paid admission to enter the park are not mere tourists, but rather "the audience." Virtually everyone who visits the Disney parks is impressed with the consistently friendly behavior of its staff, a reflection of the power of words in creating culture. (Of course, a strict and strongly enforced policy concerning courtesy toward park guests also helps.)

change culture by attending to or ignoring particular issues, problems, or projects. They can modify culture through their reactions to crises, by rewarding new or different kinds of behavior, or by eliminating previous punishments or negative consequences for certain behaviors. Their general personnel policies send messages about the value of employees to the organization (e.g., cutting wages to avoid layoffs). They can use role modeling and self-sacrifice as a way to inspire or motivate others to work more vigorously or interact with each other differently. Finally, leaders can also change culture by the criteria they use to select or dismiss followers.

Changing an organization's culture, of course, takes time and effort, and sometimes it may be extremely difficult. This is especially true in very large organizations or those with strong cultures (see, for example, Highlight 11.5). New organizations, on the other hand, do not have the traditions, stories or myths, or established rites to the same extent that older companies do, and it may be easier for leaders to change culture in these organizations.

Why would a leader *want* to change an organization's culture? It all should depend on whether the culture is having a positive or a negative impact on various desirable outcomes. We remember one organization with a very "polite" culture, an aspect that seemed very positive at first. There were never any potentially destructive emotional outbursts in the organization, and there was an apparent concern for other individuals' feelings in all interactions. However, a darker side of that culture gradually became apparent. When it was appropriate to give feedback for performance appraisals or employee development, supervisors were hesitant to raise negative aspects of behavior; they interpreted doing so as not being polite. And so the organization continued to be puzzled by employee behavior that tended not to improve; the organization was a victim of its own culture.

Leaders especially need to be sensitive to how their own "brilliant ideas" may adversely impact subtle but important aspects of organizational culture. What may appear to be a major technical innovation (and therefore seemingly desirable) may also be devastating to organizational culture. For example, for hundreds of years in England, coal was mined by teams of three persons each.

John DeLorean and Counterculture at GM

Highlight 11.5

One of the more interesting stories about organizational culture and the actions taken to change a culture concerns John DeLorean (Martin & Siehl, 1983). DeLorean was a senior executive at GM, an institution with a well-established culture. One of GM's key cultural values was showing deference and respect to authority. For example, subordinates were expected to meet out-of-town superiors at the airport, carry their bags, pay their hotel and meal bills, and chauffeur them around day and night. Additionally, the more senior the executive, the bigger the traveling party would be. Some employees were so eager to please their boss that a group of Chevrolet sales people had a refrigerator put in the hotel room of a visiting senior executive after they had learned he liked to have a few cold beers and to make a sandwich before going to bed. Unfortunately, the door to the suite was too small to accommodate the refrigerator, so the Chevrolet sales personnel went so far as to hire a crane to bring in and later remove the refrigerator through the windows of the suite. A second core value at GM was communicating invisibility by visible cues. Ideal GM employees dressed identically, had the same office decor and layout, were "team players," and could easily fit in without drawing attention to themselves. The last key cultural value at GM was loyalty to one's boss. Loyalty to one's boss was clearly evident in the ritual of the retirement dinner, where a loyal subordinate was given the task of providing a detailed account of the retiree's steady rise through the corporation, counterpointed with allusions to the retiree's charming wife and family.

DeLorean took a number of actions to change the dominant culture at GM. First, DeLorean liked independence and dissent, and he modeled the behavior he wished others to emulate. He wore suits that stood out, and when appointed to head the Chevrolet division, he immediately changed the office furniture, carpeting, and decor and allowed executives to decorate their offices any way they wanted to "within reasonable limits." Second, because DeLorean believed that subordinates were more productive doing work than catering to superiors, he traveled by himself and did not greet his superiors at the airport, nor did he have his subordinates pick him up. Third, he changed the performance appraisal system within his division. Subordinates were to be rewarded on the basis of objective performance data, not subjective data that indicated a willingness to fit in. Although for a time DeLorean managed to maintain a delicate balance between culture and counterculture, his dissent was eventually met with disfavor, and he left GM to form a company of his own. Nevertheless, DeLorean's story provides several insights about the pervasiveness of organizational culture and the actions a leader might take to change culture.

In England, coal is layered in very narrow seams, most only a few feet high. In the past, the only practical means to get the coal out was to send the three-person teams of miners down into the mines to dig coal from the seam and then haul it to the surface on a tram. These mining teams had extremely high levels of group cohesiveness. A technological development called the long-wall method of coal extraction was to upset these close relationships, however. In the long-wall method, workers were arrayed all along an entire seam of coal rather than in distinct teams, and the method should have resulted in higher productivity among the miners. However, the breakdown of the work teams led to unexpected decreases in productivity, much higher levels of worker dissatisfaction, and even disruption of social life among the miners' families. Although the long-wall method was technically superior to the three-person mining team, the leaders of the coal-mining companies failed to consider the cultural consequences of this technological advancement (Emery & Trist, 1965).

After reading these examples, you may be asking whether it is better for leaders to create cultures that emphasize interpersonal relationships or organizational productivity. We can glean some insights into this question by looking at Mitchell's (1985) study of two groups of successful organizations. Mitchell compared two different groups of organizational cultures: those of organizations considered well managed, and those of organizations considered well liked by people working in the organization. The former group consisted of the 62 organizations identified in *In Search of Excellence* (Peters & Waterman, 1982), and the latter group included firms identified in *The One Hundred Best Companies to Work for in America* (Levering, Moskowitz, & Katz, 1984).

Interestingly, there was relatively little overlap between the two lists. According to Mitchell, this lack of overlap was due primarily to differences between task- and relationship-oriented organizational cultures. Cultures in the well-liked organizations emphasized making employees feel they were part of a family, reducing social distance, and making the organization a pleasant one to work in. Cultures in the well-managed organizations, on the other hand, were much more manipulative. Those firms had cultures that valued people not for themselves but as instruments of productivity. Although which type of culture is best for an organization is still under debate, it is important to note that the 62 companies deemed excellently managed by Peters and Waterman did not provide any higher returns on investments than less well managed firms (Simpson & Ireland, 1987), and many of these 62 companies and cultures look considerably less excellent today.

An Afterthought on Organizational Issues for Students and Young Leaders. Let us conclude this section by adding an afterthought about what relevance organizational issues may have for students or others at the early stages of their careers, or at lower levels of leadership within their organizations. It is unlikely that such individuals will be asked soon to redesign their organization's structure or change its culture. As noted earlier, this chapter is not intended as a how-to manual for changing culture. On the other hand, it has been our experience that younger colleagues sometimes develop biased impressions of leaders or have unrealistic expectations about decision making in organizations, based on their lack of familiarity with, and appreciation for, the sorts of organizational dynamics discussed in this section. In other words, one of the primary reasons for being familiar with such organizational variables is the context they provide for understanding the leadership process at your own level in the organization. Finally, we have worked with some senior leaders of huge organizations who have been with their company for their entire career. They have often been unable to identify *any* of the dimensions of their culture because they have never seen anything else. In these cases we were amazed by how junior managers were far better at describing the culture of the large organization. While these junior people may have had only five to eight years of total work experience, if that experience had been obtained in several different organizations, they were much better prepared to describe the characteristics of their new large organization's culture than were the senior executives.

Environmental Characteristics

We mentioned the environment earlier in the chapter as an input variable in the Congruence Model. We now return to a slightly more in-depth analysis of environmental characteristics since not attending to environmental characteristics is the root of extinction, both for the organization and for the population at large. Environmental characteristics concern situational factors outside the task or organization that still affect the leadership process. These include technological, economic, political, social, and legal forces. For example, imagine how changing economic conditions, such as threats of layoffs from a recession or a hostile takeover, would affect leaders' and followers' behavior. These factors often create anxiety, and therefore cause an increase in employees' security needs. They also tend to result in decreased training budgets for workers (Bass, 1990). Recent changes in the valuation of high-technology and telecommunication stocks cannot be ignored. Political changes also can have substantial impacts on leaders and followers. Just imagine, for example, how leaders' and followers' behaviors are changing in Eastern Europe as the various countries move from communist systems to private ownership of companies even though the changes have not gone smoothly or uniformly. Legal forces affecting Western organizations include those contributing to the growth of new industries (e.g., industrial waste disposal) or to personnel reductions in other industries due to changes in governmental rules and regulations (Ungson, James, & Spicer, 1985). Finally, technological advances are changing leader-follower relationships. For example, the advent of personal computers, fax machines, and high-speed access lines allows people to work at geographically dispersed locations.

Technology and Uncertainty

Technology affects the leadership process in other ways as well. For example, it might determine what design is best for an organization (Woodward, 1965). In environments of low **technological complexity,** workers play a large role and are able to modify their behavior depending on the situation. In environments of high technological complexity, there is a highly predictable work flow.

Examples of organizations in environments of low technological complexity are printing shops, tailor shops, and cabinetmakers. In each case, the organization is well suited to meeting specific customer orders. One of the authors of this book encountered an organization fitting this mold in trying to find an oak wall unit that would meet his requirements for a stereo system. After much frustrating shopping and finding a number of mass-produced units that would not work, he found a shop that had a variety of different units. Some of these came close to what he needed, but even the closest was not quite right. After listening in detail to the requirements, the owner agreed he didn't have anything on the floor that would work. In the next breath, however, he said, "But if you can draw it, we can build it."

A higher level of technological complexity occurs when mass production is the focus and orders are filled from inventory. An example would be furniture purchased from large warehouse stores. As opposed to the individually crafted wall unit described above, most furniture is not specifically designed and built precisely to meet special customer needs. Instead, manufacturers produce large quantities of various pieces of furniture likely to adequately meet the tastes and needs of most customers.

The highest level of technological complexity occurs when a continuous process is mechanized from beginning to end. People don't play much of a role in such organizations at all except to monitor the process flow and detect problems. Oil refining operations, chemical production plants, and nuclear power plants are all examples of continuous-process organizations. In such plants, people are merely observing and monitoring the processes and detecting anomalies that need to be corrected.

The significance of such a range of technological complexity is that different kinds of organizational structures or designs are best suited for different technological environments. An organization is most likely to be successful if the structure fits the technology. If the technological environment is one of moderately high complexity (like large furniture-manufacturing companies), a mechanistic or bureaucratic structure to the organization may be most appropriate. On the other hand, if the technological environment is one of low complexity (like the custom cabinetmaker or printer), setting up a rigid, bureaucratic structure will make it difficult for your organization to produce and "flex" as required by the different specific orders.

In addition to technology, the degree of **environmental uncertainty** also affects optimal organizational design. In stable environments where there is little change, a relatively formalized, centralized, and bureaucratic structure may be desirable. In turbulent environments, on the other hand, structures should be flexible enough to adapt to changing conditions (Burns & Stalker, 1961). In a similar fashion, flat, highly differentiated, and organic structures are most appropriate for very uncertain environments (Lawrence & Lorsch, 1967a, 1967b).

Crises

Another environmental variable that affects the leadership process is the presence or absence of **crises.** Some researchers believe crises play such an important part in charismatic leadership that certain leaders will purposely create crises in order to be perceived as being charismatic (Bass, 1985; Curphy, 1991; Roberts & Bradley, 1988). Furthermore, the behaviors associated with effective leadership during crises differ from those associated with noncrisis situations. During crises, followers are more likely to look to leaders to identify the prob-

> *I claim not to have controlled events, but confess plainly that events have controlled me.*
>
> Abraham Lincoln

lem as well as develop and implement a solution. Thus, work groups facing strong deadlines or crises generally expect their leaders to be more assertive, directive, and decisive (Mulder & Stemerding, 1963). Moreover, leaders are less apt to use participation or consultation during crises (Mulder, de Jong, Koppelaar, & Verhage, 1986; Pfeffer & Salancik, 1975). These findings make sense when contrasting emergency and nonemergency situations. For example, surgeons spend considerable time consulting with colleagues prior to conducting a difficult surgery. However, surgeons do not have time to consult with other specialists when a patient's heart has just stopped during surgery; the doctor must quickly diagnose the reason for the heart failure and coordinate the efforts of the surgical team for the patient to live. Similarly, coaches often spend considerable time consulting with other coaches and staff members when preparing for games, but during particularly close games they may consult with relatively few members of even their own staffs.

Situational Engineering

One of the most important points this chapter can make concerns the idea of **situational engineering.** Although leaders' and followers' behaviors are affected by a variety of situational factors, all too often leaders and followers completely overlook how changing the situation can help them to change their behavior. Just as a dieter can better stick to a diet by identifying bad eating habits and limiting food cues, so can a leader or follower become more effective by identifying problem areas and restructuring the situation so that these problems become easier to overcome.

Say, for example, a leader attended a leadership development program and received feedback that he did not interact enough with his subordinates. This leader might set a goal and may genuinely make an attempt to increase the level of interaction with his followers. Because his typical day is hectic and he manages a work group with a high level of lateral interdependence, however, situational demands may more or less force him to revert to his old behaviors. This leader would be likely to realize more success if he also restructured the situation in order to facilitate the accomplishment of this goal.

"*. . . Then it's agreed. As a crowd, we'll be subdued in innings one through seven, then suddenly become a factor in innings eight and nine . . .*"

He could, for example, delegate more activities to subordinates. This would give the leader more opportunities to interact with followers (by mutually setting performance goals and monitoring progress), and it would give the leader more time to engage in other activities. Moreover, the leader could project a more approachable and friendly attitude by rearranging office furniture, keeping his door open as much as possible, and building specific times into his daily schedule to "manage by wandering around" (Peters & Waterman, 1982).

There are a variety of ways in which leaders and followers can change the task, organizational, and environmental factors affecting their behaviors and attitudes. By asking questions and listening effectively, leaders may be able to redesign work using the suggestions from Hackman and Oldham's (1980) job characteristics model or Herzberg's (1966) two-factor theory in order to improve followers' satisfaction and productivity levels. Similarly, leaders might discover ways to adjust followers' workloads, responsibilities, or levels of task interdependence; rearrange office layouts; establish new or different policies or procedures; or modify reporting relationships and appraisal systems (Yukl, 1989). More senior leaders might be able to change the organization itself or work to influence changes in the environment. Perhaps the most important point regarding situational engineering is to get leaders and followers to understand that the situation is not set in concrete, and to think about how they can change the situation in order for everyone to be more satisfied and productive.

One final example may be useful not only to illustrate the powerful impact of the situational variables but also to link this section to our previous discussion of Ginnett's Team Effectiveness Leadership Model, introduced in Chapter 10. You may recall that one of the important inputs in the TELM was the organizational level where we identified four types of systems impacting team process. These systems involved rewards, information, education, and control. In one of our research projects, we were observing a series of work processes performed by teams in a highly centralized and controlled organization. No work was ever performed without specific directions which were generated by a complex computer program. Engineers, who were not in the buildings where the work was performed, would prepare the working procedures, which were then integrated in the computer system and finally printed out for each task. While engineers could change the procedures, the perception of the workers in the processing facility was that the procedures were "like the bible—and equally difficult to change." In one series of work sequences, a team would prepare a sheet of flexible insulation (according to the printed instructions) for installation by the next team. However, when we followed the insulation, we found that the first thing the installation team would do was to unfold the flexible sheet and refold it in exactly the opposite manner so that it could be installed. When we asked the preparation team if they were aware that the installation team was having to redo their work, they had no idea that was happening. Even more surprising was that when they did learn of this, both teams decided it was easier to continue their work as described on the computer task sheets than to try to change it! Using the TELM model, we were able to identify at least two systems which were creating problems. First, the interteam information system was inadequate; it should have allowed them to correct inappropriate strategies (e.g., folding it one way only to have that work undone and redone), but it didn't. Of equal impact was the teams' perception of powerlessness because of the oppressive control system in which they operated. Even after problems were discovered, the situation in which the teams operated created conditions which reduced the creative potential of those with direct knowledge of the work flow. Leadership could have changed the way work was done by these teams by improving the information system and modifying the control system. Highlight 11.6 describes one final example of dealing with situations. In this case, a young leader dealt with the stress of being in a new and dangerous situation with a team he'd only just met.

Taking Charge

Highlight 11.6

A critical period for any leader often involves those first few moments and days of assuming command. It is a time when first impressions are formed and expectations are set. It is a crucial time for any leader in any situation, but can be a matter of life or death for a young leader in a combat situation. Here are one young officer's first reactions upon arriving in Southeast Asia to command a platoon.

I was alone. That was my first sensation as a leader. The men were going about the morning's business—breaking out C rations, relieving themselves, shaving, brushing their teeth. They moved among each other comfortably, a word here, a smile there. I could hear snatches of conversation: "A good night's sleep. . ." "Only ninety days left." Occasionally a man would nod in my direction, or glance at me for a fleeting moment.

I gathered up my belongings—weapon, web gear, and rucksack—and moved toward the command post. I needed a few minutes to gather my thoughts before I made my debut as a platoon leader. I knew it was going to be a tricky business.

I had assumed that I would have a company commander nearby to give me my orders. But I had not even met him yet; I would not meet him for weeks. The fact was, I was totally on my own. What should I do? Whose advice could I ask? The platoon sergeant's? The squad leaders'? In time I would listen to their ideas and incorporate them with my own, but I could hardly begin my tour with "Well what do you think we ought to do, men?" No, I knew that the basic decisions were mine to make.

The first few moments would be crucial. Obviously, I was the object of interest that morning. Everyone was wondering what the new lieutenant would be like, and I would be telling them with my first words, my gestures, my demeanor, my eyes. I would have no grace period in which to learn my way around. This was a life and death environment. If I began with a blunder, my credibility as a leader would be shot, and so might some of the men.

I decided to begin by giving my attention to tactics. In a military environment, everything is determined by tactical considerations. Where you sleep, when you sleep, where you go, what you do, and in whose company you do it—all are dictated by underlying tactical necessities. I would communicate my style of leadership through my tactical instructions.

As I surveyed the soldiers, the nearby village, the distant rice paddies, the heavy undergrowth, the varied terrain, my mind raced back over the years of tactical training I had received. Conscious of the stares of the men, I hoped to appear composed as I fought back the panic of having to decide, both quickly and correctly.

Source: J. M. McDonough, *Platoon Leader* (San Francisco: Presidio Press, 1985), pp. 30–31. Reprinted with permission.

Summary

The situation may well be the most complex factor in the leader-follower-situation framework. Moreover, situations vary not only in complexity but also in strength. Situational factors can play such a pervasive role that they can effectively minimize the effects of personality traits, intelligence, values, and preferences on leaders' and followers' behaviors, attitudes, and relationships. Given the dynamic nature of leadership situations, finding fairly consistent results is a highly encouraging accomplishment for leadership researchers.

As an organizing framework, this chapter introduced the Congruence Model as a way to consider many of the situational factors leaders should consider. In terms of work factors, leaders need to be aware of how task interdependence, task structure, and job characteristics can affect both their own and their followers' behaviors, and how they might change these factors in order to improve followers' satisfaction and performance. Research also has shown that organizational factors, such as lateral interdependence, structure, design, and culture, play major roles in determining why certain communication problems and conflicts might exist, how work is accomplished, and why some people may be more satisfied in the organization than others. The informal organization or the organizational culture can have a profound impact on the way both leaders and followers behave—and may be the least recognizable since it is the water in the bowl where all the fish are swimming. Factors in the environment, such as legal, political, or economic forces, can also affect leaders' and followers' behaviors. Sometimes these may effectively wipe out any changes a leader may make to improve productivity or satisfaction among work-group members.

Finally, let's look back one more time at our three outstanding leaders: Colin Powell, Madeleine Albright, and Konosuke Matsushita. Except this time, change the situation they find themselves in. Imagine instead Colin Powell as the CEO of a major electronics firm with an entrepreneurial focus, Madeleine Albright as the chairman of the Joint Chiefs of Staff, and Konosuke Matsushita as the secretary of state. Consider the implications of how their personalities would impact their work in these situations and what would still make them effective. These are the kinds of questions we are continuing to ask and research as we move forward in the 21st century.

Key Terms

Questions

1. The term *bureaucratic* has a pejorative connotation to most people. Can you think of any positive aspects of a bureaucracy?
2. Think of a crisis situation you are familiar with involving a group, team, organization, or country, and analyze it in terms of the leader-follower-situation framework. For example, were the followers looking for a certain kind of behavior from the leader? Did the situation demand it? Did the situation, in fact, contribute to a particular leader's emergence?
3. Can you identify reward systems that impact the level of effort students are likely to put forth in team or group projects? Should these reward systems be different than for individual effort projects?

Skills

Leadership skills relevant to this chapter include:
• Problem solving

• Diagnosing performance problems in individuals, groups, and organizations
• Development planning

Activity

Your instructor has several exercises available which demonstrate the impact of situational factors on behavior. They are not described here since identifying the situational factors being manipulated in an exercise undercuts the purpose of that exercise.

C H A P T E R

12 CONTINGENCY THEORIES OF LEADERSHIP

Introduction

I f we were to provide an extremely short summary of the book to this point, we would say leadership is a process that involves aspects, of the leader, the followers, and the situation. In Part I we discussed the process aspects, while Part II was devoted exclusively to the leader. Part III focused on the followers, and in the previous chapter we discussed the situational components of leadership. You may have also noted that as much as we attempted to focus exclusively on the component of interest for the section, there were often overlapping areas in our leader-follower-situation (L-F-S) model. The overlap is true, and our attempts to segregate the concepts were done merely for simplicity. The world of leadership is really a rather complex one where multiple aspects of the L-F-S model will come into play. Leadership is contingent upon the interplay of all three aspects of our model, and these contingencies are the focus of this chapter.

> It is a capital mistake to theorize before one has data.
>
> Sir Arthur Conan Doyle

This chapter reviews four of the more well-known contingency theories of leadership. All four address certain aspects of the leader, the followers, and the situation. These four theories also share several other similarities. First, because they are theories rather than someone's personal opinions, these four models have been the focus of a considerable amount of empirical research over the years. Second, these theories implicitly assume that leaders are able to accurately diagnose or assess key aspects of the followers and the leadership situation. Third, with the exception of the contingency model (Fiedler, 1967), leaders are assumed to be able to act in a flexible manner. In other words, leaders can and should change their behaviors as situational and follower characteristics change. Fourth, a correct match between situational and follower characteristics and leaders' behaviors is assumed to have a positive effect on group or organizational outcomes. Thus, these theories maintain that leadership effectiveness is maximized when leaders correctly make their behaviors *contingent* on certain situational and follower characteristics. Because of these similarities, Chemers (1984) argued that these four theories were more similar than they were different. He said they differed primarily in terms of the types of situational and follower characteristics upon which various leader behaviors should be contingent.

The Normative Decision Model

Obviously, in some situations leaders can delegate decisions to subordinates or should ask subordinates for relevant information before making a decision. In other situations, such as emergencies or crises, leaders may need to make a decision with little, if any, input from subordinates. The level of input subordinates have in the decision-making process can and does vary substantially depending on the issue at hand, followers' level of technical expertise, or the presence or absence of a crisis. Although the level of participation varies due to various leader, follower, and situational factors, Vroom and Yetton (1973) maintained that leaders could often improve group performance by using an optimal amount of participation in the decision-making process. Thus, the normative decision model is directed solely at determining how much input subordinates should have in the decision-making process. Precisely because the normative decision model is limited only to decision making and is not a grand, all-encompassing theory, it is a good model with which to begin the chapter.

Levels of Participation

Like the other theories in this chapter, the **normative decision model** (Vroom & Yetton, 1973) was designed to improve some aspects of leadership effectiveness. In this case, Vroom and Yetton explored how various leader, follower, and situational factors affect the degree of subordinates' participation in the decision-making process and, in turn, group performance. To determine which situational and follower factors affect the level of participation and group performance, Vroom and Yetton first investigated the decision-making processes leaders use in group settings. They discovered a continuum of decision-making processes ranging from completely autocratic (labeled "AI") to completely democratic, where all member of the group have equal participation (labeled "GII"). These processes are listed in Highlight 12.1.

Decision Quality and Acceptance

After establishing a continuum of decision processes, Vroom and Yetton (1973) established criteria to evaluate the adequacy of the decisions made—criteria they believed would be credible to leaders and equally applicable across the five levels of participation. Although a wide variety of criteria could be used, Vroom and Yetton believed decision quality and decision acceptance were the two most important criteria for judging the adequacy of a decision.

Levels of Participation in the Normative Decision Model

Highlight 12.1

Autocratic Processes

AI: The leader solves the problem or makes the decision by him- or herself using the information available at the time.

AII: The leader obtains any necessary information from followers, then decides on a solution to the problem herself. She may or may not tell followers the purpose of her questions or give information about the problem or decision she is working on. The input provided by them is clearly in response to her request for specific information. They do not play a role in the definition of the problem or in generating or evaluating alternative solutions.

Consultative Processes

CI: The leader shares the problem with the relevant followers individually, getting their ideas and suggestions without bringing them together as a group. Then he makes a decision. This decision may or may not reflect the followers' influence.

CII: The leader shares the problem with her followers in a group meeting. In this meeting, she obtains their ideas and suggestions. Then she makes the decision, which may or may not reflect the followers' influence.

Group Process

GII: The leader shares the problem with his followers as a group. Together they generate and evaluate alternatives and attempt to reach agreement (consensus) on a solution. The leader's role is much like that of a chairman, coordinating the discussion, keeping it focused on the problem, and making sure that the critical issues are discussed. He can provide the group with information or ideas that he has, but he does not try to "press" them to adopt "his" solution. Moreover, leaders adopting this level of participation are willing to accept and implement any solution that has the support of the entire group.

Source: Adapted from V. H. Vroom and P. W. Yetton, *Leadership and Decision Making* (Pittsburgh: University of Pittsburgh Press, 1973).

Decision quality means simply that if the decision has a rational or objectively determinable "better or worse" alternative, the leader should select the better alternative. Vroom and Yetton (1973) intended quality in their model to apply when the decision could result in an objectively or measurably better outcome for the group or organization. In the for-profit sector, this criterion can be assessed in several ways, but perhaps the easiest to understand is, Would the decision show up on the balance sheet? In this case, a high-quality (or, conversely, low-quality) decision would have a direct and measurable impact on the organization's bottom line. In the public sector, one might determine if there was a quality component to a decision by asking, "Will one alternative have a greater cost saving than the other?" or "Does this decision improve services to the client?" Although it may seem that leaders should always choose the alternative with the highest decision quality, this is not always the case. Often, leaders are confronted with equally good (or bad) alternatives. At other times, the issue in question is fairly trivial, rendering the quality of the decision relatively unimportant.

Decision acceptance implies that followers accept the decision as if it were their own and do not merely comply with the decision. Acceptance of the decision outcome by the followers may be critical, particularly if it is the followers who will bear principal responsibility for implementing the decision. With such acceptance, there will be no need for superiors to monitor compliance, which can be a continuing and time-consuming activity (and virtually impossible in some circumstances, such as with a geographically dispersed sales staff).

As with quality, acceptance of a decision is not always critical for implementation. For example, most organizations have an accounting form that employees use to obtain reimbursement for travel expenses. Suppose a company's chief financial officer (CFO) has decided to change the format of the form for reimbursing travel expenses and has had the new forms printed and distributed throughout the company. Further, she has sent out a notice that effective June 1, the old forms will no longer be accepted for reimbursement—only claims made using the new forms will be processed and paid. Assuming the new form has no gross errors, problems, or omissions, our CFO really has no concern with acceptance as defined here. If people want to be reimbursed for their travel expenses, then they will use the new form. This decision, in essence, implements itself.

On the other hand, leaders sometimes assume that they do not need to worry about acceptance because they have so much power over their followers that overt rejection of a decision is not likely to occur. A corporate CEO is not apt to see a junior accountant stand up and openly challenge the CEO's decision to implement a new policy, even though the young accountant may not "buy into" the new policy at all. Because followers generally do not openly object to the decisions made by leaders with this much power, these leaders often mistakenly assume that their decisions have been accepted and will be fully implemented. This is a rather naive view of what really goes on in organizations. Just because the junior subordinate does not publicly voice his opposition does not mean he will rush right out and wholeheartedly implement the decision. In fact, the junior accountant has a lot more time to destructively undermine the policy than the CEO does to check to ensure it is being carried out to the letter.

The Decision Tree

Having settled on quality and acceptance as the two principal criteria for effective decisions, Vroom and Yetton then developed a normative decision model. (A normative model is one based on what ought to happen rather than describing what does happen.) They also developed a set of questions to protect quality and acceptance by eliminating decision processes that would be wrong or inappropriate. Generally, these questions concern the problem itself, the amount of pertinent information possessed by the leader and followers, and various situational factors.

In order to make it easier for leaders to determine how much participation subordinates should have to optimize decision quality and acceptance, Vroom and Yetton (1973) incorporated these questions into a decision tree (see Figure 12.1). To use the decision tree, one starts at the left by stating the problem and then proceeds through the model from left to right. Every time a box is encountered, the question associated with that box must be answered with either a yes or a no response. Eventually, all paths lead to a set of decision processes that, if used, will lead to a decision that protects both quality and acceptance.

Having reached a set of feasible alternatives that meet the desirable criteria for quality and acceptance among followers, the leader may then wish to consider additional criteria. One very practical consideration is the amount of time available. If time is critical, then the leader should select the alternative in the feasible set that is farthest to the *left*, again noting that the feasible set is arranged from AI through GII. It generally takes less time to make and implement

FIGURE 12.1

Vroom and Yetton's leadership decision tree

Source: Reprinted from *Leadership and Decision Making*, by Victor H. Vroom and Philip W. Yetton, by permission of the University of Pittsburgh Press, © 1973 by the University of Pittsburgh Press.

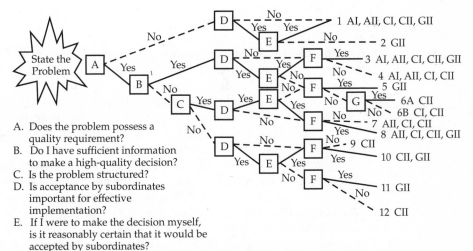

A. Does the problem possess a quality requirement?
B. Do I have sufficient information to make a high-quality decision?
C. Is the problem structured?
D. Is acceptance by subordinates important for effective implementation?
E. If I were to make the decision myself, is it reasonably certain that it would be accepted by subordinates?
F. Do subordinates share the organizational goals to be attained in solving this problem?
G. Is conflict among subordinates over preferred solutions likely?

autocratic decisions than it does to make consultative or group decisions. Nevertheless, it is important to note that the first step is to protect quality and acceptance (by using the model). Only *after* arriving at an appropriate set of outcomes should leaders consider time in the decision-making process. This tenet is sometimes neglected in the workplace by leaders who overemphasize time as a criterion. Obviously, there are some situations where time is absolutely critical, as in life-or-death emergencies. But too often, leaders ask for a decision to be made as if the situation were an emergency when, in reality, they (the leaders, not the situation) are creating the time pressure. Despite such behavior, it is difficult to imagine a leader who would knowingly prefer a fast decision that lacks both quality and acceptance among the implementers to one that is of high quality and acceptable to followers but that takes more time.

Another important consideration is follower development. Again, after quality and acceptance have been considered using the decision tree, and if the leader has determined that time is not a critical element, she may wish to follow a decision process more apt to allow followers to develop their own decision-making skills. This can be achieved by using the decision tree and then selecting the alternative within the feasible set that is farthest to the *right*. As was the case above, the arrangement of processes from AI to GII provides an increasing amount of follower development by moving from autocratic to group decisions.

Finally, if neither time nor follower development is a concern and multiple options are available in the feasible set of alternatives, the leader may select a style that best meets his or her needs. This may be the process with which the leader is most comfortable ("I'm a CII kind of guy"), or it may be a process in which he or she would like to develop more skill.

Concluding Thoughts about the Normative Decision Model

Having looked at this model in some detail, we will now look at it from the perspective of the leader-follower-situation (L-F-S) framework. To do this, we have used the different decision processes and the questions from the decision tree to illustrate different components in the L-F-S framework (see Figure 12.2). Several issues become apparent in this depiction. First, for ease of presentation we have placed each question or factor solely within one circle or another. Nevertheless, one could argue that some of the questions could or should be placed in another part of the model. For example, the question "Do I have sufficient information to make a high-quality decision?" is placed in the leader block. It might be argued, however, that no leader could answer this question without some knowledge of the situation. Strictly speaking, therefore, perhaps this question should be placed in the intersection between the leader and the situation. Nonetheless, in keeping with our theme that leadership involves interactions among all three elements, it seems sufficient at this point to illustrate them in their simplest state.

A second issue also becomes apparent when the normative decision model is viewed through the L-F-S framework. Notice how the Vroom and Yetton (1973)

> *Irrationally held truths may be more harmful than reasoned errors.*
>
> Thomas Huxley

FIGURE 12.2

Factors from the normative decision model and the interactional framework

Leader

Decision process preferences

B. Does the leader have sufficient information?

Outcomes:
Decision quality
Decision acceptance
Subordinate development

D. Acceptance important for implementation?
E. If decision made solely by leader, will it be accepted by subordinates?
F. Do subordinates share organizational goals?
G. Is conflict over preferred solution likely?

A. Quality requirement?
C. Is problem structured?

Time criticality?

Followers

Situation

model shifts focus away from the leader toward both the situation and, to an even greater degree, the followers. There are no questions about the leader's personality, motivations, values, or attitudes. In fact, the leader's preference is considered only after higher-priority factors have been considered. The only underlying assumption is that the leader is interested in implementing a high-quality decision (when quality is an issue) that is acceptable to followers (when acceptance is critical to implementation). Given that assumption and a willingness to consider aspects of the situation and aspects of the followers, the leader's behavior can be channeled into more effective decision-making processes.

A third issue is that the L-F-S framework organizes concepts in a familiar conceptual structure. This is an advantage even for a theory with as limited a focus as the normative decision model (i.e., decision making); it will be even more helpful later as we consider more complex theories.

Finally, because the normative decision model is a *leadership theory* rather than Vroom and Yetton's personal opinions, a number of empirical studies have investigated the model's efficacy. Research conducted by Field (1982) and Vroom and Jago (1974, 1988) provided strong support for the model, as these studies showed that leaders were much more likely to make effective or successful decisions when they followed its tenets than when they ignored them. Nevertheless, although leaders may be more apt to make more effective decisions when using the model, there is no evidence to show that these leaders are more effective overall than leaders not using the model (Miner, 1975). The latter findings again point out that both the leadership process and leadership effectiveness are complex phenomema; being a good decision-maker is not enough to be a good leader (although it certainly helps). Other problems with the model are that it views decision making as taking place at a single point in time (Yukl, 1989), assumes that leaders are equally skilled at using all five decision procedures (Yukl & Van Fleet, 1992), and assumes that some of the prescriptions of the model may not be the best for a given situation. For example, the normative decision model prescribes that leaders use a GII decision process if conflict may occur over a decision, but leaders may be more effective if they instead make an AI decision and avoid intragroup conflict (Couch & Yetton, 1987). Despite these problems, the normative model is one of the best supported of the four major contingency theories of leadership, and leaders would be wise to consider using the model when making decisions.

The Situational Leadership Theory

It seems fairly obvious that leaders do not interact with all followers in the same manner. For example, a leader may give general guidelines or goals to her highly competent and motivated followers but spend considerable time coaching, directing, and training her unskilled and unmotivated followers. Or leaders may provide relatively little praise and few assurances to followers with high self-confidence but high amounts of support to followers with low self-confidence. Although leaders often have different interactional styles when dealing with individual followers, is there an optimum way for leaders to adjust their behavior with different followers and thereby increase their likelihood of success? And if there is, then what factors should the leader base his behavior on—the follower's intelligence? Personality traits? Values? Preferences? Technical competence? Hersey and Blanchard (1969, 1977, 1982) developed the **situational leadership theory (SLT)** to answer these two important leadership questions.

Leader Behaviors

Situational leadership theory has evolved over time. Its roots are in the Ohio State studies, in which the two broad categories of leader behaviors, initiating structure and consideration, were initially identified (see Chapter 8). As SLT evolved, so did the labels (but not the content) for the two leadership behavior categories. Initiating structure changed to **task behaviors,** which were defined as the extent to which the leader spells out the responsibilities of an individual or group. Task behaviors include telling people what to do, how to do it, when to do it, and who is to do it. Similarly, consideration changed to **relationship**

FIGURE 12.3

The SLT prescriptions for the most appropriate leader behaviors based on follower maturity

Source: Paul Hersey and Kenneth Blanchard, *Management of Organizational Behavior: Utilizing Human Resources,* 4th ed. (Englewood Cliffs, NJ: Prentice Hall, 1982), p. 152. Adapted by permission.

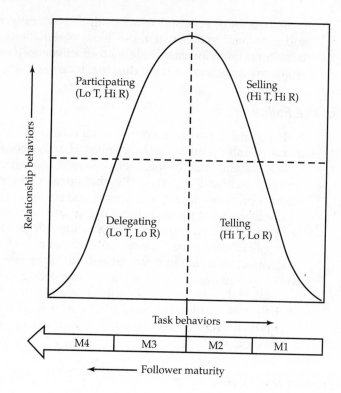

behaviors, or how much the leader engages in two-way communication. Relationship behaviors include listening, encouraging, facilitating, clarifying, and giving socioemotional support.

When the behavior of actual leaders was studied, there was little evidence to show these two categories of leader behavior were consistently related to leadership success; the relative effectiveness of these two behavior dimensions often depended on the situation. Hersey and Blanchard (1969, 1977, 1982) proposed a model to explain why leadership effectiveness varied across these two behavior dimensions and situations. First, they arrayed the two orthogonal dimensions as in the Ohio State studies, and then they divided each of them into high and low segments (see Figure 12.3). According to Hersey and Blanchard, depicting the two leadership dimensions this way indicated that certain combinations of task and relationship behaviors may be more effective in some situations than in others. For example, in some situations high levels of task behaviors but low levels of relationship behaviors were effective; in other situations, just the opposite was true. So far, however, we have not considered the key follower or situational characteristics with which these

> *The real world is a messy place—yet, even a messy place can (should?) be attacked systematically.*
>
> Alex Cornell

combinations of task and relationship behaviors were most effective. Hersey and Blanchard stated that these four combinations of task and relationship behaviors would increase leadership effectiveness if they were made contingent on the maturity level of the individual follower.

Maturity of the Follower

Follower maturity consists of two components: job maturity and psychological maturity. **Job maturity** is the amount of *task-relevant* knowledge, experience, skill, and ability that the follower possesses. In a sense, job maturity is much the same as technical expertise. **Psychological maturity** is the follower's self-confidence, commitment, motivation, and self-respect *relative to the task* at hand. Notice that both of these elements of maturity are meaningful only with regard to a particular task. Someone with a medical degree and years of experience as a surgeon might be rated as extremely mature at performing open-heart surgery. That same person might have virtually no job or psychological maturity for the tasks of designing and building a house, piloting a hot-air balloon, or counseling a suicidal patient. It is impossible to assess either job or psychological maturity if the task is unknown. Similarly, because most of us perform multiple tasks, there is no universal level of maturity. Both job and psychological maturity vary according to the task at hand.

Prescriptions of the Theory

Now that the key contingency factor, follower maturity, has been identified, let us move on to another aspect of the figure—combining follower maturity levels with the four combinations of leader behaviors described earlier. The horizontal bar or arrow in Figure 12–3 depicts follower maturity as increasing from right to left (not in the direction we are used to seeing). There are four segments along this continuum, ranging from M1 (the least mature) to M4 (the most mature). Along this continuum, however, the assessment of follower maturity can be fairly subjective. A follower who possesses high levels of both job and psychological maturity relative to the task would clearly fall in the M4 category, just as a follower with neither job nor psychological maturity would fall in M1. The discriminating factors for categories M2 and M3 are less clear, however.

To complete the model, Hersey and Blanchard (1982) added a curved line that represents the leadership behavior that will most likely be effective given a particular level of follower maturity. In order to use SLT, leaders should first assess the maturity level (M1–M4) of the follower relative to the task to be accomplished. Next, a vertical line should be drawn from the center of the maturity level up to the point where it intersects with the curved line in Figure 12–3. The quadrant in which this intersection occurs represents the level of task and relationship behavior that has the best chance of producing successful outcomes. For example, imagine you are a fire chief and have under your command a search-and-rescue team. One of the team members is needed to rescue a backpacker who has fallen in the mountains, and you have selected a particular follower to accomplish the task. What leadership behavior should you exhibit? Assuming this is a responsible and psychologically mature follower who has both substantial training and experience in this type of rescue, you would assess his maturity level as M4. A vertical line from M4 would intersect the curved line in the quadrant where both low-task and low-relationship behaviors by the leader are most apt to be successful. As the leader, you should exhibit a low level of task and relationship behaviors and delegate this task to the follower. On the other hand, you may have a brand-new member of the fire department who still has to learn the ins and outs of firefighting. Because this particular follower has low job and psychological maturity (M1), SLT maintains that the leader should use a high level of task behaviors and a low level of relationship behaviors when initially dealing with this follower.

Hersey and Blanchard suggested one further step leaders may wish to consider. The model described above helps the leader select the most appropriate behavior given the current level of follower maturity. However, there may be cases when the leader would like to see the followers increase their level of maturity. Because more mature followers are generally more effective than less mature followers, leaders may wish to implement a series of **developmental interventions** to help boost follower maturity levels. The process would begin by first assessing the follower's current level of maturity and then determining the leader behavior that best suits that follower in that task. Instead of using the behavior prescribed by SLT, however, the leader would select the next-higher leadership behavior. Another way of thinking about this would be for the leader to select the behavior pattern that would fit the follower if that follower were one level higher in maturity. This intervention is designed to help followers in their maturity development, hence its name (see Highlight 12.2, on developmental interventions).

Concluding Thoughts about the Situational Leadership Theory

In Figure 12.4, we can see how the factors in SLT fit within the L-F-S framework. In comparison to the Vroom and Yetton model, there are fewer factors to be considered in each of the three elements. The only situational consideration is knowledge of the task, and the only two follower factors are job and psychological maturity. On the other hand, the theory goes well beyond decision making, which was the sole domain of the normative decision model. In fact, Hersey and Blanchard have suggested that their model can even be extended to other applications, such as parenting.

Situational leadership theory is usually appealing to students and practitioners because of its commonsense approach as well as its ease of understanding. Unfortunately, there is little research to support the predictions of SLT in the workplace (Vecchio, 1987; Yukl & Van Fleet, 1992). Moreover, follower maturity is poorly defined (Graeff, 1983), and the model provides inadequate rationale or sufficiently specific guidance about *why* or *how* particular levels of task and relationship behaviors correspond to each of the follower

A Developmental Intervention Using SLT

Highlight 12.2

Dianne is a resident assistant in charge of a number of students in a university dorm. One particular sophomore, Michael, has volunteered to work on projects in the past but never seems to take the initiative to get started on his own. Michael seems to wait until Dianne gives him explicit direction, approval, and encouragement before he will get started. Michael can do a good job, but he seems to be unwilling to start without some convincing that it is all right, and unless Dianne makes explicit what steps are to be taken. Dianne has assessed Michael's maturity level as M2, but she would like to see him develop, both in task maturity and in psychological maturity. The behavior most likely to fit Michael's current maturity level is selling, or high task, high relationship. But Dianne has decided to implement a developmental intervention to help Michael raise his maturity level. Dianne can be most helpful in this intervention by moving up one level to participating, or low task, high relationship. By reducing the amount of task instructions and direction while encouraging Michael to lay out a plan on his own and supporting his steps in the right direction, Dianne is most apt to help Michael become an M3 follower. This does not mean the work will get done most efficiently, however. Just as we saw in the Vroom and Yetton model earlier, if part of the leader's job is development of followers, then time may be a reasonable and necessary trade-off for short-term efficiency.

maturity levels (Yukl, 1989). Furthermore, Hersey and Blanchard have simply defined leadership effectiveness as those leader behaviors that match the prescriptions of SLT. They have not presented any evidence that leaders who behave according to the model's prescriptions actually have higher unit performance indexes, better-performing or more satisfied subordinates, or a more favorable organizational climate (Vecchio, 1987). Nevertheless, even with these shortcomings, SLT is a useful way to get leaders to think about how leadership effectiveness may depend somewhat on being flexible with different subordinates, not on acting the same way toward them all.

The Contingency Model

Although leaders may be able to change their behaviors toward individual subordinates, leaders also have dominant behavioral tendencies. Some leaders may be generally more supportive and relationship-oriented, whereas others may be

FIGURE 12.4

Factors from the situational leadership theory and the interactional framework

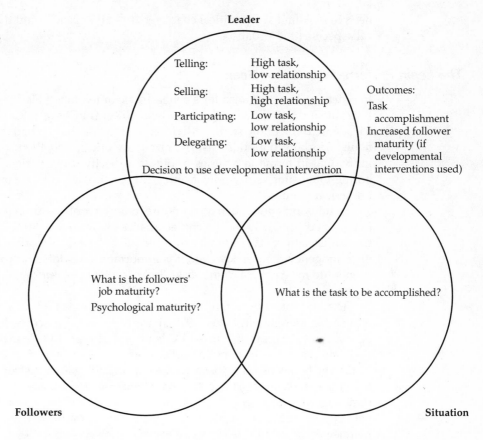

more concerned with task or goal accomplishment. The contingency model (Fiedler, 1967) recognizes that leaders have these general behavioral tendencies and specifies situations where certain leaders (or behavioral dispositions) may be more effective than others.

Fiedler's (1967) **contingency model** of leadership is probably the earliest and most well-known contingency theory, and is often perceived by students to be almost the opposite of SLT. Compared to the contingency model, SLT emphasizes flexibility in leader behaviors, whereas the contingency model maintains that leaders are much more consistent (and consequently less flexible) in their behavior. Situational leadership theory maintains that leaders who *correctly base their behaviors* on follower maturity will be more effective, whereas the contingency model suggests that leader effectiveness is primarily determined by *selecting the right kind of leader for a certain situation or changing the situation* to fit the particular leader's style. Another way to say this is that leadership effectiveness depends on both the leader's style and the favorableness of the leadership situation. Some leaders are better than others in some situations but less effective in other situations. To understand contingency theory, therefore, we need to look first at the critical characteristics of the leader and then at the critical aspects of the situation.

The Least-Preferred-Coworker Scale

In order to determine a leader's general style or tendency, Fiedler developed an instrument called the **least-preferred-coworker (LPC) scale.** The scale instructs a leader to think of the single individual with whom he has had the greatest difficulty working (i.e., the least-preferred coworker) and then to describe that individual in terms of a series of bipolar adjectives (e.g., friendly-unfriendly, boring-interesting, sincere-insincere). Those ratings are then converted into a numerical score.

In thinking about such a procedure, many people assume that the score is determined primarily by the characteristics of whatever particular individual the leader happened to identify as his least-preferred co-worker. In the context of contingency theory, however, it is important to understand that the score is thought to *represent something about the leader, not the specific individual the leader evaluated.*

The current interpretation of these scores is that they identify a leader's motivation hierarchy (Fiedler, 1978). Based on their LPC scores, leaders are categorized into two groups: **low-LPC leaders** and **high-LPC leaders.** In terms of their motivation hierarchy, low-LPC leaders are primarily motivated by the task, which means that these leaders primarily gain satisfaction from task accomplishment. Thus, their dominant behavioral tendencies are similar to the initiating structure behavior described in the Ohio State research or the task behavior of SLT. However, if tasks are being accomplished in an acceptable manner, then low-LPC leaders will move to their secondary level of motivation, which is forming and maintaining relationships with followers. Thus, low-LPC leaders will focus on improving their relationships with followers *after* they are assured that assigned tasks are being satisfactorily accomplished. As soon as tasks are no longer being accomplished in an acceptable manner, however, low-LPC leaders will refocus their efforts on task accomplishment and persist with these efforts until task accomplishment is back on track.

In terms of motivation hierarchy, high-LPC leaders are primarily motivated by relationships, which means that these leaders are primarily satisfied by establishing and maintaining close interpersonal relationships. Thus, their dominant behavioral tendencies are similar to the consideration behaviors described in the Ohio State research or the relationship behaviors in SLT. If high-LPC leaders have established good relationships with their followers, then they will move to their secondary level of motivation, which is task accomplishment. As soon as leader-follower relations are jeopardized, however, high-LPC leaders will cease working on tasks and refocus their efforts on improving relationships with followers.

You can think of the LPC scale as identifying two different sorts of leaders with their respective motivational hierarchies depicted in Figure 12.5. Lower-

FIGURE 12.5

*Motivational
hierarchies for
low- and high-
LPC leaders*

Low-LPC leader motivational hierarchy

High-LPC leader motivational hierarchy

level needs must be satisfied first. Low-LPC leaders will move "up" to satisfying relationship needs when they are assured the task is being satisfactorily
accomplished. High-LPC leaders will move "up" to emphasizing task accomplishment when they have established good relationships with their followers.

Because all tests have some level of imprecision, Fiedler (1978) suggested
that the LPC scale cannot accurately identify the motivation hierarchy for those
individuals with certain intermediate scores. Research by Kennedy (1982) suggested an alternative view. Kennedy has shown that individuals within the
intermediate range of LPC scale scores may more easily or readily switch
between being task- or relationship-oriented leaders than those individuals
with more extreme scale scores. They may be equally satisfied by working on
the task or establishing relationships with followers.

Situational Favorability

The other critical variable in the contingency model is **situational favorability,**
which is the amount of control the leader has over the followers. Presumably,
the more control a leader has over followers, the more favorable the situation is,
at least from the leader's perspective. Fiedler included three subelements in situation favorability. These were leader-member relations, task structure, and
position power.

Leader-member relations is the most powerful of the three subelements in determining overall situation favorability. It involves the extent to which relationships
between the leader and followers are generally cooperative and friendly or
antagonistic and difficult. Leaders who rate leader-member relations as high
would feel they had the support of their followers and could rely on their loyalty.

Task structure is second in potency in determining overall situation favorability. Here the leader would objectively determine task structure by assessing whether there were detailed descriptions of work products, standard operating procedures, or objective indicators of how well the task is being accomplished. The more one could answer these questions affirmatively, the higher the structure of the task.

Position power is the weakest of the three elements of situational favorability. Leaders who have titles of authority or rank, the authority to administer rewards and punishments, and the legitimacy to conduct follower performance appraisals have greater position power than leaders who lack them.

The relative weights of these three components, taken together, can be used to create a continuum of situational favorability. When using the contingency model, leaders are first asked to rate items that measure the strength of leader–member relations, the degree of task structure, and their level of position power. These ratings are then weighted and combined to determine an overall level of situational favorability facing the leader (Fiedler & Chemers, 1982). Any particular situation's favorability can then be plotted on a continuum Fiedler divided into octants representing distinctly different levels of situational favorability. The relative weighting scheme for the subelements and how they make up each of the eight octants can be seen in Figure 12.6.

You can see that the octants of situational favorability range from 1 (highly favorable) to 8 (very unfavorable). The highest levels of situational favorability occur when leader–member relations are good, the task is structured, and position power is high. The lowest levels of situational favorability occur when there are high levels of leader–member conflict, the task is unstructured or unclear, and the leader does not have the power to reward or punish subordinates. Moreover, the relative weighting of the three subelements can easily be seen by their order of precedence in Figure 12.6, with leader–member relations appearing first, followed by task structure and then position power. For example, because leader–member relations carry so much weight, it is impossible for leaders with good leader–member relations to have anything worse than moderate situational favorability, regardless of their task structure or position power. In other words, leaders with good leader–member relations will be in a situation that has situational favorability no worse than octant 4; leaders with poor

FIGURE 12.6

Contingency model octant structure for determining situational favorability

High < Overall situation favorability							Low

Leader-member relations	Good				Poor			
Task structure	Structured		Unstructured		Structured		Unstructured	
Position power	High	Low	High	Low	High	Low	High	Low
Octant	1	2	3	4	5	6	7	8

leader-member relations will be facing a leadership situation with situational favorability no better than octant 5.

Prescriptions of the Model

Fiedler and his associates have conducted numerous studies to determine how different leaders (as described by their LPC scores) have performed in different situations (as described in terms of situational favorability). Figure 12.7 describes which type of leader (high or low LPC) Fiedler found to be most effective, given different levels of situation favorability. The solid dark line represents the relative effectiveness of a low-LPC leader, and the dashed line represents the relative effectiveness of a high-LPC leader. It is obvious from the way the two lines cross and recross that there is some interaction between the leader's style and the overall situation favorability. If the situational favorability is moderate (octants 4, 5, 6, or 7), then those groups led by leaders concerned with establishing and maintaining relationships (high-LPC leaders) seem to do best. However, if the situation is either very unfavorable (octant 8) or highly favorable (octants 1, 2, or 3), then those groups led by the task-motivated (low-LPC) leaders seem to do best.

Fiedler suggested that leaders will try to satisfy their primary motivation when faced with unfavorable or moderately favorable situations. This means that low-LPC leaders will concentrate on the task and high-LPC leaders will concentrate on relationships when faced with these two levels of situational favorability. Nevertheless, leaders facing highly favorable situations know that their primary motivations will be satisfied and thus will move to their secondary motivational state. This means that *leaders will behave according to their secondary motivational state only when faced with highly favorable situations* (see Highlight 12.3).

FIGURE 12.7

Leader effectiveness based on the contingency between leader LPC score and situation favorability

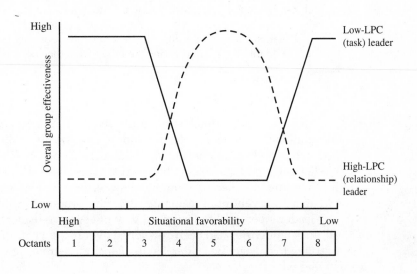

High- and Low-LPC Leaders and the Contingency Model

Highlight 12.3

Suppose we had two leaders, Tom Low (a low-LPC or task-motivated leader) and Brenda High (a high-LPC or relationship-motivated leader). In unfavorable situations, Tom will be motivated by his primary level and will thus exhibit task behaviors. In similar situations, Brenda will also be motivated by her primary level and as a result will exhibit relationship behaviors. Fiedler found that in unfavorable situations, task behavior will help the group to be more effective, so Tom's behavior would better match the requirements of the situation. Group effectiveness would not be aided by Brenda's relationship behavior in this situation.

In situations with moderate favorability, both Tom and Brenda are still motivated by their primary motivations, so their behaviors will be precisely the same as described: Tom will exhibit task behaviors and Brenda will exhibit relationship behaviors. Because the situation has changed, however, group effectiveness no longer requires task behavior. Instead, the combination of situational variables leads to a condition where a leader's relationship behaviors will make the greatest contribution to group effectiveness. Hence, Brenda will be the most effective leader in situations of moderate favorability.

In highly favorable situations, the explanation provided by Fiedler gets more complex. When leaders find themselves in highly favorable situations, they no longer have to be concerned about satisfying their primary motivations. In highly favorable situations, leaders switch to satisfying their secondary motivations. Because Tom's secondary motivation is to establish and maintain relationships, in highly favorable situations he will exhibit relationship behaviors. Similarly, Brenda will also be motivated by her secondary motivation, so she would manifest task behaviors in highly favorable situations. Fiedler believed that leaders who manifested relationship behaviors in highly favorable situations helped groups to be more effective. In this case, Tom is giving the group what they need to be more effective.

There are several interesting implications of Fiedler's (1967) model worthy of additional comment. Because leaders develop their distinctive motivation hierarchies and dominant behavior tendencies through a lifetime of experiences, Fiedler believed these hierarchies and tendencies would be difficult to change through training. Fiedler maintained it was naive to believe that sending someone to a relatively brief leadership training program could substantially alter any leader's personality or typical way of acting in leadership situations; after all, such tendencies had been developed over many years of experience. Instead of trying to change the leader, Fiedler concluded, training would be more effec-

FIGURE 12.8

*Factors from
Fiedler's
contingency
theory and the
interactional
framework*

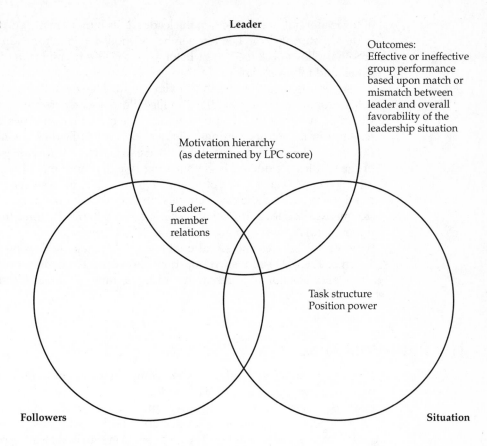

Leader

Outcomes:
Effective or ineffective
group performance
based upon match or
mismatch between
leader and overall
favorability of the
leadership situation

Motivation hierarchy
(as determined by LPC score)

Leader-
member
relations

Task structure
Position power

Followers

Situation

tive if it showed leaders how to recognize and change key situational characteristics to better fit their personal motivational hierarchies and behavioral tendencies. Thus, according to Fiedler, the content of leadership training should emphasize situational engineering rather than behavioral flexibility in leaders.
Relatedly, organizations could become more effective if they matched the characteristics of the leader (in this case LPC scores) with the demands of the situation (i.e., situational favorability) than if they tried to change the leader to fit the
situation. These suggestions imply that high- or low-LPC leaders in mismatched
situations should either change the situation or move to jobs that better match
their motivational hierarchies and behavioral patterns.

Concluding Thoughts about the Contingency Model

Before reviewing the empirical evidence, perhaps we can attain a clearer understanding of the contingency model by examining it through the L-F-S framework. As seen in Figure 12.8, task structure is a function of the situation and LPC
scores are a function of the leader. Because position power is not a characteristic

of the leader but of the situation the leader finds him- or herself in, it is included in the situational circle. Leader-member relations is a joint function of the leader and the followers; thus, it best belongs in the overlapping intersection of the leader and follower circles.

As opposed to the dearth of evidence for Hersey and Blanchard's (1969, 1982) situational theory, Fiedler and his fellow researchers have provided considerable evidence that the predictions of the model are empirically valid, particularly in laboratory settings (Fiedler, 1978, 1995; Fiedler & Chemers, 1982; Peters, Hartke, & Pohlmann, 1985; Strube & Garcia, 1981). However, a review of the studies conducted in field settings yielded only mixed support for the model (Peters, Hartke, & Pohlmann, 1985). Moreover, researchers have criticized the model for the uncertainties surrounding the meaning of LPC scores (Kennedy, 1982; Rice, 1978; Schriesheim & Kerr, 1977), the interpretation of situational favorability (Jago & Ragan, 1986a, 1986b), and the relationships between LPC scores and situational favorability (Jago & Ragan, 1986a, 1986b, Vecchio, 1983). Despite such questions, however, the contingency model has stimulated considerable research and is the most validated of all leadership theories.

The Path-Goal Theory

Perhaps the most sophisticated (and comprehensive) of the four contingency models is path-goal theory. The underlying mechanism of **path-goal theory** deals with expectancy, a cognitive approach to understanding motivation where people calculate effort-to-performance probabilities (If I study for 12 hours what is the probability I will get an A on the final exam?), performance-to-outcome probabilities (If I get an A on the final what is the probability of getting an A in the course?), and assigned valences or values to outcome (How much do I value a higher GPA?). Theoretically at least, people were assumed to make these calculations on a rational basis, and the theory could be used to predict what tasks people will put their energies into, given some finite number of options.

Path-goal theory uses the same basic assumptions as expectancy theory. At the most fundamental level, the effective leader will provide or ensure the availability of valued rewards for followers (the "goal") and then help them find the best way of getting there (the "path"). Along the way, the effective leader will help the followers identify and remove roadblocks, and avoid dead ends; the leader will also provide emotional support as needed. These "task" and "relationship" leadership actions essentially involve increasing followers' probability estimates for effort-to-performance and performance-to-reward expectancies. In other words, the leader's actions should strengthen followers' beliefs that if they exert a certain level of effort, then they will be more likely to accomplish a task, and if they accomplish the task, then they will be more likely to achieve some valued outcome.

Although not very complicated in its basic concept, the model added more variables and interactions over time. Evans (1970) is credited with the first version of path-goal theory, but we will focus on a later version developed by House and Dressler (1974). Their conceptual scheme is ideally suited to the L-F-S framework because they described three classes of variables, which include leader behaviors, followers, and the situation. We will examine each of these in turn.

Leader Behaviors

The four types of leader behavior in path-goal theory can be seen in Table 12–1. Like SLT, path-goal theory assumes that leaders not only may use varying styles with different subordinates but might very well use differing styles with the same subordinates in different situations. Path-goal theory suggests that depending on the followers and the situation, these different leader behaviors can increase followers' acceptance of the leader, enhance their level of satisfaction, and raise their expectations that effort will result in effective performance, which in turn will lead to valued rewards.

TABLE 12–1   The Four Leader Behaviors of Path-Goal Theory

Directive leadership. These leader behaviors are very similar to the task behaviors from SLT. They include telling the followers what they are expected to do, how to do it, when it is to be done, and how their work fits in with the work of others. This behavior would also include setting schedules, establishing norms, and providing expectations that followers will adhere to established procedure and regulations.

Supportive leadership. Supportive leadership behaviors include having courteous and friendly interactions, expressing genuine concern for the followers' well-being and individual needs, and remaining open and approachable to followers. These behaviors, which are very similar to the relationship behaviors in SLT, also are marked by attention to the competing demands of treating followers equally while recognizing status differentials between the leader and the followers.

Participative leadership. Participative leaders engage in the behaviors that mark the consultative and group behaviors described by Vroom and Yetton (1973). As such, they tend to share work problems with followers; solicit their suggestions, concerns, and recommendations; and weigh these inputs in the decision-making process.

Achievement-oriented leadership. Leaders exhibiting these would be seen as both demanding and supporting in interactions with their followers. In the first place, they would set very challenging goals for group and follower behavior, continually seek ways to improve performance en route, and expect the followers to always perform at their highest levels. But they would support these behaviors by exhibiting a high degree of ongoing confidence that subordinates can put forth the necessary effort; will achieve the desired results; and, even further, will assume even more responsibility in the future.

The Followers

Path-goal theory contains two groups of follower variables. The first relates to the *satisfaction of followers,* and the second relates to the *followers' perception of their own abilities* relative to the task to be accomplished. In terms of followers' satisfaction, path-goal theory suggests that leader behaviors will be acceptable to the followers to the degree followers see the leader's behavior either as an immediate source of satisfaction or as directly instrumental in achieving future satisfaction. In other words, followers will actively support a leader as long as they view the leader's actions as a means for increasing their own levels of satisfaction. However, there is only so much a leader can do to increase followers' satisfaction levels, as satisfaction also depends on characteristics of the followers themselves.

A frequently cited example of how followers' characteristics influence the impact of leader behaviors on followers' levels of satisfaction involves the trait of locus of control. People who believe they are "masters of their own ship" are said to have an internal locus of control; people who believe they are (relatively speaking) "pawns of fate" are said to have an external locus of control. Mitchell, Smyser, and Weed (1975) found that follower satisfaction was not directly related to the degree of participative behaviors manifested by the leader (i.e., followers with highly participative leaders were not any more satisfied than followers with more autocratic leaders). However, when followers' locus-of-control scores were taken into account, a contingency relationship was discovered. As can be seen in Figure 12.9, internal-locus-of-control followers, who believed outcomes were a result of their own decisions, were much more satisfied with leaders who exhibited participative behaviors than they were with leaders who were directive. Conversely, external-locus-of-control followers were more satisfied with directive leader behaviors than they were with participative leader behaviors.

FIGURE 12.9

Interaction between followers' locus of control scores and leader behavior in decision making

Source: Adapted from T. R. Mitchell, C. M. Smyser, and S. E. Weed, "Locus of Control: Supervision and Work Satisfaction," *Academy of Management Journal* 18 (1975), pp. 623–30.

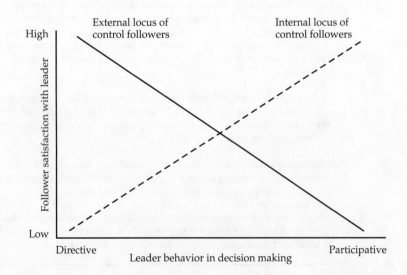

Followers' perceptions of their own skills and abilities to perform particular tasks can also affect the impact of certain leader behaviors. Followers who believe they are perfectly capable of performing a task are not as apt to be motivated by, or as willing to accept, a directive leader as they would a leader who exhibits participative behaviors. Using the same rationale as for locus of control, one can predict the opposite relationship for followers who do not perceive they have sufficient abilities to perform the task. Once again, the acceptability of the leader and the motivation to perform are in part determined by followers' characteristics. Thus, path-goal theory suggests that both leader behaviors and follower characteristics are important in determining outcomes.

The Situation

Path-goal theory considers three situational factors that impact or moderate the effects of leader behavior on follower attitudes and behaviors. These include the *task, the formal authority system, and the primary work group.* Each of these three factors can influence the leadership situation in one of three ways. These three factors can serve as an independent motivational factor, as a constraint on the behavior of followers (which may be either positive or negative in outcome), or as a reward.

However, it should also be increasingly apparent that these variables can often affect the impact of various leader behaviors. For example, if the task is very structured and routine, the formal authority system has constrained followers' behaviors, and the work group has established clear norms for performance, then leaders would be serving a redundant purpose by manifesting directive or achievement-oriented behaviors. These prescriptions are similar to some of those noted in substitutes for leadership theory (Kerr & Jermier, 1978), as everything the follower needs to understand the effort-to-performance and performance-to-reward links is provided by the situation. Thus, redundant leader behaviors might be interpreted by followers as either a complete lack of understanding or empathy by the leader, or an attempt by the leader to exert excessive control. Neither of these interpretations is likely to enhance the leader's acceptance by followers or increase their motivation.

Although we have already described how follower characteristics and situational characteristics can impact leader behaviors, path-goal theory also maintains that follower and situational variables can impact each other. In other words, situational variables, such as the task performed, can also impact the influence of followers' skills, abilities, or personality traits on followers' satisfaction. Although this seems to make perfect sense, hopefully you are beginning to see how complicated path-goal theory can be when one starts considering how situational variables, follower characteristics, and leader behaviors interact in the leadership process.

> *Although people object when a scientific analysis traces their behavior to external conditions and thus deprives them of credit and the chance to be admired, they seldom object when the same analysis absolves them of blame.*
>
> B. F. Skinner

Prescriptions of the Theory

In general, path-goal theory maintains that leaders should first assess the situation and select a leadership behavior appropriate to situational demands. By manifesting the appropriate behaviors, leaders can increase followers' effort-to-performance expectancies, performance-to-reward expectancies, or valences of the outcomes. These increased expectancies and valences will improve subordinates' effort levels and the rewards attained, which in turn will increase subordinates' satisfaction and performance levels and the acceptance of their leaders. Perhaps the easiest way to explain this fairly complicated process is through the use of an example. Suppose we have a set of followers who are in a newly created work unit and do not have a clear understanding of the requirements of their positions. In other words, the followers have a reasonably high level of role ambiguity. According to path-goal theory, leaders should exhibit a high degree of directive behaviors in order to reduce the role ambiguity of their followers. The effort-to-performance link will become clearer when leaders tell followers what to do and how to do it in ambiguous situations, which in turn will cause followers to exert higher effort levels. Because role ambiguity is assumed to be unpleasant, these directive leader behaviors and higher effort levels should eventually result in higher satisfaction levels among followers. Figure 12.10 illustrates this process. Similarly, leaders may look at the leadership situation and note that followers' performance levels are not acceptable. The leader may also conclude that the current situation offers few, if any, incentives for increased performance. In this case, the leader may use directive behaviors to increase the value of the rewards (or valence), which in turn will increase followers' effort levels and performance.

FIGURE 12.10

Examples of applying path-goal theory

Situation	Leader	Followers	Outcomes
Newly formed work unit	Directive behaviors (tell followers what to do and how to do it)	Reduced role ambiguity (clearer effort-to-perfomance links)	Higher effort / Higher satisfaction
Substandard performance (no rewards for performance)	Directive behaviors (make rewards available and contingent on performance)	Clearer perfomance-to-reward links (increased valence)	Higher effort / Higher satisfaction

Concluding Thoughts about the Path-Goal Theory

Before getting into the research surrounding path-goal theory, you may wish to examine the theory using the L-F-S framework. As seen in Figure 12.11, the components of path-goal theory fit quite nicely into the L-F-S model. The four leader behaviors fit nicely in the leader circle, the characteristics of the followers fit into the follower circle, and the task and the formal authority system fit into the situation circle. Of all the components of path-goal theory, the only "mismatch" with the L-F-S model deals with the primary work group. The norms, cohesiveness, size, and stage of development of groups is considered to be part of the follower function in the L-F-S model but is part of the situation function in path-goal theory. In that regard, we hasten to note we use the L-F-S framework primarily for heuristic purposes. Ultimately, the concepts described in these four theories are sufficiently complex and ambiguous that there probably is no right answer to any single depiction.

In terms of research, the path-goal theory has received only mixed support to date (Schriesheim & DeNisi, 1981; Schriesheim & Kerr, 1977; Yukl, 1989).

FIGURE 12.11

Factors from path-goal theory and the interactional framework

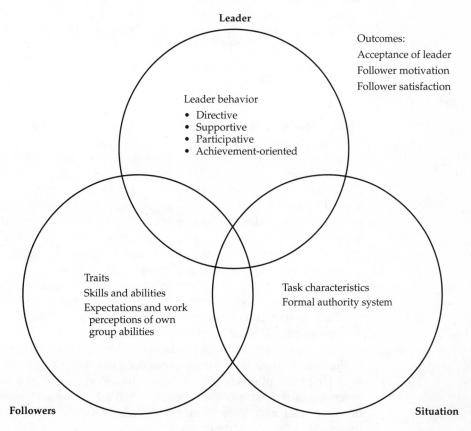

Although many of these mixed findings may be due to the fact that the path-goal theory excludes many of the variables found to impact the leadership process, that may also be due to problems with the theory. Yukl (1989) maintained that most of these criticisms deal with the methodology used to study path-goal theory and the limitations of expectancy theory. Moreover, the path-goal theory assumes that the only way to increase performance is to increase followers' motivation levels. The theory ignores the roles leaders play in selecting talented followers, building their skill levels through training, and redesigning their work (Yukl & Van Fleet, 1992).

Nonetheless, path-goal theory is useful for illustrating two points. First, as noted by Yukl (1989), "path-goal theory has already made a contribution to the study of leadership by providing a conceptual framework to guide researchers in identifying potentially relevant situational moderator variables" (p. 104). Path-goal theory also illustrates that as models become more complicated, they may be more useful to researchers and less appealing to practitioners. Our experience is that pragmatically oriented students and in-place leaders want to take something from a model that is understandable and can be applied in their work situation right away. This does not mean they prefer simplicity to validity—they generally appreciate the complexity of the leadership process. But neither do they want a model that is so complex as to be indecipherable.

> *To act is easy; to think is hard.*
>
> Goethe

Summary

This chapter is designed to provide an overview of four of the more well-known contingency theories of leadership, which include the normative decision model (Vroom & Yetton, 1973), the situational leadership model (Hersey & Blanchard, 1984), the contingency model (Fiedler, 1967), and the path-goal theory (House & Dessler, 1974). All four models are fairly similar in that they specify that leaders should make their behaviors contingent on certain aspects of the followers or the situation in order to improve leadership effectiveness. In addition, all four theories implicitly assume that leaders can accurately assess key follower and situational factors. However, as the material regarding perception in Chapter 3 shows, it is entirely possible that two leaders in the same situation may reach very different conclusions about followers' level of knowledge, maturity, the strength of leader-follower relationships, the degree of task structure, or the level of role ambiguity being experienced by followers. These differences in perception could lead these two leaders to reach different conclusions about the situation, which may in turn cause them to take very different actions in response to the situation. Furthermore, these actions may be in accordance or in conflict with the prescriptions of any of these four theories. Also, the fact that leaders' perceptions may have caused them to act in a manner not prescribed by a particular model may be an underlying reason why these four theories have reported conflicting findings, particularly in field settings.

Another reason these theories have generally found mixed support in field settings concerns the fact that they are all fairly limited in scope. Many of the factors that affect leader and follower behaviors in work group, team, or volunteer committee settings are not present in laboratory studies but often play a substantial role in field studies. For example, none of the models take into account how levels of stress, organizational culture and climate, working conditions, technology, economic conditions, or type of organizational design affect the leadership process. Nevertheless, the four contingency theories have been the subject of considerable research, and even if only mixed support for the models has been found, this research has succeeded in adding to our body of knowledge about leadership and has given us a more sophisticated understanding of the leadership process.

Key Terms

normative decision model   358
autocratic processes   359
consultative processes   359
group process   359
decision quality   359
decision acceptance   360
situational leadership theory (SLT)   364
task behaviors   364
relationship behaviors   364
job maturity   366
psychological maturity   366

developmental interventions   367
contingency model   369
least-preferred-coworker (LPC) scale   370
low-LPC leaders   370
high-LPC leaders   370
situational favorability   371
path-goal theory   376
directive leadership   377
supportive leadership   377
participative leadership   377
achievement-oriented leadership   377

Questions

1. Given the description of the leadership situation facing the airplane crash survivors described in Chapter 1, how would the normative decision model, the situational leadership theory, the contingency model, and path-goal theory prescribe that a leader should act?

2. Can leaders be flexible in how they interact with others? Do you believe leaders can change their behavior? Their personalities?

3. Think of a leadership situation you are fairly familiar with. Apply each of the theories in this chapter to the situations; which theory best fits the interaction of the leader, followers, and situation in your example? Does any theory allow you to predict a likely or preferred outcome for a current challenge?

Skills

Leadership skills relevant to this chapter include:
- Diagnosing performance problems in individuals, groups, and organizations

- Development planning

Activity

Tower Building

Purpose:

Observe decision-making skills in a leaderless group challenged to build a freestanding tower out of Tinker-Toys. Process how situational leadership theory was applied — how the group reacted to a skilled worker. Have the group determine the situational favorability for the task.

Summary:

Divide the class into small groups of approximately 8 to 10 students each. Each group will need its own container of Tinker-Toys. Additionally, it is especially worthwhile in this exercise to appoint at least one observer for each group.

Each group receives identical instructions:

Your task is to build the tallest freestanding tower you can, using the materials in this container (i.e., the Tinker-Toys). You will have 20 minutes to plan your tower and 40 seconds to actually build it. During the planning phase, you may examine your materials but you may not connect any pieces. If you do so, those pieces will be removed and you will not be allowed to use them to construct your tower. The instructor will announce when the planning phase begins and when it ends. At the end of the planning phase, all of the pieces must be returned to the container; the pieces must be in the container when the building phase begins. As with the planning phase, the instructor will announce when the building period starts and when it ends. When the instructor says "Stop" you must cease all construction. (If there are any questions, reread the relevant portion of the instructions.)

13 LEADERSHIP AND CHANGE

Introduction

Old is easy, new is hard.
David B. Peterson and Mary Dee Hicks, *Personnel Decisions International*

Organizations today face a myriad of potential challenges. To be successful they must cope effectively with the implications of new technology, globalization, changing social and political climates, new competitive threats, shifting economic conditions, industry consolidation, swings in consumer preferences, and new performance and legal standards. Think how these factors affected Matsushita from the 1920s to the 1990s, and how the company had to change the products and services provided; the organizational structure; and the purchasing, manufacturing, distribution, and sales processes over this 70-year period. Not only did Konosuke Matsushita have to change his leadership style and skills as the company went from a small shop to a multibillion-dollar global organization, but also he had to change the equipment, systems, and skills of the people working in the company. The same holds true for Colin Powell. The U.S. military underwent dramatic technological and organizational changes during the time between Vietnam and Desert Storm, and the mission changed from stemming the tide of communism to intervening in regional conflicts. As secretary of state, Madeleine Albright had to cope not only with the long-standing regional conflicts in Northern Ireland and the Middle East, but also with the breakup of the Soviet Union; regional conflicts in Somalia, Rwanda, and Yugoslavia; the two embassy bombings in Africa; NAFTA; and the impact of China and the European Union on world affairs. It is highly unlikely that members of Matsushita, the U.S. military, or the State Department could have acted the same way they did in the 1920s and been successful in the new millennium. These three leaders had to change the organizations they led, and leading change is perhaps the most difficult challenge facing any leader. Yet it may be that this skill is the best differentiator of managers from leaders, and of mediocre from exceptional leaders. The best leaders are those who recognize the situational and follower factors inhibiting or facilitating change, paint a compelling vision of the future, and formulate and execute a plan that moves their vision from a dream to reality.

The scope of any change initiative varies dramatically. Leaders can use goal setting, coaching, mentoring, delegation, or empowerment skills to effectively change the behaviors and skills of individual direct reports. But what would you need to do if you led a pharmaceutical company of 5,000 employees, and you had just received FDA approval to introduce a revolutionary new drug into the marketplace? How would you get the research and development, marketing, sales, manufacturing, quality, shipping, customer service, accounting, and information technology departments to work together to ensure a profitable product launch? Or what would you do if you had to reduce company expenses by 40 percent for the next two years, or deal with a recent acquisition of a competitor? Obviously, change on this scale involves more than individual coaching and mentoring. Because this chapter builds on much of the content of the previous chapters, it is fitting that it appears at the end of the text. To successfully lead larger-scale change initiatives, leaders need to attend to the situational and follower factors affecting their group or organization (Chapters 10–12). They then must use their intelligence, problem-solving skills, creativity, and values to sort out what is important and formulate solutions to the challenges facing their group (Chapters 6–8). But solutions in and of themselves are no guarantee for change; leaders must use their power and influence, personality traits, coaching and planning skills, and knowledge of motivational techniques and group dynamics in order to drive change (Chapters 5, 7–10). Finally, leaders can use some of the measures described in Chapter 4 to monitor the progress of their change initiatives.

As an overview, this chapter begins by revisiting the leadership versus management discussion from Chapters 1 and 2. We then describe a rational approach to organizational change and spell out what leaders can do if they are to be successful with their change efforts. This model also provides a good diagnostic framework for understanding why many change efforts fail. We conclude the chapter with a discussion of an alternative approach to change—charismatic and transformational leadership. The personal magnetism, heroic qualities, and spellbinding powers of these leaders can have unusually strong effects on followers, which often leads to dramatic organizational, political, or societal change. Unlike the rational approach to change, the charismatic and transformational leadership framework places considerable weight on followers' heightened emotional levels to drive organizational change. Much of the leadership research over the past 20 years has helped us to better understand the situational, follower, and leader characteristics needed for charismatic or transformational leadership to occur. The chapter concludes with an overview of these factors and a review of the predominant theory in the field, Bass's (1985) theory of transformational and transactional leadership.

Leadership and Management: Revisited Again

Earlier in this text we described leadership as "the process of influencing an organized group toward accomplishing its goals" (Roach & Behling, 1984). We also differentiated leadership from management, with leadership being more concerned with doing the right thing and management more concerned with doing things right. Bennis (1989) stated that leaders inspire and develop others, challenge the status quo, ask what and why questions, and are more apt to take a long-term view. Managers administer programs, control budgets and costs, maintain the status quo, and are more likely to take a short-term view. Building on Bennis's distinctions, one could say that leadership involves changing the way things are, whereas management involves maintaining the current state of affairs. This distinction between leadership and management is more clearly depicted in Table 13–1. Much like a driver uses the gas, brakes, clutch, gears, and steering wheel to control the speed and direction of a car, a manager uses various accounting, information, hiring, performance management, compensation, training, planning, quality, and inventory systems to align the behavior of followers toward the accomplishment of team or organizational goals. If followers are over budget on travel expenses or fail to come to work on time, then managers use various levers in the accounting or performance management system to correct the situation. These systems help followers to behave in both a consistent and an efficient manner. Organizations tend to be more successful when followers exhibit those behaviors most closely aligned with organizational goals. And organizations that need fewer resources to deliver goods and services tend to be more profitable (i.e., efficient) than those

> *A manager is a person who directs the work of employees and is responsible for results. An effective manager brings a degree of order and consistency to tasks. A leader, by contrast, inspires employees with a vision and helps them cope with change.*
>
> D. Hellriegel, J. Slocum Jr., and R. Woodman,
> *Organizational Behavior* (7th ed.)

TABLE 13–1   **Leadership versus Management**

Leadership = Change	*Management = Control*
Vision	Plan
Inspire	Reward
Empower	Direct
Coach	Train
Revenues	Expenses
Forecasts	Budgets
Possibilities	Systems and procedures
Opportunity	Schedule
Synergy	Coordinate

needing more resources to do the same thing. There is nothing inherently good or bad with organizational systems, but to some degree the quality of these systems dictates the ease with which a manager can do his or her job.

Although there are several benefits to organizational systems, one of their inherent problems is that they are fairly resistant to change. And well they should be, as they are specifically designed to minimize variability in the way expenses are paid, how software packages are used, the quality of goods and services provided, and so forth. Adding to this resistance is the tendency of people to fall in love with their systems. Whole bureaucracies and departments are designed to do nothing but support organizational systems. Oftentimes the people working in the accounting, information technology, or quality departments invented the relevant systems used throughout the organization, and pride of ownership may get in the way of needed changes. Likewise, the users of these systems may not want to learn new graphics programs, accounting procedures, sales models, or six sigma quality processes. Even if current systems are inefficient and dysfunctional, people know how to use them, and with this knowledge comes a certain degree of stability and predictability. Learning new systems and behaviors requires some tolerance for ambiguity and can take a considerable amount of patience, persistence, and hard work. All things being equal, many followers may prefer to have a predictable path rather than risk their success on some uncharted course for the future (O'Toole, 1995).

> *The definition of neurotic management is to continue to do the same thing but expect a different result.*
>
> Anonymous

So where does leadership come into play in the car analogy? A leader is a person who takes the car down a different road, has a different final destination, or determines whether a car is even the right vehicle. Because technology, globalization, market conditions, consumer preferences, and demographic changes can have big impact on any team or organization, leadership is the key to aligning organizational systems and follower behaviors around a new organizational vision. Whereas managers focus on compliance with existing procedures, leaders take a step back and ask why a system even exists. They create and align systems around a new set of goals for the organization, rather than having existing systems dictate what the organization can and cannot do. Successful leaders are also able to align followers' behaviors with this new vision and systems. But changing followers' behaviors and organizational systems, structure, and goals takes a tremendous amount of skill and effort. You will see that it takes a combination of both leadership and management skills to successfully implement any team or organizational change effort. The rest of this chapter describes some of the pertinent research and the steps leadership practitioners must take if they wish to use either the rational or the emotional approach to drive organizational change.

The Rational Approach to Organizational Change

A number of authors have written about organizational change, including Burns (1978), Kanter (1983), Bennis and Nanus (1985), Tichy and Devanna (1986), Bridges (1991), O'Toole (1995), Kotter (1996), Collins and Porras (1997), Treacy and Wiersma (1997), Beer (1988, 1999), and Fryer (2001). All of these authors have unique perspectives on leadership and change, but they also share a number of common characteristics. Beer (1988, 1999) has offered a rational and straightforward approach to organizational change that addresses many of the issues raised by the other authors. Beer's model also provides a road map for leadership practition-

> *Seventy percent of TQM and reengineering initiatives fail to live up to the expectations of senior management.*
>
> Michael Beer,
> Harvard Business School

ers wanting to implement an organizational change initiative, as well as a diagnostic tool for understanding why change initiatives fail. According to Beer:

$$C = D \times M \times P > R$$

The D in this formula represents followers' **dissatisfaction** with the current status quo. M symbolizes the **model** for change, and includes the leader's vision of the future as well the goals and systems that need to change to support the new vision. P represents **process:** This is concerned with developing and implementing a plan that articulates the who, what, when, where, and how of the change initiative. R stands for **resistance;** people resist change because they fear a loss of identity or social contacts, and good change plans address these sources of resistance. Finally the C corresponds to the **amount of change.** Notice that leaders can increase the amount of change by increasing the level of dissatisfaction, increasing the clarity of vision, developing a well-thought-out change plan, or decreasing the amount of resistance in followers. You should also note that the DxMxP is a multiplicative function—increasing dissatisfaction but having no plan will result in little change. Likewise, if followers are content with the status quo, then it may be very difficult for leaders to get followers to change, no matter how compelling their vision or change plan may be. This model maintains that organizational change is a very systematic process, and large-scale changes can take months if not years to implement (Beer, 1988, 1999). Leadership practitioners who possess a good understanding of the model should be able to do a better job developing change initiatives and diagnosing where their initiatives may be getting stuck. Because change is an important component of leadership, we will go into more detail on each of the components of Beer's model.

Dissatisfaction

Followers' level of satisfaction is an important ingredient in a leader's ability to drive change. Followers who are relatively content are not apt to change; malcontents are much more likely to do something to change the situation. Although employee satisfaction is an important outcome of leadership, leaders who want to change the status quo may need to take action to *decrease* employee satisfaction levels. Follower's

> *The ultimate curse is to be a passenger on a large ship, to know that the ship is going to sink, to know precisely what to do to prevent it, and to realize that no one will listen.*
>
> Myron Tribus, Massachusetts Institute of Technology

emotions are the fuel for organizational change, and change often requires a considerable amount of fuel. The key for leadership practitioners is to increase dissatisfaction (D) to the point where followers are inclined to take action, but not so much that they decide to leave the organization. So what can leaders do to increase follower dissatisfaction levels? Probably the first step is to determine just how satisfied followers are with the current situation. This information can be gleaned from employee satisfaction surveys, grievance records, customer complaints, or conversations with followers. To increase dissatisfaction, leaders can talk about potential competitive, technology, or legal threats or employee concerns about the status quo. They can also capitalize on or even create some type of financial or political crisis, or substantially increase performance standards. All of these actions can potentially heighten followers' emotional levels; however, leaders must ensure that these emotions are channeled toward the leader's vision for the organization.

Model

There are four key components to the model (M) variable in the change formula, and these include environmental scanning, a vision, identifying needed system changes, and new goals. As discussed earlier, organizations are constantly bombarded with economic, technological, competitive, legal, and social challenges. Good leaders are constantly scanning the external environment to assess the seriousness of these threats. They are also adept at internal scanning; they understand where the organization is doing well and falling short. Thus, keeping up to date on current events, spending time reviewing organizational reports, and taking time to listen to followers' concerns are some of the techniques leaders use to conduct external and internal scans (O'Toole, 1995; Kotter, 1996; Beer, 1999). This information in turn is used to formulate a vision for the change initiative. What would a new organization look like if it were to successfully counter the gravest external threats, take advantage of new market opportunities, and overcome organizational shortcomings? What would be the purpose of the new organization and why would people want to work in it? A good vision statement should answer these questions. The good news about a vision statement is that it does not have to be a solo effort on the part of the leader. Oftentimes leaders will either solicit followers for ideas or work with a team of followers to craft a vision statement (Bennis & Nanus, 1985; Tichy & Devanna, 1996). Both of these actions can help to increase followers' commitment to the new vision.

> *A vision is only a dream if it does not have the commitment and support of the people involved.*
> David Lee and Lou Quast, Personnel Decisions International

It is important to understand the difference between an organization's vision and goals. Just as the ancient mariners used the stars to navigate, so too should a vision provide guidance for an organization's actions. A vision helps the organization make choices about what it should and should not do, the kind of people it should hire and retain, the rules by which it should operate, and so on (Treacy & Wiersma, 1997). But just as the stars were

> *There can be no leadership without vision.*
> Manfred Kets de Vries, INSEAD

not the final destination for the ancient mariners, so too is a vision not the final destination for an organization. An organization's goals are the equivalent of the ancient mariner's final destination, and they should spell out specifically what the organization is trying to accomplish and when they will get done (Collins & Porras, 1997; O'Toole, 1995). Depending on the organization, these goals might concern market share, profitability, revenue or customer growth, quality, the implementation of new customer service or information technology systems, the number of patents awarded, school test scores, fund-raising targets, or the reduction of crime rates. Thus, an organization's goals can be externally or internally focused or both, depending on the results of the environmental scan and the vision of the organization. Highlight 13.1 provides an example of a vision statement and organizational goals for a human resource consulting firm.

Before determining goals, however, the leader will need to determine which systems need to change in order for the organization to fulfill its vision and accomplish its goals. In other words, how do the marketing, sales, manufacturing, quality, human resource, shipping, accounting, or customer service systems need to change if the organization is to succeed? And does the current organizational structure or culture support or interfere with the new vision? Leaders

---

An Example of a Vision Statement and Organizational Goals

Highlight 13.1

Vision Statement

We believe that an organization will only be as good as its leaders. Our vision is to increase our clients' productivity, profitability, and shareholder value by enhancing their ability to attract, develop, promote, and retain leadership talent.

Selected Year End Goals

- Increase revenues from $16,300,000 to $19,300,000.
- Successfully implement the new sales model and compensation plan by April 1.
- Acquire 100 new clients with at least $50,000 in annual billings.
- Ensure all consultants achieve their billable hour, client management, and business development goals.
- Improve customer loyalty ratings from 65.5 percent to 75.0 percent.
- Reduce annual turnover from 22.3 percent to 15 percent.

wanting their organizational change initiatives to succeed will need to take a systems thinking approach (Senge, 1994) before setting organizational goals. A **systems thinking approach** asks leaders to think about the organization as a set of interlocking systems, and explains how changes in one system can have intended and unintended consequences for other parts of the organization. For example, if a company wanted to grow market share and revenues, then it might change the compensation system to motivate salespeople to go after new customers. However, this approach could also cause a number of problems in the manufacturing, quality, shipping, accounting, and customer service departments. Leaders who anticipate these problems make all of the necessary systems changes in order to increase the odds of organizational success. Leaders may need to set goals and put action plans in place for each of these system changes. These actions can be contrasted to **siloed thinking,** where leaders act to optimize their part of the organization at the expense of suboptimizing the organization's overall effectiveness (Senge, 1994). For example, the vice president of sales could change the sales compensation plan if she believed her sole concern was annual revenues. This belief could be reinforced if her compensation was primarily based on hitting certain revenue targets. If she is a siloed thinker, she would also believe that profitability, quality, or customer service were not her concern. However, this mode of thinking could ultimately lead to her downfall, as quality and order fulfillment problems may cause customers to leave at a faster rate than new customers are buying products.

> *The most important component of organizational change is not the seed—it's the soil.*
>
> Michael Beer, Harvard Business School

Figure 13.1 is a graphic depiction of a systems model for leadership practitioners. All of the components of this model interact with and affect all the other components of the model. Therefore, leaders changing organizational vision or goals will need to think through the commensurate changes in the organization's structure, culture, systems, and leader and follower capabilities. Similarly, changes in the information or hiring systems can affect the organization's capabilities, culture, structure, or ability to meet its goals. One of the keys to successful organizational change is ensuring that all components in Figure 13.1 are in alignment. A common mistake for many leaders is to change the organization's vision, structure, and systems and overlook the organization's culture and leader and follower capabilities. This makes sense in that it is relatively easy to create a new vision statement, organization chart, or compensation plan. Leaders either discount the importance of organizational culture and capabilities, falsely believe they are easy to change, or believe they are a given because they are so difficult to change. It is possible to change the culture and capabilities of an organization, but it takes considerable time and focused effort (Dickson, Smith, Grojean, & Ehrhart, 2001). Unfortunately, about 70 percent of change initiatives fail, and the underlying cause for many of these failures is the leader's inability or unwillingness to address these culture and capabilities issues (Beer, 1999; Marks & Mirvis, 2001).

FIGURE 13.1

The components of organizational alignment

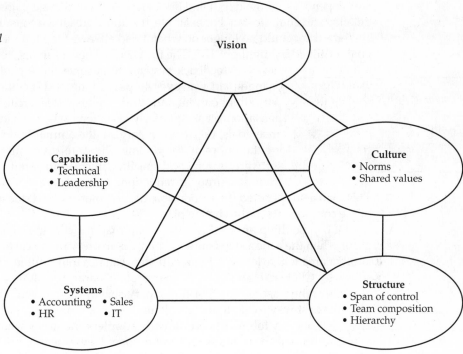

Process

At this point in the change process, the leader may have taken certain steps to increase follower dissatisfaction. She may also have worked with followers to craft a new vision statement, set new team or organizational goals, and determined what organizational systems, capabilities, or structures need to change. In many ways, the D and M components of the change model are the easiest for leadership practitioners to accomplish. The process (P) component of the change model is where the change initiative becomes tangible and actionable because it consists of the development and execution of the **change plan.** Good change plans outline the sequence of events, key deliverables, timelines, responsible parties, metrics, and feedback mechanisms needed to achieve the new organizational goals. It may also include the steps needed to increase dissatisfaction and deal with anticipated resistance, an outline of training and resource needs, and a comprehensive communication plan to keep all relevant parties informed.

Organizational change initiatives will only succeed when the changes are specified down to the individual employee level. Employees need to understand which old attitudes and behaviors are to be discarded and which new ones are to be acquired.

Jerry Jellison,
University of Southern California

Depending on the depth and breadth of change, change plans can be fairly detailed and complicated. For example, the human resource consulting firm discussed earlier could no longer do what it had always done if it were to reach its goals outlined in Highlight 13.1. The firm needed new systems, behaviors, metrics, and feedback systems to achieve these goals. The firm's change plan was over 40 pages long and included marketing data about current and future clients, sales territories and compensation plans, quarterly sales forecasts, individual performance goals, productivity targets, the annual budget, the implementation plan for a new client relationship management software system, and specific information about the consultant training, turnover reduction, and customer loyalty initiatives. This plan also specified the responsible parties, metrics, and due dates for each of the components in the change plan.

> *Communication is the currency of leadership.*
> David Lee,
> Personnel Decisions International

Of course the plan itself is only a road map for change. Change will only occur when the action steps outlined in the plan are actually carried out. This is another area where leadership practitioners can run into trouble. One of the reasons why CEOs fail is an inability to execute (Charan & Colvin, 1999), and it is also one of the reasons why first-line supervisors through executives derail. Perhaps the best way to get followers committed to a change plan is to have them create it. This way followers become early adopters and know what, why, when, where, who, and how things are to be done. Nevertheless, many times it is impossible for all the followers affected by the change to be involved with the creation of the plan. In these cases follower commitment can be increased if the new expectations for behavior and performance are explicit, the personal benefits of the change initiative is made clear, and followers already have a strong and trusting relationship with their leader. Even after taking all of these steps, leadership practitioners will still need to spend considerable time holding people accountable for their roles and responsibilities in the change plan. Followers face competing demands for the time and effort, and a lack of follow-through will cause many followers to drop the change initiative off of their radar screens. Leaders should also anticipate shifts in followership styles once the change plan is implemented. Exemplary followers may shift to become alienated followers, conformist to passive followers, or passive to alienated followers. Leaders who address these shifts in styles and inappropriate follower behaviors in a swift and consistent manner are more likely to succeed with their change initiatives.

Resistance

So why would followership styles shift as a result of a change initiative? One reason is that it may take some time before the benefits of change are realized. Many times leaders, followers, and other stakeholders assume that that performance, productivity, or customer service will immediately improve upon the acquisition of new equipment, systems, behaviors, and so on. However, there is often a temporary drop in performance or productivity as followers learn new systems and skills (Jellison, 2000). This difference between initial expectations and reality can be the source of considerable frustration (see Figure 13.2). If not managed properly, it can spark resistance (R), causing followers to revert back to old behaviors and systems to get things done. Leadership practitioners can help

> *Everybody resists change, particularly those who have to change the most.*
>
> James O'Toole, Aspen Institute

followers deal with their frustration by setting realistic expectations, demonstrating a high degree of patience, and ensuring followers gain proficiency with the new systems and skills as quickly as possible. Good change plans address the expectation-performance gap by building in training and coaching programs to improve follower skill levels.

Another reason why followers resist change is a fear of loss (Beer, 1988). Because of the change, followers are afraid of losing power, close relationships with others, valued rewards, and their sense of identity or, on the other hand, being seen as incompetent. According to Beer (1999), the fear of loss is a predictable and legitimate response to any change initiative, and some of a leader's responses to these fears can be found in Table 13–2. Change initiatives are more likely to be successfully adopted if their change plans identify potential and address these areas of resistance. People also seem to go through some very predictable reactions when confronted with change. An example might help to clarify the typical stages people go through when coping with change. Suppose you were working for a large company that needed to lay off 30 percent of the workforce due to a slowdown in

FIGURE 13.2

The expectation-performance gap

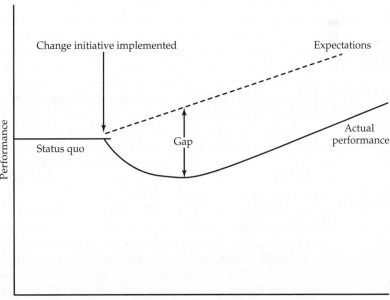

TABLE 13–2   Common Losses with Change

Loss of:	Possible Leader Actions
Power	Demonstrate empathy, good listening skills, and new ways to build power.
Competence	Coaching, mentoring, training, peer coaching, job aids, and so forth.
Relationships	Help employees build new relationships before change occurs, or soon thereafter.
Rewards	Design and implement new reward system to support change initiative.
Identity	Demonstrate empathy; emphasize value of new roles.

Source: M. Beer, *Leading Change* (Boston: Harvard Business School Press, 1988).

the economy and declining profits. If you were one of the people asked to leave, your first reaction might be shock or surprise. You may not have been aware that market conditions were so soft, or that you would be among those affected by the layoff. Next you would go through an anger stage. You may be angry that you had dedicated many long evenings and weekends to the company, and now the company no longer wanted your services. After anger comes the rejection stage. In this stage, you start to question whether the company really knew what it was doing by letting you go, and perhaps rationalize that they will probably be calling you back. In the final stage, acceptance, you realize that the company is not going to ask you back and you start to explore other career options. These four reactions to change—shock, anger, rejection, and acceptance—make up what is known as the **SARA model** (Kubler-Ross, 1981). It is important to note that most people go through these four stages whenever they get passed over for a promotion, receive negative feedback on a 360-degree report, get criticized by their boss, and so on.

But what should a leadership practitioner do with the SARA model? Perhaps the first step is to simply recognize the four reactions to change. Second, leaders need to understand that individual followers can take more or less time to work through the four stages. Leaders can, however, accelerate the pace in which followers work though the four stages by maintaining an open door policy, demonstrating empathy, and listening to concerns. Third, they also need to understand that where people are in the SARA model often varies according to organization level. Usually the first people to realize that a change initiative needs to be implemented are the organization's top leaders. Like everyone else, they go through the four stages, but they are the first to do so. The next people to hear the news are middle managers, followed by first-line supervisors and individual contributors. These three groups also go through the emotional stages of the SARA model, but do so at different times. These differences in emotional reactions by organizational level are depicted in Figure 13.3. What is interesting in Figure 13.3 is that just when top executives have reached the acceptance stage, first-line supervisors and individual contributors are in the shock or anger stages. By this time top leaders are ready to get on with the implementation of the change initiative and may not understand why the rest of the organization is still struggling. Because they are already at the acceptance stage, top

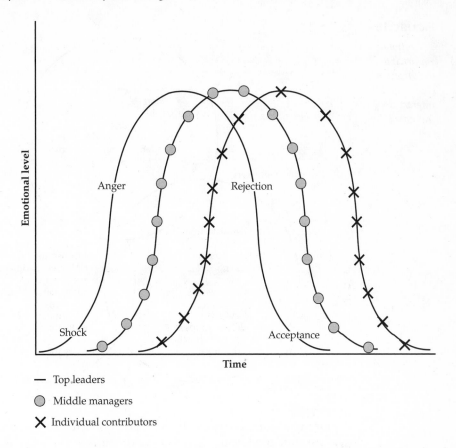

FIGURE 13.3

Reactions to change

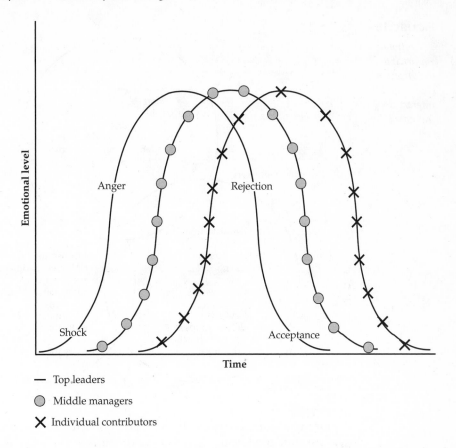

leaders may fail to demonstrate empathy and listening skills, and this may be another reason for the depressed performance depicted in Figure 13.2.

Concluding Comments about the Rational Approach to Organizational Change

The situational, follower, and leader components of the rational approach to organizational change are shown in Figure 13.4. Although organizational vision, goals, and change plans are often a collaborative effort between the leader and followers, they are the primary responsibility of the leader. Leaders also need to think about the importance of critical mass for driving change. They may be more successful by initially focusing their change efforts on early adopters and those on the fence rather than on those followers who are the most adamant about maintaining the status quo. Once critical mass is reached, the adopters can then exert peer pressure on those followers

> *Commitment is nice, but doses of compliance may be necessary.*
> Michael Beer,
> Harvard Business School

FIGURE 13.4

The rational approach to organization change and the interactional framwork

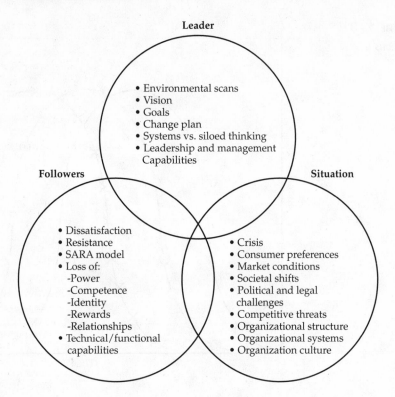

reluctant to change (Beer, 1999). This approach also maintains that the leader needs both good leadership and good management skills if a change initiative is to be successful over the long term. Leadership skills are important for determining a new vision for the organization, increasing dissatisfaction, coaching followers on how to do things differently, and overcoming resistance. Management skills are important when setting new goals and creating and implementing the change plan. Both sets of skills not only are important components in organizational change but also may play a key role in determining whether a new company will succeed or fail. Because of their strong leadership skills, entrepreneurs are often very good at starting up new organizations, such as dotcoms. Many of these leaders can get followers excited about the leader's vision for the new company. However, if entrepreneurial leaders fail to possess or appreciate the importance of management skills, they may not create the systems, policies, and procedures necessary to keep track of shifting consumer preferences, revenues, customer satisfaction, quality, and costs. As a result, these leaders may not have the information needed to make good operational and financial decisions, and their companies may eventually have to file for bankruptcy. On the other hand, it is hard to see how planning and execution skills alone will result in the formation of a new company or drive organizational change. It is almost impossible to start up a new company—or an organization

TABLE 13–3 Eight Reasons Why Change Efforts Succeed or Fail

1. Demonstrate a sense of urgency.	1. Allow too much complacency.
2. Form a strong change coalition.	2. Fail to create a strong change coalition.
3. Envision the future and build strategy.	3. Underestimate the power of vision.
4. Constantly communicate the vision.	4. Undercommunicate the vision by a factor of 10.
5. Remove barriers and align the organization.	5. Permit obstacles to block the vision.
6. Build on early successes.	6. Fail to create short-term wins.
7. Maintain (or increase) the pace of change.	7. Declaring victory too soon.
8. Put systems in place to reinforce change.	8. Neglect to anchor changes in the culture.

Source: J. P. Kotter, *Leading Change* (Boston: Harvard Business School Press, 1996).

to successfully change—if the person in charge does not have a compelling vision or fails to motivate others to do something different. As seen in Table 13–3, many of the other reasons why organizational change initiatives succeed or fail also have their roots in underdeveloped leadership or management skills.

Although both sets of skills are important, leadership practitioners should recognize that there is a natural tension between leadership and management skills. In many ways management skills help to maintain the status quo; they help to ensure consistency in behaviors and results. Leadership skills are often used to change the status quo; they help to change the purpose and processes by which an organization gets things done. Leaders who overuse or overemphasize either set of skills are likely to suboptimize team or organizational performance. The first part of this chapter was designed to help leadership practitioners better understand when to use these skills in the change process, and education and experience can help leadership practitioners to improve both sets of skills.

The Emotional Approach to Organizational Change: Charismatic and Transformational Leadership

Although the rational approach provides a straightforward model for organizational change, it seems like many of the large-scale political, societal, or organizational changes were not this formulaic. For example, it is doubtful that Jesus Christ, Muhammad, Joan of Arc, Vladimir Lenin, Adolf Hitler, Mahatma Gandhi, Mao Zedong, Martin Luther King, Jr., the Ayatollah Khomeini, or Nelson Mandela followed some change formula or plan, yet these individuals were able to fundamentally change their respective societies. Although these leaders differ in a number of important ways, one distinct characteristic they all share is charisma. Charismatic leaders are passionate, driven individuals who are able to paint a compelling vision of the future.

> *Leadership is the art of getting someone else to do something you want done because he wants to do it.*
>
> Dwight D. Eisenhower

Through this vision they are able to generate high levels of excitement among followers and build particularly strong emotional attachments with them. The combination of a compelling vision, heightened emotional levels, and strong personal attachments often compels followers to put forth greater effort to meet organizational or societal challenges. The enthusiasm and passion generated by charismatic leaders seems to be a dual-edged sword, however. Some charismatic movements can result in positive and relatively peaceful organizational or societal changes; some more recent examples might include the Falun Gong movement in China, Louis Farrakhan's Million Man March, or Gloria Steinem's feminist movement. On the downside, when this passion is used for selfish or personal gains, history mournfully suggests it can have an equally devastating effect on society. Examples here might include David Koresh of Waco infamy, Adolf Hitler, or the Serbian leader Slobodan Milosevic.

So what is it about charismatic leadership that causes followers to get so excited about future possibilities that they may willingly give up their lives for a cause? Even though many people conjure up images of charismatic individuals when thinking about leadership, the systematic investigation of charismatic leadership is relatively recent. The remainder of this chapter begins with a historical review of the research on charismatic leadership and the leader-follower-situation components of charismatic leadership. We will then review the most popular conceptualization of charisma, Bass's (1985) theory of transformational and transactional leadership. We conclude this chapter by comparing and contrasting the rational and emotional approaches to organizational change.

Charismatic Leadership: A Historical Review

Prior to the mid-1970s charismatic leadership was studied primarily by historians, political scientists, and sociologists. Of this early research, Max Weber (1947) arguably wrote the single most important work. Weber was a sociologist interested primarily in how authority, religious, and economic forces affected societies over time. Weber maintained that societies could be categorized into one of three types of authority systems: traditional, legal-rational, and charismatic.

In the **traditional authority system,** the traditions or unwritten laws of the society dictate who has authority and how this authority can be used. The transfer of authority in such systems is based on traditions such as passing power to the first-born son of a king after the king dies. Historical examples would include the monarchies of England from the 1400s to 1600s or the dynasties of China from 3000 B.C. to the 1700s. Although few nations are currently ruled by monarchies, there are a number of modern-day examples of the traditional authority system. Many CEOs in privately held companies or publicly traded companies that are controlled by a majority shareholder are often the children or relatives of the previous CEO. Examples include Ford, Anheuser-Busch, Coors, Amway, and Carlson Companies (owners of T.G.I.F. restaurants and Radisson Hotels). In the **legal-rational authority system** a person possesses authority not because of tradition or birthright, but because of the laws that govern the position occupied. For example, elected officials and most leaders in nonprofit or publicly traded companies are authorized to take certain actions because of the position they occupy. The power is in the position itself, rather than in the person who occupies the position.

These two authority systems can be contrasted to the **charismatic authority system,** in which persons derive authority because of their exemplary characteristics. Charismatic leaders are thought to possess superhuman qualities or powers of divine origin that set them apart from ordinary mortals. The locus of authority in this system rests with the individual possessing these unusual qualities; it is not derived from birthright or laws. According to Weber, charismatic leaders come from the margins of society and emerge as leaders in times of great social crisis. These leaders serve to focus society both on the problem it faces and on the revolutionary solutions proposed by the leader. Thus, charismatic authority systems are usually the result of a revolution against the traditional and legal-rational authority systems. Examples of these revolutions might be the overthrow of the shah of Iran by the Ayatollah Khomeini, the ousting of the British in India by Mahatma Gandhi, and the success of Martin Luther King, Jr., in changing the civil rights laws in the United States. Unlike traditional or legal-rational authority systems, charismatic authority systems tend to be short-lived. Charismatic leaders must project an image of success in order for followers to believe they possess superhuman qualities; any failures will cause followers to question the divine qualities of the leader and in turn erode the leader's authority.

> *It's better to burn out than it is to rust.*
>
> Neil Young, songwriter

A number of historians, political scientists, and sociologists have commented on various aspects of Weber's conceptualization of charismatic authority systems. Of all these comments, however, probably the biggest controversy surrounding Weber's theory concerns the locus of charismatic leadership. Is charisma primarily the result of the situation or social context facing the leader, the leader's extraordinary qualities, or the strong relationships between charismatic leaders and followers? A number of authors argued that charismatic movements could not take place unless the society was in a crisis (Blau, 1963; Chinoy, 1961; Wolpe, 1968). Along these lines, Friedland (1964), Gerth and Mills (1946), and Kanter (1972) argued that before a leader with extraordinary qualities would be perceived as charismatic, the social situation must be such that followers recognize the relevance of the leader's qualities. Others have argued that charismatic leadership is primarily a function of the leader's extraordinary qualities, not the situation (Tucker, 1968; Dow, 1969). These qualities include having extraordinary powers of vision, the rhetorical skills to communicate this vision, a sense of mission, high self-confidence and intelligence, and setting high expectations for followers. Finally, several authors have argued that the litmus test for charismatic leadership does not depend on the leader's qualities or the presence of a crisis, but rather on followers' reactions to their leader (Clark, 1972; Deveraux, 1955; Downton, 1973; Marcus, 1961; Shils, 1965). According to this argument, charisma is attributed only to those leaders who can develop particularly strong emotional attachments with followers.

The debate surrounding charismatic leadership shifted dramatically with the publication of James MacGregor Burns's, *Leadership* (1978). Burns was a prominent political scientist who had spent a career studying leadership in the national political arena. He believed that leadership could take one of two forms. **Transactional leadership** occurred when leaders and followers were in some type of exchange relationship in order to get needs met. The exchange could be economic, political, or psychological in nature, and examples might include exchanging money for work, votes for political favors, loyalty for consideration, and so forth. Transactional leadership is very common but tends to be transitory, in that there may be no enduring purpose to hold parties together once a transaction is made. Burns also noted that while this type of leadership could be quite effective, it did not result in organizational or societal change and instead tended to perpetuate and legitimize the status quo.

> *Some men see things as they are and ask why? I dream things that never were and ask, why not?*
>
> Edward Kennedy, U.S. Senator, in the eulogy to his brother, Robert F. Kennedy

The second form of leadership is **transformational leadership,** which serves to change the status quo by appealing to followers' values and their sense of higher purpose. Transformational leaders articulate the problems in the current system and have a compelling vision of what a new society or organization could be. This new vision of society is intimately linked to the values of both the leader and the followers; it represents an ideal that is congruent with their value systems. According to Burns, transformational leadership is ultimately a moral exercise in that it serves to raise the standard of human conduct. This implies that the acid test for transformational leadership might be the answer to the question, "Do the changes advocated by the leader advance or hinder the development of the organization or society?" Transformational leaders are also adept at **reframing** issues; they point out how the problems or issues facing followers can be resolved if they fulfill the leader's vision of the future. These leaders also teach followers how to become leaders in their own right and incite them to play active roles in the change movement (see Highlight 13.2).

It is important to note that all transformational leaders are charismatic, but not all charismatic leaders are transformational. Transformational leaders are charismatic because they are able to articulate a compelling vision of the future and form strong emotional attachments with followers. However, this vision and these relationships are aligned with followers' value systems and help them get their needs met. Charismatic leaders who are *not* transformational can convey a vision and form strong emotional bonds with followers, but they do so in order to get their own (i.e., the leader's) needs met. Both charismatic and transformational leaders strive for organizational or societal change; the difference is whether the changes are for the benefit of the leader or the followers. This distinction can be appreciated more fully by reading Highlight 13.3. Finally, transformational leaders are always controversial. Charismatic leadership almost inherently raises conflicts over values or definitions of the social "good." Controversy also arises because the people with the most to lose in any

An Example of a Transformational Leader: Nelson Mandela

Highlight 13–2

South Africa was ruled by a white minority government for much of the past 200 years. Although blacks made up over 75 percent of the populace, whites owned most of the property, ran most of the businesses, and controlled virtually all of the country's resources. Moreover, blacks did not have the right to vote and often worked under horrible conditions for little or no wages. Seeing the frustration of his people, Nelson Mandela spent 50 years working to overturn white-minority rule. He started by organizing the African National Congress, a nonviolent organization that protested white rule through work stoppages, strikes, and riots. Several whites were killed in the early riots, and in 1960 the police killed or injured over 250 blacks in Sharpeville. Unrest over the Sharpeville incident caused 95 percent of the black workforce to go on strike for two weeks, and the country declared a state of emergency. Mandela then orchestrated acts of sabotage to further pressure the South African government to change. The organization targeted installations and took special care to ensure no lives were lost in the bombing campaign. Mandela was arrested in 1962 and spent the next 27 years in prison. While in prison he continued to promote civil unrest and majority rule, and his cause eventually gained international recognition. He was offered but turned down a conditional release from prison in 1985. After enormous international and internal pressure, South African President F. W. de Klerk "unbanned" the ANC and unconditionally released Nelson Mandela from prison. Nonetheless, South Africa remained in turmoil, and in 1992 four million workers went on strike to protest white rule. Because of this pressure, Mandela forced de Klerk to sign a document outlining multiparty elections. Mandela won the 1994 national election and was the first truly democratically elected leader of the country.

Sources: M. Fatima, *Higher than Hope: The Authorized Biography of Nelson Mandela* (New York: Harper & Row, 1990); S. Clark, *Nelson Mandela Speaks: Forming a Democratic, Nonracist South Africa* (New York: Pathfinder Press, 1993).

existing system will put up the most resistance to a transformational change initiative. The emotional levels of those resisting the transformational leadership movement are often just as great as those who embrace it, and this may be the underlying cause for the violent ends to Martin Luther King, Jr., John F. Kennedy, Mahatma Gandhi, Joan of Arc, or Jesus Christ. Burns stated that transformational leadership always involves conflict and change, and transformational leaders must be willing to embrace conflict, make enemies, exhibit a high level of self-sacrifice, and be thick-skinned and focused in order to perpetuate the cause.

An Example of a Charismatic Leader: David Koresh

Highlight 13.3

In April 1993 approximately 85 people died at a religious compound outside Waco, Texas. Many of them died from the fire that consumed the compound, but a single shot in the head had killed others. Twenty-five of the deceased were children. How did this happen? The story of David Koresh is a classic example of what can go wrong when the situational, follower, and leadership elements necessary for charismatic leadership are in place but the leader exploits followers for his own selfish purposes. As a child, David's nickname was Sputnik—he was smart, inquisitive, energetic, but also had a strong need for security. When David turned nine his mother decided to attend the local Seventh-day Adventist church. Apparently David loved church and religion—he would be spellbound during sermons and spend hours listening to religious programs on the radio. David had a strong need to be the center of attention and spent time convincing others that he was special and worthwhile. He did so by reciting long passages of Scripture during church meetings and by telling others that God was talking to him. He eventually joined the Branch Davidians, a splinter group of the Seventh-day Adventists. Over the next four years David consolidated his hold on leadership, and convinced his fellow sect members that he was a living prophet and that Armageddon was at hand. To meet the challenge of Armageddon, he and fellow Branch members acquired a large cache of handguns, assault weapons, and explosives. During this time David's behavior became increasingly temperamental and violent. He made fellow members watch violent war movies, listen to his rock and roll sessions, and put them through long fasts and strange diets. This bizarre behavior continued until the Alcohol, Tobacco, and Firearms raid in February 1993.

Source: K.R. Samples; E.M. deCastro; R. Abanes; and R.J. Lyle, *Prophets of the Apocalypse: David Koresh and Other American Messiahs* (Grand Rapids, MI: Baker Books, 1994).

Yukl (1999), Hunt (1999) and Conger and Hunt (1999) all maintained that the publication of *Leadership* (Burns, 1978) played a key role in renewing interest in the topic of leadership. As a result, research over the past 25 years has explored cross-cultural, gender, succession, leader, follower, situational, and performance issues in charismatic or transformational leadership. From these efforts we now know that charismatic or transformational leadership is both common and rare. It is common because it can occur in almost every social stratum across every culture. For example, a high school student leader in France, a military cadet leader at the United States Air Force Academy, a Kenyan community leader, an Indonesian hospital leader, or a Russian business executive could all be perceived as charismatic or transformational leaders (Bass, 1999; Den Hartog, Hanges, Dorfman, Ruitz-Quintana & Associates, 1999). But it is also rare because most people in positions of authority are not perceived to be charismatic or transformational leaders. We also know that females such as Margaret Thatcher, Mary Kay Ash, or Anita Roddick tend to be perceived as more charismatic than their male counterparts, and that transformational leadership results in higher group performance than transactional leadership (Eagly, 1987; Rosener, 1990; Druskat, 1994; Bass, Avolio, & Atwater, 1996; Ross & Offermann, 1991; Avolio & Bass, 2000; Bass, 1999, 2000; Waldman, Ramirez, House, & Puranam, 2001). Although charismatic or transformational leadership often results in large-scale organizational change and higher organizational performance, there is little evidence that these changes remain permanent in business settings after the leader moves on (Conger, 1999).

As a result of this research, we also have three newer theories of charismatic or transformational leadership. Conger and Kanungo (1998) used a stage model to differentiate charismatic from noncharismatic leaders. Charismatic leaders begin by thoroughly assessing the current situation and pinpointing problems with the status quo. They then articulate a vision that represents a change from the status quo. This vision represents a challenge to and is a motivating force for change for followers. The vision must be articulated in such a way that increases dissatisfaction with the status quo and compels followers to take action. In the final stage, leaders build trust in their vision and goals by personal example, risk taking, and their total commitment to the vision. The theory developed by House and his colleagues (House, 1977; House & Shamir, 1993; Shamir, House, & Arthur, 1993) describes how charismatic leaders achieve higher performance by changing followers' self-concepts. Charismatic leaders are believed to motivate followers by changing their perceptions of work itself, offering an appealing vision of the future, developing a collective identity among followers, and increasing their confidence in getting the job done. Avolio and Bass's (2000) theory of transactional and transformational leadership is essentially an extension of Burns's theory. Unlike Burns, who viewed transactional and transformational leadership as the extremes of a single continuum, Avolio and Bass viewed these two concepts as independent leadership dimensions. Thus, leaders can be transformational and transactional, transactional but not transformational, and so on. Transformational leaders are believed to achieve stronger results because they heighten followers' awareness of goals and the means to achieve them, they convince followers to take action for the collective good of the group, and their vision of the future helps followers satisfy higher-order needs. Because Avolio and Bass created a questionnaire to assess a leader's standing on transactional and transformational leadership, this theory is by far the most thoroughly researched and will be discussed in more detail later in this chapter.

What Are the Common Characteristics of Charismatic and Transformational Leadership?

Although there are some important differences in the theories offered by Conger and Kanungo (1998), House (1977), and Avolio and Bass (2000), in reality they are far more similar than different. It is also important to note that these

> *We've long believed that when the rate of change inside an institution becomes slower than the rate of change outside, the end is in sight. The only question is when.*
>
> Jack Welch, General Electric

researchers either do not differentiate charismatic from transformational leadership, or see charisma as a component of transformational leadership. Therefore, we will use the terms somewhat interchangeably in the next section, although we acknowledge the fundamental difference between these two types of leadership. A review of the common leader, follower, and situational factors from Burns and the three more recent theories can be found in Figure 13.5. Like the past debates surrounding charismatic leadership, modern researchers are divided on whether charismatic leadership is due to the leader's superhuman qualities, a special relationship between leaders and followers, the situation, or some combination of these factors. Irrespective of the locus of charismatic leadership, the research does provide overwhelming support for the notion that transformational leaders are effective at large-scale societal or organizational change.

FIGURE 13.5

Factors pertaining to charismatic leadership and the interactional framework

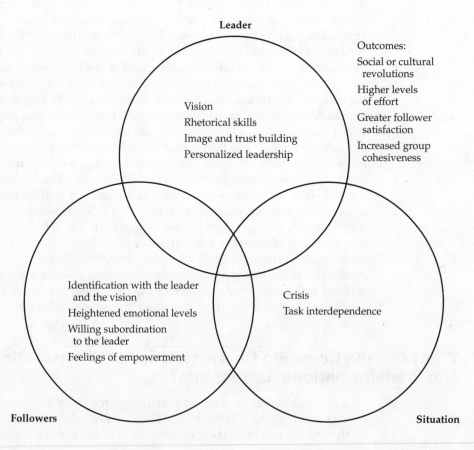

Leader

Vision
Rhetorical skills
Image and trust building
Personalized leadership

Outcomes:

Social or cultural
 revolutions

Higher levels
 of effort

Greater follower
 satisfaction

Increased group
 cohesiveness

Identification with the leader
 and the vision
Heightened emotional levels
Willing subordination
 to the leader
Feelings of empowerment

Crisis
Task interdependence

Followers

Situation

Leader Characteristics

Leadership researchers have spent considerably more time and effort trying to identify the unique characteristics of charismatic leaders than they have exploring follower or situational factors (Conger, 1999). This is partly because some researchers believe that it is possible to drive higher levels of organizational change or performance through the selection or training of charismatic leaders (Avolio & Bass, 1998, 2000; Bass, 1999; Hooijberg & Choi, 2000; Ross & Offermann, 1997; Zacharatos, Barling, & Kelloway, 2000). Although some scholars have argued that the leader's personal qualities are the key to charismatic or transformational leadership (Boal & Bryson, 1987; C. W. Hill, 1984, Kets de Vries, 1977, 1993; Sashkin, 1988; Zeleznik, 1974), we do not believe the leader's qualities alone result in charismatic leadership. We do, however, acknowledge several common threads in the behavior and style of both charismatic and transformational leaders, and these

> *Charismatic leaders are meaning makers. They pick and choose from the rough materials of reality and construct pictures of great possibilities. Their persuasion then is of the subtlest kind, for they interpret reality to offer us images of the future that are irresistible.*
>
> Jay Conger, University of Southern California

include their vision and values, rhetorical skills, ability to build a particular kind of image in the hearts and minds of their followers, and personalized style of leadership.

Vision.   Both transformational and charismatic leaders are inherently future-oriented. They involve helping a group move "from here to there." Charismatic leaders perceive fundamental discrepancies between the way things are and the way things can (or should) be. They recognize the shortcomings of a present order and offer an imaginative vision to overcome them. Several aspects of vision are worth elaboration. First, vision is not limited to grand social movements; leaders can use vision to help drive organizational change and performance in any kind or level of organization. Second, both Bennis and Nanus (1985) and Tichy and Devanna (1986) reported that the leader's vision of the future is often a collaborative effort; the genius of the leader is his or her ability to synthesize seemingly disparate issues and problems and develop a vision that ties all of these concerns together. Paradoxically, the magic of a leader's vision is often that the more complicated the problem, the more people may be drawn to simplistic solutions. Third, values play a key role in the leader's vision, and serve as a moral compass for aligning the actions of leaders and followers with change initiatives (Ket de Vries, 1993; Shamir, Arthur, & House, 1994; Shamir, House, & Arthur, 1993; Bass, 1999; Bass & Steidlmeier, 1999). As noted previously, this is one way transformational leaders differ from "mere" charismatic leaders: the former builds a vision based on *followers'* values whereas the latter's vision is based solely on their *own* values. Fourth, the leader's vision helps followers interpret events and actions in terms of a common perceptual framework

FIGURE 13.6

A leader's vision of the future can align efforts and help groups accomplish more

Source: Adapted from P. M. Senge *The Fifth Discipline* (New York: Doubleday, 1990)

Groups that lack vision

Groups with vision

(Wofford & Goodwin, 1994; Fairhurst & Sarr, 1996; Gardner & Avolio, 1998). Fifth, Berlew (1974, 1992) maintained that the vision of the charismatic leader had both a stimulating and a unifying effect on the efforts of followers. As seen in Figure 13.6, these effects can help drive greater organizational change and higher performance levels by followers.

Facts tell, but stories sell.

Bob Whelan, NCS Pearson

Rhetorical Skills.   In addition to *having* vision, charismatic leaders are gifted in *sharing* their vision. As discussed earlier, charismatic and transformational leaders have superb **rhetorical skills** that heighten followers', emotional levels and inspire them to embrace the vision. As it turns out, both the content of a transformational leader's speeches and the way they are delivered are vitally important. Charismatic leaders make extensive use of metaphors, analogies, and stories rather than abstract and colorless rational discourse to reframe issues and make their points. Moreover, these stories and metaphors can be particularly effective when they invoke potent cultural symbols and elicit strong emotions. Transformational leaders are adept at tailoring their language to particular groups, thereby better engaging them mentally and emotionally. Many transformational or charismatic religious and political leaders effectively use speech techniques like repetition, rhythm, balance, and alliteration to strengthen the impact of their messages (Conger, 1989; Holladay & Coombs, 1994; Shamir, Arthur, & House, 1994; Den Hartog & Verburg, 1997; Awamleh & Gardner, 1998; Berson, Shamir, Avolio, & Popper, 2001; Gargiulo, 2001). Often the delivery of the speech is even more important than the content itself, as poor delivery can detract from compelling content. Adolf Hitler mastered his delivery techniques so well that his speeches can have a hypnotizing power even to

"I Have a Dream"

Highlight 13.4

This will be the day when all of God's children will be able to sing with new meaning—"my country 'tis of thee, sweet land of liberty, of thee I sing; land where my fathers died, land of the pilgrim's pride; from every mountain side, let freedom ring"—and if America is to be a great nation, this must become true. So let freedom ring from the prodigious hilltops of New Hampshire. Let freedom ring from the mighty mountains of New York. Let freedom ring from the snow-capped Rockies of Colorado. Let freedom ring from the curvaceous slopes of California. But not only that. Let freedom ring from Stone Mountain of Georgia. Let freedom ring from Lookout Mountain of Tennessee. Let freedom ring from every hill and molehill of Mississippi, from every mountainside, let freedom ring. And when we allow freedom to ring, when we let it ring from every village and every hamlet, from every state and every city, we will be able to speed up that day when all of God's children—Black and White men, Jews and Gentiles, Protestants and Catholics—will be able to join hands and to sing in the words of the old Negro spiritual: "Free at last, free at last; thank God Almighty, we are free at last."

Source: Martin Luther King, Jr., "I Have a Dream" speech.

people who do not understand German (Willner, 1984). Similarly, many people consider Martin Luther King, Jr.'s "I Have a Dream" speech one of the most moving speeches they have ever heard. Note his use of different speech techniques and his masterful evocation of patriotic and cultural themes in the excerpt presented in Highlight 13.4.

> *Setting an example is not the main means of influencing another; it is the only means.*
>
> Albert Einstein

Image and Trust Building.   Transformational leaders build trust in their leadership and the attainability of their goals through an **image** of seemingly unshakable self-confidence, strength of moral conviction, personal example and self-sacrifice, and unconventional tactics or behavior (House, 1977; Conger, 1989; Bass & Avolio, 1994; Bass, 1997; Gardner & Avolio, 1998; Bass & Steidlmeier, 1999; Conger, 1999; Yorges, Weiss, & Strickland, 1999; Choi & Mai-Dalton, 1999). They are perceived to have unusual insight and ability and act in a manner consistent with their vision and values. Some charismatic leaders even seem to place more importance on creating the *appearance* of success than on success per se (House, 1977). Whereas transformational leaders **build trust** by showing commitment to

> One of the first assignments I give my lieutenants is to have them go down to the motor pool and stand in front of a tank. I then tell them to yell out, "Right face!" Of course, the tank doesn't move. I don't care how fancy or sophisticated your equipment or systems are, if you don't have motivated people to operate it, then it doesn't really matter. Leadership isn't about systems; it's about people.
>
> H. Norman Schwarzkopf,
> U.S. Army

followers' needs over self-interest, some charismatic leaders are not beyond taking credit for others' accomplishments or exaggerating their expertise (Conger, 1989).

Personalized Leadership.   One of the most important aspects of charismatic and transformational leadership is the personal nature of the leader's power. These leaders share strong, personal bonds with followers, even when the leader occupies a formal organizational role (Yagil, 1998; Conger, 1999; Avolio & Bass, 2000). It is this **personalized leadership** style that seems to be responsible for the feelings of empowerment notable among followers of charismatic or transformational leaders, and it has three important components. First, charismatic leaders are more sensitive to the emotional states of followers (Judge & Bono, 2000). They seem to be more adept at picking up social cues and tailoring their messages accordingly. Second, they also tend to be emotionally expressive, especially through such nonverbal channels as their eye contact, posture, movement, gestures, tone of voice, and facial expressions (Bass, 1990; Den Hartog & Verburg, 1997). It is partly through their ability to pick up on emotional cues and their nonverbal behaviors that some people are perceived to have a "magnetic" personality. Third, transformational leaders empower followers by building their self-efficacy. They do this by giving followers tasks that lead to successively greater success experiences and heightened self-confidence, encouraging followers to continually upgrade their skills, and creating an environment of heightened expectations and positive emotions (Larmore & Ayman, 1998; Bass, 1997; Bass & Avolio, 1994; Conger & Kanungo, 1998; Rost, 1991).

Follower Characteristics

If charismatic leadership were defined solely by a leader's characteristics, then it would be relatively easy to identify those individuals with good visioning, rhetorical, and impression management skills, and place them in leadership positions. Over time we would expect that a high percentage of followers would embrace and act on the leader's vision. However, a number of leaders appear to possess these attributes, yet are not seen as charismatic. They may be good, competent leaders in their own right, but they seem unable to evoke strong feelings in followers or to get followers to do more than they thought possible. In reality, charisma is probably more a function of the followers' reactions to a leader than of the leader's personal characteristics. If followers do not accept the leader's vision or become emotionally attached to the leader, then the leader simply will not be perceived to be either charismatic or transformational. Thus, **charisma** is in the eyes and heart of the beholder; it is a particularly strong emotional reaction to, identification with, and belief in

> Nothing great was ever achieved without enthusiasm.
> Ralph Waldo Emerson

some leaders by some followers. It is important to note that this definition is value-free—leaders seen as charismatic may or may not share the same values as their followers or meet Burns's criteria for transformational leadership. Many of the more popular conceptualizations of charisma and charismatic leadership today also define charisma in terms of followers' reactions to the leader (Bass, 1985, 1997; Avolio & Bass, 2000; Conger & Kanungo, 1998; Shamir, House, & Arthur, 1993; Howell, 1988; Willner, 1984). Defining charisma as a reaction that followers have toward leaders makes it reasonable to turn our attention to the four unique characteristics of these reactions.

> *To be an effective leader, one must become a leader of leaders. . . The ultimate measure of Christ's leadership is that the movement he founded continued to spread after his death. In fact, from the moment of his first conversions, Christianity belonged not to Christ but to the Christians.*
>
> James O'Toole,
> The Aspen Institute

Identification with the Leader and the Vision. Two of the effects associated with charismatic leadership include a strong affection for the leader and a similarity of follower beliefs with those of the leader. These effects describe a sort of bonding or **identification with the leader** personally, and a parallel psychological investment to a goal or activity (a "cause") bigger than oneself. Followers bond with a leader because they see the implementation of the vision as a solution to all of their problems. Followers may be intensely dissatisfied with the status quo but unsuccessful in developing a satisfactory solution on their own. Charismatic leaders capitalize on this dissatisfaction and on the belief that most people want to make a difference in their organizations or society. Followers' identities or self-concepts also become defined in terms of the leader. Being like the leader, or approved by the leader, becomes an important part of one's self-worth (Ehrhart & Klein, 2001; Lord & Brown, 2001). Effects like these go well beyond what might be expected from the typical contractual or exchange relationships between most supervisors and subordinates.

Heightened Emotional Levels. Charismatic leaders are able to stir followers' feelings, and this **heightened emotional level** results in increased levels of effort and performance. Emotions are often the fuel driving large-scale initiatives for change, and charismatic leaders will often do all they can to maintain them, including getting followers to think about their dissatisfaction with the status quo or making impassioned appeals directly to followers. There are several dangers with increasing followers' emotional levels, however. The leader must ensure that followers' emotions are channeled toward the change initiative, otherwise followers will find some other outlet for their feelings and efforts. In addition, the people alienated by a charismatic leader

> *We're not worthy; we're not worthy!*
>
> Wayne and Garth,
> *Wayne's World*

and the movement can have emotions just as intense as those of the followers of the vision. This polarizing effect of charismatic leaders may be one reason why they tend to have violent deaths, as those alienated by a charismatic leader are just as likely to act on their emotions as followers within the movement (House, Woycke, & Fodor, 1988).

Willing Subordination to the Leader.   Whereas the preceding factor dealt with followers' emotional and psychological closeness to the leader, **willing subordination to the leader** involves their deference to his or her authority. Charismatic leaders often seem imbued with superhuman qualities. As a result, followers often naturally and willingly submit to the leader's apparent authority and superiority. Followers seem to suspend their critical thinking skills; they have few if any doubts about the intentions or skills of the leader, the correctness of the vision or change initiative, or the actions they need to take in order achieve the vision.

> *Never tell people how to do things. Tell them what to do, and they will surprise you with their ingenuity.*
> George Patton, U.S. Army

Feelings of Empowerment.   Followers of charismatic leaders are moved to expect more of themselves, and they work harder to achieve these higher goals. Charismatic leaders capitalize on the Pygmalion Effect: They set high expectations while boosting the self-confidence of followers by expressing confidence in their abilities and providing ongoing encouragement and support (Dvir, Eden, Avolio, & Shamir, 1999; Larmore & Ayman, 1998; Bass & Avolio, 1994). Somewhat paradoxically, followers feel stronger and more powerful at the same time they willingly subordinate themselves to the charismatic leader. Charismatic leaders are able to make their followers feel more powerful without any diminution or threat to their own status. These **feelings of empowerment,** when combined with heightened emotional levels and a leader's vision of the future, often result in increases in organizational, group, or team performance or significant social change.

Situational Characteristics

Most of the research up to now has focused on identifying the leader attributes associated with charismatic leadership. There is considerably more to learn about the underlying attributes of followers and the situational characteristics of charismatic or transformational leadership (Beyer, 1999; Conger, 1999). Despite this gap in knowledge, some researchers believe that situational factors do play an important role in determining whether a leader will be perceived as charismatic (Bradley, 1987; Roberts & Bradley, 1988; Westley & Mintzberg, 1988; Gardner & Avolio, 1998; Conger, 1999; Hunt, Boal, & Dodge, 1999; Shamir & Howell, 1999; Waldman, Ramirez, House, & Puranam, 2001). It may be that individuals possessing the qualities of charismatic leaders will be perceived as charismatic *only when confronting certain types of situations.* It may also be that the more favorable the situation is for charismatic leadership, the fewer qualities

Saving Continental Airlines

Highlight 13.5

By all accounts, Continental Airlines was ready to go under in 1993. The company ranked last in customer service of the 10 major airlines, it lost $600 million in 1994, and employees were so disgruntled that they tore the Continental Airlines logos off their uniforms. The company had gone through 10 CEOs in as many years, and had no vision or strategy in place to pull out of its nosedive. Because of the crisis facing the company, Gordon Berthune from Boeing and Greg Brenneman from Bain & Company were asked in early 1994 to be the next in line to turn Continental Airlines around. Fortunately for the customers, employees, and shareholders, these two leaders have been remarkably successful with their change efforts. But how were they able to turn around such a company facing such a crisis? They did so through a combination of rational and emotional change approaches. They started with a thorough assessment of the situation facing the company. They then built a vision and implemented a set of strategies to improve financial and customer service results. Some of these strategies included changing the Continental Airlines brand, eliminating nonprofitable routes, improving maintenance and operational performance, tracking cash flow, building employee trust and morale through constant communication and numerous "town hall" meetings, eliminating 7,000 positions (of 50,000 employees), and aligning the compensation system around desired employee behaviors. None of these changes were easy—Brenneman likened them to having a 12-hour surgery without anesthesia. However, during the time that these two leaders were on board, Continental Airlines' revenues doubled, the company made a profit every year from 1995 to 2000, stock prices increased fivefold, employee morale soared, and customer satisfaction ratings placed the airline among the best in the industry.

Source: G. Brenneman, *Right Away and All at Once: How We Saved Continental.* Reprint No. 98503 (Boston: Harvard Business School Publishing Division, 1998).

leaders will need before they are perceived to be charismatic (Conger, 1999). Because the situation may play an important role in the attribution of charisma, it will be useful to review some of the situational factors believed to affect charismatic leadership (see also Highlight 13.5).

Crises.   Perhaps the most important situational factor associated with charismatic leadership is the presence or absence of a **crisis.** Followers who are content with the status quo are relatively unlikely to perceive a need for a charismatic leader or be willing to devote great effort to fundamentally change an organization or society. On the other hand, a crisis—whether reflected by the failure of traditional social institutions or a corporation's imminent financial failure—often creates a "charisma hunger" in followers; they are looking for a leader to alleviate or resolve their crisis (Madsen & Snow, 1983; Trice & Beyer, 1986). Leaders are given considerably more latitude and autonomy and may temporarily (or sometimes permanently) suspend accepted rules, policies, and procedures in order to pull the organization out of the crisis. Some researchers even believe that some leaders purposely create or manufacture crises to increase followers' acceptance of their vision, the range of actions they can take, and followers' level of effort (Pawar & Eastman, 1997; Avolio & Bass 1988; Boal & Bryson, 1987; Kets de Vries, 1977). Although a crisis situation does not necessarily make every leader look charismatic, such a situation may "set the stage" for particular kinds of leader behaviors to be effective (Hunt, Boal, & Dodge, 1999; Waldman, Ramirez, House, & Puranam, 2001).

Task Interdependence.   It may be easier for leaders to be seen as charismatic when the tasks performed by their followers require a high level of interdependent rather than independent effort (Curphy, 1991a, 1992a). With **task interdependence,** for example, it may be easier for leaders to be perceived as charismatic when they are leading a software design team rather than a sales team because each individual programmer's code could be affected by the code developed by the other programmers. However, a sales representative with a defined territory will probably not be affected by efforts of the other sales representatives on the team.

Other Situational Characteristics.   Several other situational characteristics may help or hinder the emergence of a charismatic leader. Howell and Avolio (1993) found that organizations placing a premium on innovation were much more supportive of transformational leadership than those less committed to innovation. Another situational factor that may affect charismatic leadership is organizational downsizing. In the minds of many peoples, downsizing has destroyed the implicit contract between employer and employee, and left many employees disillusioned with corporate life (Church, 1994). On the one hand, because charismatic or transformational leadership is intensely relational in nature, destroying the implicit contract between leaders and followers could greatly diminish the odds of charismatic leadership emergence. On the other hand, this disillusionment has caused many talented managers to leave large organizations to form their own companies. Employees are drawn to these start-up organizations precisely because the company's vision is consistent with their own personal values. But of all the situational variables affecting charismatic leadership, perhaps the most important and overlooked variable is time. Charismatic or transformational leadership does not happen overnight. It takes time for leaders to develop and articulate their vision, heighten followers' emotional levels, build trusting relationships with followers, and direct and empower followers to fulfill the vision. It may be that a crisis compresses the amount of time while relatively stable situations lengthen the amount of time needed for charismatic leadership to emerge.

Concluding Thoughts about the Characteristics of Charismatic and Transformational Leadership

Several final points about the characteristics of charismatic leadership need to be made. First, although we defined charisma as a quality attributed to certain leaders based on the relationships they share with followers, charismatic leadership is most fully understood when we also consider how leader and situational factors affect this attribution process. The special relationships charismatic leaders share with followers do not happen by accident; rather, they are often the result of interaction between the leader's qualities, leader and follower values, and the presence of certain situational factors. Second, it seems unlikely that all the characteristics of charismatic leadership need to be present before charisma is attributed to a leader. The bottom line for charisma seems to be the relationships certain leaders share with followers, and there may be a variety of ways in which these relationships can develop. This also implies that charisma may be more of a continuum than an all-or-nothing phenomenon. Some leaders may be able to form particularly strong bonds with a majority of followers, others with a few followers, and still others may get along with most but not form particularly strong bonds with any followers. Third, it does seem that charismatic leadership can happen anywhere—schools, churches, communities, businesses, government organizations, and nations—and does not happen only on the world stage.

Fourth, given that there are a number of ways to develop strong emotional attachments with followers, one important question is whether it is possible to attribute charisma to an individual based solely on his or her position or celebrity status (Etzioni, 1961; Hollander, 1978; Bass, 1990). Some individuals in positions of high public visibility and esteem (e.g., film stars, musicians, athletes, television evangelists, and politicians) can develop (even cultivate) charismatic images among their fans and admirers. In these cases, it is helpful to recognize that charismatic leadership is a two-way street. Not only do followers develop strong emotional bonds with leaders, but leaders also develop strong emotional bonds with followers and are concerned with follower development (Burns, 1978; Dvir, Eden, Avolio, & Shamir, 1999). It is difficult to see how the one-way communication channels of radio and television can foster these two-way relationships or enhance follower growth. Thus, although we sometimes view certain individuals as charismatic based on media manipulation and hype, this is not transformational leadership in the truest sense.

So what can leadership practitioners take from this research if they want to use an emotional approach to drive organizational change? They will probably be more successful at driving organizational change if they capitalize on or create a crisis. They also need to be close enough to their followers to determine the sources of discontent and ensure their vision is aligned with followers' values and paints a compelling picture of the future. Leaders must passionately articulate their vision of the future; it is difficult to imagine followers being motivated toward a vision that is unclear or presented by a leader who does not seem to really care about it. Leadership practitioners also need to understand that they alone cannot make the vision a reality; they need their followers' help and support to create organizational or societal changes. Along these lines, they will need to be a role model and coach followers on what they should (and should not) be doing, provide feedback and encouragement, and persuade followers to take on more responsibilities as their skills and self-confidence grow. Finally, leadership practitioners using this approach to organizational change also need to be thick skinned, resilient, and patient. They will need to cope with the polarization effects of charismatic leadership and understand that it takes time for the effects of this type of leadership to yield results. However, the rewards appear to be well worth the efforts. There appears to be overwhelming evidence that charismatic or transformational leaders are more effective than their noncharismatic counterparts, whether they be presidents of the United States (Deluga, 1998), CEOs (Waldman, Ramirez, House, & Puranam, 2001), military cadets and officers (Bass, 2000; Curphy, 1991a; Clover, 1990; Adams, Price, Instone, & Rice, 1984), college professors (Labak, 1973), or first-line supervisors and middle-level managers in a variety of public and private sector companies (Avolio & Bass, 2000).

Bass's Theory of Transformational and Transactional Leadership

Much of what we know about the leader, follower, and situational characteristics associated with charismatic or transformational leaders comes from research on Bass's (1985, 1997) **Theory of Transformational and Transactional Leadership.** Bass believed that transformational leaders possessed those leader characteristics described earlier; he used perceptions or reactions of subordinates' to determine whether or not a leader was transformational. Thus, transformational leaders possess good visioning, rhetorical, and impression management skills, and they use these skills to develop strong emotional bonds with followers. Transformational leaders are believed to be more successful at driving organizational change because of followers' heightened emotional levels and their willingness to work toward the accomplishment of the leader's vision (Avolio & Bass, 2000; Bass, 1997; Bass & Avolio, 1996). In contrast, transactional leaders do not possess these leader characteristics, nor are they able to develop strong emotional bonds with followers or inspire followers to do more than followers thought they could. Instead, transactional leaders were believed to motivate followers by setting goals and promising rewards for desired performance. Avolio and Bass (1987, 1988) maintained that transactional leadership could have positive effects on follower satisfaction and performance levels, but they also stated that these behaviors were often underutilized because of time constraints, a lack of leader skills, and a disbelief among leaders that rewards could boost performance. Bass (1997) also maintained that transactional leadership only perpetuates the status quo; a leader's use of rewards does not result in the long-term changes associated with transformational leadership.

Like the "initiating structure" and "consideration" behaviors described in Chapter 8, Bass hypothesized that transformational and transactional leadership comprised two independent leadership dimensions. Thus, individuals could be high transformational but low transactional leaders, low transformational and low transactional leaders, and so on. Bass developed a questionnaire, known as the **Multifactor Leadership Questionnaire (MLQ),** to assess the extent to which leaders exhibited transformational or transactional leadership and the extent to which followers were satisfied with their leader and believed their leader was effective. The MLQ is a 360-degree feedback instrument that assesses five transformational and three transactional factors and a nonleadership factor (Bass & Avolio, 2000; Bass, 1997). The transformational leadership factors assess the degree to which the leader instills pride in others, displays power and confidence, makes personal sacrifices or champions new possibilities, considers the ethical or moral consequences of decisions, articulates a compelling vision of the future, sets challenging standards, treats followers as individuals, and helps followers understand the problems they face. The three transactional leadership factors assess the extent to which leaders set goals, make rewards contingent on performance, obtain necessary resources, provide rewards when performance goals have been met, monitor followers' performance levels, and intervene when problems occur. The MLQ also assesses another factor called laissez-faire leadership, which assesses the extent to which leaders avoid responsibilities, fail to make decisions, are absent when needed, or fail to follow up on requests.

Research Results of Transformational and Transactional Leadership

To date, over 200 studies have used the MLQ to investigate transformational and transactional leadership across a wide variety of situations. These results indicated that transformational leadership can be observed in all countries, institutions, and organizational levels, but it was more prevalent in public institutions and at lower organizational levels (Avolio & Bass, 2000; Bass, 1999, 2000; Lowe, Kroeck, & Sivasubramaniam, 1996). In other words, there seemed to be more transformational leaders in the lower levels of the military or other public sector organizations than anywhere else. Second, there is overwhelming evidence that transformational leadership is a significantly better predictor of organizational effectiveness than transactional or laissez-faire leadership. Transformational leaders, whether they are U.S. presidents, CEOs, school administrators, or plant managers, seem to be more effective at driving organizational change and getting results than transactional leaders. Avolio and Bass (2000) also believed that transformational leadership augments performance above and beyond what is associated with transactional leadership. Third, as expected, laissez-faire leadership was negatively correlated with effectiveness.

Given that the MLQ can reliably identify transformational leaders and that these leaders can drive higher levels of organizational change and effectiveness than their transactional counterparts, it seems reasonable to ask whether it is possible to train or select charismatic leaders. Fortunately, Avolio (1999), Avolio and Bass (1998; 2000), Bass (1999), and Barling, Weber, and Kelloway (1996) have all looked at the effects of transformational leadership training on the performance of military, public sector, and private industry leaders in the United States, Canada, and Israel. Usually these training programs consisted of a one-to five-day initial training session where participants learned about the Theory of Transformational and Transactional Leadership; received MLQ feedback on the extent to which they exhibit transformational, transactional, and laissez-faire leadership; and then went through a series of skill-building exercises and activities to improve their leadership effectiveness. At the end of the initial session, participants were asked to create a development plan to improve specific transformational or transactional leadership skills. Approximately 6 to 24 months after the initial program, participants attended a second training session that also provided a second round of MLQ feedback. The time 1 and time 2 MLQ results allowed researchers to determine quantitatively whether the training program improved the transformational and transactional leadership skills of the participants. These results indicated that improving transactional leadership skills is fairly easy; participants who targeted these skills for improvement reported higher time 2 MLQ scores on the transactional leadership factor. There were also modest gains in the time 2 MLQ transformational leadership factor scores for those participants who targeted these skills in their development plan. Moreover, those areas that were not targeted for improvement saw no commensurate increase in time 2 MLQ scores. Thus, the higher time 2 scores were not due to some general effect, but rather were limited only to those skills that were part of a participant's development plan. These results provided strong evidence that it is possible for leaders to systematically develop their transformational and transactional leadership skills.

An alternative to training leaders to be more transformational is to select leaders with the propensity to be transformational or charismatic in the first place. Several researchers have looked at the importance of childhood experiences, leadership traits, and even genetics in transformational leadership. Zacharatos, Barling, and Kelloway (2000) reported that adolescents who were rated by coaches and peers to be more transformational were also more likely to have parents who were transformational leaders. There is also evidence that certain leadership traits differentiate transformational from transactional leaders. Hogan, Curphy, and Hogan (1994), Curphy and Nilsen (1995), Nilsen (1995), House, Spangler, and Woycke (1991), House, Woycke, and Fodor (1988), Ross and Offermann (1991), and Judge and Bono (2000) all showed that certain Five Factor Model (FFM) leadership traits (Chapter 7) could be reliably used to identify transformational leaders. Some of the most compelling evidence comes from Nilsen (1995), who looked at the relationships between FFM personality traits and 125 CEOs. As seen in Table 13–4, not only are the FFM personality dimensions strongly correlated with certain components of transformational leadership, but the pattern of high and low correlations seems to make sense.

TABLE 13–4   **Correlations between Five Factor Model Dimensions and Charismatic Leadership Characteristics for 125 Corporate CEOs and Presidents**

Transformational Leadership Characteristics

Personality Dimension	Visionary Thinking	Empowering Others	Inspiring Trust	High Impact Delivery
Surgency	.32	.33	.16	.47
Dependability	−.08	−.01	.06	−.04
Agreeableness	.02	.52	.48	.35
Adjustment	−.03	.29	.38	.22
Intellectance	.47	.30	.14	.40

Source: D. Nilsen, "Using Self and Observers' Ratings for Personality to Predict Leadership Performance." Unpublished doctoral dissertation, University of Minnesota, Minneapolis, 1995.

Given that certain leadership traits are related to transformational leadership, and that leadership traits have a genetic component, then it is not surprising that some researchers also believe that some aspect of transformational leadership is also heritable (Hooijberg & Choi, 2000).

Despite this evidence that it may be possible to select and train transformational leaders, the fact remains that charisma ultimately exists in the eyes of the beholder. Thus, there never could be any guarantee that leaders who had the right stuff and were schooled in the appropriate techniques will be seen as charismatic by followers. As discussed earlier, follower and situational variables will play a key role in determining whether leaders are perceived to be transformational and drive organizational change. Certain leaders may get higher transformational leadership scores as a result of a training program, but do they actually heighten followers' emotional levels, get followers to exert extra effort, and as a result achieve greater organizational change or performance after the program? Furthermore, while it may be possible to train some leaders to improve their visioning, impression management, and rhetorical skills, leaders who have relatively low scores on certain personality traits or other individual differences (e.g., intelligence, creativity, surgency, agreeableness, adjustment, and intellectance) may not benefit much from transformational leadership training. Bass (1985), Curphy (1991a), and Segal (1985) have all stated that personality is going to have a big effect on whether a leader will be seen as charismatic. Given what we know about individual differences and leadership skills training, it seems likely that a leader's personality will also play a major role in determining whether he or she will benefit from such training.

Finally, several other important comments about the Theory of Transformational and Transactional Leadership are worth noting. First, and perhaps most important, this theory has generated a considerable amount of interest among leadership researchers. This research has helped leadership practitioners to better understand the leader, follower, and situational components of charismatic or transformational leadership, whether transformational leaders are born or made, and so forth. Nevertheless, much of the research is based on surveys and correlational studies; the handful of experiments exploring the effects of transformational and transactional leadership have involved college students, not leadership practitioners (Hunt, 1999; Yukl, 1999). Third, this approach to leadership seems to have a strong bias toward people, in that measures such as the MLQ may be more a reflection of socially desirable leadership behaviors than the full range of skills needed by leaders (Beyer, 1999). For example, it seems likely that business leaders wanting to drive organizational change or performance need to have a good understanding of the industry, business operations, market trends, finance, strategy, and technical/functional knowledge; they also need to effectively cope with stress, negotiate contracts with vendors, demonstrate good planning skills, and develop and monitor key metrics. Yet none of these attributes and skills are directly measured by the MLQ. Relatedly, Beyer (1999) and Yukl (1999) pointed out that the primary problem with this theory is that there is only one way to be an effective leader, and that is by demonstrating transformational leadership skills. The contingency theories of leadership no longer matter, and situational or follower factors have little impact on leadership effectiveness. In this regard Beyer and Yukl may be right; leaders probably need to do more than exhibit only transformational leadership skills if they wish to achieve greater organizational change and performance.

Summary

This chapter began by revisiting the topic of leadership and management. Management skills are important to ensure compliance with existing systems, processes, and procedures; they are used to help preserve the status quo, improve consistency and efficiency, and maintain control. Leadership skills are needed when changes need to be made to existing systems and processes; they are used to create new systems and drive organizational change. The chapter then reviewed two major approaches to organizational change. Although independent lines of research were used to develop the rational and emotional approaches to change, in reality these approaches have several important similarities. With the rational approach, leaders increase follower dissatisfaction by pointing out problems with the status quo, systematically identifying areas of needed change, developing a vision of the future, and developing and implementing a change plan. In the emotional approach, leaders develop and articulate a vision of the future, heighten the emotions of followers, and empower followers to act on their vision. Charismatic leaders are also more likely to emerge during times of uncertainty or crisis, and may actually manufacture a crisis to improve the odds that followers will become committed to their vision of the future. The rational approach puts more emphasis on analytic, planning, and management skills whereas the emotional approach puts more emphasis on leadership skills, leader–follower relationships, and the presence of a crisis to drive organizational change. This chapter described the steps leadership practitioners must take if they wish to drive organizational change. There is ample evidence to suggest that either the rational or the emotional approach can result in organizational change, but the effectiveness of the change may depend on which approach leadership practitioners are most comfortable with and the skill with which they can carry it out.

Key Terms and Concepts

$C=DxMxP>R$ 389
dissatisfaction   389
model   389
process   389
resistance   389
amount of change   389
systems thinking approach   392
siloed thinking   392
change plan   393
SARA model   396
traditional authority system   400
legal-rational authority system   400
charismatic authority system   401
transactional leadership   402
transformational leadership   402
reframing   402

vision   407
rhetorical skills   408
image   409
build trust   409
personalized leadership   410
charisma   410
identification with the leader   411
heightened emotional level   411
willing subordination to the leader   412
feelings of empowerment   412
crisis   413
task interdependence   414
Theory of Transformational and Transactional leadership   416
Multifactor Leadership Questionnaire (MLQ)   417

Questions

1. Is Colin Powell a transformational or charismatic leader? What data would you need to gather to answer this question?
2. Is Osama bin Laden a charismatic or transformational leader? Would your answer differ if you were sympathetic to his cause?
3. Research shows that females are seen as more transformational leaders, yet hold relatively few top leadership positions compared to men. Why do you think this is the case? What, if anything, could you do to change this situation?

4. Research shows that charismatic and transformational leaders need to project an image of success, but muckraking and negativity in political campaigns are at an all-time high. Which leader, follower, or situational components of charismatic leadership do political advertisements attempt to undermine? Given these ads, is it even possible for a political leader today to be seen as charismatic?
5. Can leaders possess the dark side personality traits described in Chapter 7 and still be seen as charismatic?

Skills

Leadership skills relevant to this chapter include:
- Communication
- Setting goals
- Credibility
- Coaching
- Empowerment

Activity

1. Break up into teams and identify something that needs to change at your school or at work. Use the rational approach to change (C=DxMxP) to develop a plan for your change initiative.

V   LEADERSHIP SKILLS

One reason any person can improve his or her leadership effectiveness is that part of leadership involves skills, and skills can be practiced and developed. A further advantage of looking at leadership skills is that most people are less defensive about deficits in skills (which can be improved) than about suggested deficits in, say, personality. Our rationale for this final portion of the book is that (1) certain skills do contribute to leadership effectiveness, and (2) they can be learned.

Presenting the skills in this final section does not, however, indicate we believe they should not be covered until the preceding material in the book has been completed. Quite the contrary. We believe it will be most useful to intersperse work on these skills with the other chapters. We also trust that professors and students in a particular course will know better for themselves what order of coverage of the various skills will work best in their unique circumstances. We have taken the liberty, however, of categorizing the skills into two broad groups of basic and more advanced leadership skills. While even this categorization is inherently somewhat arbitrary, it may provide a useful starting point for the reader. Furthermore, as you have seen throughout the text, the end of each chapter contains a list of skills which we believe relate directly to the content of that chapter.

LIST OF SKILLS IN PART V

BASIC LEADERSHIP SKILLS

Learning from Experience

Creating Opportunities to Get Feedback
Taking a 10 Percent Stretch
Learning from Others
Keeping a Journal
Having a Developmental Plan

Leadership practitioners can enhance the learning value of their experiences by *(a)* creating opportunities to get feedback, *(b)* taking a 10 percent stretch, *(c)* learning from others, *(d)* keeping a journal of daily leadership events, and *(e)* having a developmental plan.

Creating Opportunities to Get Feedback

It may be difficult for leaders to get relevant feedback, particularly if they occupy powerful positions in an organization. Yet leaders often need feedback more than subordinates do. Leaders may not learn much from their leadership experiences if they get no feedback about how they are doing. Therefore, they may need to create opportunities to get feedback, especially with regard to feedback from those working for them.

First of all, leaders should not assume they have invited feedback merely by saying that they have an open-door policy. A mistake some bosses make is presuming that others perceive them as open to discussing things just because they say they are open to discussing things. How truly open a door is, clearly, is in the eye of the beholder. In that sense, the key to constructive dialogue (i.e., feedback) is not just expressing a policy but also being perceived as approachable and sincere in the offer.

Some of the most helpful information for developing your own leadership can come from asking for feedback from others about their perceptions of your behavior and its impact on your group's overall effectiveness. Leaders who take psychological tests and use periodic surveys or questionnaires will have greater access to feedback than leaders who fail to systematically solicit feedback from their followers. Unless leaders ask for feedback, they may not get it.

Taking a 10 Percent Stretch

Learning always involves stretching. Learning involves taking risks and reaching beyond one's comfort zone. This is true of a toddler's first unsteady steps, a student's first serious confrontation with divergent worlds of thought, and leadership development. The phrase *10 percent stretch* conveys the idea of voluntary but determined efforts to improve leadership skills. It is analogous to physical exercise, though in this context stretching implies extending one's behavior, not muscles, just a bit beyond the comfort zone. Examples could include making a point to converse informally with everyone in the office at least once each day, seeking an opportunity to be chairman of a committee, or being quieter than usual at meetings (or more assertive, as the case may be). There is much to be gained from a commitment to such ongoing "exercise" for personal and leadership development.

Several positive outcomes are associated with leaders who regularly practice the 10 percent stretch. First, their apprehension about doing something new or different gradually decreases. Second, leaders will broaden their repertoire of leadership skills. Third, because of this increased repertoire, their effectiveness will likely increase. And finally, leaders regularly taking a 10 percent stretch will model something very valuable to others. Few things will send a better message to others about the importance of their own development than the example of how sincerely a leader takes his or her own development.

One final aspect of the 10 percent stretch is worth mentioning. One reason the phrase is so appealing is that it sounds like a measurable yet manageable change. Many people will not offer serious objection to trying a 10 percent change in some behavior, whereas they might well be resistant (and unsuccessful) if they construe a developmental goal as requiring fundamental change in their personality or interpersonal style. Despite its nonthreatening connotation, though, an actual 10 percent change in behavior can make an enormous difference in effectiveness. In many kinds of endeavor the difference between average performers and exceptional performers is 10 percent. In baseball, for example, many players hit .275, but only the best hit over .300—a difference of about 10 percent.

Learning from Others

Leaders learn from others, first of all, by recognizing they *can* learn from others and, importantly, from *any* others. That may seem self-evident, but in fact people often limit what and whom they pay attention to, and thus what they may learn from. For example, athletes may pay a lot of attention to how coaches handle leadership situations. However, they may fail to realize they could also learn a lot by watching the director of the school play and the band conductor. Leaders should not limit their learning by narrowly defining the sorts of people they pay attention to.

Similarly, leaders also can learn by asking questions and paying attention to everyday situations. An especially important time to ask questions is when leaders are new to a group or activity and have some responsibility for it. When possible, leaders should talk to the person who previously had the position to benefit from his or her insights, experience, and assessment of the situation. In addition, observant leaders are able to extract meaningful leadership lessons from everyday situations. Something as plain and ordinary as a high school car wash or the activities at a fast-food restaurant may offer an interesting leadership lesson. Leaders can learn a lot by actively observing how others react to and handle different challenges and situations, even very common ones.

Keeping a Journal

Another way leaders can mine experiences for their richness and preserve their learning is by keeping a journal (Csikszentmihalyi, 1990). Journals are similar to diaries, but they are not just accounts of a day's events. A journal should include entries that address some aspect of leaders or leadership. Journal entries may include comments about insightful or interesting quotes, anecdotes, newspaper articles, or even humorous cartoons about leadership. They may also include reflections on personal events, such as interactions with bosses, coaches, teachers, students, employees, players, teammates, roommates, and so on. Such entries can emphasize a good (or bad) way somebody handled something, a problem in the making, the differences between people in their reactions to situations, or people in the news, a book, or a film. Leaders should also use their journals to "think on paper" about leadership readings from textbooks or formal leadership programs or to describe examples from their own experience of a concept presented in a reading.

There are at least three good reasons for keeping a journal. First, the very process of writing increases the likelihood that leaders will be able to look at an event from a different perspective or feel differently about it. Putting an experience into words can be a step toward taking a more objective look at it. Second, leaders can (and should) reread earlier entries. Earlier entries provide an interesting and valuable autobiography of a leader's evolving thinking about leadership and about particular events in his or her life. Third, journal entries provide a repository of ideas that leaders may later want to use more formally for papers, pep talks, or speeches. As seen in Highlight LFE.1, good journal entries provide leaders with a wealth of examples that they may use in speeches, presentations, and so on.

Having a Developmental Plan

Leadership development almost certainly occurs in ways and on paths that are not completely anticipated or controlled. That is no reason, however, for leaders to avoid actively directing some aspects of their own development. A systematic

Sample Journal Entries

Highlight LFE.1

I went skiing this weekend and saw the perfect example of a leader adapting her leadership style to her followers and situation. While putting on my skis I saw a ski instructor teaching little kids to ski. She did it using the game "red light, green light." The kids loved it and seemed to be doing very well. Later that same day, as I was going to the lodge for lunch, she was teaching adults, and she did more demonstrating than talking. But when she talked she was always sure to encourage them so they did not feel intimidated when some little kid whizzed by. She would say to the adults that it's easier for children, or that smaller skis are easier. She made the children laugh and learn, and made the adults less self-conscious to help them learn too. . .

Today may not exactly be a topic on leadership, but I thought it would be interesting to discuss. I attended the football game this afternoon and could not help but notice our cheerleaders. I was just thinking of their name in general, and found them to be a good example (of leadership). Everyone gets rowdy at a football game, but without the direction of the cheerleaders there would be mayhem. They do a good job of getting the crowd organized and the adrenaline pumping (though of course the game is most important in that too!). It's just amazing to see them generate so much interest that all of the crowd gets into the cheering. We even chant their stupid-sounding cheers! You might not know any of them personally, but their enthusiasm invites you to try to be even louder than them. I must give the cheerleaders a round of applause. . .

I've been thinking about how I used to view/understand leadership, trying to find out how my present attitudes were developed. It's hard to remember past freshman year, even harder to go past high school. Overall, I think my father has been the single most important influence on my leadership development—long before I even realized it. Dad is a strong "Type A" person. He drives himself hard and demands a great deal from everyone around him, especially his family and especially his only son and oldest child. He was always pushing me to study, practice whatever sport I was involved in at the time, get ahead of everybody else in every way possible.

plan outlining self-improvement goals and strategies will help leaders take advantage of opportunities they otherwise might overlook. Developing a systematic plan also will help leaders prioritize the importance of different goals so that their efforts can be put into areas with the greatest relative payoffs. Leaders who carefully choose which seminars and conferences to attend may help themselves maximize their contribution to their personal developmental goals. Leaders should look for opportunities on the job or in volunteer work for responsibilities that may further their growth. Leaders should recognize, however, that they may experience conflict—both internal and external—between doing more of what they already do well and stretching developmentally.

The following is an example of such a conflict. Suppose Sheila is an accountant who has just joined the board of a local charity. Because handling financial records is something many people do not enjoy, and because Sheila has a demonstrable knack for and interest in it, others on the board may well ask her to become the treasurer. Almost certainly Sheila would do as good a job as anyone else on the board. But suppose Sheila's personal goals included developing her public speaking skills. In such a case, doing what she does best (and what others want her to do) might stand in the way of growth in another area.

Sheila has several alternatives. She could refuse the job of treasurer because she has had her fill of accounting. Alternatively, she could accept the job of treasurer and look for yet another activity in which to develop her public speaking skills. Unfortunately, both of these options may present their own problems. Still another alternative would be to negotiate to expand the role of treasurer to allow greater opportunity to blend the role with her own developmental goals. For example, Sheila might choose to make regular oral reports to the board instead of submitting solely written reports. Additionally, she might take on a larger share of speaking at local service clubs for the purpose of public education about the charity and her own expert view of its needs with regard to fundraising and financial support. The point here is that leaders simply need to be deliberate in seeking opportunities to put their personal development plans into action. Leaders should exercise control over events to the extent they can; they should not let events exercise a counterproductive control over them.

A leader's first step in exercising control over his personal development is to identify what his goals actually are. The example above presumed Sheila already had identified public speaking as a skill she wanted to improve. But what if a leader is uncertain about what he or she needs to improve? As described earlier, leaders should systematically collect information from a number of different sources. One place a leader can get information about where to improve is through a review of current job performance, if that is applicable. Ideally, leaders will have had feedback sessions with their own superiors, which should help them identify areas of relative strength and weakness. Leaders should treat this feedback as a helpful perspective on their developmental needs. Leaders also should look at their interactions with peers as a source of ideas about what they might work on. Leaders should especially take notice if the same kind of problem comes up in their interactions with different individuals in separate situations. Leaders need to look at their own role in such instances as objectively as they can; there might be clues about what behavioral changes might facilitate better working relationships with others. Still another way to identify developmental objectives is to look ahead to what new skills are needed to function effectively at a higher level in the organization, or in a different role than the leader now has. Finally, leaders can use formal psychological tests and questionnaires to determine what their relative strengths and weaknesses as a leader may be.

On a concluding note, there is one activity leaders should put in their developmental plans whatever else might be included in them: a program of personal reading to broaden their perspectives on leadership. This reading can include the classics as well as contemporary fiction, biographies and autobiographies of successful leaders, essays on ethics and social responsibility, and assorted self-improvement books on various leadership and management issues. A vital part of leadership development is intellectual stimulation and reflection, and an active reading program is indispensable to that. Leaders might even want to join (or form) a discussion group that regularly meets to exchange ideas about a book everyone has read.

Communication

Know What Your Purpose Is

Choose an Appropriate Context and Medium

Send Clear Signals

Actively Ensure That Others Understand the Message

Bass (1990) defined communication effectiveness as the degree to which someone tells others something and ensures they understand what was said. In an even more general sense, **effective communication** involves the ability to transmit and receive information with a high probability that the intended message is passed from sender to receiver. Few skills are more vital to leadership. Studies show that good leaders communicate feelings and ideas, actively solicit new ideas from others, and effectively articulate arguments, advocate positions, and persuade others (Bennis & Nanus, 1985; Kanter, 1983; Parks, 1985). It seems likely the same can be said of good followers, though far less study has gone into that question. Moreover, the quality of a leader's communication is positively correlated with subordinate satisfaction (Klimoski & Haynes, 1980) as well as with productivity and quality of services rendered (Snyder & Morris, 1984). Effective communication skills are also important because they provide leaders and followers with greater access to information relevant to important organizational decisions (Fiechtner & Krayer, 1986).

A systems view of communication is depicted in Figure C.1. Communication is best understood as a process beginning with an intention to exchange certain information with others. That intention eventually takes form in some particular expression, which may or may not adequately convey what was intended. The next stage is reception. Just as with a weak or garbled radio signal or malfunctioning antenna, what is received is not always what was sent. Reception is followed by interpretation. If a driver asks, "Do I turn here?" and a passenger answers, "Right," did the passenger mean *yes* or *turn right*? Finally, it is not enough merely to receive and interpret information; others' interpretations may or may not be consistent with what was intended at the outset. Therefore, it always helps to have a feedback loop to assess any communication's overall effectiveness.

FIGURE C.1

A systems view of communication

Intention	Expression	Reception	Interpretation
What do you want to accomplish?	What medium?	Was it seen?	Was it understood?
Is your purpose clear?	Consistent verbally and nonverbally?	Was it heard?	Do the receiver's ego needs interfere with understanding?
Who needs to hear you?	Expressed with receiver's frame of reference in mind?	Were there competing messages or other "noise"?	Do the receiver's biases or assumptions interfere with understanding?

New Intentions

Expressed in terms receiver will understand?

Too much information expressed too quickly?

Important points emphasized?

Might message be ambiguous to others?

Is message confounded by sender's feelings?

Biases or invalid assumptions about receiver?

Are you communicating directly with the receiver or through others?

Are there reasons the receiver wittingly or unwittingly may have filtered the information?

Has time or the medium of transmittal diluted or changed the message?

Feedback
Did you communicate what you intended?

History of prior communications
Context of relationships and common practices
Concurrent events

We also can use the scheme in Figure C.1 to think about the knowledge, behaviors, and criteria used to evaluate communication skills. According to this model, the knowledge component of communication skills concerns the intentions of the leader, knowing what medium is most effective, and knowing whether the message was heard and understood. The behavioral component of communication skills concerns the behaviors associated with communicating verbally and nonverbally. Feedback concerning whether or not

FIGURE C.2

Breakdowns in communication sometimes lead to finger pointing

the message was understood by the receiver constitutes the evaluative component of communication skills. An important aspect regarding feedback is that it is an outcome of the previous steps in the communication process. In reality, the effectiveness of the communication process depends on the successful integration of all of the steps in the communication process. Effectiveness in just one step (e.g., speaking ability) is not enough. Successful communication needs to be judged in terms of the effective operation of the whole system.

The model also suggests a number of reasons why communication breakdowns might occur. For example, communication breakdowns can occur because the purpose of the message was unclear, the leader's or follower's verbal and nonverbal behaviors were inconsistent, the message was not heard by the receiver, or because someone may have misinterpreted another's message. Most people see themselves as effective communicators, and senders and receivers of messages often seem disposed to believe communication breakdowns are the other person's fault. Communication breakdowns often lead to blaming someone else for the problem, or "finger pointing" (see Figure C.2). One way to avoid the finger pointing associated with communication breakdowns is to think of communication as a process, not as a set of discrete individual acts (i.e., giving instructions to someone). By using the communication model, leadership practitioners can minimize the conflict typically associated with communication breakdowns.

The model in Figure C.1 can provide leadership practitioners with many ideas about how to improve communication skills. They can do so by *(a)* determining the purpose of their communication before speaking, *(b)* choosing an appropriate context and medium for the message, *(c)* sending clear signals, and *(d)* actively ensuring that others understand the message. The following is a more detailed discussion of some of the different ways in which leaders can improve their communication skills.

Know What Your Purpose Is

One will communicate more effectively with others if one is clear about what one intends to communicate. By knowing purpose, a leader or follower can better decide whether to communicate publicly or privately, orally or in writing, and so on. These decisions may seem trivial, but often the specific content of a message will be enhanced or diminished by how and where it is communicated.

Choose an Appropriate Context and Medium

There is a rule of thumb that says leaders should praise followers in public and punish them in private. It points out the importance of selecting physical and social settings that will enhance the effectiveness of any communication. If the leader has an office, for example, then how much communication with subordinates should occur in her office and how much in the followers' workplace?

Sometimes, of course, an office is the best place to talk. Even that decision, however, is not all a leader needs to consider. The arrangement of office furniture can enhance or interfere with effective communication. Informal, personal communications are enhanced when two people sit at a 90-degree angle and are relatively close to each other; more formal communication is enhanced when the follower remains standing when the leader is sitting or if the leader communicates across his desk to followers.

Additionally, a leader's communications often take place in a whole organizational context involving broader existing practices, policies, and procedures. Leaders need to take care that their words and deeds do not inadvertently undercut or contradict such broader organizational communications, including their own bosses. Organizational factors also help determine whether any particular communication is most appropriately expressed orally or in writing. Oral communication is the most immediate, the most personal, the most dynamic, and often the most impactive; it is ideal when communication needs to be two-way or when the personalized aspect is especially important. At the other extreme, a more permanent modality is probably most appropriate when the leader needs a record of the communication or when something needs to be expressed in a particular way to different people, at different times, in different settings.

Send Clear Signals

Leaders and followers can enhance the clarity of their communications in several ways. First, it is helpful to be mindful of others' level of expertise, values, experiences, and expectations and how these characteristics affect their **frames of reference.** For example, the leader may brief a new organizational policy to followers, and they may come up with different interpretations of this policy based on different values and expectations. By being sensitive to followers' frames of reference and modifying messages accordingly, leaders can minimize communication breakdowns. Another way to clarify messages is to create a common frame of reference for followers before communicating a message. For example, consider the following passage:

> With hocked gems financing him, our hero bravely defied all scornful laughter that tried to prevent his scheme. "Your eyes deceive," he had said. "An egg, not a table, correctly typifies this unexplored planet." Now, three sisters sought sturdy proof. Forging along, sometimes through calm vastness, yet more often over turbulent peaks and valleys, days became weeks as many doubters spread fearful rumors about the edge. At last, welcome winged creatures appeared signifying momentous success. (Sanford & Garrod, 1981)

Many are slow to recognize that the passage is about Christopher Columbus. Once the correct frame of reference is known, however, the previously confusing elements become sensible. Followers more readily understand new or ambiguous material when leaders paint a common frame of reference prior to introducing new material.

Another way to send clear signals is to use familiar terms, jargon, and concepts. This can serve to clarify and abbreviate messages when receivers are familiar with the terms. However, messages containing jargon can also be confusing to receivers unfamiliar with those terms. For example, a freshman cadet at the United States Air Force Academy might say to another, "I hope we get an ONP this weekend, because after three GRs, a PCE, and a SAMI, I'll need it." Because the second cadet understands this organizational jargon, he or she would have no difficulty understanding what was said. However, a person unfamiliar with the Air Force Academy would not have the slightest idea what this conversation meant. Leaders should make sure followers understand any jargon they use—especially if the followers are relatively inexperienced. (In case you were wondering, the cadet said, "I hope we get a pass to go downtown this weekend, because after three academic tests, a military test, and a room inspection, I'll need it.")

Two other ways to improve the clarity of messages are to use unambiguous, concrete terms and to send congruent verbal and nonverbal signals. For example, a leader who tells a follower, "Your monthly sales were down 22 percent last month" will more effectively communicate her concerns and cause less follower defensiveness than a leader who states, "Your performance has been poor." Thus, the more specific the message, the less likely receivers will be confused over what it means. In addition, leaders will be more effective communicators if their nonverbal signals match the content of the message. Followers, like everyone, can get confused, and tend to believe nonverbal signals when leaders send mixed verbal and nonverbal messages (Remland, 1981). Similarly, followers may send mixed messages to leaders; communication goes both ways.

One particularly destructive form of incongruent verbal and nonverbal signals is sarcasm. It is not the anger of the message per se but rather the implicit message conveyed by dishonest words that drives a wedge in the trust between leaders and followers. It is not a wise idea for leaders to always share their transitory feelings with subordinates, but if the leader is going to share his or her feelings, it is important to do so in a congruent manner. Similarly, it can be just as unwise for followers to share transitory feelings with leaders; but if it's done, it's important for verbal and nonverbal behaviors to be congruent.

Actively Ensure That Others Understand the Message

Leaders and followers can ensure that others understand their messages by practicing two-way communication and by paying attention to the others' emotional responses. Effective leaders and followers tend to actively engage in two-way communication (though this usually is more under the control of the leader than the follower). They can do so in many ways: by seeking feedback, by mingling in each other's work areas, and, in the case of leaders, by being sincere about having an open-door policy (Luthans & Larsen, 1986).

Although such steps appear to be straightforward, leaders typically believe they utilize two-way communication more frequently than their followers perceive them to be using it (Sadler & Hofstede, 1972). Leaders can get clues about the clarity of their messages by paying attention to the nonverbal signals sent by their followers. When followers' verbal and nonverbal messages seem to be incongruent, it may be because the message sent to them was unclear. For example, followers may look confused when they verbally acknowledge that they understand a particular task. In this case, leaders may find it useful to address the mixed signals directly in order to clear up such confusion.

Listening

Demonstrate Nonverbally That You Are Listening
Actively Interpret the Sender's Message
Attend to the Sender's Nonverbal Behavior
Avoid Becoming Defensive

Our systems view of communication emphasized that effectiveness depends upon both *transmitting and receiving* information. It may seem inconsistent, therefore, to distinguish the topic of listening from the more general topic of communication. Isn't listening *part* of communication, you may ask? Of course, and we do not intend to imply it's not. Our separate treatment of listening is simply for emphasis. It seems to us most discussions of communication emphasize the transmission side and neglect the receiving side. Good leaders and followers recognize the value of two-way communication. Listening to others is just as important as expressing oneself clearly to them. People in leadership roles are only as good as the information they have, and much of their information comes from watching and listening to what goes on around them.

At first, it may seem strange to describe listening as a skill. Listening may seem like an automatic response to things being said, not something one practices to improve, like free throws. However, the best listeners are **active listeners,** not passive listeners (Davis, Hellervik, & Sheard, 1989). In passive listening, someone may be speaking but the receiver is not focused on understanding the speaker. Instead, the receiver may be thinking about the next thing he will say or how bored he is in listening to the speaker. In either case, the receiver is not paying attention to what the sender is saying. To truly get the fullest meaning out of what someone else says, one needs to practice active listening. Individuals who are listening actively exhibit a certain pattern of nonverbal behaviors, do not disrupt the sender's message, try to put the sender's message into their own words, and scan the sender for various nonverbal signals. Knowing what nonverbal signals to send and correctly interpreting the sender's nonverbal signals are the knowledge component of listening skills. One's nonverbal signals are the behavioral component, and how well one can paraphrase a sender's message makes up the evaluative component of listening skills.

In addition to helping one understand others better, active listening is a way to visibly demonstrate that one respects others. People, particularly those with high self-monitoring scores, can often sense when others are not truly paying attention to what they are saying. Followers will quickly decide it is not worth their time to give their leader information if they perceive they are not being listened to. Leaders may do the same. To avoid turning off others, leaders and followers can improve their active listening skills in a number of ways. Some of these tips include learning to *(a)* model nonverbal signals associated with active listening, *(b)* actively interpret the sender's message, *(c)* be aware of the sender's nonverbal behaviors, and *(d)* avoid becoming defensive. The following is a more detailed discussion of these four ways to improve active listening skills.

Demonstrate Nonverbally That You Are Listening

Make sure your nonverbal behaviors show that you have turned your attention entirely to the speaker. Many people mistakenly assume that listening is a one-way process. Although it seems plausible to think of information flowing only from the sender to the receiver, the essence of active listening is to see all communication, even listening, as a two-way process. Listeners show they are paying attention to the speaker with their own body movements. They put aside, both mentally and physically, other work they may have been engaged in. Individuals who are actively listening establish eye contact with the speaker, and they do not doodle, shoot rubber bands, or look away at other things. They show they are genuinely interested in what the speaker has to say.

Actively Interpret the Sender's Message

The essence of active listening is trying to understand what the sender truly means. It is not enough merely to be (even if you could) a perfect human tape recorder. One must look for the meaning behind someone else's words. In the first place, this means one needs to keep one's mind open to the sender's ideas. This, in turn, implies not interrupting the speaker and not planning what to say while the speaker is delivering the message. In addition, good listeners withhold judgment about the sender's ideas until they have heard the entire message. This way, they avoid sending the message that their mind is made up and avoid jumping to conclusions about what the sender is going to say. Another reason to avoid sending a closed-minded message is that it may lead others to *not* bring up things one definitely needs to hear.

Another valuable way to actively interpret what the sender is saying is to **paraphrase** the sender's message. By putting the speaker's thoughts into their own words, leaders can better ensure that they fully understand what their fol-

Communication Leads for Paraphrasing and Assuring Mutual Understanding

Highlight L.1

From your point of view . . .
It seems you . . .
As you see it . . .
You think . . .
What I hear you saying is . . .
Do you mean . . .?
I'm not sure I understand what you mean; is it . . .?
I get the impression . . .
You appear to be feeling . . .
Correct me if I'm wrong, but . . .

lowers are saying, and vice versa. The value of paraphrasing even a simple idea is apparent in the following dialogue:

> *Sarah:* "Jim should never have become a teacher."
>
> *Fred:* "You mean he doesn't like working with kids? Do you think he's too impatient?"
>
> *Sarah:* "No, neither of those things. I just think his tastes are so expensive he's frustrated with a teacher's salary."

In this example, Fred indicated what he thought Sarah meant, which prompted her to clarify her meaning. If he had merely said, "I know what you mean," Fred and Sarah mistakenly would have concluded they agreed when their ideas were really far apart. Paraphrasing also actively communicates your interest in what the other person is saying. Highlight L.1 offers various "communication leads" that may help in paraphrasing others' messages to improve your listening skills.

Attend to the Sender's Nonverbal Behavior

People should use all the tools at their disposal to understand what someone else is saying. This includes paraphrasing senders' messages, and being astute at picking up on senders' nonverbal signals. Much of the social meaning in messages is conveyed nonverbally, and when verbal and nonverbal signals conflict, people often tend to trust the nonverbal signals. Thus, no one can be an effective listener without paying attention to nonverbal signals. This requires listening to more than just the speaker's words themselves; it requires listening for feelings expressed via the speaker's loudness, tone of voice, and pace of speech as well as watching the speaker's facial expressions, posture, gestures, and so on. These behaviors convey a wealth of information that is immensely richer in meaning than the purely verbal content of a message, just as it is richer to watch actors in a stage play rather than merely read their script (Robbins, 1989). Although there may not be any simple codebook of nonverbal cues with which one can decipher what a sender "really" feels, listeners should explore what a sender is trying to say whenever they sense mixed signals between the sender's verbal and nonverbal behaviors.

Avoid Becoming Defensive

Defensive behavior is most likely to occur when someone feels threatened (Gibb, 1961). Although it may seem natural to become defensive when criticized, defensiveness lessens a person's ability to constructively make use of the information. Acting defensively may also decrease followers' subsequent willingness to pass additional unpleasant information on to the leader or other followers, or even the leader's willingness to give feedback to followers. Defensiveness on the part of the leader can also hurt the entire team or organization, as it includes a tendency to place blame, categorize others as morally good or bad, and generally question others' motives. Such behaviors on a leader's part hardly build a positive work or team climate.

Leaders can reduce their defensiveness when listening to complaints by trying to put themselves in the other person's shoes. Leaders have an advantage if they can empathize with how they and their policies are seen by others; they can better change their behaviors and policies if they know how others perceive them. Leaders need to avoid the temptation to explain how the other person is wrong and should instead just try to understand how he perceives things. A useful warning sign that a leader may be behaving defensively (or perhaps closedmindedly) is if he begins a conversation saying, "Yes, but . . ."

Assertiveness

> Use "I" Statements
> Speak Up for What You Need
> Learn to Say No
> Monitor Your Inner Dialogue
> Be Persistent

What is **assertive behavior,** and what are assertiveness skills? Basically, individuals exhibiting assertive behavior are able to stand up for their own rights (or their group's rights) in a way that also recognizes the concurrent right of others to do the same (see Highlight A.1). Like the skills already discussed, assertiveness skills also have knowledge, behavioral, and evaluative components. The behavioral component of assertiveness skills was mentioned already—it involves standing up for one's own or the group's rights in a constructive, nonhostile way. The knowledge component of assertiveness skills

Assertiveness Questionnaire

Highlight A.1

Do you let someone know when you think he or she is being unfair to you?

Can you criticize someone else's ideas openly?

Are you able to speak up in a meeting?

Can you ask others for small favors or help?

Is it easy for you to compliment others?

Can you tell someone else you don't like what he or she is doing?

When you are complimented, do you really accept the compliment without inwardly discounting it in your own mind?

Can you look others in the eye when you talk to them?

If you could answer most of these questions affirmatively for most situations, then you do behave assertively.

Source: Adapted from R. E. Alberti and M. L. Emmons, *Your Perfect Right* (San Luis Obispo, CA: Impact, 1974).

concerns knowing where and when not to behave assertively. People who are overly assertive may be perceived as aggressive and often may "win the battle but lose the war." Finally, the evaluative component comes into play when individuals are successful (or unsuccessful) in standing up for their own or their group's rights and continually working in an effective manner with others.

Perhaps the best way to understand assertiveness is to distinguish it from two other styles people have for dealing with conflict: acquiescence (nonassertiveness) and aggression (Alberti & Emmons, 1974). **Acquiescence** is avoiding interpersonal conflict entirely either by giving up and giving in or by expressing one's needs in an apologetic, self-effacing way. Acquiescence is *not* synonymous with politeness or helpfulness, though it is sometimes rationalized as such. People who are acquiescent, or nonassertive, back down easily when challenged. By not speaking up for themselves, they abdicate power to others and, in the process, get trampled on. Besides the practical outcome of not attaining one's goals, an acquiescent style typically leads to many negative feelings such as guilt, resentment, and self-blame, as well as a low self-image. Sometimes people justify their nonassertiveness to themselves with the idea that acquiescing to others is being polite or helpful, but this often is just a rationalization.

Aggression, on the other hand, is an effort to attain objectives by attacking or hurting others. Aggressive people trample on others, and their aggressiveness can take such direct forms as threats, verbal attacks, physical intimidation, emotional outbursts, explosiveness, bullying, and hostility—and such indirect

FIGURE A.1

*Relationships
between
assertiveness,
acquiescence,
and aggression*

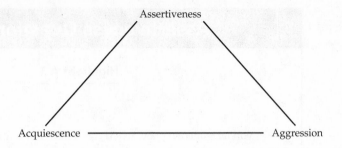

forms as nagging, passive-aggressive uncooperativeness, guilt arousal, and other behaviors that undermine an adversary's autonomy. It is important to understand that aggressiveness is not just an emotionally strong form of assertiveness. Aggressiveness tends to be reactive, and it tends to spring from feelings of vulnerability and a lack of self-confidence. Aggressive people inwardly doubt their ability to resolve issues constructively through the give-and-take of direct confrontation between mutually respecting equals. Aggressiveness is a form of interpersonal manipulation in which one tries to put oneself in a "top dog" role and others in a "bottom dog" role (Shostrom, 1967). Additionally, aggressive people have difficulty expressing positive feelings.

Assertiveness is different from both acquiescence and aggression; it is not merely a compromise between them or a midpoint on a continuum. Assertiveness involves direct and frank statements of one's own goals and feelings, and a willingness to address the interests of others in the spirit of mutual problem solving and a belief that openness is preferable to secretiveness and hidden agendas. Assertiveness is the behavioral opposite of both acquiescence and aggression, as depicted in Figure A.1. The qualitative differences between these three styles are like the differences between fleeing (acquiescence), fighting (aggression), and problem solving (assertiveness).

It may seem axiomatic that leaders need to behave assertively with subordinates. Sometimes, however, leaders also need to be assertive with their own bosses. Followers often need to be assertive with other followers and even with their leaders sometimes. For example, middle-level supervisors need to communicate performance expectations clearly and directly to subordinates, and they need to be strong advocates for their subordinates' interests with senior supervisors. Likewise, leaders sometimes need to give their own superiors bad news, and it is best to do so directly rather than hesitantly and guardedly. Followers may sometimes need to be assertive with a peer whose poor work habits are adversely impacting the work group. In addition, leaders sometimes need to be assertive with representatives of other power-holding or special-interest groups. For example, the leader of a community group seeking a new elementary school in a residential area may need to take a very assertive stand with local school board officials.

It is important to note that sometimes the hardest people to be assertive with are friends, family, and peers. Leaders who fail to be assertive with friends and peers run the risk of becoming victims of the Abilene paradox (see Highlight A.2).

The Abilene Paradox

Highlight A.2

That July afternoon in Coleman, Texas (population 5,607), was particularly hot—104 degrees according to the Rexall's thermometer. In addition, the wind was blowing fine-grained West Texas topsoil through the house. But the afternoon was still tolerable—even potentially enjoyable. A fan was stirring the air on the back porch; there was cold lemonade; and finally, there was entertainment. Dominoes. Perfect for the conditions. The game requires little more physical exertion than an occasional mumbled comment, "Shuffle 'em," and an unhurried movement of the arm to place the tiles in their appropriate positions on the table. All in all, it had the makings of an agreeable Sunday afternoon in Coleman. That is, until my father-in-law suddenly said, "Let's get in the car and go to Abilene and have dinner at the cafeteria."

I thought, "What, go to Abilene? Fifty-three miles? In this dust storm and heat? And in an unairconditioned 1958 Buick?"

But my wife chimed in with, "Sounds like a great idea. I'd like to go. How about you, Jerry?" Since my own preferences were obviously out of step with the rest, I replied, "Sounds good to me," and added, "I just hope your mother wants to go."

"Of course I want to go," said my mother-in-law. "I haven't been to Abilene in a long time."

So into the car and off to Abilene we went. My predictions were fulfilled. The heat was brutal. Perspiration had cemented a fine layer of dust to our skin by the time we arrived. The cafeteria's food could serve as a first-rate prop in an antacid commercial.

Some four hours and 106 miles later, we returned to Coleman, hot and exhausted. We silently sat in front of the fan for a long time. Then, to be sociable and to break the silence, I dishonestly said, "It was a great trip, wasn't it?"

No one spoke.

Finally, my mother-in-law said, with some irritation, "Well, to tell the truth, I really didn't enjoy it much and would rather have stayed here. I just went along because the three of you were so enthusiastic about going. I wouldn't have gone if you all hadn't pressured me into it."

I couldn't believe it. "What do you mean 'you all'?" I said. "Don't put me in the 'you all' group. I was delighted to be doing what we were doing. I didn't want to go. I only went to satisfy the rest of you. You're the culprits."

My wife looked shocked. "Don't call me a culprit. You and Daddy and Mama were the ones who wanted to go. I just went along to keep you happy. I would have had to be crazy to want to go out in heat like that."

Her father entered the conversation with one word. "Shee-it." He then expanded on what was already absolutely clear: "Listen, I never wanted to go to Abilene. I just thought you might be bored. You visit so seldom I wanted to be sure

(continued)

you enjoyed it. I would have preferred to play another game of dominoes and eat the leftovers in the icebox."

After the outburst of recrimination, we all sat back in silence. Here we were, four reasonably sensible people who—of our own volition—had just taken a 106-mile trip across a godforsaken desert in furnace-like heat and a dust storm to eat unpalatable food at a hole-in-the-wall cafeteria in Abilene, when none of us had really wanted to go. To be concise, we'd done just the opposite of what we wanted to do. The whole situation simply didn't make sense.

At least it didn't make sense at the time. But since that day in Coleman, I have observed, consulted with, and been a part of more than one organization that has been caught in the same situation. As a result, the organizations have either taken side trips or, occasionally, terminal journeys to Abilene, when Dallas or Houston or Tokyo was where they really wanted to go. And for most of those organizations, the negative consequences of such trips, measured in terms of both human misery and economic loss, have been much greater than for our little Abilene group.

I now call the tendency for groups to embark on excursions that no group member wants "the Abilene paradox." Stated simply, when organizations blunder into the Abilene paradox, they take actions in contradiction to what they really want to do and therefore defeat the very purpose they are trying to achieve. Business theorists typically believe that managing conflict is one of the greatest challenges faced by an organization, but a corollary of the Abilene paradox states that the inability to manage agreement may be the major source of organization dysfunction.

Source: Jerry B. Harvey, "The Abilene Paradox: The Management of Agreement," *Organizational Dynamics,* Summer 1974. Reprinted by permission of the publisher. American Management Association New York. http:www.amanet.org. All rights reserved.

The **Abilene paradox** (Harvey, 1974) occurs when someone suggests that the group engage in a particular activity or course of action, and no one in the group really wants to do the activity (including the person who made the suggestion). However, because of the false belief that everyone else in the group wants to do the activity, no one behaves assertively and voices an honest opinion about it. Only after the activity is over does anyone voice an opinion (and it is usually negative). For example, someone in your group of friends may suggest that the group go to a particular movie on a Friday night. No one in the group really wants to go, yet because of the false belief everyone else is interested, no one points out the movie is not supposed to be very good and the group should do something else instead. If group members' true opinions surface only *after* the movie, then the group has fallen victim to the Abilene paradox. Leaders can avoid the Abilene paradox by being assertive when suggestions about group decisions and activities are first made.

There are several things everyone can do to help themselves behave more assertively. These things include (*a*) using "I" statements, (*b*) speaking up for what you need, (*c*) learning to say no, (*d*) monitoring your inner dialogue, and (*e*) being persistent. The following is a more detailed discussion of these assertiveness tips.

Tips for Being Assertive

Highlight A.3

Examples of Good and Bad "I" Statements

Bad: Some people may not like having to maintain those new forms.

Good: I don't think these new forms are any good. I don't think they're worth the effort.

Bad: Maybe that candidate doesn't have all the qualifications we're looking for.

Good: I think his academic record looks fine, but we agreed only to consider candidates with at least five years' experience. I think we should keep looking.

Tips for Speaking Up for What You Need

Do not apologize too much or justify yourself for needing help or assistance (e.g., "I just hate to ask you, and I normally wouldn't need to, but . . .").

At the same time, giving a brief reason for your request often helps.

Be direct. Do not beat around the bush, hinting at what you need and hoping others get the message.

Do not play on someone's friendship.

Do not take a refusal personally.

Tips for Saying No

Keep your reply short and polite. Avoid a long, rambling justification.

Do not invent excuses.

Do not go overboard in apologizing because you cannot do it.

Be up-front about your limitations and about options you could support.

Ask for time to consider it if you need to.

Source: Adapted from K. Back and K. Back, *Assertiveness at Work* (New York: McGraw-Hill, 1982).

Use "I" Statements

Assertive people take responsibility for what they say. They are clear in their own minds and with others about what they believe and what they want. One of the easiest ways to do this is to use first-person pronouns when you speak. Highlight A.3 provides examples of how to be more assertive by using first-person pronouns.

Speak Up for What You Need

No one has all of the skills, knowledge, time, or resources needed to do all of the taskings assigned to their work group. Virtually everyone will need to ask superiors, peers, or subordinates for help at some time. Both effective leaders and effective followers ask for help from others when they need it. Highlight A.3 also provides guidelines when making requests for help.

Learn to Say No

No one can be all things to all people, but it takes assertiveness to say no to others. Leaders, for example, may need to say no to their own superiors at times to stand up for their subordinates' or organization's rights and to keep from spreading themselves too thin and detracting from other priorities. Additionally, people who cannot (i.e., who *do not*) say no often build up a reservoir of negative emotions, such as those associated with the feeling of being taken advantage of. Tips for assertively refusing to do something also can be found in Highlight A.3.

Monitor Your Inner Dialogue

Most of us talk to ourselves, though not out loud. Such self-talk is natural and common, though not everyone is aware of how much it occurs or how powerful an influence on behavior it can be. Assertive people have self-talk that is positive and affirming. Nonassertive people have self-talk that is negative, doubtful, and questioning. Learning to say no is a good example of the role self-talk plays in assertiveness. Suppose that someone was asked to serve on a volunteer committee he simply does not have time for and that he *wants* to say no. In order to behave assertively, the person would need to talk to himself positively. He would need to ensure that he is not defeated by his own self-talk. It would hardly help the person's resolve, for example, to have an inner dialogue that says, "They'll think I'm selfish if I don't say yes," or "If they can make time for this committee, I should be able to make time for it, too." In learning to behave more assertively, therefore, it is necessary for leaders to become more aware of their own counterproductive self-talk, confront it, and change it.

Be Persistent

Assertive individuals stick to their guns without becoming irritated, angry, or loud. They persistently seek their objectives, even in the face of another person's excuses or objections. Exchanging merchandise can provide a good occasion for assertive persistence. Suppose someone had purchased a shirt at a department store, had worn it once, and then noticed the seam was poorly sewn. A person acting assertively might have an exchange much like that found in Highlight A.4. An assertive person is similarly persistent in standing up for his own or his group's rights.

Example Exchange between a Buyer and a Clerk

Highlight A.4

Buyer: "I bought this shirt last week, and it's poorly made."

Clerk: "It looks like you've worn it. We don't exchange garments that already have been worn."

Buyer: "I understand that is your policy, but it's not that I don't like the shirt. It is obviously defective. I didn't know it had these defects when I wore it."

Clerk: "Maybe this seam came loose because of the way you wore it."

Buyer: "I didn't do anything unusual. It is defective. I want it exchanged."

Clerk: "I'm sorry, but you should have returned it earlier. We can't take it back now."

Buyer: "I understand your point, but I didn't get what I paid for. You need to return my money or give me a new shirt."

Clerk: "It's beyond my authority to do that. I don't make the policies, I just have to follow them."

Buyer: "I understand you don't think you have the authority to change the policy. But your boss does. Please tell her I'd like to see her right now."

Providing Constructive Feedback

Make It Helpful

Be Specific

Be Descriptive

Be Timely

Be Flexible

Give Positive as Well as Negative Feedback

Avoid Blame or Embarrassment

Giving constructive feedback involves sharing information or perceptions with another about the nature, quality, or impact of that person's behavior. It can range from giving feedback pertaining specifically to a person's work (i.e., performance feedback) to impressions of how aspects of that person's interpersonal behavior may be pervasively affecting relationships with others. Our use of the term *feedback* here is somewhat different from its use in the systems view of communication (Figure C.1). In the communication model, the feedback loop begins with actively checking the receiver's *interpretation* of one's own message, and then initiating or modifying subsequent communications as necessary. A simple example of that meaning of feedback might be noting another person's quizzical expression when you try to explain a complicated point, thereby realizing that you'd better say it differently. The skill of giving constructive feedback, however, inherently involves *actively giving feedback to someone else.*

Getting helpful feedback is essential to a subordinate's performance and development. Without feedback, a subordinate will not be able to tell whether she's doing a good job or whether or not her abrasiveness is turning people off and hurting her chances for promotion. And it's not just subordinates who need constructive feedback to learn and grow. Peers may seek feedback from peers, and leaders may seek feedback from subordinates. Besides fostering growth, effective supervisory feedback also plays a major role in building morale.

In many ways, the development of good feedback skills is an outgrowth of developing good communication, listening, and assertiveness skills. Giving good feedback depends on being clear about the purpose of the feedback and on choosing an appropriate context and medium for giving it. Giving good feedback also depends on sending the proper nonverbal signals and trying to detect emotional signals from whoever may be receiving the feedback. In addition, giving good feedback depends on being somewhat assertive in providing it, even when it may be critical of a person's performance or behavior. Although feedback skills are related to communication, listening, and assertiveness skills, they are not the same thing. Someone may have good communication, listening, and assertiveness skills but poor feedback skills. Perhaps this distinction can be made clearer by examining the knowledge, behavior, and evaluative components of feedback skills.

The knowledge component of feedback concerns knowing when, where, and what feedback is to be given. For example, knowing when, where, and how to give positive feedback may be very different from knowing when, where, and how to give negative feedback. The behavioral component of feedback concerns how feedback actually is delivered (as contrasted with knowing how it should be delivered). Good feedback is specific, descriptive, direct, and helpful; poor feedback is often too watered down to be useful to the recipient. Finally, one way to evaluate feedback is to examine whether recipients actually modify their behavior accordingly after receiving it. Of course, this should not be the only way to evaluate feedback skills. Even when feedback is accurate in content and delivered skillfully, a recipient may fail to acknowledge it or do anything about it.

Although most leaders probably believe that feedback is an important skill, research has shown that leaders also believe they give more feedback than their subordinates think they do (Greller, 1980). There are many reasons leaders may be reluctant to give feedback. Leaders may be reluctant to give positive feedback because of time pressures, doubts about the efficacy of feedback, or lack of feedback skills (Komacki, 1982). Sometimes supervisors are hesitant to use positive feedback because they believe subordinates may see it as politically manipulative, ingratiating, or insincere (Bass, 1990). Leaders also may give positive feedback infrequently if they rarely leave their desks, if their personal standards are too high, or if they believe good performance is expected and should not be recognized at all (Deep & Sussman, 1990). Other reasons may explain the failure to give negative feedback (Larson, 1986), such as fears of disrupting leader–follower relations (Harrison, 1982) or fear of employee retaliation (Parsons, Herold, & Leatherwood, 1985).

Although there are a number of reasons why leaders are hesitant to provide both positive and negative feedback, leaders need to keep in mind that followers, committee members, or team members will perform at a higher level if they are given accurate and frequent feedback. It is difficult to imagine how workgroup or team performance could improve without feedback. Positive feedback is necessary to tell followers they should keep doing what they are doing well, and negative feedback is needed to give followers or team members ideas on how to change other behavior to improve their performance. Although accurate and frequent feedback is necessary, there are several other aspects of feedback that everyone can work on to improve their feedback skills, including *(a)* making sure it's helpful, *(b)* being direct, *(c)* being specific, *(d)* being descriptive, *(e)* being timely, *(f)* being flexible, *(g)* giving both positive and negative feedback, and *(h)* avoiding blame and embarrassment when giving feedback. Highlight F.1 gives examples of each of these different aspects of feedback, and the following is a more complete description of ways leaders can improve their feedback skills.

Make It Helpful

The purpose of feedback is to provide others with information they can use to change their behavior. Being clear about the intent and purpose is important because giving feedback sometimes can become emotional for both the person giving it and the person receiving it. If the person giving feedback is in an emotional state (e.g., angry), she may say things that make her temporarily feel better but that only alienate the receiver. In order to be helpful, individuals need to be clear and unemotional when giving feedback, and should give feedback only about behaviors actually under the other person's control.

People can improve the impact of the feedback they give when it is addressed to a specific individual. A common mistake in giving feedback is addressing it to "people at large" rather than to a specific individual. In this case, the individuals for whom the feedback was intended may not believe the feedback pertained to them. In order to maximize the impact of the feedback, people should try to provide it to specific individuals, not large groups.

Be Specific

Feedback is most helpful when it specifies particular behaviors that are positive or negative. One of the best illustrations of the value of specific feedback is in compositions or term papers written for school. If someone turned in a draft of a paper to the instructor for constructive comments and the instructor's comments about the paper were "Good start, but needs work in several areas," then the person would have a difficult time knowing just what to change or correct.

Tips for Improving Feedback Skills

Being Helpful

Do not: "I got better scores when I was going through this program than you just did."

Do: "This seems to be a difficult area for you. What can I do to help you master it better?"

Being Direct

Do not: "It's important that we all speak loud enough to be heard in meetings."

Do: "I had a difficult time hearing you in the meeting because you were speaking in such a soft voice."

Being Specific

Do not: "Since you came to work for us, your work has been good."

Do: "I really like the initiative and resourcefulness you showed in solving our scheduling problem."

Being Descriptive

Do not: "I'm getting tired of your rudeness and disinterest when others are talking."

Do: "You weren't looking at anyone else when they were talking, which gave the impression you were bored. Is that how you were feeling?"

Being Timely

Do not: "Joe, I think I need to tell you about an impression you made on me in the staff meeting last month."

Do: "Joe, do you have a minute? I was confused by something you said in the meeting this morning."

Being Flexible

Do not (while a person is crying, or while they are turning beet-red with clenched teeth in apparent anger): "There's another thing I want to tell you about your presentation yesterday. . ."

Do: When a person's rising defenses or emotionality gets in the way of their really listening, deal with those feelings first, or wait until later to finish your feedback. Do not continue giving information.

More helpful feedback from the instructor would be specific comments like "This paragraph does not logically follow the preceding one" or "Cite an example here." The same is true of feedback in work situations. The more specifically leaders can point out which behaviors to change, the more clearly they let the other person know what to do.

Be Descriptive

In giving feedback, it is good to stick to the facts as much as possible, being sure to distinguish them from inferences or attributions. A behavior description reports actions that others can see, about which there could be little question or disagreement. Such descriptions must be distinguished from inferences about someone else's feelings, attitudes, character, motives, or traits. It is a behavior description, for example, to say that Sally stood up and walked out of a meeting while someone else was talking. It is an inference, though, to say she walked out because she was angry. However, sometimes it is helpful to describe both the behavior itself and the corresponding impressions when giving feedback. This is particularly true if the feedback giver believes that the other person does not realize how the behavior negatively affects others' impressions.

Another reason to make feedback descriptive is to distinguish it from evaluation. When a person gives feedback based mostly on inferences, he often conveys evaluations of the "goodness" or "badness" of behavior as well. For example, saying "You were too shy" has a more negative connotation than saying "You had little to say." In the former case, the person's behavior was evaluated unfavorably, and by apparently subjective criteria. Yet evaluation is often an intrinsic part of a supervisor's responsibilities, and good performance feedback may necessitate conveying evaluative information to a subordinate. In such cases, leaders are better off providing evaluative feedback when clear criteria for performance have been established. Filley and Pace (1976) described criteria that can be used to provide evaluative feedback; some are listed in Highlight F.2.

An issue related to impressions and evaluative feedback concerns the distinction between job-related (i.e., performance feedback) and more personal or discretionary feedback. Although leaders have a right to expect followers to listen to their performance feedback, that is not necessarily true concerning feedback about other behaviors. It may well be that sharing perceptions of the person's behavior could be very helpful to that person even when the behavior doesn't pertain specifically to his formal responsibilities; in such cases, however, it is the follower's choice whether to hear it or, if he hears it, whether to act on it or not.

Be Timely

Feedback usually is most effective when it is given soon after the behavior occurs. The context and relevant details of more recent events or behaviors are more readily available to everyone involved, thus facilitating more descriptive and helpful feedback.

Types of Criteria to Use for Evaluative Feedback

Highlight F.2

1. Compare behavior with others' measured performance. With this method, the subordinate's behavior is compared with that of her peers or co-workers; also called norm-referenced appraisal. For example, a subordinate may be told her counseling load is the lightest of all 10 counselors working at the center.
2. Compare behavior with an accepted standard. An example of this method would be where a counselor was told her workload was substantially below the standard of acceptable performance set at 30 cases per week. This is known as criterion-referenced appraisal.
3. Compare behavior with an a priori goal. With this method, the subordinate must participate in and agree with a goal. This is a form of criterion-referenced appraisal, with the subordinate's "ownership" and acceptance of the goal before the fact critical to the feedback procedure.
4. Compare behavior with past performance.

Source: Adapted from A. C. Filley and L. A. Pace, "Making Judgments Descriptive," in J. E. Jones and J. W. Pfeiffer, eds, *The 1976 Annual Handbook for Group Facilitators* (La Jolla, CA: University Associates Press, 1976), pp. 128–31.

Be Flexible

Although feedback is best when it is timely, sometimes waiting is preferable to giving feedback at the very earliest opportunity. In general, everyone should remember that the primary purpose of feedback is to be helpful. Feedback sessions should be scheduled with that in mind. For example, a subordinate's schedule may preclude conveniently giving him feedback right away, and it may not be appropriate to give him feedback when it will distract him from another more immediate and pressing task. Furthermore, it may not be constructive to give someone else feedback when the person receiving it is in a very emotional state (whether about the behavior in question or other matters entirely). Moreover, it is important to be attentive to the other person's emotional responses while giving feedback and to be ready to adjust one's own behavior accordingly.

A final important part of being flexible is to give feedback in manageable amounts. In giving feedback, one does not need to cover every single point at one time, as doing so would only overload the other person with information. Instead, anyone who needs to give a lot of feedback to someone else may want to spread out the feedback sessions and focus on covering only one or two points in each session.

Give Positive as Well as Negative Feedback

Giving *both* positive and negative feedback is more helpful than giving only positive or negative feedback alone. Positive feedback tells the other person or the group only what they are doing right, and negative feedback tells the other person or group only what they are doing wrong. Providing both kinds of feedback is best.

Avoid Blame or Embarrassment

Because the purpose of feedback is to give useful information to other people to help them develop, talking to them in a way merely intended (or likely) to demean or make them feel bad is not a helpful part of the development process. Followers tend to be more likely to believe feedback if it comes from leaders who have had the opportunity to observe the behavior and are perceived to be credible, competent, and trustworthy (Coye, 1982; Quaglieri & Carnazza, 1985; Stone, Guetal, & MacIntosh, 1984). Bass (1990) pointed out that followers will continue to seek feedback even if their leaders are not competent or trustworthy—though they will not seek it from their leaders. They will seek it from others they do trust, such as peers or other superiors.

Guidelines for Effective Stress Management

Monitor Your Own and Your Followers' Stress Levels
Identify What Is Causing the Stress
Practice a Healthy Lifestyle
Learn How to Relax
Develop Supportive Relationships
Keep Things in Perspective
The A-B-C Model

People use the term *stress* in a number of different ways. Sometimes people use the term to describe particular sorts of events or *environmental conditions*. For example, fans might speculate that a professional football coach's heart attack was caused by the *pressures* of his profession. Other examples might include receiving a failing grade on a physics exam, or arriving noticeably late to an important meeting, or playing a sudden-death overtime in hockey. We would acknowledge, for example, that walking in late to a meeting could be very embarrassing (i.e., stressful). Likewise for working at the service counter of a major department store on the day after Christmas; it's a *stressful job*. In each of these instances, stress refers to *characteristics of the environment*. But people also use the term in a quite different way. Sometimes it refers to the *effects* of those environments. The phrase "I'm feeling a lot of stress" might refer to various *symptoms* a person is experiencing, such as muscular tension or difficulty concentrating. Before we proceed further, therefore, it will be useful to agree upon some conventions of terminology.

We will define stress as the whole process by which we appraise and respond to events that challenge or threaten us (Myers, 1989). These responses usually include increased levels of emotional arousal and changes in physiological symptoms, such as increases in perspiration and heart rates, cholesterol levels, or blood pressure. Stress often occurs in situations that are overly complex, demanding, or unclear. Stressors are those specific characteristics in individuals, tasks, organizations, or the environment that pose some degree of threat or challenge to people (see Highlight S.1). Although all the factors in Highlight S.1 probably have an adverse impact on people, the degree of stress associated with each of them depends on one's overall level of stress tolerance and previous experience with the stressor in question (Benner, 1984). Similarly, it is important to realize that stress is in the eye of the beholder—what one person may see as challenging and potentially rewarding, another may see as threatening and distressful (McCauley, 1987; Staw, 1984).

Stress Symptoms

Highlight S.1

Are you behaving "unlike" yourself?

Has your mood become negative, hostile, or depressed?

Do you have difficulty sleeping?

Are you defensive or touchy?

Are your relationships suffering?

Have you made more mistakes or bad decisions lately?

Have you lost interest in normally enjoyable activities?

Are you using alcohol or other drugs?

Do you seem to have little energy?

Do you worry a lot?

Are you nervous much of the time?

Have you been undereating or overeating?

Have you had an increase in headaches or back pains?

This checklist can also be used to help determine the level of stress in followers.

Who do you think typically experiences greater stress—leaders or followers? In one sense, the answer is the same as that for much psychological research: it depends. The role of leader certainly can be quite stressful. Leaders face at least one major stressful event at least once a month (Ivancevich, Schweiger, & Ragan, 1986). Followers' stress levels, on the other hand, often depend on their leaders. Leaders can help followers cope with stress or, alternatively, actually increase their followers' stress levels. Many leaders recognize when followers are under a lot of stress and will give them time off, try to reduce their workload, or take other actions to help followers cope. On the other hand, about two out of three workers say their bosses play a bigger part in creating their stress than any other personal, organizational, or environmental factor (R. T. Hogan & Morrison, 1991; Shipper & Wilson, 1992). Similarly, McCormick and Powell (1988) reported that working for a tyrannical boss was the most frequently cited source of stress among workers. It is clear that leaders play a substantial role in how stressful their followers' work experience is, for good or ill.

Stress can either facilitate or inhibit performance, depending on the situation. Too much stress can take a toll on individuals and organizations that includes decreased health and emotional well-being, reduced job performance, and decreased organizational effectiveness (see Highlight S.2 for an example of how too much stress impaired one person's performance).

In order to understand the effects of stress, an analogy might be helpful. Kites need an optimal amount of wind to fly; they will not fly on windless days, and the string may break on a day that is too windy. You can think of stress as like the wind for a kite: There is a certain level that is optimal, neither too little nor too much. Another analogy is your car. Just as an automobile engine operates optimally within a certain range of revolutions per minute (RPM), most people function best at certain levels of stress. A certain amount of stress or arousal is helpful in increasing motivation and performance, but too much stress can be counterproductive. For example, it is common and probably helpful to feel a little anxiety before giving a speech, but being too nervous can destroy one's effectiveness.

The optimal level of stress depends on a number of factors. One is the level of physical activity actually demanded by the task. Another is the perceived difficulty of the task. Performance often suffers when difficult tasks are performed under stressful situations. For example, think how one's performance might differ when learning to first drive a car with an instructor who is quiet and reserved rather than one who yells a lot. Chances are, performance will be much better with the first instructor than with the second.

It is important to note that task difficulty is generally a function of experience; the more experience one has with a task, the less difficult it becomes. Thus, the more driving experience one has, the easier the task becomes. Moreover, not only do people cope with stress more readily when performing easier tasks; people often need higher levels of stress for performing them optimally. One underlying purpose behind any type of practice, be it football, marching band, soccer, or drama, is to reduce task difficulty and help members or players to

Stress on a TV Game Show

Highlight S.2

The television game show *Wheel of Fortune* pits contestants against each other in trying to identify common sayings. By spinning a wheel, contestants determine varying dollar amounts to be added to their potential winnings.

The game is similar to the game of "Hangman" you may have played as a child. It begins with spaces indicating the number of words in a saying and the number of letters in each word. One player spins the wheel, which determines prize money, and then guesses a letter. If the letter appears somewhere in the saying, then the player spins the wheel again, guesses another letter, and so on. The letters are "filled in" as they are correctly identified. A player may try to guess the saying after naming a correct letter.

If a player names a letter which does not appear in the saying, then that prize money is not added to the contestant's potential winnings and play moves on to another contestant.

One day a contestant was playing for over $50,000 to solve the puzzle below. Perhaps because of the stress of being on television and playing for so much money, the contestant could not accurately name a letter for one of the four remaining spaces. Most people, not experiencing such stress, easily solve the problem. Can you? For the answer, see the bottom of the box.

```
T  H  E     T  H  R  I  __  __
O  F     __  I     T  O  R  Y
   A  N  D     T  H  E
   A  G  O  N  Y     O  F
      D  E  F  E  A  T
```

Answer: The Thrill of Victory and the Agony of Defeat

perform at an even higher level when faced with the stress of key performances and games.

Although stress can have positive effects, research has focused on the negative implications of too much stress on health and work. In terms of health, stress has been linked to heart disease (Friedman & Ulmer, 1984), immune system deficiencies (Pomerleau & Rodin, 1986), and the growth rates of tumors (Justice, 1985). In terms of work behaviors, both Latack (1986) and Quayle (1983) reported that work-related stress has caused a dramatic increase in drug and alcohol use in the workplace, and Jamal (1984) found that stress was positively related to absenteeism, intentions to quit, and turnover. Relatedly, Quayle (1983) and Albrecht (1979) estimated the economic impact of stress to companies in the Unites States to be somewhere between $70 billion and $150 billion annually. Stress can also affect the decision-making process. Although leaders need to act decisively in stressful situations (i.e., crises), they may not make good decisions under stress (Fiedler, 1992; Gibson, 1992; Mulder, de Jong, Koppelaar, & Verhage, 1986). According to Weschler (1955) and Tjosvold (1985), people make poor decisions when under stress because they revert to their intuition rather than think rationally about problems.

As we have noted, too much stress can take a toll on individuals and their organizations. For individuals, the toll can be in terms of their health, mental and emotional well-being, job performance, or interpersonal relationships. For organizations, the toll includes decreased productivity and increased employee absenteeism, turnover, and medical costs. It stands to reason, then, that leaders in any activity should know something about stress. Leaders should understand the nature of stress because the leadership role itself can be stressful and because leaders' stress can impair the performance and well-being of followers. To prevent stress from becoming so excessive that it takes a toll in some important dimension of your own or your followers' lives, the following guidelines for effective stress management are provided.

Monitor Your Own and Your Followers' Stress Levels

One of the most important steps in managing stress is to *monitor your own and your followers' stress levels.* Although this seems straightforward, a seemingly paradoxical fact about stress is that it often takes a toll without one's conscious awareness. A person experiencing excessive stress might manifest various symptoms apparent to everyone but him or her. For that reason, it is useful to develop the habit of regularly attending to some of the warning signs that your stress level may be getting too high. Some of the warning signs of stress are in Highlight S.1. If you answered yes to any of these questions, then your own or your followers' stress levels may be getting too high and it would probably be a good idea to put some of the following stress management strategies into practice right away. On the other hand, answering some of the questions affirmatively does not necessarily mean your stress level is too high. There could, for example, be some other physiological explanation.

Identify What Is Causing the Stress

Monitoring your stress will reduce the chances that it will build to an unhealthy level before you take action, but monitoring is not enough. Leaders also need to *identify what is causing the stress.* It may seem at first that the causes of stress always will be obvious, but that is not true. Sometimes the problems are clear enough even if the solutions are not (e.g., family finances or working in a job with a high workload and lots of deadlines). At other times, however, it may be difficult to identify the root problem. For example, a coach may attribute his anger to the losing record of his team, not recognizing that a bigger cause of his emotional distress may be the problems he is having at home with his teenage son. A worker may feel frustrated because her boss overloads her with work, not realizing that her own unassertiveness keeps her from expressing her feelings to her boss. Problem solving can be applied constructively to managing stress, but only if the problem is identified properly in the first place. Once the problem is identified, then a plan for minimizing stress or the effects of the stressor can be developed.

Practice a Healthy Lifestyle

Practicing a healthy lifestyle is one of the best ways to minimize stress. There are no substitutes for balanced nutrition, regular exercise, adequate sleep, abstention from tobacco products, and drinking only moderate amounts of alcohol (if at all) as keys to a healthy life. A long-term study of the lifestyles of nearly 7,000 adults confirmed these as independent factors contributing to wellness and the absence of stress symptoms (Wiley & Camacho, 1980). Insufficient sleep saps energy, interferes with alertness and judgment, increases irritability, and lowers resistance to illness. Exercise, besides being a valuable part of any long-term health strategy, is also an excellent way to reduce tension.

Learn How to Relax

Believe it or not, some people just do not know how to relax. Although physical exercise is a good relaxation technique, sometimes you will need to relax but not have an opportunity to get a workout. Having practiced other relaxation techniques will come in handy when the situation prevents strenuous exercise. Also, of course, some people simply prefer alternative relaxation techniques to exercise. *Deep-breathing techniques, progressive muscle relaxation, and thinking of calming words and images* can be powerful on-the-spot calming techniques to reduce arousal level. They are applicable in stressful situations ranging from job interviews to sports. The effectiveness of these techniques is somewhat a matter of personal preference, and no single one is best for all purposes or all people.

Develop Supportive Relationships

Another powerful antidote to stress is having a *network of close and supportive relationships* with others (Berkman & Syme, 1979). People who have close ties to others through marriage, church membership, or other groups tend to be healthier than those with weaker social ties. Also, social supports of various kinds (e.g., the supportiveness of one's spouse, co-workers, or boss) can buffer the impact of job stress (Cummings, 1990; Jayaratne, Himle, & Chess, 1988), and unit cohesion is believed to be a critical element of soldiers' ability to withstand even the extreme physical and psychological stresses of combat (West Point

Associates, 1988). Leaders can play a constructive role in developing mutual supportiveness and cohesiveness among subordinates, and their own open and frank communication with subordinates is especially important when a situation is ambiguous as well as stressful.

Keep Things in Perspective

As we noted earlier, the stressfulness of any event depends partly on the way one interprets it, not just on the event itself. For example, a poor grade on an examination may be more stressful for one student than for another, just as a rebuke from a boss may be more stressful for one worker than for another. This is partly due, of course, to the fact individuals invest themselves in activities to different degrees because they value different things. A problem in an area of heavy personal investment is more stressful than one in an area of little personal investment. It goes deeper than that, however. Managing stress effectively depends on *keeping things in perspective.* This is difficult for some people because they have a style of interpreting events that aggravates their felt stress.

Individuals who have relatively complex self-concepts, as measured by the number of different ways they describe or see themselves, are less susceptible to common stress-related complaints than are people with lesser degrees of "self-complexity" (Linville, 1987). Take, for example, someone who has suffered a setback at work, such as having lost out to a colleague for a desired promotion. Someone low in self-complexity (e.g., a person whose self-concept is defined solely in terms of professional success) could be devastated by the event. Low self-complexity implies a lack of resilience to threats to one's ego. Consider, on the other hand, someone with high self-complexity facing the same setback. The person could understandably feel disappointed and perhaps dejected about work, but if she were high in self-complexity, then the event's impact would be buffered by the existence of relatively uncontaminated areas of positive self-image. For example, she might base her feelings of professional success on more criteria than just getting (or not getting) a promotion. Other criteria, such as being highly respected by peers, may be even more important bases for her feelings of professional success. Furthermore, other dimensions of her life (e.g., her leadership in the local Democratic Party, support to her family) may provide more areas of positive self-image.

The A-B-C Model

Unfortunately, because there are no shortcuts to developing self-complexity, it is not really a viable stress management strategy. There are other cognitive approaches to stress management, however, that can produce more immediate results. These approaches have the common goal of changing a person's self-talk about stressful events. One of the simplest of these to apply is called the A-B-C model (Ellis & Harper, 1975; Steinmetz, Blankenship, Brown, Hall, & Miller, 1980).

To appreciate the usefulness of the A-B-C model, it is helpful to consider the chain of events that precedes feelings of stress. Sometimes people think of this as a two-step sequence. Something external happens (i.e., a stressful event), and then something *internal* follows (i.e., symptoms of stress). We can depict the sequence like this:

A. Triggering Event (e.g., knocking your boss's coffee onto his lap)
C. Feelings and Behaviors (e.g., anxiety, fear, embarrassment, perspiration)

In other words, many people think their feelings and behaviors result directly from external events. Such a view, however, leaves out the critical role played by our thoughts, or self-talk. The actual sequence looks like this:

A. Triggering Event (knocking your boss's coffee onto his lap)
B. Your Thinking ("He must think I'm a real jerk.")
C. Feelings and Behaviors (anxiety, fear, embarrassment, perspiration)

From this perspective you can see the causal role played by inner dialogue, or self-talk, in contributing to feelings of stress. Such inner dialogue can be rational or irrational, constructive or destructive—and which it will be is under the individual's control. People gain considerable freedom from stress when they realize that by changing their own self-talk, they can control their emotional responses to events around them. Consider a different sequence for our scenario:

A. Triggering Event (knocking your boss's coffee onto his lap)
B. Your Thinking ("Darn it! But it was just an accident.")
C. Feelings and Behavior (apologizing and helping clean up)

Thus, a particular incident can be interpreted in several different ways, some likely to increase feelings of stress and distress, and others likely to maintain self-esteem and positive coping. You will become better at coping with stress as you practice listening to your inner dialogue and changing destructive self-talk to constructive self-talk. Even this is not a simple change to make, however. Changing self-talk is more difficult than you might think, especially in emotionalized situations. Because self-talk is covert, spontaneous, fleeting, and reflexive (McKay, Davis, & Fanning, 1981), it, like any bad habit, can be difficult to change. Nevertheless, precisely because self-talk is just a habit, you can change it.

Finally, leaders need to recognize their role in their followers' stress levels. A leader in a stressful situation who is visibly manifesting some of the symptoms found in Highlight S–1 is not going to set much of an example for followers. On the contrary, because followers look to leaders for guidance and support, these behaviors and symptoms could become contagious and may serve to increase followers' stress levels. Leaders need to recognize the importance of role modeling in reducing (or increasing) followers' stress levels. Leaders also need to make sure their style of interacting with subordinates does not make the leaders "stress carriers."

Building Technical Competence

Determining How the Job Contributes to the Overall Mission

Becoming an Expert in the Job

Seeking Opportunities to Broaden Experiences

Technical competence concerns the knowledge and repertoire of behaviors one can bring to bear to successfully complete a task. For example, a highly skilled surgeon possesses vast knowledge of human anatomy and surgical techniques and can perform an extensive set of highly practiced surgical procedures; a highly skilled volleyball player has a thorough understanding of the rules, tactics, and strategies of volleyball and can set, block, and serve effectively. Individuals usually acquire technical competence through formal education or training in specialized topics (i.e., law, medicine, accounting, welding, carpentry), on-the-job training, or experience (Yukl, 1989), and many studies have documented the importance of technical competence to a person's success and effectiveness as both a leader and a follower. This section describes why technical competence is important to followers and leaders; it also provides readers with ideas about how to increase their own technical competence.

There are many reasons why followers need to have a high level of technical competence. First, performance is often a function of technical competence (Borman, Hanson, Oppler, & Pulakos, 1993; Schmidt & Hunter, 1992). Relatedly, research has shown that technical expertise plays a key role in supervisors' performance appraisal ratings of subordinates (Borman, White, Pulakos, & Oppler, 1991; J. Hogan, 1992b). Second, followers with high levels of technical competence have a lot of expert power, and at times can wield more influence in their groups than the leader does (Bugental, 1964; Farris, 1971). Third, individuals with high levels of technical competence may be more likely to be a member of a leader's in-group (Duchon, Green, & Taber, 1986). Relatedly, followers with high levels of technical competence are more likely to be delegated tasks and asked to participate in the decision-making process. Conversely, supervisors are more likely to use a close, directive leadership style when interacting with subordinates with poor technical skills (Dewhirst, Metts, & Ladd, 1987; Leana, 1987; Lowin & Craig, 1968; Rosen & Jerdee, 1977). Similarly, Blau (1968) noted that organizations with relatively high numbers of technically competent members tended to have a flatter organizational structure; organizations with relatively fewer qualified members tended to be more centralized and autocratic. Thus, if followers wish to earn greater rewards, exert more influence in their groups, and have greater say in the decision-making process, then they should do all they can to enhance their technical competence.

There are also many reasons why it benefits leaders to have high levels of technical competence. First, technical competence has been found to be consistently related to managerial promotion rates. Managers having higher levels of technical competence were much more likely to rise to the top managerial levels at AT&T than managers with lower levels of technical competence (Howard, 1986; Howard & Bray, 1989). Second, having a high level of technical competence is important because many leaders, particularly first-line supervisors, often spend considerable time training followers (Wexley & Latham, 1981). Perhaps nowhere is the importance of technical competence in training more readily apparent than in coaching; little is as frustrating as having a coach who knows less about the game than the team members. Third, leaders with high levels of technical competence seem to be able to reduce the level of role ambiguity and conflict in their groups (Podsakoff, Todor, & Schuler, 1983; Walker, 1976), and followers are generally more satisfied with leaders who have high rather then average levels of technical competence (Bass, 1985; Penner, Malone, Coughlin, & Herz, 1973). Finally, leaders who have a high level of technical competence may be able to stimulate followers to think about problems and issues in new ways, which in turn has been found to be strongly related to organizational climate ratings and followers' motivation to succeed (Avolio & Bass, 1988; Curphy, 1991a). Given these findings for both leaders and followers, below is some practical advice for improving technical competence.

Determining How the Job Contributes to the Overall Mission

The first step in building technical competence is to determine how one's job contributes to the overall success of the organization. By taking this step, individuals can better determine what technical knowledge and which behaviors are most strongly related to job and organizational success. Next, people should evaluate their current level of technical skills by seeking verbal feedback from peers and superiors, reviewing past performance appraisal results, or reviewing objective performance data (e.g., golf scores, team statistics, the number of products rejected for poor quality). These actions will help individuals get a better handle on their own strengths and weaknesses, and in turn can help people be certain that any formal education or training program they pursue is best suited to meet their needs.

Becoming an Expert in the Job

Becoming an expert in one's primary field is often the springboard for further developmental opportunities. There are a number of ways in which individuals can become experts in their field, and these include enrolling in formalized education and training programs, watching others, asking questions, and teaching others. Attending pertinent education and training courses is one way to acquire technical skills, and many companies often pay the tuition and fees associated with these courses. Another way to increase expertise in one's field is by being a keen observer of human behavior. Individuals can learn a lot by observing how others handle work-coordination problems, achieve production goals, discipline team members, or develop team members with poor skills. However, merely observing how others do things is not nearly as effective as observing and reflecting about how others do things. One method of reflection is trying to explain others' behaviors in terms of the concepts or theories described in this book. Observers should look for concepts that cast light on both variations and regularities in how others act and think about the reasons why a person might have acted a certain way. Additionally, observers can develop by trying to think of as many different criteria as possible for evaluating another person's actions.

It is also important to ask questions. Because everyone makes inferences regarding the motives, expectations, values, or rationale underlying another person's actions, it is vital to ask questions and seek information likely to verify the accuracy of one's inferences. By asking questions, observers can better understand why team practices are conducted in a particular way, what work procedures have been implemented in the past, or what really caused someone to quit a volunteer organization. Finally, perhaps nothing can help a person become a technical expert more than having to teach someone else about the equipment, procedures, strategies, problems, resources, and contacts associated with a job, club, sport, or activity. Teachers must have a thorough understanding of the job or position in order to effectively teach someone else. By seeking opportunities to teach others, individuals enhance their own technical expertise as well as that of others.

Seeking Opportunities to Broaden Experiences

Individuals can improve their technical competence by seeking opportunities to broaden their experiences. Just as a person should try to play a variety of positions in order to better appreciate the contributions of other team members, so should a person try to perform the tasks associated with the other positions in his or her work group in order to better appreciate how the work contributes to organizational success. Similarly, people should visit other parts of the organization in order to gain an understanding of its whole operation. Moreover, by working on team projects, people get a chance to interact with members of other work units and often get the opportunity to develop new skills. Additionally, volunteering to support school, political, or community activities is another way to increase one's organization and planning, public speaking, fund-raising, and public relations skills, all of which may be important aspects of technical competence for certain jobs.

Building Effective Relationships with Superiors

Understanding the Superior's World

Adapting to the Superior's Style

As defined here, superiors are those individuals with relatively more power and authority than the other members of the group. Thus, superiors could be teachers, band directors, coaches, team captains, heads of committees, or first-line supervisors. Needless to say, there are a number of advantages to having a good working relationship with superiors. First, superiors and followers sharing the same values, approaches, and attitudes will experience less conflict, provide higher levels of mutual support, and be more satisfied with superior–follower relationships than superiors and followers having poor working relationships (Duchon, Green, & Taber, 1986; Porter, 1992). Relatedly, individuals having good superior–follower relationships are often in the superior's in-group and thus are more likely to have a say in the decision-making process, be delegated interesting tasks, and have the superior's support for career advancement (Yukl, 1989). Second, followers are often less satisfied with their supervisor and receive lower performance appraisal ratings when superior–follower relationships are poor (Pulakos & Wexley, 1983; Weiss, 1977).

Although the advantages of having a good working relationship with superiors seem clear, one might mistakenly think that followers have little, if any, say in the quality of the relationship. In other words, followers might believe their relationships with superiors are a matter of luck; either the follower has a good superior or a bad one, or the superior just happens to like or dislike the follower, and there is little if anything the follower can do about it. However, the quality of a working relationship is not determined solely by the superior, and effective subordinates do not limit themselves to a passive stance toward superiors. Effective subordinates have learned how to take active steps to strengthen the relationship and enhance the support they provide their superior and the organization (Gabarro & Kotter, 1980; Kelley, 1988).

Wherever a person is positioned in an organization, an important aspect of that person's work is to help his superior be successful, just as an important part of the superior's work is to help followers be successful. This does not mean that followers should become apple-polishers, play politics, or distort information just to make superiors look good. It does mean, however, that followers should think of their own and their superior's success as interdependent. It means that followers are players on their superior's team and should be evaluated on the basis of the team's success, not just their own. If the team succeeds, then both the coach and the team members should benefit; if the team fails, then the blame should fall on both the coach and the team members. Because team, club, or organizational outcomes depend to some extent on good superior–follower relationships, understanding how superiors view the world and adapting to superiors' styles are two things followers can do to increase the likelihood their actions will have positive results for themselves, their superiors, and their organizations (Gabarro & Kotter, 1980).

Understanding the Superior's World

There are a number of things followers can do to better understand their superior's world. First, they should try to get a handle on their superior's personal and organizational objectives. Loyalty and support are a two-way street, and just as a superior can help subordinates attain their personal goals most readily by knowing what they are, so can subordinates support their superior if they understand the superior's goals and objectives. Relatedly, knowing a superior's values, preferences, and personality can help followers better understand why superiors act the way they do and can give followers insights into how they might strengthen relationships with superiors.

Second, followers need to realize that superiors are not supermen or superwomen; superiors do not have all the answers, and they have both strengths and weaknesses. Subordinates can make a great contribution to the overall success of a team by recognizing and complementing a superior's weaknesses, and understanding his constraints and limitations. For example, a highly successful management consultant might spend over 200 days a year conducting executive development workshops, providing organizational feedback to clients, or giving speeches at various public events. This same consultant, however, might not be skilled in designing and making effective visual aids for presentations, or she might dislike having to make her own travel and accommodation arrangements. A follower could make both the consultant and the consulting firm more successful through his own good organization and planning, attention to detail, computer graphics skills, and understanding that the consultant is most effective when she has at least a one-day break between engagements. A similar process can take place in other contexts, as when subordinates help orient and educate a newly assigned superior whose expertise and prior experience may have been in a different field or activity.

In an even more general sense, subordinates can enhance superior–follower relationships by keeping superiors informed about various activities in the work group or new developments or opportunities in the field. Few superiors like surprises, and any news should come from the person with responsibility for a particular area—especially if the news is potentially bad or concerns unfavorable developments. Followers wishing to develop good superior–follower relationships should never put their superior in the embarrassing situation of having someone else know more about her terrain than she does (her own boss, for instance). As Kelley (1988) maintained, the best followers think critically and play an active role in their organizations, which means that followers should keep their superiors informed about critical information and pertinent opinions concerning organizational issues.

Adapting to the Superior's Style

Research has shown that some executives fail to get promoted (i.e., are derailed) because they are unable or unwilling to adapt to superiors with leadership styles different from their own (McCall & Lombardo, 1983). Followers need to keep in mind that it is their responsibility to adapt to their superior's style, not vice versa. For example, followers might prefer to interact with superiors face-to-face, but if their superior appreciates written memos, then written memos it should be. Similarly, a follower might be accustomed to informal interactions with superiors, but a new superior might prefer a more businesslike and formal style. Followers need to be flexible in adapting to their superiors' decision-making styles, problem-solving strategies, modes of communication, styles of interaction, and so on.

One way followers can better adapt to a superior's style is to clarify expectations about their role on the team, committee, or work group. Young workers often do not appreciate the difference between a job description and one's role in a job. A job description is a formalized statement of tasks and activities; a role describes the personal signature an incumbent gives to a job. For example, the job description of a high school athletic coach might specify such responsibilities as selecting and training a team or making decisions about lineups. Two different coaches, however, might accomplish those basic responsibilities in quite different ways. One might emphasize player development in the broadest sense, getting to know her players personally and using sports as a vehicle for their individual growth; another might see his role simply to produce the most winning team possible. Therefore, just because followers know what their job is does not mean their role is clear.

Although some superiors take the initiative to explicitly spell out the roles they expect subordinates to play, most do not. Usually it is the subordinate's task to discern his or her role. One way followers can do this is to make a list of major responsibilities and use it to guide a discussion with the superior about different ways the tasks might be accomplished and the relative priorities of the tasks. Relatedly, followers will also find it helpful to talk to others who have worked with a particular superior before.

Finally, followers interested in developing effective relationships with superiors need to be honest and dependable. Whatever other qualities or talents a subordinate might have, a lack of integrity is an absolutely fatal flaw. No one—superior, peer, or subordinate—wants to work with someone who is untrustworthy. After integrity, superiors value dependability. Superiors value workers who have reliable work habits, accomplish assigned tasks at the right time in the right order, and do what they promise (Kouzes & Posner, 1987).

Building Effective Relationships with Peers

Recognizing Common Interests and Goals

Understanding Peers' Tasks, Problems, and Rewards

Practicing a Theory Y Attitude

The phrase *influence without authority* (Cohen & Bradford, 1990) captures a key element of the work life of increasing numbers of individuals. More and more people are finding that their jobs require them to influence others despite having no formal authority over them. No man is an island, it is said, and perhaps no worker in today's organizations can survive alone. Virtually everyone needs a co-worker's assistance or resources at one time or another. Along these lines, some researchers have maintained that one of the fundamental requirements of leadership effectiveness is the ability to build strong alliances with others, and groups of peers generally wield more influence (and can get more things done) than individuals working separately (R. T. Hogan, J. Hogan, & Curphy, 1992). Similarly, investing the time and effort to develop effective relationships with peers not only has immediate dividends but also can have long-term benefits if a peer ends up in a position of power in the future. Many times, leaders are selected from among the members of a group, committee, club, or team and, having previously spent time developing a friendly rather than an antagonistic relationship with other work group members, will lay the groundwork for building effective relationships with superiors and becoming a member of superiors' ingroups. Given the benefits of strong relationships with peers, the following are a few ideas about how to establish and maintain good peer relationships.

Recognizing Common Interests and Goals

Although Chapters 5 through 8 described a variety of ways people vary, one of the best ways to establish effective working relationships with peers is to acknowledge shared interests, values, goals, and expectations (Cohen & Bradford, 1990). In order to acknowledge shared aspirations and interests, however, one must know what peers' goals, values, and interests actually are. Establishing informal communication links is one of the best ways to discover common interests and values. To do so, one needs to be open and honest in communicating one's own needs, values, and goals, as well as being willing to acknowledge others' needs, aspirations, and interests. Little can destroy a relationship with peers more quickly than a person who is overly willing to share his own problems and beliefs but unwilling to listen to others' ideas about the same issues. Moreover, although some people believe that participating in social gatherings, parties, committee meetings, lunches, company sport teams, or community activities can be a waste of time, peers with considerable referent power often see such activities as opportunities to establish and improve relationships with others. Thus, an effective way to establish relationships with other members of a team, committee, or organization is to meet with them in contexts outside of normal working relationships.

Understanding Peers' Tasks, Problems, and Rewards

Few things reinforce respect between co-workers better than understanding the nature of each other's work. Building a cooperative relationship with others depends, therefore, on knowing the sorts of tasks others perform in the organization. It also depends on understanding what their problems and rewards are. With the former, one of the best ways to establish strong relationships is by lending a hand whenever peers face personal or organizational problems. With the latter, it is especially important to remember that people tend to repeat those behaviors that are rewarded and are less likely to repeat behaviors that go unrewarded. A person's counterproductive or negative behaviors may be due less to his personal characteristics (e.g., "He is just uncooperative") than to the way his rewards are structured. For example, a teacher may be less likely to share successful classroom exercises with others if teachers are awarded merit pay on the basis of classroom effectiveness. To secure cooperation from others, it helps to know which situational factors reinforce both positive and negative behaviors in others (Cohen & Bradford, 1990). By better understanding the situation facing others, people can determine whether their own positive feedback (or lack thereof) is contributing to, or hindering the establishment of, effective relationships with peers. People should not underestimate the power of their own sincere encouragement, thanks, and compliments in positively influencing the behavior of their colleagues.

Practicing a Theory Y Attitude

Another way to build effective working relationships with peers is to view them from a Theory Y perspective (see Chapter 6). When a person assumes that others are competent, trustworthy, willing to cooperate if they can, and proud of their work, peers will look on that person in the same light. Even if one practices a Theory Y attitude, however, it may still be difficult to get along with a few co-workers. In such cases, it is easy to become preoccupied with the qualities one dislikes. This should be resisted as much as possible. A vicious cycle can develop in which people become enemies, putting more and more energy into criticizing each other or making the other person look bad than into doing constructive work on the task at hand. The costs of severely strained relationships also can extend beyond the individual parties involved. Cliques, or sides, can develop among other co-workers as well, which can impair the larger group's effectiveness. The point here is not to overlook interpersonal problems, but rather to not let the problems get out of hand.

Practicing Theory Y does *not* mean looking at the world through rose-colored glasses, but it *does* mean recognizing someone else's strengths as well as weaknesses. Nevertheless, sometimes peers will be assigned to work on a task together when they don't get along with each other, and the advice "Practice a Theory Y attitude" may seem too idealistic. At such times, it is important to decide whether to focus energy first on improving the relationship (before addressing the task) or to focus it solely on the task (essentially ignoring the problem in the relationship).

Cohen and Bradford (1990) suggested several guidelines for resolving this problem. They said it is best to work on the task if there is little animosity between the parties, if success can be achieved despite existing animosities, if group norms inhibit openness, if success on the task will improve the feelings between the parties, if the other person handles directness poorly, or if you handle directness poorly. Conversely, they said it is best to work on the relationship if there is great animosity between the parties, if negative feelings make task success unlikely, if group norms favor openness, if feelings between the parties are not likely to improve even with success on the task, if the other person handles directness well, *and* if you handle directness well.

Setting Goals

Goals Should Be Specific and Observable

Goals Should Be Attainable but Challenging

Goals Require Commitment

Goals Require Feedback

The Roman philosopher Seneca wrote, "When a man does not know what harbor he is making for, no wind is the right wind." Setting goals and developing plans of action to attain them are important for individuals and for groups. For example, the purpose or goal is often the predominant norm in any group. Once group goals are agreed on, they serve to induce member compliance, act as a criterion for evaluating the leadership potential of group members, and become the criteria for evaluating group performance (Bass, 1990).

Perhaps the most important step in accomplishing a personal or group goal is stating it right in the first place. The reason many people become frustrated with the outcomes of their New Year's resolutions is not any character flaw on their part (e.g., "I don't have any willpower"), but that their resolutions are so vague or unrealistic they are unlikely to ever lead to demonstrable results. It is possible to keep New Year's resolutions, but one must set them intelligently. In a more general sense, some ways of writing goal statements increase the likelihood that someone will successfully achieve the desired goals. Goals should be specific and observable, attainable and challenging, based on top-to-bottom commitment, and designed to provide feedback to personnel about their progress toward them. The following is a more detailed discussion of each of these points.

Goals Should Be Specific and Observable

As described in Chapter 9, research provides strong support for the idea that specific goals lead to higher levels of effort and performance than general goals. General goals do not work as well because they often do not provide enough information regarding which particular behaviors are to be changed or when a clear end-state has been attained. This may be easiest to see with a personal example.

Assume that a student is not satisfied with her academic performance and wants to do something about it. She might set a very general goal, such as "I will do my best next year" or "I will do better in school next year." At first, such a goal may seem fine; after all, as long as she is motivated to do well, what more would be needed? However, on further thought you can see that "do my best" or "do better" are so ambiguous as to be unhelpful in directing her behavior and ultimately assessing her success. General goals have relatively little impact on energizing and directing immediate behavior, and they make it difficult to assess, in the end, whether someone has attained them or not. A better goal statement for this student would be, for example, to attain a B average or to get no deficient grades this semester. Specific goals like these make it easier to chart one's progress. A more business-oriented example might deal with improving productivity at work. Specific goal statements in this case might include a 20 percent increase in the number of products being produced by the work unit over the next three months or a 40 percent decrease in the number of products being returned by quality control next year.

The idea of having specific goals is closely related to that of having observable goals. It should be clear to everyone when the goal has or has not been reached. It is easy to say your goal is to go on a diet, but a much better goal is "to lose 10 pounds by March." Similarly, it is easy to say the team should do better next season, but a better goal is to say the team will win more than half of next season's games. It is important to note that specific, observable goals are also time limited. Without time limits for accomplishing goals, there would be little urgency associated with them. Neither would there be a finite point at which it is clear a person or group has or has not accomplished the goals. For example, it is better to set a goal of improving the next quarter's sales figures than just improving sales.

Goals Should Be Attainable but Challenging

Some people seem to treat goals as a sort of loyalty oath they must pass, as if it would be a break with one's ideals or be a reflection of insufficient motivation if any but the loftiest goals were set for oneself or one's organization. Yet to be useful, goals must be realistic. The struggling high school student who sets a goal of getting into Harvard may be unrealistic; but it may be realistic to set a goal of getting into the local state university. A civil rights activist may wish to eliminate prejudice completely, but a more attainable goal might be to eliminate racial discrimination in the local housing project over the next five years. A track team is not likely to win every race, but it may be realistic to aim to win the league championship.

The corollary to the preceding point is that goals should also be challenging. If goals merely needed to be attainable, then there would be nothing wrong with setting goals so easy that accomplishing them would be virtually guaranteed. As we have seen previously, setting easy goals does not result in high levels of performance; higher levels of performance come about when goals stretch and inspire people toward doing more than they thought they could. Goals need to be challenging but attainable to get the best out of oneself and others.

Goals Require Commitment

There is nothing magical about having goals; having goals per se does not guarantee success. Unless supported by real human commitment, goal statements are mere words. Organizational goals are most likely to be achieved if there is commitment to them at both the top and the bottom of the organization. Top leadership needs to make clear that it is willing to put its money where its mouth is. When top leadership sets goals, it should provide the resources workers need to achieve the goals and then should reward those who do. Subordinates often become committed to goals simply by seeing the sincere and enthusiastic commitment of top leadership to them. Another way to build subordinate acceptance and commitment to goals is to have subordinates participate in setting the goals in the first place. Research on the effects of goal setting demonstrates that worker acceptance and satisfaction tend to increase when workers are allowed to participate in setting goals (Erez, Earley, & Hulin, 1985; Locke, Latham, & Erez, 1987).

On the other hand, research is less conclusive about whether participation in goal setting actually increases performance or productivity. These mixed findings about participation and performance may be due to various qualities of the group and the leader. In terms of the group, groupthink may cause highly cohesive groups to commit to goals that are unrealistic and unachievable. Group members may not have realistically considered equipment or resource constraints, nor have the technical skills needed to successfully accomplish the goal. In addition, group members may not have any special enthusiasm for accomplishing a goal if the leader is perceived to have little expert power or is unsupportive, curt, or inept (House, 1984; Latham & Lee, 1986; Locke, Latham, & Erez, 1987). However, if leaders are perceived to be competent and supportive, then followers may have as much goal commitment as they would if they had participated in setting the goal. Thus, participation in goal setting often leads to higher levels of commitment and performance if the leader is perceived to be incompetent, but it will not necessarily lead to greater commitment and performance than is achieved when a competent leader assigns a goal. Again, these findings lend credence to the importance of technical competence in leadership effectiveness.

Goals Require Feedback

One of the most effective ways to improve any kind of performance is to provide feedback about how closely a person's behavior matches some criterion, and research shows that performance was much higher when goals were accompanied by feedback than when either goals or feedback were used alone. Goals that are specific, observable, and time limited are conducive to ongoing assessment and performance-based feedback, and leaders and followers should strive to provide and/or seek feedback on a fairly regular basis. Moreover, people should seek feedback from a variety of sources or provide feedback using a variety of criteria. Often, different sources and criteria can paint very different pictures about goal progress, and people can get a better idea of the true level of their progress by examining the information provided and integrating it across the different sources and criteria.

Punishment

Myths Surrounding the Use of Punishment
Punishment, Satisfaction, and Performance
Administering Punishment

In an ideal world, perhaps everyone would be dependable, achievement oriented, and committed to the organization's goals. The fact is, however, that leaders sometimes will need to deal with followers who are openly hostile or insubordinate, create conflicts among co-workers, do not work up to standards, or openly violate important rules or policies. In such cases leaders may need to administer punishment to change the follower's behavior.

Of all of the different aspects of leadership, few are as controversial as punishment. Some of the primary reasons for this controversy stem from myths surrounding the use of punishment, as well as the lack of knowledge regarding the effects of punishment on followers' motivation, satisfaction, and performance. This section is designed to shed light on the punishment controversy by (*a*) addressing several myths about the use of punishment, (*b*) reviewing research findings concerning the relationships between punishment and various organizational variables, and (*c*) providing leadership practitioners with advice on how to properly administer punishment.

Myths Surrounding the Use of Punishment

We should begin by repeating the definition of punishment stated earlier in the book. Punishment is the administration of an aversive event or the withdrawal of a positive event or stimulus, which in turn *decreases* the likelihood a particular behavior will be repeated (Arvey & Ivancevich, 1980). Examples of punishment might include verbal reprimands, being moved to a less prestigious office, having pay docked, being fired, being made to run several laps around the athletic field, or losing eligibility for a sport entirely. We should note that according to this definition, only those aversive events administered on a contingent basis are considered to be forms of punishment; aversive events administered on a noncontingent basis may constitute harsh and abusive treatment but are not punishment. Additionally, punishment appears to be in the eye of the beholder; aversive events that effectively change the direction, intensity, or persistence of one follower's behavior may have no effect on another's (Curphy, Gibson, Asiu, McCown, & Brown, 1992). It is even possible that some followers may find the administration of a noxious event or the removal of a positive event to be reinforcing. For example, it is not uncommon for some children to misbehave if that increases the attention they receive from parents, even if the latter's behavior outwardly may seem punishing to others. (To the children, some parental attention of any kind may be preferable to no attention.) Similarly, some followers may see the verbal reprimands and notoriety they receive by being insubordinate or violating company policies as forms of attention. Because these followers enjoy being the center of attention, they may find this notoriety rewarding. From an operant perspective, they may be even more likely to be insubordinate in the future.

We will examine four myths surrounding the use of punishment. Three of these myths were reviewed by Arvey and Ivancevich (1980) and included beliefs that the use of punishment resulted in undesirable emotional side effects on the part of the recipient, was unethical and inhumane, and rarely worked anyway (i.e., seldom eliminated the undesirable behavior).

B. F. Skinner's (1938) work in behavioral psychology lent support to the idea that punishment was ineffective and caused undesirable side effects. He based his conclusions on the unnatural behaviors manifested by rats and pigeons punished in various conditioning experiments. Despite the dangers of generalizing from the behavior of rats to humans, many people accepted Skinner's contention that punishment was a futile and typically counterproductive tool for controlling human behavior. This was so despite the fact that considerable research regarding the emotional effects of punishment on humans did not support Skinner's claim (Kazdin, 1975; Johnston, 1972; Solomon, 1964). Parke (1972), for example, suggested that undesirable emotional side effects of punishment might occur only when punishment was administered indiscriminately or was particularly harsh.

With respect to the myth that punishment is unethical or inhumane, Arvey and Ivancevich (1980) maintained there is an ethical distinction between "future-oriented" and "past-oriented" punishment. Future-oriented punishment, intended to help improve behavior, may be effective in diminishing or eliminating undesirable behavior. Past-oriented punishment, or what we commonly think of as retribution, on the other hand, is simply a payback for past misdeeds. This sort of punishment may be more questionable ethically, especially when it is intended *only* as payback and not, say, as deterrent to others. Moreover, when considering the ethics of administering punishment, one must also consider the ethics of *failing* to administer punishment. The costs of *failing* to punish a potentially harmful behavior, such as unsafe workplace practices, may far outweigh those associated with the punishment itself (Arvey & Ivancevich, 1980).

A third myth concerns the efficacy of punishment. Skinner (1938, 1985), and more recently Campbell (1977) and Luthans (1989), claimed that punishment did not result in a permanent behavior change but instead only temporarily suppressed behavior. Evidence to support this claim was found by Huberman (1964), who reported that incarcerated prisoners had a recidivism rate of 85 percent. However, this high recidivism rate may be due to the fact that criminals may have received punishment primarily for retribution rather than for corrective purposes. Judicious administration of sanctions, combined with advice about how to avoid punishment in the future, may successfully eliminate undesirable behaviors on a more permanent basis (Arvey & Ivancevich, 1980). Furthermore, it may be a moot point to argue (as Skinner did) that punishment only temporarily suppresses behavior; so long as sanctions for misdeeds remain in place, their impact on behavior should continue. In that regard, it's relevant to note that the "temporary" effects of punishment on behavior are no different from the "temporary" effects of reinforcement on behavior.

Punishment, Satisfaction, and Performance

It appears that properly administered punishment does not cause undesirable emotional side effects, is not unethical, and may effectively suppress undesirable behavior. However, we also should ask what effect punishment has on followers' satisfaction and performance. Most people probably would predict that leaders who use punishment more frequently will probably have less-satisfied and lower-performing followers. Interestingly, this does not appear to be the case—at least when punishment is used appropriately. Let us look a little more closely at this issue.

Several researchers have looked at whether leaders who administer punishment on a contingent basis also administered rewards on a contingent basis. Generally, researchers have found that there is a moderate positive relationship between leaders' contingent reward behaviors and contingent punishment behaviors (Arvey, Davis, & Nelson, 1984; Podsakoff & Todor, 1985; Strasser, Dailey, & Bateman, 1981). There also are consistently strong negative correlations found between leaders' contingent reward and noncontingent punishment behaviors. Thus, leaders meting out rewards on a contingent basis were also more likely to administer punishment only when followers behaved inappropriately or were not performing up to standards.

Keller and Szilagyi (1976, 1978) maintained that punishment can serve several constructive organizational purposes. They said it can help clarify roles and expectations, as well as reduce role ambiguity. Several other authors have found contingent punishment either was unrelated to followers' satisfaction with their supervisor ratings or had a low positive relationship with it (Arvey, Davis, & Nelson, 1984; Podsakoff, Todor, Grover, & Huber, 1984). In other words, leaders who follow certain rules in administering punishment need not have dissatisfied subordinates. As a matter of fact, judicious and appropriate use of punishment by leaders may result in somewhat *higher* satisfaction of followers overall. These findings make sense when the entire work unit is considered; failing to use punishment when it seems called for in most followers' eyes may lead to perceptions of inequity, which may in turn lead to lower group cohesiveness and satisfaction (Curphy et al., 1992; Dobbins & Russell, 1986).

With respect to followers' work behaviors, Arvey and Jones (1985) reported that punishment has generally been found to reduce absenteeism and tardiness rates. Nevertheless, the evidence about punishment's impact on performance appears mixed. Some authors report a strong positive relationship between punishment and performance (Beyer & Trice, 1984; Katz, Maccoby, Gurin, & Floor, 1951; Podsakoff & Todor, 1985; Schnake, 1986), whereas others found either no relationship between punishment and performance or a negative one (Curphy et al., 1992; Curtis, Smith, & Smoll, 1979).

Despite such mixed findings, there are several points about the relationship between punishment and performance findings still worth noting. First, the level of punishment as well as the manner in which it was administered across studies could have differed dramatically, and these factors could have affected the results. Second, of the studies reporting positive results, Schnake's (1986) experiment of the vicarious effects of punishment is by far the most provocative. Schnake hired college students for a temporary job, and after several hours at work, publicly reduced the pay or threatened to reduce the pay of a confederate in the work group. As predicted, the more severe the punishment witnessed (either the threat of reduced pay or the reduction of pay), the higher the subsequent performance of other work-group members.

Although these findings demonstrated that merely witnessing rather than receiving punishment could result in increased performance, these results should be interpreted with some caution. Because most of the individuals in the experiment did not know each other and had only been working together for several hours, there was probably not enough time for group cohesiveness or norms to develop. It is not at all clear whether members of cohesive groups or groups with strong norms would react in the same way if they had observed another group member being punished (Curphy et al., 1992).

Third, of the studies reporting less favorable punishment-performance results, the Curtis, Smith, and Smoll (1979) study made an important point about the opportunities to punish. Curtis, Smith, and Smoll examined the relationships between Little League coaches' behaviors and their teams' win–loss records. They found coaches who punished more often had less-successful teams. These coaches also, however, had less-talented players and therefore had many more opportunities to use punishment. Coaches of successful teams had little if any reason to use punishment. Fourth, many behaviors that do get punished may not have a direct link to job performance. For example, being insubordinate, violating company dress codes, and arriving late to meetings are all punishable behaviors that may not be directly linked to solving work-related problems or producing goods or services.

Finally, almost all these studies implicitly assumed punishment enhanced performance (by correcting problem behaviors), but Curphy and his associates (1992) were the only researchers who actually tested this assumption. They collected over 4,500 incidents of documented punishment and performance data from 40 identical organizations over a three-month period. (The punishment and performance data were collected monthly.) They found that low performance led to higher levels of punishment. Moreover, they found that inexperienced leaders administered almost twice as much punishment as experienced leaders. The authors hypothesized that inexperienced leaders used punishment (i.e., relied on their coercive power) more frequently because by being the newest arrivals to the organization, they lacked knowledge of the organizational norms, rules, and policies (i.e., expert power); had not yet established relationships with followers (i.e., referent power); and were severely limited in the rewards they could provide to followers (i.e., reward power).

In summary, the research evidence shows that punishment can lead to positive organizational outcomes if administered properly. When administered on a contingent basis, it may help increase job satisfaction; may decrease role ambiguity and absenteeism rates; and depending on the behaviors being punished, may have a positive effect on performance. However, administering intense levels of punishment in a noncontingent or capricious manner can have a devastating effect on the work unit. Group cohesiveness may suffer, followers are likely to become more dissatisfied and less apt to come to work, and they may perform at a lower level in the long term. Thus, learning how to properly administer punishment may be the key to maximizing the benefits associated with its use.

Administering Punishment

Usually, leaders administer punishment in order to rectify some type of behavioral or performance problem at work. However, not every behavior or performance problem is punished, and leaders probably weigh several different factors before deciding whether or not to administer punishment. Green and Mitchell (1979) maintained that leaders' decisions concerning punishment depended on whether leaders made internal or external attributions about a subordinate's substandard performance. Leaders making internal attributions were more likely to administer punishment; leaders making external attributions were more likely to blame the substandard performance on situational factors beyond the follower's control.

Attribution theory (Mitchell, Green, & Wood, 1981; Mitchell & Wood, 1980) maintains that leaders weigh three factors when making internal or external attributions about a follower's substandard performance. More specifically, leaders would be more likely to make an internal attribution about a follower's substandard performance (and administer punishment) if the follower had previously completed the task before, if other followers had successfully completed the task, and if the follower had successfully completed other tasks in the past. Moreover, Mitchell, Green, and Wood (1981) and Mitchell and Wood (1980) reported that leaders were biased toward making internal attributions about followers' poor performance (i.e., the fundamental attribution error) and thus more likely to use punishment to modify a follower's behavior.

Because leaders are biased toward making internal attributions about followers' substandard performance, leaders can administer punishment more effectively by being aware of this bias and getting as many facts as possible *before* deciding whether or not to administer punishment. Leaders also can improve the manner or skill with which they administer punishment by using tips provided by Arvey and Ivancevich (1980), who said punishment is administered most effectively when it focuses on the act, not the person. Followers probably cannot change their personalities, values, or preferences, but they can change their behaviors. By focusing on specific behaviors, leaders minimize the threat to followers' self-concepts. Also, punishment needs to be consistent across *both* behaviors and leaders; the same actions need to have the same consequences across work groups, or feelings of inequity and favoritism will pervade the organization. One way to increase the consistency in punishment is through the establishment of clearly specified organizational policies and procedures.

Administering punishment properly depends on effective two-way communication between the leader and follower. Leaders need to provide a clear rationale for punishment and indicate the consequences for unacceptable behavior in the future. Finally, leaders need to provide followers with guidance about how to improve. This guidance may entail role-modeling proper behaviors for followers, suggesting followers take additional training courses, or just giving followers accurate feedback about their behavior at work (Arvey & Ivancevich, 1980).

Overall, it may be the manner in which punishment is administered, rather than the level of punishment, that has the greatest effect on followers' satisfaction and performance. Leaders need to realize that they may be biased toward administering punishment to rectify followers' substandard performance, and the best way to get around this bias is to collect as much information as possible before deciding whether or not to punish. By collecting the facts, leaders will be better able to focus on the act, not the person; be able to administer a punishment consistent with company policy; provide the rationale for the punishment; and give guidance to followers on how to improve.

A final caution which leaders need to be aware of concerns the reinforcing or rewarding nature of punishment. As stated earlier in the discussion of the operant approach to motivation, behaviors that are rewarded are likely to be repeated. When leaders administer punishment and subsequently see improvement in a follower's behavior, the leader will be rewarded and be more apt to use punishment in the future. Over time, this may lead to an overreliance on punishment and an underemphasis of the other motivational strategies as the means for correcting performance problems. Again, by collecting as much information as possible and by carefully considering the applicability of goal setting, the operant approach, job characteristics theory, and so on, to the problem, leaders may be able to successfully avoid having only one tool in their motivational tool kit.

Conducting Meetings

Determine Whether It Is Necessary

List the Objectives

Stick to the Agenda

Provide Pertinent Materials in Advance

Make It Convenient

Encourage Participation

Keep a Record

Meetings are a fact of organizational life. It is difficult to imagine a leader who could (or should) avoid them, particularly when groups, committees, or teams have high levels of task or lateral interdependence. Well-planned and well-led meetings are a valuable mechanism for accomplishing diverse goals and are an important way of exchanging information and keeping open lines of communication within and between work groups or volunteer organizations (Bass, 1990; O'Reilly, 1977). Although meetings have many advantages, they also cost time and money. The annual cost of meetings in the corporate sector alone may well be in the billions of dollars. Furthermore, unnecessary or inefficient meetings can be frustrating and are often a source of dissatisfaction for participants. Given the investment of time and energy meetings require, leaders have a responsibility to make them as productive as possible. Guth and Shaw (1980) provided seven helpful tips for running meetings, which are discussed in the following paragraphs.

Determine Whether It Is Necessary

Perhaps the most important step in conducting a meeting is to take the time to *determine whether or not a meeting is really necessary*. If you are evaluating whether or not to have a meeting, assess what it can accomplish. Have a meeting only if the potential benefits outweigh the costs. As part of this process, get the opinions of the other participants beforehand if that is possible. Moreover, if meetings are regularly scheduled, then you should have significant business to conduct in each meeting. If not, then these meetings should probably be scheduled less frequently.

List the Objectives

Once you have decided that a meeting is necessary, you should then *list your objectives for the meeting and develop a plan for attaining them* in an orderly manner. Prioritize what you hope to accomplish at the meeting. It is often helpful to indicate approximately how much time will be spent on each agenda item. Finally, get the agenda and issues to be covered to the participants well in advance; also let them know who else will be attending.

Stick to the Agenda

Once the meeting gets started, is it important for leaders to *stick to the agenda*. It is easy for groups to get sidetracked by tangential issues or good-natured storytelling. Although you should try to keep a cooperative and comfortable climate in the meeting, it is better to err on the side of being organized and businesslike than being lax and laissez-faire. If items were important enough to put on the agenda, they are important enough to get to in the time allotted for the meeting.

Provide Pertinent Materials in Advance

Besides having an agenda, a meeting is often more effective if leaders also provide the other participants with *pertinent reports or support materials well in advance*. Passing out materials and waiting for people to read them at the meeting itself wastes valuable time. Most people will come prepared, having read relevant material beforehand, if you have given it to them, and almost everyone will resent making a meeting longer than necessary doing work that could and should have been done earlier. In a similar vein, prepare well in advance for any presentations you will make. If you did not provide reports before the meeting, then it is often helpful to provide an outline of your presentation for others to take notes on. Finally, of course, be sure the information you pass out is accurate.

Make It Convenient

Another way to maximize the benefits of meetings is to *pick a time and place as convenient as possible for all participants.* Besides maximizing attendance, this will also keep key participants from being distracted with thoughts of other pressing issues. Similarly, choose a place that is convenient for the participants and suitable for the nature of the meeting. Be sure to consider whether you need such things as a table for the meeting (with seating around it for all participants); a blackboard, an overhead projector, or similar audiovisual aids; coffee or other refreshments; and directions on how to find the meeting place. And start on time; waiting for stragglers is unfair to those who were punctual, and it sends the wrong signal about the seriousness of the meeting. Also plan and announce a time limit on the meeting beforehand and stick to it.

Encourage Participation

Leaders have a responsibility to *encourage participation;* everyone at the meeting should have an opportunity to be heard and should feel some ownership in the meeting's outcome. In some cases, you may need to solicit participation from quieter participants at the meeting, as these members often make valuable contributions to the group when given the chance. Furthermore, ensuring that the quieter members participate will also help you to avoid interpreting someone's quietness as implied consent or agreement. By the same token, you sometimes may need to curtail the participation of more verbal and outspoken participants. You can do this respectfully by merely indicating that the group has a good idea of their position and that it would be useful also to hear from some others. You also help encourage relevant participation by providing interim summaries of the group's discussion.

Keep a Record

During a meeting, the points of discussion and various decisions or actions taken may seem clear to you. However, do not trust your memory to preserve them all. *Take minutes for the record* so you and others can reconstruct what the participants were thinking and why you did or did not take some action. Record decisions and actions to be taken, including *who* will be responsible for doing it and *when* it is supposed to be accomplished. Such records are also very useful for preparing future meeting agendas.

By following the preceding simple steps, both leaders and followers are likely to get much more out of their meetings, as well as appear well organized and effective.

ADVANCED LEADERSHIP SKILLS

Delegating

Why Delegating Is Important
Common Reasons for Avoiding Delegation
Principles of Effective Delegation

Although delegation is a relatively simple way for leaders to free themselves of time-consuming chores; provide followers with developmental opportunities; and increase the number of tasks accomplished by the work group, team, or committee, delegation is often an overlooked and underused management option (Bass, 1990; Leana, 1986). Delegation implies that one has been empowered by one's leader, boss, or coach to take responsibility for completing certain tasks or engaging in certain activities (Bass, 1990). Delegation gives the responsibility for decisions to those individuals most likely to be affected by or to implement the decision, and delegation is more concerned with autonomy, responsibility, and follower development than with participation (Leana, 1987).

Research has shown that leaders who delegate authority more frequently often have higher-performing businesses (Miller & Toulouse, 1986), but followers are not necessarily happier when their leaders frequently delegate tasks (Stogdill & Shartle, 1955). Bass (1990) maintained that the latter findings were due to subordinates who felt they were (a) not delegated the authority needed to accomplish delegated tasks, (b) monitored too closely, or (c) only delegated tasks leaders did not want to do. Nevertheless, Wilcox (1982) showed that leaders who delegated skillfully had more satisfied followers than leaders who did not delegate well. Because leaders who delegate skillfully often have more satisfied and higher-performing work groups, teams, or committees, the following suggestions from Taylor (1989) are provided to help leadership practitioners delegate more effectively and successfully. Taylor provided useful ideas about why delegating is important, common reasons for avoiding delegation, and principles of effective delegation.

Why Delegating Is Important

Delegation Frees Time for Other Activities.   The essence of leadership is achieving goals through others, not trying to accomplish them by oneself. Learning to think like a leader partly involves developing a frame of mind wherein one thinks in terms of the whole group's or organization's capabilities and not just one's own. This requires a new frame of reference for many individuals, especially those whose past successes resulted primarily from personal achievement in interpersonally competitive situations. Still, leaders typically have so many different responsibilities they invariably must delegate some of them to others.

It is not just the mere quantity of work that makes delegation necessary. There is a qualitative aspect, too. Because leaders determine what responsibilities will be delegated, the process is one by which leaders can ensure that their time is allocated most judiciously to meet group needs. The leader's time is a precious commodity that should be invested wisely in those activities for which the leader is uniquely suited or situated to accomplish and that will provide the greatest long-term benefits to the group. What the leader *can* delegate, the leader *should* delegate.

Delegation Develops Followers.   Developing subordinates is one of the most important responsibilities any leader has, and delegating significant tasks to them is one of the best ways to support their growth. It does so by providing opportunities for initiative, problem solving, innovation, administration, and decision making. By providing practical experience in a controlled fashion, delegation allows subordinates the best training experience of all: learning by doing.

Delegation Strengthens the Organization.   Delegation is an important way to develop individual subordinates, but doing so also strengthens the entire organization. For one thing, an organization that uses delegation skillfully will be a motivating one to work in. Delegation sends an organizational signal that subordinates are trusted and their development is important. Moreover, skillful delegation inherently tends to increase the significance and satisfaction levels of most jobs, thus making subordinates' jobs better. Delegation also can be seen as a way of developing the entire organization, not just the individuals within it. To the extent that a whole organization systematically develops its personnel using delegation, its overall experience level, capability, and vitality increase. Finally, delegation stimulates innovation and generates fresh ideas and new approaches throughout the whole organization.

Common Reasons for Avoiding Delegation

Delegation Takes Too Much Time.   Delegation saves time for the leader in the long run, but it costs time for the leader in the short run. It takes time to train a subordinate to perform any new task, so it often really does take less time for a leader to do the task herself than to put in the effort to train someone else to do it. When a task is a recurring or repetitive one, however, the long-term savings will make the additional effort in initial training worth it—both for the leader and for the subordinate.

Delegation Is Risky.   It can feel threatening to delegate a significant responsibility to another person because doing so reduces direct personal control over the work one will be judged by (Dewhirst, Metts, & Ladd, 1987). Delegation may be perceived as a career risk by staking one's own reputation on the motivation, skill, and performance of others. It is the essence of leadership, though, that the leader will be evaluated in part by the success of the entire team. Furthermore, delegation need not and should not involve a complete loss of control by the leader over work delegated to others. The leader has a responsibility to set performance expectations, ensure that the task is understood and accepted, provide training, and regularly monitor the status of all delegated tasks and responsibilities (Bass, 1990).

The Job Will Not Be Done as Well.   Often the leader can do many specific tasks or jobs better than anyone else. That is not surprising, as the leader is often the most experienced person in the group. This fact, however, can become an obstacle to delegation. The leader may rationalize not delegating a task to someone else because the follower lacks technical competence and the job would subsequently suffer (Dewhirst, Metts, & Ladd, 1987). However, this may be true only in the short term, and letting subordinates make a few mistakes is a necessary part of their development, just as it was for the leader at an earlier stage in her own development. Few things are likely to be so stifling to an organization as a leader's perfectionistic fear of mistakes. When thinking about delegating tasks to others, leaders should remember what their own skill levels used to be, not what they are now. Leaders should assess subordinates' readiness to handle new responsibilities in terms of the former, not the latter.

The Task Is a Desirable One.   A leader may resist delegating tasks that are a source of power or prestige. He may be quite willing to delegate relatively unimportant responsibilities but may balk at the prospect of delegating a significant one having high visibility (Bass, 1990; Dewhirst, Metts, & Ladd, 1987). The greater the importance and visibility of the delegated task, though, the greater will be the potential developmental gains for the subordinate. Furthermore, actions always speak louder than words, and nothing conveys trust more genuinely than a leader's willingness to delegate major responsibilities to subordinates.

Others Are Already Too Busy.   A leader may feel guilty about increasing a subordinate's already full workload. It is the leader's responsibility, though, to continually review the relative priority of all the tasks performed across the organization. Such a review might identify existing activities that could be eliminated, modified, or reassigned. A discussion with the subordinate about her workload and career goals would be a better basis for a decision than an arbitrary and unilateral determination by the leader that the subordinate could not handle more work. The new responsibility could well be something the subordinate wants and needs, and she might also have some helpful ideas about alternative ways to manage her present duties.

Principles of Effective Delegation

Decide What to Delegate.   The first step leaders should take when deciding what to delegate is to identify all of their present activities. This should include those functions regularly performed and decisions regularly made. Next, leaders should estimate the actual time spent on these activities. This can be done fairly easily by developing and maintaining a temporary log. After collecting this information, leaders need to assess whether each activity justifies the time they are spending on it. In all likelihood, at least some of the most time-consuming recurring activities should be delegated to others. This process will probably also identify some activities that could be done more efficiently (either by the leader or someone else) and other activities that provide so little benefit they could be eliminated completely.

Decide Whom to Delegate To.   There might be one individual whose talent and experience makes her the logical best choice for any assignment. However, leaders must be careful not to overburden someone merely because that individual always happens to be the best worker. Additionally, leaders have a responsibility to balance developmental opportunities among all their followers. Leaders should look for ways to optimize, over a series of assignments, the growth of all subordinates by matching particular opportunities to their respective individual needs, skills, and goals.

Make the Assignment Clear and Specific.   As with setting goals, leaders delegating an assignment must be sure the subordinate understands just what the task involves and what is expected of him. Nevertheless, at times leaders provide too brief an explanation of the task to be delegated. A common communication error is overestimating one's own clarity, and in the case of delegation this can happen when the leader already knows the ins and outs of the particular task. Some of the essential steps or potential pitfalls in an assignment that seem self-evident to the leader may not be as obvious to someone who has never done the assignment before. Leaders should welcome questions and provide a complete explanation of the task. The time leaders invest during this initial training will pay dividends later on. When giving an assignment, leaders should ensure that they cover all of the points listed in Highlight D.1.

Points to Cover When Delegating a Task

Highlight D.1

How does the task relate to organizational goals?

When does the subordinate's responsibility for the task begin?

How has the task been accomplished in the past?

What problems were encountered with the task in the past?

What sources of help are available?

What unusual situations might arise in the future?

What are the limits of the subordinate's authority?

How will the leader monitor the task (e.g., provide feedback)?

Finally, in covering the above points, always convey high confidence and expectations.

Assign an Objective, Not a Procedure.   Indicate what is to be accomplished, not *how* the task is to be accomplished. End results are usually more important than the methods. It is helpful to demonstrate procedures that have worked before, but not to specify rigid methods to follow in the future. Leaders should not assume their ways always were and always will be best. Leaders need to be clear about the criteria by which success will be measured, but allowing subordinates to achieve it in their own ways will increase their satisfaction and encourage fresh ideas.

Allow Autonomy, but Monitor Performance.   Effective delegation is neither micromanagement of everything the subordinate does nor laissez-faire indifference toward the subordinate's performance. Leaders need to give subordinates a degree of autonomy (as well as time, resources, and authority) in carrying out their new responsibilities, and this includes the freedom to make certain kinds of mistakes. An organizational climate where mistakes are punished suppresses initiative and innovation. Furthermore, mistakes are important sources of development. Knowing this, one wise executive reassured a subordinate who expected to be fired for a gigantic mistake by saying, "Why should I fire you when I've just invested $100,000 in your development?" (McCall, Lombardo, & Morrison, 1988, p. 154).

Once a task has been delegated, even though the subordinate's training and development are continuing, the leader should be cautious about providing too much unsolicited advice or engaging in "rescue" activities. An exception would be when a subordinate's mistake would put significant organizational assets at risk. On the other hand, the leader needs to establish specific procedures for periodically reviewing the subordinate's performance of the delegated task. Leaders need to maintain good records of all the assignments they have delegated, including appropriate milestone and completion dates for each one.

Give Credit, Not Blame. Whenever leaders delegate, they must give subordinates *authority* along with responsibility. In the final analysis, however, leaders always remain fully responsible and accountable for any delegated task. If things should go wrong, then *leaders* should accept responsibility for failure fully and completely and never try to pass blame on to subordinates. On the other hand, if things go well, as they usually will, then leaders should give all the public credit to the subordinates. Also, when providing performance feedback privately to a subordinate, emphasize what went right rather than what went wrong. Leaders should not ignore errors in judgment or implementation, but they need not dwell on them, either. One helpful approach to performance feedback is called the sandwich technique. With this technique, negative feedback is placed in between two "pieces" of positive feedback. It affirms the subordinate's good work, puts the subordinate at least somewhat at ease, and keeps the ratio of positive and negative comments in balance. The idea of a sandwich, however, should not be taken too literally. There is nothing magical about two pieces of positive feedback for one piece of negative feedback. In fact, from the receiver's point of view the balance between positive and negative feedback may seem "about right" when the ratio is considerably higher than 2:1.

In summary, Taylor (1989) has provided useful insight about the importance of delegation as well as specific and helpful suggestions for delegating more effectively.

Managing Conflict

What Is Conflict?
Is Conflict Always Bad?
Conflict Resolution Strategies

We read or hear every day in the news about various types of negotiations. Nations often negotiate with each other over land or fishing rights, trade agreements, or diplomatic relations. Land developers often negotiate with city councils for variances on local zoning laws for their projects. Businesses often spend considerable time negotiating employee salaries and fringe benefits with labor unions. In a similar fashion, negotiations go on every day about matters ranging from high school athletic schedules to where a new office copying machine will be located. In one sense, all these negotiations, big or small, are similar. In every case, representatives from different groups meet to resolve some sort of conflict. Conflict is an inevitable fact of life and an inevitable fact of leadership. Researchers have found that first-line supervisors and middle-level managers can spend more than 25 percent of their time dealing with conflict (Thomas & Schmidt, 1976), and resolving conflicts has been found to be an important factor in leadership effectiveness (Morse & Wagner, 1978). In fact, successfully resolving conflicts is so important that it is a central theme in some of the literature about organizations (Brown, 1983; Ouchi, 1981; Peters & Waterman, 1982). Moreover, successfully resolving conflicts will become an increasingly important skill as leadership and management practice moves away from authoritarian directives and toward cooperative approaches emphasizing rational persuasion, collaboration, compromise, and solutions of mutual gain.

What Is Conflict?

There are times in life when we confront values worth fighting for. This is one such time.

George Bush (before the Allied attack on Iraq)
Time, January 21,1991.

Should the Americans become embroiled, we will make them swim in their own blood.

Saddam Hussein (before the Allied attack on Iraq)
Time, January 21, 1991.

Conflict occurs when two opposing parties have interests or goals that appear to be incompatible (Robbins, 1986). There are a variety of sources of conflict in team, committee, work-group, and organizational settings. For example, conflict can occur when group or team members *(a)* have strong differences in values, beliefs, or goals; *(b)* have high levels of task or lateral interdependence; *(c)* are competing for scarce resources or rewards; *(d)* are under high levels of stress; or *(e)* face uncertain or incompatible demands—that is, role ambiguity and role conflict (Yukl, 1989). Conflict can also occur when leaders act in a manner inconsistent with the vision and goals they have articulated for the organization (Kets de Vries & Miller, 1984). Of these factors contributing to the level of conflict within or between groups, teams, or committees, probably the most important source of conflict is the lack of communication between parties (Thomas & Schmidt, 1976). Because many conflicts are the result of misunderstandings and communication breakdowns, leaders can minimize the level of conflict within and between groups by improving their communication and listening skills, as well as spending time networking with others (Yukl, 1989).

Before reviewing specific negotiation tips and conflict resolution strategies, it is necessary to describe several aspects of conflict that can have an impact on the resolution process. First, the size of an issue (bigger issues are more difficult to resolve), the extent to which parties define the problem egocentrically (how much they have personally invested in the problem), and the existence of hidden agendas (unstated but important concerns or objectives) can all affect the conflict resolution process. Second, seeing a conflict situation in win–lose or either/or terms restricts the (perceived) possible outcomes to either total satisfaction or total frustration. A similar but less-extreme variant is to see a situation in zero-sum terms. A zero-sum situation is one in which intermediate degrees of satisfaction are possible (i.e., not either/or), but increases in one party's satisfaction inherently decrease the other party's satisfaction, and vice versa. Still another variant can be when parties perceive a conflict as unresolvable. In such cases neither party gains at the expense of the other, but each continues to perceive the other as an obstacle to satisfaction (Thomas, 1976).

Is Conflict Always Bad?

So far, we have described conflict as an inherently negative aspect of any group, team, committee, or organization. This certainly was the prevailing view of conflict among researchers during the 1930s and 1940s, and it probably also represents the way many people are raised today (i.e., most people have a strong value of minimizing or avoiding conflict). Today, researchers studying group effectiveness have come to a different conclusion. Some level of conflict may be helpful in order to bolster innovation and performance (Robbins, 1986). Conflict that enhances group productivity is viewed as useful, and conflict that hinders group performance is viewed as counterproductive (Robbins, 1986). Various possible positive and negative effects of conflict are listed in Highlight MC.1.

Along these lines, researchers have found that conflict can cause a radical change in political power (Bass, 1985; Weber, 1947; Willner, 1984), as well as dramatic changes in organizational structure and design, group cohesiveness, and group or organizational effectiveness (Roberts & Bradley, 1988; Kanter, 1983). Nevertheless, it is important to realize that this current conceptualization of conflict is still somewhat limited in scope. For example, increasing the level of conflict within a group or team may enhance immediate performance but may also have a disastrous effect on organizational climate and turnover. As we noted in

Possible Effects of Conflict

Highlight MC.1

Possible Positive Effects of Conflict	Possible Negative Effects of Conflict
Increased effort	Reduced productivity
Feelings get aired	Decreased communication
Better understanding of others	Negative feelings
Impetus for change	Stress
Better decision making	Poorer decision making
Key issues surfaced	Decreased cooperation
Critical thinking stimulated	Political backstabbing

FIGURE MC.1

Five conflict-handling orientations, plotted according to party's desire to satisfy own and other's concerns

Source: K. W. Thomas, "Conflict and Conflict Management," in *Handbook of Industrial and Organizational Psychology*, ed. M. D. Dunnette (Chicago: Rand McNally, 1976). Used by permission of Marvin D. Dunnette.

Chapter 4, however, leaders may be evaluated in terms of many criteria, only one of which is group performance. Thus, leaders should probably use criteria such as turnover and absenteeism rates and followers' satisfaction or organizational climate ratings in addition to measures of group performance when trying to determine whether conflict is good or bad. Leaders are cautioned against using group performance alone, as these indices may not reveal the overall effects of conflict on the group or team.

Conflict Resolution Strategies

In addition to spending time understanding and clarifying positions, separating people from the problem, and focusing on interests, there are five strategies or approaches leaders can use to resolve conflicts. Perhaps the best way to differentiate between these five strategies is to think of conflict resolution in terms of two independent dimensions: cooperativeness/uncooperativeness and assertiveness/unassertiveness (see Figure MC.1). Parties in conflict do vary in their commitment to satisfy the other's concerns, but they also vary in the extent to which they assertively stand up for their own concerns (Thomas, 1976). Thus, conflict resolution can be understood in terms of how cooperative or uncooperative the parties are and how assertive or unassertive they are.

Using this two-dimension scheme, Thomas (1976) described five general approaches to managing conflict:

1. **Competition** reflects a desire to achieve one's own ends at the expense of someone else. This is domination, also known as a win–lose orientation.

2. **Accommodation** reflects a mirror image of competition, entirely giving in to someone else's concerns without making any effort to achieve one's own ends. This is a tactic of appeasement.

3. **Sharing** is an approach that represents a compromise between domination and appeasement. Both parties give up something, yet both parties get something. Both parties are moderately, but incompletely, satisfied.

4. **Collaboration** reflects an effort to fully satisfy both parties. This is a problem-solving approach that requires the integration of each party's concerns.

5. **Avoidance** involves indifference to the concerns of both parties. It reflects a withdrawal from or neglect of any party's interests.

Does one of these approaches seem clearly a better method than the other to you? Each of them does, at least, reflect certain culturally valued modes of behavior (Thomas, 1977). For example, the esteem many people hold for athletic, business, and military heroes reflects our cultural valuation of competition. Valuation of a pragmatic approach to settling problems is reflected in the compromising approach. Cultural values of unselfishness, kindness, and generosity are reflected in accommodation, and even avoidance has roots in philosophies that emphasize caution, diplomacy, and turning away from worldly concerns. These cultural roots to each of the approaches to managing conflict suggest that no single one is likely to be the right one all the time. There probably are circumstances when each of the modes of conflict resolution can be appropriate. Rather than seeking to find some single best approach to managing conflict, it may be wisest to appreciate the relative advantages and disadvantages of all approaches, and the circumstances when each may be most appropriate. A summary of experienced leaders' recommendations for when to use each strategy is presented in Highlight MC.2 (Thomas, 1977).

Negotiation

Prepare for the Negotiation

Separate the People from the Problem

Focus on Interests, Not Positions

Negotiation is an approach that may help resolve some conflicts. The following negotiating tips, from Fisher and Ury (1981), include taking the time to prepare for a negotiating session; keeping the people and problems separate; focusing on issues, not positions; and seeking win–win outcomes.

Situations in Which to Use the Five Approaches to Conflict Management

Highlight MC.2

Competing

1. When quick, decisive action is vital—e.g., emergencies.
2. On important issues where unpopular actions need implementing—e.g., cost cutting, enforcing unpopular rules, discipline.
3. On issues vital to company welfare when you know you're right.
4. Against people who take advantage of noncompetitive behavior.

Collaborating

1. To find an integrative solution when both sets of concerns are too important to be compromised.
2. When your objective is to learn.
3. To merge insights from people with different perspectives.
4. To gain commitment by incorporating concerns into a consensus.
5. To work through feelings which have interfered with a relationship.

Compromising

1. When goals are important, but not worth the effort or potential disruption of more assertive modes.
2. When opponents with equal power are committed to mutually exclusive goals.
3. To achieve temporary settlements of complex issues.
4. To arrive at expedient solutions under time pressure.
5. As a backup when collaboration or competition is unsuccessful.

Avoiding

1. When an issue is trivial or more important issues are pressing.
2. When you perceive no chance of satisfying your concerns.
3. When potential disruption outweighs the benefits of resolution.
4. To let people cool down and regain perspective.
5. When gathering information supersedes immediate decision.
6. When others can resolve the conflict more effectively.
7. When issues seem tangential to or symptomatic of other issues.

Accommodating

1. When you find you are wrong—to allow a better position to be heard, to learn, and to show your reasonableness.
2. When issues are more important to others than yourself—to satisfy others and maintain cooperation.
3. To build social credits for later issues.
4. To minimize loss when you are outmatched and losing.
5. When harmony and stability are especially important.
6. To allow subordinates to develop by learning from mistakes.

Source: K. W. Thomas, "Toward Multidimensional Values in Teaching: The Example of Conflict Management," *Academy of Management Review* 2, no. 3 (1977), pp. 484–90. Used with permission.

Prepare for the Negotiation

To successfully resolve conflicts, leaders may need to *spend considerable time preparing for a negotiating session.* Leaders should anticipate each side's key concerns and issues, attitudes, possible negotiating strategies, and goals.

Separate the People from the Problem

Fisher and Ury (1981) also advised negotiators to *separate the people from the problem.* Because all negotiations involve substantive issues and relationships between negotiators, it is easy for these parts to become entangled. When that happens, parties may inadvertently treat the people *and* the problem as though they were the same. For example, a group of teachers angry that their salary has not been raised for the fourth year in a row may direct their personal bitterness toward the school board president. However, reactions such as these are usually a mistake, as the decision may be out of the other party's hands, and personally attacking the other party often only serves to make the conflict even more difficult to resolve.

There are several things leaders can do to separate the people from the problem. First, leaders should not let their fears color their perceptions of each side's intentions. It is easy to attribute negative qualities to others when one feels threatened. Similarly, it does no good to blame the other side for one's own problems (Blake, Shepard, & Mouton, 1964). Even if it is justified, it is still usually counterproductive. Another thing leaders can do to separate the people from the problem is to communicate clearly. Earlier in this text, we suggested techniques for active listening. Those guidelines are especially helpful in negotiating and resolving conflicts.

Focus on Interests, Not Positions

Another of Fisher and Ury's (1981) main points is to *focus on interests, not positions.* Focusing on interests depends on understanding the difference between interests and positions. Here is one example. Say Raoul has had the same reserved seats to the local symphony every season for several years and he was just notified he will no longer get his usual tickets. Feeling irate, he goes to the ticket office to complain. One approach he could take would be to demand the same seats he has always had; this would be his *position.* A different approach would be to find alternative seats that are just as satisfactory as his old seats had been; this would be his *interest.* In negotiating, it is much more constructive to satisfy interests than to fight over positions. Furthermore, it is important to focus both on your counterpart's interests (not position) and on your own interests (not position).

Finally, winning a negotiation at your counterpart's expense is likely to be only a short-term gain. Leaders should attempt to work out a resolution by looking at long-term rather than short-term goals, and they should try to build a working relationship that will endure and be mutually trusting and beneficial beyond the present negotiation. Along these lines, leaders should always seek win–win outcomes, which try to satisfy both sides' needs and continuing interests. It often takes creative problem solving to find new options that provide gains for both sides. Realistically, however, not all situations may be conducive to seeking win–win outcomes (see Highlight N.1).

Problem Solving

Identifying Problems or Opportunities for Improvement
Analyzing the Causes
Developing Alternative Solutions
Selecting and Implementing the Best Solution
Assessing the Impact of the Solution

Identifying Problems or Opportunities for Improvement

The first step in problem solving is to state the problem so that everyone involved in developing a solution has an informed and common appreciation and understanding of the task. This is a critical stage in problem solving and will take time and probably group discussion. It is dangerous to assume that everyone (or anyone!) knows at the outset what the problem is. A hurried or premature definition of the problem (e.g., as a result of groupthink) may lead to considerable frustration and wasted effort. In counseling and advising, for example, a significant portion of the work with a client is devoted to clarifying the problem. A student may seek help at the school counseling center to improve his study skills because he is spending what seems to be plenty of time studying yet is still doing poorly on

How to Swim with Sharks

Highlight N.1

It is dangerous to swim with sharks, but not all sharks are found in the water. Some people may behave like sharks, and a best-selling book for executives written a few years ago took its title from that theme. However, an article appeared in the journal *Perspectives in Biology and Medicine* nearly three decades ago claiming to be a translated version of an essay written in France more than a century earlier for sponge divers (Cousteau, 1973). The essay notes that while no one wants to swim with sharks, it is an occupational hazard for certain people. For those who must swim with sharks, it can be essential to follow certain rules. See if you think the following rules for interacting with the sharks of the sea serve as useful analogies for interacting with the sharks of everyday life.

Rule 1: *Assume any unidentified fish is a shark.* Just because a fish may be acting in a docile manner does not mean it is not a shark. The real test is how it will act when blood is in the water.

Rule 2: *Don't bleed.* Bleeding will prompt even more aggressive behavior and the involvement of even more sharks. Of course, it is not easy to keep from bleeding when injured. Those who cannot do so are advised not to swim with sharks at all.

Rule 3: *Confront aggression quickly.* Sharks usually give warning before attacking a swimmer. Swimmers should watch for indications an attack is imminent and take prompt counteraction. A blow to the nose is often appropriate since it shows you understand the shark's intentions and will respond in kind. It is particularly dangerous to behave in an ingratiating manner toward sharks. People who once held this erroneous view often can be identified by a missing limb.

Rule 4: *Get out of the water if anyone starts bleeding.* Previously docile sharks may begin attacking if blood is in the water. Their behavior can become so irrational, even including attacking themselves, that it is safest to remove yourself entirely from the situation.

Rule 5: *Create dissension among the attackers.* Sharks are self-centered and rarely act in an organized fashion with other sharks. This significantly reduces the risk of swimming with sharks. Every now and then, however, sharks may launch a coordinated attack. The best strategy then is to create internal dissension among them since they already are quite prone to it; often sharks will fight among themselves over trivial or minor things. By the time their internal conflict is settled, sharks often have forgotten about their organized attack.

Rule 6: *Never divert a shark attack toward another swimmer.* Please observe this final item of swimming etiquette.

examinations. A little discussion, however, may reveal that he is having difficulty concentrating on schoolwork because of problems at home. If the counselor had moved immediately to develop the client's study skills, the real cause of his difficulties would have gone untreated, and the client might have become even more pessimistic about his abilities and the possibility that others can help him. Or consider the case of a police chief who is concerned about the few volunteers willing to serve on a citizen's advisory committee to her department. There are many problems she might identify here, such as citizen apathy or poor publicity concerning the need and importance of the committee. The real problem, however, might be her own reputation for rarely listening to or heeding recommendations made by similar advisory committees in the past. If the chief were to take the time to explore and clarify the problem at the outset, then she *could* discover this important fact and take steps to solve the *real* problem (her own behavior). If, on the other hand, she pressed ahead aggressively, trusting her own appraisal of the problem, then nothing likely would change.

The reason it helps to take time to define a problem carefully is that sometimes people mistake symptoms for causes. In the case of the student, his poor studying was a symptom of another cause (family difficulties), not the cause of his poor grades. In the case of the police chief, lack of citizen participation on the advisory committee was a symptom of a problem, not the problem itself. If a plan addresses a symptom rather than the causes of a problem, the desired results will not be attained. It also is important during this stage to avoid scapegoating or blaming individuals or groups for the problem, which may just engender defensiveness and reduce creative thinking. This is a stage where conflict resolution techniques and negotiating skills can be very important. Finally, the statement of a problem should not imply that any particular solution is the correct one.

As an application of these considerations, let us consider two pairs of problem statements that a teacher might present to his class as a first step in addressing what he considers to be an unsatisfactory situation. These samples of dialogue touch on many aspects of communication, listening, and feedback skills addressed earlier in this book. Here, however, our focus is on differences in defining problems. In each case, the second statement is the one more likely to lead to constructive problem solving.

A: I don't think you care enough about this course. No one is ever prepared. What do I have to do to get you to put in more time on your homework?

B: What things are interfering with your doing well in this course?

A: Your test grades are too low. I'm going to cancel the field trip unless they improve. Do you have any questions?

B: I'm concerned about your test scores. They're lower than I expected them to be, and I'm not sure what's going on. What do you think the problem is?

Another aspect of this first stage of problem solving involves identifying those factors that, when corrected, are likely to have the greatest impact on improving an unsatisfactory situation. Since there are almost always more problems or opportunities for improvement than time or energy to devote to them all, it is crucial to identify those whose solutions offer the greatest potential pay-

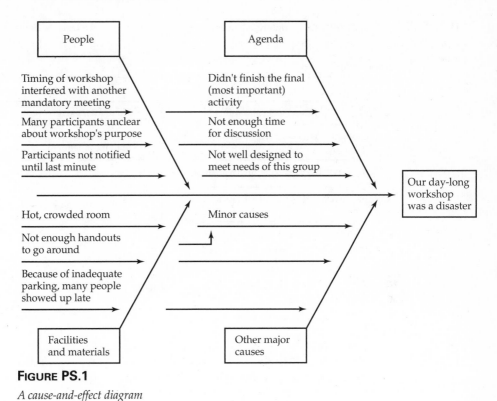

FIGURE PS.1

A cause-and-effect diagram

off. A useful concept here is known as the Pareto principle. It states that about 80 percent of the problems in any system are the result of about 20 percent of the causes. In school, for example, most of the discipline problems are caused by a minority of the students. Of all the errors people make on income tax returns, just a few kinds of errors (e.g., forgetting to sign them) account for a disproportionately high percentage of returned forms. We would expect about 20 percent of the total mechanical problems in a city bus fleet to account for about 80 percent of the fleet's downtime. The Pareto principle can be used to focus problem-solving efforts on those causes that have the greatest overall impact.

Analyzing the Causes

Once a problem is identified, the next step is to analyze its causes. Analysis of a problem's causes should precede a search for its solutions. Two helpful tools for identifying the key elements affecting a problem situation are the cause-and-effect diagram (also called the "fishbone" diagram because of its shape, or the Ishikawa diagram after the person who developed it) and force field analysis. The cause-and-effect diagram uses a graphic approach to depict systematically the root causes of a problem, the relationships between different causes, and potentially a prioritization of which causes are most important (see Figure PS.1).

FIGURE PS.2

*Force field
analysis
example:
Starting
personal
exercise
program*

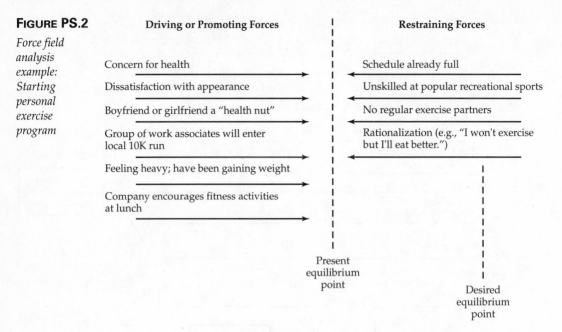

Force field analysis (see Figure PS.2) also uses a graphic approach, this time to depict the opposing forces that tend to perpetuate a present state of affairs. It is a way of depicting any stable situation in terms of dynamic balance, or equilibrium, between those forces that tend to press toward movement in one direction and those other forces that tend to restrain movement in that direction. So long as the net sum of all those forces is zero, no movement occurs. When a change is desirable, force field analysis can be used to identify the best way to upset the balance between positive and negative forces so that a different equilibrium can be reached.

Developing Alternative Solutions

Several ideas we've examined previously are relevant here (e.g., brainstorming), as is the importance of solutions meeting criteria for quality and acceptance. A procedure called Nominal Group Technique (NGT) is another way to generate a lot of ideas pertinent to a problem (Delbecq, Van de Ven, & Gustafson, 1975). This procedure is similar to brainstorming in that it is an idea-generating activity conducted in a group setting. With NGT, however, group members write down ideas on individual slips of paper, which are later transferred to a blackboard or flipchart for the entire group to work with.

Selecting and Implementing the Best Solution

The first solution one thinks of is not necessarily the best solution, even if everyone involved finds it acceptable. It is better to select a solution on the basis of established criteria. These include such questions as the following: Have the advantages and disadvantages of all possible solutions been considered? Have all the possible solutions been evaluated in terms of their respective impacts on the whole organization, not just a particular team or department? Is the information needed to make a good decision among the alternatives available?

Assessing the Impact of the Solution

One should not assume that just by going through the preceding steps the actions implemented will solve the problem. The solution's continuing impact must be assessed, preferably in terms of measurable criteria of success that all parties involved can agree on.

Improving Creativity

Seeing Things in New Ways
Using Power Constructively
Forming Diverse Problem-Solving Groups

Seeing Things in New Ways

There are several things leaders can do to increase their own and their followers' creativity. Some of these facilitating factors have already been discussed and include assuring adequate levels of technical expertise, delaying and minimizing the evaluation or judgment of solutions, focusing on the intrinsic motivation of the task, removing unnecessary constraints on followers, and giving followers more latitude in making decisions. One popular technique for stimulating creative thinking in groups is called brainstorming (see Highlight IC.1).

An additional thing leaders can do to enhance creativity is to *see things in new ways*, or to look at problems from as many perspectives as possible. This is, though, easier said than done. It can be difficult to see novel uses for things we are very familiar with, or to see such in novel ways. Psychologists call this kind of mental block functional fixedness (Duncker, 1945). Creative thinking depends on overcoming the functional fixedness associated with the rigid and stereotyped perceptions we have of the things around us.

One way to see things differently is to think in terms of analogies. Thinking in terms of analogies is a practical extension of Cronbach's (1984) definition of creativity—making fresh observations, or seeing one thing as something else. In this case, the active search for analogies is the essence of the problem-solving method. In fact, finding analogies is the foundation of a commercial creative-problem-solving approach called Synectics (W. J. J. Gordon, 1961). An actual example of use of analogies in a Synectics problem-solving group concerned designing a new roofing material that would adjust its color to the season,

Steps for Enhancing Creativity through Brainstorming

Highlight IC.1

Brainstorming is a technique designed to enhance the creative potential of any group trying to solve a problem. Leaders should use the following rules when conducting a brainstorming session:

1. Groups should consist of five to seven people: Fewer than five limits the number of ideas generated, but more than seven often can make the session unwieldy. It may be more important to carefully decide who should attend a session than how many people should attend.
2. Everybody should be given the chance to contribute. The first phase of brainstorming is idea generation, and members should be encouraged to spontaneously contribute ideas as soon as they get them. The objective in the first phase is quantity, not quality.
3. No criticism is allowed during the idea generation phase. This helps to clearly separate the activities of imaginative thinking and idea production from idea evaluation.
4. Freewheeling and outlandish ideas should be encouraged. With some modification, these ideas may be eventually adopted.
5. "Piggybacking" off others' ideas should be encouraged. Combining ideas or extending others' ideas often results in better solutions.
6. The greater the quantity and variety of ideas, the better. The more ideas generated, the greater the probability a good solution will be found.
7. Ideas should be recorded. Ideally, ideas should be recorded on a blackboard or butcher paper so that members can review all of the ideas generated.
8. After all of the ideas have been generated, each idea should be evaluated in terms of pros and cons, costs and benefits, feasibility, and so on. Choosing the final solution often depends on the results of these analyses.

Source: A. F. Osborn, *Applied Imagination* (New York: Scribner's, 1963).

turning white in the summer to reflect heat and black in the winter to absorb heat. The group's first task was to find an analogy in nature, and it thought of fishes whose colors change to match their surroundings. The mechanism for such changes in fish is the movement of tiny compartments of pigments closer to or farther away from the skin's surface, thus changing its color. After some discussion, the group designed a black roof impregnated with little white plastic balls which would expand when it is hot, making the roof lighter, and contract when it is cold, making the roof darker (W. J. J. Gordon, 1961).

Another way to see things differently is to try putting an idea or problem into a picture rather than into words. Feelings or relationships that have eluded verbal description may come out in a drawing, bringing fresh insights to an issue.

Using Power Constructively

In addition to getting followers to see problems from as many perspectives as possible, a leader can also *use her power constructively to enhance creativity.* As noted earlier, groups may suppress creative thinking by being overly critical or by passing judgment during the solution generation stage. This effect may be even more pronounced when strong authority relationships and status differences are present. Group members may be reluctant to take the risk of raising a "crazy" idea when superiors are present, especially if the leader is generally perceived as unreceptive to new ideas, or they may be reluctant to offer the idea if they believe others in the group will take potshots at it in front of the leader. Leaders who wish to create a favorable climate for fostering creativity need to use their power to encourage the open expression of ideas and to suppress uncooperative or aggressive reactions (overt or covert) between group members. Further, leaders can use their power to encourage creativity by rewarding successes and by not punishing mistakes. Leaders can also use their power to delegate authority and responsibility, relax followers' constraints, and empower followers to take risks. By taking these steps, leaders can help followers to build idiosyncratic credits, which in turn will encourage them to take risks and to be more creative. Along these same lines, the entire climate of an organization can be either more or less conducive to creative thinking, differences that may be due to the use of power within the organization. In an insightful turn of the familiar adage, "Power corrupts," Kanter (1982) noted how powerlessness also corrupts. She pointed out how managers who feel powerless in an organization may spend more energy guarding their territory than collaborating with others in productive action. The need to actively support followers' creativity may be especially important for leaders in bureaucratic organizations, as such organizations tend to be so inflexible, formalized, and centralized as to make many people in them feel relatively powerless.

Forming Diverse Problem-Solving Groups

Leaders can enhance creativity by *forming diverse problem-solving groups.* Group members with similar experiences, values, and preferences will be less likely to create a wide variety of solutions and more apt to agree on a solution prematurely than more diverse groups. Thus, selecting people for a group or committee with a variety of experiences, values, and preferences should increase the creativity of the group, although these differences may also increase the level of conflict within the group and make it more difficult for the leader to get consensus on a final solution. One technique for increasing group diversity and, in turn, creativity in problem-solving groups involves the use of the four preference dimensions of the Myers-Briggs Type Indicator (MBTI). Actual evidence to support this specific approach appears scanty (Thayer, 1988), but perhaps preferences only assume significance after certain other conditions for group creativity already have been met. For example, diversity cannot make up for an absence of technical expertise. Although the MBTI dimensions may be useful in selecting diverse groups, this instrument should only be used after ensuring that all potential members have high levels of technical expertise. Choosing members based solely on MBTI preferences ignores the crucial role that technical expertise and intrinsic motivation play in creativity. Another aspect of the relationship between creativity and leadership is described in Highlight IC.2.

Diagnosing Performance Problems in Individuals, Groups, and Organizations

Expectations

Capabilities

Opportunities

Motivation

In many ways leaders will only be as effective as the followers and teams they lead. Along these lines, one of the more difficult issues leaders must deal with is managing individuals or teams that are not performing up to expectations. What makes this issue even more difficult is that although the lack of performance may be obvious, the reasons for it may not. Leaders who correctly determine why a follower or team is exhibiting suboptimal performance are much more likely to implement an appropriate intervention to fix the problem. Unfortunately, many leaders do not have a model or framework for diagnosing performance problems at work, and as a result many do a poor job of dealing with problem performers. The model in Figure DPP.1 provides leaders with a pragmatic framework for understanding why a follower or team may not be performing up to expectations and what the leader can do to improve the situation. This model maintains that performance is a function of expectations, capabilities, opportunities, and motivation and integrates concepts discussed in more detail earlier in this book.

Figure DPP.1

A model of performance

Performance $= f$ (Expectations $\times$ Capabilities $\times$ Opportunities $\times$ Motivation)

The model is also a modification of earlier models developed by J. P. Campbell (1977), Campbell, McCloy, Oppler, and Sager (1993), and Ramstad and Boudreau (2000). As a multiplicative rather than a compensatory model, a deficit in any one component should result in a substantial decrement in performance that

Managing Creativity

Highlight IC.2

T. Hogan and Morrison (1993) maintained that people who are seen as more creative tend to have several distinguishing personality characteristics. In general, creative people are open to information and experience, have high energy, can be personally assertive and even domineering, react emotionally to events, are impulsive, are more interested in music and art than in hunting and sports, and finally are very motivated to prove themselves (i.e., are concerned with personal adequacy). Thus, creative people tend to be independent, willful, impractical, unconcerned with money, idealistic, and nonconforming. Given that these tendencies may not make them ideal followers, the interesting question raised by Hogan and Morrison is: How does one lead or manage creative individuals? This question becomes even more interesting when considering the qualities of successful leaders or managers. As discussed earlier, successful leaders tend to be intelligent, dominant, conscientious, stable, calm, goal-oriented, outgoing, and somewhat conventional. Thus, one might think that the personalities of creative followers and successful leaders might be the source of considerable conflict and make them natural enemies in organizational settings. Because many organizations depend on creativity to grow and prosper, being able to successfully lead creative individuals may be a crucial aspect of success for these organizations. Given that creative people already possess technical expertise, imaginative thinking skills, and intrinsic motivation, Hogan and Morrison suggested that leaders take the following steps to successfully lead creative followers:

1. Set goals. Because creative people value freedom and independence, this step will be best accomplished if leaders use a high level of participation in the goal-setting process. Leaders should ask followers what they can accomplish in a particular time frame.
2. Provide adequate resources. Followers will be much more creative if they have the proper equipment to work with, as they can devote their time to resolving the problem rather than spending time finding the equipment to get the job done.
3. Reduce time pressures, but keep followers on track. Try to set realistic milestones when setting goals, and make organizational rewards contingent on reaching these milestones. Moreover, leaders need to be well organized to acquire necessary resources and to keep the project on track.
4. Consider nonmonetary as well as monetary rewards. Creative people often gain satisfaction from resolving the problem at hand, not from monetary rewards. Thus, feedback should be aimed at enhancing their feelings of personal adequacy. Monetary rewards perceived to be controlling may decrease rather than increase motivation toward the task.

(continued)

5. Recognize that creativity is evolutionary, not revolutionary. Although followers can create truly novel products (such as the Xerox machine), often the key to creativity is continuous product improvement. Making next year's product faster, lighter, cheaper, or more efficient requires minor modifications that can, over time, culminate in major revolutions. Thus, it may be helpful if leaders think of creativity more in terms of small innovations than major breakthroughs.

Source: R. T. Hogan and J. Morrison, "Managing Creativity," in *Create & Be Free: Essays in Honor of Frank Barron*, ed. A. Montouri (Amsterdam: J. C. Gieben, 1993).

cannot be easily made up by increasing the other components. An example might help to illuminate this point. Recently one of the authors was asked to help the manager of a nuclear power plant fix several safety and operational issues affecting the plant. Apparently many plant personnel did not feel they had to comply with governmental regulations regarding the proper use of safety equipment. An investigation into the problem revealed that the expectations for compliance were clear, everyone had been trained on the proper use of safety equipment, and the equipment was readily available. However, many personnel felt the equipment and procedures were a nuisance and unnecessary. The plant manager's initial attempt to rectify this problem was to run all plant personnel through a three-day nuclear safety training program. Much to the manager's surprise, the training program actually appeared to have a negative impact on safety compliance! This was due to the fact that the underlying issue was not expectations, capabilities, or opportunities but rather motivation. Even if the staff had 30 days of training it still would not have positively affected motivation, which was the underlying barrier to performance. Because there were few if any positive or negative consequences for the staff for properly using the equipment, the problem did not improve until the manager implemented a system of rewards and punishments for safety compliance. A more thorough explanation of the components of the model and what leaders can do to improve performance can be found below.

Expectations

Performance problems often occur because individuals or groups do not understand what they are supposed to do. There are many instances where talented, skilled groups accomplished the wrong objective because of miscommunication or sat idly by while waiting for instructions that never arrived. It is the leader's responsibility for ensuring that followers understand their roles, goals, performance standards, and the key metrics for determining success. More information about goal setting and clarifying team goals and roles can be found in the "Setting Goals" and "The Building Blocks of Team Building" sections in Part V of this text.

Capabilities

Just because followers understand what they are supposed to do does not necessarily mean they can do it. Sometimes followers and teams lack the capabilities needed to achieve a goal or perform above expectations. Abilities and skills are the two components that make up capabilities. Ability is really another name for raw talent, and includes such individual difference variables as athleticism, intelligence, creativity, and personality traits. As such, abilities are characteristics that are relatively difficult to change with training. Because abilities are relatively insensitive to training interventions, sending people who lack the required abilities to more training or motivating them to work harder will have relatively little impact on performance. Instead, the best remedy for this situation is to select those individuals with the abilities needed for performance.

Although followers may have the raw talent needed to perform a task, they still may lack the skills needed to perform at a high level. Such is the case with many athletic teams or musical groups at the beginning of the season or when a work group gets a new set of equipment or responsibility for tasks they have no previous experience with. As discussed in the "Leadership Behavior" chapter (8), skills consist of a well-defined body of knowledge and a set of related behaviors. Unlike abilities, skills are very amenable to training, and leaders with high levels of relevant expertise may coach others in the development of skills, see that they are obtained in other ways on the job, or send their followers to training programs in order to improve followers' skill levels. More information about selecting people with the right abilities can be found in Chapter 4. See Chapters 3 and 9 and the sections on "Building Technical Competence," "Coaching," and "Development Planning" in Part V for more information on building skills.

Opportunities

Performance can also be limited when followers lack the resources needed to get the job done. At other times followers may lack the opportunity to demonstrate acquired skills. Such is the case when passengers are hungry but flight attendants do not have any meals to pass out during the flight. In this situation the flight attendants could have very high levels of customer service goals, capabilities, and motivation but will still not be able to satisfy customer needs. Leaders must ensure that followers and teams have the needed equipment, financial resources, and the opportunities to exhibit their skills if they want to eliminate this constraint on performance. More about opportunities can be found in The Building Blocks of Team Building section in Part V of this text.

Motivation

Many performance problems can be attributed to a lack of motivation. The two critical issues here are whether followers or groups choose to perform or exhibit the level of effort necessary to accomplish a task. If this does not occur, then the leader should first try to learn why people are unmotivated. Sometimes the task may involve risks the leader is not aware of. At other times individuals or groups may simply run out of steam to perform the task or there are few consequences for superior or unsatisfactory performance. Leaders have several options to resolve motivation problems in followers and teams. First, they can select followers who have higher levels of achievement or intrinsic motivation for the task. Second, they can set clear goals or do a better job providing feedback about performance. Third, they can reallocate work across the team or redesign the task to improve skill variety, task significance, and task identity. Fourth, they can restructure rewards and punishments so they are more closely linked to performance levels. See the "Motivation, Satisfaction, and Performance" chapter (9) for more information about motivating followers.

Concluding Comments on the Diagnostic Model

In summary, this model provides an integrative framework for many of the topics affecting performance previously reviewed in this text. It reviews some of the factors that affect performance and suggests ideas for rectifying performance problems. It should be emphasized, however, that this model only addresses follower, group, and organizational performance. Leaders need to be mindful that there are other desirable outcomes, too, such as organizational climate and job satisfaction, and that actions to increase performance (especially just in the short term) may adversely impact these other desirable outcomes.

Team Building for Work Teams

Team-Building Interventions
What Does a Team-Building Workshop Involve?
Examples of Interventions

Few activities have become more commonplace in organizations these days than "team-building workshops." One reason for this level of activity is the powerful shift that has occurred in the workplace from a focus primarily on individual work to team-centered work. Unfortunately, however, they do not always achieve their objectives. As noted earlier in this text, it doesn't make sense to hold teams responsible for work if nothing else in the organizational environment changes. Team-building interventions, at the team level, may help team members understand why they are having so much difficulty in achieving team objectives, and even suggest coping strategies for an intolerable situation. They are not, however, very likely to remove root causes of the problem. In order to better understand the importance of looking at teams this way, let's use an example of this kind of erroneous thinking from a quite different context.

Team-Building Interventions

Suppose you have decided that the next car you drive must have outstanding ride and handling characteristics. Some cars you test, such as some huge American-made automobiles, have outstanding ride characteristics, but you are not happy with their handling. They sway and "float" in tight slalom courses. Other cars you test have just the opposite characteristics. They are as tight and as stable as you could hope for in turns and stops, but their ride is so hard that your dental work is in serious jeopardy. But you do find one car that seems to meet your requirements. In fact, a Mercedes-Benz does provide both an extremely comfortable ride and tremendous road handling characteristics in high-performance situations. There is, however, one small problem. The Mercedes costs a lot of money up front—more than you are willing to put into this project. So you arrive at an alternative solution. You find a used Yugo, a little car built in Yugoslavia and no longer imported into the United States, largely because of inferior quality. But it is really cheap, and after purchasing it, you know you will have lots of money left over to beef up the suspension, steering, and braking systems to provide you with the Mercedes-Benz ride you really want.

Ludicrous! Obviously, you are never going to get a Mercedes-Benz ride unless you are willing to put in considerable money and effort *up front* rather than doing little up front and putting all your money into repair work. But that is precisely what many organizations are attempting to do with teams. They do not seem willing to create the conditions necessary for teamwork to occur naturally (a point we will discuss in the section "Team Building at the Top"), but when the teams struggle in a hostile environment, as they invariably will, the leaders seem more than willing to pour tremendous amounts of money into team-building interventions to fix the problem. (And there are lots of team-building consultants out there willing to take their money.) These types of team-building problems are those we would categorize as "top-down."

An equally vexing problem occurs when organizations are committed to teamwork, are willing to change structures and systems to support it, but are not committed to the "bottom-up" work that will be required. This is best illustrated in the rationale for team training shown in Figure TW.1. In our work with organizations, we are frequently asked to help teams that are struggling. In Figure TW.1

FIGURE TW.1

A rationale for individual, interpersonal, team, and organizational training

we would place these requests at the "TEAM" level, which is the third platform up from the bottom. We believe this type of intervention will work only if the team members have achieved a stable platform from which to work. In this case, that would include the two previous platforms in Figure TW.1. If the foundation is not well established, the solely team-based intervention often leads to intrateam competition or apathy and withdrawal.

As a basis for any work at the team level, individual team members must first be comfortable with themselves. They must be able to answer the questions, "What do *I* bring to the team?" and "What do *I* need from the team?" Not to answer these questions breeds inherent fear and mistrust. When these questions have been answered, team members are then in a position to begin dealing at the interpersonal level, where they may now comfortably ask, "What do *you* bring to the team and what do *you* need from the team?" Not to resolve these issues results in caution in dealing with other members, and interactions at the "polite-façade" level rather than at the level of truth and understanding. If the first- and second-level platforms are in place, a true team-building intervention can be useful. (Incidentally, just because team members have not stabilized themselves at levels 1 and 2 does not mean an intervention can not be conducted. Rather, it means a more extensive intervention will be required than a solely team-based effort.)

What Does a Team-Building Workshop Involve?

There are literally hundreds, if not thousands, of team-building interventions that are being conducted today. There are many good sources, such as the *Team and Organization Development Sourcebook*, which contain team-based activities such as conflict resolution, problem solving, development of norms, building trust, or goal setting, to name but a few. Rather than trying to describe all of these suggestions, however, we will give you a few recommendations that we have found to be useful and then share a few examples of interventions we have used.

At the Center for Creative Leadership, staff are frequently asked to design custom team interventions for mid- to upper-level teams. While we enter these design meetings with no agenda of activities, neither do we enter with a completely blank slate. We believe an intervention at the team level must meet three general requirements to be successful, and at least one activity must be included in the intervention pertaining to each of those three requirements.

The first requirement involves awareness raising. As we noted in our previous chapters, not all cultures are equally prepared or nurtured in the concepts of teamwork. In fact, many of the lessons we think we have learned about teams are incorrect. So we believe we need to dispel such myths and include a healthy dose of team-based research findings about how teams *really* work as a critical element of a workshop. Second, we need some diagnostic, instrument-based feedback so team members can have a reasonably valid map of where they and their teammates now are located. Finally, each intervention must include a practice field, to use Senge's (1990) term. Practice is necessary for athletic success, and it is necessary in organizations too. It would be foolish to design a whole new series of plays for a hockey team to implement, talk about them in the locker room, but never actually practice any of them before expecting the team to implement them in a game. Similarly, if you are asking people to change their behaviors in the way they interact to improve teamwork, then it is only fair to provide them with a practice field upon which they can test their new behaviors in a reasonably risk-free, protected environment. This is where experiential exercises can be extremely useful. And it is here that the quality of the team-building facilitator is most critical. Conducting a pencil-and-paper exercise in the classroom does not require the same facilitator skill set as that required to conduct, say, a team-rappelling exercise off the face of a cliff—few facilitators get those requirements wrong and we have seldom discovered problems here. Where we have seen a significant breakdown in facilitator skills is in being able to make the link between the exercise that is conducted and the real world in which the team will be asked to perform. Here facilitators must have not only a good sense of real-time team dynamics, but also a sense of the business in which the team operates. They must help the participants make the links back to team dynamics that occur on the manufacturing floor or in the boardroom, and this seems to be the skill that separates highly effective facilitators from the pack.

Examples of Interventions

Now let us provide a few examples of the range of interventions that can be included in team building. Ginnett (1984) conducted an intervention with three interdependent teams from a state youth psychiatric hospital. The teams included members of the administrative services, the professional staff, and the direct care providers. The members of each team were dedicated to their roles in providing high-quality service to the youths under their care, but the three groups experienced great difficulty in working with each other. Extensive diagnosis of the groups revealed two underlying problems. First, each group had a very different vision of what the hospital was or should be. Second, each of the groups defined themselves as "care givers," thus making it very difficult for them to ask others for help since, in their minds, asking for help tended to put them in the role of their patients. We conducted a series of workshops to arrive at a common vision for the hospital, but the second problem required considerably more work. Since the staff members needed to experientially understand that asking for help did not place them in an inherently inferior position, a "Wilderness Experience" was designed where the entire staff was asked to spend four days together in a primitive wilderness environment with difficult hiking, climbing, and mountaineering requirements. By the end of the experience, everyone had found an occasion to ask someone else for help. Even more important, everyone found that actually asking others for help—something they had previously resisted—moved the overall team much higher in its ability to perform. Considerable time was spent each evening linking the lessons of the day with the work in the hospital.

In one of the more interesting programs we've conducted, a team of senior executives spent a week together at a ranch in Colorado. Each morning, the team met for a series of awareness sessions and data feedback sessions. Afternoons were reserved by the chief operating officer for fun and relaxation, with the only requirement being that attendees participate in them as a team or subteams. As facilitators, we actively participated with the teams, and related their team experiences each day to the lessons of the next morning, and to challenges facing the team in its normal work. In interventions like this we have learned that team building can be fun, and that the venues for it are almost limitless. Second, we have learned that being able to observe and process team activity in a real-time mode is critical for team-building facilitators. There is no substitute for first-hand observation as a basis for discerning group dynamics and noting the variety of revealing behaviors that emerge in unstructured team activities.

The Building Blocks of Team Building

Purpose
Teamwork
Empowerment
Implications of the High Performance Team Model

As stated throughout this text, leadership is not an individual process. Rather, it involves influencing a group of people to pursue some type of overarching goal. From Chapter 10 we do know that teams vary on a number of important factors, such as group size, norms, development stages, and cohesion. We also know that leaders need to take these factors into consideration when creating and leading teams. The Team Effectiveness Leadership Model in Chapter 10 provides a very

FIGURE BBTB.1

*The high
performance
team model*

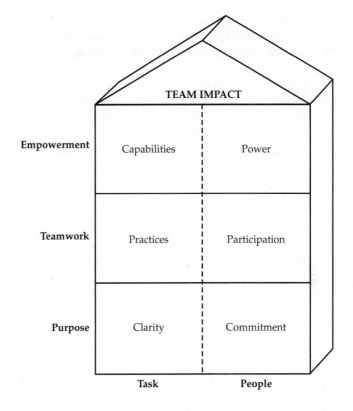

comprehensive description of team dynamics and what leaders must do if they want to create high performing teams. What follows is a description of a much simpler but perhaps more pragmatic model of team effectiveness. The **High Performance Team Model** (Quast, Hazucha, and Johnson, 1993; Curphy, 1999, 2000) provides leaders with an easy-to-follow road map for creating and leading teams. This model can also be used as a diagnostic tool for understanding where teams are falling short and what a leader needs to do to get a team back on track.

The High Performance Team Model is based on extensive research on teams in the pharmaceutical, retail, manufacturing, software, telecommunications, utilities, and financial services industries. The model has been used with executive level teams at The Home Depot and Level 3 Communications, midmanagement teams at 3M and Medtronic, and project teams at Qwest Communications and Hewlett-Packard. The model seems to work equally well with different types of teams and industries. Line managers in particular like the model because of its straightforward and pragmatic approach to team building.

A graphic of the High Performance Team Model can be found in Figure BBTB.1. As depicted in the graphic, building a team can be analogous to building a house. Just as builders start with the foundation when building a house, leaders need to start with the Clarity and Commitment components when building a team. Once the Clarity and Commitment components have been addressed, leaders should then work on the Practices and Participation components of the model, and so on. Research has shown that the teams with the most impact are usually those who report a high level of functioning on all six components of the High Performance Team Model. Teams reporting a high level of functioning in only some of the components often report mediocre performance, and those reporting a low level of functioning on all six components often have little if any impact on team goals. The model not only provides a road map for leaders when building a new team, it can also serve as a diagnostic model to understand where existing teams are falling short. The following is a more in-depth description of the seven components of the High Performance Team Model.

Purpose

When building a new team, the first thing a leader needs to do to work with the team is to clarify the overall vision or mission, outline team objectives, determine team member roles and set high performance standards, and ensure that individual goals roll up to overall team objectives. Thus the **Clarity** component of the High Performance Team Model is concerned with setting a common direction for the team. Like the notion of organizational shells, in some cases the leader works closely with team members to work out these issues; in other cases the leader may make these determinations; and in some other cases the organization may make these decisions. For this component of the model, who makes these decisions is not as important as ensuring that everyone on the team understands what the team is trying to accomplish and how they personally contribute to team success. Teams with this common understanding often experience lower levels of role ambiguity and conflict.

If we were to apply the High Performance Team Model to a learning team in a Leadership course, then the first thing the team should do is to clarify what the team wants to accomplish. This might include such things as everyone on the team getting an A on the midterm, final exam, and overall course. Once the overall mission and team objectives are determined, the learning team would then need to decide who would do what and what the performance standards would be for each team member.

The next component of the model is **Commitment.** Just because team members understand the team's mission and objectives and their roles doesn't necessarily mean they will automatically buy in to them. Teams with high levels of commitment have team members who believe in what the team is trying to accomplish and enthusiastically pursue their individual roles and goals. Teams with lower commitment often have team members who may explicitly agree with the team's objectives and roles but do little to ensure these objectives are achieved. Because people prefer to make choices as opposed to being told what to do, one way to enhance team commitment is to involve team members in the team clarity process. Having input into what the team is trying to accomplish, team roles, and performance standards can go a long way toward improving team commitment. Nevertheless, leaders who set the overall mission, goals, and roles for a team can generate high levels of team commitment, provided team members see them as having a high degree of relevant experience, credibility, and respect.

In our learning team example, team commitment would likely be enhanced if the team got together and jointly determined their mission, objectives, roles and goals. Team commitment might be somewhat lower if the instructor determined the learning team's mission, objectives, and individual team member goals and roles. Because Clarity and Commitment are the foundational components of the High Performance Team Model, leaders must ensure that these components are adequately addressed before working to improve the other components of the model. Many teams in the corporate world fail because team members are unclear of what the team is trying to accomplish, or what their role is on the team, or are not particularly committed to team success.

Teamwork

If team members have a clear understanding and are committed to what the team is trying to accomplish, leaders then need to address the **Practices** component of the High Performance Team Model. This component of the model is concerned with determining how work should actually get done within the team. Some of the issues to be addressed here include decision making, workflow processes, internal communication processes, feedback loops, the frequency and content of team meetings, and so forth. Many of these issues concern authority dynamics, setting team norms, maximizing social facilitation, and minimizing process loss. In the learning team example, the team would need to decide how they would prepare for the midterm exam, what the format and quality of the prep materials should be, how often and where they would meet to prepare for the exam, what they would do both in and outside of the preparation meetings, and how they would use the results of the midterm exams to adjust their preparation for the final exam. Corporate teams often fail because they do not explicitly set decision-making, meeting, or communication norms or ask themselves if the processes they have adopted are still working or need to be improved.

Just because individual team members understand what the team is trying to accomplish, are committed to achieving team objectives, and understand how the team gets work done doesn't necessarily mean they will all get along with each other. Teams that report high levels of **Participation** tend to effectively deal with interpersonal conflict and have high levels of morale and cohesion. This does not mean that highly cohesive teams do not experience interpersonal conflict. Instead, teams with high Participation scores have learned how to get conflict out in the open and deal with it in an effective manner. One way leaders can improve Participation is to work with team members to determine the rules or norms for addressing team conflict. On the other hand, some of the best techniques for destroying team morale are for leaders to either ignore interpersonal conflict or simply tell people to "quit fighting and just get along." Because of personality conflicts, work load inequities, miscommunication, and unfulfilled expectations, it is highly likely that our learning team will experience some level of interpersonal conflict. If the learning team wanted to improve cohesiveness, then it would have to discuss how they were going to address conflict in the group. These discussions should happen relatively early in the group's formation and team conflict should be a regular topic at team meetings.

Empowerment

Teams with too many or few people or with team members lacking needed skills often report lower **Capabilities** scores than teams having the right number of people with the right skills. Selecting the right kinds of people and continuously developing their skills are two key leadership activities in this component of the model. In the learning team example, Capabilities would come into play if team leaders selected their teammates and then worked to improve their test preparation and test-taking skills. If the leader were to do this right, then they should pick people with proven track records (i.e., high GPAs) who also get along with others. They would then need to assess what skills team members still needed to develop and work to ensure that the team improved in these areas. The latter could be accomplished through coaching, training programs, practice sessions, and so on. Of course, this scenario assumes the leader gets to pick the team members. Many times leaders do not have this luxury. This situation places even more importance on assessing and developing team member skills.

The **Power** component of the High Performance Team Model concerns the latitude and resources the team has to make decisions. Teams reporting high levels of power have considerable decision-making autonomy and all of the equipment, facilities, or funds they need to get things done. They also consist of team members who are highly confident that the team can accomplish its goals and objectives. Teams with low Power often lack necessary equipment and funding, have little decision-making authority, and often consist of team members who lack confidence in the team's ability to accomplish its objectives. To improve this component of the model, team leaders need to work stakeholders and decision-makers outside the team in order to secure needed resources and expand the decision-making authority of the team. They will also need to exhibit a positive, "can do" attitude as a role model for the rest of the team. The leader of the learning team may need to secure a room or facility in order to conduct study sessions, computer resources for team members, or even work with the instructor to see if the team could take group rather than individual exams. The learning team leader would also need to express optimism and confidence in the team as it works toward team goals.

Some teams are very successful, whereas others have a very difficult time accomplishing team objectives. **Impact** is a measure of the quality and quantity of team outputs and is usually tied to team objectives. Teams producing more high-quality goods and services have more impact than those who produce lower quality and quantities of goods and services. Therefore, learning teams achieving high grades in the Leadership course would have more impact than those receiving lower grades. It is important to note that leaders cannot directly affect Impact. Instead, leaders must optimize the other six components of the High Performance Team Model if they wish to maximize team outputs.

Implications of the High Performance Team Model

There are several interesting implications of the High Performance Team Model. First, many corporate teams report having very low Participation scores and often take some kind of action to improve team morale. Usually these actions include sending the team to some kind of conflict management or experiential course. In almost all cases these interventions have little if any long-term effect on team morale, the reason being that the Participation component is often a symptom of a deeper team problem. If the team is not getting along, it often is the result of unclear goals and objectives; a lack of buy-in; poor communication or decision-making processes; or a lack of skills or resources. When team morale is low, leaders should look at the other components of the model to determine root causes.

Second, when building a new team or determining where an existing team is falling short, leaders should always start with the Clarity and Commitment components before moving to the other parts of the model. Just as a house needs a solid foundation, so does a team need a solid foundation to be successful. Along these lines, the Team Assessment Survey (Curphy, 2000) was designed to provide teams with feedback on where they stand with respect to the six components of the High Performance Team Model. The results of the survey provide teams with both normative data and insights about which team components need to be improved if they want to enhance their overall impact. A copy of the Team Assessment Survey can be found in the Instructor's Manual.

Third, the components of the High Performance Team Model roughly correspond to Tuckman's (1965) four development stages of groups. According to Tuckman, forming is the first stage teams go through. Team leaders can help teams to successfully work through this stage by focusing on the Clarity and Commitment phases of the High Performance Team Model. Tuckman maintained that teams then go into the storming phase, during which team leaders should concentrate on the Practices and Participation components of the model. Team leaders should focus on the Capabilities and Power components when teams are in the norming phase, and the performing phase corresponds to the Impact component of the High Performance Team Model.

Team Building at the Top

Executive Teams Are Different
Applying Individual Skills and Team Skills
Tripwise Lessons

In certain ways, executive teams are similar to any other teams. For example, just about any group of senior executives that has faced a dire crisis and survived will note that teamwork was essential for their survival. In a nutshell, then, *when teamwork is critical,* all the lessons of the previous section apply. More specifically, to really be able to benefit from a team-building intervention, individual members must be comfortable with their own strengths and weaknesses and the strengths and weaknesses of their peers. But this raises a question: If all this is true, why do we include a separate section on team building for top teams? Because there are two critical differences between most teams and "teams at the top" that should be addressed.

Executive Teams Are Different

As opposed to other kinds of work teams, not all the work at the executive level requires all (or even any) of the team to be present. An example might help. In our research on teams we studied the air crews who fly the B-1 bomber. These are four-person teams comprising an aircraft commander, a copilot, an offensive systems officer, and a defensive systems officer. While each has individual responsibilities, in every single bombing run we observed, it was absolutely essential that the team work together to accomplish the mission. They had all of the components of a true team (complex and common goal, differentiated skills, interdependence), and no individual acting alone could have achieved success. But this is not always the case for executive teams.

As Katzenbach (1998) has observed, many top leadership challenges do not really require teamwork at all. Furthermore, many top leadership challenges that do constitute real team opportunities do not require or warrant full involvement by everyone who is officially on the team. In fact, an official "team at the top" rarely functions as a collective whole involving all the formal members. Thus, the real trick for executive teams is to be able to apply both the technical individual skills that probably got the individuals to the team in the first place *and* the skills required for high-performance teamwork when a team situation presents itself.

Applying Individual Skills and Team Skills

There are two critical requirements if this is to work. First, one must have the diagnostic skills to discern whether the challenge presenting itself involves an individual situation or a team situation. Then, it requires that leaders "stay the course" when a team situation is present. This means, for example, when pressure for results intensifies, not slipping back into the traditional modes of assigning work to an individual (e.g., one member of that top team), but rather allowing the team to complete the work *as a team.* Again, Katzenbach (1998) stated this clearly:

> Some leadership groups, of course, err in the opposite way, by attempting to forge a team around performance opportunities that do not call for a team approach. In fact, the increasing emphasis that team proponents place on "team-based organizations" creates real frustrations as top leadership groups try to rationalize good executive

leadership instincts into time-consuming team building that has no performance purpose. Catalyzing real team performances at the top does not mean replacing executive leadership with executive teams; it means being rigorous about the distinction between opportunities that require single-leader efforts and those that require team efforts—and applying the discipline that fits.

To summarize this point, executives do not always need to perform as a team to be effective. But when they do need to perform as a team, the same lessons of team building discussed earlier can be very useful in helping them to enhance their team performance.

The second difference with executive teams is that they have an opportunity to enhance teamwork throughout their organization that few others have. It is our experience that *only the executive team can change organizational systems.* Recall from a chapter earlier in the book that we described the Team Effectiveness Leadership Model and mentioned there were four system issues critical to team performance. These systems were all located at the organizational level and consisted of reward systems, education systems, information systems, and control systems. The impact of these systems can be so pervasive across the entire organization that a small change in a system can have monumental impact in the organization. In a sense, then, the executive team has within its control the power to do widespread "team building" in a very different manner than we have discussed to this point. Just consider the impact of changing a compensation system (one element of a reward system) from an individual-based bonus plan to a team-based bonus plan!

Tripwire Lessons

Finally, our experience in working with executives has taught us that leaders at this level have some important lessons to learn about team building at the top. Richard Hackman, in preparing the huge editorial task of having many people produce one coherent book (by his own admission, not necessarily the best of team tasks), assembled the various authors at a conference center. As one of the contributors, one of this text's authors (RCG) recalls a most frustrating task of attempting to put together the simple checklist of steps to ensure a team developed properly. As this arduous process dragged on and tempers flared, it became obvious that "Teamwork for Dummies" was never going to emerge. But something else did start to emerge. It became clear *that some behaviors leaders engaged in could virtually guarantee failure for their teams.* While not our intent, this experience yielded a worthwhile set of lessons. A condensed version of those lessons, labeled "tripwires" by Hackman (1990), concludes our discussion of team building at the top.

Trip Wire 1: Call the Performing Unit a Team but Really Manage Members as Individuals. One way to set up work is to assign specific responsibilities to specific individuals and then choreograph individuals' activities so their products coalesce into a team product. A contrasting strategy is to assign a team responsibility and accountability for an entire piece of work and let members decide among themselves how they will proceed to accomplish the work. While either of these strategies can be effective, a choice must be made between them. A mixed model, in which people are *told* they are a team but are *treated* as individual performers with their own specific jobs to do, sends mixed signals to members, is likely to confuse everyone, and in the long run is probably untenable.

To reap the benefits of teamwork, one must actually build a team. Calling a set of people a team or exhorting them to work together is insufficient. Instead, explicit action must be taken to establish the team's boundaries, to define the task as one for which members are collectively responsible and accountable, and to give members the authority to manage both their internal processes and the team's relations with external entities such as clients and co-workers. Once this is done, management behavior and organizational systems gradually can be changed as necessary to support teamwork.

Trip Wire 2: Create an Inappropriate Authority Balance.   The exercise of authority creates anxiety, especially when one must balance between assigning a team authority for some parts of the work and withholding it for other parts. Because both managers and team members tend to be uncomfortable in such situations, they may collude to "clarify" them. Sometimes the result is the assignment of virtually all authority to the team—which can result in anarchy or a team that heads off in an inappropriate direction. At other times, managers retain virtually all authority, dictating work procedures in detail to team members and, in the process, losing many of the advantages that can accrue from teamwork. In both cases, the anxieties that accompany a mixed model are reduced, but at significant cost to team effectiveness.

To achieve a good balance of managerial and team authority is difficult. Moreover, merely deciding how much authority will be assigned to the group and how much will be retained by management are insufficient. Equally important are the domains of authority that are assigned and retained. Our findings suggest that managers should be unapologetic and insistent about exercising their authority about *direction*—the end states the team is to pursue—and about *outer-limit constraints* on team behavior—the things the team must always do or never do. At the same time, managers should assign to the team full authority for the *means* by which it accomplishes its work—and then do whatever they can to ensure that team members understand and accept their responsibility and accountability for deciding how they will execute the work.

Few managerial behaviors are more consequential for the long-term being of teams than those that address the partitioning of authority between managers and teams. It takes skill to accomplish this well, and it is a skill that has emotional and behavioral as well as cognitive components. Just knowing the rules for partitioning authority is insufficient; one also needs some practice in applying those rules in situations where anxieties, including one's own, are likely to be high. Especially challenging for managers are the early stages in the life of a team (when managers often are tempted to give away too much authority) and when the going gets rough (when the temptation is to take authority back too soon). The management of authority relations with task-performing teams is indeed much like walking a balance beam, and our evidence suggests that it takes a good measure of knowledge, skill, and perseverance to keep from falling off.

Trip Wire 3: Assemble a Large Group of People, Tell Them in General Terms What Needs to Be Accomplished, and Let Them "Work Out the Details." Traditionally, individually focused designs for work are plagued by constraining structures that have built up over the years to monitor and control employee behavior. When groups are used to perform work, such structures tend to be viewed as unnecessary bureaucratic impediments to team functioning. Thus, just as managers sometimes (and mistakenly) attempt to empower teams by relinquishing all authority to them, so do some attempt to get rid of the dysfunctional features of existing organizational structures simply by taking down all the structures they can. Apparently, the hope is that removing structures will release teams and enable members to work together creatively and effectively.

Managers who hold this view often wind up providing teams with less structure than they actually need. Tasks are defined only in vague, general terms. Group composition is unclear or fluid. The limits of the team's authority are kept deliberately fuzzy. The unstated assumption is that there is some magic in the group interaction process and that, by working together, members will evolve any structures that the team actually needs.

It is a false hope; there is no such magic. Indeed, our findings suggest the opposite: groups that have appropriate structures tend to develop healthy internal processes, whereas groups with insufficient or inappropriate structures tend to have process problems. Worse, coaching and process consultation are unlikely to resolve these problems, precisely because they are rooted in the team structure. For members to learn how to interact well within a flawed or underspecified structure is to swim upstream against a very strong current.

Trip Wire 4: Specify Challenging Team Objectives, but Skimp on Organizational Supports. Even if a work team has clear, engaging direction and an enabling structure, its performance can go sour—or, at least, it can fall below the group's potential—if the team is not well supported. Teams in high-commitment organizations (Walton, 1985) fall victim to this trip wire when given "stretch" objectives but not the wherewithal to accomplish them; high initial enthusiasm soon changes into disillusionment.

It is no small undertaking to provide these supports to teams, especially in organizations designed to support work by individuals. Corporate compensation policy, for example, may make no provision for team bonuses and, indeed, may explicitly prohibit them. Human resource departments may be primed to identify individuals' training needs and provide first-rate courses to fill those needs, but training in team skills may not be available at all. Existing performance appraisal systems, which may be state-of-the-art for measuring individual contributions, are likely to be wholly inappropriate for assessing and rewarding work done by teams. Information systems and control systems may provide managers with the data they need to monitor and control work processes, but they may be neither available nor appropriate for use by work teams. Finally, the material resources required for the work may have been prespecified by those who originally designed it, and there may be no procedure in place for a team to secure the special configuration of resources it needs to execute the particular performance strategy it has developed.

To align existing organizational systems with the needs of teams often requires managers to exercise power and influence upward and laterally in the organization.

An organization set up to provide teams with full support for their work is noticeably different from one whose systems and policies are intended to support and control individual work, and many managers may find the prospect of changing to a group-oriented organization both unsettling and perhaps even vaguely revolutionary.

It is hard to provide good organizational support for task-performing teams, but generally it is worth the trouble. The potential of a well-directed, well-structured, well-supported team is tremendous. Moreover, to stumble over the organizational support trip wire is, perhaps, the saddest of all team failures. When a group is both excited about its work and all set up to execute it superbly, it is especially shattering to fail merely because the organizational supports required cannot be obtained. It is like being all dressed up and ready to go to the prom only to have the car break down en route.

Trip Wire 5: Assume That Members Already Have All the Competence They Need to Work Well as a Team.   Once a team is launched and operating under its own steam, managers sometimes assume their work is done. As we have seen, there are indeed some good reasons for giving a team ample room to go about its business in its own way: inappropriate or poorly timed managerial interventions impaired the work of more than one group in our research. However, a strict, hands-off managerial stance also can limit a team's effectiveness, particularly when members are not already skilled and experienced in teamwork.

Development Planning

Conducting a GAPS Analysis

Identifying and Prioritizing Development Needs: Gaps of GAPS

Bridging the Gaps: Building a Development Plan

Reflecting on Learnings: Modifying Development Plans

Transfer Learnings to New Environments

Change before you have to.

Jack Welch
General Electric CEO

Development planning is the systematic process of building knowledge and experience or changing behavior. Two people who have done a considerable amount of cutting-edge research in the development-planning process are Peterson and Hicks (1995). These two researchers believe development planning consists of five interrelated phases. The first phase of development planning is identifying development needs. Here leadership practitioners identify career goals, assess their abilities in light of career goals, seek feedback about how their behaviors are affecting others, and review the organizational standards pertaining to their career goals. Once this information has been gathered, the second phase consists of analyzing this data to identify and prioritize development needs. The prioritized development needs in turn are used to create a highly focused and achievable development plan, the third phase of this process. To help ensure permanent behavioral change takes place, the plan itself must utilize many of the best-practices techniques described in Chapter 8. Some of these best practices include having a plan that is limited to no more than two or three objectives, that capitalizes on on-the-job activities, and that incorporates multiple sources of feedback. The fourth phase in development planning is periodically reviewing the plan, reflecting on learnings, and modifying or updating the plan as appropriate. As you might expect, the Action-Observation-Reflection (AOR) model, described in Chapter 3, is a key component during this phase of the development planning process. The last phase in development planning is transferring learnings to new environments. Just because a leadership practitioner can successfully delegate activities to his 3-person team may not mean he will effectively delegate tasks or utilize his staff efficiently when he is leading a group of 25 people. In that case, the leader will need to build and expand on the delegation skills he learned when leading a much smaller team. These five phases are well grounded in research—Hazucha, Hezlett, and Schneider (1993), Peterson (1993b), and Hezlett and Koonce (1995) show that approximately 75 percent of the leadership practitioners adopting these phases were successful in either changing their behaviors permanently or developing new skills. Because these five phases are so important to the development planning process, the remainder of this section will describe each phase in more detail.

Conducting a GAPS Analysis

The first phase in the development-planning process is to conduct a GAPS (Goals, Abilities, Perceptions, Standards) analysis. A GAPS analysis helps leadership practitioners to gather and categorize all pertinent development planning information. A sample GAPS analysis for an engineer working in a manufacturing company can be found in Figure DP.1. This individual wants to get promoted to a first-line supervisor position within the next year, and all of the information pertinent to this promotion can be found in her GAPS analysis. The specific steps for conducting a GAPS analysis are as follows:

- *Step 1: Goals.* The first step in a GAPS analysis is to clearly identify what you want to do or where you want to go with your career over the next year or so. This does not necessarily mean moving up or getting promoted to the next

FIGURE DP.1

A sample GAPS analysis

Sources: D. B. Peterson and M. D. Hicks, *Leader as Coach* (Minneapolis: Personnel Decisions International, 1996); and G. J. Curphy, *Career and Development Planning Workshop: Planning for Individual Development* (Minneapolis: Personnel Decisions International, 1998).

Goals: Where do you want to go?	Abilities: What can you do now?
Step 1: Career objectives: Career strategies:	*Step 2:* What strengths do you have for your career objectives? *Step 3:* What development needs will you have to overcome?
Standards: What does your boss or the organization expect?	Perceptions: How do others see you?
Step 5: Expectations:	*Step 4:* 360 and Performance Review Results, and feedback from others: • *Boss* • *Peers* • *Direct Reports*

level. An alternative career objective might be to master one's current job, as you may have just gotten promoted and advancing to the next level is not as important at the moment. Other career objectives might include taking on more responsibilities in your current position, taking a lateral assignment in another part of the company, taking an overseas assignment, or even cutting back on job responsibilities to gain more work-life balance. This latter career objective may be very appropriate for leaders who are just starting a family or are taking care of loved ones who are suffering from poor health. The two most important aspects of this step in the GAPS analysis are that leadership practitioners will have a lot more energy to work on development needs that are aligned with career goals, and in many cases advancing to the next level may not be a viable or particularly energizing career goal. This latter point may be especially true with organizations that have been recently downsized.

Management positions often bear the brunt of downsizing initiatives, resulting in fewer available positions for those wishing to advance.

- *Step 2: Abilities.* People bring a number of strengths and development needs to their career goals. Over the years, you may have developed specialized knowledge or a number of skills that have helped you to be successful in your current and previous jobs. Similarly, you may also have received feedback over the years that there are certain skills you need to develop or behaviors you need to change. Good leaders know themselves—over the years they know which strengths they need to leverage and which skills they need to develop.
- *Step 3: Perceptions.* The perceptions component of the GAPS model concerns how your abilities, skills, and behaviors impact others. What are others saying about your various attributes? What are their reactions to both your strengths and your development needs? A great way of obtaining this information is by asking others for feedback or through performance reviews or 360-degree feedback instruments.
- *Step 4: Standards.* The last step in a GAPS analysis concerns the standards your boss or the organization has for your career objectives. For example, your boss may say that you may need to develop better public speaking, delegation, or coaching skills before you can get promoted. Similarly, the organization may have policies stating that people in certain overseas positions must be proficient in the country's native language, or it may have educational or experience requirements for various jobs.

When completing a GAPS analysis you may discover that you do not have all the information you need. If you do not, then you need to get it before you complete the next step of the development-planning process. Only you can decide upon your career objectives, but you can solicit advice from others on whether these objectives are realistic given your abilities, the perceptions of others, and organizational standards. You may find that your one-year objectives are unrealistic given your development needs, organizational standards, or job opportunities. In this case, you may need to either reassess your career goals or consider taking a number of smaller career steps that will ultimately help you achieve your career goal. If you are lacking information about the other quadrants, then you can ask your boss or others whose opinions you value about your abilities, perceptions, or organizational standards. Getting as much up-to-date and pertinent information for your GAPS analysis will help ensure that your development plan is focusing on high-priority objectives.

Identifying and Prioritizing Development Needs: Gaps of GAPS

As seen in Figure DP.2, the Goals and Standards quadrants are future oriented; these quadrants ask where you want to go and what your boss or your organization expects of people in these positions. The Abilities and Perceptions quadrants are focused on the present; what strengths and development needs do you currently have and how are these attributes affecting others? Given what you currently have and where you want to go, what are the gaps in your GAPS? In other words, after looking at all of the information in your GAPS analysis, what

FIGURE DP.2

A gaps-of-the-GAPS analysis

Sources: D. B. Peterson and M. D. Hicks, *Leader as Coach* (Minneapolis, Personnel Decisions International, 1996); and G. J. Curphy, *The Leadership Development Process Manual* (Minneapolis, Personnel Decisions International, 1998).

Where you want to go

Goals

Where you are now

Abilities

←——— Gaps? ———→

Standards

Perceptions

Developmental Objectives

Current Position: _____

_____

_____

_____

_____

_____

Next Proposed Position: _____

_____

_____

_____

_____

_____

are your biggest development needs? And how should these development needs be prioritized? You need to review the information from the GAPS model, look for underlying themes and patterns, and determine what behaviors, knowledge, experiences, or skills will be the most important to change or develop if you are to accomplish your career goals.

Bridging the Gaps: Building a Development Plan

A gaps-of-the-GAPS analysis helps leadership practitioners identify high-priority development needs, but does not spell out what leaders need to do to overcome these needs. A good development plan is like a road map; it clearly describes the final destination, lays out the steps or interim checkpoints, builds in regular feedback to keep people on track, identifies where additional resources are needed, and builds in reflection time so that people can periodically review progress and determine whether an alternative route is needed. (See page 229 for a sample development plan.) The specific steps for creating a high-impact development plan are as follows:

- *Step 1: Career and Development Objectives.* Your career objective comes directly from the Goals quadrant of the GAPS analysis; it is where you want to be or what you want to be doing in your career a year or so in the future. The development objective comes from your gaps-of-the-GAPS analysis; it should be a high-priority development need pertaining to your career objective. People should be working on no more than two to three development needs at any one time.
- *Step 2: Criteria for Success.* What would it look like if you developed a particular skill, acquired technical expertise, or changed the behavior outlined in your development objective? This can be a difficult step in development planning, particularly with "softer" skills, such as listening, managing conflict, or building relationships with others.
- *Step 3: Action Steps.* The focus in the development plan should be on the specific, on-the-job action steps leadership practitioners will take in order to overcome their development need. However, sometimes it is difficult for leaders to think of the on-the-job action steps to overcome their development needs. Three excellent resources that provide on-the-job action steps for overcoming a variety of development needs are two books, *The Successful Manager's Handbook* (Davis, Skube, Hellervik, Gebelein, & Sheard, 1996) and *For Your Improvement* (Lombardo & Eichinger, 1996), and the development planning and coaching software *DevelopMentor* (PDI, 1995). These three resources can be likened to restaurant menus in that they provide leadership practitioners with a wide variety of action steps to overcome just about any development need.
- *Step 4: Whom to Involve and Reassess Dates.* This step in a development plan involves feedback—whom do you need to get it from and how often do you need to get it? This step in the development plan is important as it helps to keep you on track. Are your efforts being noticed? Do people see any improvement? Are there things you need to do differently? Do you need to refocus your efforts?
- *Step 5: Stretch Assignments.* When people reflect on when they have learned the most, they often talk about situations where they felt they were in over their heads. These situations stretched their knowledge and skills and often are seen as extremely beneficial to learning. If you know of a potential assignment, such as a task force, a project management team, or a rotational assignment, that would emphasize the knowledge and skills you need to develop and accelerate your learning, you should include it in your development plan.
- *Step 6: Resources.* Oftentimes people find it useful to read a book, attend a course, or watch a videotaped program to gain foundational knowledge about a particular development need. These methods generally describe the how-to steps for a particular skill or behavior.

- *Step 7: Reflect with a Partner.* In accordance with the Action-Observation-Reflection model of Chapter 3, people should periodically review their learnings and progress with a partner. The identity of the partner is not particularly important, as long as you trust his or her opinion and the partner is familiar with your work situation and development plan.

Reflecting on Learnings: Modifying Development Plans

Just as the development plan is a road map, this phase of development planning helps leaders to see whether the final destination is still the right one, if an alternative route might be better, and whether there is need for more resources or equipment. Reflecting on your learnings with a partner is also a form of public commitment, and people who make public commitments are much more likely to fulfill them. All things considered, in most cases it is probably better to periodically review your progress with your boss. Your boss should not be left in the dark with respect to your development, and periodically reviewing progress with your boss will help ensure there are no surprises at your performance appraisal.

Transfer Learnings to New Environments

The last phase in development planning concerns ongoing development. Your development plan should be a "live" document; it should be changed, modified, or updated as you learn from your experiences, receive feedback, acquire new skills, and overcome targeted development needs. There are basically three ways to transfer learnings to new environments. The first way is to constantly update your development plan. Another way to enhance your learning is to practice your newly acquired skills to a new environment. A final way to hone and refine your skills is to coach others in the development of your newly acquired skills. Moving from the student role to that of a master is an excellent way to reinforce your learnings.

Credibility

The Two Components of Credibility
Building Expertise
Building Trust
Expertise × Trust

Leaders know that while their position may give them authority, their behavior earns them respect. Leaders go first. They set an example and build commitment through simple, daily acts that create progress and momentum.

Jim Kouzes and Barry Posner

Interviews with thousands of followers as well as the results of over half a million 360-degree feedback reports indicate that credibility may be one of the most important components of leadership success and effectiveness (Kouzes & Posner, 1987, 1996; PDI, 1992). Employees working for leaders they thought were credible were willing to work longer hours, felt more of a sense of ownership in the company, felt more personally involved in work, and were less likely to leave the company over the next two years (Kouzes & Posner, 1996). Given the difficulties companies are having finding and retaining talented leaders and workers and the role intellectual capital and bench strength play in organizational success, it would appear that credibility could have a strong bottom-line impact on many organizations. Credibility is a little like leadership in that many people have ideas of what credibility is (or is not), but there may not be a lot of consensus on one "true" definition of credibility. This section will define what we believe credibility is, present the two components of credibility, and explore what leadership practitioners can do (and avoid doing) if they want to build their credibility.

The Two Components of Credibility

Credibility can be defined as the ability to engender trust in others. Leaders with high levels of credibility are seen as trustworthy; they have a strong sense of right and wrong, stand up and speak up for what they believe in, protect confidential information, encourage ethical discussions of business or work issues, and follow through with commitments. Sometimes dishonest leaders, personalized charismatic leaders, or power wielders can initially be seen by followers to be credible, but their selfish and self-serving interests usually come to light over time. Credibility is made up of two components, which include expertise and trust. Followers will not trust leaders if they feel their leaders do not know what they are talking about. Similarly, followers will not trust leaders if they feel confidential information will be leaked, if their leaders are unwilling to take stands on moral issues, or if their leaders do not follow through with their promises. Much about these two components of credibility have already been discussed in the sections on "Building Technical Competence," "Building Effective Relationships with Superiors," and "Building Effective Relationships with Peers." What follows is a brief overview of these three skills as well as some additional considerations that can help leadership practitioners build their credibility.

Building Expertise

Expertise consists of technical competence as well as organizational and industry knowledge, so building expertise means increasing your knowledge and skills in these three areas. Building technical competence, described earlier in Part V, concerns increasing the knowledge and repertoire of behaviors one can bring to bear to successfully complete a task. To build technical competence, leadership practitioners must determine how their job contributes to the overall mission of the company or organization, become an expert in the job through formal training or teaching others, and seek opportunities to broaden their technical expertise.

Nonetheless, building expertise takes more than just technical competence. Leaders also need to understand the company and the industry they are in. Many followers are not only looking for leaders to coach them on their skills, they are also looking to their leaders to provide some context for organizational, industry, and market events. Building one's organizational or industry knowledge may be just as important as building technical competence. However, the ways in which leadership practitioners build these two knowledge bases is somewhat different from building technical competence. Building technical competence often takes more of a hands-on approach to development, but it is hard to do this when building organizational or industry knowledge. One way to build your organizational or industry knowledge is by regularly reading industry-related journals, annual reports, *The Wall Street Journal, Fortune, Inc.,* or various websites. Many leaders spend 5–10 hours a week building their industry and organizational knowledge bases using this approach. Getting a mentor or being coached by your boss is another way to build these knowledge bases. Other leadership practitioners have taken stretch assignments where they work on special projects with senior executives. Often these assignments allow them to work closely with executives, and through this contact they better understand the competitive landscape, the organization's history and business strategies, and organizational politics. The bottom line is that your learning is not over once you have obtained your degree. In many ways, it will have just started.

Finally, it is important to remember that expertise is more than experience. As noted previously, some leaders get one year's worth of experience out of five years' work, whereas others get five years' worth of experience after one year's work. Leaders who get the most from their experience regularly discuss what they have been learning with a partner, and they frequently update their development plans as a result of these discussions.

Building Trust

The second component of credibility is building trust, which can be broken down into clarifying and communicating your values, and building relationships with others. In many ways leadership is a moral exercise. For example, one of the key differences between charismatic and transformational leaders is that the latter base their vision on their own and their followers' values, whereas the former base their vision on their own possibly selfish needs. Having a strong values system is an important component both in the Building Blocks Model of Skills and in leadership success. Because of the importance of values and relationships in building trust, the remainder of this section explores these two topics in more depth.

Chapter 6 defined values as generalized behaviors or states of affairs that an individual considers to be important. Provided that leaders make ethical decisions and abide by organizational rules, however, differences in values among leaders and followers may be difficult to discern. Since people do not come to work with their values tattooed to their foreheads, others typically make inferences about a leader's values based on their day-to-day behaviors (or just as importantly, their absence of certain day-to-day behaviors). Unfortunately, in many cases leaders' day-to-day behaviors are misaligned with their personal values; they are not living their life (at work, at least) in a manner consistent with their values.

An example of a leader not living life according to his values might be illustrative. An executive with an oil and gas firm was responsible for all exploration (i.e., drilling) operations in western Canada. Because he felt the discovery of new oil and gas fields was the key to the company's long-term success, he worked up to 18 hours a day, pushed his followers to work similar sorts of hours, had little patience for and would publicly disparage those oil rig operators who were behind schedule, and almost fired a manager who gave one of his followers a week off to see the birth of his son back in the United States. As these behaviors continued over time, more and more of his followers either requested transfers or quit to join other companies. Because of these problems with turnover and morale, he was asked to participate in a formal coaching program. Not surprisingly, his 360-degree feedback showed that his boss, peers, and followers found him very difficult to work with or for. These results indicated that he put a premium on getting results, getting ahead, and economic rewards, yet when he was asked to name the things he felt were most important to him as a leader, his priorities were his family, his religion, getting along with others, and developing his followers (altruism). Obviously, there was a huge gap between what he truly believed in and how he behaved. He felt the company expected him to hold people's feet to the fire and get results no matter what the cost, yet neither the boss nor his peers felt that this was the case. The executive had misconstrued the situation and was exhibiting behaviors that were misaligned with his values.

Although the case above was somewhat extreme, it is not unusual to find leaders acting in ways that are misaligned with their personal values. One way to assess the degree to which leaders are living their lives according to their personal values is by asking what they truly believe in and what they spend their time and money on. For example, you could write down the five things you believe most strongly in (i.e., your top five values), and then review your calendar, daytimer, checkbook, and credit card statements to determine where you spend your time and money. If the two lists are aligned, then you are likely to be living your life according to your values. If not, then you may be living your life according to how others think you should act. And if there is some level of discrepancy between the two lists, what should you do? Of course, some level of discrepancy is likely to occur, as situational demands and constraints can often influence the way leaders behave. On the other hand, large discrepancies between the lists may indicate that you are not living life consistently with your values, and those you interact with may infer that you have a very different set of values than those you personally believe in. A good first step in clarifying this discrepancy is to craft a personal mission statement or a leadership credo, a statement that describes what you truly believe in as a leader.

Examples of different leadership credos for managers across corporate America can be found in Highlight CR.1. There are several aspects of leadership

Sample Leadership Credos

Highlight CR.1

As a leader, I . . .
. . . believe in the concept of whole persons and will seek to use the full range of talents and abilities of colleagues whenever possible.
. . . will seek to keep people fully informed.
. . . will more consistently express appreciation to others for a job well done.
. . . will take risks in challenging policies or protocol when they do not permit us to effectively serve our customers.
. . . will selectively choose battles to fight—rather than trying to fight all of the possible battles.
. . . will actively support those providing the most effective direction for our company.
. . . will seek to change the things I can in a positive direction and accept those things I have no chance or opportunity to change.

Source: *Impact Leadership* (Minneapolis: Personnel Decisions International, 1995).

credos worth additional comment. First, leadership credos are personal and are closely linked with a leader's values—a credo should describe what the leader believes in and will (or will not) stand for. Second, it should also describe an ideal state. A leader's behavior may never be perfectly aligned with his or her personal mission statement, but it should be a set of day-to-day behaviors that he or she will strive to achieve. Third, leadership credos should be motivating; leaders should be passionate and enthusiastic about the kind of leader they aspire to be. If the leader does not find his or her personal mission statement to be particularly inspiring, then it is hard to see how followers will be motivated by it. Much of the inspiration of a leadership credo stems from its being personal and values-based. Fourth, personal mission statements should be made public. Leaders need to communicate their values to others, and a good way to do this is to display their leadership credos prominently in their offices. This not only lets others know what you as a leader think is important, it also is a form of public commitment to your leadership credo.

Another key way to build trust is to form strong relationships with others. There is apt to be a high level of mutual trust if leaders and followers share strong relationships; if these relationships are weak, then the level of mutual trust is apt to be low. Techniques for building relationships with peers and superiors have already been described in this section of the text. Perhaps the best way

FIGURE CR.1

The credibility matrix

Source: G. J. Curphy, *Credibility: Building Your Reputation throughout the Organization* (Minneapolis: Personnel Decisions International, 1997).

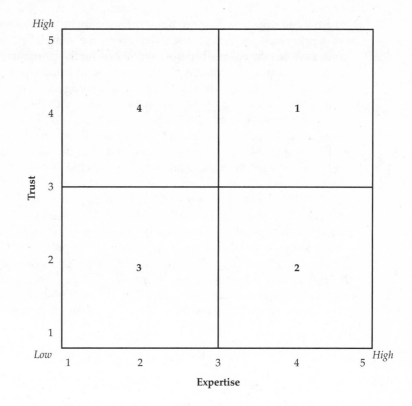

to build relationships with followers is to spend time listening to what they have to say. Because many leaders tend to be action oriented and get paid to solve (rather than listen to) problems, some leaders overlook the importance of spending time with followers. Yet leaders who take the time to build relationships with followers are much more likely to understand their followers' perspectives of organizational issues, intrinsic motivators, values, level of competence for different tasks, or career aspirations. Leaders armed with this knowledge may be better able to influence and get work done through others. More on building relationships with followers can be found in the "Coaching" section of Part V.

Expertise × Trust

Leaders vary tremendously in their levels of both expertise and trust, and these differences have distinct implications for leaders wanting to improve their credibility. Take leaders who fall into the first quadrant of Figure CR.1. These individuals have a high level of trust and a high level of expertise; they would likely be seen by others as highly credible. Individuals falling into the second quadrant might include leaders who have spent little time with followers, who do not follow through with commitments, or who are new to the organization and have had little time to build relationships with co-workers. In all three cases, leaders wanting to improve their credibility should include building relationships with co-workers as key development objectives. Leaders falling into the third quadrant may be new college hires or people joining the company from an entirely different industry. It is unlikely that either type of leader would have the technical competence, organizational or industry knowledge, or time to build relationships with co-workers. These leaders may be in touch with their values and have a personal mission statement, but they will need to share their statement with others and act in a manner consistent with this statement in order to build their credibility. Other development objectives could include building expertise and strong relationships with others. Leaders falling into the fourth quadrant might include those promoted from among peers or transferring from another department within the company. Both sets of leaders may be in touch with their values, have a leadership credo, share strong relationships with co-workers, and have organizational and industry knowledge, but the former may need to develop leadership knowledge or skills and the latter technical competence if they wish to increase their credibility. Finally, it is important to note that leadership credos and development plans also have credibility implications because leaders who do not strive to live up to their ideals or fail to follow through with their developmental commitments are likely to be seen as less trustworthy than those who do.

Coaching

Forging a Partnership
Inspiring Commitment: Conducting a GAPS Analysis
Growing Skills: Creating Development and Coaching Plans
Promoting Persistence: Helping Followers Stick to Their Plans
Transferring Skills: Creating a Learning Environment
Concluding Comments

People who are coaches will be the norm. Other people won't get promoted.

Jack Welch
General Electric CEO

A key success factor in most organizations today is having leaders and followers with the right knowledge and skills. More and more, companies are looking at "bench strength" as a competitive advantage moving into the next century. There are essentially two ways to acquire bench strength; employers can either buy (i.e., hire) the talent they need, or they can build their existing talent through development and coaching programs. Given that many employers face a labor shortage in certain critical positions, many are looking to build their own internal talent (Tichy & Cohen, 1997). Much of this talent is being developed through informal coaching. As we noted in Chapter 8, most leaders engage in some form of informal coaching. But how good of a coach are they? The authors' conversations with a multitude of leaders indicate that almost every single one was unsure what to do as a coach. Some thought it involved directing their employees on how to do tasks. Others thought it involved counseling employees on personal problems. One stated that his only example of coaching came from his high school football coach, and he wouldn't want to wish that on anyone.

Two thought leaders in this area are Peterson and Hicks (1996), who described coaching as the "process of equipping people with the tools, knowledge, and opportunities they need to develop themselves and become more successful" (p. 14). According to Peterson and Hicks, good coaches orchestrate rather than dictate development. Good coaches help followers clarify career goals, identify and prioritize development needs, create and stick to development plans, and create environments that support learning and coaching. To some extent, many of the steps to coaching have been described under some of the other skills in Part V. Thus, coaching is really a blend of several different leadership skills. Being a good coach means having well-developed skills, determining where a follower is in the coaching process, and intervening as appropriate. The five steps of coaching provide leaders with both a good road map and a diagnostic model for improving the bench strength of their followers.

Peterson and Hicks (1996) pointed out that this model works particularly well for high performers—individuals who tend to benefit the most from, but are often overlooked by, leaders when coaching. We noted in Chapter 9 that high performers produce 20–50 percent more than average employees (Hunter, Schmidt, & Judiesch, 1990), so coaching can have a considerable impact on the bottom line if it is targeted at high performers. Further support for the idea that top performers may benefit the most from coaching comes from athletics. If you watched any of the Sydney Olympics in 2000, then you would have seen that many of the world's top athletes had at least one and sometimes two or three coaches. If these world-class athletes feel that coaching can enhance their performance, then it is likely that good coaches can also enhance the performance of any organization's top employees. Although the five-step model also works with poorly performing employees, more appropriate interventions might also include diagnosing performance problems, goal setting, providing rewards and constructive feedback, and punishing these individuals, particularly if informal coaching is not achieving desired results.

Forging a Partnership

The first step in informal coaching involves establishing a relationship built on mutual trust and respect with a follower. If a follower does not trust or respect her leader, then it will be very unlikely that she will pay much attention to his ideas for her development. There are several things leaders can do to forge a partnership with coachees. First, it will be much easier for leaders with high credibility to build strong partnerships with followers than for leaders with low credibility. Therefore, leaders need to determine where they are on the credibility matrix (Figure CR.1), and they may need to take appropriate developmental steps to improve their credibility before their coaching suggestions will have much impact. These developmental steps may include building technical and organizational knowledge as well as building strong relationships with the individuals they want to coach. Having an understanding of the context in which the employee operates can be as important as the relationship the leader shares with the employee. In the "Credibility" section, we noted that leaders will also need to spend time listening to their coachees; they need to understand coachees' career aspirations, values, intrinsic motivators, view of the organization, and current work situation. Good coaches can put themselves in their coachees' shoes, and can understand how coachees may view issues or opportunities differently from themselves. While forging a partnership, leaders can also provide coachees with realistic career advice, as sometimes coachees have unrealistic estimations of their skills and opportunities. For example, a new graduate from a top MBA program might want to be a partner at a consulting firm after two years with the company, but company policy may dictate that this decision will not be made until she has been with the firm for at least eight years. Her coach should inform her of this policy, and then work with her to map out a series of shorter-term career objectives that would help her become a partner in eight years. If coaches do not know what drives their coachees' behaviors, then another step to forging a partnership is to start asking a lot of questions. This is an excellent opportunity for leaders to practice their listening skills so as to better understand their coachees' career aspirations and intrinsic motivators.

Inspiring Commitment: Conducting a GAPS Analysis

This step in the coaching process is very similar to the GAPS analysis and the gaps-of-the-GAPS analysis, discussed in "Development Planning." The only difference is that these two analyses are now done from the coachee's perspective. Figure CH.1 might help to clarify this difference in perspective. Thus, in the Goals quadrant of the GAPS analysis the leader should write down the coachee's career objectives, and in the Perceptions quadrant the leader would write down how the coachee's behavior is impacting others. It is entirely possible that the leader may not be able to complete all of the quadrants of the GAPS for a coachee. If so, then the leader will need to gather more information before going any further. This information gathering may include discussing career goals and abilities with the coachee, reviewing the coachee's 360-degree feedback results, asking peers about how the coachee comes across or impacts others, or asking human resources about the educational or experience standards relevant to the coachee's career goals. One way to gather additional information is to have both the leader and the coach complete a GAPS analysis independently, and then get together and discuss areas of agreement and disagreement. This can help ensure that the best information is available for the GAPS analysis and also help to build the partnership between the leader and coachee. During this discussion the leader and coachee should also do a gaps-of-the-GAPS analysis to identify and prioritize development needs. Usually leaders will get more commitment to development needs if coachees feel they had an important

FIGURE CH.1

A GAPS analysis for an employee

Source: D. B. Peterson, and M. D. Hicks, *Leader as Coach* (Minneapolis: Personnel Decisions International, 1996); and G. J. Curphy, *The Leadership Development Process Manual* (Minneapolis: Personnel Decisions International, 1998).

Goals: What does the employee want to do?	**Abilities:** What can the employee do now?
Step 1: Career objectives: —To become an Engineering Supervisor	*Step 2:* What strengths does the employee have for his or her career objectives? — Understand operational side of the business — Good planning skills — Good job function definition skills — Set clear individual and team goals *Step 3:* What development needs will he or she have to overcome? — Multidirection communication; may need to improve listening skills — May need to improve conflict resolution skills
Standards: What do you or the organization expect?	**Perceptions:** How do others see the employee?
Step 5: Expectations: • Boss: To be promoted, will need to: — Get along better with peers — Develop stronger listening skills	*Step 4:* PPRP and feedback from others: • *Boss* — Good technician — Develops good plans and holds people accountable — More interested in own rather than others' ideas • *Peers* — Can be counted on to get the job done — Can be too set in ways; too argumentative • *Direct Reports* — Has clear goals — Understands technical side of business — Doesn't value our ideas and opinions

role in determining these needs, and a gaps-of-the-GAPS discussion is a way to build buy-in. This discussion can also help ensure that development needs are aligned with career goals.

Growing Skills: Creating Development and Coaching Plans

Once the coachee's development needs are identified and prioritized, coachees will need to build development plans to overcome targeted needs. These plans are identical to those described in the "Development Planning" section. Leaders generally do not build development plans for their coachees. Instead, they may want to go over a sample (or their own) development plan and coach their coachees on the seven steps in building a plan. They can then either jointly build

TABLE CH–1   Development Plan Checklist

Objectives:
❏ One-year career objective identified?
❏ No more than a total of two or three development goals?
❏ Areas in which the employee is motivated and committed to change and develop?

Criteria for Success:
❏ Is the new behavior clearly described?
❏ Can the behavior be measured or observed?

Action Steps:
❏ Specific, attainable, and measurable steps?
❏ Mostly on-the-job activities?
❏ Includes a variety of types of activities?
❏ Are activities divided into small, doable steps?

Seek Feedback and Support:
❏ Involvement of a variety of others?
❏ Includes requests for management support?
❏ Are reassess dates realistic?

Stretch Assignments:
❏ Do the stretch assignments relate to the employee's career objectives?

Resources:
❏ Uses a variety of books, seminars, and other resources?

Reflect with a Partner:
❏ Includes periodic reviews of learnings?

Source: G. J. Curphy, *The Leadership Development Process Manual* (Minneapolis: Personnel Decisions International, 1998).

a plan or have the coachee individually build a plan for the leader to review. Providing coachees with an important role in development planning should increase their level of commitment to the plan. Once a draft development plan is created, the leader and coach can then use the development planning checklist in Table CH–1 to review the plan.

In addition to the development plan, leaders will need to build a coaching plan that outlines the actions they will take to support their coachees' development. Some of these actions might include meeting with the coachees on a regular basis to provide developmental feedback, identifying developmental resources or opportunities, or helping the coachee reflect on what they have learned. As with development plans, leaders should share their coaching plans so that coachees know what kind of support they will be getting. This will also publicly commit the leaders to the coachees' development, which will make it more likely that they will follow through with the coaching plan.

Promoting Persistence: Helping Followers Stick to Their Plans

Just because development and coaching plans are in place is no guarantee that development will occur. Sometimes coachees build development plans with great enthusiasm, but then never take any further action. This step in the coaching process is designed to help coachees "manage the mundane." An example of managing the mundane might be illustrative. One of the authors successfully completed a triathlon. The most difficult part of this accomplishment was not the event itself, but rather doing all of the training needed to successfully complete the event. Similarly, the inability to stick to a diet or keep a New Year's resolution is primarily due to an inability to manage the mundane; people are initially committed to these goals but have a difficult time sticking to them. The same is true with development planning. Conducting a GAPS analysis and creating a development plan are relatively easy; sticking to the plan is much more difficult. From the leader's perspective, a large part of coaching is helping followers stick to their development plan.

Several development-planning steps were specifically designed to promote persistence. For example, ensuring alignment between career and development objectives, getting feedback from multiple sources on a regular basis, and reflecting with a partner can help keep coachees focused on their development. If the leader is a coachee's developmental partner, then reflection sessions can help followers persist with their development. If leaders are not designated as partners in the development plan, then they should commit to meeting regularly with the coachees to discuss progress, what the leaders can do to support development, developmental opportunities, developmental feedback, and so forth.

Leaders can also help to promote persistence by capitalizing on coachable moments. Say a coachee was working on listening skills, and the leader and coach were in a staff meeting together. If the leader provides feedback to the coachee about her listening skills immediately after the staff meeting, then the leader has capitalized on a coachable moment. To capitalize on a coachable moment, leaders must know the followers' developmental objectives, be in situations where they can observe followers practicing their objectives, and then provide immediate feedback on their observations. Few coaches capitalize on coachable moments, but they can go a long way toward promoting persistence in coachees. It is important to note that capitalizing on coachable moments should take little time, often less than two minutes. In the example above, the leader could provide feedback to the coachee during their walk back to the office after the staff meeting.

Transferring Skills: Creating a Learning Environment

To build bench strength, leaders need to create a learning environment so that personal development becomes an ongoing process rather than a one-time event. As Tichy and Cohen (1997) aptly point out, the most successful organizations are those that emphasize the learning and teaching process—they focus on constantly creating leaders throughout the company. In reality, leaders have quite a bit of control over the kind of learning environments they want to create for their followers, and there are several interventions they can take to ensure that development becomes an ongoing process. Perhaps the most important intervention is for leaders to role-model development. In that regard, if leaders are not getting regular feedback from followers, then they are probably not doing a good job of role-modeling development. By regularly soliciting feedback from followers, leaders are also likely to create a feedback-rich work environment. Once feedback becomes a group norm, people will be much more willing to help build team member skills, which in turn can have a catalytic effect on group performance. It is important to note that the leader will play a large role in this group norm, because if the leader is feedback averse, it will be difficult to see how this norm will be adopted by followers.

Leaders can also create learning environments by regularly reviewing their followers' development. Perhaps the easiest way to do this is by making leaders and followers development partners; then both parties can provide regular feedback and on-going support. During these discussions leaders and followers should review and update their development plans to capitalize on new development opportunities or acquire new skills. Leaders and followers can also review coaching plans to see what is and is not working and make the necessary adjustments.

Concluding Comments

Perhaps one of the greatest misperceptions of coaching, and the primary reason why leaders state they do not coach others, is that it takes a lot of time. In reality, nothing could be further from the truth. Leaders are working to build credibility, build relationships with followers, and understand followers' career aspirations and view of the world. Although these do take time, they are also activities leaders should be engaged in even if they are not coaching followers. Doing a GAPS analysis, identifying and prioritizing development needs, helping followers create development plans, and creating coaching plans often takes less than four hours. Although leaders will need to take these steps with all their followers, these four hours can be spread out over a four- to six-week period. As stated earlier, meeting with followers on a regular basis to review development (perhaps monthly) and capitalizing on coachable moments also take little time. Finally, many of the actions outlined in "Create a Learning Environment" either take little time or are extensions of actions outlined earlier. The bottom line is that coaching really can take little additional time; it is really more a function of changing how you spend time with followers so that you can maximize their development.

Another note about the coaching model is that good coaches are equally versatile at all five steps of coaching. Some leaders are very good at forging a partnership, but then fail to carry development to the next level by conducting a GAPS analysis or helping followers build a development plan. Other leaders may help followers build a development plan but do not do anything to promote persistence or create a learning environment. Just as leaders need to develop their technical skills, so might they need to assess and in turn develop certain coaching skills. It is also important to remember that coaching is a very dynamic process—good coaches assess where followers are in the coaching process and intervene appropriately. By regularly assessing where they are with followers, they may determine that the relationship with a particular follower is not as strong as they thought, and this lack of relationship is why followers are not sticking to their development plan. In this case, a good coach would go back to forging a partnership with the follower and, once a trusting relationship had been created, go through another GAPS analysis, and so forth.

Finally, it is important to note that people can and do develop skills on their own. Nevertheless, leaders who commit to the five steps of informal coaching outlined above will both create learning organizations and help to raise development to a new level. Given the competitive advantage of companies that have a well-developed and capable workforce, in the future it will be hard to imagine leadership excellence without coaching. Good leaders are those who create successors, and coaching may be the best way to make this happen.

Empowerment

What Is Empowerment?
The Psychological Components of Empowerment
Six Best Practices of Empowerment

Do what you can, where you are at, with what you have.

Teddy Roosevelt

Inside every old company is a new company waiting to be born.

Alvin Toffler

Empowerment has become a very popular concept over the past 10 years. Many companies have embarked on various types of empowerment programs to improve results, yet the success of these programs has been mixed at best (Howard, 1996). One of the reasons for the mixed results is that empowerment often means different things to different people. This section describes what empowerment is (and is not), as well as some of the psychological constructs underlying empowerment and some of the best practices of empowering others.

What Is Empowerment?

In general, people seem to fall into one of two camps with respect to empowerment. Some people believe empowerment is all about delegation and accountability, a top-down process where senior leaders articulate a vision and specific goals, and hold followers responsible for achieving them. Others believe empowerment is more of a bottom-up approach that focuses on intelligent risk taking, growth, change, trust, and ownership; followers act as entrepreneurs and owners that question rules and make intelligent decisions. Leaders tolerate mistakes and encourage cooperative behavior in this approach to empowerment (Quinn & Spreitzer, 1997). Needless to say, these two conceptualizations of empowerment have very different implications for leaders and followers. And it is precisely this conceptual confusion which has caused empowerment programs to fail in many organizations (Quinn & Spreitzer, 1997). Because of the conceptual confusion surrounding empowerment, companies such as Motorola will not use this term to describe programs that push decision making to lower organizational levels. These companies would rather coin their own terms to describe these programs, thus avoiding the confusion surrounding empowerment.

We define empowerment as having two key components. For leaders to truly empower employees, they must delegate leadership and decision making down to the lowest level possible. Employees are often the closest to the problem and have the most information, and as such can often make the best decisions. A classic example was the UPS employee who ordered an extra 737 aircraft to haul presents that had been forgotten in the last-minute Christmas rush. This decision was clearly beyond the employee's level of authority, but UPS praised his initiative for seeing the problem and making the right decision. The second component of empowerment, and the one most often overlooked, is equipping followers with the resources, knowledge, and skills necessary to make good decisions. All too often companies adopt an empowerment program and push decision making down to the employee level, but employees have no experience creating business plans, submitting budgets, dealing with other departments within the company, or directly dealing with customers or vendors. Not surprisingly, ill-equipped employees often make poor, uninformed decisions, and managers in turn are likely to believe that empowerment was not all it was cracked up to be. The same happens with downsizing, as employees are asked to take on additional responsibilities but are provided with little training or support. As we stated in Chapter 9, this "forced" empowerment may lead to some short-term stock gains but tends to be disastrous in the long run. Thus, empowerment has both delegation and developmental components; delegation without development is often perceived as abandonment, and development without delegation can often be perceived as micromanagement. Leaders wishing to empower followers must determine what followers are capable of doing, enhance and broaden these capabilities, and give followers commensurate increases in authority and accountability.

The Psychological Components of Empowerment

The psychological components of empowerment can be examined at both macro and micro levels. There are three macro psychological components underlying empowerment, and these are motivation, learning, and stress (Howard, 1996). As a concept, empowerment has been around since at least the 1920s, and the vast majority of companies that have implemented empowerment programs have done so to increase employee motivation and, in turn, productivity. As a motivational technique, however, empowerment has not lived up to its promise; empowered workers may not be any more productive than unempowered workers (Howard, 1996). There are several reasons why this may be the case. First, senior leaders tend to see empowerment through rose-colored glasses. They hear about the benefits an empowerment program is having in another company, but do not consider the time, effort, and changes needed to create a truly empowered workforce. Relatedly, many empowerment programs are poorly implemented—the program is announced with great fanfare, but little real guidance, training, or support is provided and managers are quick to pull the plug on the program as soon as followers start making poor decisions. Adopting an effective empowerment program takes training, trust, and time (Offermann, 1996), but companies most likely to implement an empowerment program (as a panacea for their poor financial situation) often lack these three attributes. Third, as described in Chapter 9, worker productivity and job dissatisfaction in the United States are at an all-time high. Many companies are dealing with high levels of employee burnout, and adding additional responsibilities to already overfilled plates is likely to be counterproductive. As reported by Xie and Johns (1995), some empowerment programs create positions that are just too big for a person to handle effectively, and job burnout is usually the result.

Although the motivational benefits of empowerment seem questionable, the learning and stress reduction benefits of empowerment seem more clear-cut. Given that properly designed and implemented empowerment programs include a strong developmental component, one of the key benefits to these programs is that they help employees learn more about their jobs, company, and industry. These knowledge and skill gains increase the intellectual capital of the company and can be a competitive advantage in moving ahead. In addition to the learning benefits, well-designed empowerment programs can actually help to reduce burnout. People can tolerate high levels of stress when they have a high level of control. Given that many employees are putting in longer hours than ever before and work demands are at an all-time high, empowerment can help followers gain some control over their lives and better cope with stress. Although an empowered worker may have the same high work demands as an unempowered worker, the empowered worker will have more choices on how and when to accomplish these demands and as such will suffer from less stress. And because stress is a key component of dysfunctional turnover, giving workers more control over their work demands can reduce turnover and in turn positively impact the company's bottom line.

There are also four micro components of empowerment. These components can be used to determine whether employees are empowered or unempowered, and include self-determination, meaning, competence, and influence (Quinn & Spreitzer, 1997; Spreitzer, 1995). Empowered employees have a sense of self-determination; they can make choices about what they do, how they do it, and when they need to get it done. Empowered employees also have a strong sense of meaning; they believe what they do is important to them and to the company's

Figure EM.1

The empowerment continuum

Empowered Employees ◄――――――――――► Unempowered Employees	
• Self-determined	• Other-determined
• Sense of meaning	• Not sure if what they
• High competence	do is important
• High influence	• Low competence
	• Low influence

success. Empowered employees have a high level of competence in that they know what they are doing and are confident they can get the job done. Finally, empowered employees have an impact on others and believe that they can influence their teams or work units and that co-workers and leaders will listen to their ideas. In summary, empowered employees have latitude to make decisions, are comfortable making these decisions, believe what they do is important, and are seen as influential members of their team. Unempowered employees may have little latitude to make decisions, may feel ill equipped and may not want to make decisions, and may have little impact on their work unit, even if they have good ideas. Most employees probably fall somewhere in between the two extremes of the empowerment continuum, depicted in Figure EM.1. Leaders wanting to create more empowered followers may want to adopt some of the best practices techniques outlined below.

Six Best Practices of Empowerment

Do We Really Want or Need Empowerment?   Perhaps the first question leaders should ask before adopting an empowerment program is whether the company wants or needs empowerment. Leaders may agree that empowerment is important but may have fundamental differences as to the actions leaders need to take to create an empowered organization. Having a clear initial understanding of just what empowerment is will make the implementation of the program that much easier.

Leaders wanting to adopt an empowerment program must also consider how their own jobs and roles will be affected. They may need to fundamentally change their leadership style to better tolerate employee mistakes, play more of a coaching than directing role, and be willing to be challenged on a regular basis. Because empowered employees have access to considerably more information, they will be much more likely to question past or current decisions, and leaders will need to exert more personal power in order to get decisions adopted. Leaders feeling that this role transition is too much of a stretch will not enthusiastically embrace an empowerment program, making companywide adoption of the program difficult.

Creating a Clear Vision, Goals, and Accountabilities.   Once a decision is made to develop and implement an empowerment program, top management must ensure that the company's vision, business strategies, and operational goals are clear and are understood by everyone in the company. It is difficult to ask employees to make wise decisions if they do not know where the company is headed. Employees should know what the company and work unit are trying to accomplish and how these accomplishments will be measured, and they should be given regular feedback on progress. In addition, employees will need to understand how their own goals are related to work unit and company goals.

Developing Others.   Just because employees have a clear understanding of their work goals does not mean they have the knowledge, skills, and resources necessary to get them accomplished. Leaders will need to determine what employees can currently do, what they need to be able to do, and how they will help employees bridge the gaps between current and future capabilities. Perhaps the best way to do this is for leaders to adopt the five steps described in the "Coaching" section of Part V. A key component of empowerment is trust, and leaders can build trust by taking the actions prescribed in "Forging a Partnership." Leaders can identify and prioritize development needs through a GAPS analysis, and can work to increase knowledge and skills through development plans, coaching plans, and the actions outlined under "Promote Persistence" and "Transferring Skills." The five steps of informal coaching give leaders a road map for improving the bench strength of their followers and systematically equipping them to meet the increased challenges of empowerment. Taking these development steps helps with the competence component of empowerment.

Delegating Decision Making to Followers.   Once followers are starting to develop the skills, knowledge, and experience necessary to make wise decisions, leaders must systematically increase the degree of latitude and autonomy employees are given to make decisions. Although this sounds fairly straightforward, in practice it can be fairly difficult. Some of the typical mistakes leaders make in this area are pushing followers into decision making too quickly, holding on to decision-making power too long, or taking decision-making power away from followers during a crisis. Other difficulties include the fact that many leaders associate decision making with leadership and may feel personally threatened by delegating decision-making authority to others. This may be particularly true when organizations have recently gone through a downsizing or when the level of trust between leaders and followers is low. Some followers may also feel reluctant to take on increased decision-making responsibility, as their level of skill may be exposed in ways it never had before (Offermann, 1996). Another complication is that some employees may feel that because they are taking on additional responsibilities, they should be paid more. This is particularly true when empowerment programs are introduced in union environments.

One way to determine how much latitude and authority to provide followers is to use the Situational Leadership Theory, described in Chapter 12. This theory provides a useful heuristic for developing employees and determining when they are ready to take on additional decision-making responsibilities. Another way to effectively delegate decision making to followers is to provide clear boundaries around the decisions they make. For example, employees at the Ritz-Carlton hotels have fixed limits on the amounts employees can spend to satisfy disgruntled guests. As the level of followers' knowledge and experience increases, the scope of the decisions can be increased and their boundaries loosened. Leaders delegating tasks and responsibilities should also follow the tenets of setting goals and delegating described earlier in this section of the text. Because followers will not be very skilled in making wise decisions, leaders will need to be prepared to tolerate followers' mistakes and help them learn from these experiences. The actions outlined under this best practice will help with the self-determination and influence components of empowerment.

Leading by Example.   Leaders must be an example of empowerment if they want to successfully empower their employees. An illustration of how a leader could role-model empowerment will be useful. A multimillion-dollar consulting firm, run by one of the authors, was facing an acute labor shortage. Customer requests for additional services created enough work for four new positions. The office had a strong financial track record, and financial analyses provided solid support for the additional positions. Moreover, employee workload was extremely high, and the office was in desperate need of additional help. Armed with these facts, the author submitted job requisitions for the four additional positions to corporate headquarters. But after two months and numerous phone calls to corporate staff, the positions did not seem to be any closer to being approved. The author went ahead and hired the four additional staff, and informed corporate headquarters of his decision once the new personnel were onboard. Although the author took a considerable amount of heat from the COO and the vice president of human resources, the office continued to be financially successful, office morale dramatically improved, and the author sent a clear signal to his staff to seek forgiveness rather than permission.

Quinn and Spreitzer (1997) have claimed that it is nearly impossible for unempowered leaders to empower followers. Although there is some truth to this statement, empowerment needs to start somewhere, and it is all too easy for leaders to say that "they" are not allowing us to empower our followers. All too often "they" are very same people who are making these statements, and it is their own preconceived notions of leadership and misunderstandings of empowerment that are getting in the way. When this occurs, it is all too easy for leaders to waste time finger-pointing and overlook the areas where they *can* empower followers. In the above example the author was not empowered to make these hiring decisions, yet he went ahead and did it anyway. This could have been a career-ending decision for the author, but he weighed the consequences of failing to hire additional help and thought the benefits were greater than the political costs. There is a certain amount of risk taking to leadership, and good leaders are those who themselves take, and allow their followers to take, intelligent risks. Like UPS and the employee who ordered the additional 737, good leaders reward intelligent risk taking and do not punish decisions that were well thought out but failed.

Empowerment Must Be Systemic to Be Successful. Although individual leaders who take initiative can empower their followers, it will be much easier and more effective if senior leadership embraces empowerment as a key business strategy. When reward and performance appraisal systems, selection systems, work processes, training programs, organizational structure, and information systems are strongly aligned with the organization's definition of empowerment, then all these programs will be very successful. On the other hand, merely introducing an empowerment program but failing to make the necessary adjustments in the organizational systems, processes, and structure will likely be a recipe for failure.

REFERENCES

Aberman, R. "Emotional Intelligence." Paper presented at the Quarterly Meeting of the Minnesota Human Resource Planning Society, Minneapolis, MN, November 29, 2000.

Adams, J.; H. T. Prince; D. Instone; and R. W. Rice. "West Point: Critical Incidents of Leadership." *Armed Forces and Society* 10 (1984), pp. 597–611.

Adams, J. L. *Conceptual Blockbusting*. New York: W. W. Norton, 1979.

Adams, J. S. "Inequity in Social Exchange." In *Advances in Experimental Social Psychology*. Ed. L. Berkowitz. Vol. 2. New York: Academic Press, 1965, pp. 267–96.

———. "Toward an Understanding of Inequity." *Journal of Abnormal and Social Psychology* 67 (1963), pp. 422–36.

Adler, S., and H. M. Weiss. "Criterion Aggregation in Personality Research: A Demonstration Looking at Self-Esteem and Goal Setting." *Human Performance* 1, no. 2 (1988), pp. 99–109.

Aguayo, R. *Dr. Deming: The Man Who Taught the Japanese about Quality*. New York: Carol Publishing, 1990.

Alberti, R. E., and M. L. Emmons. *Your Perfect Right*. San Luis Obispo, CA: Impact, 1974.

Albrecht, K. *Stress and the Manager*. Englewood Cliffs, NJ: Prentice Hall, 1979.

Alderfer, C. P. "An Empirical Test of a New Theory of Human Needs." *Organizational Behavior and Human Performance* 4 (1969), pp. 142–75.

———. "Group and Intergroup Relations." In *Improving Life at Work*. Ed. J. R. Hackman and J. L. Suttle, Santa Monica, CA: Goodyear, 1977.

Aldrich, H. E. *Organizations and Environments*. Englewood Cliffs, NJ: Prentice Hall, 1979.

Allen, T. H. "Situational Management Roles: A Conceptual Model." *Dissertation Abstracts International* 42, no. 2A (1981), p. 465.

Allport, G. W., and H. S. Odbert, "Trait-names: A Psycho-Lexical Study." *Psychological Monographs* 47 (1936), 171–220.

Amabile, T. M. "Beyond Talent: John Irving and the Passionate Craft of Creativity." *American Psychologist* 56, no. 4 (2001), pp. 333–36.

Amabile, T. M. "Motivation and Creativity: Effects of Motivation Orientation on Creative Writers." *Journal of Personal and Social Psychology* 48 (1985), pp. 393–99.

———. "The Motivation to Be Creative." In *Frontiers in Creativity: Beyond the Basics*. Ed. S. Isaksen. Buffalo, NY: Bearly, 1987.

———. *The Social Psychology of Creativity*. New York: Springer-Verlag, 1983.

Amabile, T. M., and R. Conti. "Changes in the Work Environment for Creativity during Downsizing." *Academy of Management Journal* 42, no. 6 (1999), pp. 630–40.

Amabile, T. M., and R. Conti. "What Downsizing Does to Creativity." *Issues & Observations* 15, no. 3 (1995), pp. 1–6.

Amabile, T. M., and S. S. Gryskiewicz. "Creativity in the R&D Laboratory." (Tech Report No. 30). Greensboro, N.C.: Center for Creative Leadership, 1987.

Amabile, T. M., and B. A. Hennessey. "The Motivation for Creativity in Children." In *Achievement and Motivation: A Social-Developmental Perspective*. Ed. A. K. Boggiano and T. Pittman. New York: Cambridge University Press, 1988.

Anastasi, A. *Psychological Testing*. 5th ed. New York: Macmillian, 1982.

Anderson, C. R., and C. E. Schneier. "Locus of Control, Leader Behavior, and Leader Performance among Management Students." *Academy of Management Journal* 21 (1978), pp. 690–98.

Andrews, P. H. "Performance, Self-Esteem and Perceptions of Leadership Emergence: A Comparative Study of Men and Women."

Western Journal of Speech Communication 48 (1984), pp. 1–13.

Andrews, R. L., and R. Soder. "Principal Leadership and Student Achievement." *Educational Leadership* 44 (1987), pp. 9–11.

Argyris, C. *Increasing Leadership Effectiveness.* New York: John Wiley, 1976.

Armour, S. "Bosses Held Liable for Keeping Workers." *USA Today*, April 12, 2000, p. 1B.

Arvey, R. D., et al. "Mainstream Science on Intelligence." *The Wall Street Journal*, December 13, 1994.

Arvey, R. D.; T. J. Bouchard, Jr.; N. L. Segal; and L. M. Abraham. "Job Satisfaction: Environmental and Genetic Components." *Journal of Applied Psychology* 74 (1989), pp. 187–92.

Arvey, R. D.; G. A. Davis; and S. M. Nelson. "Use of Discipline in an Organization: A Field Study." *Journal of Applied Psychology* 69 (1984), pp. 448–60.

Arvey, R. D., and J. M. Ivancevich. "Punishment in Organizations: A Review, Propositions, and Research Suggestions." *Academy of Management Review* 5 (1980), pp. 123–32.

Arvey, R. D., and A. P. Jones. "The Use of Discipline in Organizational Settings; A Framework for Future Research." In *Research in Organizational Behavior.* Ed. L. L. Cummings and B. M. Staw. Vol. 7. Greenwich, CT: JAI, 1985, pp. 367–408.

Arvey, R. D., and K. R. Murphy. "Performance Evaluation in Work Settings." *Annual Review of Psychology* 49 (1998), pp. 141–68.

Astin, H. S., and C. Leland. *Women of Influence, Women of Vision.* San Francisco: Jossey-Bass, 1991.

Atkinson, J. W. "Motivational Determinants of Risk Taking Behavior." *Psychological Review* 64 (1957), pp. 359–72.

Atwater, L. E; C. Ostroff; F. J. Yammarino; and J. W. Fleenor. "Self-Other Agreement: Does It Really Matter?" *Personnel Psychology* 51, no. 3 (1998), pp. 577–98.

Atwater, L. E; D. Waldman; D. Atwater; and P. Cartier. "An Upward Feedback Field Experiment: Supervisors' Cynicism, Reactions, and Commitment to Subordinates." *Personnel Psychology* 53, no. 2 (2000), pp. 275–97.

Atwater, L.; P. Roush; and A. Fischthal. "The Influence of Upward Feedback on Self- and Follower Ratings of Leadership." *Personnel Psychology* 48, no. 1 (1995), pp. 35–60.

Austin, J. S.; E. J. Conlon; and R. L. Daft. "Organizing for Effectiveness: A Guide to Using Structural Design for Mission Accomplishment." LMDC-TR-84-3-0. Maxwell AFB, AL: Leadership and Management Development Center, Air University, 1986.

Avolio, B. J. *Full Leadership Development: Building the Vital Forces in Organizations.* Thousand Oaks, CA: Sage, 1999.

Avolio, B. J., and B. M. Bass. "Charisma and Beyond." In *Emerging Leadership Vistas.* Ed. J. G. Hunt, B. R. Baliga, H. P. Dachler, and C. A. Schriesheim. Lexington, MA: D. C. Heath, 1987.

———. *Developing A Full Range of Leadership Potential: Cases on Transactional and Transformational Leadership.* Binghamton: State University of New York at Binghamton, 2000.

———. "Transformational Leadership, Charisma, and Beyond." In *Emerging Leadership Vista.* Ed. J. G. Hunt, B. R. Baliga, and C. A. Schriesheim. Lexington. MA: D. C. Heath, 1988.

———. "You Can Drag a Horse to Water but You Can't Make It Drink Unless It Is Thirsty." *Journal of Leadership Studies* 5, no. 1 (1998), pp. 1–17.

Avolio, B. J., and T. C. Gibbons. "Developing Transformational Leaders: A Life Span Approach." In *Charismatic Leadership: The Elusive Factor in Organizational Effectiveness.* Ed. J. A. Conger and R. N. Kanungo. San Francisco: Jossey-Bass, 1988.

Awamleh, R., and W. L. Gardner. "Perceptions of Leader Charisma and Effectiveness: The Effects of Vision Content, Delivery, and Organizational

Performance." *Leadership Quarterly* 10, no. 3 (1998), pp. 245–374.

Ayman R., and M. M. Chemers. "The Effect of Leadership Match on Subordinate Satisfaction in Mexican Organizations: Some Moderating Influences of Self-Monitoring." *Applied Psychology: An International Review* 40, no. 3 (1991), pp. 229–314.

Azar, B. "Corporations Seek Help Fitting Goals Together." *APA Monitor,* July 1997, pp. 14–15.

———. "Searching for Intelligence Beyond G." *APA Monitor* 26, no. 1 (1995), p. 1.

———. "Which Traits Predict Job Performance?" *APA Monitor,* July 1995, pp. 30–31.

Back, K., and K. Back. *Assertiveness at Work.* New York: McGraw-Hill, 1982.

Badin, I. J. "Some Moderator Influences on Relationships between Consideration, Initiating Structure, and Organizational Criteria." *Journal of Applied Psychology* 59 (1974), pp. 380–82.

Bales, R. F. "Task Roles and Social Roles in Problem-Solving Groups." In *Readings in Social Psychology.* Ed. E. E. Maccoby, T. M. Newcomb, and E. L. Hartley. New York: Holt, 1958.

Baltzell, E. D. *Puritan Boston and Quaker Philadelphia.* New York: Free Press, 1980.

Bandura, A. "Self-Efficacy: Toward a Unifying Theory of Behavioral Change." *Psychological Review* 84 (1977), pp. 191–215.

Bar-On, R. *The Emotional Quotient Inventory (EQi).* Toronto, Canada: Multi-Health Systems, 1996.

Barling, J.; T. Weber; and E. K. Kelloway. "Effects of Transformational Leadership Training on Attitudinal and Financial Outcomes: A Field Experiment." *Journal of Applied Psychology* 81, no. 6, (1996), pp. 827–32.

Barnes, F. "Mistakes New Presidents Make" *Reader's Digest,* January 1989, p. 43.

Barnum, D. F. "Effective Membership in the Global Business Community." In *New Traditions in Business.* Ed. J. Renesch. San Francisco: Berrett-Koehler, 1992.

Barrick, M. R. "Answers to Lingering Questions about Personality Research." Paper presented at the 14th Annual Conference of the Society of Industrial and Organizational Psychology, Atlanta, GA, 1999.

Barrick, M. R., and M. K. Mount. "The Big Five Personality Dimensions and Job Performance: A Meta-analysis." *Personal Psychology* 44 (1991), pp. 1–26.

———. "Effects of Impression Management and Self-Deception on the Predictive Validity of Personality Constructs." *Journal of Applied Psychology* 81, no. 3 (1996), pp. 261–72.

B. M. Bass. *Bass and Stogdill's Handbook of Leadership.* 3rd ed. New York: Free Press, 1990.

———. "Does the Transactional-Transformational Leadership Paradigm Transcend Organizational and National Boundaries?" *American Psychologist* 52, no. 3 (1997), pp. 130–39.

———. "Evolving Perspectives of Charismatic Leadership." In *Charismatic Leadership: The Elusive Factor in Organizational Effectiveness.* Ed. J. A. Conger and R. N. Kanungo. San Francisco: Jossey-Bass, 1988.

———. *Leadership, Psychology, and Organizational Behavior.* New York: Harper, 1960.

———. *Leadership and Performance beyond Expectations.* New York: Free Press, 1985.

———. "Thoughts and Plans." In *Cutting Edge: Leadership 2000.* Eds. B. Kellerman and L. R. Matusak. Carbondale: Southern Illinois University Press, 2000, pp. 5–9.

———. "Two Decades of Research and Development in Transformational Leadership." *European Journal of Work and Organizational Psychology* 8, no. 1 (1999), pp. 9–32.

Bass, B. M., and B. J. Avolio, eds. *Increasing Organizational Effectiveness through Transformational Leadership.* Thousand Oaks, CA: Sage, 1994.

———. *The Multifactor Leadership Questionnaire Report.* Palo Alto, CA: Mind Garden, 1996.

Bass, B. M., and P. Steidlmeier. "Ethics, Character, and Authentic Transformational Leadership Behavior." *Leadership Quarterly* 10, no. 2 (1999), pp. 181–218.

Bass, B. M., and F. J. Yammarino. *Long-term Forecasting of Transformational Leadership and Its Effects among Naval Officers: Some Preliminary Findings.* Technical Report No. ONR-TR-2. Arlington, VA: Office of Naval Research, 1988.

Bedeian, A. G., and A. A. Armenakis. "The Cesspool Syndrome: How Dreck Floats to the Top of Declining Organizations." *Academy of Management Executive* 12, no. 1 (1998), pp. 58–63.

Beer, M. "Developing Organizational Fitness: Towards a Theory and Practice of Organizational Alignment." Paper presented at the 14th Annual Conference of the Society of Industrial and Organizational Psychology, Atlanta, GA, 1999.

———. *Leading Change.* Reprint No. 9-488-037. Boston: Harvard Business School Publishing Division, 1988.

Behar, K; D. Arvidson; W. Omilusik; B. Ellsworth; and B. Morrow. *Developing Husky Oil Leaders: A Strategic Investment,* Calgary, Canada: Husky Energy, 2000.

Benne, K. D., and P. Sheats. "Functional Roles of Group Members." *Journal of Social Issues* 4 (1948), pp. 41–49.

Benner, P. E. *Stress and Satisfaction on the Job.* New York: Praeger, 1984.

Bennis, W. G. "Leadership Theory and Administrative Behavior: The Problem of Authority." *Administrative Science Quarterly* 4 (1959), pp. 259–260.

———. *On Becoming a Leader.* Reading, MA: Addison-Wesley, 1989.

Bennis, W. G., and B. Nanos. *Leaders: The Strategies for Taking Charge.* New York: Harper & Row, 1985.

Berkman, L., and S. L. Syme. "Social Networks, Host Resistance, and Mortality: A Nine-Year Follow-up Study of Alameda County Residents." *American Journal of Epidemiology* 109 (1979), pp. 186–204.

Berlew, D. E. "Leadership and Empowerment." Workshop presented at the 7th Annual Society for Industrial and Organizational Psychologists Convention, Montreal, May 1992.

———. "Leadership and Organizational Excitement." In *Organizational Psychology: A Book of Readings.* Ed. D. A. Kolb, I. M. Rubin, and J. M. McIntyre. 2nd ed. Englewood Cliffs, NJ: Prentice Hall, 1974.

Bernardin, H. J., and R. W. Beatty. *Performance Appraisal: Assessing Human Behavior at Work.* Boston: Kent, 1984.

Berry, J. K. "Linking Management Development to Business Strategies." *Training and Development Journal,* August 1990, pp. 20–22.

Berson, Y.; B. Shamir; B. J. Avolio; and M. Popper. "The Relationship between Vision Strength, Leaders Style, and Context." *Leadership Quarterly* 12, no. 1 (2001), pp. 53–74.

Bettencourt, L. A.; K. P. Gwinner; and M. L. Meuter. "A Comparison of Attitude, Personality, and Knowledge Predictors of Service-Oriented Organizational Citizenship Behaviors." *Journal of Applied Psychology,* 86, no. 1 (2001), pp. 29–41.

Betz, E. L. "Two Tests of Maslow's Theory of Need Fulfillment." *Journal of Vocational Behavior* 24 (1984), pp. 204–20.

Beyer, J. M. "Training and Promoting Charisma to Change Organizations." *Leadership Quarterly* 10, no. 2 (1999), pp. 307–30.

Beyer, J. M., and H. M. Trice. "A Field Study in the Use and Perceived Effects of Discipline in Controlling Work Performance." *Academy of Management Journal* 27 (1984), pp. 743–64.

Bickman, L. "The Social Power of a Uniform." *Journal of Applied Social Psychology* (1974), pp. 47–61.

Blake, P. "Walt Disney World: No Mere Amusement Park." *Architectural Forum* 136, no. 5 (1972), pp. 24–40.

———. "The Lessons of the Parks." In *The Art of Walt Disney: From Mickey Mouse to the Magic*

Kingdom. Ed. C. Finch. New York: Harry N. Abrams, 1973, pp. 423–49.

Blake, R. J. "Relations between Worker Satisfactories and Personality." In R. T. Hogan (chair), *Personality and Organizational Behavior.* Symposium presented at the 104th Annual Meeting of the American Psychological Association, Toronto, Canada, 1996.

Blake, R. J., and E. H. Potter III. "Novice Leaders, Novice Behaviors, and Strong Culture: Promoting Leadership Change beyond the Classroom." In *Impact of Leadership.* Ed. K. E. Clark, M. B. Clark, and D. P. Campbell. Greensboro, NC: Center for Creative Leadership, 1992.

Blake, R. R., and A. A. McCanse. *Leadership Dilemmas—Grid Solutions.* Houston, TX: Gulf, 1991.

Blake, R. R., and J. S. Mouton. *The Managerial Grid.* Houston, TX: Gulf, 1964.

———. *The Managerial Grid III.* Houston, TX: Gulf, 1985.

Blake, R. R.; H. A. Shepard; and J. S. Mouton. *Managing Intergroup Conflict in Industry.* Houston, TX: Gulf, 1964.

Blanchard, K.; P. Zigami; and P. Zigami. *Leadership: The One Minute Manager.* New York: Morrow, 1985.

Blank, T. O. "What High School Leaders Think of Leadership." *High School Journal* 63 (1986), pp. 207–13.

Blankenship, L. V., and R. E. Miles. "Organizational Structure and Managerial Decision Behavior." *Administrative Science Quarterly* 13 (1968), pp. 106–20.

Blau, P. M. "Critical Remarks on Weber's Theory of Authority." *American Political Science Review* 57, no. 2 (1963), pp. 305–15.

———. "The Hierarchy of Authority in Organizations." *American Journal of Sociology* 73 (1968), pp. 453–67.

Block, P. *Stewardship.* San Francisco: Berrett-Koehler, 1993.

Bloom, M. "The Performance Effects of Pay Dispersions on Individuals and Organizations." *Academy of Management Journal* 42, no. 1 (1999), pp. 25–40.

Bloom, M., and G. T. Milkovich. "Relationships among Risk, Incentive Pay, and Organizational Performance." *Academy of Management Journal* 41, no. 3 (1998), pp. 283–97.

Blum, R. E.; J. A. Butler; and N. L. Olson. "Leadership for Excellence: Research-based Training for Principals." *Educational Leadership* 45, no. 1 (1987), pp. 25–29.

Boal, K. M., and J. M. Bryson. "Charismatic Leadership: A Phenomenal and Structural Approach." In *Emerging Leadership Vista.* Ed. J. G. Hunt, B. R. Baliga, H. P. Dachler, and C. A. Schriesheim. Lexington, MA: D.C. Heath, 1988.

Borman, W. C.; M. A. Hanson; S. H. Oppler; and E. D. Pulakos. "The Role of Early Supervisory Experience in Supervisor Performance." *Journal of Applied Psychology* (in press).

Borman, W. C.; L. A. White; E. D. Pulakos; and S. A. Oppler. "Models Evaluating the Effects of Rated Ability, Knowledge, Proficiency, Temperament, Awards, and Problem Behavior on Supervisor Ratings." *Journal of Applied Psychology* 76 (1991), pp. 863–72.

Bottger, P. C. "Expertise and Air Time as Bases of Actual and Perceived Influence in Problem-Solving Groups." *Journal of Applied Psychology* 69 (1984), pp. 214–21.

Boudreau, J. W.; W. R. Boswell; T. A. Judge; and R. D. Bretz, Jr. "Personality and Cognitive Ability as Predictors of Job Search among Employeed Managers." *Personnel Psychology* 54, no. 1 (2001), pp. 25–50.

Bowers, D. G., and S. E. Seashore. "Predicting Organizational Effectiveness with a Four Factor Theory of Leadership." *Administrative Science Quarterly* 11 (1966), pp. 238–63.

Boyatzis, R. E., and F. R. Skelly. "The Impact of Changing Values on Organizational Life." In *Organizational Behavior Readings.* Ed. D. A. Kolb, I. M. Rubin, and J. Osland. 5th Ed. Englewood Cliffs, NJ: Prentice Hall, 1991, pp. 1–16.

Bracken, D. W. "Straight Talk about Multi-rater Feedback." *Training & Development*, September 1994.

Bracken, D. W; C. W. Timmreck; and A. H. Church. *The Handbook of Multisource Feedback.* San Francisco: Jossey-Bass, 2000.

Bradley, R. T. *Charisma and Social Power: A Study of Love and Power, Wholeness and Transformation.* New York: Paragon, 1987.

Brandt, R. "On Leadership and Student Achievement: A Conversation with Richard Andrews." *Educational Leadership* 45, no. 1 (1987), pp. 9–16.

Bray, D. W.; R. J. Campbell; and D. L. Grant. *Formative Years in Business: A Long-term AT&T Study of Managerial Lives.* New York: Wiley-Interscience, 1974.

Bray, D. W., and A. Howard. "The AT&T Longitudinal Study of Managers. In *Longitudinal Studies of Adult Psychological Development.* Ed. K. W. Schaiel. New York: Guilford, 1983.

Brenner, O. C.; J. Tomkiewicz; and V. E. Schein. "The Relationship between Sex Role Stereotypes and Requisite Management Characteristics Revisited." *Academy of Management Journal* 32 (1989), pp. 662–69.

Bridges, W. *Managing Transitions: Making the Most of Change.* Reading, MA: Addison-Wesley, 1991.

Brief, A. P.; R. S. Schuler; and M. Van Sell. *Managing Job Stress.* Boston: Little, Brown, 1981.

Brinkmeyer, K. R., and R. T. Hogan. "An Exploration of the Structure of Individual Differences." In R. T. Hogan (chair), *Personality Applications in the Workplace: Thinking outside the Dots.* Symposium presented at the 12th Annual Conference of the Society of Industrial and Organizational Psychology, St. Louis, MO, 1997.

Brockner, J., and L. Adsit. "The Moderating Impact of Sex on the Equity-Satisfaction Relationship." *Journal of Applied Psychology* 71 (1986), pp. 585–90.

Brody, N. *Intelligence.* San Diego: Academic Press, 1992.

———. "Intelligence, Schooling, and Society." *American Psychologist* 52, no. 10 (1997), pp. 1046–50.

Brown, A. D. "Narcissism, Identity, and Legitimacy." *Academy of Management Review* 22, no. 3 (1997), pp. 643–86.

Brown, L. D. *Managing Conflict at Organizational Interfaces.* Reading, MA: Addison-Wesley, 1983.

Brumback, G. "Institutionalizing Ethics in Government." *Public Personnel Management* 20, no. 3 (1991), pp. 353–64.

Brungardt, C. "Benchmarking Employee Attitudes." *Training and Development,* June 1992, pp. 49–53.

———. "The Making of Leaders: A Review of the Research in Leadership Development and Education." *Journal of Leadership Studies* 3, no. 3. (1996), pp. 81–95.

Bugental, D. E. "A Study of Attempted and Successful Social Influence in Small Groups as a Function of Goal-Relevant Skills." *Dissertation Abstracts* 25 (1964), p. 660.

Bunker, K. A., & Webb, A. *Learning How to Learn from Experience: Impact of Stress and Coping.* Report No. 154. Greensboro, NC: Center for Creative Leadership, 1992.

Burke, M. J., and R. R. Day. " A Cumulative Study of the Effectiveness of Managerial Training." *Journal of Applied Psychology* 71 (1986), pp. 242–45.

Burke, P. J. "The Development of Task and Socio-Emotional Role Differentiation." *Sociometry* 30 (1967), pp. 379–92.

Burns, J. M. *Leadership.* New York: Harper & Row, 1978.

Burns, T., and G. M. Stalker. *The Management of Innovation.* London: Tavistock, 1961.

Butorac, T. "Recruitment and Retention: The Keys to Profitability at Carlson Companies." Presentation given at Personnel Decisions International, Minneapolis, MN, June 11, 2001.

Calder, B. J. and B. M. Staw. "Self-Perception of Intrinsic and Extrinsic Motivation." *Journal of Personality and Social Psychology* 31 (1975), pp. 599–605.

Caldwell, D. F., and J. M. Burger. "Personality Characteristics of Job Applicants and Success in Screening Interviews." *Personnel Psychology* 51, no. 1 (1998), pp. 119–36.

Caliguiri, P. M. "The Big Five Personality Characteristics as Predictors of Expatriot's Desire to Terminate the Assignment and Supervisor-Rated Performance." *Personnel Psychology* 53, no. 1 (2000), pp. 67–88.

Campbell, D. P. *Campbell Leadership Index Manual.* Minneapolis, MN: National Computer Systems, 1991.

———. *Handbook for the Strong Vocational Interest Blank.* Stanford, CA: Stanford University Press, 1971.

———. "The Psychological Test Profiles of Brigadier Generals: Warmongers or Decisive Warriors?" Invited address presented to Division 14 of the American Psychological Association, New York, 1987.

Campbell, D. P.; G. J. Curphy; and T. Tuggle. *360 Degree Feedback Instruments: Beyond Theory.* Workshop presented at the Tenth Annual Conference of the Society for Industrial and Organizational Psychology. Orlando, FL, May 1995.

Campbell, D. P., and S. Hyne. *Manual for the Revised Campbell Organizational Survey.* Minneapolis, MN: National Computer Systems, 1995.

Campbell, D. P.; S. Hyne; and D. L. Nilsen. *Campbell Interests and Skill Survey Manual.* Minneapolis, MN: National Computer Systems, 1992.

Campbell, J. P. "The Cutting Edge of Leadership: An Overview." In *Leadership: The Cutting Edge.* Ed. J. G. Hunt and L. L. Larson. Carbondale: Southern Illinois University Press, 1977.

———. "Training Design for Performance Improvement." In *Productivity in Organizations: New Perspectives from Industrial and Organizational Psychology.* Ed. Campbell, J. P.; R. J.

Campbell; and associates. San Francisco: Jossey-Bass, 1988, pp. 177–216.

Campbell, J. P.; R. A. McCloy; S. H. Oppler; and C. E. Sager. "A Theory of Performance." In *Frontiers in Industrial/Organizational Psychology and Personnel Selection.* Ed. N. Schmitt and W. C. Borman. San Francisco: Jossey-Bass, 1993, pp. 35–70.

Campbell, J. P., and R. D. Pritchard. "Motivation Theory in Industrial and Organizational Psychology." In *Handbook for Industrial and Organizational Psychology.* Ed. M. D. Dunnette. Chicago: Rand McNally, 1976, pp. 60–130.

Cascio, W. F. *A Guide to Responsible Restructuring.* Washington, DC: U.S. Government Printing Office, 1995.

Case, T.; L. Dosier; G. Murkison; and B. Keys. "How Managers Influence Superiors: A Study of Upward Influence Tactics." *Leadership and Organization Development Journal* 9, no. 4 (1988), pp. 4, 25–31.

Ceci, S. J., and W. M. Williams. "Schooling, Intelligence, and Income." *American Psychologist* 52, no. 10 (1997), pp. 1051–58.

Chaleff, I. *The Courageous Follower.* San Francisco: Berrett-Koehler, 1995.

Chandler, A. D. *Scale and Scope: The Dynamics of Industrial Capitalism.* Cambridge: Harvard University Press, 1990.

Charan, R., and G. Colvin. Why CEOs Fail. *Fortune,* June 21, 1999, pp. 69–82.

Charan, R.; S. Drotter; and J. Noel. *The Leadership Pipeline: How to Build the Leadership-Powered Company.* San Francisco: Jossey-Bass, 2001.

Charters, W. W., and N. J. Pitner. "The Application of the Management Behavior Survey to the Measurement of Principle Leadership Behaviors." *Education and Psychological Measurement* 46 (1986), pp. 811–25.

Chemers, M. M. "The Social, Organizational, and Cultural Contest of Effective Leadership." In *Leadership: Multidisciplinary Perspectives.* Ed. B. Kellerman. Englewood Cliffs, NJ: Prentice Hall, 1984.

Chen, X. P.; C. Hui; and D. J. Sego. "The Role of Organizational Citizenship Behavior in Turnover: Conceptualization and Preliminary Tests of Key Hypotheses." *Journal of Applied Psychology* 83, no. 6 (1998), pp. 922–31.

Chinoy, E. *Society.* New York: Random House, 1961.

Chitayat, G., and I. Venezia. "Determinates of Management Styles in Business and Nonbusiness Organizations." *Journal of Applied Psychology* 69 (1984), pp. 437–47.

Choi, Y., and R. R. Mai-Dalton. "The Model of Followers' Responses to Self-Sacrificial Leadership: An Empirical Test." *Leadership Quarterly* 10, no. 3 (1999), pp. 397–422.

Chueng, G. W. "Multifaceted Conceptions of Self-Other Ratings Disagreement." *Personnel Psychology* 52, no. 1 (1999), pp. 1–36.

Church, A. H. "Do Higher Performing Managers Actually Receive Better Ratings?" *Consulting Psychology Journal* 52, no. 2 (2000), pp. 99–116.

———. "From Both Sides Now: The Utility of Individual Personality Theory in I/O Psychology." *Industrial-Organizational Psychologist* 31, no. 3 (1994), pp. 108–16.

———. "From Both Sides Now: The Utility of Individual Personality Theory in I/O Psychology." *Industrial-Organizational Psychologist* 32, no. 3 (1995), pp. 55–63.

———. "Managerial Self-Awareness in High-Performing Individuals in Organizations." *Journal of Applied Psychology* 82, no. 2 (1997) pp. 281–92.

Church, A. H., and J. Waclawski. "A Five-Phase Framework for Designing a Successful Multisource Feedback System. *Consulting Psychology Journal* 53, no. 2 (2001), pp. 82–95.

Cialdini, R. B. *Influence.* New York: William Morrow, 1984.

Clark, B. R. "The Organizational Saga in Higher Education." *Administrative Science Quarterly* 17 (1972), pp. 178–84.

Cleland, D. I. *Strategic Management of Teams.* New York: John Wiley, 1996.

Cleveland, H. *The Knowledge Executive: Leadership in an Information Society.* New York: Dutton, 1985.

Clover, W. H. "Transformational Leaders: Team Performance Leadership Ratings and Firsthand Impressions." In *Measures of Leadership.* Ed. K. E. Clark and M. B. Clark. West Orange, NJ: Leadership Library of America, 1990.

———. "At TRW, Executive Training Contributes to Quality." *Human Resources Professional,* Winter 1991, pp. 16–20.

Clutterbuck, D. "How Much Does Success Depend upon a Helping Hand from Above?" *International Management* 37 (1982), pp. 17–19.

Cohen, A. R., and D. L. Bradford. *Influence without Authority.* New York: John Wiley, 1990.

Collins, J. C., and J. I. Porras. *Built to Last: Successful Habits of Visionary Companies.* Reading, MA: Perseus Books, 1997.

Colquitt, J. A. "On the Dimensionality of Organizational Justice: A Construct Validation of a Measure." *Journal of Applied Psychology* 86, no. 2 (2001), pp. 386–400.

Colquitt, J. A.; D. E. Conlon; M. J. Wesson; C. O. L. H. Porter; and K. Y. Ng. "Justice at the Millennium: A Meta-Analytic Review of 25 Years of Organizational Justice Research." *Journal of Applied Psychology* 86, no. 2 (2001), pp. 425–45.

Conference Board. "Global Management Teams: A Perspective." *HR Executive Review* 4 (1996).

Conger, J. "Can We Really Train Leadership?" *Strategy, Management, Competition,* Winter 1996, pp. 52–65.

Conger, J. A. "Charismatic and Transformational Leadership in Organizations: An Insider's Perspective on These Developing Streams of Research." *Leadership Quarterly* 10, no. 2 (1999), pp. 145–80.

Conger, J. A. *The Charismatic Leader.* San Francisco: Jossey-Bass, 1989.

Conger, J. A. "Qualitative Research as the Cornerstone Methodology for Understanding Leadership. *Leadership Quarterly* 9, no. 1 (1998), pp. 107–122.

Conger, J. A., and J. G. Hunt. "Charismatic and Transformational Leadership: Taking Stock of the Present and Future." *Leadership Quarterly* 10, no. 2 (1999), pp. 121–28.

Conger, J. A., and R. N. Kanungo. *Charismatic Leadership: The Elusive Factor in Organizational Effectiveness.* San Francisco: Jossey-Bass, 1988.

Conger, J. A., and R. N. Kanungo. *Charismatic Leadership in Organizations.* Thousand Oaks, CA: Sage, 1998.

Connelly, M. S.; Gilbert, J. A.; Zaccaro, S. J.; Threlfell, K. V.; Marks, M. A.; and M. D. Mumford. "Exploring the Relationship of Leadership Skills and Knowledge to Leader Performance." *The Leadership Quality,* 11(1), 2000, pp. 65–80.

Connolly, J. J., and C. Viswesvaran. *Affectivity and Job Satisfaction: A Meta-Analysis.* Presentation given at the 13th Annual Conference of the Society of Industrial and Organizational Psychology, Dallas, TX, April 1998.

Cornwell, J. M. "A Meta-Analysis of Selected Trait Research in the Leadership Literature." Paper presented at the Southeastern Psychological Association, Atlanta, GA, 1983.

Cosell, H. *I Never Played the Game.* New York: William Morrow, 1985.

Costa, R. R., and P. T. McCrae. "The Stability of Personality: Observations and Evaluations." *Current Directions in Psychological Science* 3, no. 6 (1994), pp. 173–175.

Couch, A., and P. W. Yetton. "Manager Behavior, Leadership Style, and Subordinate Performance: An Empirical Extension of the Broom-Yetton Conflict Rule." *Organizational Behavior and Human Decision Processes* 39 (1987), pp. 384–96.

Cousteau, V. "How to Swim with Sharks: A Primer." *Perspectives in Biology and Medicine,* Summer 1973, pp. 525–28.

Coye, R. W. "Subordinate Responses to Ineffective Leadership." *Dissertation Abstracts International* 43, 6A (1982), p. 2070.

Cronbach, L. J. *Essentials of Psychological Testing.* 4th ed. San Francisco: Harper & Row, 1984.

Cronshaw, S. F., and R. J. Ellis. "A Process Investigation of Self-Monitoring and Leader Emergence." Paper presented at the Academy of Management Annual Meeting, San Francisco, 1990.

Csikszentmihalyi, M. *Flow: The Psychology of Optimal Experience.* New York: Harper & Row, 1990.

Cudney, M. R., and R. E. Hardy. *Self-Defeating Behaviors.* San Francisco: HarperCollins, 1993.

Cummings, R. C. "Job Stress and the Buffering Effect of Supervisory Support." *Group and Organizational Studies* 15, no. 1 (1990), pp. 92–104.

Cummings, W. H. "Age Group Differences and Estimated Frequencies of the MBTI Types: Proposed Changes." *Proceedings of the Psychology in the Department of Defense Thirteenth Symposium.* Colorado Springs, CO: U. S. Air Force Academy, April 1992.

Curphy, G. J. "Career and Development Planning." Television presentation at National Technical University. Ft. Collins, CO, 1997b.

Curphy, G. J. "A Commentary on Moral Character Screening." In W. Sellman (chair). *Moral Character Screening: Sorting Good and Bad Apples.* Symposium presented at the 105th Annual Meeting of the American Psychological Association, Chicago, 1997d.

Curphy, G. J. "Concluding Remarks on Executive Assessment and Development." In *The Role of I/O Psychology in Executive Assessment and Development,* G. J. Curphy (chair). Symposium presented at the 15th Annual Conference of the Society for Industrial and Organizational Psychology, New Orleans, LA, 2000.

Curphy, G. J. "Early Leadership Talent Identification and Development." Paper presented at the Conference for Executives of Saudi Aramco, Dhahran, Saudi Arabia, October 2001.

Curphy, G. J. "A Roadmap for Creating High Performing Teams." Presentation given at the Strategic Staff Meeting of the Mid-Atlantic Division of the Home Depot, Atlantic City, NJ, September 2000.

————. "The Effects of Transformational and Transactional Leadership on Organizational Climate, Attrition, and Performance." In *Impact of Leadership*. Ed. K. E. Clark, M. B. Clark, and D. P. Campbell. Greensboro, NC: Center for Creative Leadership, 1992a.

————. "An empirical investigation of Bass' (1985) theory of transformational and transactional leadership." Ph.D. dissertation, University of Minnesota, 1991a.

————. "Executive Coaching: How to Achieve Long-Term Leadership Behavioral Change." Panel presentation at the 15th Annual Applied Behavioral Sciences Symposium, United States Air Force Academy, Colorado Springs, CO, 1996.

————. "In-Depth Assessments, 360-Degree Feedback, and Development: Key Research Results and Recommended Next Steps." Presentation at the Annual Conference for HR Managers at U S WEST Communications, Denver, CO, January 1998a.

————. "New Directions in Personality." In R. T. Hogan (chair). *Personality and Organizational Behavior.* Symposium presented at the 104th Annual Meeting of the American Psychological Association, Toronto, Canada, 1996b.

————. "Personality and Work: Some Food for Thought." In R. T. Hogan (chair). *Personality Applications in the Workplace: Thinking outside the Dots.* Symposium presented at the 12th Annual Conference of the Society of Industrial and Organizational Psychology, St. Louis, MO, 1997c.

————. "Personality, Intelligence, and Leadership." Presentation given to the Pioneer Leadership Program at Denver University, Denver, CO, 1997a.

————. "Some Closing Remarks about the Use of Self- and Other-Ratings of Personality and Behaviors." In *Multirater Assessment Systems: What We've Learned.* M. D. Dunnette, chair. Symposium conducted at the 99th American Psychological Association Convention, San Francisco, August 1991b.

————. The Team Assessment Survey. Minneapolis, MN. Personnel Decisions International, 1999.

————. "Transformational, Charismatic, and Transactional Leadership: A Literature Review." Unpublished manuscript. University of Minnesota, Department of Psychology, Minneapolis, 1990.

————. *Users Guide and Interpretive Report for the Leadership Personality Survey.* Minneapolis, MN: Personnel Decisions International, 1998b.

————. "Using Low Fidelity Simulations to Predict Future Leadership Success." In *Selections in Leadership: Some New Research Directions.* R. T. Hogan, chair. Symposium conducted at the 13th Biennial Psychology in the Department of Defense Conference, United States Air Force Academy, 1992b.

Curphy, G. J., F. W. Gibson; B. Asiu; J. Horn; and G. Macomber. *The Attaché & Selection Project.* Technical Report No. 94-2. Colorado Springs, CO: U.S. Air Force Academy, 1994.

Curphy, G. J.; F. W. Gibson; B. W. Asiu; C. P. McCown; and C. Brown. "A Field Study of the Causal Relationships between Organizational Performance, Punishment, and Justice," working paper, 1992.

Curphy, G. J., and K. D. Osten. *Technical Manual for the Leadership Development Survey.* Technical Report No. 93-14. Colorado Springs, CO: U.S. Air Force Academy, 1993.

Curphy, G. J., Osten, K. D., and Voetberg, J. "Research on the Leadership Personality Survey. " Panel presentation at the 15th Annual Behavior Sciences Symposium, United States Air Force Academy, Colorado Springs, CO, 1996.

Curtis, B.; R. E. Smith; and F. L. Smoll. "Scrutinizing the Skipper: A Study of Behaviors in the Dugout." *Journal of Applied Psychology* 64 (1979), pp. 391–400.

Dalton, M. A. "Using 360-Degree Feedback Successfully." *Leadership in Action* 18, no. 1 (1998), pp. 2–11.

Dansereau, F., Jr.; G. Graen; and J. W. Haga. "A Vertical Dyad Linkage Approach to Leadership within Formal Organizations: A Longitudinal Investigation of the Role Making Process." *Organizational Behavior and Human Performance* 13 (1975), pp. 46–78.

Davidson, O. B., and D. Eden. "Remedial Self-Fulfilling Prophecy: Two Field Experiments to Prevent Golem Effects among Disadvantaged Women." *Journal of Applied Psychology* 83, no. 3 (2000), pp. 386–98.

Davis, B. L.; L. W. Hellervik; and J. L. Sheard. *The Successful Manager's Handbook.* 3rd ed. Minneapolis, MN: Personnel Decisions, 1989.

Davis, B. L.; C. J. Skube; L. W. Hellervik; S. H. Gelelein; and J. L. Sheard. *The Successful Manager's Handbook.* Minneapolis, MN: Personnel Decisions, 1992.

Davis, R. C. *The Fundamentals of Top Management.* New York: Harper, 1942.

Deary, J. J. "A (Latent) Big-Five Personality Model in 1915? A Reanalysis of Webb's Data." *Journal of Applied Psychology* 71, no. 5 (1996), pp. 992–1005.

DeBolt, J. W.; A. E. Liska; and B. R. Weng, "Replications of Associations between Internal Locus of Control and Leadership in Small Groups." *Psychological Reports* 38 (1976), p. 470.

Deci, E. L. "Effects of Contingent and Noncontingent Rewards and Controls on Intrinsic Motivation." *Organizational Behavior and Human Performance* 22 (1972), pp. 113–20.

———. *Intrinsic Motivation.* New York: Plenum, 1975.

———. *The Psychology of Self-Determination.* Lexington, MA: Lexington Books, 1980.

Deci, E. L., and R. M. Ryan. "The Support of Autonomy and the Control of Behavior." *Journal of Personality and Social Psychology* 53 (1987), pp. 1024–37.

Decker, P. J. "Social Learning Theory and Leadership." *Journal of Management* 5 (1986), pp. 46–58.

Deep, S., and L. Sussman. *Smart Moves.* Reading MA: Addison-Wesley, 1990.

Delbecq, A. L.; A. H. Van de Ven; and D. H. Gustafson. *Group Techniques for Program Planning: A Guide to Nominal and Delphi Processes.* Glenview, IL: Scott, Foresman, 1975.

Deluga, R. J. "American Presidential Proactivity, Charismatic Leadership and Rated Performance." *Leadership Quarterly* 9, no. 2 (1998), 265–92.

Den Hartog, D. N., and R. M. Verburg. Charisma and Rhetoric: Communicative Techniques of International Business Leaders." *Leadership Quarterly* 8, no. 4 (1997), pp. 355–92.

Den Hartog, D. N.; R. J. House; P. J. Hanges; S. A. Ruiz-Quintanilla; P. W. Dorfman; and Associates. "Culture Specific and Cross-Culturally Generalizable Implicit Leadership Theories: Are Attributes of Charismatic/Transformational Leadership Universally Endorsed?" *Leadership Quarterly* 10, no. 2 (1999), pp. 219–56.

DeNisi, A. S., and A. N. Kluger. "Feedback Effectiveness: Can 360-Degree Appraisals Be Improved?" *Academy of Management Executive* 14, no. 1 (2000), pp. 129–39.

Dessler, G. "How to Earn Your Employees' Commitment." *Academy of Management Executive* 13, no. 2 (1999), pp. 58–67.

Deveraux, G. "Charismatic Leadership and Crisis." In *Psychoanalysis and the Social Sciences.* Ed. W. Muensterberger and S. Axelrod. New York: International University Press, 1955.

Dewhirst, H. D.; V. Metts; and R. T. Ladd. "Exploring the Delegation Decision: Managerial Responses to Multiple Contingencies." Paper presented at the Academy of Management Convention, New Orleans, LA, 1987.

Dickson, M. W.; D. B. Smith; M. W. Grojean; and M. G. Ehrhart. "An Organizational Climate regarding Ethics: The Outcome of Leader Values and the Practices That Reflect Them." *Leadership Quarterly* 12, no. 2 (2001), pp. 197–218.

Dienesch, R. M., and R. C. Liden. "Leader-Member Exchange Model of Leadership: A Critique and Further Development." *Academy of Management Review* 11 (1986), pp. 618–34.

Dobbins, G. H., and J. M. Russell. "The Biasing Effects of Subordinate Likeableness on Leaders' Responses to Poor Performance." *Personnel Psychology* 39 (1986), pp. 759–77.

Donley, R. E., and D. G. Winter. "Measuring the Motives of Public Officials at a Distance: An Exploratory Study of American Presidents." *Behavioral Science* 15 (1970), pp. 227–36.

Donno, D. "Introduction." In *The Prince and Selected Discourses: Machiavelli.* Ed. and trans., D. Dunno. New York: Bantam, 1966.

Dosier, L.; T. Case; and B. Keys. "How Managers Influence Subordinates: An Empirical Study of Downward Influence Tactics." *Leadership and Organization Development Journal* 9, no. 5 (1988), pp. 22–31.

Dow, T. E. "The Theory of Charisma." *Sociological Quarterly* 10 (1969), pp. 306–18.

Downton, J. V. *Rebel Leadership: Commitment and Charisma in the Revolutionary Process.* New York: Free Press, 1973.

Druskat, V. U. "Gender and Leadership Style: Transformational and Transactional Leadership in the Roman Catholic Church." *Leadership Quarterly* 5, no. 1 (1994), pp. 99–120.

Druskat, V. U., and S. B. Wolff. "Building the Emotional Intelligence of Groups." *Harvard Business Review,* March 2001, pp. 80–91.

Dubois, P. H. "A Test Dominated Society: China 1115 BC–1905. In *Testing Problems in Perspective.* Ed. A. Anastasi. American Council on Education, 1964.

Duchon, D.; S. G. Green; and T. D. Taber. "Vertical Dyad Linkage: A Longitudinal Assessment of Antecedents, Measures, and Consequences." *Journal of Applied Psychology* 71 (1986), pp. 56–60.

Dukerich, J. M.; M. L. Nichols; D. R. Elm; and D. A. Vollrath. "Moral Reasoning in Groups: Leaders Make a Difference," *Human Relations* 43 (1990), pp. 473–93.

Dumaine, B. "Creating a New Company Culture." *Fortune,* 1990, pp. 127–131.

Duncker, K. "On Problem Solving." *Psychological Monographs* 58, no. 5, 1945.

Durand, D. E., and W. R. Nord. "Perceived Leader Behavior as a Function of Personality Characteristics of Supervisors and Subordinates." *Academy of Management Journal* 19 (1976), pp. 427–38.

Dvir, T.; D. Eden; B. J. Avolio; and B. Shamir. "Impact of Transformational Leadership Training on Follower Development and Performance: A Field Experiment." Paper presented at 14th Annual Conference of the Society for Industrial and Organizational Psychology, Atlanta, GA, 1999.

Eagly, A. H. *Sex Differences in Social Behavior: A Social Role Interpretation.* Hillsdale, NJ: Erlbaum. 1987.

Eden, D., and A. B. Shani. "Pygmalion Goes to Boot Camp: Expectancy, Leadership, and Trainee Performance." *Journal of Applied Psychology* 67 (1982), pp. 194–99.

Eden, D.; D. Geller; A. Gewirtz; R. Gordon-Terner; I. Inbar; M. Liberman; Y. Pass; I. Salomon-Segev; and M. Shalit. "Implanting Pygmalion Leadership Style through Workshop Training: Seven Field Experiments." *Leadership Quarterly* 11, no. 2 (2000), pp. 171–210.

Edwards, B. *Drawing on the Artist Within.* New York: Simon & Schuster, 1986.

———. *Drawing on the Right Side of the Brain.* Los Angeles, CA: J. P. Tarcher, 1979.

Edwards, M. R., and A. J. Ewen. *360 Degree Feedback: The Powerful New Model for Employee Assessment and Performance Improvement.* New York. American Management Association, 1996.

Ehrhart, M. G., and K. J. Klein. "Predicting Followers' Preferences for Charismatic Leadership: The Influence of Followers Values and Personality." *Leadership Quarterly* 12, no. 2 (2001), pp. 153–80.

Ehrlichman, J. *Witness to Power.* New York: Simon & Schuster, 1982.

Einstein, A. *On Education, Ideas and Opinions.* New York: Bonanza Books, 1954.

Eisenberger, R., and J. Cameron. "Detrimental Effects of Reward: Reality or Myth?" *American Psychologist* 51, no. 11 (1996), pp. 1153–66.

Ellis, A., and R. Harper. *A New Guide to Rational Living.* Englewood Cliffs, NJ: Prentice Hall, 1975.

Ellis, R. J.; R. S. Adamson; G. Deszca; and T. F. Cawsey. "Self-Monitoring and Leadership Emergence." *Small Group Behavior* 19 (1988), pp. 312–24.

Elovainio, M.; M. Kivimaki; and K. Helkama. "Organizational Justice Evaluations, Job Control, and Occupational Strain." *Journal of Applied Psychology* 86, no. 2 (2001), pp. 418–24.

Emery, F. E., and E. L. Trist. "The Causal Texture of Organizational Environments." *Human Relations* 18 (1965), pp. 21–32.

———. *Towards a Social Ecology.* London: Plenum, 1973.

England, G. W., and R. Lee. "The Relationship between Managerial Values and Managerial Success in the United States, Japan, India, and Australia." *Journal of Applied Psychology* 59 (1974), 411–19.

Erez, M.; P. C. Earley; and C. L. Hulin. "The Impact of Participation on Goal Acceptance and Performance: A Two-Step Model." *Academy of Management Journal* (1985), pp. 359–72.

Etzioni, A. *A Comparative Analysis of Complex Organizations.* New York: Free Press, 1961.

Evans, M. G. "The Effects of Supervisory Behavior on the Path-Goal Relationship." *Organizational Behavior and Human Performance* 5 (1970), pp. 277–98.

Fairholm, G. W. *Values Leadership.* Praeger: New York, 1991.

Fairhurst, G. T., and R. A. Sarr. *The Art of Framing: Managing the Language of Leadership.* San Francisco, CA: Jossey-Bass, 1996.

Farris, G. F. "Colleagues' Roles and Innovation in Scientific Teams." Working paper No. 552-71. Cambridge, MA: Alfred P. Sloan School of Management, MIT., 1971.

Feldman, D. C. "The Development and Enforcement of Group Norms," *Academy of Management Review,* January 1984, pp. 47–53.

Ferlise, W. G. "Violence in the Workplace." *Labor and Employment Newsletter,* Washington, DC: Semmes, Bowen, & Semmes, Winter 1995.

Ferris, G. R. "Role of Leadership in the Employee Withdrawal Process: A Constructive Replication." *Journal of Applied Psychology* 70 (1985), pp. 777–81.

Fiechtner, B., and J. J. Krayer, "Variations in Dogmatism and Leader-Supplied Information: Determinants of Perceived Behavior in Task-Oriented Groups." *Group and Organizational Studies* 11 (1986), 403–18.

Fiedler, F. E. "Cognitive Resources and Leadership Performance." *Applied Psychology: An International Review* 44, no. 1 (1995), pp. 5–28.

———. "The Contingency Model and the Dynamics of the Leadership Process." In *Advances in Experimental Social Psychology.* Ed. L. Berkowitz. New York: Academic Press, 1978.

———. "The Effect and Meaning of Leadership Experience: A Review of Research and a Preliminary Model." In *Impact of Leadership.* Ed. K. E. Clark, M. B. Clark, and D. P. Campbell. Greensboro, NC: Center for Creative Leadership, 1992.

———. "Reflections by an Accidental Theorist." *Leadership Quarterly* 6, no. 4 (1995), pp. 453–61.

———. *A Theory of Leadership Effectiveness.* New York: McGraw-Hill, 1967.

Fiedler, F. E., and M. M. Chemers. *Improving Leadership Effectiveness: The Leader Match Concept,* 2nd ed. New York: John Wiley, 1982.

Fiedler, F. E., and J. E. Garcia. *New Approaches to Leadership: Cognitive Resources and Organizational Performance.* New York: John Wiley, 1987.

Field, R. H. G. "A Test of the Vroom-Yetton Normative Model of Leadership." *Journal of Applied Psychology* 67 (1982), pp. 523–32.

Filley, A. C., and L. A. Pace. "Making Judgments Descriptive." In *The 1976 Annual Handbook for Group Facilitators.* Ed. J. E. Jones and J. W. Pfeiffer. La Jolla, CA: University Associates Press, 1976.

Fishbein, M., and I. Azjen. *Belief, Attitude, Intention, and Behavior: An Introduction to Theory and Research.* Reading, MA: Addison-Wesley, 1975.

Fisher, C. D. "The Effects of Personal Control, Competence, and Extrinsic Reward Systems on Intrinsic Motivation." *Organizational Behavior and Human Performance* 21 (1978), pp. 273–88.

Fisher, C. D., and R. Gitleson. "A Meta-Analysis of the Correlates of Role Conflict and Ambiguity." *Journal of Applied Psychology* 68 (1983), pp. 320–33.

Fisher, R., and W. Ury. *Getting to Yes.* Boston: Houghton Mifflin, 1981.

Flanagan, J. C. "Defining the Requirements of the Executive's Job." *Personnel* 28, no. 1 (1951), pp. 28–35.

Fleenor, J. W.; C. D. McCauley; and S. Brutus. "Self-Other Rating Agreement and Leader Effectiveness." *Leadership Quarterly* 7, no. 4 (1996), pp. 487–506.

Fleishman, E. A. *Examiner's Manual for the Leadership Opinion Questionnaire.* Rev. ed. Chicago: Science Research Associates, 1989.

———. *Examiner's Manual for the Supervisory Behavior Description Questionnaire.* Washington, DC: Management Research Institute, 1972.

———. "Twenty Years of Consideration and Structure." In *Current Developments in the Study of Leadership.* Ed. E. A. Fleishman and J. G. Hunt. Carbondale: Southern Illinois University Press, 1973.

"Focus on Personality Tests." *Individual Employment Rights.* Washington, DC: Bureau of National Affairs, April 23, 1996, p. 4.

Fodor, E. "Motive Pattern as an Influence on Leadership in Small Groups." Paper presented at the meeting of the American Psychological Association, New York, August, 1987.

Folkman, S., and R. S. Lazarus. "An Analysis of Coping in a Middle-Aged Community Sample." *Journal of Health and Social Behavior* 21 (1980), pp. 219–39.

Ford, J. D. "Department Context and Formal Structure as Constraints on Leader Behavior." *Academy of Management Journal* 24 (1981), pp. 274–88.

Foushee, H. C. "Dyads and Triads at 35,000 Feet: Factors Affecting Group Process and Aircrew Performance." *American Psychologist* 39 (1984), pp. 885–93.

French, J., and B. H. Raven. "The Bases of Social Power." In *Studies of Social Power.* ed. D. Cartwright. Ann Arbor, MI: Institute for Social Research, 1959.

Freud, S. *Group Psychology and the Analysis of the Ego.* Trans. J. Strachey. 2nd ed. *The Standard Edition of the Complete Psychological Works of Sigmund Freud,* Vol. 2. London: Hogarth Institute for Psychoanalysis.

Friedland, W. H. "For a Sociological Concept of Charisma." *Social Forces,* no. 1 (1964), pp. 18–26.

Friedman, M., and D. Ulmer. *Treating Type A Behavior—and Your Heart.* New York: Knopf, 1984.

Fry, L.; W. Kerr; and C. Lee. "Effects of Different Leader Behaviors under Different Levels of Task Interdependence." *Human Relations* 39 (1986), pp. 1067–82.

Fryer, B. "Tom Seibel of Seibel Systems: High-Tech the Old-Fashioned Way." *Harvard Business Review,* March 2001, pp. 118–30.

Funder, D. C. "Errors and Mistakes: Evaluating the Accuracy of Social Judgement." *Psychological Bulletin* 101 (1987), pp. 75–90.

Gabarro, J. J., and J. P. Kotter. "Managing Your Boss." *Harvard Business Review* 58, no. 1 (1980), pp. 92–100.

Gabor, A. *The Man Who Discovered Quality.* New York: Penguin, 1990.

Gabrenya, W. K., and R. M. Arkin. "Self-Monitoring Scale: Factor Structure and Correlates." *Personality and Social Psychology Bulletin* 6 (1980), pp. 12–22.

Gal, R. *A Portrait of the Israeli Soldier.* New York: Greenwood Press, 1986.

Galbraith, J. *Designing Complex Organizations.* Menlo Park, CA: Addison-Wesley, 1973.

Ganzach, Y. "Intelligence and Job-Satisfaction." *Academy of Management Journal,* 41(5), pp. 526–539.

Ganzach, Y.; A. N. Kluger; and N. Klayman. "Making Decisions from an Interview: Expert Measurement and Mechanical Combination." *Personnel Psychology* 53 no. 1 (2000), pp. 1–20.

Gardner, H. *Frames of Mind: The Theory of Multiple Intelligences.* New York: Basic Books, 1983.

Gardner, J. W. "The Antileadership Vaccine." Essay in the Carnegie Corporation of New York annual report, 1965.

———. *On Leadership.* New York: Free Press, 1990.

———. The Tasks of Leadership. Leadership paper No. 2. Washington, DC: Independent Sector, 1986.

Gardner, W. L., and B. J. Avolio. "The Charismatic Relationship: A Dramaturgical Perspective." *Academy of Management Review* 23, no. 1 (1998), pp. 32–58.

Garforth, F. I. De la P. "War Office Selection Boards." *Occupational Psychology* 19 (1945), pp. 97–108.

Gargiulo, T. F. *Making Stories: A Practical Guide for Organizational Leaders and Human Resource Specialists.* Westport, CT: Greenwood Publishing, 2001.

Gaugler, B. B.; D. B. Rosenthal; G. C. Thornton III; and C. Bentson. "Meta-Analysis of Assessment Center Validity." *Journal of Applied Psychology* 72 (1987), pp. 493–511.

Gebelein, S. H. "Multi-rater Performance Appraisal: The Promise, the Pitfalls, and the Steps." Paper presented at the American Society of Training and Development Convention. Anaheim, CA, May 1994.

———. "360-Degree Feedback Goes Strategic." *PDI Portfolio,* Summer 1996, pp. 1–3.

General Accounting Office. "Managerial Practices—U.S. Companies Improve Performance through Quality Efforts," 1990.

Gerth, H. H., and C. W. Mills. *Max Weber: Essays in Sociology.* New York: Oxford University Press, 1946.

Ghiselli, E. E. "Intelligence and Managerial Success." *Psychological Reports* 12 (1963), p. 89.

Ghorpade, J. "Managing Six Paradoxes of 360-Degree Feedback." *Academy of Management Executive* 14, no. 1 (2000), pp. 140–150.

Gibb, C. A. "Leadership." In *The Handbook of Social Psychology.* Ed. G. Lindzey and E. Aronson. Vol. 4. 2nd ed. Reading, MA: Addison-Wesley, 1968, pp. 205–82.

Gibb, J. R. "Defensive Communication." *Journal of Communication* 13, no. 3 (1961), pp. 141–48.

Gibbard, G. S.; J. J. Hartman; and R. D. Mann. *Analysis of Groups: Contribution to the Theory, Research, and Practice.* San Francisco: Jossey-Bass, 1974.

Gibble, J. L., and J. D. Lawrence. "Peer Coaching for Principals." *Educational Leadership* 45 (1987), pp. 72–73.

Gibson, F. W. "A Taxonomy of Leader Abilities and Their Influence on Group Performance as a Function of Interpersonal Stress." In *Impact of Leadership*. Ed. K. E. Clark, M. B. Clark, and D. P. Campbell. Greensboro, NC: Center for Creative Leadership, 1992.

Gibson, F. W., and G. J. Curphy. "The MBTI: Skewering A Sacred Cow." Presentation given to the Colorado Organizational Development Network, Denver, CO, 1996.

Ginnett, R. C. "Airline Cockpit Crew." In *Groups That Work (and Those That Don't)*. Ed. J. Richard Hackman. San Francisco: Jossey-Bass, 1990.

————. "Behavioral Characteristics of Effective Crew Leaders." *Human Error Avoidance Techniques: Proceedings of the Second Conference*. Herndon, VA: Society of Automotive Engineers, 1989.

————. "Cockpit Crew Effectiveness from the Inside Out: A Micro-Analysis Leading to Macro Considerations." *Proceedings of the Eleventh Psychology in the Department of Defense Symposium*. Colorado Springs, CO, 1988.

————. "Crews as Groups: Their Formation and Their Leadership." In *Cockpit Resource Management*. Ed. E. Wiener, B. Banki, and R. Helmreich. Orlando, FL: Academic Press, 1993.

————. "Effectiveness Begins Early: The Leadership Role in the Formation of Intra-Organizational Task Groups." (unpublished manuscript, 1992).

————. "The Formation Process of Airline Flight Crews." *Proceedings of the Fourth International Symposium on Aviation Psychology*. Columbus, OH, 1987.

————. "Interaction of Traits and Motivational Factors in the Determination of the Success of Managers." *Journal of Applied Psychology* 52 (1968), pp. 480–83.

————. "Team Effectiveness Leadership Model: Identifying Leverage Points for Change." *Proceedings of the 1996 National Leadership Institute Conference*. College Park, MD: National Leadership Institute, 1996.

————. "To the Wilderness and Beyond: The Application of a Model for Transformal Change." *Proceedings of the 9th Psychology in the Department of Defense Symposium*. Colorado Springs, CO, 1984.

Gilligan, C. *In a Different Voice*. Cambridge: Harvard University Press, 1982.

Glasser, W. *The Quality School*. New York: Harper & Row, 1990.

Goff, M. *Critical Leadership Skills Valued by Every Organization*. Minneapolis, MN: Personnel Decisions International, 2000.

Goldstein, I. L. *Training in Organizations: Needs Assessments, Development, and Evaluation*. 2nd ed. Monterey, CA: Brooks/Cole, 1986.

Goleman, D. *Emotional Intelligence*. New York: Bantam Doubleday Dell, 1995.

————. *Working with Emotional Intelligence*. New York: Bantam Doubleday Dell, 1998.

Goodstadt, B. E., and L. A. Hjelle. "Power to the Powerless: Locus of Control and the Use of Power." *Journal of Personality and Social Psychology* 27 (1973), pp. 190–96.

Goodstadt, B. E., and D. Kipnis. "Situational Influences on the Use of Power." *Journal of Applied Psychology* 54 (1970), pp. 201–07.

Gordon, L. V. *Measurement of Interpersonal Values*. Chicago: Science Research Associates, 1975.

Gordon, W. J. J. *Synectics*. New York: Harper & Row, 1961.

————. "A Managerial Potential Scale for the California Psychological Inventory." In *Measures of Leadership*. Ed. K. E. Clark and M. B. Clark. West Orange, NJ: Leadership Library of America, 1989.

Graeff, C. L. "The Situational Judgement Theory: A Critical Review." *Academy of Management Journal* 8 (1983), pp. 285–96.

Graen, G. B., and J. F. Cashman. "A Role-Making Model of Leadership in Formal Organizations: A Developmental Approach." In *Leadership*

Frontiers. Ed. J. G. Hunt and L. L. Larson. Kent, OH: Kent State University Press, 1975.

Graen, G. B.; R. C. Linden; and W. Hoel. "Role of Leadership in the Employee Withdrawal Process." *Journal of Applied Psychology* 67 (1982), pp. 868–72.

Graen, G. B. and T. A. Scandura. "Toward a Psychology of Dyadic Organizing." In *Research in Organizational Behavior.* Vol. 9. Ed. L. L. Cummings and B. M. Staw. Greenwich, CT: JAI Press, 1987.

Grant, L. "Happy Workers, High Returns." *Fortune,* January 12, 1998, p. 81.

Green, S. G.; G. T. Fairhurst; and B. K. Snavely. "Chains of Poor Performance and Supervisory Control." *Organizational Behavior and Human Decision Processes* 38 (1986), pp. 7–27.

Green, S. G., and T. R. Mitchell. "Attributional Processes of Leaders in Leader-Member Interactions." *Organizational Behavior and Human Performances* 23 (1979), pp. 429–58.

Greguras, G. J., and C. Robie. "A New Look at Within-Source Interrater Reliability of 360-Degree Feedback Ratings." *Journal of Applied Psychology* 83, no. 6 (1998), pp. 960–68.

Greller, M. M. "Evaluation of Feedback Sources as a Function of Role and Organizational Development." *Journal of Applied Psychology* 65 (1980), pp. 24–27.

Grey, R. J. and G. G. Gordon. "Risk-Taking Managers: Who Gets the Top Jobs?" *Management Review* 67 (1978), pp. 8–13.

Griffin, R. W.; A. Welsh; and G. Moorehead. "Perceived Task Characteristics and Employee Performance: A Literature Review." *Academy of Management Review* 6 (1981), pp. 655–64.

Guilford, J. P. *The Nature of Human Intelligence.* New York: McGraw-Hill, 1967.

Guion, R. M. "Personnel Assessment, Selection, and Placement." In *Handbook of Industrial and Organizational Psychology.* Vol. 2. Ed. M. D. Dunnette and L. M. Hough. Palo Alto, CA: Consulting Psychologists Press, 1991, pp. 327–98.

Guion, R. M., and R. F. Gotter. "Validity of Personality Measures in Personnel Selection." *Personnel Psychology* 18 (1965), pp. 135–64.

Guth, C. K., and S. S. Shaw. *How to Put on Dynamic Meetings.* Reston, VA: Reston, 1980.

Guzzo, R. A.; P. R. Yost; R. J. Campbell; and G. P. Shea. "Potency in Teams: Articulating a Construct." *British Journal of Social Psychology* 32 (1993), pp. 87–106.

Hackman, J. R. "Group Influences on Individuals." In *Handbook of Industrial and Organizational Psychology.* Ed. M. D. Dunnette. Chicago: Rand McNally, 1976.

————. "Group Level Issues in the Design and Training of Cockpit Crews." In *Proceedings of the NASA/MAC Workshop on Cockpit Resource Management.* Ed. H. H. Orlady and H. C. Foushee. Moffett Field, CA: NASA Ames Research Center, 1986.

————. *Groups That Work (and Those That Don't).* San Francisco: Jossey-Bass, 1990.

Hackman, J. R., and G. R. Oldham. "Motivation through the Design of Work: Test of a Theory." *Organizational Behavior and Human Performance* 16 (1976), pp. 250–79.

————. *Work Redesign.* Reading, MA: Addison-Wesley, 1980.

Hales, D., and R. E. Hales. "Is Work Driving You Mad?" *Parade Magazine,* March 18, 2001, pp. 8–9.

Hall, J., and S. M. Donnell. "Managerial Achievement: The Personal Side of Behavioral Theory." *Human Relations* 32 (1979), pp. 77–101.

Hallam, G. L., and D. P. Campbell. "Selecting Team Members? Start with a Theory of Team Effectiveness." Paper presented at the Seventh Annual Meeting of the Society of Industrial/Organizational Psychologists, Montreal, Canada, May 1992.

Hallam, S. *Leadership Matters: Research about Leadership Is Important.* Akron, OH: University of Akron, 2001.

Halpin, A. W., and B. J. Winer. "A Factorial Study of the Leader Behavior Descriptions." In *Leader Behavior: Its Descriptions and Measurement.* Ed. R. M. Stogdill and A. E. Coons. Columbus: Ohio State University, Bureau of Business Research, 1957.

Hambrick, D. C. "Environment, Strategy and Power within Top Management Teams." *Administrative Science Quarterly* 26 (1981), pp. 253–75.

Hambuger, K. E. "Leadership in Combat." Unpublished report. Department of History, U. S. Military Academy, 1984.

Hammer, M., and J. Champy. *Reengineering the Corporation.* New York: HarperBusiness, 1993.

Hammer, T. H., and J. Turk. "Organizational Determinants of Leader Behavior and Authority." *Journal of Applied Psychology* 71 (1987), pp. 674–82.

Haney, C.; C. Banks; and P. G. Zimbardo. "Interpersonal Dynamics in a Simulated Prison." *International Journal of Criminology and Penology* 1 (1973), pp. 69–97.

Hansen, J. C., and D. P. Campbell. *Manual for the Strong Interest Inventory.* 4th ed. Stanford, CA: Stanford University Press, 1985.

Harris, T. A. *I'm OK—You're OK: A Practical Guide to Transactional Analysis.* New York: Harper & Row, 1967.

Harrison, E. L. "Training Supervisors to Discipline Effectively." *Training and Development Journal* 36, no. 11 (1982), pp. 111–13.

Hart, M. H. *The 100: A Ranking of the Most Influential Persons in History.* New York: Hart, 1978.

Hart, P. M. "Predicting Employee Life Satisfaction: A Coherent Model of Personality, Work and Nonwork Experiences, and Domain Satisfactions." *Journal of Applied Psychology* 84, no. 4 (1999), pp. 564–83.

Harvey, J. B. "The Abilene Paradox: The Management of Agreement." *Organizational Dynamics* 3 (1974), pp. 63–80.

Hazucha, J. F. *PDI Indicator: Competence, Potential, and Jeopardy. What Gets Managers Ahead May Not Keep Them out of Trouble.* Minneapolis, MN: Personnel Decisions, September 1992.

Hazucha, J. F.; S. A. Hezlett; and R. J. Schneider. "The Impact of 360-Degree Feedback on Management Skills Development." *Human Resource Management* 32 (1993), pp. 325–51.

Health, Education, and Welfare Task Force. *Work in America.* Cambridge, MA: MIT Press, 1973.

Heckman, R. J., and B. W. Roberts. "Personality Profiles of Effective Managers across Functions: A Person-Centered Approach." In R. T. Hogan (chair). *Personality Applications in the Workplace: Thinking outside the Dots.* Symposium presented at the 12th Annual Conference of the Society of Industrial and Organizational Psychology, St. Louis, MO, 1997.

Hegarty, W. H., and H. P. Sims. "Organizational Philosophy, Policies, and Objectives Related to Unethical Decision Behavior: A Laboratory Experiment." *Journal of Applied Psychology* 64 (1979), pp. 331–38.

———. "Some Determinants of Unethical Decision Behavior: An Experiment." *Journal of Applied Psychology* 63 (1978), pp. 451–57.

Heine, D. "Using I/O Psychology to Turn Around a Business." In *The Role of I/O Psychology in Executive Assessment and Development,* G. J. Curphy (chair). Symposium presented at the 15th Annual Conference of the Society for industrial and Organizational Psychology, New Orleans, LA, 2000.

Heller, T., and J. Van Til. "Leadership and Followership: Some Summary Propositions." *Journal of Applied Behavioral Science* 18, 405–14.

Hemphill, J. K. "The Leader and His Group." *Journal of Educational Research* 28 (1949), pp. 225–29, 245–46.

Hemphill, J. K., and A. E. Coons. "Development of the Leader Behavior Description Questionnaire." In *Leader Behavior: Its Description and Measurement.* Ed. R. M. Stogdill and A. E. Coons. Columbus: Ohio State University, Bureau of Business Research, 1957.

Herrnstein, R. J., and C. Murray. *The Bell Curve: Intelligence and Class Structure in American Life.* New York: Free Press, 1994.

Hersey, P., and K. H. Blanchard. "Life Cycle Theory of Leadership." *Training and Development Journal* 23 (1969), pp. 26–34.

————. *Management of Organizational Behavior: Utilizing Human Resources.* 3rd ed. Englewood Cliffs, NJ: Prentice Hall, 1977.

————. *Management of Organizational Behavior: Utilizing Human Resources.* 4th ed. Englewood Cliffs, NJ: Prentice Hall, 1984.

Herzberg, F. "The Motivation-Hygiene Concept and Problems of Manpower." *Personnel Administrator* 27 (1964), pp. 3–7.

————. *Work and the Nature of Man.* Cleveland, OH: World Publishing, 1966.

Hezlett, S. A., and B. A. Koonce. "Now That I've Been Assessed, What Do I Do? Facilitating Development after Individual Assessments." Paper presented at the IPMA Assessment Council Conference on Public Personnel Assessment, New Orleans, LA, June 1995.

Hill, C. W. "Leadership and Symbolic Authority in Psychoanalysis." In *Multidisciplinary Perspectives.* Ed. B. Kellerman. Englewood Cliffs, NJ: Prentice Hall, 1984.

Hill, N. "Self-Esteem: The Key to Effective Leadership." *Administrative Management* 40, no. 9, (1985), pp. 71–76.

Hinkin, T. R., and C. A. Schriesheim. "Development and Application of New Scales to Measure the French and Raven (1959) Bases of Social Power." *Journal of Applied Psychology* 74 (1989), pp. 561–67.

Hirsh, S. K., and J. M. Kummerow. *Introduction to Type in Organizations.* Palo Alto, CA: Consulting Psychologists Press, 1990.

Hogan, J. "The Mask of Integrity." Paper presented at the 13th Biennial Psychology in the Department of Defense Symposium, United States Air Force Academy, Colorado Springs, CO, 1992a.

————. "Personality and Personality Measurement." In *Handbook of Industrial and Organizational Psychology.* Vol. 2. Ed. M. D. Dunnette and L. M. Hough. Palo Alto, CA: Consulting Psychologists Press, 1991, pp. 873–919.

————. "The View from Below." In *The Future of Leadership Selection.* R. T. Hogan (chair). Symposium conducted at the 13th Biennial Psychology in the Department of Defense Conference, United States Air Force Academy, Colorado Springs, CO, 1992b.

Hogan, R. T. "The Role of Big Five Personality Traits in Executive Selection." In G. J. Curphy (chair). *The Role of I/O Psychology in Executive Assessment and Development.* Paper presented at the 15th Annual Conference of the Society of Industrial and Organizational Psychology, New Orleans, LA, 2000.

Hogan, R. T.; G. J. Curphy; and J. Hogan. "What Do We Know about Personality: Leadership and Effectiveness?" *American Psychologist* 49 (1994), pp. 493–504.

Hogan, R. T., and J. Hogan. *Manual for the Hogan Personality Inventory.* Tulsa, OK: Hogan Assessment Systems, 1992.

Hogan, R. T.; J. Hogan; and B. W. Roberts. "Personality Measurement and Employment Decisions: Questions and Answers." *American Psychologist* 51, no. 5 (1996), pp. 469–77.

Hogan, R. T., and A. M. Morrison. "The Psychology of Managerial Incompetence." Paper presented at a joint conference of the American Psychological Association–National Institute of Occupational Safety and Health. Washington, DC, October 1991.

Hogan, R. T., and J. Morrison. "Managing Creativity," In *Create to Be Free: Essays in Honor of Frank Barron.* Ed. A. Montouri. Amsterdam: J. C. Gieben, 1993.

Hogan, R. T.; J. Morrison; and G. J. Curphy. *The Necessary and Sufficient Traits for Leadership Effectiveness.* Manuscript submitted for publication.

Hogan, R. T.; R. Raskin; and D. Fazzini. "The Dark Side of Charisma." In *Measures of Leadership.*

Ed. K. E. Clark and M. B. Clark. West Orange, NJ: Leadership Library of America, 1989.

Holladay, S. J., and W. T. Coombs. "Speaking of Visions and Visions Being Spoken: An Exploration of the Effects of Content and Delivery on Perceptions of Leader Charisma." *Management Communication Quarterly* 7 (1994), pp. 165–89.

Hollander, E. P. *Leadership Dynamics: A Practical Guide to Effective Relationships.* New York: Free Press, 1978.

———. "Leadership and Power." In *Handbook of Social Psychology.* Ed. G. Lindzey and E. Aronson. Vol. 2. 3rd ed. New York: Random House, 1985.

———. "Relationships between Subordinate Perceptions of Supervisory Influence Tactics and Attributed Bases of Supervisory Power." *Human Relations* 43 (1990), pp. 221–37.

Hollander, E. P., and J. W. Julian. "Contemporary Trends in the Analysis of Leadership Processes." *Psychological Bulletin* 71 (1969), pp. 387–91.

Hollander, E. P., and L. R. Offermann. "Power and Leadership in Organizations." *American Psychologist* 45 (1990), pp. 179–89.

Holloman, C. R. "Leadership and Headship: There Is a Difference." *Personal Administration* 31, no. 4 (1968), pp. 38–44.

Hooijberg, R., and J. Choi. "Which Leadership Roles Matter to Whom? An Examination of Rater Effects on Perceptions of Effectiveness." *Leadership Quarterly* 11, no. 3 (2000), pp. 341–64.

Hooijberg, R., and J. Choi. "From Selling Peanuts and Beer in Yankee Stadium to Creating a Theory of Transformational Leadership: An Interview with Bernie Bass." *Leadership Quarterly* 11, no. 2 (2000), pp. 291–300.

Hoppock, R. *Job Satisfaction.* New York: Harper, 1935.

Hough, L. "Personality Measurement, Response Distortion, and Issues of Implementation." In J. Hogan (chair). *Personality Measurement and Employment Decisions: Questions and Answers.* Symposium presented at the 12th Annual Conference of the Society of Industrial and Organizational Psychology, St. Louis, MO, 1997.

Hough, L. M. "The Big Five Personality Variables—Construct Confusion: Description Versus Prediction." *Human Performance* 5 (1992), pp. 139–55.

House, R. J. "A 1976 Theory of Charismatic Leadership." In *Leadership: The Cutting Edge.* Ed. J. G. Hunt and L. L. Larson. Carbondale: Southern Illinois University Press, 1977.

———. "Power in Organizations: A Social Psychological Perspective." Unpublished manuscript, University of Toronto, 1984.

House, R. J., and G. Dressler. "The Path-Goal Theory of Leadership: Some Posthoc and A Priori Tests." In *Contingency Approaches to Leadership.* Ed. J. G. Hunt and L. L. Larson. Carbondale: Southern Illinois University Press, 1974.

House, R. J., and T. R. Mitchell. "Path-Goal Theory of Leadership." *Contemporary Business* 3 (Fall 1974), pp. 81–98.

House, R. J.; R. S. Schuler; and E. Levanoni. "Role Conflict and Ambiguity Scales: Reality or Artifact?" *Journal of Applied Psychology* 68 (1983), pp. 334–37.

House, R. J., and B. Shamir. "Toward an Integration of Transformational, Charismatic, and Visionary Theories." In *Leadership Theory and Research Perspective and Directions.* Ed. M. Chemers and R. Ayman. Orlando, FL: Academic Press, 1993, pp. 577–94.

House, R. J.; W. D. Spangler; and J. Woycke. "Personality and Charisma in the U.S. Presidency: A Psychological Theory of Leadership Effectiveness." *Administrative Science Quarterly* 36 (1991), pp. 364–96.

House, R. J.; J. Woycke; and E. M. Fodor. "Charismatic and Noncharismatic Leaders: Differences in Behavior and Effectiveness." In *Charismatic Leadership: The Elusive Factor in Organizational Effectiveness.* Ed. J. A. Conger and R. N. Kanungo. San Francisco: Jossey-Bass, 1988, pp. 98–121.

Howard, A. "College Experiences and Managerial Performance." *Journal of Applied Psychology* 71 (1986), pp. 530–52.

Howard, A., and D. W. Bray. "Predictors of Managerial Success over Long Periods of Time." In *Measures of Leadership.* Ed. M. B. Clark and K. E. Clark. West Orange, NJ: Leadership Library of America, 1989.

Howard, A; T. A. Judge; E. A. Locke; C. C. Durham; and A. N. Kluger. "Dispositional Effects on Job and Life Satisfaction: The Role of Core Evaluations." *Journal of Applied Psychology* 83, no. 1 (1998), pp. 17–34.

Howard, P. J., and J. M. Howard. "Buddy, Can You Paradigm?" *Training & Development,* September 1995, pp. 28–34.

Howell, J. M., and B. J. Avolio. "Transformational Leadership, Transactional Leadership, Focus of Control, and Support for Innovation: Key Predictors of Consolidated Business Unit Performance." *Journal of Applied Psychology* 78 (1993), pp. 891–902.

Howell, J. M., and P. Frost. "A Laboratory Study of Charismatic Leadership." *Organizational Behavior and Human Decision Processes* 43 (1988), pp. 243–69.

Howell, J. P., and P. W. Dorfman. "Leadership and Substitutes for Leadership among Professional and Nonprofessional Workers." *Journal of Applied Behavioral Science* 22 (1986), pp. 29–46.

———. "Substitute for Leadership: Test of a Construct." *Academy of Management Journal* 24 (1981), pp. 714–28.

Huberman, J. "Discipline without Punishment." *Harvard Business Review,* July–August 1964, p. 62.

Hughes, R. L., and R. LaScala. *Helper Effectiveness Learning Program.* Chicago: Instructional Dynamics, 1977.

Humphreys, L. G. "General Intelligence." In *Perspectives on Bias in Mental Testing.* Ed. C. R. Reynolds and R. T. Brown. New York: Plenum, 1984, pp. 221–47.

———. "Intelligence: Three Kinds of Instability and Their Consequences for Policy." In *Intelligence: Measurement, Theory, and Public Policy.*

Ed. R. L. Linn. Chicago: University of Illinois Press, 1989, pp. 193–216.

Hunt, J. G. "Transformational/Charismatic Leadership's Transformation of the Field: An Historical Essay." *Leadership Quarterly,* 10, no. 2 (1999), pp. 129–44.

Hunt, J. G.; K. B. Boal; and G. E. Dodge. "The Effects of Visionary and Crisis-Responsive Charisma on Followers: An Experimental Examination of Two Kinds of Charismatic Leadership." *Leadership Quarterly* 10, no. 3 (1999), pp. 423–48.

Hunt, J. G., and R. N. Osborn. "Toward a Macro-oriented Model of Leadership: An Odyssey." In *Leadership: Beyond Establishment Views.* Ed. J. G. Hunt, U. Sekaran, and C. A. Schriesheim. Carbondale: Southern Illinois University Press, 1982, pp. 196–221.

Hunter, J. E., and R. F. Hunter. "Validity and Utility of Alternative Predictors of Job Performance." *Psychological Bulletin* 96 (1984), pp. 72–98.

Hunter, J. E.; F. L. Schmidt; and M. K. Judiesch. "Individual Differences in Output Variability as a Function of Job Complexity." *Journal of Applied Psychology* 74 (1990), pp. 28–42.

Hurtz, G. M., and J. J. Donovan. "Personality and Job Performance: The Big Five Revisited." *Journal of Applied Psychology* 85, no. 6 (2000), pp. 869–79.

Huselid, M. A. "The Impact of Human Resource Practices on Turnover, Productivity, and Corporate Financial Performance." *Academy of Management Journal* 38, no. 4 (1995), pp. 635–72.

Hymowitz, C. "Five Main Reasons Why Managers Fail." *The Wall Street Journal.* May 2, 1988.

Iacocca, L., with W. Novack. *Iacocca: An Autobiography.* New York: Bantam, 1984.

Iaffaldano, M. T., and P. M. Muchinsky. "Job Satisfaction and Job Performance: A Meta-Analysis." *Psychological Bulletin* 97 (1985), pp. 251–73.

Imai, M. *Kaizen: The Key to Japan's Competitive Success.* New York: Random House, 1986.

Indik, B. P. "Organizational Size and Member Participation: Some Empirical Tests of Alternative Explanations." *Human Relations* 18 (1965), pp. 339–50.

Instone, D.; B. R. Major; and B. B. Bunker. "Gender, Self-Confidence, and Social Influence Strategies: An Organizational Simulation." *Journal of Personality and Social Psychology* 44 (1983), pp. 322–33.

Ivancevich, J. M.; D. M. Schweiger; and J. W. Ragan. "Employee Stress, Health, and Attitudes: A Comparison of American, Indian, and Japanese Managers." Paper presented at the Academy of Management convention, Chicago, 1986.

Jago, A. G. "Leadership: Perspectives in Theory and Research." *Management Science* 28 (1982), pp. 315–36.

Jago, A. G., and J. W. Ragan. "The trouble with LEADER MATCH Is That It Doesn't Match Fiedler's Contingency Model." *Journal of Applied Psychology* 71 (1986a), pp. 555–59.

―――. "Some Assumptions Are More Troubling than Others: Rejoinder to Chemers and Fiedler." *Journal of Applied Psychology* 71 (1986b), pp. 564–65.

Jamal, M. "Job Stress and Job Performance Controversy: An Empirical Assessment." *Organizational Behavior and Human Performance* 33 (1984), pp. 1–21.

Janda, K. F. "Towards the Explication of the Concept of Leadership in Terms of the Concept of Power." *Human Relations* 13 (1960), pp. 345–63.

Janis, I. L. *Groupthink.* 2nd ed. Boston: Houghton Mifflin, 1982.

―――. *Stress and Frustration.* New York: Harcourt Brace Jovanovich, 1971.

Jaques, E. "Assessing Creative Leaders." In *Proceedings of the Creativity and Innovation Symposium.* Ed. V. E. Hendrix, D. B. Chapla, and W. Mizzle. Washington, DC: National Defense University, 1985, pp. 145–56.

Jayaratne, S.; D. Himle; and W. A. Chess. "Dealing with Work Stress and Strain: Is the Perception of Support More Important than Its Use?" *Journal of Applied Behavioral Science* 24, no. 2 (1988), pp. 34–45.

Jellison, J. "Leading Agile Organizations in Turbulent Times." Presentation given at The Saint Paul Companies, St. Paul, MN, October, 2000.

Jenkins, G. D.; A. Mitra; N. Gupta; and J. D. Shaw. "Are Financial Incentives Related to Performance? A Meta-Analytic Review of Empirical Research." *Journal of Applied Psychology* 83, no. 5 (1998), pp. 777–87.

Jennings, G. *The Mobile Manager.* New York: McGraw-Hill, 1971.

Jones, D. "Firms Spend Billions to Fire Up Workers— With Little Luck." *USA Today,* May 10, 2001, pp. 1–2A.

Johnson, A. L.; F. Luthans; and H. W. Hennessey. "The Role of Locus of Control in Leader Influence Behavior." *Personal Psychology* 37 (1984), pp. 61–75.

Johnson, C. "Japanese-Style Management in America." *California Management Review* 30 (1988), pp. 34–45.

Johnson, J. "Towards a Taxonomy of Managerial Profiles." *Human Performance,* in press.

Johnson, J. C., and M. D. Dunnette. "Validity and Test-Retest Stability of the Nash Managerial Effectiveness Scale on the Revised Form of the Strong Vocational Interest Blank." *Personnel Psychology* (1968), pp. 283–93.

Johnson, K., and J. Johnson. *Economic Value of Performance Change after 360 Degree Feedback.* Minneapolis, MN: Personnel Decisions International, 2001.

Johnson, S. *Who Moved My Cheese?* New York: Putnam, 1999.

Johnston, J. M. "Punishment of Human Behavior." *American Psychologist* 27 (1972), pp. 1033–54.

Jones, E. E. "Interpreting Interpersonal Behavior: The Effects of Expectancies." *Science* 234 (1986), pp. 41–46.

Jones, E. E., and R. E. Nisbett. "The Actor and the Observer: Divergent Perceptions of the Causes of Behavior." In *Attribution: Perceiving the Causes of Behavior.* Ed. E. E. Jones, D. E. Kanouse, H. H. Kelley, R. E. Nisbett, S. Valins, and B. Weiner. Morristown, NJ: General Learning Press, 1972.

Jones, J. E. "Criteria of Effective Goal-Setting: The Spiro Model." In *The 1972 Annual Handbook for Group Facilitators.* Ed. J. E. Jones and J. W. Pfeiffer. La Jolla, CA: University of Associates Press, 1972, pp. 133–34.

Judge, T. A., and J. E. Bono. "Five-Factor Model of Personality and Transformational Leadership." *Journal of Applied Psychology,* 85, no. 5 (2000), pp. 751–65.

Judge, T. A.; J. W. Boudreau; R. D. Bretz. "Job and Life Attitudes of Male Executives." *Journal of Applied Psychology* 79 (1994), pp. 767–82.

Judge, T. A.; C. A. Higgins; C. J. Thoresen; and M. R. Barrick. "The Big Five Personality Traits, General Mental Ability, and Career Success across the Life Span." *Personnel Psychology* 52, no. 3 (1999), pp. 621–52.

Judge, T. A., and C. L. Hulin. "Job Satisfaction as a Reflection of Disposition: A Multiple Source Causal Analysis." *Organizational Behavior and Human Decision Processes* 56 (1993), pp. 388–421.

Judge, T. A.; C. J. Thoresen; V. Pucik; and T. W. Welbourne. "Managerial Coping with Change: A Dispositional Perspective." *Journal of Applied Psychology* 84, no. 1 (1999), pp. 107–22.

Judge, T. A., and E. A. Locke. "Effect of Dysfunctional Thought Processes on Subjective Well-Being and Job Satisfaction." *Journal of Applied Psychology* 78 (1993), pp. 475–490.

Judge, T. A.; J. E. Bono; and E. A. Locke. "Personality and Job Satisfaction: The Mediating Role of Job Characteristics." *Journal of Applied Psychology* 85, no. 2 (2000), pp. 237–49.

Judge, T. A., and S. Watanabe. "Another Look at the Job Satisfaction–Life Satisfaction Relationship." *Journal of Applied Psychology* 78 (1993), pp. 939–48.

Jung, C. G. *Psychological Types.* Trans. R. F. C. Hall. Princeton, NJ: Princeton University Press, 1971.

Juran, J. M. *Juran on Leadership for Quality.* New York: Free Press, 1989.

———. "The QC Circle Phenomenon." *Industrial Quality Control,* January 1967, pp. 329–36.

Justice, A. "Review of the Effects of Stress on Cancer in Laboratory Animals: Importance of Time of Stress Application and Type of Tumor." *Psychological Bulletin* 98 (1985), pp. 108–38.

Kanfer, R. "Motivation Theory in Industrial and Organizational Psychology." In *Handbook of Industrial and Organizational Psychology.* Vol. 1. Ed. M. D. Dunnette and L. M. Hough. Palo Alto, CA: Consulting Psychologists Press, 1990, pp. 75–170.

Kanter, R. M. *The Change Masters.* New York: Simon & Schuster, 1983.

———. *Commitment and Community.* Cambridge: Harvard University Press, 1972.

Kaplan, R. E. "The Warp and Woof of the General Manager's Jobs." In *Facilitating Work Effectiveness.* Ed. B. Schneider and D. Schoorman. Lexington, MA: Lexington Books, 1986.

Kaplan, R. S., and D. P. Norton. *The Balanced Scorecard: Translating Strategy into Action.* Boston: Harvard Business School Press, 1996.

Karp, D. A., and W. C. Yoels. *Symbols, Selves, and Society.* New York: Lippincott, 1979.

Katz, D.; N. Maccoby; G. Gurin; and L. G. Floor. *Productivity, Supervision, and Morale Among Railroad Workers.* Ann Arbor: University of Michigan, Survey Research Center, Institute of Social Research, 1951.

Katzell, R. A., and R. A. Guzzo. "Psychological Approaches to Productivity Improvement." *American Psychologist* 38 (1983), pp. 468–72.

———. "Dilemmas of Managing Participation." *Organizational Dynamics* 11, no. 1 (1982), pp. 5–27.

———. *Teams at the Top.* Boston: Harvard Business School Press, 1998.

Katzenbach, J. R., and B. K. Smith. *The Wisdom of Teams.* Boston: HarperBusiness, 1994.

Kazdin, A. E. *Behavior Modification in Applied Settings.* Homewood, IL: Dorsey, 1975.

Keller, G. "Increasing Quality on Campus." *Change* 24, no. 3 (1992), pp. 48–51.

Keller, R. T. *Toward a Contingency Theory of Leader Behavior and Creative versus Incremental Innovative Outcomes in Research and Development Project Groups: Report on the First Wave of Data.* Bethlehem, PA: Lehigh University, Center for Innovative Management, 1989.

Keller, R. T., and A. D. Szilagyi. "Employee Reactions for Leader Reward Behavior." *Academy of Management Journal* 19 (1976), pp. 619–27.

———. "A Longitudinal Study of Leader Reward Behavior, Subordinate Expectancies, and Satisfaction." *Personnel Psychology* 11 (1978), pp. 119–29.

Kelley, R. *The Power of Followership.* New York: Doubleday Currency, 1992.

Kelley, R. E. "In Praise of Followers." *Harvard Business Review* 66, no. 6 (1988), pp. 142–48.

Kelly, G. *The Psychology of Personal Constructs.* New York: W. W. Norton, 1955.

Kennedy, J. K. "Middle LPC Leaders and the Contingency Model of Leader Effectiveness." *Organizational Behavior and Human Performance* 30 (1982), pp. 1–14.

Kerr, S., and J. M. Jermier. "Substitutes for Leadership: Their Meaning and Measurement." *Organizational Behavior and Human Performance* 22 (1978), pp. 375–403.

Kets de Vries, M. F. R. "Crises Leadership and the Paranoid Potential: An Organizational Perspective." *Bulletin of the Menninger Clinic* 41 (1977), pp. 349–65.

Kets de Vries, M. F. R., and D. Miller. "Managers Can Drive Their Subordinates Mad." In *The Irrational Executive: Psychoanalytic Explorations in Management.* Ed. M. F. R. Kets de Vries. New York: International Universities Press, 1984.

Keys, B.; T. Case; T. Miller; K. E. Curran; and C. Jones. "Lateral Influence Tactics in Organizations." *International Journal of Management* 4 (1987), pp. 425–37.

Kilmann, R. H., and M. J. Saxton. *Organizational Cultures: Their Assessment and Change.* San Francisco: Jossey-Bass, 1983.

Kincheloe, J. L. *Measured Lies: The Bell Curve Examined.* New York: St. Martins, 1996.

King, A. W.; S. W. Fowler; and C. P. Zeithaml. "Managing Organizational Competencies for Competitive Advantage: The Middle-Management Edge." *Academy of Management Executive* 15, no. 2 (2001), pp. 95–106.

Kinni, T. B. "The Empowered Workforce." *Industry Week,* September 19, 1994, pp. 37–41.

Kipnis, D. "Technology, Power, and Control." *Research in the Sociology of Organizations* 3 (1984a), pp. 125–56.

———. "The View from the Top." *Psychology Today* 18, no. 12 (1984b), pp. 30–36.

Kipnis, D., and S. M. Schmidt. "The Language of Persuasion." *Psychology Today* 19, no. 4 (1985), pp. 40–46.

———. *Profiles of Organizational Strategies.* Form M. San Diego, CA: University Associates, 1982.

Kipnis, D.; S. M. Schmidt; and I. Wilkinson. "Intraorganizational Influence Tactics: Explorations in Getting One's Way." *Journal of Applied Psychology* 65 (1980), pp. 440–52.

Kirkpatrick, D. L. "Evaluation of Training." In *Training and Development Handbook.* Ed. R. L. Craig and L. R. Bittel. New York: McGraw-Hill, 1967.

Kirkpatrick, S. A., and E. A. Locke. "Direct and Indirect Effects of Three Core Charismatic Leadership Components on Performance and Attitudes." *Journal of Applied Psychology* 81, no. 1, 1996, pp. 36–51.

Kirton, M. J. *Test Manual for the Kirton Adaptation-Innovation Inventory.* Hatfield, U.K.: Occupational Research Centre, 1987.

Kleiman, C. "Majority of Management Rates Salary as Very Good." *Denver Post,* January 4, 1998b, p. L-1.

———. "Survey: Job Satisfaction Can Be Costly to Employers." *Denver Post,* June 22, 1997, p. J-4.

Klein, H. J.; M. J. Wesson; J. R. Hollenbeck; and B. J. Alge. "Goal Commitment and the Goal-Setting Process: Conceptual Clarification and Empirical Synthesis." *Journal of Applied Psychology* 84, no. 6 (1999), pp. 885–96.

Klein, S. B. *Learning.* 2nd ed. New York: McGraw-Hill, 1991.

Klimoski, R. J., and N. J. Hayes. "Leader Behavior and Subordinate Motivation." *Personnel Psychology* 33 (1980), pp. 543–55.

Kohl, L. R. *Survival Kit for Overseas Living.* 2nd ed. Yarmouth, ME: Intercultural Press.

Kohlberg, L. *The Philosophy of Moral Development: Essays on Moral Development.* Vol. 1. San Francisco: Harper & Row, 1981.

———. *The Psychology of Moral Development: Essays on Moral Development.* Vol. 2. San Francisco: Harper & Row, 1984.

Kohn, A. "It's Hard to Get Left Out of a Pair." *Psychology Today,* October 1987, pp. 53–57.

Kohn, A. "Why Incentive Plans Cannot Work." *Harvard Business Review,* September–October 1993, pp. 54–63.

Kojimoto, C. "The Kids-Eye View of Effective Principals." *Educational Leadership,* September 1987, pp. 69–74.

Kolb, D. *Experiential Learning: Experience as the Source of Learning and Development.* Englewood Cliffs, NJ: Prentice Hall, 1983.

Komacki, J. L. "Toward Effective Supervision: An Operant Analysis and Comparison of Managers at Work." *Journal of Applied Psychology* 71 (1986), pp. 270–79.

———. "Why We Don't Reinforce: The Issues." *Journal of Organizational Behavior Management* 4, nos. 3–4 (1982), pp. 97–100.

Komacki, J. L.; S. Zlotnick; and M. Jensen. "Development of an Operant-based Taxonomy and Observational Index on Supervisory Behavior." *Journal of Applied Psychology* 71 (1986), pp. 260–69.

Kossler, M., and S. Prestridge. "Geographically Dispersed Teams." *Issues and Observations* 16 (1996), pp. 2–3.

Kotter, J. *Matsushista Leadership.* New York: Free Press, 1997.

Kotter, J. P. *Leading Change.* Boston: Harvard Business School Press, 1996.

Kotter, J. R. "Power and Influence: Beyond Formal Authority. *Macmillan Executive Summary Program,* September 1985, pp. 1–8.

———. "What Leaders Really Do." *Harvard Business Review,* May–June 1990, pp. 103–111.

Kouzes, J. M., and B. Z. Posner. *The Credibility Factor.* San Francisco: Jossey-Bass, 1996.

———. *The Leadership Challenge: How to Get Extraordinary Things Done in Organizations.* San Francisco: Jossey-Bass, 1987.

Koys, D. J. "The Effects of Employee Satisfaction, Organizational Citizenship Behavior, and Turnover on Organizational Effectiveness: A Unit-Level, Longitudinal Study." *Personnel Psychology* 54, no. 1 (2001), pp. 101–14.

Kozlowski, S. W. J., and M. L. Doherty. "Integration of Climate and Leadership: Examination of a Neglected Issue." *Journal of Applied Psychology* 74 (1989), pp. 546–53.

Kraiger, K.; J. K. Ford; and E. Salas. *Integration of Cognitive, Behavioral, and Affective Theories of Learning into New Methods of Training Evaluation.* Manuscript submitted for publication.

Kroeger, O., and J. M. Thuesen. *Type Talk.* New York: Delacourt, 1988.

Kubler-Ross, E. *Living with Death and Dying.* New York: Macmillan, 1981.

Kuhn, R. *The Structure of Scientific Revolutions.* Chicago: University of Chicago Press, 1962.

Kuncel, N. "Personality and Cognitive Differences among Management Levels." Unpublished manuscript. Minneapolis, MN: Personnel Decisions International, 1996.

Kurke, L. B., and H. E. Aldrich. "Mintzberg Was Right! A Replication and Extension of 'The Nature of Managerial Work.'" *Management Science* 29 (1983), pp. 975–84.

Labak, A. S. "The Study of Charismatic College Teachers." *Dissertation Abstracts International* 34 (1973), pp. 1258B.

Lall, R. "Mentoring Experiences of Retired Navy Admirals." Paper presented at Personnel Decisions International, Denver, CO, May 6, 1999.

Landy, F. J. *Psychology of Work Behavior.* 3rd ed. Homewood, IL: Dorsey, 1985.

Larmore, A., and R. Ayman. "Empowering Leadership, Transformational Leadership, and Feelings of Empowerment: A Multi-Level Analysis." Paper presented at the 13th Annual Conference of the Society of Industrial and Organizational Psychology, Dallas, TX, 1998.

Larson, J. R., Jr. "Supervisors' Performance Feedback to Subordinates: The Impact of Subordinate Performance Valence and Outcome Dependence." *Organizational Behavior and Human Decision Processes* 37 (1986), pp. 391–408.

Latack, J. C. "Coping with Job Stress: Measures and Future Decisions for Scale Development." *Journal of Applied Psychology* 71 (1986), pp. 377–85.

Latane, B.; K. Williams; and S. Harkins. "Social Loafing." *Psychology Today* (1979), p. 104.

Latham, G. P., and T. W. Lee. "Goal Setting." In *Generalizing from Laboratory to Field Settings.* Ed. E. A. Locke. Lexington, MA: Lexington Books, 1986.

Lawler, E. E. III. *Motivation in Work Organizations.* Pacific Grove, CA: Brooks/Cole, 1973.

Lawrence, P. R., and J. W. Lorsch. "Differentiation and Integration in Complex Organizations." *Administrative Science Quarterly* 12 (1967a), pp. 1–47.

———. *Organization and Environment.* Boston: Harvard University Press, 1967b.

———. *Organization and Environment: Managing Differentiation and Integration.* Homewood, IL: Irwin, 1969.

Lazarsfeld, P. F. "The American Soldier: An Expository Review." *Public Opinion Quarterly* 13 (1949), pp. 377–404.

Leana, C. R. "Power Relinquishment vs. Power Sharing: Theoretical Clarification and Empirical Comparison of Delegation and Participation." *Journal of Applied Psychology* 72 (1987), pp. 228–33.

———. "Predictors and Consequences of Delegation." *Academy of Management Journal* 29 (1986), pp. 754–74.

Lee, David B. "War Gaming: Thinking for the Future." *Airpower Journal* 3 (1990), pp. 40–51.

Leib, J. "Poor Management Blamed on Most New-Airline Failures." *Denver Post,* July 1, 1998, p. 10C.

Lepper, M. R.; D. Greene; and R. E. Nisbett. "Undermining Children's Intrinsic Interests with Extrinsic Rewards: A Test of the 'Overjustification' Hypothesis." *Journal of Personality and Social Psychology* 28 (1973), pp. 128–37.

Lepsinger, R., and A. D. Lucia. *The Art and Science of 360° Feedback.* San Francisco: Pfeiffer, 1997.

Levering, R.; M. Moskowitz; and M. Katz. *The 100 Best Companies to Work for in America.* Reading, MA: Addison-Wesley, 1984.

Levy, J. "Right Brain, Left Brain: Fact and Fiction." *Psychology Today,* May 1985, pp. 38–44.

Levy-Leboyer, C. "Leadership Performance: Towards a More Complex Model." *Applied Psychology: An International Review* 44, no. 1 (1995), pp. 43–44.

Lewis, R.; D. L. Nilsen; C. Robie; and G. J. Curphy. "Organizational Decision Making with Multirater Instruments." Roundtable discussion at the 16th Annual Conference of the Society for Industrial and Organizational Psychology, San Diego, CA, 2001.

Liden, R. C, and G. B. Graen. "Generalizability of the Vertical Dyad Linkage Model of Leadership." *Academy of Management Journal* 23 (1980), pp. 451–65.

Liden, R. C.; R. W. Sparrowe; R. T. Wayne; and S. J. Wayne. "Leader-Member Exchange Theory: The Past and Potential for the Future." In *Research in Personnel and Human Resource Management.* Vol. 15. Ed. G. R. Ferris. Greenwich, CT: JAI Press, 1997.

Likert, R. *New Patterns of Management.* New York: McGraw-Hill, 1961.

Lindsley, D. H.; D. J. Brass.; and J. B. Thomas. "Efficacy-Performance Spirals: A Multilevel Perspective." *Academy of Management Review* 20 (1995), pp. 645–78.

Linn, R. L., Ed. *Intelligence: Measurement, Theory, and Public Policy.* Chicago: University of Illinois Press, 1989.

Linville, P. W. "Self-Complexity as a Cognitive Buffer against Stress-Related Illness and Depression." *Journal of Personality and Social Psychology* 52, no. 4 (1987), pp. 663–76.

Lipnack, J., and J. Stamps. *Virtual Teams: Reaching across Space, Time and Organizations with Technology.* New York: John Wiley, 1997.

Lippitt, R. "The Changing Leader-Follower Relationships of the 1980s." *Journal of Applied Behavioral Science* 18 (1982), pp. 395–403.

Litzinger, W., and T. Schaefer. "Leadership through Followership." *Business Horizons* 25, no. 5 (1982), pp. 78–81.

Locke, E. A., and G. P. Latham. *Goal Setting: A Motivational Technique that Works.* Englewood Cliffs, NJ: Prentice Hall, 1984.

———. "Work Motivation and Satisfaction: Light at the End of the Tunnel." *Psychological Science* 1 (1990), pp. 240–46.

Locke, E. A.; G. P. Latham; and M. Erez. "Three-way Interactive Presentation and Discussion; A Unique Approach to Resolving Scientific Disputes; Designing Crucial Experiments." Papers presented at the Society of Industrial and Organizational Psychology Convention, Atlanta, GA, 1987.

Locke, E. A.; S. J. Motowidlo; and P. Bobko. "Using Self-Efficacy Theory to Resolve the Conflict between Goal-Setting Theory and Expectancy Theory in Organizational Behavior and Industrial/Organizational Psychology." *Journal of Social and Clinical Psychology* 4 (1985), pp. 280–89.

Lombardo, M. M., and R. W. Eichinger. *Eighty-eight Assignments for Development in Place: Enhancing the Developmental Challenge of Existing Jobs.* Greensboro, NC: Center for Creative Leadership, 1990.

———. *For Your Improvement: A Development and Coaching Guide.* Minneapolis, MN: Lominger, 1996.

Lombardo, M. M., M. N. Ruderman; and C. D. McCauley. "Explorations of Success and Derailment in Upper-Level Management Positions." Paper presented at meeting of the Academy of Management, New York, 1987.

London, M., and J. W. Smither. "Can Multisource Feedback Change Perceptions of Goal Accomplishment, Self-Evaluations, and Performance-Related Outcomes? Theory-Based Applications and Directions for Research." *Personnel Psychology* 48, no. 4 (1995), pp. 803–39.

Lord, R. G., and D. J. Brown. "Leadership, Values, and Subordinate Self-Concepts." *Leadership Quarterly* 12, no. 2 (2001), pp. 133–52.

Lord, R. G.; C. L. DeVader; G. M. Allinger. "A Meta-Analysis of the Relationship between Personality Traits and Leadership Perceptions: An Application of Validity Generalization Procedures." *Journal of Applied Psychology* 71 (1986), pp. 402–10.

Lowe, K. B.; K. G. Kroeck; and N. Sivasubramaniam. "Effectiveness Correlates of Transformational and Transactional Leadership: A

Meta-Analytic Review of the MLQ Literature." *Leadership Quarterly* 7, no. 3 (1996), pp. 385–425.

Lowin, A., and J. R. Craig. "The Influence of Level of Performance on Managerial Style: An Experimental Object-Lesson in the Ambiguity of Correlational Data." *Organizational Behavior and Human Performance* 3 (1968), pp. 68–106.

Lundin, S. C., and L. C. Lancaster. "Beyond Leadership . . . The Importance of Followership." *The Futurist*, May–June 1990, pp. 18–22.

Luthans, F. 1989. *Organizational Behavior.* 5th ed. New York: McGraw-Hill, 1992.

Luthans, F., and R. Kreitner. *Organizational Behavior Modification and Beyond: An Operant and Social Learning Approach.* Glenview, IL: Scott, Foresman, 1985.

Luthans, F., and J. K. Larsen. "How Managers Really Communicate." *Human Relations* 39 (1986), pp. 161–78.

Luthans, F.; S. A. Rosenkrantz; and H. W. Hennessey. "What Do Successful Managers Really Do? An Observational Study of Managerial Activities." *Journal of Applied Behavioral Science* 21 (1985), pp. 255–70.

Luthans, F., and A. D. Stajkovic. "Reinforce for Performance: The Need to Go Beyond Pay and Even Rewards." *Academy of Management Executive* 13, no. 2 (1999), pp. 49–57.

Lytle, C. F., ed. *Leaves of Gold.* Williamsport, PA: Coslett, 1948.

Maccoby, M. "Management: Leadership and the Work Ethic." *Modern Office Procedures* 28, no. 5 (1983), pp. 14, 16, 18.

MacKenzie, R. A. "The Management Process in 3-D." *Harvard Business Review* 47, no. 6 (1969s), pp. 80–87.

Macrorie, K. *Twenty Teachers.* Oxford: Oxford University Press, 1984.

Madsen, D., and P. G. Snow. "The Dispersion of Charisma." *Comparative Political Studies* 16, no. 3 (1983), pp. 337–62.

Mahoney, T. A.; T. H. Jerdee; and S. J. Carroll. "The Job(s) of Management." *Industrial Relations* 4 (1965), pp. 97–110.

Main, J. "Is the Baldrige Overblown?" *Fortune,* July 1, 1991, pp. 62–65.

Malinkowski, C. I., and C. P. Smith. "Moral Reasoning and Moral Conduct: An Investigation Prompted by Kohlberg's Theory." *Journal of Personality and Social Psychology* 49 (1985), pp. 1016–27.

Mann, F. C. "Toward an Understanding of the Leadership Role in a Formal Organization." In *Leadership and Productivity.* Ed. R. Dubin. San Francisco: Chandler, 1965.

Mann, R. D. "A Review of the Relationships between Personality and Performance in Small Groups." *Psychological Bulletin* 56 (1959), pp. 241–70.

Manz, C. C. "Self-Leadership: Toward an Expanded Theory of Self-Influence Process in Organizations." *Academy of Management Review* 11 (1986), pp. 585–600.

Marcus, J. T. "Transcendence and Charisma." *Western Political Quarterly* 16 (1961), pp. 236–41.

Marentette, D. *SHRM/PD1 2000 Performance Management Survey.* Minneapolis, MN: Personnel Decisions International, 2000.

Margerison, C. J. "Action Learning and Excellence in Management Development." *Journal of Management Development* 7 no. 2 (1983), pp. 52–64.

Marks, M. L., and P. H. Mirvis. "Making Mergers and Acquisitions Work." *Academy of Management Executive* 15, no. 2 (2001), pp. 80–94.

Maslow, A. H. *Motivation and Personality.* New York: Harper & Row, 1954.

Massey, M. *The People Puzzle: Understanding Yourself and Others.* Reston: VA: Reston, 1979.

Mayer, R. E. *Thinking, Problem Solving, Cognition.* New York: W. H. Freeman, 1983.

Maynard, H. B., and S. E. Mehrtens. *The Fourth Wave: Business in the 21st Century.* San Francisco: Berrett-Koehler, 1993.

Mayo, E. *The Human Problems of an Industrial Civilization.* New York: Macmillan, 1933.

McCall, M. W., Jr., and M. M. Lombardo. "Off the Track: Why and How Successful Executives Get Derailed." Technical Report No. 21. Greensboro, NC: Center for Creative Leadership, 1983.

———. "Using Simulation for Leadership and Management Research: Through the Looking Glass." *Management Science* 28 (1982), pp. 533–49.

McCall, M. W. Jr.; M. M. Lombardo; and A. M. Morrison. *The Lessons of Experience: How Successful Executives Develop on the Job.* Lexington, MA: Lexington Books, 1988.

McCarley, N., and T. G. Carskadon. "Test-Retest Reliabilities of Scales and Subscales of the Myers-Briggs Type Indicator and of Criteria for Clinical Interpretive Hypothesis Involving Them." *Research in Psychological Type* 6 (1983), pp. 24–36.

McCauley, C. D.; "Stress and the Eye of the Beholder." *Issues & Observations* 7, no. 3 (1987), pp. 1–16.

McCauley, C. D.; Ruderman, M. N.; Ohlott, P. J.; and J. E. Morrow "Assessing the Developmental Components of Managerial Jobs." *Journal of Applied Psychology* 79, no. 4(1994), pp. 544–60.

McCaulley, M. H. "The Myers-Briggs Type Indicator and Leadership." In *Measures of Leadership.* Ed. K. E. Clark and M. B. Clark. Greensboro, NC: Center for Creative Leadership, 1988.

McClelland, D. C. *Human Motivation.* Glenview, IL: Scott Foresman, 1985.

———. "Intelligence Is Not the Best Predictor of Job Performance." *Current Directions in Psychological Science* 2, no. 1 (1993), pp. 5–6.

———. *Power: The Inner Experience.* New York: Irvington, 1975.

McClelland, D. C., and R. E. Boyatzis. "Leadership Motive Pattern and Long-Term Success in Management." *Journal of Applied Psychology* 67 (1982), pp. 737–43.

McClelland, D. C., and D. H. Burnham. "Power Is the Great Motivator." *Harvard Business Review,* 54, no. 2 (1976), pp. 100–110.

McCormick, J., and B. Powell. "Management for the 1990s" *Newsweek,* April 1988, pp. 47–48.

McCrae, R. R., and Costa, P. T. "The Stability of Personality: Observations and Evaluations." *Current Directions in Psychological Science* 3, no. 6, (1994), pp. 173–75.

McDaniel, S. L. "The Dark Side of the Big Five: New Perspectives for Personnel Selection." Paper presented at the 14th Annual Conference of the Society of Industrial and Organizational Psychology, Atlanta, GA, 1999.

McElreath, J., and A. R. Bass. *Development of a Biodata Measure of Leadership Effectiveness: A Life History Essay Approach.* Paper Presented at the 14th Annual Conference of the Society for Industrial and Organizational Psychology, Atlanta, GA, May 1999.

McFarlin, D. B., and P. D. Sweeney. "Distributive and Procedural Justice as Predictors of Satisfaction with Personal and Organizational Outcomes." *Academy of Management Journal* 35 (1992), pp. 626–37.

McGrath, J. E. *Leadership Behavior: Some Requirements for Leadership Training.* Washington, DC: Office of Career Development, U.S. Civil Service Commission, 1964.

McGregor, D. *Leadership and Motivation.* Cambridge, MA: MIT Press, 1966.

McGue, M., and T. J. Bouchard, Jr. "Genetic and Environmental Determinants of Information Processing and Special Mental Abilities: A Twin Analysis." In *Advances in the Psychology of Human Intelligence.* Ed. R. J. Sternberg. Hillsdale, NJ: Erlbaum, 1989, pp. 7–45.

McKay, H. "Author Encourages Creativity, Risk Taking on Road to Success." *Denver Post,* December 21, 1997, p. J-8.

McKay, M.; M. Davis; and P. Fanning. *Thoughts and Feelings: The Art of Cognitive Stress Intervention.* Richmond, CA: New Harbinger, 1981.

McNatt, D. B. "Ancient Pygmalion Joins Contemporary Management: A Meta-Analysis of the Result." *Journal of Applied Psychology* 83, no. 2 (2000), pp. 314–21.

Meindl, J. R., and S. B. Ehrlich. "The Romance of Leadership and the Evaluation of Organizational Performance." *Academy of Management Journal* 30 (1987), pp. 90–109.

Meindl, J. R.; S. B. Ehrlich; and J. M. Dukerich. "The Romance of Leadership." *Administrative Science Quarterly* 30 (1985), pp. 78–102.

Merton, R. K. "The Social Nature of Leadership." *American Journal of Nursing,* 69 (1969), pp. 2614–18.

———. *Social Theory and Social Structure.* New York: Free Press, 1957.

Michel, R., and R. T. Hogan. "Personality and Organizational Behavior." In R. T. Hogan (chair). *Personality and Organizational Behavior.* Symposium presented at the 104th Annual Meeting of the American Psychological Association, Toronto, Canada, 1996.

Michener, H. A., and M. R. Burt. "Use of Social Influence under Varying Conditions of Legitimacy." *Journal of Personality and Social Psychology* 32 (1975), pp. 398–407.

Milgram, S. "Behavioral Study of Obedience." *Journal of Personality and Social Psychology* 67 (1963), pp. 371–78.

Miller, D. D. *The Story of Walt Disney.* New York: Henry Holt, 1956.

Miller, D., and J. M. Toulouse. "Strategy, Structure, CEO Personality and Performance in Small Firms." *American Journal of Small Business,* Winter 1986, pp. 47–62.

Miller, D. T., and M. Ross. "Self-Serving Biases in the Attribution of Causality: Fact or Fiction?" *Psychological Bulletin* 82 (1975), pp. 213–25.

Miller, W. R., and S. Rollnick. *Motivational Interviewing: Preparing People to Change Addictive Behavior.* New York: Guilford Press, 1991.

Mills, V. "Longer Hours, Extra Work" *Orlando Sentinel,* June 16, 1999, p. 3C.

Mindell, M., and W. Gorden. *Employee Values in a Changing Society: An AMA Management Briefing.* New York: American Management Associations, 1981.

Miner, J. B. "If You're Not Serving Bill or Barbara, Then You're Not Serving Leadership." In *Leadership: Beyond Establishment Views.* Ed. J. G. Hunt, U. Sekaran, and C. A. Schriesheim. Carbondale: Southern Illinois University Press, 1982.

———. "Student Attitudes toward Bureaucratic Role Prescriptions and the Prospects for Managerial Shortages." *Personnel Psychology* 27 (1974), pp. 605–13.

———. "Twenty Years of Research on Role Motivation Theory of Managerial Effectiveness." *Personnel Psychology* 31 (1978), pp. 739–60.

———. "The Uncertain Future of the Leadership Concept: An Overview." In *Leadership Frontiers.* Ed. J. G. Hunt and L. L. Larson. Kent, OH: Kent State University, 1975.

Mitchell, R. R.; C. M. Smyser; and S. E. Weed. "Locus of Control: Supervision and Work Satisfaction." *Academy of Management Journal.* 18 (1975), pp. 623–30.

Mitchell, T. R. "Review of *In Search of Excellence* versus *The 100 Best Companies to Work for in America:* A Question of Perspective and Values." *Academy of Management Review* 10 (1985), pp. 350–55.

Mitchell, T. R.; S. G. Green; and R. E. Wood. "An Attributional Model of Leadership and the Poor Performing Subordinate: Development and Validation." In *Research in Organizational Behavior.* Ed. B. M. Staw and L. L. Cummings. Greenwich, CN: JAI 1981, pp. 197–234.

Mitchell, T. R., and R. E. Wood. "Supervisors' Responses to Subordinate Poor Performance: A Test of an Attributional Model." *Organizational Behavior and Human Performance* 25 (1980), pp. 123–38.

Moore, L. I. "The FMI: Dimensions of Follower Maturity." *Group and Organizational Studies* 1 (1976), pp. 203–22.

Moorman, R. H. "Relationships between Organizational Justice and Organizational Citizenship Behaviors: Do Fairness Perceptions Influence Employee Citizenship?" *Journal of Applied Psychology* 76 (1991), pp. 845–55.

Morabito, M. A., and B. L. Dilla. "Leadership Development of USAF Aircraft Maintenance Officers." Paper presented at the 27th Annual Meeting of the Military Testing Association, San Diego, CA, October 1985.

Moreno, J. L. *Sociodrama: A Method of Analysis for Social Conflicts.* Beacon, NY: Beacon House, 1955.

Morical, K. E. "A Product Review: 360 Assessments." *Training & Development,* April 1999, pp. 43–47.

Morrison, A. M.; R. P. White; and E. Van Velsor. *Breaking the Glass Ceiling.* Reading, MA: Addison-Wesley, 1987.

Morse, J. J., and F. R. Wagner. "Measuring the Process of Managerial Effectiveness." *Academy of Management Journal* 21 (1978), pp. 23–35.

Motowidlo, S. J.; M. D. Dunnette; and G. W. Carter. "An Alternative Selection Procedure: The Low-Fidelity Simulation." *Journal of Applied Psychology* 75 (1990), pp. 640–47.

Mount, M. K.; M. R. Barrick; and J. K. Strauss. "Validity of Observers Ratings of the Big Five Personality Factors." *Journal of Applied Psychology* 79 (1994), pp. 272–80.

Mount, M. K.; T. A. Judge; S. E. Scullen; M. R. Sytsma; and S. A. Hezlett. "Trait, Rater, and Level Effects in 360-Degree Performance Ratings." *Personnel Psychology* 51, no.3 (1998), pp. 557–77.

Mount, M. K.; M. R. Sytsma; J. F. Hazucha; and K. E. Holt. "Rater-Ratee Effects in Development Performance Ratings of Managers." *Personnel Psychology* 50, no. 1, pp. 51–70. 1997

Mowday, R. T. "Leader Characteristics, Self-Confidence, and Methods of Upward Influence in Organizational Decision Situations." *Academy of Management Journal* 22, no. 4 (1979), pp. 709–25.

Mulder, M., R. D. de Jong; L. Koppelar; and J. Verhage. "Power, Situation, and Leaders' Effectiveness: An Organizational Study." *Journal of Applied Psychology* 71 (1986), pp. 566–70.

Mulder, M. and A. Stemerding. "Threat, Attraction to Group, and Need for Strong Leadership." *Human Relations* 16 (1963), pp. 317–34.

Mumford, M. D.; S. J. Zaccaro; J. F. Johnson; M. Diana; J. A. Gilbert; and K. V. Threlfall. "Patterns of Leader Characteristics: Implications for Performance and Development." *Leadership Quarterly* 11, no. 1 (2000), pp. 115–36.

Munson, C. E. "Style and Structure in Supervision." *Journal of Education for Social Work* 17 (1981), pp. 65–72.

Murphy, A. J. "A Study of the Leadership Process." *American Sociological Review* 6 (1941), pp. 674–87.

Murray, H. A., and D. W. MacKinnon. "Assessment of OSS Personnel." *Journal of Consulting Psychology* 10 (1946), pp. 76–80.

Murray, M., and M. A. Owen. *Beyond the Myths and Magic of Mentoring.* San Francisco: Jossey-Bass, 1991.

Mussen, P. H., and L. W. Porter, "Personal Motivations and Self-Conceptions Associated with Effectiveness and Ineffectiveness in Emergent Groups." *Journal of Abnormal and Social Psychology* 59 (1959), pp. 23–27.

Myers, D. G. *Psychology.* 2nd ed. New York: Worth, 1989.

Myers, I. *Gifts Differing.* Palo Alto, CA: Consulting Psychologists Press, 1980.

Myers, I. B. *Introduction to Type.* Palo Alto, CA: Consulting Psychologists Press, 1976.

———. *The Myers-Briggs Type Indicator: Supplementary Manual.* Palo Alto, CA: Consulting Psychologists Press, 1977.

Myers, I. B., and K. C. Briggs. *The Myers-Briggs Type Indicator.* Palo Alto, CA: Consulting Psychologists Press, 1943/1962.

Myers, I. B., and B. H. McCaulley. *Manual: A Guide to the Development and Use of the Myers-Briggs Type Indicator.* Palo Alto, Calif.: Consulting Psychologists Press, 1985.

Naisbitt, J., and P. Aburdene. *Megatrends 2000.* New York: William Morrow, 1990.

————. *Re-inventing the Corporation.* New York: Warner Books, 1985.

Nash, A. N. "Vocational Interests of Effective Managers: A Review of the Literature." *Personnel Psychology* 18 (1965), pp. 21–37.

Neilson, E. H., and J. Gypen. "The Subordinate's Predicament." *Harvard Business Review* 57, no. 5 (1979), pp. 133–43.

Neisser, U.; G. Boodoo; T. J. Bouchard; A. W. Boykin; N. Brody; S. J. Ceci, D. F. Halpern; J. C. Loehlin; R. Perloff; R. J. Sternberg; and S. Urbina. "Development of a SVIB Key for Selecting Managers." *Journal of Applied Psychology* 50 (1966), pp. 250–54.

————. "Intelligence: Knowns and Unknowns." *American Psychologist* 51, no. 2 (1996), pp. 77–101.

Nevins, M., and S. Stumpf. "21st–Century Leadership: Redefining Management Education. *Strategy, Management, Competition,* 3rd quarter 1999, pp. 41–51.

Nierenberg, G. I. *The Art of Creative Thinking.* New York: Simon & Schuster, 1982.

Nilsen, D. L. "Using Observer Judgments for Selection." In *The Future of Leadership Section.* Chair, R. L. Hughes. Symposium conducted at the 13th Biennial Psychology in the Department of Defense Conference, U.S. Air Force Academy, April 1992.

————. *Using Self and Observers' Rating of Personality to Predict Leadership Performance.* Unpublished doctoral dissertation, University of Minnesota, 1995.

Nixon, R. M. *Leaders.* New York: Warner Books, 1982.

Nutt, P. C. "Surprising but True: Half the Decisions in Organizations Fail." *Academy of Management Executive* 13, no. 4 (1999), pp. 75–90.

Nystrom, P. C. "Comparing Beliefs of Line and Technostructure Managers." *Academy of Management Journal* 29 (1986), pp. 812–19.

O'Brien, B. "Designing an Organization's Governing Ideas." In *The Fifth Discipline Fieldbook.* Ed. P. Senge, A. Kleiner, C. Roberts, R. Ross, and B. Smith. New York: Doubleday, 1994.

O'Connor, J.; M. D. Mumford; T. C. Clifton; T. L. Gessner; and M. S. Connelly. "Charismatic Leaders and Destructiveness: An Historiometric Study." *Leadership Quarterly* 6, no. 4 (1995), pp. 529–40.

Offermann, L. R. "Leading and Empowering Diverse Followers." In *The Balance of Leadership and Followership.* Ed. E. P. Hollander and L. R. Offerman. Kellogg Leadership Studies Project. College Park: University of Maryland Press, 1997, pp. 31–46.

Ohlott, P. "Change and Leadership Development: The Experience of Executive Women." *Leadership in Action* 19, no. 5 (1999), pp. 8–12.

Oldham, G. R., and A. Cummings. "Employee Creativity: Personal and Contextual Factors at Work." *Academy of Management Journal* 39 (1996), pp. 607–34.

Ones, D. S.; M. K. Mount; M. R. Barrick; and J. E. Hunter. "Personality and Job Performance: A Critique of Tett, Jackson, and Rothstein (1991) Meta-Analysis." *Personnel Psychology* 47 (1994), pp. 147–56.

Ones, D. S.; C. Viswesvaran; and A. D. Reiss. "Role of Social Desirability in Personality Testing for Personnel Selection: The Red Herring." *Journal of Applied Psychology* 81, no. 6 (1996), pp. 660–79.

O'Reilly, B. "360-Degree Feedback Can Change Your Life." *Fortune,* October 17, 1994.

O'Reilly, C. A. "Supervisors and Peers as Informative Sources, Group Supportiveness, and Individual Decision-Making Performance." *Journal of Applied Psychology* 62 (1977), pp. 632–35.

Organ, D. W., and K. Ryan. "A Meta-Analytic Review of Attitudinal and Dispositional Predictors of Organizational Citizenship Behavior." *Personnel Psychology* 48 (1995), pp. 775–802.

Osborn, A. F. *Applied Imagination.* New York: Scribner's, 1963.

O'Toole, J. *Leading Change.* San Francisco: Jossey-Bass, 1995.

Ouchi, W. G. *How American Business Can Meet the Japanese Challenge.* Reading, MA: Addison-Wesley, 1981.

———. *Theory Z.* Reading, MA: Addison-Wesley, 1981.

Paajanen, G. E.; T. L. Hansen; and R. A. McLellan. *PDI Employment Inventory and PDI Customer Service Inventory Manual.* Minneapolis, MN: Personnel Decisions, 1993.

Page, R. C., and W. W. Tornow. "Managerial Job Analysis: Are We Any Further Along?" Paper presented at a meeting of the Society of Industrial Organizational Psychology, Atlanta, GA, 1987.

Parke, R. D. "Some Effects of Punishment on Children's Behavior." In *The Young Child: Reviews of Research.* Vol. 2. Ed. W. W. Hartup. Washington, DC: National Association for the Education of Young Children, 1972.

Parks, M. R. "Interpersonal Communication and the Quest for Personal Competence." In *Handbook of Interpersonal Communication.* Ed. M. L. Knapp and G. R. Miller. Beverly Hills, CA: Sage, 1985.

Parsons, C. K.; D. M. Herold; and M. L. Leatherwood. "Turnover during Initial Employment: A Longitudinal Study of the Role of Causal Attributions." *Journal of Applied Psychology* 70 (1985), pp. 337–41.

Paunonen, S. V. "Sense, Nonsense, and the Big Five Factors of Personality." *The Score* 16, no. 1 (1993), pp. 8–9.

Pawar, B. S., and K. K. Eastman. "The Nature and Implications of Contextual Influences on Transformational Leadership: A Conceptual Examination." *Academy of Management Review* 22, no. 1 (1997), pp. 80–109.

Pearson, C. S. *The Hero Within.* San Francisco: HarperCollins, 1986.

Peiperl, M. A. "Getting 360-Degree Feedback Right." *Harvard Business Review,* January 2001, pp. 142–48

Penner, D. D.; D. M. Malone; T. M. Coughlin; and J. A. Herz. *Satisfaction with U.S. Army Leadership.* Leadership Monograph Series, no. 2. U.S. Army War College, 1973.

Perkins, D. N. "Thinking Frames." *Educational Leadership* 43 (1986), pp. 4–10.

Person, H. S. "Leadership as a Response to Environment." *Educational Record Supplement* no. 6 (1928), pp. 9–21.

Personnel Decisions Inc. *The Management Skills Profile.* Minneapolis, MN: Author, 1983.

———. *Managerial Job Satisfaction.* Minneapolis, MN: Author, 1991.

———. *PROFILOR® Certification Workshop Manual.* Minneapolis, MN: Author, 1992.

———. *Successful Managers Handbook: Development Suggestions for Today's Managers.* Minneapolis, MN: Author, 1983.

Personnel Decisions International. *Develop Mentor: Assessment, Development, and Coaching Software.* Minneapolis, MN: Personnel Decisions International, 1995.

———. *The Evolution of Assessment over the Past Three Decades.* Minneapolis, MN: Author, 2001.

———. *The Successful Manager's Handbook.* Minneapolis, MN: Author, 2000.

Peter, L., and R. Hull. *The Peter Principle.* New York: Morrow, 1969.

Peters, L. H.; D. D. Hartke; and J. T. Pohlmann. "Fielder's Contingency Theory of Leadership:

An Application of the Meta-Analytic Procedures of Schmidt and Hunter." *Psychological Bulletin* 97 (1985), pp. 274–85.

Peters, T. *The Circle of Innovation: You Can't Shrink Your Way to Greatness.* New York: Random House. 1997.

Peters, T. J., and R. H. Waterman. *In Search of Excellence.* New York: Harper & Row, 1982.

Peterson, D. B. "Executive Coaching at Work: The Art of One-on-One Change." *Consulting Psychology Journal* 48 no. 2 (1996), pp. 78–86.

———. *Individual Coaching Services: Coaching That Makes a Business Difference.* Minneapolis, MN: Personnel Decisions International, 1999.

———. "Making the Break from Middle Manager to a Seat at the Top." *The Wall Street Journal*, July 7, 1998, p. B16.

———. *Positive Coaching Manual.* Unpublished manuscript. Minneapolis, MN: Personnel Decisions, 1994.

———. *A Psychometric Approach to Evaluating Individual Training Outcomes.* Paper presented at the Eighth Annual Conference of the Society of Industrial and Organizational Psychology. San Francisco, April, 1993a.

———. *The Science and Art of Self-Development.* Paper presented at the Arabian States Human Resource Management Society Annual Conference, Bahrain, October 2001.

———. "Skill Learning and Behavioral Change in an Individually Tailored Management Coaching and Training Program." Unpublished doctoral dissertation. University of Minnesota, 1993b.

Peterson, D. B., and M. D. Hicks. "Coaching across Borders: It's Probably a Long Distance Call." *Development Matters* no. 9, (1997), pp. 1–4.

———. *Development FIRST: Strategies for Self-Development.* Minneapolis, MN: Personnel Decisions International, 1995.

Peterson, D. B., and M. D. Hicks. *Leader as Coach: Strategies for Coaching and Developing Others.* Minneapolis, MN: Personnel Decisions International, 1996.

Peterson, D. B., and M. D. Hicks. *Professional Coaching: State of the Art, State of the Practice.* Minneapolis, MN: Personnel Decisions International, 1998.

Petrick, J. A., and G. E. Manning. "Developing an Ethical Climate for Excellence." *Journal of Quality and Participation,* March 1990, pp. 13–18.

Petty, R. E., and J. T. Cacioppo. *Attitudes and Persuasion: Classic and Contemporary Approaches.* Dubuque, IA: Wm. C. Brown, 1981.

Pfeffer, J. "The Ambiguity of Leadership." In *Leadership: Where Else Can We Go?,* Ed. M. W. McCall, Jr., and M. M. Lombardo. Durham, NC: Duke University Press, 1977.

Pfeffer, J., and G. R. Salancik. "Determinants of Supervisory Behavior: A Role Set Analysis." *Human Relations* 28 (1975), pp. 139–54.

Phillips, J. M.; E. A. Douthitt; and M. M. Hyland. "The Role of Justice in Team Member Satisfaction with the Leader and Attachment to the Team." *Journal of Applied Psychology* 86, no. 2 (2001), pp. 316–25.

Pitt, L. F. "Managerial Attitudes Towards Corruption: A Pilot Study." *South African Journal of Business Management* 16 (1985), pp. 27–30.

Pittman, T. S.; W. E. Rosenbach; and E. H. Potter. "Followers as Partners: Taking the Initiative for Action." In *Contemporary Issues in Leadership.* 4th ed. Ed. W. E. Rosenback and R. L. Taylor. Boulder, CO: Westview Press, 1998.

Ployhart, R. E., and A. M. Ryan. "Applicants' Reactions to the Fairness of Selection Procedures: The Effects of Positive Rule Violations and Time of Measurement." *Journal of Applied Psychology* 83, no. 1 (1998), pp. 3–16.

Podsakoff, P. M. "Determinants of a Supervisor's Use of Rewards and Punishments: A Literature Review and Suggestions for Future Research." *Organizational Behavior and Human Performance* 29 (1982), pp. 58–83.

Podsakoff, P. M., and C. A. Schriesheim. "Field Studies of French and Raven's Bases of Power: Critique, Reanalysis, and Suggestions for Future Research." *Psychological Bulletin* 97 (1985), pp. 387–411.

Podsakoff, P. M., and W. D. Todor. "Relationships between Leader Reward and Punishment Behavior and Group Process and Productivity." *Journal of Management* 11 (1985), pp. 55–73.

Podsakoff, P. M.; W. D. Todor; R. A. Grover; and V. L. Huber. "Situational Moderators of Leader Reward and Punishment Behaviors: Fact or Fiction?" *Organizational Behavior and Human Performance* 34 (1984), pp. 21–63.

Podsakoff, P. M.; W. D. Todor; and R. S. Schuler. "Leadership Expertise as a Moderator of the Effects of Instrumental and Supportive Leader Behaviors." *Journal of Management* 9 (1983), pp. 173–85.

Podsakoff, P. M.; W. D. Todor; and R. Skov. "Effects of Leader Contingent and Noncontingent Reward and Punishment Behaviors on Subordinate Performance and Satisfaction." *Academy of Management Journal* 25 (1982), pp. 810–25.

Podsakoff, P. M., and L. J. Williams. "The Relationship between Job Performance and Job Satisfaction." In *Generalizing from Laboratory to Field Setting*. Ed. E. A. Locke. Lexington, MA: Lexington, 1986.

Polanyi, M. *Personal Knowledge.* Chicago: University of Chicago Press, 1962.

Pomerleau, O. F., and J. Rodin. "Behavioral Medicine and Health Psychology." In *Handbook of Psychotherapy and Behavior Change.* 3rd ed. Ed. S. L. Garfield and A. E. Bergin. New York: John Wiley, 1986.

Popper, M.; O. Landau; and U. M. Gluskinos. "The Israeli Defense Forces: An Example of Transformational Leadership." *Leadership and Organizational Development Journal*, 13, no. 1 (1992), pp. 3–8.

Porter, D. A. "Student Course Critiques: A Case Study in Total Quality in the Classroom." In *Proceedings of the 13th Biennial Psychology in Department of Defense Conference.* Colorado Springs, CO: U.S. Air Force Academy, 1992, pp. 26–30.

Porter, D. B.; M. Bird; and A. Wunder. "Competition, Cooperation, Satisfaction, and the Performance of Complex Tasks among Air Force Cadets." *Current Psychology Research and Reviews* 9, no. 4 (1991), pp. 347–54.

Porter, L. W., and E. E. Lawler, III. *Managerial Attitudes and Performance.* Homewood, IL: Dorsey, 1968.

Posner, B. Z., and J. M. Kouzes. "Leadership Practices: An Alternative to the Psychological Perspective." In *Measures of Leadership.* Ed. K. E. Clark and M. B. Clark. West Orange, NJ: Leadership Library of America, 1990, pp. 205–15.

Posner, B. Z.; and W. H. Schmidt. "Values and the American Manager: An Update." *California Management Review* 3 (1984), pp. 206–16.

Potter, E. H.; W. E. Rosenbach; and T. S. Pittman. "Leading the New Professional." In *Military Leadership*, 3rd ed., Ed. R. L. Taylor and W. E. Rosenbach. Boulder, CO: Westview Press, 1996.

Powell, C., with Joe Pirsico. *My American Journey.* New York: Random House, 1995.

Prince, G. M. "Creative Meetings through Power Sharing." *Harvard Business Review* 50, no. 4 (1972), pp. 47–54.

Pritchard, R. D.; J. Hollenback; P. J. DeLeo. "The Effects of Continuous and Partial Schedules of Reinforcement of Effort, Performance, and Satisfaction." *Organizational Behavior and Human Performance* 16 (1976), pp. 205–30.

Pritchard, R. D.; S. D. Jones; P. L. Roth; K. K. Stuebing; and S. E. Ekeberg. "Effects of Group Feedback, Goal Setting, and Incentives on Organizational Productivity." *Journal of Applied Psychology* 73, no. 2 (1988), pp. 337–58.

Pryer, M. W., and M. K. DiStefano. "Perceptions of Leadership Behavior, Job Satisfaction, and Internal-External Control across Three Nursing Levels." *Nursing Review* 20 (1971), pp. 534–37.

Pulakos, E. D., and K. N. Wexley. "The Relationship among Perceptual Similarity, Sex, and Performance Ratings in Manager-Subordinate Dyads." *Academy of Management Journal* 26 (1983), pp. 129–39.

Quaglieri, P. L., and J. P. Carnazza. "Critical Inferences and the Multidimensionality of Feedback." *Canadian Journal of Behavioral Science* 17 (1985), pp. 284–93.

Quast, L. N., and T. L. Hansen. *The Relationship between MBTI Expanded Analysis Report (EAR) Scores and Leaders' Management Behaviors.* Minneapolis, MN: Personnel Decisions International, 1996.

Quast, L. N., Hazucha, J. F., and Johnson, C. *The Leadership Effect.* Minneapolis, MN: Personnel Decisions International, 1993.

Quayle, D. "American Productivity: The Devastating Effect of Alcoholism and Drug Use." *American Psychologist* 38 (1983), pp. 454–58.

Quigley, A. "President's Message." *Personnel Testing Council Newsletter* 35, no. 1 (2001).

Quinn, R. E., and G. M. Spreitzer. "The Road to Empowerment: Seven Questions Every Leader Should Consider." *Organizational Dynamics,* Autumn 1997, pp. 37–49.

Quirk, M. P., and P. M. Fandt. *The Second Language of Leadership.* Mahwah, NJ: Erlbaum, 2000.

Ragins, B. R., and J. L. Cotton. "Mentoring Functions and Outcomes: A Comparison of Men and Women in Formal and Informal Mentoring Relationships." *Journal of Applied Psychology* 84, no. 4 (1999), pp. 529–500.

Ragins, B. R.; J. L. Cotton; and J. S. Miller. "Marginal Mentoring: The Effects of Types of Mentor, Quality of Relationship, and Program Design of Work and Career Attitudes." *Academy of Management Journal,* 43, no. 6 (2000), pp. 1177–94.

Ragins, B. R.; B. Townsend; and M. Mattis. "Gender Gap in the Executive Suite: CEOs and Female Executives Report on Breaking the Glass Ceiling." *Academy of Management Executive* 12, no. 1 (1998), pp. 28–42.

Rath, G. J., and K. S. Stoyanoff. "Understanding and Improving Communication Effectiveness." In *The 1982 Annual for Facilitators, Trainers, and Consultants.* Ed. J. W. Pfeiffer and L. D. Goodstein. San Diego, CA: University Associates, 1982.

Read, P. P. *Alive.* New York: J. B. Lippincott, 1974.

Reason, J., and K. Mycielska. *Absent-Minded? The Psychology of Mental Lapses and Everyday Errors.* Englewood Cliffs, NJ: Prentice Hall, 1982.

Ree, M. J., and J. A. Earles. "G Is to Psychology What Carbon Is to Chemistry: A Reply to Sternberg and Wagner, McClelland, and Calfee." *Current Directions in Psychological Science* 2, no. 1 (1993), pp. 11–12.

———. "Intelligence Is the Best Predictor of Job Performance." *Current Directions in Psychological Science* 1, no. 3 (1992), pp. 86–89.

Remland, M. S. "Developing Leadership Skills in Nonverbal Communication: A Situation Perspective." *Journal of Business Communication* 18, no. 3 (1981), pp. 17–29.

Rest, J. "Research on Moral Judgment in College Students." In *Approaches to Moral Development, New Research and Emerging Themes.* Ed. A. Garrod. New York: Teachers College Press, Columbia University, 1993, pp. 201–13.

Reykowski, J. "Social Motivation." *Annual Review of Psychology* 33 (1982), pp. 123–54.

Rice, R. W. "Construct Validity of the Least Preferred Co-Worker Score." *Psychological Bulletin* 85 (1978), pp. 1199–1237.

Richardson, R. J., and S. K. Thayer. *The Charisma Factor: How to Develop Your Natural Leadership Ability.* Englewood Cliffs, NJ: Prentice Hall. 1993.

Rizzo, J. R.; R. J. House; and S. I. Lirtzman. "Role Conflict and Ambiguity in Complex Organizations." *Administrative Science Quarterly* 15 (1970), pp. 150–63.

Roach, C. F., and O. Behling. "Functionalism: Basis for an Alternate Approach to the Study of Leadership." In *Leaders and Managers: International Perspectives on Managerial Behavior and Leadership.* Ed. J. G. Hunt, D. M. Hosking, C. A. Schriesheim, and R. Stewar. Elmsford, NY: Pergamon, 1984.

Robbins, S. P. *Organizational Behavior: Concepts, Controversies, and Applications.* Englewood Cliffs, NJ: Prentice Hall, 1986.

———. *Training in Interpersonal Skills.* Englewood Cliffs, NJ: Prentice Hall, 1989.

Roberts, B. W. "An Alternative Perspective on the Relation between Work and Psychological Functioning: The Reciprocal Model of Person-Environment Interaction." In R. T. Hogan (chair). *Personality and Organizational Behavior.* Symposium presented at the 104th Annual Meeting of the American Psychological Association, Toronto, Canada, 1996.

Roberts, N. C., and R. T. Bradley. "Limits of Charisma." In *Charismatic Leadership: The Elusive Factor in Organizational Effectiveness.* Ed. J. A. Conger and R. N. Kanungo. San Francisco: Jossey-Bass, 1988, pp. 253–75.

Robie, C.; K. Kanter; D. L. Nilsen; and J. Hazucha. *The Right Stuff: Understanding Cultural Differences in Leadership Performance.* Minneapolis, MN: Personnel Decisions International, 2001.

Roethlisberger, F. J.; and W. J. Dickson. *Management and the Worker: An Account of a Research Program Conducted by the Western Electric Company, Hawthorne Works, Chicago.* Cambridge: Harvard University Press, 1939.

Rogers, C., and R. E. Farson. "Active Listening." In *Organizational Psychology.* Ed. D. A. Kolb, I. M. Rubin, and J. M. McIntyre. Englewood Cliffs, NJ: Prentice Hall, 1984, pp. 255–66.

Rokeach, M. *The Nature of Human Values.* New York: Free Press, 1973.

Rorabaugh, W. J. *Berkeley at War.* New York: Oxford University Press, 1989.

Rosen, B., and T. H. Jerdee. "Influence of Subordinate Characteristics on Trust and Use of Participative Decision Strategies in a Management Simulation." *Journal of Applied Psychology* 59 (1977), pp. 9–14.

Rosenbach, W. E. "Mentoring: A Gateway to Leader Development." In *Contemporary Issues in Leadership.* 2nd ed. Ed. W. E. Rosenbach and R. L. Taylor. Boulder, CO: Westview, 1989, pp. 139–48.

Rosenbach, W. E.; T. S. Pittman; and E. H. Potter. "The Performance and Relationship Questionnaire." Gettysburg College, Gettysbury, PA: 1997.

Rosener, J. B. "Ways Women Lead." *Harvard Business Review* 68 (1990), pp. 119–25.

Ross, L. "The Intuitive Psychologist and His Shortcomings." *Advances in Experimental Social Psychology.* Vol. 10. Ed. L. Berkowitz. New York: Academic Press, 1977.

Ross, S., and G. J. Curphy. *Foundations of Leadership Executive Overview.* Presentation given to executives at Williams-Sonoma Inc., San Francisco, April 24, 2000.

Ross, S. M., and L. R. Offermann. "Transformational Leaders: Measurement of Personality Attributes and Work Group Performance." Paper presented at the Sixth Annual Society of Industrial and Organizational Psychologists Convention, St. Louis, MO, April 1991.

Rost, J. C. *Leadership in the 21st Century.* New York; Praeger, 1991.

Rotter, J. B. "Generalized Expectancies for Internal versus External Control of Reinforcement." *Psychological Monographs* 80, no. 609 (1966).

Roush, P. E. "The Myers-Briggs Type Indicator and Perceptions of Leadership Effectiveness." Paper presented at the Center for Creative Leadership's Impact of Leadership Conference, Colorado Springs, CO, July 1991.

Rushton, J. P. "Race, IQ, and the APA Report on the Bell Curve." *American Psychologist* 52, no. 1 (1997), pp. 69–70.

Rutan, J. S., and C. A. Rice. "The Charismatic Leader: Asset or Liability?" *Psychotherapy: Theory, Research, and Practice* 18 (1981), pp. 487–92.

Ryan, E. M.; V. Mims; and R. Koestner. "Relation of Reward Contingency and Interpersonal Context to Intrinsic Motivation: A Review and Test Using Cognitive Evaluation Theory." *Journal of Personality and Social Psychology* 45 (1983), pp. 736–50.

Rybicki, S. L., and D. D. Klippel. "Exploring the Impact of Personality Syndromes on Job Performance." In R. T. Hogan (chair). *Personality Applications in the Workplace: Thinking outside the Dots.* Symposium presented at the 12th Annual Conference of the Society of Industrial and Organizational Psychology, St. Louis, MO, 1997.

Rynes, S. L.; J. M. Bartunek; and R. L. Daft. "Across the Great Divide: Knowledge Creation and Transfer between Practitioners and Academics." *Academy of Management Journal* 44, no. 2 (2001), pp. 340–55.

Saal, F. E., and P. A. Knight. *Industrial Organizational Psychology: Science and Practice.* Belmont, CA: Brooks/Cole, 1988.

Sadler, P. J., and G. H. Hofstede. "Leadership Styles: Preferences and Perceptions of Employees of an International Company in Different Countries." *Mens en Onderneming* 26 (1972), pp. 43–63.

Safire, W., and L. Safir, eds. *Leadership.* New York: Simon & Schuster, 1990.

Sales, C. A.; E. Levanoni; and D. H. Saleh. "Satisfaction and Stress as a Function of Job Orientation, Style of Supervision, and the Nature of the Task." *Engineering Management International* 2 (1984), pp. 145–53.

Salgado, J. F. "The Five-Factor Model of Personality and Job Performance in the European Community." *Journal of Applied Psychology* 82, no. 1 (1997), pp. 30–43.

Salovey, P., and J. D. Mayer. "Emotional Intelligence." *Imagination, Cognition, and Personality* 9 (1990), pp. 185–211.

Sandal, G. M.; I. M. Endresen; R. Vaernes; and H. Ursin. "Personality and Coping Strategies during Submarine Missions." *Military Psychology* 11, no. 4 (1999), pp. 381–404.

Sanford, A., and S. Garrod. *Understanding Written Language.* New York: John Wiley, 1981.

Sarason, I. "Stress, Anxiety, and Cognitive Interference: Reactions to Stress." *Journal of Personality and Social Psychology* 46 (1986), pp. 929–39.

Sarchione, C. D.; M. J. Cuttler; P. M. Muchinsky; and R. O. Nelson-Grey. "Prediction of Dysfunctional Job Behaviors among Law Enforcement Officers." *Journal of Applied Psychology* 83, no. 6 (1998), pp. 904–12.

Sashkin, M. *A Manager's Guide to Performance Management.* New York: American Management Association, 1986.

———. "A New Vision of Leadership." *Journal of Management Development* 6, no. 4 (1987), pp. 19–28.

———. "The Visionary Leader." In *Charismatic Leadership: The Elusive Factor in Organizational Effectiveness.* Ed. J. A. Conger and R. N. Kanungo. San Francisco: Jossey-Bass, 1988.

Sashkin, M., and G. Huddle. "Recruit Top Principals." *School Administrator* 45, no. 2 (1988), pp. 8–15.

Sayles, L. *Leadership: What Effective Managers Really Do . . . and How They Do It.* New York: McGraw-Hill, 1979.

Scandura, T. A; G. B. Graen; and M. A. Novak. "When Managers Decide Not to Decide Autocratically: An Investigation of Leader-Member Exchange and Decision Influence." *Journal of Applied Psychology* 52 (1986), pp. 135–47.

———. "When Managers Decide Not to Decide Autocratically: An Investigation of Leader-Member Exchange and Decision Influence." *Journal of Applied Psychology* 71 (1986), pp. 579–84.

Scarr, S. "Protecting General Intelligence: Constructs and Consequences for Interventions." In *Intelligence: Measurement, Theory, and Public Policy.* Ed. R. L. Linn. Chicago: University of Illinois Press, 1989.

Schein, E. *Career Dynamics: Matching Individual and Organizational Needs.* Reading, MA: Addison-Wesley, 1978.

Schein, E. H. *Organizational Culture and Leadership: A Dynamic View.* San Francisco: Jossey-Bass, 1985.

Schein, V. E. "The Relationship Between Sex-Role Stereotypes and Requisite Management Characteristics: A Cross-Cultural Look." Paper presented at the 22nd International Congress of Applied Psychology, Kyoto, Japan, July 1990.

Schellenbarger, S. "Investors Seem Attracted to Firms with Happy Employees." *The Wall Street Journal,* March 19, 1997, p. I2.

Schmidt, F. L.; I. Gast-Rosenberg; and J. E. Hunter. "Validity Generalization Results for

Computer Programmers." *Journal of Applied Psychology* 65 (1980), pp. 643–61.

Schmidt, F. L., and J. E. Hunter. "Development of a Causal Model of Job Performance." *Current Directions in Psychological Science* 1, no. 3 (1992), pp. 89–92.

———. "Tacit Knowledge, Practical Intelligence, General Mental Ability and Job Knowledge." *Current Directions in Psychological Science* 2, no. 1 (1993), pp. 8–9.

Schmidt, M. J.; J. A. Kihm; and C. Robie. "Development of a Global Measure of Personality." *Personnel Psychology* 53, no. 1 (2000), pp. 153–92.

Schmidt, W. H., and B. Z. Posner. "Values and Expectations of Federal Service Executives." *Public Administrative Review* 46 (1986), pp. 447–54.

Schnake, M. E. "Vicarious Punishment in a Work Setting." *Journal of Applied Psychology* 71 (1986), pp. 343–45.

Schneider, B. "Interactional Psychology and Organizational Behavior." In *Research in Organizational Behavior*. Ed. L. L. Cummings and B. M. Staw. New York: Praeger, 1983, pp. 106–28.

Schneider, J. "The Cultural Situation as a Condition for the Condition of Fame." *American Sociology Review* 2 (1937), pp. 480–91.

Schonpflug, W. "The Noncharismatic Leader-Vulnerable." *Applied Psychology: An International Review* 44, no. 1 (1995), pp. 39–42.

Schriesheim, C. A., and A. S. DeNisi. "Task Dimensions as Moderators of the Effects of Instrumental Leadership: A Two Sample Replicated Test of Path-Goal Leadership Theory." *Journal of Applied Psychology* 66 (1981), pp. 589–97.

Schriesheim, C. A., and T. R. Hinkin. "Influence Tactics Used by Subordinates: A Theoretical and Empirical Analysis and Refinement of the Kipnis, Schmidt, and Wilkinson Subscales." *Journal of Applied Psychology* 75 (1990), pp. 246–57.

Schriesheim, C. A., and S. Kerr. "Theories and Measures of Leadership: A Critical Appraisal of Current and Future Directions." In *Leadership: The Cutting Edge*. Ed. J. G. Hunt and L. L. Larson. Carbondale: Southern Illinois University Press, 1977.

Schriesheim, C. A.; R. T. Mowday; and R. M. Stogdill. "Crucial Dimensions in Leader-Group Interactions." In *Cross-Currents in Leadership*. Ed. J. G. Hunt and L. L. Larsen. Carbondale: Southern Illinois University Press, 1979.

Schwartz, T. "How Do You Feel?" *Fast Company*, June 2000, pp. 297–312.

Schwarzkopf, N. *It Doesn't Take a Hero: The Autobiography of General H. Norman Schwarzkopf.* New York: Bantam Books, 1993.

Scully, J. A.; H. P. Sims, Jr.; J. D. Olian; E. R. Schneell; and K. A. Smith. "Tough Times Make Tough Bosses: A Meso-Analysis of CEO Leader Behavior." *Leadership Quarterly* 5 (1994), pp. 59–83.

Segal, D. "Management, Leadership, and the Future Battlefield." In *Leadership on the Future Battlefield*. Ed. J. Hunt and J. Blair. Washington, DC: Permagon-Brassey, 1985, pp. 201–13.

Seldes, G., Ed. *The Great Quotations*. Secaucus, NJ: Citadel, 1983.

Senge, P. M. *The Fifth Discipline: The Art and Practice of the Learning Organization*. New York: Doubleday/Currency, 1994.

Shamir, B.; M. B. Arthur; and R. J. House. "The Rhetoric of Charismatic Leadership: A Theoretical Extension, a Case Study, and Implications for Research." *Leadership Quarterly* 5 (1994), pp. 25–42.

Shamir, B.; R. J. House; and M. B. Arthur. "The Motivation Effects of Charismatic Leadership: A Self-Concept Based Theory." *Organizational Science* 4 (1993), pp. 577–94.

Shamir, B., and J. M. Howell. "Organizational and Contextual Influences on the Emergence and Effectiveness of Charismatic Leadership." *Leadership Quarterly*, 10, no. 2 (1999), pp. 257–84.

Shaver, K. G. *Principles of Social Psychology.* 2nd ed. Hillsdale, NJ: Erlbaum, 1985.

Shaw, M. *Group Dynamics: The Psychology of Small Group Dynamics.* 3rd ed. New York: McGraw-Hill, 1981.

Shephard, J. E. "Thomas Becket, Ollie North, and You." *Military Review* 71, no. 5 (1991), pp. 20–33.

Sheppard, B. H.; R. J. Lewicki; and J. W. Minton. *Organizational Justice: The Search for Fairness in the Workplace.* New York: Lexington Books, 1972.

Shils, E. "Charisma, Order, and Status." *American Sociological Review* 30 (1965), pp. 199–213.

Shipper, F., and C. L. Wilson. "The Impact of Managerial Behaviors on Group Performance, Stress, and Commitment." In *Impact of Leadership.* Ed. K. E. Clark, M. B. Clark, D. P. Campbell. Greensboro, NC: Center for Creative Leadership, 1992.

Shippmann, J. S.; R. A. Ash; M. Battista; L. Carr; L. D. Eyde; B. Hesketh; J. Kehoe; K. Pearlman; E. P. Prien; and J. I. Sanchez. "The Practice of Competency Modeling." *Personnel Psychology* 53, no. 3 (2000), pp. 703–740.

Shostrom, E. L. *Man, the Manipulator.* New York: Bantam, 1967.

Siegall, M., and L. L. Cummings. "Task Role Ambiguity, Satisfaction, and the Moderating Effect of Task Instruction Source." *Human Relations* 39 (1986), pp. 1017–32.

Silberman, M. *Team and Organization Development Sourcebook.* New York: McGraw-Hill, 1996, 1997, 1998.

Simon, H. A. "Making Management Decisions: The Role of Intuition and Emotion." *Academy of Management Executive* 1 (1987), pp. 57–64.

Simoneit, M. *Grundris de Charakterologischen Diagnostik.* Leipzig: Teubner, 1944.

Simonton, D. "Creativity and Leadership: Convergence and Divergence." In *National Defense University, Proceedings of the Creativity and Innovation Symposium.* Ed. V. E. Hendrix, D. B. Chapla, and W. Mizzelle. Washington, DC: National Defense University, 1985, pp. 157–70.

———. "Presidential Style: Personality, Biography, and Performance." *Journal of Personality and Social Psychology* 55 (1988), pp. 928–36.

Simpson, W. G., and T. C. Ireland. "Managerial Excellence and Shareholder Returns." *American Association of Individual Investors Journal* 9 (1987), pp. 4–8.

Sims, H. P., and A. D. Szilagyi. "Leader Reward Behavior and Subordinate Satisfaction and Performance." *Organizational Behavior and Human Performance* 14 (1975), pp. 426–38.

Sirota Consulting. *Establishing the Linkages between Employee Attitudes, Customer Attitudes, and Bottom-Line Results.* Chicago: Author, 1998.

Skinner, B. F. *The Behavior of Organisms.* New York: Appleton-Century-Crofts, 1938.

———. *Walden Two.* New York: MacMillan, 1948.

Slater, R. *Jack Welch and the GE Way.* New York: McGraw-Hill Professional Publishing, 1998.

Sloane, E. B.; S. A. Hezlett; N. R. Kuncel; and M. R. Systma. "Performance, Potential, and Peril: What It Takes to Succeed at the Top." Paper presented at the 11th Annual Conference of the Society for Industrial and Organizational Psychology, San Diego, CA, April 1996.

Slovic, P., and B. Fischoff. "On the Psychology of Experimental Surprises." *Journal of Experimental Social Psychology* 22 (1977), pp. 544–51.

Smith, F. J.; K. D. Scott; and C. L. Hulin. "Trends in Job-Related Attitudes in Managerial and Professional Employees." *Academy of Management Journal* 20 (1977), pp. 454–60.

Smith, J. E.; K. P. Carson; and R. A. Alexander. "Leadership: It Can Make a Difference." *Academy of Management Journal* 27 (1984), pp. 765–76.

Smith, K. W.; E. Salas; and M. T. Brannick. "Leadership Style as a Predictor of Teamwork Behavior: Setting the Stage by Managing Team

Climate." Paper presented at the Ninth Annual Conference of the Society for Industrial and Organizational Psychology, Nashville, TN, 1994.

Smith, L. "The Executive's New Coach." *Fortune*, December 27, 1993.

Smith, M. J. *When I Say No I Feel Guilty*. New York: Dial, 1975.

Smith, P. C. "Behaviors, Results, and Organizational Effectiveness: The Problem of Criteria." In *Handbook of Industrial and Organizational Psychology*. Ed. M. D. Dunnette. Chicago: Rand McNally, 1976.

Smither, J. W.; M. London; N. L. Vasilopoulis; R. R. Reilly; R. E. Millsap; and N. Salvemini. "An Examination of the Effects of an Upward Feedback Program over Time." *Personnel Psychology* 48, no. 1 (1995), pp. 1–34.

Snyder, M. "Self-Monitoring of Expressive Behavior." *Journal of Personality and Social Psychology* 30 (1974), pp. 526–37.

Snyder, N. H.; J. J. Dowd; and D. M. Houghton. *Vision, Values, and Courage*. New York: Free Press, 1994.

Snyder, R. A., and J. H. Morris. "Organizational Communication and Performance." *Journal of Applied Psychology* 69 (1984), pp. 461–65.

Solomon, R. L. "Punishment." *American Psychologist* 19 (1964), pp. 239–53.

Sparrowe, R. T., and R. C. Liden. "Process and Structure in Leader-Member Exchange." *Academy of Management Review* 22 (1997).

Spector, B., and M. Beer. "Beyond TQM Programmes." *Journal of Organizational Change Management* 7 (1994), pp. 63–70.

Sperry, R. W. "Some Effects of Disconnecting the Cerebral Hemispheres." *Science* 217 (1968), pp. 1223–26.

Spiller, G. "The Dynamics of Greatness." *Sociological Review* 21 (1929), pp. 218–32.

Spitzberg, I. J. "Paths of Inquiry into Leadership." *Liberal Education* 73, no. 2 (1987), pp. 24–28.

Spreitzer, G. M. "Psychological Empowerment in the Workplace: Dimensions, Measurement, and Validation." *Academy of Management Journal* 38, no. 5 (1995), pp. 1442–65.

Springer, S.; and G. Deutsch. *Left Brain, Right Brain*. San Francisco: W. H. Freeman, 1981.

Stahl, M. J. "Achievement, Power, and Managerial Motivation: Selecting Managerial Talent with the Job Choice Exercise." *Personnel Psychology* 36 (1983), pp. 775–89.

Staines, G. L., and R. P. Quinn. "American Workers Evaluate the Quality of Their Jobs." *Monthly Labor Review* 102, no. 1 (1979), pp. 3–12.

Stajkovic, A. D., and F. Luthans. "Differential Effects of Incentive Motivators on Performance." *Academy of Management Journal* 44, no. 3 (2001), 580–90.

Stamps, D. "Are We Smart for Our Jobs?" *Training*, April 1996, pp. 44–50.

Staw, B. M. "Organizational Behavior: A Review and Reformulation of the Field's Outcome Variables." *Annual Review of Psychology* 35 (1984), pp. 627–66.

Stech, E. L. *Leadership Communication*. Chicago: Nelson-Hall, 1983.

Steele, R. S. "Power Motivation, Activation, and Inspirational Speeches." *Journal of Personality* 45 (1977), pp. 53–64.

Steinberg, A. G., and D. M. Foley. "Mentoring in the Army: From Buzzword to Practice." *Military Psychology* 11, no. 4 (1999), pp. 365–380.

Steiner, I. D. *Group Process and Productivity*. New York: Academic Press, 1972.

Steinmetz, J.; J. Blankenship; L. Brown; D. Hall; and G. Miller. *Managing Stress Before It Manages You*. Palo Alto, CA: Bull, 1980.

Sternberg, R. J. *Beyond IQ: A Triarchic Theory of Human Intelligence*. New York: Cambridge University Press, 1985.

———. "The Concept of Intelligence: Its Role in Lifelong Learning and Success." *American Psychologist* 52, no. 10 (1997), pp. 1030–37.

———. "What Is the Common Thread of Creativity? Its Dialectical Relationship to Intelligence and Wisdom." *American Psychologist* 56, no. 4 (2001), pp. 360–62.

Sternberg, R. J., and N. K. Dees. "Creativity for the New Millenium." *American Psychologist* 56, no. 4 (2001), p. 332.

Sternberg, R. J., and E. L. Grigorenko. "Are Cognitive Styles Still in Style?" *American Psychologist* 51, no. 7 (1996), pp. 677–88.

Sternberg, R. J., and T. I. Lubart. "Investing in Creativity." *American Psychologist* 52, no. 10 (1997), pp. 1046–50.

Sternberg, R. J.; R. K. Wagner; W. M. Williams; and J. A. Horvath. "Testing Common Sense." *American Psychologist* 50, no. 11 (1995), pp. 912–927.

Stewart, R. *Choices for the Manager: A Guide to Understanding Managerial Work*. Englewood Cliffs, NJ: Prentice Hall, 1982.

———. *Contrasts in Management*. Maidenhead, England: McGraw-Hill UK, 1976.

———. *Managers and Their Jobs*. London: MacMillan, 1967.

Stock, G. *The Book of Questions: Business, Politics, and Ethics*. New York: Workman Publishing, 1991.

Stogdill, R. M. "Group Productivity, Drive, and Cohesiveness." *Organizational Behavior and Human Performance* 8 (1972), pp. 26–43.

———. *Handbook of Leadership*. New York: Free Press, 1974.

———. *Individual Behavior and Group Achievement*. New York: Oxford University Press, 1959.

———. "Personal Factors Associated with Leadership: A Review of the Literature." *Journal of Psychology* 25 (1948), pp. 35–71.

Stogdill, R. M.; O. S. Goode; and D. R. Day. "The Leader Behavior of Presidents of Labor Unions." *Personnel Psychology* 17 (1964), pp. 49–57.

Stogdill, R. M., and C. L. Shartle. *Methods in the Study of Administrative Performance*. Columbus: Ohio State University, Bureau of Business Research, 1955.

Stone, A. "Army Sees Leaders of the Future Leaving Today." *USA Today*, April 18, 2000, p. 10A.

Stone, D. L.; H. G. Gueutal; and B. MacIntosh. "The Effects of Feedback Sequence and Expertise of Rater of Perceived Feedback Accuracy." *Personal Psychology* 37 (1984), pp. 487–506.

Strasser, S.; R. C. Dailey; and T. S. Bateman. "Attitudinal Moderators and Effects of Leaders' Punitive Behavior." *Psychological Reports* 49 (1981), pp. 695–98.

Strauss, G. "Workers Hone the Fine Art of Revenge: Acts of Violence, Harassment toward Boss on Rise in Corporate World." *Denver Post*, August 24, 1998, p. 6E.

Strickland, B. R. "Internal-External Expectancies and Health-Related Behaviors." *Journal of Consulting and Clinical Psychology* 46 (1978), pp. 1192–1211.

Strube, M. J., and J. E. Garcia. "A Meta-Analytic Investigation of Fielder's Contingency Model of Leadership Effectiveness." *Psychological Bulletin* 90 (1981), pp. 307–21.

Sutherland, E. *Bosses Encouraged to Play Nice*. Minneapolis, MN: Personnel Decisions International, 2000.

Sutton, C. D., and R. W. Woodman. "Pygmalion Goes to Work: The Effects of Supervisor Expectations in the Retail Setting." *Journal of Applied Psychology* 74 (1989), pp. 943–50.

Swets, J. A.; and R. A. Bjork. "Enhancing Human Performance: An Evaluation of "New Age" Techniques Considered by the U.S. Army." *Psychological Science* 1, no. 2 (1990), pp. 85–96.

Taylor, H. L. *Delegate: The Key to Successful Management*. New York: Warner Books, 1989.

Tellegen, A.; D. T. Lykken; T. J. Bouchard; K. J. Wilcox; N. L. Segal; and S. Rich. "Personality Similarity in Twins Reared Apart and

Together." *Journal of Personality and Social Psychology* 54 (1988), pp. 1031–39.

Tepper, B. J. "Consequences of Abusive Supervision." *Academy of Management Journal* 43, no. 2 (2000), pp. 178–90.

Terborg, J. R.; C. H. Castore; and J. A. DeNinno. "A Longitudinal Field Investigation of the Impact of Group Composition on Group Performance and Cohesion." Paper presented at the annual meeting of the Midwestern Psychological Association, Chicago, 1975.

Tett, R. P.; H. A. Guterman; A. Bleier; and P. J. Murphy. "Development and Content Validation of a 'Hyperdimensional' Taxonomy of Managerial Competence." *Human Performance* (in press).

Tett, R. P., and J. P. Meyer. "Job Satisfaction, Organizational Commitment, Turnover Intention, and Turnover: Path Analyses Based on Meta-Analytic Findings." *Personnel Psychology* 44 (1991), pp. 703–42.

Tett, R. P.; D. N. Jackson; M. Rothstein; J. R. Reddon. "Meta-Analysis of Personality-Job Performance Relations: A Reply on Ones, Mount, Barrick, and Hunter, 1994" *Personnel Psychology* 47 (1994), pp. 157–79.

Thayer, P. W. "The Myers-Briggs Type Indicator and Enhancing Human Performance." Report prepared for the Committee on Techniques for the Enhancement of Human Performance of the National Academy of Sciences, 1988.

Thomas, B. *Walt Disney.* New York: Simon & Schuster, 1976.

Thomas, D. A. "The Truth about Mentoring Minorities: Race Matters." *Harvard Business Review*, April 2001, pp. 98–111.

Thomas, K. W. "Conflict and Conflict Management." In *Handbook of Industrial and Organizational Psychology.* Ed. M. D. Dunnette. Chicago: Rand McNally, 1976.

———. "Toward Multidimensional Values in Teaching: The Example of Conflict Manage-

ment." *Academy of Management Review* 2, no. 3 (1977), pp. 484–90.

Thomas, K. W.; and W. H. Schmidt. "A Survey of Managerial Interests with Respect to Conflict." *Academy of Management Journal* 19 (1976), pp. 315–18.

Thurstone, L. L. "The Factors of the Mind." *Psychological Review* 41 (1934), pp. 1–32.

Tichy, N. M., and E. Cohen. *The Leadership Engine: How Winning Companies Build Leaders at Every Level.* New York: HarperCollins, 1997.

Tichy, N. M., and M. A. Devanna. *The Transformational Leader.* New York: John Wiley, 1986.

Tierney, P.; S. M. Farmer; and G. B. Graen. "An Examination of Leadership and Employee Creativity: The Relevance of Traits and Relationships." *Personnel Psychology* 52, no. 3 (1999), pp. 591–620.

Tjosvold, D. "Stress Dosage for Problem Solvers." *Working Smart*, August 1995, p. 5.

Toffler, A. *Future Shock.* New York: Random House, 1970.

Tolman, E. C. *Purposeful Behavior in Animals and Men.* New York: Appleton-Century-Crofts, 1932.

Tornow, W. W., and M. London. *Maximizing the Value of 360-Degree Feedback.* San Francisco, CA: Jossey-Bass, 1998.

Treacy, M., and F. Wiersma. *The Discipline of Market Leaders.* Reading, MA: Perseus Books, 1997.

Trevino, L. K. "The Social Effects of Punishment in Organizations: A Justice Perspective." *Academy of Management Review* 17 (1992), pp. 647–76.

Trevino, L. K., and S. A. Youngblood. "Bad Apples in Bad Barrels: A Causal Analysis of Ethical Decision-Making Behavior." *Journal of Applied Psychology* 75 (1990), pp. 378–85.

Trice, H. M., and J. M. Beyer. "Charisma and Its Routinization in Two Social Movement Organizations." In *Research in Organizational Behavior.* Vol. 8. Ed. B. M. Staw and L. L. Cummings. Greenwich, CN: JAI Press, 1986.

Trist, E. L., and K. W. Bamforth. "Some Social and Psychological Consequences of the Longwall Method of Goal Setting." *Human Relations* 4 (1951), pp. 1–38.

Tsui, A. "A Role Set Analysis of Managerial Reputation." *Organizational Behavior and Human Performance* 34 (1984), pp. 64–96.

Tucker, R. C. "The Theory of Charismatic Leadership." *Daedalus* 97 (1968), pp. 731–56.

Tuckman, B. W. "Developmental Sequence in Small Groups." *Psychological Bulletin* 63 (1965), pp. 384–99.

Udell, J. G. "An Empirical Test of Hypotheses Relating to Span of Control." *Administrative Science Quarterly* 12 (1967), pp. 420–39.

Uecker, M. E., and B. L. Dilla. "Mentoring as a Leadership Development Tool in the United States Air Force." *Proceedings of the 26th Annual Meeting of the Military Testing Association,* Munich, Germany, 1985, pp. 423–28.

Ulrich, D.; J. Zenger; and N. Smallwood. *Results-Based Leadership.* Boston: Harvard Business School Press, 1999.

Ungson, G. R.; C. James; and B. H. Spicer. "The Effects of Regulatory Agencies on Organizations in Wood Products and High Technology/ Electronics Organizations." *Academy of Management Journal* 28 (1985), pp. 426–45.

Urwick, L. F. *Notes on the Theory of Organization.* New York: American Management Association, 1952.

Van Velsor, E., and J. B. Leslie. "Why Executives Derail: Perspectives across Time and Cultures." *Academy of Management Executive* 9, no. 4 (1995), pp. 62–71.

Vecchio, R. P. "Assessing the Validity of Fiedler's Contingency Model of Leadership Effectiveness: A Closer Look at Strube and Garcia." *Psychological Bulletin* 93 (1983), pp. 404–08.

——. "Predicting Worker Performance in Inequitable Settings." *Academy of Management Review* 7 (1982), pp. 103–10.

——. "Situational Leadership Theory: An Examination of a Prescriptive Theory." *Journal of Applied Psychology* 72 (1987), pp. 444–51.

Vroom, V. H. *Work and Motivation.* New York: John Wiley, 1964.

Vroom, V. H., and A. G. Jago. "Leadership and Decision Making: A Revised Normative Model." Paper presented at the Academy of Management Convention, Boston, MA, 1974.

——. *The New Theory of Leadership: Managing Participation in Organizations.* Englewood Cliffs, NJ: Prentice Hall, 1988.

Vroom, V. H., and P. W. Yetton. *Leadership and Decision Making.* Pittsburgh, PA: University of Pittsburgh Press, 1973.

Wagner, J. A. "Participation's Effect on Performance and Satisfaction: A Reconsideration of Research Evidence." *Academy of Management Review* 19 (1994), pp. 312–30.

Wainer, H. A., and I. M. Rubin. "Motivation of Research and Development Entrepreneurs: Determinants of Company Success." *Journal of Applied Psychology* 53 (1969), pp. 178–84.

Wakabayashi, M., and G. B. Graen. "The Japanese Career Progress Study: A Seven-Year Follow-Up." *Journal of Applied Psychology* 69 (1984), pp. 603–14.

Wakin, M. M. "Ethics of Leadership." In *Military Leadership.* Ed. J. H. Buck and L. J. Korb. Beverly Hills, CA: Sage, 1981.

Waldman, D. A.; G. G. Ramirez; R. J. House; and P. Puranam. "Does Leadership Matter? CEO Leadership Attributes and Profitability under Conditions of Perceived Environmental Uncertainty." *Academy of Management Journal,* 44, no. 1 (2001), pp. 134–43.

Walker, A. and J. W. Smither. "A Five-Year Study of Upward Feedback: What Managers

Do with Their Results Matters." *Personnel Psychology* 52, no. 2 (1999), pp. 395–423.

Walker, T. G. "Leader Selection and Behavior in Small Political Groups." *Small Group Behavior* 7 (1976), pp. 363–68.

Wall, T. D.; N. J. Kemp; P. R. Jackson; and C. W. Clegg. "Outcomes of Autonomous Work Groups: A Long-Term Field Experiment." *Academy of Management Journal* 29 (1986), pp. 280–304.

Wallas, G. *The Art of Thought.* New York: Harcourt Brace, 1926.

Wanous, J. P.; T. L. Keon; and J. C. Latack. "Expectancy Theory and Occupational/ Organizational Choices: A Review and Test." *Organizational Behavior and Human Performance* 32 (1983), pp. 66–86.

Wayne, S. J.; L. M. Shore; and R. C. Liden. "Perceived Organizational Support and Leader-Member Exchange: A Social Exchange Perspective." *Academy of Management Journal* 40 (1997), pp. 82–111.

Weber, J. "Managers' Moral Meaning: An Exploratory Look at Managers' Responses to the Moral Dilemmas." *Proceedings of the Academy of Management Convention*, Washington, DC, 1989, pp. 333–37.

Weber, M. *The Theory of Social and Economic Organization.* Ed. and trans. A. M. Henderson and T. Parsons. (Original work published in 1923). New York: Free Press.

Weber, M. *The Theory of Social and Economic Organization.* Ed. Talcott Parsons; trans. A. M. Henderson and T. Parsons. New York: Free Press, 1964.

Weiss, H. M. "Subordinate Imitation of Supervisor Behavior: The Role of Modeling in Organizational Socialization." *Organizational Behavior and Human Performance* 19 (1977), pp. 89–105.

Welbourne, T. M., and L. A. Cyr. "The Human Resource Executive Effect in Initial Public Offering Firms." *Academy of Management Journal* 42, no. 6 (1999), pp. 616–29.

Wenzel, L. H. "Understanding Managerial Coaching: The Role of Manager Attributes and Skills in Effective Coaching." Unpublished doctoral dissertation, Colorado State University, 2000.

Weschler, D. *Weschler Adult Intelligence Scale: Manual.* New York: Psychological Corporation, 1955.

West, M. A., and N. R. Anderson. "Innovation in Top Management Teams." *Journal of Applied Psychology* 81, no. 6, (1996), pp. 680–93.

West Point Associates, the Department of Behavior Sciences and Leadership, United States Military Academy. *Leadership in Organizations.* Garden City Park, NY: Avery, 1988.

Westley, F. R., and H. Mintzberg. "Profiles of Strategic Vision: Levesque and Iacocca." In *Charismatic Leadership: The Elusive Factor in Organizational Effectiveness.* Ed. J. A. Conger and R. N. Kanungo. San Francisco: Jossey-Bass, 1988.

Wexley, K. N., and G. P. Latham. *Developing and Training Human Resources in Organizations.* Glenview, IL: Scott, Foresman, 1981.

Wheelan, S. A. *Group Processes.* Needham Heights, MA: Allyn & Bacon, 1994.

White, S. S., and E. A. Locke. "Problems with the Pygmalion Effect and Some Proposed Solutions." *Leadership Quarterly* 11, no. 3 (2000), pp. 389–416.

Whitely, W.; T. W. Dougherty; and G. F. Dreher. "The Relationship of Mentoring and Socioeconomic Origin to Managers' and Professionals' Early Career Progress." *Proceedings of the Academy of Management.* Anaheim, CA: 1988, pp. 58–62.

Whiteside, D. E. *Command Excellence: What It Takes to Be the Best!* Department of the Navy. Washington, DC: Leadership Division, Naval Military Personnel Command, 1985.

Wilcox, W. H. "Assistant Superintendents' Perceptions of the Effectiveness of the Superintendent, Job Satisfaction, and Satisfaction with the Superintendent's Supervisory Skills." Ph.D. dissertation, University of Missouri, Columbia, 1982.

Wiley, J., and T. Comacho. "Life-Style and Future Health: Evidence from the Alameda County Study." *Preventive Medicine* 9 (1980), pp. 1–21.

Willerman, L. *The Psychology of Individual and Group Differences.* San Francisco: W. H. Freeman, 1979.

Willner, A. R. *The Spellbinders: Charismatic Political Leadership.* New Haven: Yale University Press, 1984.

Wilson, J. A., and N. S. Elman. "Organizational Benefits of Mentoring." *Academy of Management Executive* 4 (1990), pp. 88–93.

Wilson, P. R. "The Perceptual Distortion of Height as a Function of Ascribed Academic Status." *Journal of Social Psychology* 74 (1968), pp. 97–102.

Winter, D. G. "Leader Appeal, Leader Performance, and the Motive Profiles of Leaders and Followers: A Study of American Presidents and Elections." *Journal of Personality and Social Psychology* 52 (1987), pp. 196–202.

Wofford, J. C., and V. L. Goodwin. "A Cognitive Interpretation of Transformational and Transactional Leadership Theories." *Leadership Quarterly* 5 (1994), pp. 161–86.

Wolpe, H. "A Critical Analysis of Some Aspects of Charisma." *Sociological Review* 16 (1968), pp. 305–18.

Wood, G. "The Knew-It-All-Along Effect." *Journal of Experimental Psychology: Human Perception and Performance* 4 (1979), pp. 345–53.

Woodward, J. *Industrial Organization.* London: Oxford University Press, 1965.

Xie, J. L., and G. Johns. "Job Scope and Stress: Can Job Scope Be Too High?" *Academy of Management Journal* 38, no. 5 (1995), pp. 1288–1309.

Yagil, D. "Charismatic Leadership and Organizational Hierarchy: Attribution of Charisma to Close and Distance Leaders." *Leadership Quarterly* 9, no. 2 (1998), pp. 161–76.

Yammarino, F. J., and A. J. Dubinsky. "Transformational Leadership Theory: Using Levels of Analysis to Determine Boundary Conditions." *Personnel Psychology* 47 (1994), pp. 787–812.

Yammarino, F. J.; W. D. Spangler; and B. M. Bass. "Transformational Leadership and Performance: A Longitudinal Investigation." *Leadership Quarterly* 4 (1993), pp. 81–102.

Yorges, S. L.; H. M. Weiss; and O. J. Strickland. "The Effect of Leader Outcomes on Influence, Attributions, and Perceptions of Charisma." *Journal of Applied Psychology,* 84, no. 3 (1999), pp. 428–36.

Yoshida, K. "Deming Management Philosophy: Does It Work in the U.S. as Well as in Japan?" *Columbia Journal of World Business* (1989), pp. 10–16.

Yukl, G. "An Evaluation of Conceptual Weaknesses in Transformational and Charismatic Leadership Theories." *Leadership Quarterly* 10, no. 2 (1999), pp. 285–306.

———. *Leadership in Organizations.* 2nd ed. Englewood Cliffs, NJ: Prentice Hall, 1989.

———. "Reflections and Directions in Leadership Research." Paper presented at the 14th Annual Conference of the Society of Industrial and Organizational Psychologists, Atlanta, GA, May 1999.

Yukl, G. A., and C. M. Falbe. "Importance of Different Power Sources in Downward and Lateral Relations." *Journal of Applied Psychology* 76 (1991), pp. 416–23.

Yukl, G. A., and D. D. Van Fleet. "Cross-Situational Multi-Method Research on Military Leader Effectiveness." *Organizational Behavior and Human Performance* 30 (1982), pp. 87–108.

———. "Theory and Research on Leadership in Organizations." In *Handbook of Industrial & Organizational Psychology.* Vol. 3. Ed. M. D. Dunnette and L. M. Hough. Palo Alto, CA: Consulting Psychologists Press, 1992, pp. 1–51.

Yukl, G. A.; R. Lepsinger; and T. Lucia. "Preliminary Report on the Development and Validation of the Influence Behavior Questionnaire." In *Impact of Leadership.* Ed. K. E. Clark,

M. B. Clark, and D. P. Campbell. Greensboro, NC: Center for Creative Leadership, 1992.

Yukl, G. A.; S. Wall; and R. Lepsinger. "Preliminary Report on Validation of the Managerial Practices Survey." In *Measures of Leadership*. Ed. K. E. Clark and M. B. Clark. Greensboro, NC: Center for Creative Leadership, 1989.

Zaccaro, S. J. "Leader Resources and the Nature of Organizational Problems." *Applied Psychology: An International Review* 44, no. 1 (1995), pp. 32–36.

Zaccaro, S. J.; R. J. Foti; and D. A. Kenny. "Self-Monitoring and Trait-Based Variance in Leadership: An Investigation of Leader Flexibility across Multiple Group Situations." *Journal of Applied Psychology* 76 (1991), pp. 308–15.

Zacharatos, A.; J. Barling; and E. K. Kelloway. "Development and Effects of Transformational Leadership in Adolescents." *Leadership Quarterly* 11, no. 2 (2000), pp. 211–26.

Zajonc, R. "Social Facilitation." *Science* 149 (1965), pp. 269–74.

Zaleznik, A. "Charismatic and Consensus Leaders: A Psychological Comparison." *Bulletin of the Menninger Clinic* 38 (1974), pp. 22–38.

———. "The Leadership Gap." *Washington Quarterly* 6, no. 1 (1983), pp. 32–39.

Zey, M. G. *The Mentor Connection*. Homewood, IL: Dow Jones-Irwin, 1984.

Zhou, J. "Feedback Valence, Feedback Style, Task Autonomy, and Achievement Orientation: Interactive Effects on Creative Performance." *Journal of Applied Psychology* 83, no. 2 (1998), pp. 261–76.

Zimbardo, P.; C. Haney; W. Banks; and D. Jafe. "The Mind Is a Formidable Jailer: A Pirandellian Prison." *New York Times Magazine*, April 8, 1973, pp. 38–60.